MR. SMITH, THE SYBARITE
Who Also Was A Teacher

By

Warren Allen Smith

Mr. Smith, The Sybarite Who Was Also a Teacher

By

Warren Allen Smith

Published by
Warren Allen Smith
31 Jane Street (Suite 10-D)
New York, NY 10014
wasm@mac.com

Copyright 2014 by Warren Allen Smith
ISBN 978-1-312-38522-1
First Edition, Revision 2

Also by the Author

Who's Who in Hell - Hell, a theological invention, does not exist
    (NY: Barricade Books, 2000, 1,249 pages, $125.00)
Cruising the Deuce - written pseudonymously as Allen Windsor
    (NY: chelCbooks, 2005), 164 pages, paperback
    (NY: chelCbooks, 2010), 164 pages, re-issue, paperback
    (NY: chelCbooks, 2010), eBook
    (NY: chelCbooks, 2013, eBook
    (NY: chelCbook, 2014, oral sociological project
Gossip From Across the Pond - British column, 1996 to 2005
    (NY: chelCbooks, 2005, 158 pages), paperback
    (NY: chelCbooks, 2010, 158 pages), re-issue, paperback
    (NY: chelCbooks, 2010), eBook
Celebrities in Hell – celebrities who are non-believers
    (NY: Barricade Books, 2002, 288 pages), 1st Edition
    (NY: chelCbooks, 2010, 422 pages), 2nd Edition, paperback
    NY: chelCbooks, 2010), eBook
In the Heart of Showbiz, A Triography
    (NY: chelCbooks, 2011), Volume 1), autobiography
    (NY: chelCbooks, 2011), paperback
    (NY: chelCbooks, 2011), eBook
    (NY: chelCbooks, 2011), Volume 2, autobiography
    (NY: chelCbooks, 2011), Volume 2, eBook
    (NY: chelCbooks, 2011), Volume 3, autobiography
    (NY: chelCbooks, 2011), Volume 3, eBook
Unforgettable New Canaanites
    (NY: chelCbooks, 2012, 309 pages), paperback
    (NY: chelCbooks, 2013, eBook

On the Cover: Photo by Ted Nelson, when he was 15
        Bentley School students Alan Noble and George Gould

For

Commandant and Madame René Picard,
who adopted me as
Jacques-François Picard,
the American sergeant, 1944-1945

and

the 2 girls and 6 boys,
who adopted me
as their surrogate dad,
1960-2002

Contents

1 Hello

    Some Irreverent Memories

2 Festschrift (1920s to 2000s)

    The Teacher at War (1940 - 1945)

3 Subjects

4 Individuals

5 Twilight to Dusk

    Obituary

1

When I taught writing, I emphasized that an author starts by determining who the audience will be.

Although the present audience that I have in mind will be the eight kids who have adopted me as their surrogate dad, the present book's audience also will be students and parents where I taught over three decades as well as friends and foes who befriended me in the past 93 years.

In a 3-volume autobiography called *In the Heart of Showbiz* (chelCbooks, 2011), at the age of almost 90, I ambitiously wrote about my life experiences since being born to a South Dakota farmer's daughter – **Ruth Marion Miles Smith** (1891 - 1975) and an Iowa-born grain dealer – **Harry Clark Smith** (1887-1975) – who played for and was a decorated World War I veteran and a scout for the Chicago Cubs' Portland farm team (.400 batting average).

For the record, I also taught for a few months in West Chester, Iowa (population 218), upon graduating in mid-year with my B.A. from Iowa State Teachers College; taught in New York City at Bentley School, 1949 - 1954, a private and one of the first progressive schools in Manhattan after receiving my M.A. from Teachers College, Columbia University; taught for one year at Teachers College, Columbia University; and taught at New Canaan High School in New Canaan, Connecticut, from 1954 to 1986. That totals over 37 ½ years

Ruth and Harry

Some Irreverent Memories of New Canaan

A major memory that I have of New Canaan is that *The Advertiser* editors wrote about the town's being the next station to Heaven because of its parks and churches, its schools and clubs, and its proximity to New York City. But the town's newspaper seldom wrote about the teachers who made its schools so noteworthy. (Capitalizing "Heaven" is questionable but common in standard English.)

If **tragedy** inspires,
comedy amuses, and
pathos does not inspire,

here are some examples:

Admiral Chester Nimitz Jr. and his wife Joan

The Nimitzes were two inspiring parents whose children I taught in New Canaan. When in their late 80s, and in poor health, they committed suicide.

Joan was blind, and the son of Admiral Chester Nimitz Sr. left a suicide note:

> "Our decision was made over a considerable period of time and was not carried out in acute desperation. Nor is it the expression of a mental illness. We have consciously, rationally, deliberately, and of our own free will taken measures to end our lives today because of the physical limitations on our quality of life placed upon us by age, failing vision, osteoporosis, back and painful orthopedic problems."

Joan could not see, and Chester had lost 30 pounds because of a prolonged stomach disorder. He also suffered from congestive heart failure. They ingested a quantity of sleeping pills.

David Letterman

Letterman, the former New Canaanite who has been the host of late night television for over three decades, is the grouchy, mischievous, and humorous comedian who is scheduled to be replaced in 2015 by Stephen Colbert.

It was no joke when, after marrying college classmate Michelle Cook in 1969 and divorcing her in 1977, he married Regina Lasko in 2009 and in 2003 they had a child, Harry. when his mother was a 43-year-old and his father was a 58-year-old.

In his home town, Indianapolis, Indiana, as a wacky weatherman, he has been documented by Wikipedia and other sources as having made up cities that did not exist ("Eight inches of snow in Bingree and surrounding areas"). During one broadcast, he once erased state borders from a weather map. For a little while he anchored the evening news and hosted a news/talk radio show. But he was too funny to play it serious. In a late night "Freeze-Dried Movies" telecast, he quit, loaded his possessions into a truck, and before he was 30 left Indiana.

While he was in New Canaan, a lady stalked his residence and was arrested several times for breaking in, stealing his car, and claiming to be his wife. After writing him hundreds of letters, she knelt in front of a freight train in 1998. He has had at least two other stalkers and reportedly has bulletproof glass in his office window.

Adolf Hitler

The pathetic Führer of Nazi Germany, Hitler became known in progressive secular nations as the most hated man in the world.

He was and is an uninspiring figure, the ultimate of pathos.

I once had dinner with Admiral Chester Nimitz Jr., his wife Joan, his mother-in-law Mrs. Chester Nimitz Sr., and his daughters, Sarah and Betsy . . .

. . . I would have enjoyed having had dinner with David Letterman . . .

. . . and, as an enlisted man during World War II, I helped Hitler go to his grave without dinner.

2

You can either cock a snook or take a test to see if you know why I . . .

- spent two days in Sing Sing Prison
- had two girlfriends; and had two paramours who died of AIDS
- was mooned by *Screw* editor Al Goldstein
- met a castrato in Iowa and later met him in a Paris church
- was "adopted" from 1944-1945 as Jacques-François Picard
  by a French commandant, his wife, his daughter, and his son
- was "adopted" by two girls and six guys as their surrogate dad
- had my class taught by Guyana's ambassador to the UN, making
  the students think I was a substitute teacher who just sat there
- edited a paper about voodoo for Haiti's first psychiatrist
- became the teacher for a girl hit by the A-bomb in Hiroshima
- had a student who was a Pulitzer Prize winner
- had a student who became deputy mayor of New York City
- had a student who developed his own television sitcom
- had a student who became a director of the NY Federal Reserve Board
- lent a wireless microphone for Sammy Davis Jr. to hide in his crotch
- helped a cop catch a thieving addict on 42nd Street
- was described in 2009 as as one of "Iowa's Famous Iowans"
- had recording clients such as Jerry Bock, Paddy Chayevsky, Chubby
  Checker, Celia Cruz, Loretta Devine, Marvin Hamlisch, Helen
  Hayes, Frankie Lane, Lorna Luft, Meadowlark Lemon, Ethel
  Merman, Arthur Miller, Liza Minnelli, Earl Monroe, Tito Puente,
  Quincy Jones, Sun Ra and his Arkestra, Paul Simon, Jimmy Smits,
  Tiny Tim, Vangellis, Sarah Vaughan, Robert Whitehead, Stefan
  Wolpe, and Stevie Wonder
- was snookered by the daughter of Indonesia's dictator
- never shot a gun during my 3½ years in the army
- managed the memorials for Broadway star Gilbert Price and the off-
  Broadway star who was Big Bubba Smith's gay brother
- while owning Anita Weschler's lightweight fiberglass statue of a man,
  The Humanist, carried it on my back, hailed a taxi, asked the driver
  to take us to the Shubert Theater, and we tied up 8th Avenue traffic
  that serenaded us with a cacophony of noise

Festschrift 1920s to 2000s

MEMORIES

A FESTSCHRIFT FOR

WARREN ALLEN SMITH

ON HIS 85TH BIRTHDAY, 27 OCTOBER 2006

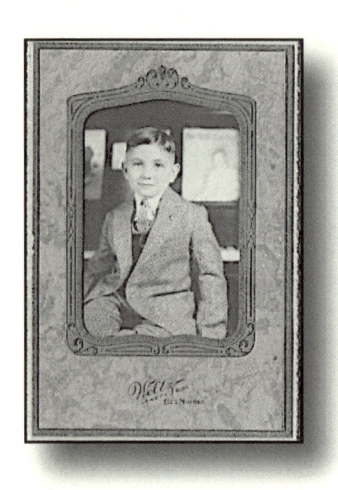

Minburn, Iowa
Population 328
1920s
Warren's $25 piano

Manhattan, New York City
Population 8,000,000+
Before 9/11/2001
The Two World Towers are still there

Warren Allen Smith was born in Minburn, Iowa, October 27, 1921. He graduated from Minburn High School in 1938; took a post-graduate high school course in business at the Rippey, Iowa, High School; after Omaha Beach in 1944, was Chief Clerk of an Adjutant General's Office, Hq. Oise, Reims, France; received his B.A. from the University of Northern Iowa, Cedar Falls, in 1948; received his M.A. from Columbia University in 1949; taught English at Bentley School, New York City, 1949-1954; taught English at New Canaan (Connecticut) High School, 1954-1986; was book review editor of *The Humanist*, 1953-1958); co-founded Variety Recording Studio with Fernando Vargas, 1961-1990; instructor, Teachers College, Columbia University, 1961-1962; President, Taursa Mutual Fund, 1971-1973; syndicated columnist "Manhattan Scene," in West Indian newspapers; Bertrand Russell Society (Director 1973 - 2013 ; Vice

President 1977-1980); Mensa Investment Club (Director, 1973-2001); Signer, *Humanist Manifesto II*, 1973; Signer *Humanist Manifesto 2000*; signer *Humanist Manifesto III*; Author, *Who's Who in Hell: A Handbook and International Directory for Freethinkers, Humanists, Naturalists, Rationalists, and Non-Theists* (Barricade Books, 2000); *Celebrities in Hell* (Barricade Books, 2002); *Gossip From Across the Pond* (chelCbooks, 2005); *Cruising the Deuce* (chelCbooks, 2005); originator in 2005, Philosopedia.org.

Following is a collection of memories by individuals who, over the years, have known Warren Allen Smith (also known as "Smitty" and "wasm").

They were asked to submit their recollections of him at the time they knew him. The dates below represent the decade in which they first met.

Submit your own memories prior to October 27th, his 85th birthday.

Dr. Donald Souden
New Canaan, Connecticut

1920s

Warren,
when he weighed 8 pounds

Harry Smith, his water jug to take to work,
and his cowboy son

The Smiths' New 1928 Chrysler,
Mr. Rowe's Department Store

16

Warren Allen Smith, Minburn, Iowa

(1929) To Warren Smiths' most respectful parents **Harry C. Smith, Ruth Smith**, from their orphan, **Warren Smith**. Important. Notice. To the effortless parents of Warren Smiths'. I didn't suppose you would do such a thing to your own boy. I appreciate how much you care for me. It would have been different if you would have made some sort of an effort to let me go with you, not leave me back. Of course I should have come home at 5:30. I came home at 6:00. You could have come down and got me for I could have went as I was or you should have sent John down to tell me. I wasn't hungry for I didn't feel exactly right.

Will go to bed before 7:00 more than likely for I am so upset. I am terribly disappointed in you folks. I hope that you had a nice time. I won't have to go to school tomorrow, so just call me up in time to get the mail. Your most loving boy, **Warren**.

P.S. The track meet was very poor and I left at 6:00 because I didn't like it.

Thelma Crawford Pohl, 221 Rockwood Bl #514, Spokane, WA 99202
[She was a graduate of Minburn High School in 1926 and was Warren's 3rd grade teacher. For several decades, he has edited *The Pinhooker*, a newsletter for all graduates of the school. In 2006 Mrs. Pohl has Alzheimer's.]

(15 January 2002) I'm off to a bad start this morning! While the washer and dryer *are* going I'll try to get a couple notes written. Part of my problem is that I just got this machine home from "surgery" and I have forgotten how it works!

I love the picture Warren sent his old 3rd grade teacher - my, how he has grown!!! But handsome as ever! Penny - my daughter - is waiting for me to go on errands - so this will be brief! Another reason is because of the great distance between you and me, thus our subjects to discuss are limited!

Now the telephone is jangling - so I must answer! You are wonderful to keep me posted on all my old friends - and I know they appreciate all the time spent on us! Keep us *all* posted - and accept my thanks! Love to all. **Miss Crawford**, your teacher in 1928.

1930s

Minburn's Bicycle Club was presided over by **Warren** (standing at extreme right, arms folded). He fingerprinted everyone and gave them membership cards. At this time, his goal was to become a police detective.

l to r:

1 to 4 ?
5 Mary Ann Bever (on tricycle)
6 ?
7 John Hinchliff (with visor cap)
8 Billy Clement
9 ?
10 Warren Allen Smith (with straw hat, arms folded)
11 Helen Schaefer
12 Loren Nissly (?)

(1931 - Warren's comments in a town-wide study of who lived where in every house in town): Yes, there was a preacher by the name of **Rev. Wholsapple**. Also **Paul McDade** was there in the 1930s, followed by **William Warren**. The reason in the 1920s that my parents, **Ruth and Harry C. Smith** (manager of the Clark Brown Grain Elevator), switched from the "other" church to the Methodist was that it had had a schism. That church's denomination was the same one once belonged to by **Ronald Reagan** (who bought a Nash in a Des Moines showroom the same day my dad bought a less-expensive Lafayette. . . . For 25 cents when I was in high school), I was paid by **Ed Hill** to take him to Perry for his weekly haircut. I have more stories if **Marjorie Joslin** would e-mail me. **Clarence Hill** once told me he found the **Frank and Jesse James** group bathing in the river, and they bought provisions because they weren't recognized as being robbers.

[On July 22, 1931, when Warren was 9 and sleeping on a hot night in the front yard of his place, three bank robbers shot and killed Minburn's Town Marshal, **Virgil Untied** (father of his friends **Mildred, Doris,** and **Afton**) just a block or so away. Although many shots were fired, one of which was found a few feet above Warren's head on a wooden wall of Mr. Rowe's department store next door, neither Warren nor his parents heard anything until all the commotion the following morning. Warren's dad drew a circle around where the shot had landed on the wall, a few feet above where Warren was sleeping in his sleeping bag. Neighbors came by for weeks to see where the bullet had hit.]

Night Marshal Shot Down By Three Minburn Bandits

FIVE WOUNDS SUFFERED IN STREET FIGHT

Virgil United, 33, Near Death, Robbers Escape in Car.

Paul Senter, a friend later on who lived in Rippey, had these recollections: (16 June 2006):

"The Barrow Gang (Bonnie & Clyde) had a big shoot-out with the law near Dexter, which was near Minburn. One of the gang died at Perry Hospital and his wife was there, too. She probably went to prison. I dated **Louise Feller**, a cousin of **Bob Feller**, summer of '42. Her folks were held hostage at their farm not far from the shoot-out. Therefore, I heard about that one. Her dad and Bob Feller's dad were brothers. I think that was probably around 1935. The gang also stole a vehicle from in front of one of the Stoner brothers that was parked in front of his house in Perry."

[Warren remembers that famed baseball star **Bob Feller** played on the 8th grade basketball team against Minburn's Little Scorpions, a team coached by **Jim Duncan** (after whom the Drake Relays track was later named), members of which included **Bob Shirley**, **Harold Gottschalk**, **Theora Burke**, **Loren Nissly**, and **Warren Smith**.]

[For obtaining a large number of new customers on his *Des Moines Register & Tribune* paper route, **Warren** when a teenager in Minburn was rewarded with a trip in an autogiro (a predecessor of helicopters). He thinks papers cost his customers 15 cents per week.]

In 2003 he wrote to **B. Doktorov**, a researcher about photographer **George Yates**]:

"With about 50 customers in our town of 328 people, I collected $7.50/week, for which I rode my bicycle for miles in hot weather and during blizzards, always pursued by barking dogs. I don't really remember my profit, but it could have been 5 cents per customer per week plus maybe another 5 cents for the Sunday paper. In short, I earned my spending money of maybe $5/week "the old-fashioned way." The good thing was that everyone in town knew me. The bad thing was that everyone in town knew me – I was slowed considerably by getting to listen to house-to-house gossip. Also, some people knew how to stiff a kid – I had a long list of people who didn't pay."

"However, a memorable reward for working for the Cowles papers was that I got to sit in the pilot's seat of the R & T's autogiro, a new-fangled single-rotary-wing aircraft that was a teenager's dream in those days but soon became replaced by helicopters. Mention the name Gardner Cowles, and I immediately think about my getting to sit in the autogiro pilot's seat. Cowles's sales people were outstanding, and we paper boys got prizes if we could talk more customers into buying. What a practical way to learn about business!"

An autogiro, like the *Des Moines Register and Tribune*'s

To **Mr. Doctorov**, Warren also wrote:

"A memorable time each year was when my parents took me to the Iowa State Fair. One year in front of the grandstand in highly advertised 'Thrill Day' events, crackups of locomotives would be staged. Or cars smashing into each other. Or parachutists would come down from the skies and land right in front of us. Auto racing was always the main event. But what I liked was eluding my parents and going alone to the freak shows' conjurers and city slicker-types, who talked us small town kids and naive farmers into paying to see the bearded lady, the giant, the pinhead, the dwarf, the elephant man, and others whom today I call 'exceptional people,' not freaks."

Paul Senter, West Grand Towers, 3663 Grand Ave. (#206), Des Moines, IA 50312-4336, a farm boy 5 days younger, accompanied Warren to the Iowa State Fair, August 30th, 1939.

Paul Senter
and Warren Allen Smith
at Iowa State Fairgrounds

23

"**Harry Smith** parked in a lot a distance away, and as he, Mrs. Smith, Warren, and I headed for the ticket booths we witnessed a Piper Cub flying low near the main auditorium and race track. Too low, it clipped some wires on a pole and crashed right in front of us.

With cameras, we rushed over and took a photo of the two still in the cabin, alive but bleeding.

We took photos from all angles, then after getting permission from Warren's parents raced to the newspaper's fairgrounds office which was always at the same spot (and near one that annually featured a cow made of butter).

We raced up to the desk of the man we recognized as **George Yates** and explained about the pictures we'd just shot.

Yates had lots of questions, but when he heard Radio WHO announce word of the crash he asked if the people were dead. No, we didn't think so.

So he said something like, "Good job, kids, here's money ($2?), take a taxi and rush to the R&T building downtown."

We ran to the main entrance to get a taxi.

But what do teenagers from a small town know about taxis!

So we took a 5-cent streetcar and got on board with Mr. Yates's money and sped away.

Stopped at the newspaper's front desk downtown, we dropped the name, "George Yates sent us!"

Someone took the film, thanked us, and we got back to the streetcar and the fairgrounds, having missed some thrills but secretly pocketing the change.

Following are two of the photos:

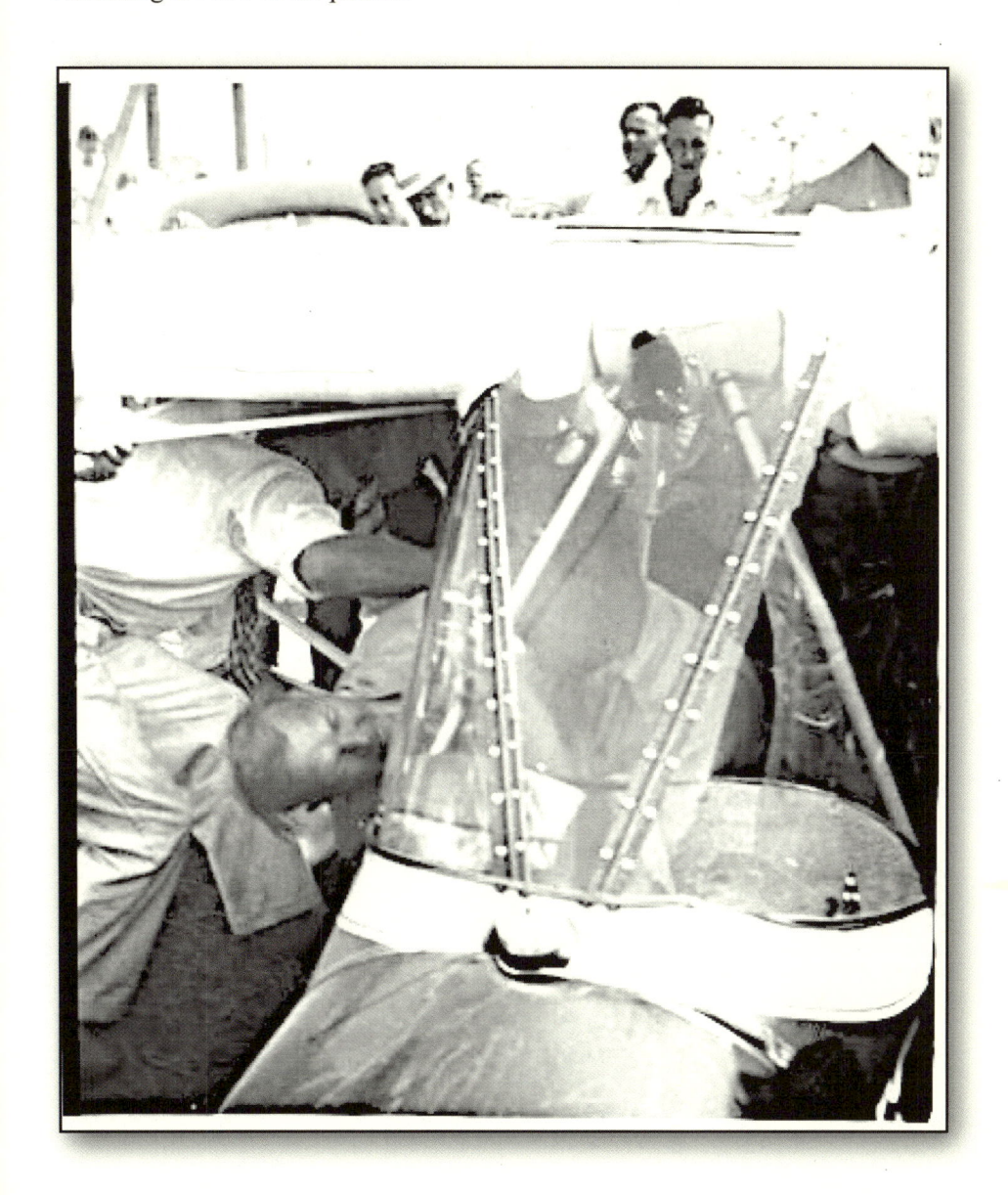

Photo by Warren Smith and Paul Senter

Photo by Paul Senter and Warren Smith
Thrill Day, Iowa State Fair, 1939

Following is Paul's June 2006 recollection:

> Believe the day was called "Thrill Day" at the Grandstand.
>
> I also have poor pictures of activities like Jimmie Lynch driving through flaming wall. Driving cars with one side on ramp and on driving on two wheels. Cars jumping over trucks. Also circus acts.
>
> The plane, as I recall, was to land in front of Grandstand as one of the final acts for the day.
>
> At the time of the crash around noon he was practicing touching down on track, then circle around and do it again.
>
> Believe we were standing east of Grandstand, and as he came around he could not gain enough altitude to clear the wires along the north side of track.
>
> He then attempted to go under the wires; however, he struck the top of cars and crashed on roadway about 50 feet from cars he had hit the tops of.
>
> We took off running to crash site which was only probably 200 feet at most. He sort of flew over our heads.
>
> I think we were at the east end of racetrack to get a better look at his practicing to land later on in day. We then headed to the R & T Building with our picture and downtown.
>
> Came back for the afternoon Grandstand performance that started at 2 in those days."

Paul thinks no picture was ever published, but Warren clearly remembers seeing the one they took that shows people trying to get the plane's occupant out.

Fred Meyer, 401 4th Avenue North, Humboldt, Iowa 50548

Mr. Meyer and a Rippey High School student, Vada Smith (daughter of Harry Smith - the *other* Harry Smith who lived in Rippey)

(June 13, 2006; **Mr. Meyer** telephoned):

Yes, Warren, I remember you in my typing and business classes when Supt. **Cale Ransom** allowed you to take a post-grad year at Rippey High School after you graduated from Minburn High School and your dad took the new job of managing the grain elevator in Rippey. It was in 1949, and then Mr. Ransom put you in a car and got you enrolled at Iowa State Teachers College in Cedar Falls, where he and I also had attended. I'm glad to hear that his son, Lowell, is still alive and was a librarian at the University of Wisconsin. Yes, I remember **Paul Senter** – you say he's the one who told you my address? That's interesting.

You say I'm your oldest living teacher? Well, that's interesting. No, I no longer type and I don't have a computer. I do remember you were a fast typist but also that you were the best pianist in town. You played at school and also for the Methodists. You were one of many I took home with me on weekends to meet my family and see the movie theater we owned. It's still going strong, and I sell tickets three times a week there.

I'm 90, going on 91, so I guess I'm only 5 years older than you. Rippey was my first job after I graduated. I now have grandchildren. My wife, who taught in the grades at Rippey, died two years ago. During the war, I was in the quartermaster's part of **General Patton**'s office, traveling with him all across France. Fortunately, I never got shot, and I got to Paris and took my typewriter everywhere I went. My job included taking orders for supplies from everyone in our command – clothing, gas, food, for example.

Where did we get our supplies? What do you mean? Are you saying that we got everything from Hq. Oise, where you were Chief Clerk of the Adjutant General's Office? Now, that's interesting. You mean that if Patton's 3rd needed gas or any other supplies, it was your headquarters in Reims that got the order and filled it? Now, that's interesting. I never knew that. You say you never studied business except with me in high school, and you got into the book, *Who's Who in Business and Finance*? I didn't know that.

I didn't know you had a recording studio. Didn't know you taught English. I have my family around me here, I help at Christmas when the busloads of people come to our special programs, and I have lots of grandchildren.

Sorry I didn't understand at the beginning when you said you were absent from my class today and you wondered if I had noticed – I couldn't figure out who was calling. Yes, do call again. I enjoyed talking with you tonight.

Goodnight, and call again.

At the age of 96, Mr. Meyer died on 9 February 2012, survived by his children, Ken Meyer of Dakota City, Jerry (Shirley) Meyer of Humboldt, and Joalyn (Monte) Cunningham of Humboldt. He was preceded in death by his parents, and his wife, Margery.

1940s

I enlisted into the U. S. Army in Jefferson, Iowa, on 27 June 1942 and served until 7 January 1946. I served 3 years, 6 months, and 11 days.

Florence Dellagnola, c/o Chalon Whyte, 1643 Warnall Ave., Los Angeles, CA 90024

> [A response by her daughter upon learning that Sgt. Dellagnola, one of Warren's WAC clerks at Hq. Oise in the Adjutant General's Office, of which he was Chief Clerk, had died of liver cancer in 1988.]

(August 15, 2005) I was absolutely delighted to receive in the mail today a letter that you sent to my cousin, **David Dellagnola**. The original letter was dated 8/10/04 with a follow-up note in your handwriting, dated 7/11/05. I am Florence's daughter, Chalon. My husband and I live in Los Angeles. My brother, **Dennis**, who is two years older than me, lives in Salt Lake City.

Florence died of liver cancer in 1988. She was at home when she died and my brother and I were with her. Since I returned home to Los Angeles right after her funeral, I never got ahold of her address book to let her friends know about her passing. I do remember mom telling me that she had several good friends that she spent time with when she was stationed in France. Even though she grew up in the same small town as my father, **Daniel**, she didn't get to know him well until they met in France and started dating. When they were discharged from the service in 1945, they got married and settled down in Salt Lake City. **Dennis** was born in 1946 and I came along in 1948. They named me after a small town in France near where my dad was stationed. Did you ever meet Dad?

Unfortunately, my mom and I were not that close when I was growing up and I moved away from home when I was 20, so we never got to know each other as adults. Also, if you have any other questions about her, I would be glad to try to answer them. Thank you so much for making the effort to contact us.

[Warren responded to Flo's daughter.]

(August 16, 2005) That's beautiful to learn. I also knew about Chalons, once having been sent by the Adjutant General to stop a flood there (or maybe it was Epernay), one that was going to damage the new postal depot we were setting up. So how do you stop a flood? You follow your general's orders, of course. I took several dozen Nazi prisoners to the building, which formerly had been a motorcycle garage. They filled sand bags and I formed them into a Henry Ford line – the one at the head of the line handed the bags to #2, and on down the line to the last guy (one who was not cooperative, so he had the toughest job because the rest would complain if he held things up) – at noon I had them heat K-rations in a kettle of hot water so everyone had a hot meal, all but the one guy, who got a cold can.

Flo and I frequently had drinks after work, and maybe we were close because, although WACs were all considered promiscuous (the soldiers hoped, although there was little evidence, not that I was looking for it), your mom was comfortable around me – at that time, I didn't know I was gay. I can still in my mind's eye see us going night after night to the same little bar near our Reims caserne, the bartender-owner loved us, he suggested champagne as a chaser for our favorite stiff drink, which we called White Lightning (maybe Cointreau?). As the Adjutant General's chief clerk, I carried all kinds of secrets because our office had the personnel files. I had to tell someone some secrets, of course, so Flo was the one. "Brown has just been made G-2 in addition to AG," I told her once. "This means he's also in charge of all the military police." Your mom was a good listener. "And he's asked me to take his Packard and drive up to Belgium to pick up his British girlfriend." Your mom and I knew this was illegal, but an AG has great power and also being G-2 knew which border patrol guard for me to pass through. So I did drive the Packard up to Bruxelles, I called his girlfriend and lied that the car had broken down and needed two days to be fixed, and learned she was happy because she wasn't quite ready to go anyway. So I picked her up two days later, after enjoying the sites and sights of Belgium's capital city and enjoying being able to get something the French didn't have: ice cream. The car, of course, had always worked beautifully.

So what did the AG do to Sgt. Smith when he returned late? Why, of course, he promoted me. That's the way life works.

[Warren also had written to Florence's son, **Dennis Caulfield**, 8968 North Cove Drive, Park City, Utah 84098]:

(24 August 1996): Your mom and I exchanged year-end greetings from 1946 or so until perhaps the 1980s. If I recall correctly, she complained about her health in a 1961 letter. Well, yes, Florence had a life before becoming your mother. And if I take some time to reminisce, it's because she was one of the few of the GIs I kept in touch with after the war. Incidentally, in 1994 on the anniversary of D-Day, I returned to Omaha Beach (with Hillary, Bill, quite a few kings, queens, presidents, and the like, including Walter Cronkite). A Norman family near the beach (**Dadda Abdesalem**, 99 Rue Andre Malraux, 14400, Bayeux, France) volunteered to let me stay with them, and it was quite an experience (inasmuch as the father was a black Moroccan, the mother a white Normandy gal with two children, and no one else spoke English – their new un-named cat I had the privilege of naming **Pepsi**). I journeyed on to Reims, where I was able to see **Jean-Marie Picard**, my little buddy (now a retired executive of Moët Champagne), the one to whom I taught English as well as to his sister, **Simone**.

She and I worked in Headquarter Oise, the group responsible for supplying the various divisions (including captured Poles as well as the French, English, etc., in our area of Europe). Although I'm not sure when your mother arrived in Reims, I was picked from a replacement depot (a "repple depple") by the Adjutant General on the basis of my being able to type over 113 wpm on a non-electric!

So I was one of the first into the building on Rue Voltaire (named after my favorite philosopher, it turns out; although if I recall correctly Florence was a churchgoer; I had "none" as my religion on my dogtags and was a true "atheist in a foxhole."). I am not sure if Florence was in my department (with the Adjutant General) or in another – our friend **Joe Sczesny** was in G-4 supply), and **Guy Ansbach** was in another office altogether. At any rate, it's possible that Florence was somewhere in the AG's big department. She must have had a clerical job, in short. In fact, I used to tease her that I could type faster.

We lived at first in a caserne near a champagne company's cellars. When "bedcheck Charlie" (a Nazi small plane that simply flew over in the middle of the night to wake the entire city up, and the most he ever dropped were flares) appeared, the air raid signals would go off. We got to go into the champagne cellars until the all-clear. Except early on, the company complained to our commandant that they were missing some bottles. The major, of course, called us all out at 04:30 and demanded that the culprit(s) step forward. No one did. We all got docked and from then on had to stay above ground during air raids! Perhaps Florence told you that story, for gossip had it that it was the WACs who'd done the damage.

You must have heard about the WACs. Two summers ago at Omaha Beach, I heard from many nurses and other members of the Women's Army Corps that they never revealed to folks back home that they'd been a WAC. The general consensus was that all WACs were either lesbians or prostitutes. Being a Voltaire man, of course, I seldom agreed with the general consensus. And the only two WACs I particularly remember were Florence and **Corporal Fuqua** (who took a beating on the pronunciation!). Both were hard-working, **ambitious**, patriotic gals with excellent reputations and certainly not sexually active, I'm sure you'll be interested in hearing. Then again, perhaps they chummed with me because I didn't represent a threat – I didn't at that time actually understand what homosexuality was, but I would never have made a pass at either. (Groping a fellow guy, well, that was another matter. But no one but no one suspected this at that time, nor have I mentioned it to other GIs since.)

Our caserne may have changed once, and as I recall both males and females lived in the same buildings except there was no mingling. Florence would, like all of us, have probably gotten up at 06:00, had a very big breakfast in the mess hall, and been at our desks by 08:00. Meanwhile, thousands of guys were sleeping out in the rain with sleeping bags and fighting real live enemies 24 hours a day.

Florence and our office group, however, slept between sheets, had clean clothing, and lived a fairly normal life.

At 17:00 or so, Florence and I would meet with perhaps a few of the others I've named, and we'd head for the evening mess but would stop at a little French bar first. I was the most fluent in French, so I'd order "white lightning" with champagne for a chaser. Reims is the center of the champagne country, and champagne was ridiculously cheap. We'd sit around the little bar and shoot the breeze, telling stories about the officers or what happened during the day or how a *kermesse* (a street fair) might be occurring somewhere.

This became a nightly habit, stopping by the bar, and the owner loved to see us because we were the ones who'd kicked the Nazis out of town, etc., and he'd ask for the latest news – our *Stars and Stripes* newspaper was far more accurate than the local journals. I'd love to be able to find that same bar, for I've many good memories of sitting with your mom, hearing about Mormons in Utah, etc. It was a small place like something out of a French movie, and a cigarette always dangled from the owner's moistened lip (if we'd supply him with our cigarettes). He'd converse without removing the cigarette.

When I met 15-year-old **Jean-Marie Picard**, who wanted to learn English and had come to the caserne on the pretense of wanting to play Bridge, I eventually got invited to his home and met his parents. Papa (**René Picard**) was a *commandant* (major) who had served in the French Foreign Legion and, when captured by the Nazis, fled from a railroad train taking him to Buchenwald and successfully eluded his captors. Maman (**Marie Thèrése Picard**) was a loving intellectual. **Simone** was an awkward but friendly gal (who married a major in our G-2 office and eventually accompanied him to the U. of Virginia, where he taught French). One day I somehow got the AG's chauffeur (**Poole Jones**) to get not only the grocery supplies for the general but also to get some extras so we could have a party at the Picards' house. When I took an entire ham, a bag of potatoes, coffee, oranges, etc., to Papa Picard's place, he was scared to death, not having seen so much food since before the war. In fact, he told me to leave, that surely the GIs would knock on the door, much as the Nazis had, and search the house. Eventually, I convinced him all was OK and that Florence, Guy, the chauffeur, and I would come the following night and we'd devour all the stolen booty. Surely enough, we had the party. But we made a point of not eating much, and the Picards had enough for the rest of the week!

I remember Florence sitting at the piano with me, for she hadn't known I play. Papa, in fact, got out his violin and we performed Beethoven together. But he was a severe and law-abiding man, not too happy at what was happening (stolen food), and he was a 101% Catholic (in charge of the St. Vincent de Paul charities at the Reims Cathedral, the fantastic building in which all the kings of France had been crowned)!

I won him over by writing to a hometown Iowa newspaper and getting farmers to send literally a ton of food and clothing for Papa's *veuves* (widows) and other destitute people. When he introduced me to the **Archbishop**, His Excellency was surprised that I did not bow or kiss the ring etc. "*Vous êtes Protestant?*" No. "*Juif?*" No. "Then why have you helped?" So I told him I was a Unitarian (like Jefferson and Emerson) whose favorite philosopher was Voltaire.

It would have made a great scene in a movie, for everyone else was quite uncomfortable, and I was having a great time! Incidentally, the Archbishop was possibly gay . . . but not, aha, my type! To explain, I didn't really get into gay matters until after the war when I went to Columbia University . . . and met a Costa Rican the very first week, and we lived together for 40 years until his death in 1989).

So, Dennis Caulfield, these are my two main memories of your mom: our nightly tete-a-tetes at the colorful little bar, and the party at the Picards. However, I remember her as being a true buddy, an upstanding gal, a person with a marvelous laugh, one who listened intently to whoever was talking, one that everyone respected. We critics hesitate to be so positive without adding some negatives in order to balance. But, Dennis, I can't really think of one negative. You're brilliant to have chosen her as your mom, Dennis. There must have been *something* wrong with her that I could relate, but I honestly, honestly can't think of one thing. Now, about everyone else I've cited in this letter, well, I could dish for pages!

Sgt. Smith at the head of the 40 & 8 railroad cars

I am the Acting 1st Sergeant, and the train is waiting for another one going the other way and filled with Nazi prisoners caught in north Africa to pass on their way back to the beach to be shipped to England for jailing.

The 40 & 8 French boxcars could hold 40 men or 8 horses.

Guy Ansbach, 679 Maryland Ave., York, PA 17404
[Sgt. Ansbach, who worked in Oise Hq's G-4, is the only Army buddy that Warren knows is alive. However, ever since he sent him an atheistic Christmas card one year, Ansbach has refused to respond to any mail. During the war, the two traveled in a jeep to Maastricht, Holland; Aachen, Germany; and Luxembourg City all in one day. On other occasions, he and Sgt. Sczesny commandeered a Postal Service jeep and spent weekends free in Paris.]

Warren driving Sgt. Ansbach in a commandeered Peep
(smaller than a Jeep)

Sgt. Smith on an errand for the Adjutant General,
about to pass into Belgium
with the AG's Packard.

A Department of Champagne rural highway,
like nothing back in Iowa.
Staff Sergeant Smith wears the Hq. Oise insignia.

Warren with other visiting GIs
at the Arc de Triomphe

A pisser at a pissoir

Fernando Rodolfo de Jesus Vargas Zamorra, 244 West 103rd St., New York, NY 25
[A letter to Warren's parents in Iowa, July 15, 1952]

Dear Ruth and Harry, Thank you for the nice time I had in Rippey. Warren was good to stop the car every time we saw pigs. I liked riding the bicycle in town and in the country. I am glad I met your sister, **Hazel** from South Dakota.

We made it back in our little Renault with the motor in back. I am sorry I spilled the watermelon onto your clean kitchen floor. When you come to New York, I will take Harry out to see dose Dodgers. Where we now live is *apartmento* of mistress of former **Costa Rica Presidente Calderón**. **Warren** is always typing. Come see us. **Fernando**

AUGUST, 1953

"Ioway, Ioway, *that's* where the tall corn grows!"

Although entombed in Costa Rica, some of Fernando's cremains are to be mixed in with Warren's at the Smith plot in Waukee, Iowa.

41

Fernando and Warren
(1950?)

[A letter from Warren's father to Fernando, dated 12 18 62. **Harry Clark Smith** (1887-1975) played third base for the Portland farm team of Chicago Cubs in the 1910s and had a .400 batting average.]

     Dear Fernando: - This is the time of year when we seem to think more about and of our dearest friends, and cannot help but be reminded of the years that have rolled around since that Sunday afternoon that you and I spent in Brooklyn, especially the very interesting and instructive ramblings through that park, & of course to finish off the afternoon with Dem Dodgers.
     We are having lots of base-ball in Rippey in the last few years, with always having a real good Town Team, which had an exceptionally good team this last year, and then with Rippey's wonderful baseball grounds, & being centrally located in the State, we get a lot of the State High School tournaments, in fact we have had three years in the last 6 years of the final State Championship games for high school.
     Well I had thought that we would surely have been back to see you & Warren before this, maybe this next year.

     As ever, **Harry** (Secretary, Elmo Lodge No. 465, A. F. & A. M., Rippey Iowa)

Fernando in the Wasmobile

Warren's girlfriend **Mary Womboldt**, ISTC's 1940s beauty queen.

Warren and English Teacher **Judy Repplier**
They drove her Beatle from New Canaan to Iowa
to meet Warren's parents, then on to Boulder, Colorado, to
meet her parents.

1950s

Warren and **Yakimo**,
1940s in Montana

Bill Keller (son of ex-Police Chief Henry E. "Red" Keller), 26622 Via Noveno, Mission Viejo, CA 92691 (949) 830-4657

[Following is a 1997 letter to Warren Allen Smith.]

Back in 1958, I was in an English class I thought I'd never pass. It was the first class that ever really challenged me, and I vividly remember a teacher who among a few others set the course for the rest of my life! I wrote a term paper, "The Violent Skills of Ice Hockey," tough work and of average quality, but I knew it made an impact because you and a raccoon coat and a little MG roadster never missed a game of ours.

Your interest in my becoming the best that I could directed me to teach, and I have never been sorry for that choice in the past 33 years.

[It is believed that Bill went to Springfield College, then the U of Southern California, earning an M.S. in biology. A laureate in DNA research, he became a teacher and a coach at Mission Viejo High School in Mission Viejo, California.

Married to **Janet Fox** ('62 NCHS). They have a 6' 5" soccer goalie son at Point Loma college in San Diego who wants to be a teacher like his dad. On Smith's first day in Connecticut, he parked his car in front of the postoffice and got a parking ticket from one of Chief Keller's officers.]

Below, Smith in New Canaan's smallest house, the home that he called not a 2- or a 1-room but a ½ room.

Also, with his parents, **Ruth and Harry C. Smith**, at their home in Iowa.

1960s

July 9, 1960, "Trade Winds" in *Saturday Review of Literature* – a column by John G. Fuller (1913-1990), a New Canaan Resident

John G. Fuller

Not long ago, we received a note from the **Hvmanist Book Clvb, XXVII Millport Avenue, New Canaan, Connecticut** – Lucretius, President; Jun Sczesnoczkawasm, Relations; Fernando Jesus Vargas, Sales:

    Dear Mr. Fuller: One of our more dissident customers has posed a problem which apparently only you can settle. She is one of your fans, I take it, for she refuses to take our money and insists that it be sent to you. Hazel Blek, of Watertown, S.D., ordered $14.50 worth of books and sent us a check, swearing that she qualified for our club because (1) she had resigned from two other book clubs, (2) had written at least one nasty letter to a book club.
    However, we have standards, too. One of our requirements is that customers must take discounts on all books whose prices would have been lower had the book clubs not gotten there first (10% off list price; 15% off orders of over $15; 25% off over $25 worth of books, all postpaid). Thus Mrs. Blek has $1.45 coming from us, but she refuses to accept it, saying she already has her money's worth. We decided we would let her remain a customer if she would donate the amount to some worthy cause. She has chosen you for, in her words, your "wit must surely go unappreciated in the more provincial cities like New York."
    Although we first thought of granting you credit, this would mean your name would go on our mailing lists, and we have no way of telling if you satisfy our stringent requirements for membership. Thus, will you kindly cash the enclosed check?

Thank you. Thine, (Signed) **Lucretius**

Since we had never heard before of the Hvmanist Book Clvb, to say nothing of Mrs. Blek, we tried to find more about an organization which defies every rule of business ethics so brilliantly. A mimeographed catalogue indicated that the club offers serious books exclusively (Bertrand Russell, Sigmund Freud, Camus, Fromm, Dewey, etc.), but has no phone listing whatever. The check, signed "Lucretius," seemed bona fide enough, drawn as it was on the Fairfield County Trust Company. We confirmed the fact that there was such an account, and that the mere signature "Lucretius" was entirely valid and acceptable. With some difficulty, we were able to find a phone number at the "XXVII" address, and were greeted by a pleasant, disembodied voice at the other end of the wire, which cautiously admitted that the Hvmanist Book Clvb "uses my mailbox" for their venture. The voice was amply informed, however, on the operation of the business.

"As I understand it," the voice said, "the book club is more or less a satire on big business, and the way it's run. Most of the customers are college professors, who enjoy a good joke while they buy the books they need. When the club gets a letter from the Harvard University Press, the greeting is always *Salve*! Lucretius, of course, always signs his letters "Thine" – although he has to admit begrudgingly that he stole the idea from Archibald MacLeish. He also likes to break all the rules, and to insult customers politely. There's nothing he likes better than to scold a buyer for a poor choice of books. He also insists that customers must write witty letters when they order, or at least *try*. His best-sellers are Walter Kaufmann's *The Critique of Religion and Philosophy*, Bertrand Russell's *Why I Am Not A Christian*, and *The Book of Job as a Greek Tragedy*.

"Lucretius is always mumbling about being Chairman of the Committee to Re-Institute Single Names by Abolishing Praenomens and Cognomens, and he's very sensitive and easily miffed. He hates to talk, that's why he doesn't have a phone. One customer drove all the way from Ohio to see if there were Roman numerals on the doorway. There aren't."

Even though we were able to talk only to the disembodied voice, who denied being Lucretius, we are at least able to report: (1) Yes, Virginia, there *is* a Hvmanist Book Clvb; (2) It has some of the most prominent writers and educators here and abroad as its customers; and (3) Its checks are good in spite of being signed only "Lucretius."

John G. Fuller   Author, *The UFO Incident*

[Mr. Smith claims the $1.45 cost of sub-rosa advertising in a major literary journal was well-worth it.]

In 1967, as the English Department chairman during which called "the Golden Age," with his department he devised the following summer reading list for all students.

Honor and AP students over the summer are required to read and report on a minimum of 4 books; academic students 3; track-2 students, 2; all others, 1.

Although each grade had optional books that could be read, the following were "required" and would be included in tests:

9th : *Huckleberry Finn, Great Expectations, The Odyssey* (Fitzgerald)
10th : *Iliad; Antigone; Oedipus Rex; Julius Caesar (*or *Romeo and Juliet; Cyrano de Bergerac; Old Man and the Sea*
11th : *Red Badge of Courage; Ben Franklin's Autobiography; Death of a Salesman; Macbeth; Walden; Great Gatsby*
12th : *Tess* or *Return of the Native; Animal Farm; Hamlet; any Shaw play; Fathers and Children; Brave New World; Metamorphosis;* Hayakawa's *Language in Thought and Action*

In 1961, Fernando Vargas and Warren founded Variety Recording Studio on 46th Street, recording **Liza Minnelli**'s first demo plus **Paul Simon, Barry Manilow, David Amram**, etc.; burned by arsonists in 1968, the studio became a 48-track on 42nd Street just off Broadway

1970s

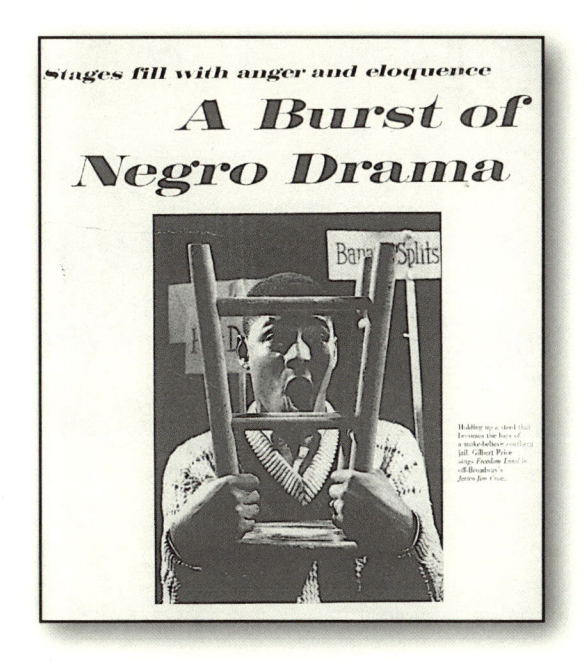

(An article in *Life*)

Gilbert Price, 2075 Second Ave., (14B), NYC 10029

Gilbert Price, *Jericho-Jim Crow* [*Life*]; Sweater loaned by Warren Allen Smith (1964).

"*Timbuktu*" (1978), Gown by **Geoffrey Holder**.

(28 February 1978, handwritten note): "Warren, rent a limo and pick Mom and my aunt and uncle up tomorrow night. Take them to the Hellinger, park, then get back before the opening. Afterwards Geoffrey [Holder] is going to want us to go to Sardi's, and I think I'm not going – y'know, Melba's [Moore] monkeying with my mike and the polyps I got. Mom will be furious. Instead, take them afterwards over near the river downtown to the Boondocks, which has live music, OK? Counting on ya!" Gil

[Gil and Warren were paramours from 1964 until his accidental death from asphyxiation in Austria by a faulty propane heater. Price was a 3-time Tony Award nominee: *Roar of the Greasepaint* (1965); *The Night That Made America Famous* (1972); and *Timbuktu* (1978)].

Premier Edward O. LeBlanc of Dominica in the West Indies – his Canadian biographer, **Judge Irving W. André,** asked Warren to write the book's foreword.

Simon Blanc, whom Warren helped bring here from Dominica in 1976. He earned his G.E.D. and got his Bachelor of Science at a Connecticut university.

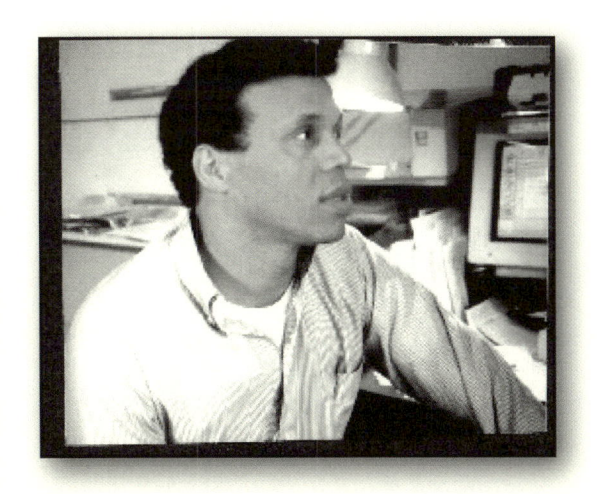

1980s

Heather Beutel Fortinbery, California, {NCHS '83}

Unfortunately I don't recall any stories or anecdotal portrayals of Mr. Smith other than he scared the #$@% out of me because of the tightly wrapped intellectual air that seemed to permeate around his head.

He was certainly the one high school teacher who brought me to my knees, as if in prayer, with me bowing reverently, hoping that he might extend to me a similar respect. **Heather**

Geoff Cox, PMP, MBA, BSEE, Virginia
[Director of Project Management, GridPoint, Inc.; Member, National Association of Realtors; Editor & Coordinator, M-**Investment** Club; Member, Washington Area Mensa; President, Lochewood Manor HOA]

I remember Warren as a friend for years through the M-Investment Club, where we traded roles back and forth between newsletter editor and chairman of the Mensa interest group. I never actually met him in person until his 80th Birthday Party in DC, where I recall he showed up looking spiffy in his tux, but without any studs!   :)   **Geoff**

Robert DePasquale, Manhattan, New York [Fellow humanist]

I first met Warren decades ago while he was publishing his humanist newsletter, *Pique*. Warren was working on his amazing book, *Who's Who In Hell*, and needed help with computer problems. I let Warren borrow a 2-volume edition of *History of Freethought, Ancient and Modern* (2 vols, 1915) by J. M. Robertson. (I bought the set from a street vendor in New York City!) I helped with typo's and spellings in his original text. Warren graciously gave me a credit and included a quote of mine in the book!

Warren Smith is a brilliant man, a great influence, and a great teacher. Thank you, Warren, for being.   **Robert**

Thom Weidlich, Manhattan, New York City
[Author; reporter, *Bloomfield News*]

Here's a sad fact: I don't remember when I met Warren! It would have been at a Bertrand Russell Society meeting. I joined in 1986. He was probably at the first meeting I was, which was in New York.

I have very fond memories of Warren at BRS meetings. He's always interesting and interested and always has something fun to say. He has been kind enough to chauffeur me around at meetings, since he usually rents a car. A few years ago we drove together from New York to the meeting in New Hampshire. I was afraid he'd drive too slow. He drove too fast! But we lived to tell the tale (and made it safely to the meeting).

One time about four years ago I was up at Warren's apartment with some others. Tim Madigan was there. We went up to Warren's roof, which has a great view of the city. All of a sudden, things went dark. There was a fire in the Con Edison plant on 14th Street and the electricity went out in the West Village, including in his building. We had to walk all the way down the stairs in the dark. Warren took it all in with his usual nonchalance and aplomb. Happy birthday, Warren!

Thom

1990s

[Warren wrote book jacket blurbs for **Isaac Asimov**'s *It's Been A Good Life* (2002) and wife **Janet Jeppson Asimov**'s *Notes for a Memoir on Isaac Asimov, Life, and Writing* (2006). Both attended meetings in the 1990s of the Secular Humanist Society of New York, of which Warren was President.]

Janet J. Asimov, New York City

Warren is a wonderful, accomplished human who is smarter, more talented, and a few years older than I am. I don't mind. What I mind is that he LOOKS YOUNGER than I do. Ah well, Warren, I forgive you. Happy Birthday and many more,

Janet

The **"Rochester gang"** of fellow Bertrand Russell Society members at an international BRS meeting, Lake Forest College in Illinois, 2004:

Phil Ebersole is on the left, middle row
Peter Stone is 2nd from the left, middle row
Alan Bock is 3rd from the left, middle row
David White is 4th from the left, middle row
Tim Madigan is 2nd from the right, middle row
Warren is at the end on the right, middle row

Tim Madigan, Rochester, New York
[Dr. Madigan teaches philosophy and religion at several Rochester, New York, colleges]

I first met Warren "in the heart of showbiz" when I visited his recording studio on 42nd Street. He was organizing a secular humanist group for New York City subscribers to *Free Inquiry* magazine, which I was helping to edit at the time. This was during the heyday of "the Deuce's" sleazy era and Warren kindly led me – like Virgil leading Dante in *The Inferno* – through many explorations of the area before Mayor Giuliani so unkindly cleaned everything up. It was an historic time.

I have since made it my business to visit Warren as often as I can, and he also visited me in Buffalo and Rochester on several occasions. We've traveled together to various places, from San Jose, Costa Rica, to New Orleans, Louisiana (pre-Katrina), to Minburn, Iowa. He is the perfect traveling companion – always with a quip on his lips, a desire to investigate every nook and cranny, and, best of all, an impeccable sense of direction.

It has been my pleasure to act as Warren's editor on several occasions, particularly when he wrote a regular gossip column for *Free Inquiry*, and I was delighted to be invited by him to write the foreword to his magnum opus, *Who's Who in Hell*. A fascinating compendium of facts, speculations and autobiographical ramblings, the book ranks with *Tristram Shandy* as an unclassifiable, multi-faceted tour de force.

To me, Warren is the quintessential New Yorker – sophisticated, blasé, witty, and never fazed by anything. I have learned more about *the* City from my gallivanting about with him than any other way, and I've seen some sights that very few tourists ever get to see! But I've also had the pleasure – along with my colleague **Dr. David White** – of going across Warren's native state of Iowa with him, seeing his birthplace, his first college, and a good part of the land from whence he came. I have to say, the old song "How You Gonna Keep 'Em Down on the Farm" came to mind. Thank "god" the G. I. Bill brought Warren to the Big Apple, the only place on earth where he truly could be at home.

Warren is my inspiration. Like him, I hope that I too can become a noted sybarite and roué. But the term which most captures him – a term he has spent a good part of his long life exploring – is "humanist." He is a lover of the arts, a freethinker, a social activist, a compassionate and caring humanitarian, and a true friend. Warren Allen Smith is a humanist in every sense of the word. He's even inspired me to write a poem, which I trust captures his fascination with all things Hellish:

> There once was fellow named Warren,
> Whose life was exciting, not borin'.
> He was born in Minburn,
> And his "soul" will return
> To a land that to Heaven is foreign!

Happy 85th birthday – we'll be celebrating many subsequent ones as well.

Tim

J. Alan Bock - Rochester, NY - Attorney and Legal Editor, Retired

I understand that many of the contributors to your celebratory event or "Festschrift" are former students of yours who have recorded their edifying experiences under your tutelage.

Alas, I have no such experience to relate since I was never one of your students. And there is the rub. I wish that I could have been.

I have tentatively entitled one of the chapters of my memoirs (which I'll probably never finish) as "*Mater et Magistra*," which will describe my parochial school religious experience – an experience I subsequently had to "unlearn." How much more beneficial it would have been for me if, instead of a "*Mater et Magistra*" indoctrinating me with dubious religious doctrines, I had, instead, experienced a "*Pater et Magistra*" inculcating me with Russellian wisdom. I would never have experienced an arrested intellectual development. Oh well, better late than never.

I set forth below my brief lament for my "Smithless" education:

> My education was blighted;
> I was taught a myth;
> My path would have been lighted,
> If I'd had a Smith
> To teach me truly and well
> All the facts of Hell.

Happy 85th birthday. May you live at least as long as Bertie.

Alan

Peter Stone

Dr. Stone taught political theory at Stanford U in California.

I've been a member of the Bertrand Russell Society for 15 years, and in that time I've missed only one Annual Meeting. Warren is one of the reasons why I come back year after year. One of the best parts of attending is the unofficial philosophical salon that fills all the nooks and crannies of each meeting. And it's hard to think of anyone who belongs at a philosophical salon more than Warren. He should be on anyone's list of "top ten people to invite to a dinner party," alongside Bertrand Russell, Mark Twain, Tom Paine, Voltaire, and Tori Amos. (OK, that last one's a personal preference, I admit….)

But the salon runs year round. I've had the pleasure of seeing New York City numerous times under Warren's guidance. (He treated my wife Rachel and me to a drink at Sardi's; my mother, who was born and raised in the Big Apple but has never been to Sardi's, was green with envy when she learned of this.) He has enlivened the Greater Rochester Russell Set on many occasions, including his memorable trip to Buffalo to collect the statue, *The Humanist*. I hope it is only a matter of time before he visits us out at the Bay Area Russell Set. (I'm sure he'd love the chance to see Rachel again. He seems to find her almost as fascinating as I do.)

One can gain almost as much from Warren's books as one can from talking to him. *Who's Who in Hell* is a fun book to which I wound up contributing an entry. Quite inadvertently, I might add. Warren wrote to me at a time when I hardly knew him and asked me to go on record as to my views about God and the afterlife. The contents of my reply are in the Good Book. As an inadvertent entry-writer, I'm in the company of Bertrand Russell and Thomas Mann. One can also get a lot out of Warren's other books as well – although my dad picked up *Cruising the Deuce* a few months ago, and found it to be a little more information than he needed….

Warren has greatly enriched the lives of all those around him, myself included, with his experience, his wit, and his readiness for a little conversation. And he's had a wonderful time doing it. I can only hope to be in the same position when I'm 85. Happy Birthday, Warren.

Peter

Gunter P. Jaenicke, P O Box 612, Port Coquiliam, BC., V3B-6H9, Canada

[*Who's Who in Hell* (2000) resulted in many interviews (including one that was televised by CNN's Jeanne Moos), radio discussions, TV talks, and lectures throughout the States as well as in Costa Rica and Canada. One who heard him sent the following on 4 July 2006, "Although I never had the privilege to meet Warren, I enclose with my best wishes one of my poems."]

The Meaning of Life

Much has been written about the meaning of life . . .
As well the reason for working between nine & five...

Much has been written but little makes sense. . .
The " best we must make of" - as well as some friends...

For the believer in life after death . . . it is said
While burning in hell and gnashing of teeth the skeptic will get...

Why would one care about life "after" death...
Much more important it seems that there is life after birth is my guess...

Contrary & in spite what preachers claim and say...
That their doctrines, opinions are the only way...

They do preach water - but drink wine...
The clergy & the priesthood think it's fine...

They do preach love - but practice hate...
The dying child because unbaptised - is " denied" the pearly gate...

Life has no purpose & no meaning...
Regardless of beliefs - religious leaning...

As days & month & years go by...
As decades, life like seconds fly...

For those of us who do get old...
To learn from past mistakes will hold...
Life's only meaning is one ourselves we give...
Caring for others - loving and the way we live...
Life's only purpose is the purpose we do give...
Void of religion love makes - what is worthwhile there to live...

Mankind lives for today - not for tomorrow...
The promises for paradise and afterlife are just assumptions & are hollow...

Without those lords, gods, masters we are free...
To give life meaning it is up to us - for us to be...

The meaning of ones life - is what one does today...
While ethics, tolerance & caring must apply to every day....

Doug Fishbone, London, UK   [Warren's Greenwich Village neighbor; he is an avant-garde artist, one known for sculpting mounds of bananas in public places around the world.]

I am a friend and admirer of Warren, who is a neighbor of my mother in New York. He is a wonderful man, and a kind, warm and energetic friend. I am delighted to send my best wishes to him on his birthday, and I hope to be able to celebrate him for many such milestones in the future. He is a treasure. Good on you, Warren!

Doug

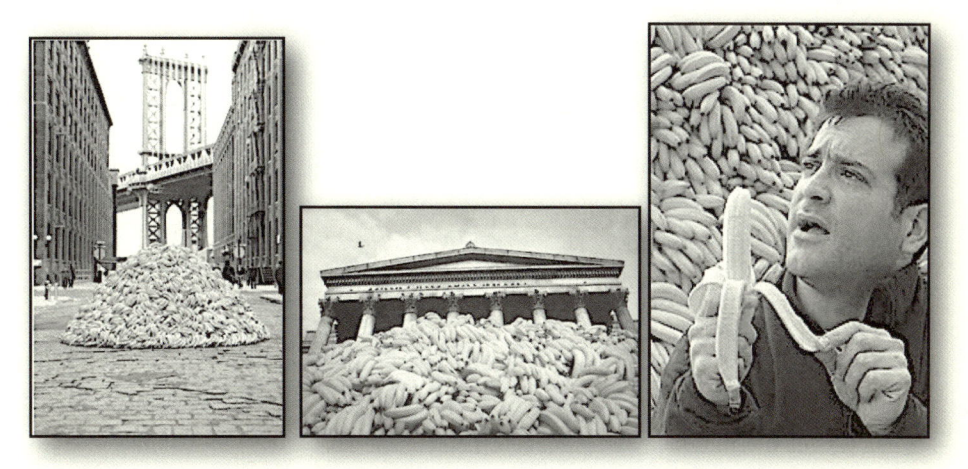

Down Under Manhattan Bridge, New York City - Trafalgar Square, London
See and eat it, too!

Anita Fishbone, Jane St., Manhattan [Doug's Mother]

Good friend. Good neighbor. Great role model. Who says you can't have your art and eat it, too?   Love, **Anita**

Taslima Nasrin

[For over a decade, Taslima has been Warren's best girlfriend and he has been her best Bengali-to-English editor. The Bangladesh physician (whom some Muslim fundamentalists want to kill because of her writing) has asked Warren to edit her prose, poetry, speeches at UN meetings, or even the wording of a possible acceptance lecture had she won the Nobel Peace Prize 2005. First meeting at a humanist convention in Mexico, he was her guest in Sweden, then she was his guest in Greenwich Village. During a BBC interview when asked where he had met her, for she had had to escape to Sweden and elsewhere, he floored them by responding, "She was hiding in a cave." He took her father and her dying mother to see the Atlantic Ocean at Coney Island, introduced her to Kurt Vonnegut, and is a close friend of her entire family.]

I met a person in a cave in Mexico. Yes, he was Warren Allen Smith and such a gentleman! It was 1996. I wanted to move to the United States of America, and because my sister lived in New York I wanted to live in New York with her. **Matt Cherry**, a British humanist and friend of both of us, told me Warren could help me about living in New York. Then I talked with Warren one evening in the lobby of the hotel where we were staying for a humanist congress. Warren was and continues to be so helpful. He attended all my talks in the congress. He has continued to help me whenever I needed it. Time has passed, the months and years have passed. and so many friends disappeared. But Warren did not disappear, he remained as a friend, he helped me correct my speeches and articles and poetry. He helped me to help my nephew and my niece. He helped me to start life in New York. He helped me in each of my difficulties, in my every problem. He laughed with me when I laughed. I feel good because I know that he is always there for me. Wherever I live, whatever I do, I know that Warren will be there for me as a best friend. Love, **Taslima**

Elaine Young and Ginny Syron Greenwich Village [Realtor, and retired Elementary Principal]

We've known him since the nineties. . . . He represents to us the ever curious, ever eccentric mind. . . . And his giving never stops. . . . We love you Warren Smith. . . . Where have all the flowers gone?

Elaine and Ginny

Robert Delford Brown, Greenwich Village

[Dadaist artist and sculptor, fellow secular humanist who hosted chapter meetings, leader of the First National Church of the Exquisite Panic, Inc., of which Warren is a member, one who converted **Sir Arthur C. Clarke** – followers cannot hope to go to Nirvana, but Brown's maps and the Theory of Pharblogence show how to use a map and get to Nevada.]

I met Warren Allen Smith at Pie Throwing Contest in Wormy Udders, Alabama, when we were both teenage dirt farmers. Since then we have both growed up and done our folks proud. Warren went to the Big City and became an intellectual. I was just happy to be a down and dirty dirt farmer. Happy 85th Birthday, Warren.
Robert Delford Brown (who is celebrating 76 years this October)

Fred Whitehead, Kansas City, Missouri   [Editor, *Freethought History*]

I am delighted to greet Warren, America's Diderot, whom unfortunately I've met only once or twice at atheist conventions. I regret that when I was a student in New York City decades ago, I had no idea of his existence. But our interests converged when I began my modest newsletter *Freethought History*, and again when some of my research provided information for his monumental work of scholarship, *Who's Who in Hell*. Speaking of which, it's truly an inspired title!!

Working by himself, Warren toiled in the intellectual vineyards and produced a work of reference of tremendous value to us all. And now he has soared into Cyberspace with an even more immense project, the Philosopedia, modeled somewhat after Wikipedia. So, I'm glad to salute him on this occasion, and to wish him many more years of health, and productive happiness!
Fred

Joe and Blodwen Piercy, Ontario, Canada [Canadian Humanist Publications]

During the 1990s we at Canadian Humanist Publications were following the story of **Taslima Nasreen**'s persecution by Bangladesh and her escape to Sweden. Joe was then editor of *Humanist in Canada*, and we published what news we found of her struggle. She had written the *Lajja* (Shame) soon after the Babri mosque at Ayodhaya, India, was demolished by Hindus, followed in turn by Muslim persecution of Hindus in Bangladesh in retaliation.

Her novel was banned for blasphemy. In fact it portrays the injustices of the Bangladesh government, particularly its failure to protect the lives of the minority Hindus.

So we were very pleased when we found out later that Warren Allen Smith, a New York humanist, was taking Taslima under his wing when she visited the city, helping her with the necessary security, etc.

We wrote to ask if he could write something for our magazine, and we were delighted to receive his interesting 1997 interview of Taslima in Sweden which went in our Summer 1998 issue.

Then, in autumn 2001, Warren came to Ottawa to speak to our local Humanist Association. It was great to meet him in person, hear his talk about his activities and events pertinent to humanists, and have a good visit at our house.

One unforgettable memory is Warren's first-hand account of the view from his apartment window of the appalling crash of the planes into the World Trade Centre just a few weeks beforehand. The kind gift of a copy of his book, *Who's Who in Hell*, is full of interesting information which we dip into at leisure – more than a memory. We hope to cross paths with him again!

Warren, our best wishes to you ahead, keeping working for a humanistic future and enjoying good health. Thanks for coming our way.

Joe and Blodwen Piercy

2000s

Muhammad Atta flew over Warren's apartment building on 9/11/2001, hitting the World Trade Center's north tower. A second plane that he saw, one flying in from the west, crashed into the south tower. From his apartment windows, Warren took the following photos. "It was as scary being at Ground Zero," he told a friend, "as it was landing on Normandy's Omaha Beach in 1944."

Photos taken from his apartment window by Warren

On his 80th birthday, **Margaret Downey** (pictured) of the Thomas Paine Foundation and the Coalition for the Community of Reason arranged an 80th birthday roast at 1 Washington Circle Hotel in Washington, D. C.

Greetings to Warren were read from humanist **Alexander Cox** in Costa Rica, author **Janet Asimov** in New York City, **Sir Arthur C. Clarke** in Sri Lanka, lecturer **Royston Ellis** on the *QE2* somewhere between Singapore and India, editor **Jim Herrick** in London, freethinker **Robbie Kirkhart** in California, **Hope Knutsson** in Iceland, **Prof. Tim Madigan** in Rochester, humanist **Lloyd L. Morain** in California, **Joe and Blodwen Piercy** in Canada, **Monica Methol** in Uruguay, Islamist critic **Ibn Warraq** somewhere in Europe, childhood chum **Robert Shirley** in Oregon, ex-faculty member **Anna Warm** in New Mexico . . . and in person **Monica Price, Cliff Palmer, August E. Brunsman, Barbara Smoker, Norm Allen, Ross Hamilton Henry, Bill Schultz, Matt Cherry, Helen and Edwin Kagin, Edd Doerr, Geoffrey Cox, Dennis Middlebrooks**, mathematics professor **Herb Silverman,** and ex-Ambassador to Nepal **Carleton Coon**, among others.

A birthday cake featuring his likeness but with devilish horns was diabolically devoured.

Herb Silverman, Mathematics Department, College of Charleston, SC [Candidate for Governor of South Carolina in 1990; president in 2006 of the Secular Coalition for America]

I had the honor to be Master of Ceremonies at Warren's 80th Birthday Party "Roast" in 2001.

I am especially proud to have been invited back by Warren to be Master of Ceremonies at his 90th Birthday Party Roast in 2011. It has given my 64-year-old body extra incentive to stay in good health so I can be around for the event.

Arthur C. Clarke – The Hotel Chelsea Plaque

The Hotel Chelsea on Manhattan's 23rd Street is where in 1964 **Arthur C. Clarke** completed a draft of *2001*. The plan was to publish the book the following year, before a Stanley Kubrick film, for which Clarke would write the screenplay, would be released in 1966. Instead, they decided he would write the novel and a film would be adapted from it. *2001: A Space Odyssey* was written while Clarke was finishing the book, which was published in 1968.

According to Warren, his friend **Gilbert Price** invited him to meet Clarke at the hotel, but he didn't actually meet him until invited by Clarke to the Chelsea in 2002 or 2003 while on his way back to Sri Lanka from Johns Hopkins Hospital in Maryland. When Clarke mentioned he was surprised no plaque on the building commemorated his having lived there, Warren wrote his publishers and biographer **Neil McAleer** about this but, receiving no follow-ups, suggested wording for the plaque to Clarke, got Clarke's approval and thanks for the HAL logo, and at his own expense hired **North Shore Monuments** to make the plaque, which was installed with hotel manager **Stanley Bard**'s help on 29 September 2004. Clarke, who had been diagnosed with post-polio syndrome in 1988 and was wheel-chaired, was knighted in 2000 but was too ill to attend – **Queen Elizabeth II** authorized the UK High Commissioner to Sri Lanka at a ceremony in Colombo to award him the title of Knight Bachelor.

Clarke e-mailed Smith on 28 December 2003:

Dear Warren,

Nice to hear from you - and best to **Stanley [Bard]** – say I'm waiting!

HAL'S red 'eye' should be widely recognisable...

Regards to **Janet [Asimov]** .... and your cybergeek **[Peter Ross]** ... what's happening on his monitor??

Do you know about **Leonard Woolf**'s Ceylon comments?

Local TV news just shown happy gay Anglican bishop - how times have changed! But I've decided that religion is the most malevolent of mind-viruses.

All best for 2004 - still can't believe [I made it past 2001]....

Arthur

Arthur with Pepsi, 1991

Warren Smith,
with the plaque he commissioned to be placed on the front of
Manhattan's Hotel Chelsea on 23rd Street

Jimi Zhivago   [5 July 2006]

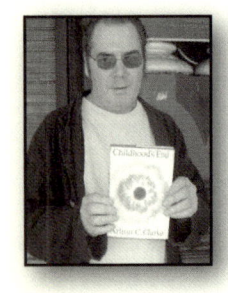

Jimi Zhivago here…..

i met Warren @ the above named hotel in NYC in 2004, when he and i were the only 2 people there for the unveiling of the plaque dedicating Sir Arthur C. Clarke, a mutual friend…..

the story's too long and weird how two most unlikely would meet..... will ring you when i'm back in NYC next week....and I'll explain myself.....best ....stay on my case about this…..as i'm real crazy busy these days.   **Jimi**

Betty Tyler Bavor, Norwalk, Connecticut [29 July 2006]

Many happy returns of the day to Warren on his 85th birthday!

I was a physical education teacher at South Elementary School in the 50's and 60's and I knew of Warren Allen Smith. However, I did not have any association with him. I do, however, appreciate all his efforts to keep the retirees of the New Canaan teaching family connected by way of the *Emeritus* publication he has edited and mailed. I have enjoyed reading it and all his clever articles are great. It is nice to have him continue to e-mail tidbits when he learns new information about past teachers. Stay well and have fun! Happy Birthday! **Betty**

Alan Scarfe, Saturna Island, Canada [Jack the Ripper's autobiographer; father of Jesus, who starred in a televised film]

To: Maestro Warren/Allen/Jun Sczesnoczkawasm/ et al.,

Alas I could not open the review .doc of *A Handbook for Attendants on the Insane: the Autobiography of 'Jack the Ripper' as revealed to Clanash Farjeon* (since I use an old Mac with no translator) – the picture and everything else came through much to my delight. Is there any other way you can send the review? Unlike yourself, I am a cyberilliterate. Nonetheless, I am planning two further novels under the names Alfresco J. Hanna and Janos LaFranche. Yes, I am hoping to attract a British or

American publisher and somehow get wider distribution. Thus my need for favorable critical comment. And thank you by the way for speaking with the local bookstore (by any chance, Partners & Crime?). I haven't done a world mailing yet – waiting for the quotes to create a flyer.

I played Hamlet (uncut) at the opening of a new theatre in Montreal in 1975. I have played many such, Lear, Othello, Faust, and on and on, mostly in my native England and Canada. But I have used Stanislavski's dressing-room at the Moscow Arts and performed in many countries in Europe; Holland, France, Spain, Poland, Russia, and twice for the Queen of Denmark.

In the US, where we lived from 1985-2000, 1985-89 in NY – I met some resistance to say the least. I played Macduff in the abominable Plummer/Jackson *Macbeth* on Broadway, a lot of off-Broadway, *Cyrano* at the Walnut Street in Philadelphia, and many years ago Harras in Zuckmayer's *Die Toefels*, *General* in Dallas under Harry Buckwitz' masterful direction. We languished the last ten years of the past century in LA doing rubbish for lots of dough and writing a dozen screenplays that sit gathering dust with different production companies there. (Two screenplays were adaptations of the novels of the long-forgotten Mississippi writer Robert Rylee – certainly the equal of Faulkner).

I found you on the web by chance (humanists connection) and was magically charmed by the wizardry of your website. I could not resist attempting to get your opinion of my book.

I have now a copy of your great work, **Who's Who in Hell**, sitting open on my desk.

One of the seminal memories of my life was listening to Ezra Pound read these lines on a scratchy recording in a scratchy sing-song – 'The thought of what America, the thought of what America, the thought of what America would be like if the classics had a wide circulation troubles my sleep.'

Why I mention this, I have no idea.

I am very grateful that you did not dismiss your staff, I am certain to retain mine also.

Yours, **Alan/Clanash/Alfresco/Janos**
Jack the Ripper's autobiographer/Jesus's (James Scarfe's) father

Edward Kagin [Kentucky attorney, Presbyterian minister's son, activist atheist]

I had met Warren Allen before 2001. But on his 80th birthday, I stood in for One who had not. To the best of my knowledge, this One (below) has not seen him since, but I have.

I last saw Warren at the American Atheists "Atheists in Foxholes" rally in Washington, D. C., on November 11, 2005. Here are two pictures taken then. One of him shows him hitting on my Helen, and one of him he's speaking at the podium. Finally, there is my photo of him with my daughter Kathryn taken in 2001. She is the one on the left wearing a Camp Quest hat with the logo she designed. Warren Allen is the one with the tie. At least he said he was Warren Allen. Best wishes to him. I am hoping to be able to take many more photos of this fine person.

Edward

God Meets Warren

Omaha Beach veteran flirts with photographer's wife.

Humanistic Naturalist praises photographer's daughter;

Atheist in Foxhole attacks Washington religious fundamentalists.

Warren discusses God on his, not His, 80th birthday

Deep   **Deeper**

Deepanjan Ghosh 2/1B, Sebak Baidya Street, Kolkata - 700029 West Bengal, India

     I am a Radio Jockey by profession, and I work for Radio Mirchi 98.3 FM, here in Kolkata (used to be called Calcutta), India. My first contact with Warren happened through Taslima Nasreen's website, when, on the 30th of December 2003, he replied to a mail that I thought I had sent to her. Eventually, through email he arranged an interview with her for me.

     I went to his site and read up about humanism, and it seems that finally I've found a school of thought with which I can align myself. However, I do have a few questions, and a few things I'd like to discuss, so I hope he will take some time out.

     Although I knew he was a colourful character, until I read his website I didn't know he was this colourful!!!! He actually fought the Nazis in Operation Overlord??? WOW!!!! So Band Of Brothers is about guys like him? He participated in the Stonewall uprising??? Awesome, man. And guys like us just sit here and quote John Osborne's "There are no great causes left to fight for"!!!........or something like that, it's been a long time since I've been in college........

     As our correspondence continued, I came to know a human being, the likes of whom I never knew existed. His sense of humor has never failed to leave me gaping; his philosophy and value systems have changed my life. Over time he has helped deal with heartbreak, death, depression, and has added so much zing and pep to my life that I really don't know how to thank him. He is 61 years older than I am, and that is what, perhaps, makes our relationship so unique. Warren is definitely one of the "coolest" people I know. Happy birthday old friend!!!   **Deep**

77

Andrew Lugg, Canada   [Wittgenstein Scholar]

Warren and I met briefly in Hamilton, Ontario, a while ago, and I just want to wish him a wonderful 85th. That's splendid.

I should also say I appreciate your messages on the Bertrand Russell list and have enjoyed reading you in other forms. All the best, **Andrew**

Edd Doerr [Former President of American Humanist Association; a frequent TV debater with religious fundamentalists, such as Jerry Falwell; President, Americans for Religious Liberty]

Although I do not know Warren well, I have only the greatest admiration for his having accomplished the impossible, producing his encyclopedic *Who's Who in Hell* and *Celebrities in Hell*.

When I had the privilege of presenting the platform address at the New York Society for Ethical Culture on 8 May 2005, the 60th anniversary of the cessation of hostilities in Europe, I began by reading General Eisenhower's communication to Allied forces to "cease active operations." The Army clerk [for Hq. Oise in Reims] who typed the message was Warren Allen Smith, who was present at my lecture. Knowing Warren has been a privilege. May he thrive for another 85 years. **Ed**

Bobbie Kirkhart, Los Angeles, California [Fellow Freethinker]

I don't really know Warren well, except in that way he treats everyone he knows like an old friend so that pretty soon you get to believe it, but I'll always remember that Sunday when we drove up from San Diego with Taslima Nasrin and a man called Peter. (Warren is old enough, as am I, to remember a movie by that name. That Peter was a preacher; this Peter is a lot of fun.)

It was the best of all possible days, a sunny Southern California fall day, drive near the beach. We had to get to an Atheists United meeting, but we stopped for coffee too near the beach, and we were late. We got there, though, and Taslima made a great speech. Then we took off to see Los Angeles. As usual Taslima couldn't stop basking in the freedom that was denied her so long, the freedom to choose her friends, the freedom to speak her mind, the freedom, just the freedom. Peter couldn't stop basking in the beauty and illustriousness of Los Angeles. But Warren, well, Warren just couldn't stop basking. Period. Warren basks in life, in freethought, and most of all in people.

It is no wonder that Warren has given us the definitive catalogue of freethought activists because Warren, more than anyone else, appreciates that the community is not made up of ideas so much as it is made up of the wonderful individuals who express those ideas.

He values most the very thing we often undervalue – each other. And he reminds us that our non-believers' movement's most important asset is, indeed, the courageous human beings who keep it going and keep it interesting.

Warren loves people, and it's no wonder that people love Warren.   **Bobbie**

Basil Fadipe, Roseau, Dominica [Surgeon-Owner, Fadipe Medical Centre]

I am a surgeon working in the Commonwealth of Dominica in the East Caribbean. Originally Nigerian, I moved here in 1991 and have founded and been the director of an 11-bed hospital called Justin Fadipe Medical Centre.

I recall meeting Warren about two years ago. I was having breakfast at one of the local hotels on a Sunday morning and my eyes caught a glimpse of this figure; it was a rather distinguished-looking figure and I couldn't help but continue looking at him, wondering who he might be. There were present many Caucasian guests in the dining room but he simply looked so different and so distinguished in all his ways for that morning. One thing I was sure of from his mien – this must be a man who 'lives by his brain'; maybe even a Nobel prize winner in the past. He looked and walked intellectual, if I could say that.

I felt happy when he came around to my table and very pleasantly introduced himself. In the course of the initial exchanges, he mentioned the name of Bertrand Russell and his level of involvement in the "Russell group" in New York.

My face lit up when he told me this because, since I first came across *Human Knowledge* in 1982 whilst still a student, I have become an avid consumer of Russell's work. Although I am not a trained philosopher or academic, I found that of every 2 lines that I read in most of his books I probably understood one. But, of the ones I did understand, I felt the need for more, and so my search for more of his works never ceased. In my hospital library, therefore, I have created a special section committed only to Russell's books.

Meeting Warren, therefore, was like a unique opportunity and I wanted never to part with it.

I took him to my hospital, and he subsequently signed me up as a member of the Russell Society along with a few others he met in the process. He has since assisted in getting more of Russell's books for our chapter here. Warren's own books also adorn our hospital library .

Warren is so easy to get along with and, with his incisive humour and broad understanding, even a fool can find a welcoming niche in the company of this astute intellectual and very, very savvy New Yorker. He is too good to make you nervous.

When I mentioned to him how my very belief in God is rooted in Russell's work, far more solidly in Russell's work than it is in the Bible or any religious work I have ever come across, he didn't seem to have any problem granting me my paradox.

I wish I could be an active member of the BRS, but currently the demands of running a hospital impose on me almost an exclusivity that deprives me of that privilege.

But I read with unyielding avidity all publications from the BRS.

As with the original Russell's work, my understanding of things is along a fifty-fifty divide. I revel in the one fifty and marvel at the other fifty, but from both I derive enough hope and *raison d'être* for the next day.

I wish Warren a very happy 85th, and I hope I get to see him again before he enters 90. **Doc**

Termonfils, Ligardy

Self Portrait, The Phoenix

Ligardy Olivier Termonfils, 1250 Halsey Street, Brooklyn, NY
[Ligardy is the 11-year-old who adopted Warren when his Haitian father (one of the five of Baby Doc Duvalier's Presidential Guards shown below) was assassinated in May 1993]

Ligardy's father, **Lima** (on the left), with four of the other Haitian Presidential Guards.

Just as I thought my Father did not leave me something after his death, I met Warren Allen Smith. He was the greatest thing that happened to me. He is like a father to me. He is also my best friend. I love this man very much. Thank you for every thing being a [tutor], father and friend.

Emmeline Termonfils, biological mother of Lima's child, brought Ligardy to meet Warren 26 August 2004. He was 5' 10" then and has been 6' tall since 9th grade.

Dinner at Fedora's Restaurant

Peter Ross, Greenwich Village, New York City [Warren's Technology Consultant, who brought him into the 21st century]

As a computer consultant in New York City, I have met many interesting people in all walks of life. But I have to say that Warren is the most interesting of all. There are people who are interested in computers for the sake of it, but he is interested in computers to figure out what will be best for completing his vast array of projects.

It's been a pleasure as his technician helping him with his projects, for he has amazed me time after time to adapt to the latest and greatest technology. He puts people half his age to shame. Happy B Day, Warren, and many more.   **Peter**

The Teacher, at War

SS John W. Brown

One of the 2,750 Liberty Ships built in the United States between 1941 and 1945

The passes and furloughs came to an end when some of the 2,500 hastily constructed new Liberty Ships became available. The fun times at last were over.

From Fort Dix, my unit was shipped either to the docks at Hoboken or those directly across the Hudson River in Manhattan. It was dark and I couldn't tell. At Dix, I was appointed an acting 1st Sergeant in charge of my company's personnel records and my own.

Our armored-trained guys were headed for Europe to replace soldiers who had been injured or had died. Just after dusk, we moved quietly through enclosed buildings on the docks up into a small Liberty Ship. Shortly thereafter, we were sailing. The Statue of Liberty was dark, for all lights were off throughout New York City. I could see what looked like a single light-bulb, or at least a very small light, in the statue's arm. By morning we were out on the ocean and were one of numerous Liberty Ships that traveled together, zigzagging back and forth to avoid German submarines. In between chows, we mainly moved around and talked – jokers told tales about a mermaid that got caught in the ship's propellers, that we'd have to go back home for a month's furlough to wait for another ship. At night we hoped a moon wouldn't divulge where we were. By day, I spent time at the rear of the ship, gazing into the bubbles the propeller was churning.

An officer one morning informed me that my company was chosen to swab the decks. So I went to the captain's station and over the loudspeaker said, "Sgt. Smith speaking. Company A will report at the front end of the boat in 5 minutes."

From every direction came officers asking who the hell had called their ship a boat – instead of one day to swab the deck, my company was penalized with an extra day. My guys weren't happy with their first sergeant. "Sarge, you can put a boat on a ship, but you can't put a ship on a boat!"

Thanksgiving was memorable, because I found a box of turkey that was Grade C, a really low grade from Argentina. I wasn't the only one who got sick, and the Liberty Ship's toilet had a dozen or so stools all built in the curvature of its rear. "Rears to the rear" got a few laughs, for landlubbers weren't all that acquainted with terms like bow, aft, and fore.

Caen Cathedral   Chartres Cathedral

Caen had much damage, many buildings exhibiting the fierce battles that had been waged. The concern was that the Chartres Cathedral with its three rose windows might have been obliterated. It had not, and during our brief stay I was able to see them up close.

On to Reims

In Chartres, at the replacement depot center (the "repple depple"), I was no longer an acting first sergeant and reverted to being just a corporal. Wanzelak and Treziak, two Polish buddies who entertained us by dancing with their *kielbasa* in hand, unabashed at showing their nude penises, were sent as replacements to General Patton, I learned. Others were sent to wherever they could fill a vacancy. I was approached by an adjutant general who, with my personnel records in hand, inquired if I really could type over 100wpm. I confirmed this, and **Floyd W. Brown** directed me to get in his chauffeured Packard and off we headed for Paris about 60 miles away.

The AG sat in the back, I in the front. The corporal who was driving explained all the **Red Ball Express** signs, for they had been posted to help Army trucks to find the fastest routes to travel across all of France. Previously posted signs in German were torn down. Truckers otherwise could come up to a junction and not have the least idea which way to turn, and time was of essence to get whatever they were hauling to their destination and fast.

The AG added that we would be in on part of the planning, that ours would be a headquarters in Reims that would plan how to supply the various divisions with literally everything they would need. In short, I would be his chief clerk in the postal section, and I would need to know how mail trucks would travel and where base post offices would need to be set up.

At times, the roads were smooth. At times, they had been bombed and were in need of being rebuilt. At all times, they led us through beautiful countrysides unlike anything I'd ever before seen. After pointing out things that interested me and finding the AG did not respond, I could see that he was not the chummy type, and I mainly helped the chauffeur find road signs as to where we should turn. Many roads were not passable, bridges had been bombed, alternate routes were not always clear, and Red Ball Express signs were not always where we needed them.

Lieutenant Colonel Brown told the driver to avoid going into Paris, telling him to find the shortest way to Reims. But that was the challenge, for there was no straight road to Reims (which I couldn't pronounce, and the AG was no help). Somehow we got almost into the city limits of Paris and headed in the direction of Reims, but there was no one to ask for advice. No, Soissons was the wrong direction. No, Epernay and Chalons were out of the way. Whenever we started down a road and had to turn back, Brown swore a blue streak. We went hit-or-miss until we felt Reims was just ahead. While searching for our destination, the

AG gave me a manual, and I learned about the chains of command. For example, we were a headquarters corps, but divisions also had their G-1s, 2s, 3s, and 4s. Yes, there was an adjutant general when I was at battalion headquarters and also when I was with Colonel Cassone in the Vehicle Department (G-3) at Fort Knox.

        G-1   Adjutant General
        G-2   Intelligence and Security
        G-3   Operations staff duties, exercise planning, training, operational requirements, combat development & tactical doctrine
        G-4   Supplies

What first? G-2 would figure how to take over the previous buildings the Nazis had used in Reims, including all the telephones. We would move into the place they had had on the 2nd floor at Rue de Voltaire, shown on the next page.

First, we found the caserne where we would be billeted. It was a 10-minute walk to my office at Rue de Voltaire. I could see the cathedral from my window, the angel blowing a horn that turned depending upon the wind. When it rained, I imagined the angel throwing spitballs at me. Across the street I could look into a family's apartment – they had a son, and every morning they would up their shades, open their windows, and exercise. Did the German who had just been stationed here, I wondered, also have seen the family each morning. But of course!

We were billeted near the Piper Heidsick champagnerie. In the mornings, we fell out for roll call, had breakfast, and I was at work in time to see the French family across the way also preparing for the day. I tried to get their attention and waved. They purposely avoided me, I felt.

But one day, the boy waved back. After several waves and several weeks, we finally motioned to each other to meet in front of his building. But he could not speak English, and I spoke French mainly with my hands. From then on, his family waved to me.

What first? G-2 would figure how to take over the previous buildings the Nazis had used in Reims, including all the telephones (that they had taken from the city's homes and businesses). We would move into the place that they had had on the 2nd floor at Rue de Voltaire.

Hq. Oise was on Rue de Voltaire before moving to the Little Red Schoolhouse.

After being there for some weeks and while leaving the caserne one morning, I was asked by a young French chap how he could get past the guard to see a person he'd talked to the day before that was going to play Bridge with him.

I had no idea how to find the un-named person but told him I'd play Bridge with him. It would be a chance to meet a teenager (their eligible soldiers had all been drafted), and I suspected what he wanted was mainly to practice English, which already was quite good.

Jean-Marie Picard

My playful friend's name sounded like *jhawnmaree*, and we made an appointment on my off-time to meet at a tennis club of which he was a member. But when the cards were dealt, we began laughing that in Iowa my parents and I played Contract Bridge, not Auction, or maybe it was the other way around.

So I'd be no help in doing what he wanted. When I asked if what he really wanted was to practice English, he smiled. Well, what I wanted also was a chance to polish up on my high school French.

When he wrote his name, it was Jean-Marie, which I thought looked like a girl's name. We met quite a few times in the private club, and at one point **Jean-Marie Picard** said he'd like me to meet his parents, **Marie and René Picard**.

But, he cautioned, his dad was a *commandant* (Major) who had served in the French Foreign Legion and wasn't too eager to meet an American enlisted man, a corporal no less.

Marie and René Picard

So Jean-Marie coached me, and when I went home with him, I said to his mother, *"Bonjour, madame et commandant, je suis très content de faire votre connaissance."* Both were happy to hear that I had almost no accent and immediately commented upon my facility. But then . . . nothing! I hadn't been coached about what to say next. Seeing their grand piano, I motioned as to whether I could play it, and Papa (it turned out, an excellent violinist) led me over and pulled up the chair. First thing I knew, he pulled his violin out and we played for half an hour. It got me their permission to return at any time, and from then on it was Maman and Papa. Papa headed the Society de St. Vincent de Paul, a charity group. Papa was high in Catholic circles, the most proper gentleman I had ever before met.

Finding that he worked with *veuves*, widows of soldiers killed in the war, I got the idea of writing to *Des Moines Register* journalist **Gordon Gammack**, suggesting that if Iowans wanted to contribute canned food or clothing, I'd turn it over to Papa. Surprisingly, several hundred packages arrived to my APO, and Papa had the problem now of delivering them and I had the problem of translating what the Iowans had written. The AG liked what I was doing so long as my work was not affected. We had loads of work every day, and I sincerely liked working the job I felt no one else could handle. I was never sick, and neither was the AG.

So it was that my parents forwarded my brown suit, which Jean-Marie later had tailored to fit him. And I risked being court-martialed for having my photo taken at the rear of the cathedral (in which all the kings of France had been crowned) – we laughed because I changed back into my Army clothes immediately after the photo, for I could have been arrested by the French police for undressing in public as well as by the Military Police for not being in uniform. I could have been court-martialed if anyone had caught me.

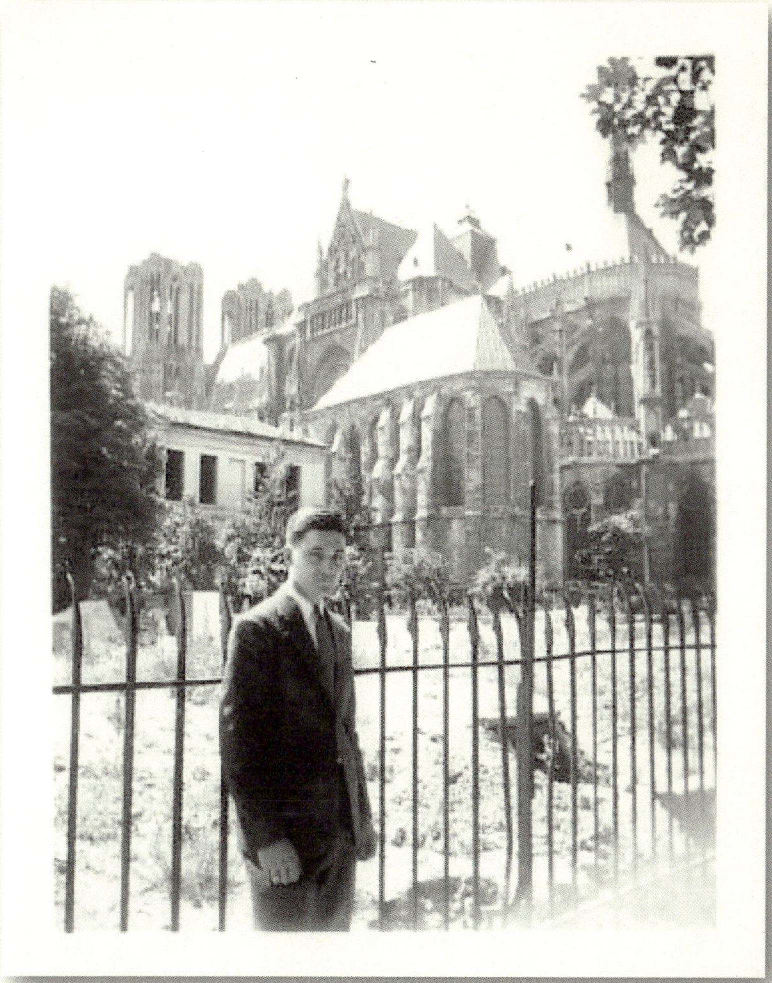

At tea with Maman and Papa Picard

Before the war, Papa and Maman Picard could afford to have a German maid. A button on the floor in the living room could be pressed to signal her to enter. Here, I'm wearing the suit my parents sent for Jean-Marie.

As often as I could, I accompanied Papa when he knocked on *veuves'* doors, had me present them with the package and translate what was in any accompanying letter. If I couldn't read the handwriting, I made it up without confessing this to proper-proper Papa. Now when a *veuve* wrote a thank-you, I had to translate that and mail it to the Iowans.

I didn't take many photos back then, but here is one taken after the war in North Carolina of Papa (on the left) and Simone (on the right).

Papa with Simone and her husband, Major Creech of G-2 after the war

Major Creech taught at the University of North Carolina in Chapel Hill after the war, and they raised a family there.

Jacques-François, Simone, and Jean-Marie Picard,
during the war

Surely enough, Jean-Marie, Papa, and I were invited for an audience with the Archbishop (who served from 1940 to 1960). He asked to meet the soldier that widows were talking about.

After waiting in a side room, we were led to a door that must have been 12' or more high and as artistic as any I'd ever before seen. When it was slowly opened for us by a uniformed guard, in the distance I saw a rather plump man rising to greet us. Papa went first, then me, then Jean-Marie. Papa and Jean-Marie did the customary genuflections, and when the archbishop looked into my eyes I kept thinking that his predecessors had gone back to the 3rd century. He had a big smile all the while, and Papa told him the details of our Iowa project.

Vous êtes catholique? He had noticed upon entering that I had not genuflected.

Non.

Vous êtes Protestant?

Non.

Ainsi, vous êtes Juif?

Non.

We were both smiling, but his expression was quizzical.

Non, mais moi suis un passionné de Voltaire. I was pro-French and liked the famous philosopher.

I disingenuously had uttered the name of an anti-Catholic, an atheist that was turning Papa's cheeks pink and Jean-Marie was stifling a laugh. I'd not meant anything wrong, and Papa continued the conversation for a short time before the Archbishop again took my hand and expressed his happiness at what I was doing for the widows. I thanked him sincerely, noticing that he wore such a big ring that it was hard to shake hands. I also noticed he reminded me of a fey individual up in the 2nd balcony of the Victory.

Come to think of it, how much did I really know about Voltaire – my intent was mainly to cite a famous French thinker.

Back at the Picards', the subject never again came up. I did wonder if the Archbishop had ever had audiences with Nazi soldiers or other Americans.

I must not forget to write about

    ... taking Simone to see *Frankenstein;*
    ... Jean-Marie's having worked as a teenager with the Free French and de-railing trains by not filling in the holes they had dug under the tracks;
    ... Jean-Marie's going to college in Lille and my sending him an onion, which was hard to obtain;
    ... our pouring water on GI's who thought the house of prostitution was at 85, not 185, Rue de Capucines;
    ... the Picards' being upset when I arranged a big delivery of meat by the AG's chauffeur from the AG's kitchen but thankful for the food;
    ... Papa's refusal to buy anything, not even bread, on the black market;
    ... my once pretending to be a Frenchman wearing an Army raincoat when stopped by American MPs for being out after curfew;
    ... how the Italian prisoners were detained in open sight without the need for walls, because they liked our food and time to comb their hair;
    ... how WAC Florence Dellagnola from Utah and I regularly had nips of Cointreau with Champagne as a chaser in a bar at the end of the day near our caserne. ...

Up at the top of some steps, the original *Mona Lisa* looked downwards at us.

Only an Iowan would pronounce it Pig Alley.

Staff Sergeant Smith touring the countryside

Ironically, of all my travels, the ones that stand our were those taken while I traveled by Jeep during the war. With violence all around, here was a road that featured trees planted by individuals who hoped that one day they would provide peace and time for meditation. Who designed the scene, who paid for the people who planted the trees, who kept the roadway so smooth, what animals and birds were in the vicinity, when had I ever before felt so relaxed!

85 Rue de Capucins

The above contemporary photo of the shuttered building on the extreme right with black ironwork is where the Picards lived.

At 185 Rue de Capucins was a house of prostitution.

Simone and I upon several occasions threw a pail of water down upon American soldiers who were ringing the doorbell.

When they complained loudly, they stopped immediately when I came to the window.

Sightseeing dogfaces at Versailles –
that's Sgt. Smith in the front row, 3rd from the left.

The guide showed us the most beautiful dwelling I had ever before seen, or seen since. We went through dozens of rooms, the sculpted garden and lawns of the Jardin des Tuilleries, the little house built especially for Marie Antoinette (for she allegedly had a wild social life apart from the king).

"There are no toilets in the entire place?" I asked. No, the guide explained, a *toilette* on wheels was brought whenever and wherever needed. Food that had been prepared downstairs was sent upstairs using a table that was lifted by using pulleys, allowing the royal family to eat casually.

Louis XIV had planned the place,
    Louis XV had enjoyed living in the place, and
        Louis XVI (and Marie) had paid for the place (with their heads).

When the AG sent me in his Packard to bring his British girlfriend in the Red Cross illegally back from Belgium, it was my tip-off that he knew I was "trustworthy."

He had dozens he could have chosen. And when I lied, teletyping him upon arriving in Belgium that I had to stay in Brussels two days for car repairs, had spoken to his girlfriend and she agreed to the delay, he knew fucking well I was lying . . . for which he gave me a promotion when I brought her back to Reims, getting through the strict Belgium border guards by using his own lies to get us through (for he also was Provost Marshal, in charge of all police).

When I arrived at the Belgian border, a smart guard approached, our picture was taken, and he was aware that I was on some kind of secret mission.

Like my limo, officer?

A soldier's life was rough, indeed, but that test I took back at Fort Leavenworth had given me an MOS that allowed me to be clerical for the entire war. At night I was always exhausted, for the job itself was important, and working for the AG was nerve-wracking. But I wasn't out in the field in the rain, a target to be zeroed in on.

One of my tasks was to fill the top drawer of the AG's desk with insignia. He might call in a major and give him hell, excusing him by saying, "That'll be all, lieutenant," and handing him the lower rank's bars. Everyone I knew thought the AG was as feared as Patton, and they wondered how I could stand working for him. Funny, but I knew the AG's IQ and his entire personnel file, and I was like a loyal and trusted family member. He liked my not being a yes-man, and I kept him informed about what I was hearing not only back at the caserne but also in the city.

His West Point training, demeanor, and work habits were such that few GIs throughout our theater of war complained about what was most important each day: mail call. Wherever you were, mail call occurred daily. Parents, sweethearts, and others who wrote or sent postal cards helped make everyone's day. The happiness of seeing whose name it was that had written helped make up for the sadness of hearing a letter was there for a soldier who had died just the day before.

Mail to be sent home was censored by officers, whose own mail was possibly censored (blanked out and initialed) by those of a higher rank. You'd be in trouble if you mentioned an officer's name that you didn't like, or divulged technical Army business, or told where you were. My parents knew I wouldn't be writing poetry to them – but I sent the following, which cleared the censor:

> Really having no problems.
>
> Everyone is friendly.
>
> I hope you're OK.
>
> Mother, don't worry about me.
>
> So nice of you to write often!

Dad was an acrostic fan, and he easily detected where I was by the first letter on a written line. Fortunately for me, I stayed in the same place for my entire European tour of duty.

The AG and I sent mail that included the time and date where we had sent them (e.g., 09:00 500 or whichever APO number we visited), in order to insure that mail was properly and quickly delivered. He kept even more complete records than I did.

Here's a 6c Monoplane Air Envelope 1944 U.S. Army Postal Service, APO 113 Reims, France, 3112th Signal Service Battalion Concession Airmail to Frederick, Maryland. The stamp in the lower left-hand corner showed the time and date and who censored the letter. Below are two that were sent from my APO 513, Hq Oise., the top one of which was censored.

Did I ever make it to Germany? Yes, I took Sczesny with me in a postal Jeep to Aachen. A *fraulein* approached, asking for chocolate and offering to *frig-frig*. We turned down her magnanimous offer and not just because we had no chocolate. She wasn't my cup of tea, and Sczesny was terrified about getting VD.

Many GIs are buried now in an American cemetery in Aachen. When we saw the badly bombed Aachen, the best part looked like this:

So here I was, unarmed, in enemy territory, traveling in a "borrowed" postal unit's Jeep, sightseeing with a fellow Hq Oise buddy.

Sgt. Sczesny also had no gun.

Neither of us smoked, and neither had any chocolate.

General Dwight David ("Ike") Eisenhower

On 7 May 1945, hard at work, I delivered the following confidential memo to the AG from a teletype received from General Dwight Eisenhower's SHAEF (Supreme Headquarters American Expeditionary Force) in the Little Red School, where they and we were headquartered. Note my initials at the bottom, confirming to the AG that I had delivered it.

```
OS FORM No. 4-b          HEADQUARTERS
                         OISE SECTION          CONFIDENTIAL
                         - I N C O M I N G -
                         TELEPRINTER MESSAGE FORM
```

Deferred		Unclassified		Date	7 May 45
Routine		Confidential	X	Time	0410B
Priority		Secret		Staff Section	
Urgent	X	Top Secret		Number	FWD-20801

ORIGINATOR: SHAEF FORWARD   AUTHENTICATION: EISENHOWER

TO: COMMANDING GENERAL OISE INTERMEDIATE SECTION

PARAGRAPH ONE COLON A REPRESENTATIVE OF THE GERMAN HIGH COMMAND SIGNED THE UNCONDITIONAL SURRENDER OF ALL GERMAN LAND CMA SEA CMA AND AIR FORCES IN EUROPE TO THE ALLIED EXPEDITIONARY FORCE AND SIMULTANEOUSLY TO THE SOVIET HIGH COMMAND AT ZERO ONE FOUR ONE HOURS CENTRAL EUROPEAN TIME CMA SEVEN MAY CMA UNDER WHICH ALL FORCES WILL CEASE ACTIVE OPERATIONS AT ZERO ZERO ZERO ONE BAKER CMA NINE MAY PD

PARAGRAPH TWO COLON EFFECTIVE IMMEDIATELY ALL OFFENSIVE OPERATIONS BY ALLIED EXPEDITIONARY FORCES WILL CEASE AND TROOPS WILL REMAIN IN PRESENT POSITIONS PD MOVES INVOLVED IN OCCUPATIONAL DUTIES WILL CONTINUE PD DUE TO DIFFICULTIES OF COMMUNICATION THERE MAY BE SOME DELAY IN SIMILAR ORDERS REACHING ENEMY TROOPS SO FULL DEFENSIVE PRECAUTIONS WILL BE TAKEN PD

PARAGRAPH THREE COLON ALL INFORMED DOWN TO AN INCLUDING DIVISIONS CMA TACTICAL AIR COMMANDS AND GROUPS CMA BASE SECTIONS CMA AND EQUIVALENT PD NO RELEASE WILL BE MADE TO THE PENDING AN ANNOUNCEMENT BY THE HEADS OF THE THREE GOVERNMENTS PD SIGNED EISENHOWER

CONFIDENTIAL

Corporal **Poole Jones**, the AG's chauffeur, had told me to wake him that morning because he had to pick up a yodeler, which I assumed was an entertainer from the USO. No, he had to pick up **General Alfred Jodl**, who was to sign the German Instrument of Surrender for **Karl Donitz**, who surprisingly had been named by **Adolf Hitler** as his successor, then committed suicide. At Nuremburg "General Doughnuts" was tried, sentenced to death, and hanged as a war criminal. (He was hanged on 16 October 1946 although he had asked for a firing squad.)

When I went to the Picards the evening of May 7th and kept smiling, they asked what was up, and I wouldn't tell. See the newspapers tomorrow, I suggested. They were able to figure why I could not tell, for rumors were spreading throughout Reims. Papa appreciated my not revealing an Army secret.

The following photo of the room, down the hall from mine in the Little Red Schoolhouse, is where **General Alfred Jodl** signed the German Instrument of Surrender for **Karl Donitz**, Hitler's successor.

The map on the wall, which had had lines showing Germans on one side and Allies on the other, now had circles indicating that the Nazi soldiers were surrounded in various areas.

The following day, 8 May 1945, Reims went wild. As soon as I got up, I joined everyone for breakfast but then we headed not to the office but to the cathedral. On the way I saw a Russian displaced person, a soldier, and together we joined hands with a French gal in the rush to assemble downtown. Passersby recognized the symbolism. The following picture (that I did not take) illustrates how easily a parade could start.

Our trio picked up a drummer, and we were in the avante-garde of one of dozens of paraders led by a drum or a musical instrument. The Russian spoke neither English nor French, the French gal spoke neither Russian nor English. I found it wasn't necessary to speak at all. Behind us came 20 or so, then 40, then 100, then who knows how many! Everyone was yelling something. A teenager with a French flag made us a foursome. Kissing strangers was a necessity, not just a sport.

All it took to gain a following was a drum, and drummers were being heard all over the large city. If you were walking alone, you listened for a drum, then walked in that direction to join that group. When the several dozens of groups got to the cathedral, the noise was ear-splitting, and I remember no attempt for the drummers to keep the same beat with other drummers.

After awhile, I dropped by the office, but few were there. The AG wasn't, so I didn't stay.

Later that night, after quite a few glasses of champagne and mingling with thousands near Joan of Arc's statue by the cathedral, I went to see what the Picards were doing. Maman and Papa were home listening to the radio, Papa opened a bottle of something, and we sang songs that I played on the grand piano until Simone arrived, accompanied by Jean-Marie.

"You knew all along," they accused. "Oui, but I couldn't divulge that I'd given Herr Jodl a black eye when I handed him the surrender pen," I joked.

When Simone translated this for her parents, they found me predictably in character. Americans always seemed so happy. Germans always seemed so suspicious, so cold. It was the French who always were mindful of their cultural and intellectual history.

The war over, on May 9th the AG met with the entire staff and discussed strategy. First, the APOs likely would be busier than before, because letter-writers back home would be writing to see how soon their friends would be coming home.

Each APO would necessarily continue until the mail slacked off, and at some point APOs could be combined in order to distribute the last letters. It wasn't easy to predict when that would be or whether the mail could be held in the U.S. and forwarded directly to individuals' homes.

Second, a point system would allow those with the longest service overseas to be discharged first. APO personnel would need to have replacements in the event a majority in any particular APO had a high number of points. The war might be over, but now we would be fighting to finish up as smoothly as possible.

I was offered a warrant officership to encourage me to stay. A warrant officer is a station between enlisted men and officers, and they had the same privileged rank that officers did. But the stipulation, in addition to a big increase in pay and benefits, included that I would have to sign on for two or some number of years.

I wanted, however, to finish my two years for the B.A. and maybe another year for the M.A.

I heard talk that a possible G. I. Bill would allow soldiers to return to college with paid benefits. Thanks, I told the AG, but no thanks. He understood and I believe seriously missed me the day I left.

Going-away Popcorn Party

My artistic going-away present: Simone doesn't want me to leave, Jean-Marie pops some Iowa popcorn, and Maman and Papa look on admiringly.

I'm not sure who drew it, but I think it was Henri, their son-in-law, an actor and artist.

To rush supplies to the 82nd and 101st Airborne divisions, Hq. Oise worked as much as 20 hours a day. On December 17th, the secret documents I handed to the AG reported that during the Battle of the Bulge as many as 90 GIs had been murdered at Malmedy by the Nazis. As many as 88 had been murdered at Baugnez.

At least two films were based on the war in that area: *Battle of the Bulge* (1965, starring Henry Fonda, Robert Shaw, and Robert Ryan) and *Saints and Soldiers* (2004, which I never saw). The best I saw was Steven Spielberg's *Saving Private Ryan* (1998), starring Tom Hanks with Matt Damon – ironically it was about an Iowan soldier from a farm area.

Little by little, friends I knew were being sent home. I had a little over three years service, but some of them had four. The system that had been devised was a fair one, and I waited for my turn.

The Stars and Stripes had news stories with photographs of victory parades on Wall Street and elsewhere. Except for a small group of expediters, we were met by no one, just hustled to transportation that would take us home.

My plane flew from New York City to Chicago, I changed to a railroad that took me back to Grand Junction, Iowa, the depot where my folks had bade me goodbye 3½ years prior.

ENLISTED RECORD AND REPORT OF SEPARATION
HONORABLE DISCHARGE

1. LAST NAME - FIRST NAME - MIDDLE INITIAL SMITH WARREN A	2. ARMY SERIAL NO. 37 421 300	3. GRADE T SGT	4. ARM OR SERVICE AGD	5. COMPONENT AUS
6. ORGANIZATION HQ DET OISE INTERMEDIATE SEC	7. DATE OF SEPARATION 7 JAN 46	8. PLACE OF SEPARATION SEPARATION CENTER- CAMP GRANT ILLINOIS		
9. PERMANENT ADDRESS FOR MAILING PURPOSES RIPPEY IA	10. DATE OF BIRTH 27 OCT 21	11. PLACE OF BIRTH MINBURN IA		
12. ADDRESS FROM WHICH EMPLOYMENT WILL BE SOUGHT SEE 9	13. COLOR EYES BROWN	14. COLOR HAIR BROWN	15. HEIGHT 5 9	16. WEIGHT 154 LBS.	17. NO. DEPEND. 0
18. RACE: WHITE X	19. MARITAL STATUS: SINGLE X	20. U.S. CITIZEN: YES X	21. CIVILIAN OCCUPATION AND NO. STUDENT	X 02

MILITARY HISTORY

22. DATE OF INDUCTION 27 JUN 42	23. DATE OF ENLISTMENT	24. DATE OF ENTRY INTO ACTIVE SERVICE 10 JUL 42	25. PLACE OF ENTRY INTO SERVICE FT LEAVENWORTH KANS	
SELECTIVE SERVICE DATA	26. REGISTERED YES X NO	27. LOCAL S.S. BOARD NO. 1	28. COUNTY AND STATE GREENE CO IA	29. HOME ADDRESS AT TIME OF ENTRY INTO SERVICE SEE 9

30. MILITARY OCCUPATIONAL SPECIALTY AND NO.
ADMINISTRATIVE NCO   502   31. MILITARY QUALIFICATION AND DATE MM W/RIFLE

32. BATTLES AND CAMPAIGNS
NORTHERN FRANCE   RHINELAND

APPLICATION FOR READJUSTMENT ALLOWANCE PUBLIC LAW #346 MADE THROUGH FCWF SECURITY STATE COMMISSION DATE 1-16-46

33. DECORATIONS AND CITATIONS
1 SERVICE STRIPE 2 OVERSEAS SERVICE BARS AMERICAN CAMPAIGN MEDAL EUROPEAN-AFRICAN-MIDDLE EASTERN THEATER RIBBON W/2 BRONZE BATTLE STARS GOOD CONDUCT MEDAL WORLD WAR II VICTORY MEDAL

34. WOUNDS RECEIVED IN ACTION
NONE

35. LATEST IMMUNIZATION DATES				36. SERVICE OUTSIDE CONTINENTAL U.S. AND RETURN		
SMALLPOX IMM JUN 44	TYPHOID STIM JAN 45	TETANUS STIM JUN 44	OTHER (specify)	DATE OF DEPARTURE 11 SEP 44 14 DEC 45	DESTINATION ETO USA	DATE OF ARRIVAL 23 SEP 44 1 JAN 46

37. TOTAL LENGTH OF SERVICE						38. HIGHEST GRADE HELD
CONTINENTAL SERVICE			FOREIGN SERVICE			
YEARS	MONTHS	DAYS	YEARS	MONTHS	DAYS	T SGT
2	2	7	1	3	21	

39. PRIOR SERVICE
NONE

40. REASON AND AUTHORITY FOR SEPARATION
CONV OF GOVT RR 1-1 (DEMOBILIZATION) AR 615-365 DATED 15 DEC 44

41. SERVICE SCHOOLS ATTENDED
AG CLERICAL ADMINISTRATION SCH

42. EDUCATION (Years)
GRAMMAR 8 HIGH SCHOOL 4 COLLEGE 2

PAY DATA VOU # 19934

43. LONGEVITY FOR PAY PURPOSES			44. MUSTERING OUT PAY		45. SOLDIER DEPOSITS	46. TRAVEL PAY	47. TOTAL AMOUNT, NAME OF DISBURSING OFFICER
YEARS 3	MONTHS 6	DAYS 11	TOTAL $ 300	THIS PAYMENT $ 100	125.00	$ 15.35	372.79 G F DOLBEAR CAPT FD

INSURANCE NOTICE

IMPORTANT IF PREMIUM IS NOT PAID WHEN DUE OR WITHIN THIRTY-ONE DAYS THEREAFTER, INSURANCE WILL LAPSE. MAKE CHECKS OR MONEY ORDERS PAYABLE TO THE TREASURER OF THE U.S. AND FORWARD TO COLLECTIONS SUBDIVISION, VETERANS ADMINISTRATION, WASHINGTON 25, D.C.

48. KIND OF INSURANCE			49. HOW PAID			50. Effective Date of Allotment Discontinuance	51. Date of Next Premium Due (One month after 50)	52. PREMIUM DUE EACH MONTH	53. INTENTION OF VETERAN TO
Nat. Serv. X	U.S. Govt.	None	Allotment X	Direct to V.A.		31 JAN 46	28 FEB 46	$ 6.50	Continue X Continue Only Discontinue

54. RIGHT THUMB PRINT

55. REMARKS (This space for completion of above items or entry of other items specified in W.D. Directives)
LAPEL BUTTON ISSUED   ASR SCORE (2 SEP 45) 60
ERC TIME FROM 27 JUN 42 TO 9 JUL 42

57. PERSONNEL OFFICER (Type name, grade and organization- signature)
JOHANNA M LOUWERENS 2ND LT WAC

56. SIGNATURE OF PERSON BEING SEPARATED
Warren A. Smith

WD AGO FORM 53-55
1 November 1944

This form supersedes all previous editions of WD AGO Forms 53 and 55 for enlisted persons entitled to an Honorable Discharge, which will not be used after receipt of this revision.

Army of the United States

Honorable Discharge

This is to certify that

WARREN A SMITH

37421300 T SGT HQ DET OISE INTERMEDIATE SEC

Army of the United States

is hereby Honorably Discharged from the military service of the United States of America.

This certificate is awarded as a testimonial of Honest and Faithful Service to this country.

Given at SEPARATION CENTER CAMP GRANT ILLINOIS

Date 7 JANUARY 1946

411

State of Iowa } ss.
Greene County
Filed for record this 30 day of January 19 46 at 10:05 o'clock A M, and recorded in Book 2 on page 350 of Greene County records

Mamie W. Kester

Rhea Smith dep.

Recorder

CHESTER A SMITH
MAJOR A C

117

The following is what my dad, a corporal, received from General Pershing at the end of World War I. Dad had been shot twice and received two Purple Hearts. I got two Battle Stars (**Battle of the Atlantic; Battle of the Bulge**) – the latter was known as the Ardennes Offensive in Belgium from 16 December 1944 to 25 January 1945.

G. H. Q.
AMERICAN EXPEDITIONARY FORCES,

GENERAL ORDERS
No. 38-A.

FRANCE, February 28, 1919.

MY FELLOW SOLDIERS:

Now that your service with the American Expeditionary Forces is about to terminate, I can not let you go without a personal word. At the call to arms, the patriotic young manhood of America eagerly responded and became the formidable army whose decisive victories testify to its efficiency and its valor. With the support of the nation firmly united to defend the cause of liberty, our army has executed the will of the people with resolute purpose. Our democracy has been tested, and the forces of autocracy have been defeated. To the glory of the citizen-soldier, our troops have faithfully fulfilled their trust, and in a succession of brilliant offensives have overcome the menace to our civilization.

As an individual, your part in the world war has been an important one in the sum total of our achievements. Whether keeping lonely vigil in the trenches, or gallantly storming the enemy's stronghold; whether enduring monotonous drudgery at the rear, or sustaining the fighting line at the front, each has bravely and efficiently played his part. By willing sacrifice of personal rights; by cheerful endurance of hardship and privation; by vigor, strength and indomitable will, made effective by thorough organization and cordial co-operation, you inspired the war-worn Allies with new life and turned the tide of threatened defeat into overwhelming victory.

With a consecrated devotion to duty and a will to conquer, you have loyally served your country. By your exemplary conduct a standard has been established and maintained never before attained by any army. With mind and body as clean and strong as the decisive blows you delivered against the foe, you are soon to return to the pursuits of peace. In leaving the scenes of your victories, may I ask that you carry home your high ideals and continue to live as you have served—an honor to the principles for which you have fought and to the fallen comrades you leave behind.

It is with pride in our success that I extend to you my sincere thanks for your splendid service to the army and to the nation.

Faithfully,

John J. Pershing

Commander in Chief.

OFFICIAL:
ROBERT C. DAVIS,
Adjutant General.

Copy furnished to

Poole Jones

Poole Jones, my Adjutant General's chauffeur, was the person who brought the VIP who would be sitting in one of the two chairs on the left in the photos.

To the *Atlanta Journal* in 2013, I submitted "Georgian from Ringgold was a Key to Bringing an End to World War II."

Corporal Poole Jones of Ringgold, Georgia, played a key role in the 1945 Nazi surrender that brought an end to World War II in Europe.

Jones, who was stationed in Reims in the Supreme Headquarters Allied Expeditionary Force (SHAEF), was Adjutant General Floyd W. Brown's chauffeur. I was one of Brown's chief clerks.

Cpl. Jones, who slept in the same caserne, asked me to be sure to wake him the following morning. It was imperative, he explained, for him to pick up a yodeler at some site and deliver him to AG Brown, who would deliver him in the same building to our general, Dwight D. Eisenhower. If one didn't follow orders, he could be shipped out to Japan where the war was still on instead of being discharged.

"A yodeler?" I asked. "An entertainer from the United Service Organization (USO)?"

Jones didn't know, but maybe entertainers Bob Hope or Bing Crosby were traveling incognito, I assumed, incorrectly.

I woke Jones as instructed, and he dutifully picked up the person who turned out to be General Alfred Jodl, who was to sign the German Instrument of Surrender on behalf of Karl Donitz, who surprisingly had been named by Adolf Hitler as his successor before committing suicide on 30 April 1945.

"That was no singer I picked up and delivered," Jones told me that afternoon with a big, big smile. "He was a Nazi bigshot general!" Jones was unsure as to why he had been given the task. We all were carrying out the chain of duty, I told him.

I informed AG Brown, who ordered both of us not to talk about it.

We didn't dare disobey.

On 7 May 1945, General Eisenhower (whom we informally called "Ike") sent a teletyped confidential memo to all his staff that the surrender would be signed by the representatives of the Oberkommando der Wehrmacht (OKW) and the Allied Expeditionary Force (AEF) together with the Soviet High Command, French representative signing as witness on 7 May, and signed again by representatives of the three armed services of the OKW and the AEF together with the Supreme

High Command of the Red Army, French, and U. S. representatives signing as witnesses on 8 May 1945.

Surrender Room

The date is known in the West as Victory in Europe Day (V-E Day, 8 May 1945), although in post-Soviet states it was signed after midnight Moscow time. Incidentally, It was President Harry Truman's 61st birthday.

On 16 October 1946 at Nuremburg, "General Doughnuts" was tried, sentenced to death, and hanged as a war criminal, although he had asked for a firing squad

The room in which the surrender was signed was near my office at SHAEF. When I returned in 1995, I visited the room at a time when a French teacher and her class were learning about the maps on the wall and where the Nazi sat to sign their surrender. For diplomatic reasons, General Eisenhower chose not to be present at the signing.

The teacher – when told that I was a GI whose office was just down the long corridor – had elementary school children ask me all kinds of questions. I got a big laugh when I told them I had just gone to the room in which I had my office from 1944 to 1945. "And it now is a boys' latrine!"

In 2013, I snail-mailed a letter to Poole Jones's daughter, Mrs. Diane Ball, 95 Shannon Drive, Ringgold, Georgia 30736 (706) 937-5089. She responded that her father, Poole Jones, and his wife had both died.

Let the record show that all soldiers who serve deserve to be remembered for their seemingly unimportant but key involvement in the international activities of which they played a part.

As a journalist who dislikes omitting the spice, before almost everyone in our group was discharged and sent home – except those who accepted the rank of Warrant Officer with more pay but who would not be immediately discharged – I was ordered to draw up papers to have Corporal Jones shipped out to Japan. That's what the Adjutant General did, made everything official by making a written record. of whatever was commanded. This I did, learning that the AG had had some disagreement with the "f-ing Southern redneck" and would deal with him roughly instead of allowing him to be discharged now that the war was over. Curious before being discharged, I wrote Jones to see what he was doing in Japan, which could have been a long stretch.

He replied, "Hey, Smith, I'm in Georgia. As soon as I got back to the States I was discharged. Tell the old fart his scheme didn't work. F him! Yes, F him again and again!"

Now, if I tell his daughter, she'll spill the beans to the *Atlanta Journal*.

I've chosen not to tell her . . . only telling you the reader. . . .

3
Alphabetized by Subject

Addicts

In 1970, when I saw an addict stealing from a car in front of my 42nd Street recording studio, I alerted a cop across the street and "we" caught him.

I'm the one in the white shirt.

In the back seat of the car was a wheelchair.

The officer, thanking me, said it was the first time a civilian had ever helped him, for I held onto the creep until the policeman got to us.

I have never been addicted to anything except coffee, which Isaac Asimov once caught me drinking, nor have I chosen addicts as friends.

Age Discrimination

At the Art Students Ball, I'm the partly nude one.

The widow of several hundred science fiction books asked me about age discrimination in September 2013. I wrote a draft to be included along with other responses received from other of her friends. They did not respond fully, alas, so she suggested that I have the following published elsewhere. Mary Renaud's Persian boy in the photo now is responding seriously.

Ageism – stereotyping and discriminating against people because of their age – I have experienced all my life.

My authoritarian father in the 1930s often said no to me because I was only a teenager. My mother who sometimes sided with me was unable to change his views.

As a collegiate I found professors older than my father surprisingly listened to me when I was in my 20s.

Serving as one of General Dwight Eisenhower's adjutant general's chief clerks from 1941 to 1942, I was one of a team. Ageism was not a concern inasmuch as final decisions at Supreme Headquarters in Reims were made openly by "Ike," whose office was just down the corridor from mine. What he ruled was accepted without question.

As a teacher in a private Manhattan progressive school in the early 1950s and also in Connecticut's New Canaan High School from 1954 until 1986, I experienced no ageism from the older female principal in the former or the older male principal in the exclusive public school. We worked on a productive academic level for over three decades.

As a business executive who headed an independent recording studio in Times Square, Manhattan, I hired engineers on the basis of their skills, not because of their gender or age. Musicians were unique in judging fellow musicians only as to how well they performed.

As a gay nonagenarian, I found that gays who bragged "No sex with under-21's" in the 1950s also bragged, "No sex with over-30's."

I met the first of my two paramours in 1948 when I was 27 and he was 20 – we remained companions for 40 years.

Paramours were different from companions, knowingly having dozens of sexual experiences. As one of the much written about Stonewall Uprising 1969ers, under a pseudonym I published *Cruising the Deuce* (2005) about such experiences in the Deuce's 42nd Street movie houses.

Paramour #2, a Broadway star and three-time Tony Award nominee, was 22 when we met and he died (faulty propane heater in Austria, although he also was HIV +) when not yet 50.

Mine was a rebellious time (See the accompanying photo, in which I was Mary Renaud's Persian boy in the Waldorf Astoria with members of the Art Students Ball). Then, if you admitted to having had sex with anyone over 30, you were ageist and not embarrassed. I became 30 in the early 1950s and my paramour #1 became 30 in the late 1950s. Paramour #2 had another #1 and both were active with others. In the 1960s, the goal was to enjoy sex as often as possible, and I was a known roué and sybarite. Yes, I got several STD's.

Genes play a big part. Queen Elizabeth is only 87. I am 3 months older than actor Betty White and 9 months older than writer-producer Norman Lear. My mother's hair had color at the time of her death when 84. My barber doubts my age even when I show him my New York State ID. Out-of-towners offer me their seat on the subway or bus. Males who are younger thank me when I offer my seat to them. The one time I visited an "old people's home," some residents' bodies showed extreme differences, many remaining on the sidelines during dances, others imitating steps mastered when they were collegiates.

I have never been, nor wanted to be, a biological father . . . but over the years eight straight kids (2 girls, 6 boys) have chosen me as their surrogate dad.

All eight (now 60 to 20 years old) keep in touch.

They had had unfortunate experiences with their own parents, and I was trusted as a counselor whether they were children of divorced parents, children with only one parent, children who disliked one parent or both parents, recovering drug addicts, epileptics, proud pot smokers, or males with wife problems.

As a retired teacher since 1986, I have not been employed by others. As a nonagenarian, I write for an international online journal, picked because I *am* old.

When I reached 80, I chose not to drive cars, but I remember passengers who implied I was old "but none of us could have gotten through that thunderstorm in the Caribbean rain forest the way you did." A friendly immigrant, for whom English is a second language, today in the West Village calls me "the old man." A noted 1950s beatnik calls me "Pops," with which term I feel comfortable except when used by non-beatniks.

The bottom line: I have pretty much avoided being hurt by ageism.

In fact, sometimes I have sometimes used it to my advantage.

Belief

To be a believer is to confess being one who disregards the facts but has "faith." My grandparents and mother believed that when they died their soul would rise to Heaven where the members of the Trinity would be with all other believers.

When I was a teenager and was told by Methodist Episcopal Bishop **Garfield Bromley Oxnam** about my and my parents' church's key beliefs, I asked about Jesus's being able to walk on water and a whale's being able to swallow a human being. It's in the sacred scripture, he lectured me, and I must believe.

The day I left home and arrived in college to major in music, I discarded "belief" for "know."

Don Cossack Chorus

Grishka, who tries to destroy the wedding ceremony of Fevronia and Prince Vsevolod. The crowd is annoyed by him, accuses all drunkards and prophesies "they will be unhappy on the earth and will never attain heaven."

The second part is the wedding song with typical sweet wedding tunes (three couplets).

Then comes the final part with its solemn, powerful chords, expressing the firmness of the city of Kitesh and the strong, unshaken faith of its inhabitants.

12. WHITE HAZEL TREE (A Russian Folk Song)
. . . . Arr. by S. Jaroff

This is a love song in which a young lad asks a maiden to come and sit with him under the white hazel tree where he can tell her of his love. The song has three couplets with solos accompanied by the chorus, and refrain.

13. THREE RUSSIAN FOLK SONGS . Arr. by I. Dobrovein

These three separate songs are combined on a musical basis only.

The first, "Between the Bluff Coasts," is a lyric song with broad melody, sung by a soloist to the accompaniment of the Chorus.

Then come two comic songs — "My Lady" in moderate tempo and "Polka" in a typical polka rhythm and primitive chord progression. The lyrics of the last two songs are replete with comic buffoonery.

14. THEIR ARMS IN THE BRIGHT
SUNSHINE BLAZING . . . . Russian Song

Monotonous is life in a provincial town. . . . When suddenly the trumpets sound, — a squadron of hussars arrives. All the girls are excited; Ah! Ah! Night comes and only greyhaired commanders sleep. The next morning the squadron marches off, leaving after it the sighing "Oh! Oh!" . . .

Arr. by C. Shvedoff
and S. Jaroff

15. DON COSSACK SONG . . . . . Arr. by S. Jaroff

At war in the Caucasian Mountains, we ride over all obstacles in our path . . . neither hard work nor sickness can stay us . . . and above the beating of the drums, our songs are heard everywhere.

These FAMOUS ARTISTS
IN THE SERIES . .

★ GLADYS SWARTHOUT, Mezzo-Soprano
Tuesday Evening, December 5, 1940.
Tickets $2.50.

★ NATHAN MILSTEIN, Violinist
Monday Evening, January 2, 1941.
Tickets $2.50.

★ MISCHA LEVITZKI, Pianist
Thursday Evening, February 13, 1941.
Tickets $2.00.

☆

Tickets for single concerts
will be sold at door only.

EXCLUSIVE MANAGEMENT:
HUROK ATTRACTIONS, INC.
30 ROCKEFELLER PLAZA, N.Y.C.

BOOKING DIRECTION:
BC ARTISTS SERVICE

CATHOLIC DAUGHTERS OF AMERICA

Presents

DON COSSACK
CHORUS

☆

WEST HIGH-SCHOOL AUDITORIUM

WEDNESDAY EVENING

November 6th, 1940

WATERLOO, IOWA, 8:15 P. M.

ANNUAL CHARITY SERIES

The Castrato

The Don Cossack Chorus performed in Waterloo, Iowa, in 1940. The Cossacks' leader was **Serge Jaroff**. The group was renowned for both the quality of the tenors and especially for the depth and resonance of the low basses.

It was reported that **Pyotr Mihailik** could reach the bottom E of the piano with little difficulty.

The group had one castrato (eunuch). On the program is a faint autograph by the leader and also the castrato.

Then a music major and a reporter on *The College Eye*, I talked with Mr. Jaroff before and after the program. "Which is the castrato?" I asked, naively wondering if he would be the shortest in the troupe.

Mr. Jaroff, who wasn't tall, pointed out the person and introduced us.

In 1944, when I was a sightseeing GI on a weekend jaunt from being an Adjutant General's chief clerk in General Eisenhower's Reims Supreme Allied Headquarters (SHAEF), I made a point of going to the first Russian Orthodox church I'd ever visited and, to my surprise, found myself standing (the large structure had no chairs) right behind Serge Jaroff, leader of the Don Cossacks whom I'd met in 1940 when his group visited a nearby high school.

During some kind of break, I introduced myself as having been an Iowa student who remembered his having introduced me to the basso profondo.

Although that person was not present, the conductor seemed to remember that I had also shown interest in the castrato, so he introduced the two of us. I found that he seemed ordinary even when he spoke.

It was a memorable time because, although I associated religious groups with various kinds and styles of music, it was not clear how religion and sex could be inter-intwined.

Jokes were rife in Iowa about the choir director's relationships with the minister's daughter or the lead soprano herself, but sex itself was a mystery throughout my first two years of college and my 3½ years in the armed forces.

The chorus's choices of music, for the Iowa program that was presented by the Catholic Daughters of America, was clearly "religious."

But I wasn't that interested in researching further.

What was unique was the frog-like sounds made by the basso profondo and the high soprano sounds that the castrato could make..

Cat Man • *Cat Man*

I'm with **Ed Hoagland**,

American Academy of Arts and Letters member,

author of *Cat Man* (May 2014)

Tico

How I become known as the cat man at 31 Jane Street

In *The New York Times Magazine* (11 August 2013), **Chuck Klosterman**'s "The Ethicist" column published my letter in which I wrote for his advice on an ethical matter . . .

http://goo.gl/zNbfte

One of my neighbors complained to my co-op board's management firm, claiming I allow my cat to exercise unsupervised in the hallway — a blatant lie. Without hearing my side, the board declared that no cats could be in the hallway, supervised or not.

Is it ethical for me to never again speak to the person who lied about my cat?

W. S., New York

. . . and Mr. Klosterman responded:

    First of all, I love the concept of a cat "exercising unsupervised," even if it never actually happened. Second, I don't see the ethical conflict in your quandary. A normal person talks to his neighbors (particularly if a neighbor initiates the conversation), but it's not a moral obligation unless the neighbor is in some kind of immediate danger. If your despised neighbor stops you in the hallway and desperately says, "I need your help," you can't walk away on account of your cat's unjust persecution.

But most of the time, day-to-day conversations aren't that intense; most of the time, you can freeze out whomever you like, for whatever reason you see fit. Friendliness is a virtue, but not a moral requirement. This behavior, however, will have its own set of discomfiting consequences. "I don't know about that guy in 6-C," your neighbors may gossip as you wordlessly skulk about the building. "He seems like an oversensitive recluse. Also, I heard that his cat has really gained weight."

Later:

Reactions, over 95% favorable, are coming in from four continents. **SAVE TICO** groups are forming. In Bangkok, it's **Mee ìt-sà-rà Teekoh!**

Already, "calling hours" have been arranged for a New York City professional journalist; for Drew University's Classics Department chairman in Madison, New Jersey; and for a professor of ethics and philosophy from St. John Fisher College in Rochester, New York – all three reasoning that the time for solace is before, not after, one's death, whether for animals or for humans.

W. S., The cat man on the 10th floor

not to be confused with **Ed Hoagland**, who wrote *Cat Man* (1955) about being in charge of lions at Ringling Brothers Circus – American Academy Member Hoagland lived on the 9th floor of the 31 Jane Street co-op building, and he and I are friends.

Hoagland won't move back until the Board hears both sides of the question and shows evidence that the complainant's physician, not a veterinarian, has supplied supporting information as to any health problems she may have.

"Ethicist" Readers' Comments

First of all, I love the concept of a cat "exercising unsupervised," even if it never actually happened. Second, I don't see the ethical conflict in your quandary. A normal person talks to his neighbors (particularly if a neighbor initiates the conversation), but it's not a moral obligation unless the neighbor is in some kind of immediate danger. If your despised neighbor stops you in the hallway and desperately says, "I need your help," you can't walk away on account of your cat's unjust persecution. But most of the time, day-to-day conversations aren't that intense; most of the time, you can freeze out whomever you like, for whatever reason you see fit. Friendliness is a virtue, but not a moral requirement. This behavior, however, will have its own set of discomfiting consequences. "I don't know about that guy in 6-C," your neighbors may gossip as you wordlessly skulk about the building. "He seems like an oversensitive recluse. Also, I heard that his cat has really gained weight." **G. Streeter, Los Angeles, CA**

I agree there is no moral requirement for friendliness or even human acknowledgement. However, not defending the truth of the matter, (assuming the cat was perhaps "stretching" under human supervision) will really fuel W.S.' anger at the neighbor and the Board. The cat is part of W.S.' life and both W.S. and the cat has been denied being heard and at least listened to. Failing to have that modicum of recognition can leave one seething. Since cats are allowed in the building, perhaps W.S. should seek out other cat lovers who can together discuss the draconian cat prohibition with the Board and appeal for a hearing on the issue. There perhaps is a way to do this through the existing Board's rules?

As for the neighbor, sounds like they either greatly dislike cats or W.S. or both... **Upstate NY**

To ethically balance the justice/injustice here, you are morally obligated to spread a lie about the man who made one about your cat and you to the board. You *must* balance it with a lie about him to those in the building, in return, and thus balance his moral debt to you, which now can be canceled and forgiven in no other way. But tell it to only one person whom you know will spread it further. As long as there are no second witnesses to your assertions, you are safe and can sleep knowing you did the right thing. **grannychi**, Grand Rapids, MI

While I don't disagree with your response to the cat owner, there are alternates with a potentially greater win-win outcome through mutual education. The person complaining, or a friend or family member, might have a health concern, or have had a bad experience with a cat, or nearly tripped over the cat. Pet owners often become blind to their animals faults, dog owners certainly seem never to hear their dogs barking. Perhaps the cat owner could approach the complainer and apologize with a comment that 'I wish you had spoken with me first, because I wasn't aware that my cat was a problem. What bothers you about him/her?' Of course that assumes the cat owner hadn't ignored multiple prior complaints before the person felt forced to approach the board ... a big assumption. Whatever, sure would be nice to live together in peace. **A**

Grannychi, the issue is not at all what you are talking about. In Heaven, all will get along in peace. The problem is that Heaven is a theological invention. **IMC** Minneapolis

"If your despised neighbor stops you in the hallway and desperately says, "I need your help," you can't walk away on account of your cat's unjust persecution."Of course you can walk away. You owe him/her nothing. **Van Bean,** Canada

Had she come to me, for I am the cat owner, instead of fingering another neighbor as the person who started what seems close to a clinical condition (personality prevarication?), I could have helped my friend of over a decade try to get a therapist's help. Instead, she fingered another neighbor as the complainer. Meanwhile, for weeks I was the accused unable to find who was my accuser. More important than my cat's no longer being allowed to continue having supervised exercizing is the lady's having snookered co-op board members and MsManagement, as I a shareholder describe my employee. The night after the complainer banged on my door, threatening to sue if I didn't stop putting information under her door asking who it is on our floor that is accusing me, she said, "Oh, hello," kindly as I passed her in the lobby. If I chose to let the cat out now, I would accompany the cat to protect it from a clinical case. **W. S.**, New York City

On the other hand, re W.S., New York, as Rodgers and Hart had it in 1937 in Babes in Arms and Lena Horne sang as nobody else: "She never bothers, with people she'd hate." A prescription I have preferred from time to time with regard to certain of my apartment neighbors, and I'm not talking about a cat, although "hate" is a bit strong. Of course, if there were a fire in the building or some other emergency, Rodgers, Hart, Horne would await another day. **JR** Pennsylvania.

If "no cats could be in the hallway, supervised or not" how are cat owners to get their cats to the vet? Is it necessary to drop the cat from a high rise window and incrementally sacrifice one of nine lives as a good health practice? **Donald Nawi** Scarsdale, NY

I'm the **W. S.** named as the cat owner in the article: Co-op residents can still exit via elevators with dogs on a leash for daily toilet duties or with cats in a container. If my Board were to come up with a rule disallowing animals on our elevators, we could lower them from our widows. Isaac Asimov formerly lived on the 33rd floor, and I only live on the 10th. New issue: Would it be ethical if you lived on the 60th floor? As the owner of the cat, which was always supervised, I did on four occasions over 12 years almost see the cat enter an open door. But a loud slap of my hands stopped him. Asked if I could help get my neighbor's Mac working, I quickly complied. No charge. Smiles all around. The person she fingered misses getting down on his hands and knees to play with the cat. He remains snookered. **W. S.**, New York City

City Guy

I've often been asked, "How did you get from an Iowa farm town of 328 individuals to Fairfield County's only town with a railroad that travels directly to Grand Central Station?"

As expected, I could only respond, "Have time to hear a long, long story?"

When I was 13, I taught myself to type on my dad's Remington, I might start, and no one had time to hear me out.

But, true, using a book I sat in my dad's office at the grain elevator and practiced the keys the same as I did to learn how to play the piano. Like many, I skipped the top line with the numbers. But upon being advanced reaching high school, I signed up for the typing class and watched the teacher when he clocked me at 60 wpm the first day. By the end of the first quarter, I typed faster than the teacher.

Upon being drafted into the Army and sent to Fort Leavenworth for all kinds of testing, I had to take a typing test, first being given a practice period to become acquainted with the typewriter. Told to start, I did . . . and the instructor accused me of including the practice period when I typed 111 wpm. "Do it again!" This time he watched, and I typed 113. That score and all the others followed me to Fort Knox, where I was sent for my basic training.

My first week of basic training, I landed in a company that needed a company clerk who could type. The good news was that I was chosen. The bad news is that I skipped basic training and never learned how to handle guns.

Had New Canaan school administrators known that I am gay, I would not have been hired. All the time I was in New Canaan, in short, I feared being found out by the puritan society.

> After leading my Armed Forces company from Fort Knox onto Omaha Beach in 1944, I became one of **General Dwight Eisenhower**'s Adjutant General's chief clerks at Supreme Headquarters (SHAEF) in Reims. We were the equivalent of the Army – rather than the Home – Depot. My job involved attempting to get every soldier her or his daily letters in time for "mail call." The task involved estimating daily where each of **General George Patton**'s troops would be the following day – they moved from Sicily to Southern France and on to the Battle of the Bulge and into Nazi Germany. When we thought nothing could stop him, an automobile accident in Heidelberg, Germany, did. But we continued to deliver

the mail. Using the G. I. Bill, I got my Bachelor's from the U of I Iowa and my Master's from Columbia University; then taught four years in one of the first "progressive education" schools, Bentley, on Manhattan's 86th Street; Teachers College, Columbia; and New Canaan High School from 1954 to 1986. I was a teacher in New Canaan for 32 years, during which few knew I had been a vet (1944 Omaha Beach and the 1969 Stonewall Uprising).

Death
"A person never dies so long as someone remembers."
Warren Allen Smith

Determinism

Determinism is like a game of cards. The hand that is dealt you is determinism. The way you play your hand is free will.

Whenever I read today about athletes and celebrities claiming to be "sex addicts," I recall my Wednesday night and weekend ventures to certain movie houses for quick sex. The excitement was pursued willingly and with forethought, and I was fully aware.

Drugstores – Cody, James J.

Picture: Max Schlusselberg

It was the meeting place of the town," said New Canaanite George Cody, whose grandfather James J. Cody owned the apothecary that was built in 1845. "Before the telephone, people would go there for telegraphs. . . .Generations have grown up knowing Cody's Drug Store."

Max Schlusselberg, in a *New Canaan Patch* (July 2010) article, wrote that what came to be known as Cody's Drug Store was not owned by the Cody family until 1918. When they closed up shop in 1965, the Cody family was contacted by the Smithsonian Institution in Washington, D. C., and the Henry Ford Museum in Detroit – both wanted to preserve the store's authentic collection of elixirs and tonics.

However, the New Canaan Historical Society would come to house the drug store's remarkable assortment of elixirs – including one of the country's largest collections of patent medicines in their original packaging.

Known as "patent medicines," they were billed as cure-all tonics for everything from diabetes to heart disease, but their active ingredients usually consisted of alcohol and narcotics.

George Cody, a New Canaan High School graduate, was quoted as saying that "People came back from the Civil War addicted to these tonics. They didn't know what was in them.

In the 1950s, an ice cream parlor with milkshakes was added. Resident and film actress Faye Emerson – who had been married to William Crawford (1938-1942;), Elliott Roosevelt (1944-1950), and musician Skitch Henderson (1950-1957) – was observed by the present author ordering a large order as she sat on one of the chairs at the place which had marble counters and chandeliers.

Wrote a new English teacher in town, "Her seat needed to have been twice as large, or her real seat needed anything but the temptation of ice cream." Her mailbox had the names Emerson, Roosevelt, and Henderson, remembers the teacher.

In 1965, to accommodate the widening of Main Street, Cody's was demolished.

Editors

An editor of a journal is responsible for selecting and preparing written, visual, audible, and film media that is used to convey information. He or she is the one responsible for the correction, condensation, and organization of information.

As is the case in any profession, some editors become known as more inspiring than others. Following is how I now grade those for whom I have worked or had a connection.

A+

Ed Wilson, Editor of *The Humanist*, 1930s to 1950s – as my first professional editor, Wilson in the 1950s taught by example as to what journalism is. His pre-computer system for compiling experts and their expertise was invaluable. I followed his way of assigning experts who could cover a variety of subjects; one expert on Freud could be expected to have a different perspective about Jung and still be objective about religious humanism.

Timothy Madigan, Executive Editor (1987–1997) and Editor (1997-1999) of *Free Inquiry*. Also, he was co-editor of *The Secular Humanist Bulletin* until 1997. Tim was independent and a superb writer and speaker.

Priscilla Robertson, editor of *The Humanist* when I was the magazine's Book Review Editor – was one of the most profound thinkers I ever worked for; she knew all the major university personnel that we could ask to review books. I worked with her from 1953 to 1958.

Royston Ellis, editor of *The Educator* in the Commonwealth of Dominica – we met deadlines and favored the aims of Premier Edward O. LeBlanc rather than in the island's establishment newspaper.

Editor of the US Virgin Islands *Daily News* – suggested the title of my "Manhattan Scene" and "Manhattan Chessboard" columns.

Barry Duke, editor of the online international journal, *The Pink Humanist*, is a Caucasian born in apartheid South Africa He lives in Spain. My column has appeared since 2012.

A

George H. Holmes was the only professor whose journalism class I ever took. In 1943 at Iowa State Teachers College (now the University of Northern Iowa) he taught fundamentals, but on the *College Eye* I had a regular column, "Smitty's Beat," about music (my minor) and also worked on *Old Gold*, the college yearbook.

Adjutant Colonel Carrusone at Fort Knox in 1942 – taught me the word "supra" for referring to information in the writing above. I had never before known the word. He also taught by example the importance of facts.

Adjutant General Floyd W. Brown at SHAEF in 1944 – was a model of separating facts from judgments, and as the adjutant's chief clerk we communicated smoothly together. I was one of the few he knew that was not afraid of his bluster.

B+

Editor of *Library Journal* – I wrote book reviews in the 1960s about humanism, philosophy, and race relations; e.g., I wrote a favorable review of Dick Gregory's *Nigger: An Autobiography* (1963); today, I believe the review was more favorable than it deserved.

C

Lincoln Anderson, Editor, *The Villager* – I wrote a few articles about Stonewall; pointed out that E. E. Cummings used capital letters when he wrote or signed his name; and pointed out that the 1969 Stonewall incident was not a riot with someone in charge but, rather, was an uprising. Anderson failed to accept my article about having been mooned by *Screw* editor Al Goldstein, one that is in the present book. He perhaps had no space but again he somehow thought the article was about two other people in an accompanying picture and did not see the connection with my mentioning the Goldstein obituary written well by the magazine's **Al Amateau**. *The Villager* has chosen to be a political, not an activist, paper as in decades past.

D

Co-editors **Dorothy McDade and Warren Allen Smith**, *The Eye Opener* (1938), Minburn Iowa – as teenagers we learned that it is best not to print any funny article about an epileptic woman in a town of 328 when one of your fathers is a businessman (grain dealer) and the other is a minister (Methodist).

The Hersam Publishing Company, founded in 1908, publishes New Canaan's *The Advertiser*. Upon arriving in New Canaan in 1954, I was asked by its editor **Carlton E. Hill** to choose which 12th grade New Canaan High School student of English would receive its annual "Best 12th Grade Student Award." The award was a $25 Savings Bond (which, only if held for ten years, was worth $25). Although I helped with supplying facts for news articles, I do not remember having a by-line. Today the company, now the Hersam Acorn Newspapers, remains a family-owned weekly company that publishes 19 weeklies.

While a resident, I subscribed to and looked forward to the news reports. Since moving to New York City, I obtain the news online and, for awhile.

shared (*Emeritus*) with fellow retirees news about former colleagues as well as called attention to *The* Advertiser's obituaries of deceased faculty members.

What I have found is that *The Advertiser*, even with its present new editor (**Joshua Fisher**), seldom writes about individual faculty members although writing that townspeople often choose to move to town because of its excellent schools.

One wonders if the Hersams have overlooked the teachers as a group and as individuals, almost all of whom cannot afford to live in town. *The Advertiser* fails to credit the dedicated educators who inspiringly teach the children of the town's parents and more than adequately prepare them for their future college, university, and professional careers.

The present book illustrates the variety of stories that *The Advertiser* did not write about.

Furthermore, *The Advertiser* has not questioned why self-published books cannot be sold in the town's book store. Similarly, Phil Kenney (who graduated from NCHS in 1967) has a brilliant book – *Radiance, A Novel* – that cannot be bought in New Canaan's book store.

How many other New Canaan authors' books are not sold in town nor reviewed in *The Advertiser*!

Nor has *The Advertiser* looked into why the town library received three copies of my *Unforgettable New Canaanites* but no longer has a copy. An investigative report could have been written as to what part the New Canaan Historical Society played in townspeople's being unable to read that book.

The Fugs

From 1963 to 1965, poets Ed Sanders and Tuli Kupferberg were joined by Ken Weaver on drums to form The Fugs (a euphemism for Fuck, one that was used in Norman Mailer's *The Naked and the Dead*).

To this day, few know of my connections.

Joining The Fugs in 1966 were bassist **John Anderson** (a New Canaan High School student where I was his English Department chairman) and in 1965-1966 guitarist **Vincent Leary**. Few knew that I hired Vinny as an engineer at Variety Recording Studio, where he was a highly skilled one.

In 2014, Leary teaches in New York at the Institute of Audio Research and has not heard from Anderson, now a lawyer in Oregon who prefers not to publicize his having been a Fug.

Stefan Grossman, Jake Jacobs, Tuli Kupferberg, Clay Cole, Vinny Leary, Ed Sanders

Haiti

In elementary school, we had to learn about all the countries of the world. In 5th grade Miss Anna Shirley was asked how far away HAH-it-ee was, and she said HAY-tee was closer than China.

Little did I know then that eventually I would get to Antigua, Barbados, Belgium, Bermuda, Canada, Costa Rica, Cuba, Denmark, Dominican Republic, France, Germany, Guadalupe, Haiti, Holland, Jamaica, Luxembourg, Martinique, Mexico, Monaco, Morocco, Nevis, Puerto Rico. Saint Kitts, Spain, Sweden, and Switzerland.

Nor could I have imagined that AW-eet-ee (as it is pronounced there) would play an important part in my life.

In 1948 when I lived in New York City's International House, I helped a fellow resident, **Dr. Louis Mars**, who lived just down the hall and became Haiti's first psychiatrist. He appreciated my help in editing some of his papers, including one on voodoo.

On one of my four trips to Haiti, I met Dr. Mars when he was Minister of Health and made him laugh when I complained that I had no physical problems whatsoever.

He wrote *The Fight Against Insanity* (1947) and *The Story of Zombi in Haiti, Crisis of Possession* (1977).

His father had been Haiti's well-known Ambassador to France.

Dr. Louis Mars

In 1977 I went to Haiti for the Mardi Gras, befriending **Lima Charles-Pierre**. **Lima**, one of Baby Doc's Presidential Guards, who became one of my unique acquaintances. To watch and take photos of a Mardi Gras parade that was a block away, I stood in front of the Presidential Palace.

"*Non, vous ne pouvez pas se tenir là*" he said (or the equivalent), pointing his gun at a spot directly between my eyes.

"What did you say?"

He explained that only Baby Doc's family and friends could stand on that side of the street, and it dawned on me that was why I was the only person there.

He asked if I was a tourist from Germany. I said I was from New York City. So he asked why I had chosen to visit Haiti. Carefully avoiding that I was a journalist, I said at my recording studio I had a friend, **Frantz Casséus**, who thought I'd like to visit, that in 1969 I had recorded his "Haitiana" and helped make its album and jacket, calling his company Afro-Carib.

Fernando made the LP and I made the LP jacket

"You recorded his *Meci bon Die*?" Yes, we recorded that. Frantz claimed that his girlfriend (Barbara Perlow) who was not Haitian, had no accent at all. She did, I smiled. I was pleasantly surprised that "Thank you, God" was such a well-known song.

A sergeant then headed toward us, and I saw an officer in the distance. So before rushing to the other side of the street, I asked the handsome Presidential Guard if he could have a beer after work. No, he said, he slept in the palace. Anyway, I gave him my guest house telephone number, happy that he no longer was pointing his gun between my eyes.

On the other side of the street, which was as packed as a rush-hour subway, not one but several grabbed my privates. White, rich, alone? I couldn't tell if the erotic ones were male or female, which is true also on the subway.

The day before leaving, while I was talking to Mr. Rouzier, the guest house's front doorbell buzzed and he almost had a heart attack upon seeing five of the President's guards standing there. Quickly, I recognized Lima and said, "*Entrez!* Arthur, please, beer, wine, liquor for everyone. *Ayons une partie!*"

When Lima (LEE-mah, on the left) brought four fellow guards in 1977 to **Arthur Rouzier**'s Guest House, it wasn't to arrest me as a journalist. It was simply to take me up on my offer to buy him a beer.

And we had a big party. But, aware that the gay residents were concerned about their safety and as I began introducing some of them to the five, down the steps with a Bette Davis swag and very large hat came Miss Belgium, making eyes at all five. She's the house entertainer, I lied. But she became handy, for she could translate everything we asked her to. For example, I searched for the words to see if on Lima's farm he had sheep and pigs or grew oats and wheat, which we had in Iowa. None of the other guards accepted invitations to come to residents' rooms (the big and oldest guard, on the right) mumbled something – but Lima came to mine so that I could give him my English-French dictionary and my postal address. We returned in a minute and it was clear there was no hanky-panky. But of course!

When I asked the best way to get to the airport the next day, Lima said he would pick me up at 08:00. No, it would cost me nothing. At the airport, he and two other guards carried my luggage up to the airline's desk, putting mine ahead of a line of tourists who also were leaving. When the airplane's wheels left the runway, several rushed to ask why I was kicked out of the country. No, I explained, the President's Guards were my friends . . . leading them to withdraw, to my amusement.

145

In 2003, Lima's brother in Brooklyn, **Renaud Charles-Pierre**, informed me that Lima had been assassinated. Thirty-seven bullets!

I have helped raise his son **Ligardy Termonfils** ever since. Ironically, Renaud has shown little interest in meeting Ligardy. He did tell me that Lima had a family, one son resembling Ligardy.

I did have many pleasant memories while in Haiti.

I asked questions of elders about their unique musical instruments.

At Freda's Bar in Port-au-Prince, I was asked to be the judge at a dance contest and made a hit by awarding 1st prize to a dwarf.

I had gone there with fellow guest house clients Chicagoan **Fred Bundy** and New Yorker **Patrick Donohue**, both of whom were looking for Haitian partners. Donohue might have brought his handsome guy to New York City for a visit or for a long-term relationship.

Just as I thought my Father did not leave me something after his death, I met Warren Allen Smith. He was the greatest thing that happened to me. He is like a father to me. He is also my best friend. I love this man very much. Thank you for every thing being a [tutor], father and friend.

Emmeline, biological mother of Lima's child, brought Ligardy to meet me on 26 August 2004. He was 5' 10" then and has been 6' tall since 9th grade.

Dinner at Fedora's Restaurant

Photo by Ligardy Termonfils

Lise Celidort (Aunt Liz) is the daughter of the sister of Ligardy's Grandmother **Yva Volmar**'s sister. She lives in the same building in the next room that Yva and Ligardy once shared and which I visited often. Since Day One all of Ligardy's family have adopted me, but this is the first holiday we dined together in Brooklyn.

I showed Lise my new iPad photos of Ligardy, including the one in his new university basketball team's suit. What a surprise when I laid the iPad down, touched its screen (dialed her cellphone), she picked up her cellphone, and there we were conversing while sitting next to each other.

How things have changed since her October birth in 1926 and mine in 1921.

The Haitian guest house was memorable. Following are some of the staff.

1958   **Matiu** – Matiu was available to everyone at Arthur Rouzier's gay guesthouse where I stayed for a week in Haiti. 7U/2 AC/DC

1958   **Eduardo** – Eduardo was popular at Rouzier's Haitian guesthouse; gentle but macho kind, he starts by ripping one's shorts off, and he knows exactly what to do then. 7U/1 bot

1958   **Fobert** (Kid) – At the Haitian guesthouse, Kid (specimen on the right) was nude and having his ears pierced. The Chicago guest at the place did the piercing, only sterilizing the needle by burning it with a match. Kid asked Benoit the artist to come with him to my room, he did, and we did. 11/U/1 bot

1958   **Benoit** – Benoit (on the left), my guide in Haiti, was the one who spoke enough English to make my visit in Haiti so special. On the last night, he brought Fobert to my room and, after quite a bit of rum, the two made the night memorable. 7/U/1

I knew about **Maya Deren**'s Guggenheim Grant and her having been in Haiti in the 1940s and 1950s to make an ethnographic film about *voudoun*, her spelling of voodoo.

Teiji Ito and Maya Deren

I was once invited to her place in Manhattan, where a truly bohemian crowd was wild with music, conversation, smoke, and drink.

I arrived alone and, after greeting me, Ms. Deren asked where my husband or wife was. I said he was at work, then asked who the Japanese guy with an ear-ring was – it was the first time I'd seen a guy with an ear-ring – I learned it was ballet composer/performer **Teiji Ito**, a teenage runaway who had married her in the late 1950s. My recollection is that Deren looked like a Russian Jew.

Standard reference sources report that in 1943 she had worked with **Marcel Duchamp** on *The Witch's Cradle* and that in 1961, Deren died from a brain hemorrhage after having taken amphetamines and sleeping pills. Deren's ashes were scattered.

Ito died from a heart attack while visiting Haiti. The Teiji Ito Collection, consisting of audio tapes, is held by the Rodgers and Hammerstein Archives of Recorded Sound in Manhattan at the New York Public Library for the Performing Arts.

Hell's Kitchen

I hitch-hiked from Iowa to Manhattan in order to take advantage of the G. I. Bill. A friendly black married couple picked me up in Pennsylvania and took me to near where they were going, 114th Street.

Because I hadn't told them I was a college student heading for Columbia University, they let me out at 110th and Amsterdam, in Harlem. No sweat, and I walked westward with my two bags to Broadway, then found where I had been assigned a temporary place to stay on 114th until the International House was ready for me.

That same week, Fernando met me on a park bench nearby in Riverside Park. Fernando had moved from his mother's and sister's apartment on nearby Claremont Avenue to room with a Costa Rican consul at 244 West 103rd Street. He was caught staying overnight with me when I was able to obtain a room at the International House, then moved with me to an apartment in the 90s on Riverside Drive. Eventually, we moved to 103rd Street. When Fernando got a job as an engineer in Times Square, we then moved in 1959 to 45th Street in Hell's Kitchen.

The move to Hell's Kitchen was an important one. The week we moved in, newspapers were filled with stories about a "cape killer" who had been caught in the playground park on 45th between 9th and 10th avenues, and on the same side of the street.

Daniel Moynihan in 1949 said of the area, "I've lived much of my life in a jungle of broken families, watching them tear out each other's minds, watching them feasting on each other's hearts. . . . I lived with the "sprawling, plodding, stupid, sluggish, ugly beautiful working people." (*NY Times*, 6 April 2003)

When Fernando and I heard about the apartment on 45th in Hell's Kitchen, I was not too happy about moving from uptown on 103rd Street to a midtown area considered dangerous near 8th and 9th avenues.

My room would be so small that even with a high-riser if I made it into a double bed there wouldn't be room to stand.

Two features appealed: its exposed brick walls and being with Fernando.

We lived here in this walk-up tenement almost 30 years, until his death 20 February 1989.

Fernando's room was on the 4th floor (left of center), the one with an air-conditioner jutting out.

The first super was a European lady, Marie, alleged to have had sex with President Herbert Hoover, which I had a problem believing.

We couldn't easily get up to the roof, but Fernando had a way of going to the basement and changing the fuse boxes so that we could use more electricity.

Hitchhiking

During and for a time after the Great Depression, hitchhiking was common. In 1940, when I went to Cedar Falls during my freshman year of college, I thumbed up rides. At a four-corner stop, I'd point my thumb to the direction in which I wanted to travel. On some occasions I'd get stuck out in nowhere.

Sometimes farmers would stop, curious to find where I was going. Sometimes they just passed slowly by, as if I might be a burglar fleeing from somewhere.

Once I got a ride with a drunk, and while going down a dangerous hill with a curve at the bottom he had a flat tire. But although stories were told about all the dangers of picking up strangers, I never had big problems.

In 1948 when my parents took me to the train, for I had a one-way ticket to New York City, I got off at Ames and hitched rides all the way to Columbia University. One lady took me to Akron, a bit miffed that I went right to sleep and didn't talk to her. In Akron, I walked over to the Goodyear building in which blimps were parked.

A black couple took me from there to Manhattan, which is where they were going. I had meant 116th and Broadway. They let me off at 116th in Harlem, but I was able to walk the distance, favorably impressed by the speed with which everything was happening.

Hymn of the Pantheist

In the Stamford Unitarian hymn book, I found,"Seek Not Afar For Beauty," an 1863 hymn by Minot Judson Savage, a 19th Century American, associated at various times with Congregational and Unitarian churches.

1. Seek not a-far for beau-ty. Lo! it glows
in dew-wet grass-es all a-bout your feet;
in birds, in sun-shine, child-ren's fac-es sweet,
in stars and moun-tain sum-mits topped with snows.
Go not a-broad for hap-pi-ness. For see,
it is a flow-er that here blooms free-ly.

2. Bring love and jus-tice home, and then no more
will you won-der where peace and joy are taught.
Dream not of no-ble ser-vice else-where wrought.
The sim-ple du-ty now waits at your door;
God's voice speaks ev-er hol-i-er com-mands:
Life's saint-ly deeds are done by com-mon hands.

3. In won-der-work-ings, or some bush a-flame,
we look for Truth, and fan-cy it con-cealed;
But in earth's com-mon things, Life stands re-vealed,
while grass and flowers and stars spell out God's Name.
Seek not a-far for beau-ty. Lo! for see
it is a flow-er that here blooms free-ly.

One Unitarian might interpret the words as meaning that it is God's gift that "all should eat and drink and take pleasure in all their toil." (*Ecclesiastes* 3:11-13.)

Instead of God, another Unitarian might use Nature and the inspiration that the natural rather than the supernatural clarifies what "beauty" is and means.

On and off, I was the Stamford church's pianist, choosing Unitarian composers' works such as Bela Bartøk's for preludes.

At some point I modified the words of the above hymn, substituting the feminine Nature for the masculine God.

At my recording studio in Times Square, I then hired studio manager José Gallegos and Mauricio Smith, a well-known Panamanian flautist, to give the music a contemporary sound, after which we recorded Broadway tenor Jimmy Justice (in the cast of *Timbuktu*) to sing the melody.

One Sunday for a prelude I played the hymn, after which I arranged that a tape recorder played the recorded tape. Those in the congregation that Sunday heard me, then heard my several variations of the melody, then the surprisingly contemporary sound of live musicians . . . and, startlingly, a 6' 1" black who had sat in the back row rose from his seat, walked slowly down the aisle, singing the hymn that finished with his incredibly high note. The applause almost never ended, many saying, "Bravo!"

But who was he? Had he ever before attended? How did he know the melody?

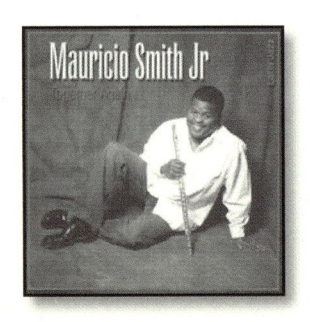

Mauricio Smith with flute   Warren, piano – José Gallegos, digital piano

No one could figure out how the dramatic scene had occurred, and everyone couldn't wait for coffee hour to happen.

HYMN OF THE PANTHEIST

Warren Allen Smith

Seek not afar for beauty. Look, it glows
In dew-wet grasses all about your feet,
In birds, in sunshine, childish faces sweet,
In stars and mountain summits topped with snows.

Go not abroad for happiness, for see
It is a flower blooming at your door.
Bring love and justice home, and then no more
Will you wonder in what dwellings joy may be.

http://wasm.us/Hymn_Pantheist.mp3

Jesus

During a gay parade, this chap willingly allowed me to photograph him.

Minburn, Iowa

In Alberta, Canada, there is a town named Minburn. It's in a county named Minburn, and they have no connection with the town in Dallas County, Iowa, named Minburn. Old-timers who claimed the place was named after the first white baby born there (Minny Burns) could never document the tale.

In 1921 the population was 328 and excluded people who lived on nearby farms. In the 2010 census, 365 were counted as living there: 98.1% white; 0.8% Native American; 0.3% African American; 0.3% Asian; 0.3% from other races; and 0.3% from two or more races. Hispanic or Latino of any race were 1.1% of the population. Only was listed as a "Notable Native": List of LGBT writers Warren Allen Smith, American author of *Cruising the Deuce* (2010), written under pseudonym Allen Windsor.

Memories, published in my *In the Heart of Showbiz*:

> The M & St L (Minneapolis & St. Louis Railroad) depot in the 1930s was where teenagers met on cold nights, because Agent Nelson did not lock the place, and a pot-bellied stove was there if someone brought firewood. I tried to gain entrance if several were inside but usually was not allowed to see what the older kids called "making out."

> In grade school when plays were performed, some teachers had everyone wear blackface. Students pretended they were niggers who sang and danced. We didn't mind when the burnt cork was rubbed on, but the creamy stuff they put on us to take it off was, I complained, for girls!

"Quick," I'd say, "so I can wash the stuff off!" We students imitated the funny way the darky radio actors in "Amos and Andy" sounded. Why some people were "coons" and we were white was never too clear, but somehow I knew it was better not to be black. "Catch a nigger by the toe – if he hollers, let 'im go," kids would say. It wasn't clear why that was so funny. Niggertoes were OK, though, except unlike peanuts you had to crack 'em, then scrape 'em to get the nut out. The nutty part seldom came out in one piece.

It is clearer if one tries to figure out how far relations between the races have come since the 1930s and 1940s.

Warren in White Pants, Leader of the Pickaninny Band

Warren (who ended up in New York)
and Loren Nissly
(who ended up in Connecticut)

When I was nine and it was Iowa-hot one night, I slept in my pj's on a blanket in the front yard between Mr. Lon Clark's place and a building that housed part of Mr. Rowe's big department store. The next morning even my parents woke up, because there was lots and lots of noise. People were running around, yelling that Virgil Untied had been killed by robbers. Virgil, who was Doris's and Afton's and Mildred's father! He was the town marshal, its only cop. It wasn't Machine Gun Kelly's or Baby Face Nelson's or Bonnie Parker's or John Dillinger's or Jesse James's gang, my mom thought, but this one had robbed several stores in town and they weren't caught. When the telephone operator (Ina Marsh, Bonnie Pestana's aunt) had heard them in the grocery store next to her, she rang Mr. Untied and his brother and Leo Hagenstein.

When they shot it out, Virgil was killed and the robbers got away. It was the most awful thing that had ever happened in the town. It was awful, too, that I didn't hear a thing and slept through it all. Why, if I'd been awake I'd have gone over to the robbers and told them to get out of town, that folks in Minburn didn't like people like them!

In the morning one of the shots was found that had hit the department store wall just a few feet above my head. Dad drew a circle around the hole, and he never dug the shell out. How I wished he could have used his mom's $1.00 Kodak Brownie to get the bad guys' picture! Meanwhile, the bad guys were never caught.

Once, when there was some kind of church social in Adel, the county seat of Dallas County, and I saw some robber put his group's ice cream freezer in a car and start to drive away, I got the license number. My dad was so proud, because the sheriff caught the guy soon afterwards, and I was rewarded with all that I could eat.

Dad was on Minburn's town council and was the most honest person in town, so at an early age I was for the good guys and against the bad ones. From *Popular Mechanics* I answered an ad for a dime and got information about how to take fingerprints. No one else in town seemed as interested in whorls.

My favorite pastime was to wave to Mr. Hungerford, who always waved back from the M. & St. L. caboose as the freight train slowly moved through town. Sometimes, Dad would purchase from Mr. Hungerford bottles of Minnehaha mineral water that he brought from Minnesota and sold along the way to St. Louis. I thought Minnehaha was the funniest word in the language.

I liked to sit on a rock near the tracks, for Mr. Hungerford in his caboose waved for him to come over to the train – he wasted no time. "Hungry" boosted me up onto the end platform, then let me peek inside, then helped me down to the ground. My parents never stopped hearing about this, the most thrilling adventure that I had ever had.

In those days, I'd not known that "M & St. L" also was called "Misery & Short Life" and "Maimed & Still Limping." I said that wasn't nice to say about Hungry's line of business.

The town library has published *The Minburn Pinhook*, and, although as kids we called ourselves Pinhookers, it has not been documented if it was a tribe of Indians. The Iowa tribes were found in Kansas, Nebraska, and Oklahoma. None of the federally recognized tribes looks or sounds similar to Pinhook.

Dad founded the first American Legion veterans' group in Minburn, and the office was just north of Shannon's ice cream shop and across from Mr. Thompson's horse-shoe place where Dolliver Thompson's dad made and attached shoes on horses.

The Perry Chief, Thursday, September 22, 2005 — 11A

s/Legals

Minburn native a member of the world's *Who's Who*

By JOSH HUTT
Staff Reporter

Warren Smith, who made the World's Who's Who list with his many accomplishments over the years, returned to Iowa to speak at a ceramony for the Waukee Hotel over the weekend.

"Dallas County is a very wonderful area," Smith said.

Born and raised in Minburn, Smith's father was a grain elevator manager. His grandfather, Spencer Smith, was one of the founders of Waukee and also built the Waukee Hotel.

After a primary graduation in 1938 from Minburn — "The best education I got was in Minburn," Smith said — Smith moved to Rippey where he would graduate from Rippey High School in 1939. His father would go on to be the mayor of Rippey and serve on the city council.

Smith's family often bought seed in Perry saying it was better than Adel seed at the time.

He was drafted into the Army and saw action on Omaha Beach during D-Day and later on during the Battle of the Bulge.

Smith took his G.I. Bill and went to Columbia and Chicago. He then come back to Cedar Falls to finish his major in journalism and English. The road led a hitch hiked path to New York.

"If you can make it in New York, you can make it anywhere," Smith said about life in the Big Apple.

Smith wound up working in the recording industry with such notable vocal talents as Liza Minnelli, Paul Simon and Steve Allen.

He Currently is the Chancellor of the African Online School of Philosphy and his column has appeared in every newspaper in the Carribbean.

Smith's return to Iowa led to 400 miles traveled in the state and 400 pictures worth of midwest memories. He stopped off at the Hotel Pattee where he had a "good strong drink."

"The surroundings were very pleasent in Perry," said Smith.

SMITH

The Perry Chief (22 September 2005) published the above.

163

On 17 July 2014, according to *The Des Moines* Register, a century-old train depot in Minburn was on the move Thursday. Literally.

"Workers spent part of the morning moving the depot about 100 yards, from near a grain elevator to next to the popular Raccoon River Valley Trail. The depot, abandoned by Union Pacific Railroad in 2004, will be transformed into a visitors center, cafe, and museum. The cost of the project is estimated at $1.2 million."It will be great for the community," Mayor Mike Pace said. "It will be great for the people riding the trail to stop and get some refreshments." The city began working on the project in 2007. Before, the depot was in the middle of the Heartland Heartland Co-op, which wasn't an ideal location for traffic, Pace said. Pace said they're hoping to have the depot fully operational by January 2015."

The photo by Mark Hinds shows the century-old Minburn train depot as it chugs along to its new location.

Physicians

I credit my parents' genes for my longevity, but where better to get sick than in New York City with its great Jewish doctors!

Thomas V. Tupper, M.D.

Dr Tupper was Fernando's and my primary doctor from the 1950s until Fernando's death, when he signed the death certificate "natural causes."

Selig Strax, M.D.

In 1958, Dr. Strax operated on me when I had a coccyx problem (pilonidal cyst near my tailbone). He died in 1999.

Brian J. Herschorn, M.D., C.M.

My opthalmologist for more than a dozen years, who was trained in Canada, removed my worst (two cataracts) and enhanced my best.

Stuart W. Haber, M.D.

My primary physician in 2014, whose Sheridan Square office is nearby in the West Village, is known by others for being a disease specialist and by me for being thorough and conscientious.

Pink Humanist

The *Pink Humanist* is a 16-page quarterly magazine launched in 2011 by the Pink Triangle Trust and edited by veteran gay journalist and photographer, Barry Duke, who lives in Benidorm on Spain's Costa Blanca.

The Trust was established as a UK registered charity in 1992 – and is the only charity of its kind in the UK.

The PTT derives its name from the pink triangle, the Nazi concentration camp badge used to identify male prisoners who were interned because of their homosexuality. Originally intended as a badge of shame, the pink triangle has been reclaimed as an international symbol of gay pride and the gay rights movement.

The PTT's principal aims, as set out in its Deed of Trust, are to promote the principles and practice of Humanism to the public, and particularly to lesbians and gay men, and to advance the education of the public, and particularly of Humanists, about all aspects of homosexuality.

Humanism is essentially a system of thought that rejects religious beliefs and centres on humans and their values, capacities, and worth.

The PTT may also assist individuals to obtain remedies under the law where they have suffered unlawful discrimination on account of their homosexuality or their absence of religious belief.

In 1990 the PTT started publishing a quarterly magazine, the *Gay and Lesbian Humanist*, which featured national and international news, feature articles and reviews. Regular contributors included journalists in the United Kingdom and abroad writing for the lesbian/gay and humanist press. The magazine was widely distributed to gay, lesbian, and Humanist organisations and stocked by gay and alternative bookshops in the UK.

An online successor was launched in 2008, but this year a decision was made by the Trust to give the magazine a make-over, and relaunch it as *The Pink Humanist*.

In 1996 the PTT started arranging secular ceremonies of love and commitment for gay and lesbian couples as the alternative to Christian "blessings" arranged – usually clandestinely – by gay clergy. The PTT ceremonies were called "affirmations". They were widely advertised, mainly in *Gay Times* and were soon in great demand.

A nationwide network of Humanist celebrants was established from Aberdeen in the North to the Channel Islands in the South and some donated part of their fee to the Trust. When London Mayor Ken Livingstone allowed ceremonies for gay and lesbian couples to be held at City Hall, the PTT was listed as providing them – and many of them were conducted by Denis Cobell, then President of the National Secular Society.

The provision of these ceremonies continued until the Civil Partnership legislation was introduced by the Labour Government in 2004 and it became possible for secular ceremonies to be held after registration at Registry Offices up and down the country. For many years the PTT provided substantial indirect funding for the Gay and Lesbian Humanist Association (GALHA) when its magazine was issued free to GALHA members. It also funded the printing cost of the GALHA newsletter which was later published in place of the magazine. It has provided funding for other LGBT and Humanist projects such as LGBT.

Scene from Across the Pond
By Warren Allen Smith

Photo credit: W WARBY

Veterans Day, an annual holiday on November 11 that honors those who served in the US Armed Forces, was celebrated with parades in towns and cities throughout the country, the largest of which was in New York City. Female as well as male veterans marched down Fifth Avenue, and politicians, notables, and members of numerous bands added to the colorful occasion.

The Villager, in downtown Greenwich Village, featured an article about a veteran – one of General Dwight D Eisenhower's adjutant generals' chief clerks – whose office in the Little Red Schoolhouse in Reims was just down the corridor from that of Eisenhower.

The reporter interviewed the technical sergeant on November 14, 2013 and illustrated the article with a 1944 photo of a now 92-year-old gay atheistic humanist who writes for The Pink Humanist, and is not a father but is a surrogate dad for eight Modern Family straight kids who know about his two paramours (one who recorded Liza Minnelli's first demo, the other a Broadway star who was nominated for three Tony Awards).

That veteran, incidentally, is your columnist – and the article explains why he never fired a rifle during World War II. You can access the report at **http://tinyurl.com/ol698xw**

FOURTEEN countries have now legalized same-sex marriage: Netherlands (2001); Belgium (2003); Spain (2005); Canada (2005); South Africa

Tech Sergeant Warren Allen Smith on his way to Verdun in 1944

(2006); Norway (2009); Portugal (2010); Iceland (2010); Argentina (2010); Denmark (2012); Brazil (2013); France (2013); Uruguay (2013); and New Zealand (2013). Britain (England and Wales) will allow same-sex marriage in Spring 2014. (see **http://tinyurl.com/opyfwf8**)

SIXTEEN states now have legal recognition of same-sex relationships: California, Connecticut, Delaware, Hawaii, Illinois, Iowa, Massachusetts, Maryland, Maine, Minnesota, New Hampshire, New Jersey, New Mexico, New York, Rhode Island and Washington. The District of Columbia, in which the Capital is located) legalized same-sex marriage in 2010. [**See http://tinyurl.com/q6o55bn**]

If 16 states grow to 26, we'll be closer to Congress making it mandatory in all 50 states.

An unofficial report card for December 2013. Gay judge appointed in 2013: Federal circuit court judge **Todd M Hughes**, US Court of Appeals for the Federal Circuit. Congress gay members: US Representative (out when first elected, male) **Jared Polis**; US Representative (out when first elected), first openly bisexual member of Congress: **Kyrsten Sinema** – elected 2012 US Representative (out when first elected), first to succeed another openly-gay officeholder in office [**Tammy Baldwin**]; Mark **Pocan**, US Representative (out when first elected). First non-white openly gay member of Congress: **Mark Takano**.

Pseudonyms

Known to my inner circle of two dozen as a roué and sybarite ("and I've never been in Sybaria"), I am called by my mailman "a man of many names" (using pseudonyms such as Rev DooDoo, Allen Windsor, Berty Russell, Guillermo Moreno, Lucretius, Iosef Kazinsky, Prometheus, Robert Shockley, Jimmy Trimble, and Jun Sczesnoczkawasm).

To the cognoscenti, I insert opinions into my writing by quoting that "a certain Manhattan wag says . . ."

Race

Although the family of eight who adopted me includes four who are black or part black, when I was in grade school I (in white pants) was chosen to lead the Pickaninny Chorus. We each had to burn some cork, then apply it to our faces in order to look like Negroes.

Have I ever used the N-word? Yes, as a book reviewer for *Library Journal*, in the 1960s I reviewed Dick Gregory's *Nigger*.

It wasn't until 24 June 2014, in a fractured decision that revealed deep divisions over what role the judiciary body should play in protecting racial and ethnic minorities, that the United States Supreme Court upheld a Michigan constitutional amendment that bans affirmative action to admissions to the state's pubic universities. The 6-2 ruling effectively endorsed similar measures in seven other states. It may also encourage more states to enact measures banning the use of race in admission or to consider race-neutral alternatives to ensure diversity.

RCA Institutes

While Fernando Vargas and I lived uptown, I helped arrange for him to study electrical engineering at RCA Institutes in Greenwich Village (pictured, at West 4th and Greenwich Street, a block away from where I now live). He received a certificate in a year.

Fernando was just learning English, and it was expedient for me to take all his classes, because everything (particularly the directions) needed to be translated. I also learned that I'd better meet him nightly at the end of classes. That way, by having a hamburger a block away, I could be certain that he would come to our apartment, not go cruising. What he learned was key to becoming an outstanding audio engineer. That led to our founding Variety Recording Studio.

Looking for employment, Fernando was interviewed by R. E. L. Lab and made a favorable impression on Edwin Armstrong after being coached about how to weld a certain item. Hired, he found Armstrong avuncular, one who confided his problems. Telling Armstrong that he lived on 109th near Columbia U, he learned that Armstrong had taught there and in 1913 had discovered regeneration.

With talk about amplifiers, feedback, and oscillators, the work turned out to be educational and enjoyable, particularly when Edwin – they soon were on a first-name basis – told of being paid only $1 by Columbia but was earning money from his patents. He allowed the military to use royalty-free his findings about FM – frequency modulation – but when the war ended RCA claimed that they, not he, had invented FM, and they were suing each other. Edwin complained to Fernando that he became nearly bankrupt from defending his patents, that his wife had left him in the middle of all this, and in 1953 his licenses and patents would all expire. He did not confide everything all at once, but on some days, when agitated, he would tell bits and pieces about having made the first portable radio and advanced AM radio, and on other days he was like a friendly uncle.

In 1954, Armstrong dressed neatly, walked to a 13th story window of the River House, 435 East 52nd Street in Manhattan, and jumped out. His body hit a third story overhang. Fernando was devastated. Later, Armstrong's wife settled with RCA for over a million dollars. What bothered Fernando was that Armstrong died believing he was a failure. Actually, he was anything but.

Headline from the front page of the New York Herald Tribune, February 2, 1954

Sing Sing

Fernando and I got sent up the river in 1972. For two days, we recorded two volumes of Eddie Palmieri's Puerto Rican band's LPs, *Eddie Palmieri, Live in Sing Sing*.

We loaded a rented truck with our needed Variety Recording Studio equipment, and I drove the two of us and engineer Johnny Taglieri to the prison . . . but we couldn't get in . . . until I stopped the truck over a pit in the road and prison officers checked to see what we might have had hidden under the truck or in all the packed cases of instruments in the truck.

The space allotted was the prison chapel, where. the musicians performed on its stage. Everyone was friendly. When I needed help to fasten down some of the electrical cables by nailing them to the floor of the chapel. a trusted guard (who might have been a convicted murderer) supplied a hammer and did the pounding inches from me. Other guards accompanied if I needed to go to the toilet (for my protection, not that of the inmates).

During some of the sessions, inmates were allowed to watch, and the Puerto Ricans who were in the majority took front rows, blacks in a side section, and whites who were in the minority didn't dare muscle in.

Palmieri and his band were first-rate.

He did other sessions at the studio, but one day I read in the tabloids that the wife of the Latin-jazz great, 73-year old Iraida, was shot by her neighbor who suspected she had made romantic advances toward her 60-year-old husband.

Out of jail it's dangerous!

Stonewall

Early in the morning of 28 June 1969, a routine police raid on the Stonewall Bar at 53 Christopher Street in New York City turned into a major happening. When police arrived at about 3 a.m., they ordered customers to leave, began arresting employees, and started to remove several "homo's" and "drag queens." Such incidents had been routine, but this morning the customers as well as those outside unexpectedly began chanting "Pigs!" at the police, who of course fought back. The police barricaded themselves inside until rescued by other officers.

For the next several evenings, further disturbances took place – the incidents have been referred to as the Stonewall Uprising; for to have been "riots" the incident would have had to have had leaders. It was the event that sparked the contemporary lesbian and gay movement which spread nationally as well as internationally.

Four secular humanists known to have been present – names associated with one of the major human rights fights of the century – later became officers or friends of the Stonewall Riot Veterans group: **Howard Cruse**, **Martin Duberman**, **Randy Wicker**, and **I**. I was the only one who actually participated the 2nd night.

The New York Times (2 June 2009) published an article, "Images Surface From Stonewall," that included some never-before published photos taken on 2 July 1969, the last day of the disturbances.

The Stonewall Veterans Organization

"Thoughts on the 40th Anniversary of the Stonewall Riots," I submitted as an article *The Villager:*

> I "outed" a straight. Not a gay. A straight! Listen up.
>
> After what some of us considered "just a happening" in June 1969 at the Stonewall, not what one day would be credited with being a turning point of the contemporary gay rights movement, several of us participants formed Veterans of Stonewall (VOS).
>
> Steven van Cline volunteered to head the group, Sylvia Rivera volunteered to help raise funds and threw a party complete with entertainment, and I volunteered to be treasurer, after finding that money from Sylvia's party was spent without any record of where it went.

Sylvia Rivera and Stephen van Cline

With the less than $50 party's profits that I was given, I started a Veterans of Stonewall checking account at Amalgamated Bank, insisting that both the President and the Treasurer had to sign all checks. Except for meeting annually and marching at the front of at least five of the annual gay parades, however, VOS transacted no further business.

Meanwhile, the bank charged monthly fees for such a small account, and when the fees represented more than the interest received, I suggested to van Cline that we close the account.

As treasurer I started by interviewing all prospective members, separating them into (a) were definitely there that week; (b) were not there but had been to the bar a little or a lot; and (c) were simply friends of our group.

Van Cline's written statement to me indicated that he clearly was in the first group:

> The first night was probably the most dramatic and the most meaningful to me, because that was the night I was directly involved. My lover and I were stunned and thrilled to see our own kind talking back, berating the cops, and throwing pennies. After seeing the gratuitous bloody beatings in front of us and being called names, we began throwing bricks and cobblestones at the bar, which suddenly became the symbol of our oppression. The second night, Saturday, which we observed from the relative safety of the Rivera Café, was more violent and chaotic with more people, including outsider agitators. The third night was reported to be less violent. I got up early Monday morning (June 30th) in my apartment, a few blocks away on 15th Street, to the sound of heavy rain. I returned to my other art gallery in the country and the rain continued through Tuesday (July 1st). Many say the rain kept people from returning to riot. It is my opinion that we were going about getting the week rolling and involved in endless discussions of the meaning of what had happened. We did not get angry again until word got around, and the newspaper reports about the riots had widely circulated. Quite a few people returned on Wednesday (July 2nd). My only direct experience with activities that night was seeing bloodied people lying on the 7th Ave. sidewalk and against the buildings around the corner from the bar. There was action on Thursday night (July 3rd).

Van Cline, however, was nowhere to be found. I could not get through to him by telephone or e-mail to sign the check. When I snail-mailed him to the addresses of van Cline & Davenport, Ltd., 1581 Route 202, Suite 179, Pomona, NY 10970; and to 3257 Route 10, Ashland, NY 12407 (518) 734-4357, asking him to phone or write. The letter to Ashland was returned, "not known."

Thus ended VOS.

My 1969 Stonewall friend **Danny Garvin** (above) had always been skeptical – he is one of the few who really were there on the first night, although hundreds claim they were. So was another veteran, **Jim Fouratt**, who believes that not even **Sylvia Rivera** was there the first night.

If you Google van Cline and his appraisal company, you'll find that he's apparently still in business. Was he threatened with death by someone who, like Sylvia, doubted he was involved except for the prospect of making money? Does he really have two children, and was he really a novelist? Journalists in the Pomona and Ashland areas might well do an investigative column about all this.

Part of the mystery was solved on 15 April 2006 when van Cline called me from (201) 337-4446 and said {I have paraphrased}:

> Yes, I am a big fake. I was trying to write a novel. I am not gay, but in order to obtain information about what it was like to have been gay in the 1960s, I joined the veterans' groups. Only **Sylvia Rivera** saw through me, and I don't know why she didn't expose me to the others of you. Not only am I not gay, I have two children who now are in their 30s. My name is not Stephen van Cline but, no, I will not tell you what it really is. My business, van Cline & Davenport, Ltd., is called that, but Davenport also does not exist. I did have an art gallery fairly near the Stonewall, so technically I was near the riots when they occurred. But I was not involved and the information I wrote for you and which you put up onto the web should be removed, for it is not true.
>
> **William Henderson**, I think, is an even bigger fake. He could have been a character in my novel, a really dangerous person who could have murdered a roommate, could have a been a real villain. Yes, you have every reason to be angry with me, and I regret that the Amalgamated Bank account was depleted because you could not find me and checks required both our signatures. At least we meant well to make sure that funds would be honestly accounted for.
>
> Yes, I have a terminal liver illness and the prognosis is that I will live only a few more years – that is why I wrote you, in order to clear my conscience. Am I religious? Well, I'm a Christian Scientist. No, I gave up on writing the novel. I did learn how difficult life was for homosexuals, but I am truly sorry to have posed as one and deceived all of you.

So what are my thoughts on the 40th anniversary? First, although I'm a gay journalist who has outed a few gays in my British column starting back in 1996, I never imagined I'd ever out a straight, if that's what van Cline is.

Second, I am honored at being called a veteran of the event that transformed the gay civil rights movement into one that caught the world's attention. It's as important as my also having been a veteran who led his company in 1944 onto Omaha Beach in Normandy.

Third, the building that houses the present Stonewall had two sections, and the original bar with the two jukeboxes was in the building just to the east of where the present bar is. It was here that many of us called home – a place where you could slow-dance with old or new friends, where we couldn't care less that it was grimy and Mafia-connected, for it was home base. Before the building's two sections are sold to a Starbucks or other chain, it is imperative that the site be purchased and re-made into a historical museum. a place worthy of representing the gay civil rights movement not only now but for decades to come.

Before Stonewall

By researching, I have found a Stonewall-before-its-time beer hall called Pfaff's, where a gay group called the "Fred Gray Association" hung out in the early 1860s. **Walt Whitman** was a member, and other members were poet and actress **Adah Isaacs Menken**, journalist and social critic **Henry Clapp**, playwright **John Brougham**, and artist **Elihu Vedder**.

Members of the **Mattachine Society** in a rare group photograph are pictured: **Harry Hay** (upper left), then (l-r) **Konrad Stevens**, **Dale Jennings**, **Rudi Gernreich**, **Stan Witt**, **Bob Hull**, **Chuck Rowland** (in glasses), **Paul Bernard**. [Photo by Jim Grube]

Although Stonewall was a turning point in the gay civil-rights movement, I maintain that the struggle originated over the years.

For example, in a Los Angeles living room in 1950, the Mattachine Society was founded. In 1965 public demonstrations and even national conventions of gay-rights groups had occurred. Immediately after the June 1969 uprising, the local chapters of the Mattachine Society and the Daughters of Bilitis organized protest marches.

"You were a veteran?" I am often asked.

"Yes," I answer. "As a clerk in Supreme Headquarters (SHAEF), Reims, France, 1944-1945. And of the Stonewall Uprising, 1969."

The Surrogate Dad and His Kids

Never a father, I was not only "adopted" by Emily Davenport while in Louisville completing my basic training, but also I was "adopted" by Commandant René Picard and his family during my entire stay in Reims during the war.

I am a dad, having been "adopted" by two girls and six guys who call me a surrogate dad, one who has filled in for a variety of reasons – their biological father may have been assassinated; their mother was divorced and they had no father figure; I was named the parent when two of them entered high school; or I was named as the person to contact if they had a problem in school; in a few cases I have helped financially.

All knew that I am gay. Several know each other. The oldest is in his sixties, the youngest is twenty-one. To my knowledge, none is gay.

Their grandparents are from the Commonwealth of Dominica, Haiti, India/Bangladesh, Puerto Rico, and Uruguay.

Teachers

For fellow New Canaan Public School teachers, I edited *Emeritus,* obtaining voluntary donations from the retirees. An example:

EMERITUS

10 December 1998

Newsletter of Ex-Faculty Members of New Canaan (CT) Schools

Deceased:

Dick Cressy (h.s. history)
Joseph Gula
Ed Lind (h.s. science)
Kathryn Rhodes (h.s. French)
Joe Sikorski (h.s. phys. ed.)
Frank Strong (Asst. Supt)
Wyatt Teurbert (b.s. English)
Daniel Krenicki (1989)
Elizabeth Moore (1989)
Norman Hague (1990)
Keith Littlefield
Lucy Herberick (29 Mar 91)
Catherine E. Cody (1906-92)
Bernice Hall (24 March 92)
Dorothy Deming (29 Apr 92)
Blanche Bowman (5 Nov 92)
Sylvia Garment (21 Apr 93)
Mary Grace Carpenter (25 Sep 93)
Warren Russell (9 Feb 94)
Lillian Mathews (7 May 93)(Sec'y to Supt.)
Marie F. Sweeney (31 May 96)
Robert Shackleton (24 June 94)
Frank Morin (June 94)

Paul Brooks (4 August 94)
Mary Reid (September 94)
Seymour Schneid (5 December 94)
Mary Beth Gilbert (30 Jan 95)
Robert W. Fraleigh (1 Feb 95)
Albert Merrill (19 Apr 95)
Harry Pelletier (18 Aug 95)
Elizabeth Sturtevant (Aug 95)
Michael P. Noto Sr (14 October 95)
Matthew J. Coyle Jr. (14 December 95)
Anthony C. LaVista (19 December 95)
Muriel K. Sleght (25 March 96)
John R. Dunn (6 April 96)
Ruth T. Kelley (3 July 96)
Harry E. Larson (23 Oct 96)
Catherine Isabel Darling (97)
Donald Hearne (4 Feb 97)
Wayne Newell (25 April 97)
Jane Hilton (6 July 98)
James Sedley Rand (11 Aug1998)

Published Annually in December

All errors of omission or commission herein have been made by the
Editor: Warren Allen Smith, 31 Jane Street (Box 10-D), New York, NY 10014
<wasm@idt.net>

Underlined = new

Address for the New Canaan Public Schools Administrative Offices:
(moved from 156 South Avenue on 31 January 1992)
39 Locust Avenue, New Canaan, CT 06840
(203) 972-4400

Emeritus (wasm@mac.com) is an annual newsletter for retirees of the entire New Canaan school system. Your present webmaster also is its newsletter editor. See Ron Donahue's letter to his former teachers by referring below to the Class of 1950.

Graduates will be sad to hear that Headmaster Kenney died 13 Aug 2001. Following is the Emeritus Jan 2002 list of deceased faculty members:

Joseph Colannino (NCHS French)
Dick Cressy (NCHS History)
Al Fabry (NCHS Art)
Joseph Gula
Al Jacobson (NCHS Art)
Ed Lind (NCHS Science)
Keith Littlefield (NCHS Math)
Kathryn Rhodes (NCHS French)
Frank Strong (Asst. Superintendent)
Joe Sikorski (NCHS Phys Ed)
Wyatt Teubert (NCHS English)
Daniel Krenicki (89)
Elizabeth Moore (89)
Norman Hague (90)
Lucy Herberick (29 Mar 91)
Catherine E. Cody (92)
Bernice Hall (24 Mar 92)
Dorothy Deming (29 Apr 92)
Blanche Bowman (5 Nov 92) Secretary
Sylvia Garment (21 Apr 93)
Mary Grace Carpenter (25 Sep 93)
Lillian Matthews (7 May 93) Secretary
Warren Russell (9 Feb 94)
Robert Shackleton (24 June 94)
Frank Morin (June 94)
Mary Reid (Sep 94)
Paul Brooks (4 Aug 94)
Seymour Schneid (5 Dec 94)
Mary Beth Gilbert (30 Jan 95)
Robert W. Fraleigh (1 Feb 95)
Gladys Herhold (Mar 95)
Albert Merrill (19 Apr 95)
Harry Pelletier (18 Aug 95)
Elizabeth Sturtevant (Aug 95)
Michael P. Noto Sr. (14 Oct 95)
Matthew J. Coyle Jr. (14 Dec 95)
Anthony C. LaVista (19 Dec 95)
Muriel K. Sleght (25 Mar 96)

John R. Dunn (6 Apr 96)
Eleanor Purcell (13 May 96)
Marie F. Sweeney (31 May 96)
Ruth T. Kelley (3 July 96)
Harry E. Larson (23 Oct 96)
Catherine Isabel Darling (97)
Donald Hearne (4 Feb 97)
Wayne Newell (25 Apr 97)
Mary R. Griffin (5 Feb 98)
Jane Hilton (6 July 98)
James Sedley Rand (11 Aug 98)
Jean Chance (West School)
Stanley E. Jaworowski (5 Jan 99)
Virginia Lord (Oct 99)
Robert Kennedy (9 Nov 99)
Madeline Murphy (29 Nov 99)
Claire Eddy (6 Dec 99)
Mary Reinhart Cox (14 Feb 00)
Stanley Twardy (23 Feb 00)
Eileen Price (Apr 00) South School Secretary
John A. Masonotti (16 May 00)
Elizabeth G. Haines (1 June 00)
Emily T. Kingsley (3 Aug 00)
Fredda Kunz (Aug 00)
Carl Howard (23 Dec 00)
Jerome Meric Pessagno (31 Dec 00)
Halford McLane (13 Jan 01)
Robert G. Larsen (8 May 01)
Sydney Bryden (13 May 01)
Janet D. Alcott (21 May 01)
Herbert W. Hammack (7 June 01)
Harold Kenney (13 Aug 01) Headmaster
Milan Daniel (20 Aug 01)
Myledred Marcely (17 Sep 01)
Harrison Coombs (13 Jun 02)
Emily C. Gower (23 Mar 03)

Variety Recording Studio

Following is a partial list of the clients of Fernando Vargas's and my Variety Recording Studio, which we founded in 1961 and owned and operated in Times Square until Fernando's death in 1989.

Afro-Carib Records
David Amram
Ansonia Records
Aviles Records
Black Roots of Dominica
Boricano of Hartford
Jerry Bock
Houston Brummit
Jerry Butler
Sammy Cahn
Franz Casseus
Catamount Records
Ray Charles
Norman Chase
Paddy Chayevsky
Steve Clayton
The Coasters
Celia Cruz
Billy Davis (5th Dimension)
Des Moines YMCA Bell Ringers
Loretta Devine
Carl Edelson
Bill Evans
Stick Evans
Fantuzzi
Sammy Fields
Bob Fosse
Jerry Fuller
Futuro Records
Garifuna de Honduras
Hal Gordon
Grand Cayman Barefoot Man
John Guare
Marvin Hamlisch
The Hardtones
Athena Hosey
Hot Cold Sweat
Mary Hurt
Etta James

Jimmy Justice
Stan Krause
Frankie Lane
David Last
Peggy Lee
Maurice Levine
Joey Luft
Lorna Luft
Mary Martin
Marilyn McCoo (5th Dimension)
Rosemary McCoy
Carmen McCrae
Fred McGriff
Ed Meta
Mic-Tone Records
Arthur Miller
Liza Minnelli
Earl Monroe
Tony Peña
The Penguins
Mary Powell
Elvis Presley Music
Gilbert Price
Harold Prince
Tito Puente
Bernard "Pretty" Purdy
Relic Rack
Sun Ra
Robert Rivera
Primitivo Santos
Paul Simon (Jerry Landis)
Jimmy Smits
Spanish World Records
The Starfires
The Starlighters
Susan Tyrell
United Jewish Appeal
Ultra Violet
Jerry Vale
Vince Vallis
Vangellis (Evangelos Odysseas Papathanassiou)
Sarah Vaughan
Harold Wheeler
Robert Whitehead
Stefan Wolpe
Stevie Wonder

Very

If it is, how can it be *very* is?

If the woman is pregnant, how can she be *very* pregnant?

If the fire is hot, why describe it as *very* hot?

If the animal is cute, is it cuter by calling it *very* cute?

I avoid *very*, which is very easy.

/was

My initials, which were on my license plate, inspired a student to devise the following:

[License plate image: "WASNT / CONNECTICUT"]

Waveny

It is officially called Waveny House. I've always called it the Waveny Castle.

In 1912, the large Tudor mansion was built for the **Lewis Lapham** family. Mr. Lapham, an American entrepreneur who made a fortune consolidating smaller businesses in the leather industry, was one of the founders of Texas Oil Company.

Born in Brooklyn, New York, he was the son of Samantha Lapham (née Vail) and Henry Griffith Lapham, who were second cousins. His father was head of a leather firm of his name, and at the age of 19 Lewis Lapham worked first in partnership with Albert Rockwell at Warren, Pennsylvania, later joining his father in Henry G. Lapham & Co.

His *New York Times* obituary included Lapham's having died of uremic poisoning at New York City's Harkness Pavilion of the Medical Center, where he had been a patient for seven weeks.

Through the discovery of oil over thirty-five years ago in a region of Pennsylvania where he had owned a tannery, Mr. Lapham entered the oil industry and helped to form the Texas Oil Company, which soon afterward changed its name to the Texas Company, and a few years ago was named the

Texas Corporation. He served on the board of directors of the two earlier corporations but never held an office.

Through his brother-in-law, the late George F. Dearborn of Maine, Mr. Lapham became interested in the American Hawaiian Steamship Company of San Francisco, the successor of an old line of clipper ships which used to sail round Cape Horn. He was a director for many years. His son, Roger, entered the employ of the company in 1905 as a clerk, and in 1925 became president. Toward the close of 1925 Mr. Lapham resigned all his directorships and since then had been virtually inactive in business.

Local and standard reference sources reported that survivors were the widow, Mrs. Antoinette Dearborn Lapham; two daughters, Mrs. Elinor Ford of Washington, D.C., and Mrs. Samuel Lloyd of Stamford, Connecticut; and two sons, Roger D. Lapham of San Francisco, president of the American Hawaiian Steamship Company, and John H. Lapham of San Antonio, Texas, a director and a member of the executive committee of the Texas Corporation. The funeral was held privately at New Canaan, Connecticut.

Lapham had Waveny House in New Canaan built as a summer residence for his family, a place to escape the city's heat. He was the father of San Francisco Mayor Roger Lapham, the grandfather of actor Christopher Lloyd, and the great-grandfather of Lewis H. Lapham of *Harper's*. In 1967, the New Canaan Planning and Zoning Commission held a hearing to discuss the acquisition of 345 acres including the Ruth Lapham Lloyd property in South Avenue.

Town Planner Daniel A. Foley, assisted by temporary assistant Donald A. Sikorski, described the current master plan dealing with such considerations as population and traffic circulation.

At the time the current population was 18,000 and the projected future population they were planning for was 28,500. The population was 19,738 according to the 2010 census.

The Lapham family gave the Town of New Canaan most of the estate land in 1967 and sold Waveny House and its surrounding 300 acres to the Town for $1,500,000.

One of the eight who adopted me as his surrogate dad was **Terry**, whose mother I had helped bring to New York City from the Commonwealth of Dominica. When I retired as a New Canaan teacher, the two of them lived in my Stamford two-bedroom apartment for awhile. I got Terry enrolled in the public school, and his mother worked in banks, eventually buying a Kia. On weekends in their new car, I drove them around the Stamford area and they visited me at my Manhattan recording studio.

As his surrogate dad, I watched as Terry succeeded in elementary and high school studies. For his Graduation, we picked out fancy suits at a Stamford shop. I chose a dark blazer jacket and tailored pants, which to this day I wear at important events. When he fell in love, I rented the entire Waveny House and grounds. The wedding was attended by over 100 at an outdoors area, and then we dined in the castle's main room, his mother and his Uncle Simon sitting at the same table with me and uncles Peter and Jimmy.

I watched as he succeeded at John Jay College in New York City, first obtaining a job on Wall Street, then obtaining one in a corporate headquarters in Stamford.

Terry's has been a success story that has made me proud. When he brought his wife and children to my Greenwich Village apartment's roof with the panoramic view of all of downtown Manhattan, no one could have guessed the long road he had so inspiringly traveled.

Yakimo

At Bob Turner's B-bar-K Ranch, owned John D. Rockefeller, I was a counselor one summer. The dude ranch, which was at the base of Teton Mountain, was eventually donated to the U. S. government.

Here I am on my sure-footed pinto, Yakimo, that the dude ranchers said would soon be sent to the glue factory.

4
Alphabetized by Individuals

Beutel, Bill

William Charles Beutel was born 12 December 1930, the son of a Cleveland, Ohio, dentist. After graduating from Dartmouth College in Hanover, New Hampshire, he went to the University of Michigan Law School, Ann Arbor, Michigan, but wrote to the journalist that he particularly liked, Edward R. Murrow, "I very much wanted to be a radio journalist." Morrow wrote back, advising him to go to Columbia University's Graduate School of Journalism in New York City. After securing a job with CBS Radio in 1957, Beutel joined ABC in 1962 as a reporter for the national news broadcast and as an anchor on the local New York news program, "The Big News." Up to then, his name had been pronounced "BOY-tel," but at the beginning of his first live broadcast on WABC-TV, the narrator pronounced it, "Byoo-TEL." The new pronunciation stuck.

In 1968, he became the London bureau chief, and in 1970 he returned to man the local evening newscast. His trademark sign-off, "Good luck and be well," closed WABC's nightly local newscast in New York City for more than 30 years.

The Beutels lived in New Canaan in the 1980s, and on her Graduation Night his daughter Heather introduced her dad to me. I was her 11th grade American Literature teacher. In the festschrift Don Souden edited for me, he knew she had written that I had been "the one high school teacher who brought [her] to [her] knees, as if in prayer, with [her] bowing reverently, hoping that [I] might extend to [her] a similar respect."

I was elated to be introduced, surprised at how short in height the well-known announcer was. "Heather told me she had a hard time with Thoreau and

Steinbeck," Beutel said in the excitement following the 1983 graduation ceremony.

"You can be extremely proud of your personable teenager," I said to him, her brother and fellow New Canaan student Peter, standing with us.

In 2001, Beutel retired as anchor of "Eyewitness News" but continued to work as a correspondent until 2003, during which time he reported on the civil war in Sierra Leone. At the age of 75 in the Pinehurst, North Carolina, home to which he had retired, Beutel died. Adair, his wife, told reporters the cause was complications from a progressive neurological disorder, Lewy Body Disease.

Beutel had been married four times, first to Gail Wilder for twenty years. His second wife was *Guiding Light* soap actress Lynn Deerfield in 1975, followed by a brief four-month marriage to his third wife in 1977. In 1980, Beutel married his fourth and last wife, Adair Atwell, a former lobbyist for the tobacco industry.

Bromley, Garfield

At a church meeting in Minburn when I asked about my and my parents' church's key beliefs, I inquired as to whether Jesus was able to walk on water and if a whale was able to swallow a human being. It's in the sacred scripture, Methodist Bishop Bromley lectured me, and I *must* believe.

The day I left home and arrived in college to major in music, I discarded "belief" for "know."

Blanc, Simon

In March of 1967, while traveling in Dominica, I learned that back of the main library in Roseau was the nation's small radio station (that was operated by a gay couple, a Dominican and an American, one of whom was among the first to die of AIDS).

Peter Gittens, a 16-year-old, told me about it and took me there to see it. He also asked how he could become an American citizen by joining the army or navy, and I advised him that I didn't think it possible.

Later, he wrote me that he was in the Virgin Islands and was volunteering into the U. S. Army, presumably having convinced officials that he was born there. When he asked as a paratrooper if I would cash a paycheck and save it for him, saying he didn't trust his family to do it for him, I agreed. When he "fell out of airplanes dozens of times" and was honorably discharged, I gave him a written accounting with the total that I had saved for him. When he got an apartment in New York City, he then asked if I'd help him bring his sister and two brothers to the States. As owner of a recording studio, I wrote a letter that the three were the sole musicians who could supply the needed "cadence-lypso," a distinctly unique *kadans* in the 1970s. The three arrived 29 August 1974, sharing Peter's one-bedroom apartment with the agreement that they owed him rent and payment of airfare.

I took them to dinner on their arrival, driving so they could see the Statue of Liberty at night.

In time, Lydia moved out, eventually working in banks.

Jimmy, the youngest, eventually married a woman with children, all of whom lived off public assistance.

Simon lived for awhile in my New York City apartment and got a job as a bartender. then lived with me in Stamford, Connecticut. He married, became a U. S. citizen, served in the National Guard, had a daughter, became a policeman in Stamford, and in 2008 was promoted to sergeant. His is the story of an immigrant who realized the American dream (one year earning more than the Mayor of Stamford, Dannel Malloy, who became Connecticut's governor in 2011.

Simon, much as if a real brother, checks many of his major decisions by consulting with me. Sometimes I have helped by editing police reports that he is required to make.

I could write a book about how, as a kid, he changed tires as well as dived into Roseau's harbor when tourists threw coins from their ship, which they realized could have resulted in the kid's drowning.

E. R. Braithwaite

Braithwaite (27 June 1912 -   ) was Guyana's representative to the United Nations. While a New Canaan resident, he was invited to teach, not just visit, an honors English class of mine. He was asked beforehand if he would mind playing a little joke by being introduced by a student who would inform him that the teacher was absent and that the adult in the room was Mr. Brown, a substitute, who would not participate in the discussion. In short, he would be the teacher, I would be the substitute who would not be expected to interrupt.

He agreed, greeted Mr. Brown the "substitute," took immediate charge as the teacher, and talked freely about his 1959 book, *To Sir With Love*, which many of the students had read.

Braithwaite told the class he had nothing but praise for Sidney Poitier, who had depicted him in the movie. The novel showed his problems as a black who was teaching unmotivated white children who he knows are anti-black, telling how he motivated them by taking trips to museums and finding about jobs they would want as adults.

The honors class members said their high school did the same, to his surprise, and they wondered how as an engineer he could have put up with what he had to do in order to earn money.

Just before the final bell rang, for the students were convinced he really thought the teacher was a substitute, he said, "Oh, and thanks, Mr. Smith, for letting us play a joke on the class."

Brown, Robert Delford

Brown (25 October 1930 - 24 March 2009), who became a noted Dadaist in the anarchic New York art scene of the 1960s, was born in Portland, Colorado. When an adolescent, he moved with his family to Long Beach, California, and he received his B.A. and M.A. degrees from the University of California, Los Angeles.

A Surrealist and Abstract Expressionist, he moved in 1959 to New York City, becoming known as one of Neo-Dadaists who billed himself as "founder, leader, prophet, president, and saint of the First National Church of the Exquisite Panic, Inc., at the Great Building Crack-Up."

What happens when we die? Who knows!

A versatile artist, he purchased a Greenwich Village building, had Yale architect Paul Rudolph "crack-up" the building by gutting it, then turned it into a combination studio and residence at 251 West 13th Street, New York, NY 10011. Passersby saw "St. Ben Turpin" in the window of the "Chapel of Pharblongence" and observed a "Map of Nevada" on a terrace floor. Brown explained that instead of people futilely trying to get to Heaven or to Nirvana, he guaranteed to get them to Nevada: he painted a roadmap, using various art forms, and showed them where to catch a bus. In 1998 he sold the building, and the new owners removed all references to the "exquisite panic."

.

Brown's work was exhibited at the Gallery of Modern Art in Washington (1965), the Kansas City Art Institute (1971), the Rhode Island School of Design (1978), and the Fondazione Mudima in Milan (1992). Brown is author of *Hanging* (1967), *Ulysses, An Altered Plagiarism* (1975), and *Teachings of the First National Church of the Exquisite Panic, Inc.* (1991).

His entry in Who's Who:

> I want the image to assume primary importance in all my work. Dazzling technique and established procedures are so often used not to enlighten but to obfuscate one's vacuity. The artist's responsibility is to tell the truth as he sees it, not to enhance his own self-importance as an expert, thereby perverting his responsibility as a moral force in society.

In 1963 he married Rhett Cone, who became his collaborator, muse, and financial backer. Mother of a daughter, Carol, she died in 1988. The couple had no children together. Upon her death, he wrote of them as "the first artist couple,"

> The most serendipitous event in my life was my meeting with Rhett Cone. She had founded the Cricket Theater on Second Ave. and Tenth St. where she showcased new material, presented Blanche Marvin's Merry Mimes children's theater, and produced and directed plays by such writers as Edward Albee, and Samuel Becket.

Brown, once a member of the Secular Humanist Society of New York, when asked why religions were started, responded in a newyorkminute,

> Religions were invented because no one could figure out how to make money from philosophy.

In the early 2000s, Brown moved to Wilmington, North Carolina, to prepare for a 2008 exhibition of his work at the Cameron Art Museum there. He was known to have been looking for a place to have an art project in the river there, one that would involve a number of rafts. He had recently had hip surgery and walked with a cane.

According to police officials, it is likely that Jones slipped, fell into the river, and drowned. His step-daughter, Carol Cone, is his only survivor.

(Expert with a Mac computer, he arranged unusual websites about Funkupaganism and the First National Church of Exquisite Panic, Inc., the latter a name for his art studio.

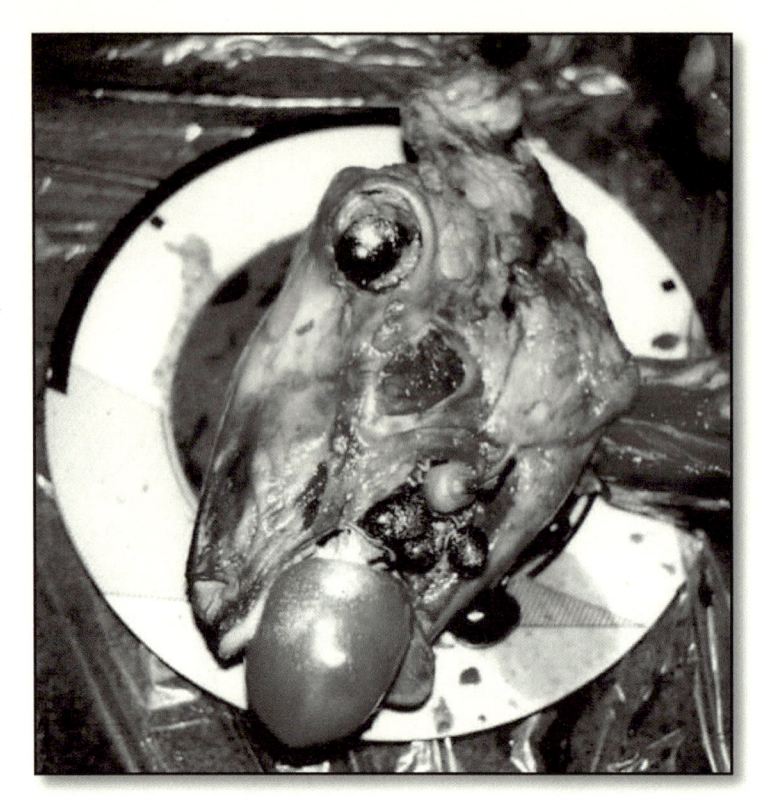

Pictured is a still frame during the making-of the "(s)AINT" video, directed by Asia Argento.

The skinned lamb (of God) on a dinner plate for ready devouring, à la the Last Supper literally interpreted.

Members of the church included dozens of his students, Sir Arthur C. Clarke, Dennis Middlebrooks, and me. The church's manifesto was amusing and described its deity, **Who**.

Asked what the future holds? "Who knows" was the answer.)

Cadmus, Paul

Cadmus and I, when he was in his 90s

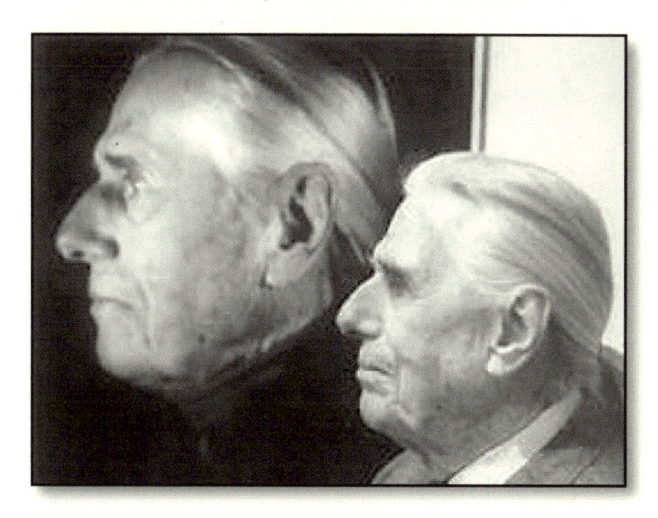

Cadmus in 1993

At an annual ceremonial of the American Academy of Arts and Letters. Mr. Cadmus noticed I was alone and wondered if I was there with a member's family. When I told him I was a journalist and worked for *The Humanist*, he showed interest in the philosophic category of "secular humanist." I stayed with him and he introduced me to members saying he was a secular humanist and that I was a journalist working for a magazine called *The Humanist*.

Following is what I wrote in his Philosopedia entry:

> Born in New York City, Cadmus (17 December 1904 - 12 December 1999) was a comparatively unknown artist until an admiral was offended by one of his works. Then, he became the controversial painter of *The Fleet's In!* and *The Seven Deadly Sins*.

The Fleet's In

Cadmus became a distinguished member of the American Academy of Arts and Letters in 1974. In 1984, he was the subject for a video-recording, "Paul Cadmus, Enfant Terrible at 80." At the time, a *New York Times' reviewer* noted,

> Recent interest in representational painting has fostered an appreciation of artists whose realist modes, long out of the stylistic and commercial mainstreams, are now receiving renewed attention. . . . For Mr. Cadmus, best known for his earlier, more accessible works, including the much reproduced New York street and restaurant scenes and Coney Island panoramas, also practices a dark, more personal, visionary magic realism in which black humor and distant allusions are endemic.

With an early lover – Jared French – Cadmus spent time on the island of Majorca, where he painted *Shore Leave* and *YMCA Locker Room*. His circle included Christopher Isherwood, W. H. Auden, George Balanchine, George

Platt Lynes, George Tooker, Lincoln Kirstein (the husband of his sister Fidelma), and E. M. Forster.

He was unsure about his ancestry: "I think my ancestors sailed from Jutland (Denmark) around 1710. My father's side may have been Dutch and, like Erasmus, Latinized the name. My mother, conceived in Spain, was born in New York. Her father was Basque, her mother Cuban. Maybe I was just a cad to begin with," he joked to me, "and the name was Latinized."

His parents, both artists, encouraged their son and their daughter, Fidelma, to study art, and Cadmus began with an interest in antiques. One day at the National Academy of Design in uptown Manhattan and knowing that older art students had nude models to work with, he peered through a peephole and saw a naked female. "I had never seen a stranger in the nude. It was a revelation," he told journalist Richard Goldstein. Naked men would follow. It was the start of his becoming the artist who painted the male body with more sensuality, Goldstein observed (*Village Voice*, 18 May 1999), than any American artist of the century:

> *The Fleet's In!* [is] the 1934 painting that made him an art star. In this knowing study of carousing sailors, there are not only buns and baskets on proud display but loose ladies admiring the briny trade and even a fey gentleman offering a cigarette to an eager gob. The navy was not amused. An outraged admiral had the painting removed before it could be shown at the Corcoran Gallery in Washington, D. C.

> A sequel, *Sailors and Floosies* (1938), featuring the angelic seaman in slumber, grasping his crotch, fared no better in San Francisco; "in the interest of national unity," it was taken off the wall. In *Shore Leave* (1933), a gay man is clearly propositioning a willing sailor, but what one notices first is the ripe women in the foreground and a recumbent swab with his bulging crotch in full view. Sometimes the queers come out to play, as in *Fantasia on a Theme by Dr. S.* (1946), which is set on Fire Island. But usually the artist's eye is drawn to what is often ignored in modern painting: a casually muscled male physique and an utterly open attitude. Looking at this pantheon of locker-room studs, seafood Sampsons, and young waifs lounging in the playground with baseball bats jammed between their legs, one sees a quality beyond the ideologically mandated worship of the working class. Call it longing. "I was fascinated by the sailors, and I used to sit on a bench and watch them all the time," Cadmus recalls. In fact, Riverside Park around 96th Street was a prime cruising ground in the 1930s, largely because it was where the warships docked. "The uniforms were so tight and form-fitting that they were an inspiration. I was young enough to be propositioned by the sailors, who would offer to take me back to the boat, but I never went. They were too unattractive, or maybe I was too timid. I don't know."

"The male nude has been a specialty of my own oeuvre," Cadmus agreed, "when I am not being concerned with the foibles of people in daily life: men, women, and children.... We are made, we are told, 'in God's image,' and we assume that He was not clothed by Armani or Brooks Brothers or, if He is She, not attired by Balenciaga or Donna Karan."

In 1992, Lincoln Kirstein, the founding director of the New York City Ballet, wrote a definitive study, *Paul Cadmus*, which described his relationship with other artists and writers, including W. H. Auden. E. M. Forster, while posing for a portrait, was said to have passed the time reading aloud passages from *Maurice*. Kirstein described Cadmus's work as being "executed with the technical virtuosity and anatomical precision of the Renaissance masters that celebrate the beauty of the human body."

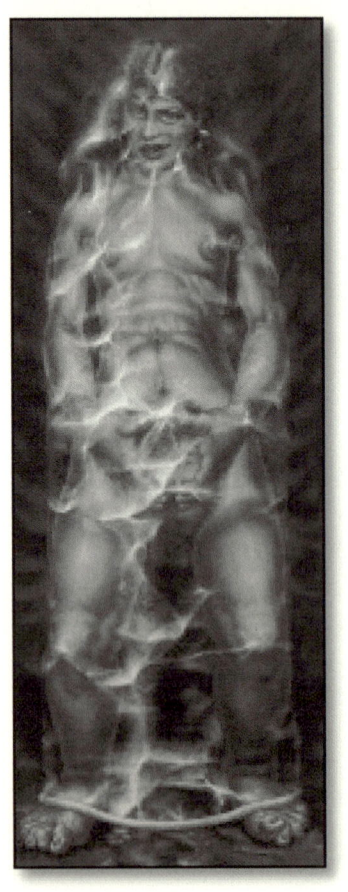

Lust, One of the Cardinal Sins

Agreeing, Guy Davenport in an introduction for *The Drawings of Paul Cadmus* (1989) stated that "Not since Michelangelo has any artist done so many studies of the male nude." He included dozens of such examples. Cadmus, who in 94 years completed over 120 paintings, delighted in such observations. "I do love Michelangelo's male forms," he has said, adding that "Michelangelo's women often look like males with grapefruits attached." "It seems that genitalia," Cadmus lamented about the public taste, "equal pornography." But not for him personally: "My penis is not the most important organ in my body. My eyes are."

In 1989, after a discussion about philosophy, he responded to a request by me for his views about humanism:

> Your request should have a worthy answer but it would take me days to try to compose one (as I used to do when I first began writing to E. M. Forster). The subject is too complicated for this feeble old mind to go into deeply. The simple description of a humanist is one who is interested in humans (not as profound as the *Oxford Universal Dictionary*'s definition, "a student of human affairs, or of human nature"). I'm no student. I guess I somewhat fit in Naturalistic Humanism #7.

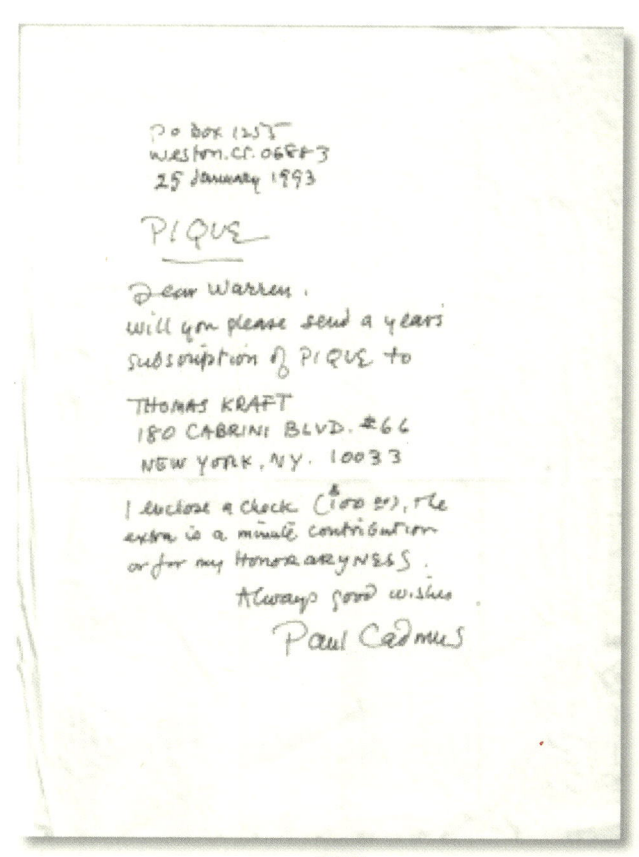

Later, in an interview at his Connecticut home, Cadmus discussed religion and his increased interest in the philosophy of naturalistic humanism. "I've always liked the story of the Albigensians," Cadmus mused, "who were besieged by the Pope at Beziers. His soldiers asked him: 'How do we know the heretics from the Christians?' The Pope replied, 'Burn them all. God will know his own.' " A devout Catholic until he was seventeen, he then "shed it all."

Cadmus is cited by Charles Kaiser in *The Gay Metropolis 1940 – 1996* (1997) as having painted key individuals and scenes of that period. Kaiser noted that Cadmus met Jon Andersson, 27, when he himself was 59 and "I never wanted to be with anyone else." That included the time he was invited to a long-ago party by Truman Capote. Capote's long-time companion Jack Dunphy told him he could not bring a male guest, that "Truman said he didn't want to ask 'a bunch of fags' to his party." This infuriated Andersson and was one of the few times the two did not appear together in public or private.

At a book signing when Kaiser referred to Cadmus as the only artist to draw so many male nudes, the then ninety-two-year-old quipped, "Well, there was Michelangelo." Kaiser quotes Cadmus as having been interviewed by Alfred Charles Kinsey: "He took homosexuality just as calmly as he did his work with wasps. He interviewed me about my sex life – how many orgasms, how big it was, measure it before and after." Kinsey even went to dinner at Cadmus's house following the interview.

Cadmus died at his home in Weston, Connecticut, five days before his 95th birthday, which he had joyously celebrated two weeks earlier with several hundred friends at the D. C. Moore Gallery in New York City.

Clarke, Arthur C.

Sir Arthur with Pepsi, 1991

Arthur C. Clarke, e-mailed 28 December 2003:

>Dear Warren,
>
>>Nice to hear from you - and best to Stanley [Bard] – say I'm waiting! HAL'S red 'eye' should be widely recognisable ...Regards to Janet [Asimov] ... and your cybergeek [Peter Ross] ... what's happening on his monitor?? Do you know about Leonard Woolf's Ceylon comments? Local TV news just shown happy gay Anglican bishop - how times have changed! But I've decided that religion is the most malevolent of mind- viruses.
>>
>>All best for 2004 - still can't believe [I made it past 2001]....
>>Arthur

Gilbert Price invited me to meet Clarke at the Chelsea Hotel, but I didn't actually meet him until Clarke invited me in 2002 or 2003 while on his way back to Sri Lanka from Johns Hopkins Hospital in Maryland. When Clarke mentioned he was surprised no plaque on the building commemorated his having lived there, I wrote his publishers and biographer Neil McAleer about this but, receiving no follow-ups, suggested wording for the plaque to Clarke, got Clarke's approval and, thanks for the HAL logo (designed by Peter Ross, my computer technician), and at my own expense hired North Shore Monuments [667 Cedar Swamp Road, Glen Head, New York] to make the plaque, which was installed with hotel manager Stanley Bard's help on 29 September 2004.

Clarke, who had been diagnosed with post-polio syndrome in 1988 and was wheel-chaired, was knighted in 2000 but was too ill to attend – Queen Elizabeth II authorized the UK High Commissioner to Sri Lanka at a ceremony in Colombo to award him the title of Knight Bachelor.

Here I am with the plaque I commissioned
to be placed on the front of Manhattan's
Hotel Chelsea on 23rd Street

Comstock, Anthony

Comstock (7 March 1844 - 21 September 1915), who became a U. S. Postal Inspector and politician dedicated to the idea of Victorian morality, was born in New Canaan, the namesake of Comstock Hill Road in town.

He has no relatives in town, but the following is a compilation of views about the person he was – in the English Department, we seldom mentioned Comstock except in derision.

> As a young man, he enlisted and fought in the 17th Connecticut Infantry from 1863 to 1865 for the Union in the American Civil War. Serving without incident, he is said to have objected to the profanity of his fellow soldiers. Afterwards, he became an active worked in the Young Men's Christian Association (YMCA) in New York City.

> In 1873, he created the New York Society for the Suppression of Vice, an institution dedicated to supervising the morality of the public. Later that year, Comstock successfully influenced the United States Congress to pass the Comstock Law, which made illegal the delivery or transportation of "obscene, lewd, or lascivious" material as well as any methods of, or information pertaining to, birth control.

> British author George Bernard Shaw used the term "comstockery," meaning "censorship because of perceived obscenity or immorality," after Comstock alerted the New York police to the content of Shaw's play *Mrs. Warren's Profession.* Shaw remarked that "Comstockery is the world's standing joke at the expense of the United States. Europe likes to hear of such things. It confirms the deep-seated conviction of the Old World that America is a

provincial place, a second-rate country-town civilization after all." Comstock thought of Shaw as an "Irish smut dealer."

The term comstockery had actually been coined by being used in a *New York Times* editorial in 1895.

Comstock's ideas of what might be "obscene, lewd, or lascivious" were quite broad. During his time of greatest power, even some anatomy textbooks were prohibited from being sent to medical students by the postal service.

Comstock aroused intense loathing from early civil liberties groups and intense support from church-based groups worried about public morals. He was a savvy political insider in New York City and was made a special agent of the United States Postal Service, with police powers up to and including the right to carry a weapon. With this power he zealously prosecuted those he suspected of either public distribution of pornography or commercial fraud. He was also involved in shutting down the Louisiana Lottery, the only legal lottery in the United States at the time, and notorious for corruption.

Comstock was despised by publishers of literature, whose works by D. H. Lawrence and Theodore Dreiser also were suppressed.

Comstock is also known for his opposition to Victoria Woodhull and Tennessee Claflin, and those associated with them. The men's journal *The Days' Doings* had popularized lewd images of the sisters for three years and was instructed by its editor (while Comstock was present) to stop producing images of "lewd character."

Comstock also took legal action against the paper for advertising contraceptives. When the sisters published an expose of an adulterous affair between Reverend Henry Ward Beecher and Elizabeth Tilton, he had the sisters arrested under laws forbidding the use of the postal service to distribute "obscene material" – specifically citing a mangled Biblical quote Comstock found obscene – though they were later acquitted of the charges.

An 1887 Letter from Comstock to Josiah Leeds:

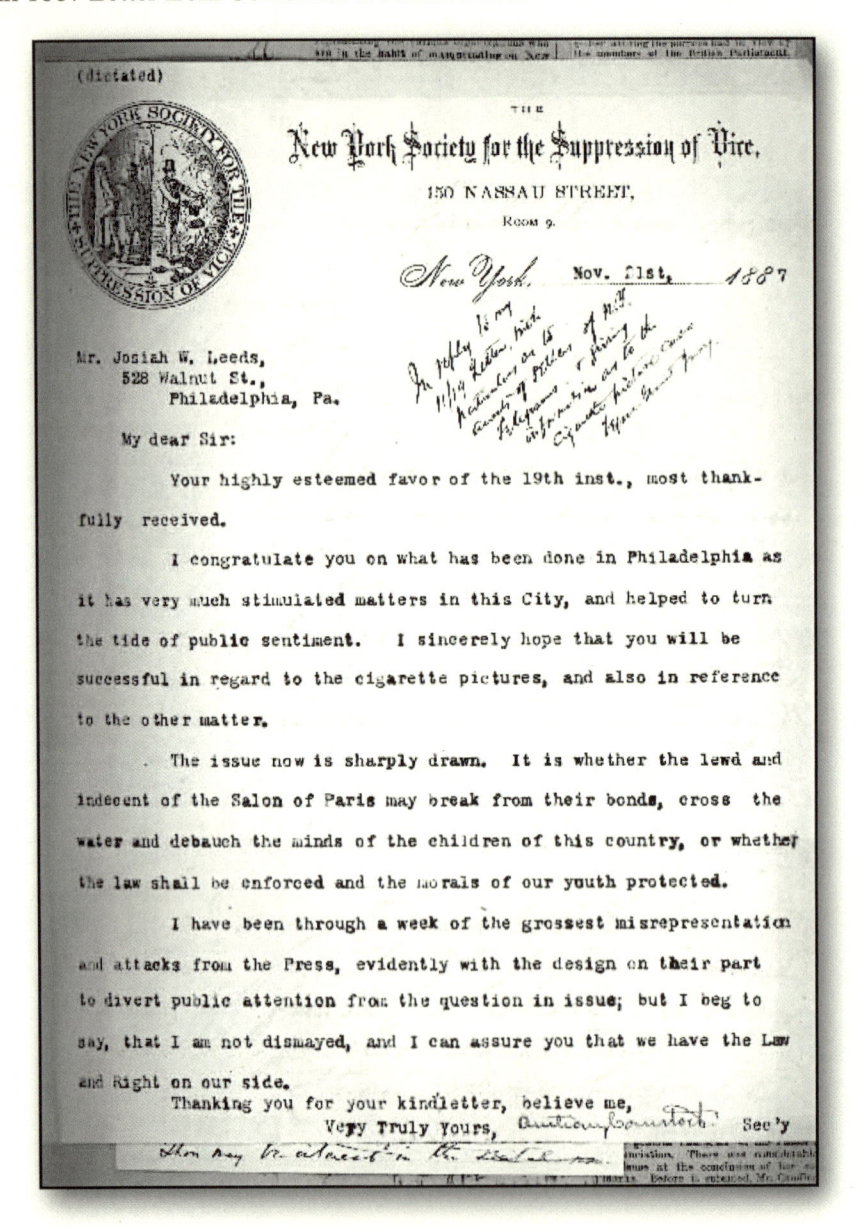

> **THE**
> **New York Society for the Suppression of Vice,**
> 150 NASSAU STREET,
> Room 9.
>
> New York, Nov. 21st, 1887
>
> Mr. Josiah W. Leeds,
> 528 Walnut St.,
> Philadelphia, Pa.
>
> My dear Sir:
>
> Your highly esteemed favor of the 19th inst., most thankfully received.
>
> I congratulate you on what has been done in Philadelphia as it has very much stimulated matters in this City, and helped to turn the tide of public sentiment. I sincerely hope that you will be successful in regard to the cigarette pictures, and also in reference to the other matter.
>
> The issue now is sharply drawn. It is whether the lewd and indecent of the Salon of Paris may break from their bonds, cross the water and debauch the minds of the children of this country, or whether the law shall be enforced and the morals of our youth protected.
>
> I have been through a week of the grossest misrepresentation and attacks from the Press, evidently with the design on their part to divert public attention from the question in issue; but I beg to say, that I am not dismayed, and I can assure you that we have the Law and Right on our side.
>
> Thanking you for your kind letter, believe me,
> Very Truly Yours, Anthony Comstock Sec'y

Less fortunate was Ida Craddock, who committed suicide on the eve of reporting to Federal prison for distributing via the U.S. Mail various sexually explicit marriage manuals she had authored. Her final work was a lengthy public suicide note specifically condemning Comstock.

Comstock claimed he drove fifteen persons to suicide in his "fight for the young." He was head vice-hunter of the New York Society for the Suppression of Vice. Comstock, the self-labeled "weeder in God's garden," arrested D. M. Bennett for publishing his "An Open Letter to Jesus Christ" and later entrapped the editor for mailing a free-love pamphlet. Bennett was prosecuted, subjected to a widely publicized trial, and imprisoned in the Albany Penitentiary.

Comstock had numerous enemies, and in later years his health was affected by a severe blow to the head from an anonymous attacker. He lectured to college audiences and wrote newspaper articles to sustain his causes. Before his death, Comstock attracted the interest of a young law student, J. Edgar Hoover, interested in his causes and methods.

During his career, Comstock clashed with Emma Goldman and Margaret Sanger. Goldman in her autobiography referred to Comstock as the leader of America's "moral eunuchs." Through his various campaigns, he allegedly destroyed 15 tons of books, 284,000 pounds of plates for printing "objectionable" books, and nearly 4,000,000 pictures. Comstock boasted that he was responsible for 4,000 arrests.

Comstock built a house in New Canaan in 1892. A Congregationalist, he died at the age of 71, cause of death unspecified.

Comstock was not buried in New Canaan but is at a Sumachs Section, Lot 95, plot in The Evergreens Cemetery, Brooklyn, New York.

Coulter, Ann [Hart]

Coulter (8 December 1961 -   ) is the daughter of John Vincent Coulter (5 May 1926 - 4 January 2008) and Nell Husbands Martin (23 February 1928 - 14 April 2009). She has two brothers, John and James M.

Her website describes her as follows:

Ann Coulter is the author of eight New York Times bestsellers —

> *Demonic: How the Liberal is Endangering America* (June 2011); *Guilty: Liberal Victims and Their Assault on America* (January 2009); *If Democrats Had Any Brains, They'd Be Republicans* (October, 2007); *Godless: The Church of Liberalism* (June 2006); *How to Talk to a Liberal (If You Must)*(October, 2004); *Treason: Liberal Treachery From the Cold War to the War on Terrorism* (June 2003); *Slander: Liberal Lies About the American Right* (June 2002); and *High Crimes and Misdemeanors:The Case Against Bill Clinton* (August 1998).

Coulter is the legal correspondent for *Human Events* and writes a popular syndicated column for Universal Press Syndicate.

She is a frequent guest on many TV shows, including *The Today Show, Good Morning America, The Early Show, The Tonight Show with Jay Leno, Hannity, The O'Reilly Factor, The Glen Beck Show, HBO's Real Time with Bill Maher*, and has been profiled in numerous publications, including *TV Guide*, the *Guardian* (UK), the *New York Observer*, *National Journal*, *Harper's Bazaar*, and *Elle*. She was the April 25, 2005, cover story of *Time*.

In 2001, Coulter was named one of the top 100 Public Intellectuals by Federal Judge Richard Posner.

A Connecticut native, Coulter graduated with honors from Cornell University School of Arts & Sciences and received her J. D. from the University of Michigan Law School, where she was an editor of *The Michigan Law Review*.

Coulter clerked for the Honorable Pasco Bowman II of the United States Court of Appeals for the Eighth Circuit and was an attorney in the Department of Justice Honors Program for outstanding law school graduates.

After practicing law in private practice in New York City, Coulter worked for the Senate Judiciary Committee, where she handled crime and immigration issues for Senator Spencer Abraham of Michigan. From there, she became a litigator with the Center For Individual Rights in Washington, D. C, a public interest law firm dedicated to the defense of individual rights with particular emphasis on freedom of speech, civil rights, and the free exercise of religion.

As described by the biography site Notable Names Database (NNDB):

> Coulter is a lawyer and author, famous for despising anyone politically left of Ronald Reagan. In college, she founded the local chapter at the Federalist Society, a conservative-libertarian group. She edited *The Michigan Review*, and she is a legal correspondent for *Human Events*. Coulter was fired from MSNBC when she told the president of the Vietnam Veterans of American Foundation, himself a disabled Vietnam veteran, "No wonder you guys lost." She was fired from the conservative *National Review* when she turned in a column offering a final solution to the Muslim problem: "We should invade their countries, kill their leaders, and convert them to Christianity."

> Political positions Coulter disagrees with are briefly, brusquely, and often inaccurately described, then dismissed, often with an insult. The same steps are repeated several times per column. The technique can be enthralling for readers already in agreement with Coulter, yet Arnold Beichman, a conservative from the Hoover Institution, reviewed *Treason* in the conservative *Washington Times*, and wrote that he had "tried to read Miss Coulter's book and failed. Life is too short to read pages and pages of rant."

Michael Tomasky, a liberal American columnist reviewing in *The New York Review of Books* (29 September 2011) Coulter's *Demonic: How the Liberal Mob Is Endangering America*, wrote:

> Ann Coulter, of course, is one of the masters of the hate genre, with many best sellers under her belt. . . . The key themes run through the book. First, Coulter tells her readers over and over again that everything – *everything* – they read and hear from the nonconservative sources is a lie. . . .

Coulter was raised in town and graduated from New Canaan High School in 1980.

Cousins, Norman

Cousins (24 June 1915 - 30 November 1990) was an American political journalist, author, professor, and world peace advocate.

As described in Philosopedia,

> Cousins was born in Union City, New Jersey, the son of Samuel and Sara Miller Cousins. At age 11, he was misdiagnosed as having tuberculosis and was placed in a sanatorium. In school, however, he engaged in athletics and claimed when young that he had "set out to discover exuberance."
>
> In New York City's Bronx, he attended Theodore Roosevelt High School, graduating on 3 February 1933. He edited the school's paper, *The Square Deal*. He earned his B.A. from Teachers College, Columbia University.
>
> He and his wife Ellen Kopf Cousins, whom he married in 1939, raised four daughters: Andrea, Amy Loveman, Candis Hitzig, and Sarah Kit.
>
> A consummate opinion maker who received over fifty honorary university and college degrees, Cousins was an essayist who was best known as the editor of the *Saturday Review of Literature* and, later, of *Saturday Review*. The latter journal drew a connection between current events and the various types of literature, showing the influence of one upon the other.

His *Good Inheritance: The Democratic Chance* (1942) spoke of the potential for greatness that exists in America. *Modern Man is Obsolete* (1945) included his ideas about humanity in the atomic age. *Anatomy of an Illness* (1979) was based upon his experience with a life-threatening illness, telling about the healing ability of the human mind and the medical value of laughter.

In the 1950s he arranged to bring a group of "Hiroshima Maidens," girls whose bodies were disfigured by the atom bomb's explosion in their city, to receive surgical and medical attention in United States hospitals. One, Shigeko Niimoto, lived at his New Canaan, Connecticut, home and became a part of his family. Members of the Society of Friends volunteered to house the other girls.

Cousins's editorials, lectures, and books on Albert Schweitzer and other subjects show him to be one of his time's major independent thinkers. He was well-known internationally and had visited Schweitzer at his African hospital. The two discussed their mutual interest in music, for both played piano and organ.

Cousins occasionally attended Unitarian and Ethical Culture meetings. For the Unitarians in Westport, Connecticut, he donated the pulpit in memory of Albert Schweitzer. Active on behalf of the World Federalists, Cousins once was sent by President Kennedy to negotiate the release of two Catholic priests with Soviet leader Nikita Khruschev, after which he visited the Pope to inform him of the project.

Cousins died of heart failure, having survived years longer than his doctors predicted: 10 years after his first heart attack, 26 years after his collagen illness, and 36 years after his doctors first diagnosed his heart disease

Cousins is buried at the Hollywood Forever Cemetery in Hollywood, California.

Among his books are

>*The Good Inheritance* (1942, nonfiction)
>*Modern Man is Obsolete* (1945, nonfiction)
>*Who Speaks for Man?* (1953, nonfiction)
>*Anatomy of an Illness as Perceived by the Patient: Reflections on Healing and Regeneration* (1979, nonfiction)
>*Human Options: An Autobiographical Notebook* (1980, memoir)
>*The Healing Heart: Antidotes to Panic and Helplessness* (1983, nonfiction)
>*Head First* (1989, nonfiction)

Crandall, Roland Dimon ("Doc")

Betty Boop

Crandall (29 August 1892 - 14 August 1972) was born in New Canaan.

Standard facts about Crandall include that he was an American animator. He is best known for his work at Fleischer Studio, especially on the Betty Boop version of *Snow White*.

He attended the Yale School of Art and was one of the first employees of Fleischer Studio, working on the early *Koko the Clown* shorts in the 1920s. Crandall's drawing ability was legendary; he provided nearly all the drawings for the 1933 *Betty Boop* animated short, *Snow White*. The film has been deemed "culturally significant" by the United States Library of Congress and selected for preservation in the National Film Registry. In 1994 it was voted #19 of the 50 Greatest Cartoons of all time by members of the animation field. The film is now public domain.

Crandall retired from animation in 1941 when Paramount Studios foreclosed on Fleischer Studios. He moved to Bridgeport, Connecticut, where he worked as a commercial illustrator.

Crandall died on August 14, 1972, in Greenwich, Connecticut.

Crawford, Cheryl

Crawford (24 September 1902 - 7 October 1986) was an American theatre producer and director. Few if any townspeople now remember her, but her standard biography is as follows:

Born in Akron, Ohio, she majored in drama at Smith College. Following graduation, she moved to New York City and enrolled at the Theatre Guild's school. By then she knew that she didn't want to pursue an acting career but saw no other way to gain access to the organization producing the highest quality theatre of its time.

Finishing their training in 1927, she was hired by Theresa Helburn, the Guild's Executive Director, as a casting secretary. She then worked her way through various backstage jobs, including assistant stage manager, to assistant to the "Board of Managers," an important administrative job.

While working at the Guild, she met Harold Clurman and Lee Strasberg, who had also been working there as play reader and actor, respectively.

She was impressed with these two young men and joined their animated discussions about the need for a radically new form of American theatre.

In 1930 Crawford urged Clurman to start giving semi-public talks to groups of like-minded actors. After he followed her suggestion and the talks attracted more people than could fit in Clurman's apartment, Crawford arranged for the use of a showroom at the Steinway Piano Company.

In 1931, Crawford, Clurman, and Strasberg announced the formation of The Group Theatre and invited 28 young actors who had been attending Clurman's talks to join them for a twelve-week-long summer of training and rehearsal at Pine Brook Country Club in Nichols, Connecticut.

Crawford had a major role in selecting the early plays produced by The Group, beginning with their first one, *The House of Connelly* by North Carolina playwright Paul Green, whom she later introduced to composer Kurt Weill. She encouraged their subsequent collaboration, Weill's first American project, the musical, *Johnny Johnson*, was the last production she worked on before resigning from The Group Theatre in 1937 to become an independent producer.

Crawford was influential in the early careers of such actors as Helen Hayes, Bojangles Robinson, Mary Martin (whose son, Larry Hagman, once lived in New Canaan), Ethel Barrymore, Ingrid Bergman, Tallulah Bankhead, and Paul Robeson, among others.

In 1946, she and Eva Le Gallienne founded the American Repertory Theatre. In 1947, together with former Group Theatre members Elia Kazan and Robert Lewis, she founded The Actor's Studio, which trained Marlon Brando, James Dean, Jerome Robbins, Shelley Winters, Jane Fonda, Bea Arthur, and others. Former partner Strasberg joined them as artistic director in 1951.

Crawford lived in New Canaan and her son, nicknamed Scoop, attended junior high school. While working on taped cues for *Yentl* (1975), Crawford phoned from her home on Chichester Road in New Canaan to my Variety Recording Studio and was not pleased that because of her low voice its owner (me) kept referring to her as "Sir."

Davenport, Basil

In 2014, using the internet, I found the following in the Yale University Library records:

> Basil (1905 - 1966) was reared in Louisville, Kentucky, the eldest of two sons born to Ira William and Emily Andrews (Davison) Davenport. A slim and personable aesthete, he never married. At the Taft School he suffered from homesickness, but won distinction as an editor of the school's literary magazine, debater, and thespian. At Yale he continued these pursuits and took up boxing before graduating in 1926.
>
> Then he studied classics for two years at Oxford and taught Greek for a year at Rutgers after returning to this country. From childhood Davenport cultivated a facility for storytelling, especially the genre of tale associated with campfires. This proclivity delighted both his peers and his elders, and subsequently it led to his numerous anthologies, especially:
>
> *Ghostly tales to be told; a collection of stories from the great masters, arranged for reading and telling aloud* (1950) and *Tales to be told in the dark; a selection of stories from the great authors, arranged for reading and telling aloud* (1953).

Other notable anthologies were: *The Portable Roman Reader* (1951) and *The Selected Works of Stephen Vincent Benét* (1942). His translations of Rostand's *L'Aiglon* (issued by the Yale Press in 1927) and Aeschylus *The Oresteia* were performed at Yale during his Freshman and Senior years respectively. Two original works were: *An Inquiry Into Science Fiction* 1955) and *An Introduction to Islandia* (1942).

After his year at Rutgers he settled in New York, contributing book reviews and feature articles to *The Saturday Review of Literature* and performing similar services for the *Book-of-the-Month Club News*. From 1936 until his death, he was associated with the latter organization, first as Editorial Assistant and from 1956-1966 as one of the five judges, at whose monthly meetings the final selections were voted.

His virtually inexhaustible store of classical and literary lore served him well on various quiz programs, notably "Down You Go." Unfortunately, it was scratched soon after he joined it, due to scandals precipitated when other programs were exposed as "fixed."

Davenport, Emily

Emily the Episcopalian and Sgt. Smith the Unitarian

I think it was Battalion Sgt. Wheat who introduced me to Mrs. Emily Davenport, a wealthy donor to the Louisville Symphony who said she'd like it if I'd warm up her Steinway grand. On my first overnight visit, I slept in her son Basil's room. In the morning, because she and her sister Mrs. Belknap (heiress of the Belknap silver fortune) had already eaten, her black 60-ish servant served breakfast. On each side of my plate were at least six pieces of silverware. I couldn't figure out which knife to pick up the butter, which utensil to pick the butter out of its container, which knife then to butter the bread. There were different spoons for the sugar and the coffee and the poached eggs. A country hick, I asked the servant which knife to use. He seemed to imply that I should know, not be asking him. It was one great breakfast, except for laughing to myself at my being so naive.

Mrs. Davenport and I had a *folie à deux* in which we would dunk cookies and determine not their IQ but their DQ. That is, how many seconds would it take for them to sink once they touched the tea. We had certain standards. If the cookie sank in 10 seconds, 60 divided by 10 gave it a DQ of 6. What sheer luxury: sitting in that grand living room, the fireplace roaring, some symphonic music in the background, and the two of us lying on a magnificent and huge Persian rug, dunking cookies and laughing!

The Steinway grand was in a large living room with high ceilings, a huge library of books, and a large fireplace at the other end of the room. She was like a mother away from home, although older than my parents, and we got along beautifully.

Mrs. Davenport was Episcopalian, and one really hot Sunday I visited and listened to her minister. I've no idea what he said, but he moved to the side of the pulpit and under his robe we could see that he had kept cool by taking off his trousers. . . .

On a following Sunday, I tried to find the same church but passed one whose Wayside Pulpit near the street entrance said the sermon by **Augustus Reccord** would be "Good Men In Hell by Augustus Reccord," and I resisted temptation and went in to see how the minister could squirm out of that topic. But he didn't, listing many non-Christian Unitarians and others like Mark Twain, Ralph Waldo Emerson, and Denis Diderot, who scoffed at the theological inventions of Heaven and Hell but not in the intellectual entities of heaven and hell.

I returned several times, eventually asking the septuagenarian Dr. Reccord how I could join. "I have no idea," he responded, for he was a retired Bostonian minister who was pinch-hitting for the regular minister, who already had volunteered as a chaplain.

But he said he'd find out if I came the following Sunday, which I did and we talked briefly about why I had rejected Methodism and was in agreement with the Rev. Ralph Waldo Emerson's unitarian views about the Oversoul. A young Speed family girl (from a prominent Louisville family) and I became members after marching down the aisle together (whispering to each other, "Will you take this man to be your illegally married husband? Yes. . . Yes!" as we walked) and simply signed a very old membership book, as witnessed by those present.

I must have written over a dozen letters against organized religion to the *Courier--Journal* editor in the weeks that followed, all published. In short, an Episcopalian led me to Unitarianism.

Davis, Sammy Jr.

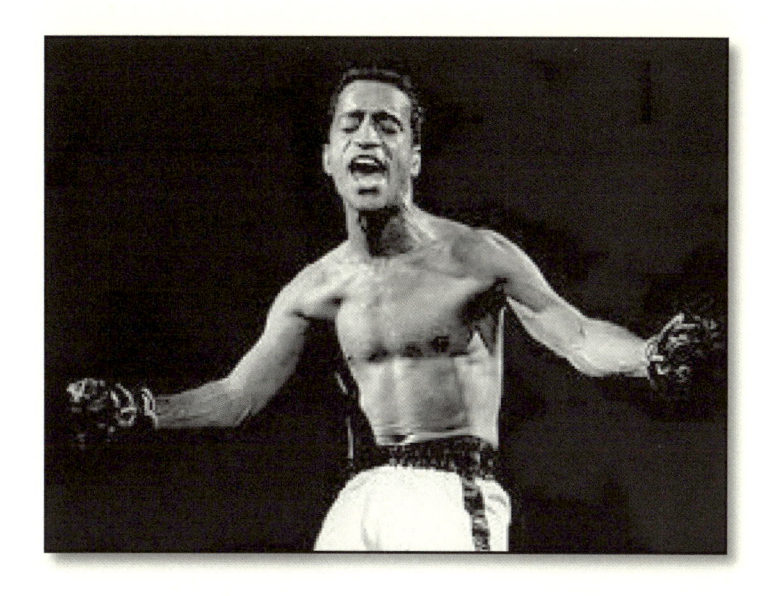

Davis is said to have joked that he was born black, then became colored, then Negro, then African-American, his handicap also being that he was "a one-eyed Negro Jew."

From the time in college that I was a counselor at the YMCA Camp in Boone, Iowa, I became acquainted and easily made friends with Negroes. Jimmy, one who took a rowboat ride up the river with me, was a kid who knew little about Caucasians much as I didn't know much about Negroes. He asked if he could feel my hair, so I felt his and both were surprised that it really did feel different. We picked up souvenir rocks as we paddled through the rapids back to camp, exchanged them, and vowed forever to remember each other. We didn't.

I don't remember seeing blacks during my war years. I thought Fernando had a condescending view of blacks until I learned he'd had sex with many, as had Harold Bonilla who claimed they all had big penises that he liked. Jimmy Justice, I figured, was an exception, or at least he always joked that God had given this 6-foot-plus black a white penis. I argued against this generalization.

Afro-American was a term I didn't much use, but I liked Afro-Cuban music, whether or not the musician wore an Afro. Black Americans had a difficult time being accepted in most gay venues even to this day, except to whites or Asians who believed blacks had big penises. This could partly have been because so many had prison or STD records.

In 1964, when Davis was in *Golden Boy,* I got a desperate call from the Majestic Theatre (247 West 44th) to see if my studio would lend them a wireless microphone. Our next few sessions would not need our only such microphone, so I carried it personally and was invited to stay and watch the show. The mike was used in a boxing scene in which Davis placed it in his crotch. We hoped it wouldn't pick up police car sounds on the street, and it didn't. But the next time it was used and the performer did what so many do, placed it too close to their mouth, I couldn't resist asking, "Do you know where that microphone was last?"

Dean, Jimmy

It was 1952.

He gave me that look from across the bar, we approached each other, and our hands had no trouble finding the sensitive areas. He said his mother was dead, that he'd been raised on an Indiana farm by his aunt and uncle. I said I'd been raised in a small Iowa farm community, that my dad was a grain dealer. We laughed about wishing we'd known each other back then when loneliness was a way of life. We both said we were not at all into religion, although he said he knew about the Friends, and I said I knew about Unitarian humanists. He didn't tell me what kind of job he had, nor did I volunteer that I was a teacher.

Now, your place or mine? Well, neither had a place. Holding hands and testicles, we slipped away into a dark area of the Julius bar in Greenwich Village. He explained he'd come to the city to become an actor. I said I'd come to attend Columbia University and get a job teaching, and we kept drinking until we got woozy. I remember the feel of his hard erection and my failure to tell him the reason I had to leave (to get home to my Costa Rican companion). As to who the handsome Midwestern chap was that I met when in my thirties, I'm unsure. Arriving home, I told Fernando I'd just met a twenty-something with playful eyes. He wasn't happy, told me about having had a fight with someone, and we fell asleep, both angry.

Jimmy Dean died fifty years ago. Born in Marion, Indiana, in 1931, he was killed 30 September 1955 in a road accident in Cholame, California. His mother died of cancer when he was nine. In 1951, with $30 earned from a Pepsi TV commercial, Dean came to New York and spent two years playing bit parts in TV dramas. In the 1950s he played an Arab street boy in André Gide's *L'immoraliste,* one who seduced a husband as well as his wife. Dean caught Elia Kazan's eye and was flown back to Hollywood to star in John Steinbeck's classic *East of Eden* (1955) and *Giant* (1956). But his claim to fame came when he played the role of Jim Stark in *Rebel Without a Cause* (1955), working with co-stars Natalie Wood and Sal Mineo. In Britain's *Guardian* (14 May 2005), Germaine Greer wrote that few would have guessed Dean was gay when he was in his prime, that his studio had him photographed often in public with starlets. But scuttlebutt around Broadway at the time was that he was definitely gay.

My never-to-be-answered question is whether or not he ever drank at Julius's bar on West 10th.

Dewey, John

Roberta Dewey was forty-five years younger than her husband and upon his death late at 11 p.m. had telephoned Donald Szantho Harrington minister of the Community (Unitarian) Church in New York City. Although John Dewey was not a member of the church, he had once told his wife that if he died she should call Harrington, that he would know what to do. Upon arriving before midnight, Harrington recalled in an article for *Religious Humanism* (Summer 1994), he found that Mrs. Dewey fainted right after opening the door. The two adopted children, Belgian war orphans John and Adrienne, sensibly found some ammonia to revive her, after which it was decided that cremation should be the following morning at Fresh Pond Crematory in Queens.

Dewey's body was covered with a sheet and blanket, the children were put to bed, and Harrington left by 2 a.m. The following morning, Harrington and Mrs. Dewey watched the coffin go into the tort for cremation. Although **David Dubinsky** and **William Heard Kilpatrick** volunteered to speak at a memorial, Mrs. Dewey did not want a long, drawn-out affair, saying Dewey hated those things, and she suggested that **Max Otto** of the University of Wisconsin in Madison should be the speaker. My notes at the funeral are as follows.

At Dewey's memorial service, held 4 June 1952, Harrington spoke of Dewey's influence on American world life and thought, of his ability as a teacher to get others to speak, and of his personal memories of having driven Dewey from Chicago to Madison and back. "I thought I would get a lot of wisdom. Instead, he . . . kept me talking. All I can remember his saying was "Possibly," and "You may be right!"

Harrington then read passages from the Bible, which surprised many in the audience, along with Matthew Arnold's "Rugby Chapel," George Eliot's "The Choir Invisible," and Samuel Taylor Coleridge's "Ode on Dejection."

George Kykhuizen recalls in *The Life and Mind of John Dewey* (1973) that Harrington referred to Dewey as "one of the intellectual and moral giants" of all time, declaring that "when the full impact of his revolutionary thought reaches the heart of our society, some generations hence, scarcely a single social institution will remain as it is today."

Norman Thomas was present, as was **William Heard Kilpatrick**, both with their distinctively white hair. Of the several speakers, Max Otto was the one with the most amusing recollection. He had stopped Dr. Dewey on the campus one day and had asked him a question pertaining to philosophy. Dewey had looked down, cogitated, looked up, had looked around, and he had not said anything for minutes and minutes . . . and yet more minutes . . . and more. Just as Dr. Otto was about to interrupt, thinking maybe Dewey was suffering some illness, there ensued a long, complex response which was uttered slowly and distinctively, one so complete Otto could scarcely believe it had not been written down beforehand. A good question deserves a good answer, Dewey was showing. But, said Otto to much laughter, "I was very, *very* careful after that whenever I questioned Dr. Dewey about anything."

Otto also said that Dewey's philosophy was like that of a mountain climber who climbs in order to see farther, and who, once he has climbed one mountain, presses on to a higher one simply to see farther yet. It was the continual quest for new vision and new vistas that marked the greatness of Dewey's mind. And what is man's purpose if he climbs *all* the mountains and there are no more to see, Dewey was once asked. Then, he responded, there would be no purpose in living.

A soloist sang "Swing Low, Sweet Chariot" and "The Balm of Gilead," the latter said to have been a favorite of Dewey's. At the end, Harrington took Mrs. Dewey with one hand and carried what appeared to be a water pitcher with the other, and the two led the audience out of the room. It was only then that I and likely others realized the cremains had been present throughout the service, that atop the altar had been a bronze urn, not a water pitcher.

Although Columbia University had wanted the ashes, Dewey's Alma Mater, the University of Vermont, received them as well as, later, Roberta Dewey's ashes. Harrington recalled that at the ceremony he had met for the first time Dewey's four children from his first marriage (one of whom was adopted), that they seemed upset and angry that they had not been consulted and involved in the funeral arrangements. Harrington, however, had left all the announcements and notifications to Roberta for completion, and, although it now was too late, Harrington became aware that the children had not approved of their father's remarriage and were critical of their having adopted the two young children.

Just before he died, John Dewey shook hands with me at a Columbia University academic meeting – he had soft, warm hands, and he looked eye-to-eye as we spoke, seemingly interested in what I had done when he sent me the $1 check for dues in the Humanist Club I founded there. For the club I published a newsletter, and because Dewey never attended he voluntarily had sent money for postage. The newsletter had the information that I had started the first such club at Iowa State Teachers College, and Dewey thought similar other university students might imitate this.

The John Dewey Society, at Southern Illinois University, has a computer in which, by entering my name, one finds that they have my correspondence to and from Dewey. They also have the (un-cashed) $1 check he gave me as dues in my 1940s Columbia University Humanist Club.

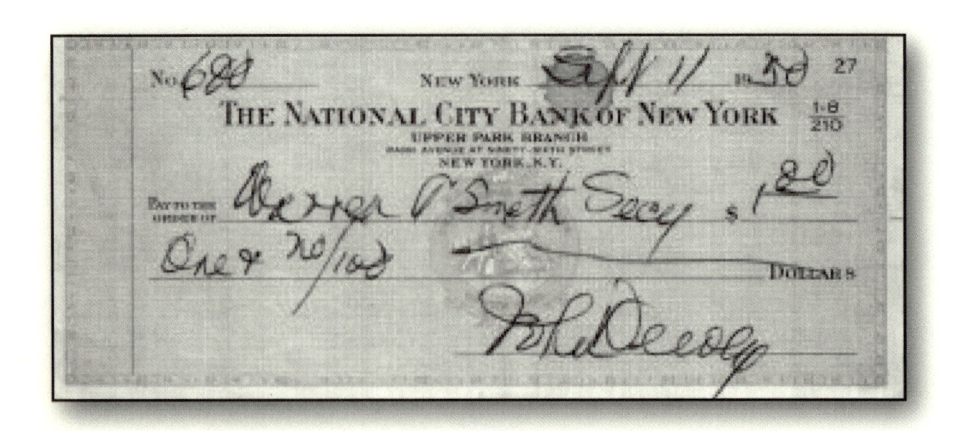

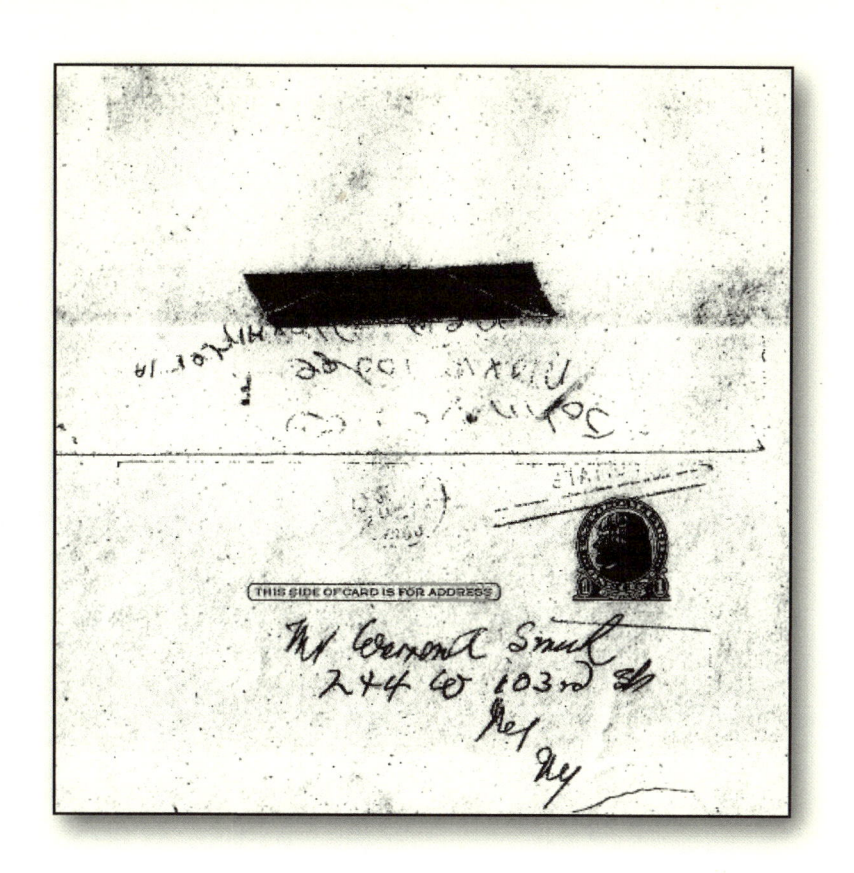

One of Dewey's children scribbled something to me.

In October 1950, Dewey sent a postcard from 1158 5th Avenue, New York City. I had asked for his mailing address

Dewey inspired me more than other contemporary educators, and I regretted not having been able to have been in any of his University of Chicago or Columbia University classes. At Iowa State Teachers in Cedar Falls, Iowa, I read about education and generally knew, as textbooks and online search engines summarize, that according to 2nd century Pausanias in his *Guide to Greece* (432.1), the **gymnasium** in Ancient Greece functioned as a training facility for competitors in public games. Also, it was a place for socializing and engaging in intellectual pursuits. The name comes from the Ancient Greek term *gymnós* (naked). Athletes competed nude, a practice said to encourage aesthetic appreciation of the male body and a tribute to the gods. *Gymnasia* and *palestrae* (wrestling schools) were under the protection and patronage of Heracles, Hermes, and, in Athens, Theseus.

The Greek gymnasium never became popular with the Romans, who believed the training of boys in gymnastics was conducive to idleness and immorality, and of little use for militaristic reasons (though in Sparta gymnastic training had been valued chiefly because it encouraged warlike tastes, promoted the bodily strength needed to use weapons, and ensured the fortitude required to endure hardship).

In the Roman Republic, games in the Campus Martius, duties of camp life, and forced marches and other hardships of warfare took the place of the gymnastic exercises of the Greeks. The first public gymnasium in Rome was built by Nero – another was built later by Commodus.

In the Middle Ages, jousting, feats of horsemanship, and field sports of various kinds became popular and the more systematic training of the body associated with the Greek gymnasium was neglected. It was no longer commonly believed that special exercises had specific therapeutic values, as Hippocrates and Galen once preached.

In Minburn High School, Mr. Jim Duncan as the principal fashioned our school on the ancient gymnasium plan.

In addition to emphasizing the sciences (general science, physics) and the humanities (literature and music), he talked about the ancient olympic games and how when we were putting the shotput, throwing the javelin, and jumping the hurdles we were experiencing how kids our age competed in ancient Greece. But, he said, the kids then did it naked. We looked at big Glen Kinney and little Dolliver Thompson and laughed, whereas Mr. Duncan remained completely serious.

In retrospect, Dewey would have told Minburn taxpayers that the salary they paid to Mr. Duncan was money well spent. I couldn't disagree but got involved only in 8th grade basketball and six-man touch football.

Dickerman, Marion

Dickerman (11 April 1890 - 16 May 1983) was an American suffragette, educator, vice-principal of the Todhunter School, an intimate of Eleanor Roosevelt, and a resident of New Canaan.

The following is from Mrs. Roosevelt's own "Papers Project":

Marion Dickerman at Val-Kill

Marion Dickerman was born 11 April 1890, in Westfield, New York. She studied for two years at Wellesley College before transferring to Syracuse University, where she was an avid supporter of woman's suffrage and campaigned for protective labor legislation for women, the abolishment of child labor, and world peace. A strong, committed student, Dickerman received her bachelor of arts in 1911 and a graduate degree in education in 1912. After a brief teaching assignment in Canisteo, New York, in 1913 Dickerman moved to Fulton, New York, where she taught American history and became reacquainted with Syracuse classmate **Nancy Cook**, who taught arts and handicrafts at Fulton High School. The two women would become lifelong partners, living together almost their entire adult lives, When they returned home the following August, Dickerman was amazed to learn that the Joint Legislative Committee and progressive Democratic leadership in Fulton had selected her to oppose Thaddeus Sweet, the anti-woman suffrage Republican speaker of the New York State Assembly. Dickerman had no chance of winning the election; however, with Cook as her manager, she siphoned away enough votes to prevent Sweet from becoming the Republican gubernatorial nominee.

In 1921, Dickerman accepted a position as dean at the New Jersey State College in Trenton and spent the summer teaching English at Bryn Mawr's Summer School for Women Workers. Unhappy, she looked for a job she loved closer to New York City, where Cook had moved to accept a position with the State Democratic Committee. By summer 1922, Dickerman had moved to New York City and joined the faculty of the Todhunter School.

Dickerman met ER in June 1922 when Dickerman accompanied Cook, then the executive secretary of the Women's Division of the State Democratic Committee, to Hyde Park for a weekend visit. The three women, sharing political ideas and tremendous energy, became fast friends, working together for the Women's Trade Union League, the League of Women Voters, and the Democratic National Committee. As ER recalled in her autobiography, "Miss Cook and Miss Dickerman and I . . . had been from the first drawn together through the work which we were doing together. This is, I think, one of the most satisfactory ways of making and keeping friends." By 1927, in addition to their political work, the three women would share the Val-Kill property, Val-Kill Industries, and the Todhunter School. Their friendship would last more than fifteen years.

Dickerman and Cook prided themselves as diplomatic workers in the sometimes difficult relationship of ER and FDR. Eventually Dickerman's allegiance appeared to ER to favor FDR. By 1932, ER had other new friends like Lorena Hickok who actively disliked Dickerman, and Dickerman, elated by FDR's victory, could not appreciate ER's great anxiety over moving into the White House. By late 1933, as ER's responsibilities introduced her to a wider world and her interests and friendships expanded, she had less time to spend with Dickerman and Cook. By 1936, when Val-Kill Industries dissolved, ER moved out of Stone Cottage, which she shared with Dickerman and Cook, and had the factory building remodeled for her private space where she could entertain without imposing on or involving Dickerman and Cook. When Dickerman sought ER's active help in securing a loan from Bernard Baruch to expand Todhunter, ER, who worried about the wisdom of expanding the school when the economy was not strong, refused to invest in the expansion and was relieved when the deal fell through. The next year, when a professional fundraiser Dickerman hired to promote the school wanted to say that ER would return to Todhunter and make it one of her major interests after the White House, ER refused to cooperate.

In the summer of 1938, FDR named Dickerman to the President's Commission to Study Industrial Relations in Great Britain and Sweden and while she was abroad, ER and Cook had a serious disagreement, "a long and tragic talk" in which the friends "said things that ought not to have been said." By October 1938, their friendship had dissolved. ER felt that they "had no difficulties in previous years" because she "had no objection to" Dickerman's "wishes." Now that she did, she thought Dickerman did not respect her opinion. Furthermore, as Blanche Cook argues, ER resented Dickerman's inference that she and Cook had helped create ER. Although Dickerman remained close to FDR, her future involvement with ER involved only Christmas and birthday gifts. The legal disentanglement of their relationship would take most of 1939. The emotional toll was just as great. As Malvina ("Tommy" Thompson wrote ER's daughter Anna, never before had she seen ER turn "her face to the wall."

Dickerman continued to be active in Democratic politics and, as an alternate delegate to the 1940 Democratic convention, helped secure an isolationist plank in the foreign policy platform sought by FDR. After FDR's death in 1945, Dickerman and Cook moved to New Canaan, Connecticut, where Dickerman directed educational programing for the Marine Museum. She died 16 May 1983 in Kennett Square, Pennsylvania.

In New Canaan, Dickerman lived outside town in a comfortable medium-sized house. She became well-known to school administrators and was free with her advice. She used the town library and from time to time visited some of the schools.

Townspeople and her neighbors found Miss Dickerman interesting and friendly, surprised when they commented that she looked and acted like the President's wife, Eleanor Roosevelt, then found that in fact she actually was her secretary and that Mrs. Roosevelt had visited her in New Canaan.

When Miss Dickerman planned to move from New Canaan, she contacted the School Superintendent and offered to give some of her books to the high school library. He contacted the high school social studies and English department chairmen who made an appointment. After warm greetings, she told them any or all books in the house could be taken that could be used in the high school library. Social Studies Chairman Richard Cressy whispered to me, the English Department chairman, that he found nothing he wanted, but when reminded that the books were not for us but for our library he helped dutifully to fill the entire back of his car.

Miss Dickerman did not object to our taking the books off her hands and, in a surprise, asked me questions about my literature classes. She once had visited, and she played a big part in the progressive advancement of the town's educational goals. "Does your old school, Bentley on 86th Street, still play Dalton?" she asked, for she remembered my having come to New Canaan from Bentley, doubling my salary because public paid better than private schools. "Yes, the Little Red School House and Friends and Dalton," I remembered, adding that "maybe Mrs. Roosevelt and definitely William Heard Kilpatrick had visited Bentley, for I took him home in a taxi." She was openly pro-progressive education, unlike most teachers at that time. I asked if she had ever met Bentley's principal, another progressive education pioneer, Irma Kaufmann, and if she had ever visited the school. She had not.

"You still have that check from John Dewey for a dollar?" she asked, still remembering that I had told her that while a student at Columbia University the eminent educator and philosopher had paid $1 dues to be a member of the Humanist Club that I founded while a student and he was not on the faculty. We laughed when I said I still had the check, that Dr. Dewey was probably still trying to balance his checking account because of the non-cashed check. I had only seen Mrs. Roosevelt once, but to me Miss Dickerman sounded, walked, and looked as if they were twins.

When Oxford University graduate Winifred Todhunter, her children now grown, chose to return to England, Miss Dickerman, the school's vice-principal, arranged with Mrs. Roosevelt and Nancy Cook to buy Todhunter School and continue it. Her "Papers Project" detailed how Mrs. Roosevelt taught American history, American literature, English, and current events to junior and seniors. Mrs. Roosevelt – like Marie Souvestre her headmistress at Allenwood boarding school outside London when 15 and her student – strove to blend a rigorous curriculum with exercises designed to encourage students to think for themselves. Her history exams had two parts: one factual and one analytical. Students had to answer questions such as: "Give your reasons for or against allowing women to actively participate in the control of the government, politics, and officials through the vote, as well as your reasons for or against women holding office in the government." "What is the object today of the inheritance, income and similar taxes?" "How are Negroes excluded from voting in the South?" In each class, she underscored the connection between the things of the past and the things of today, as well as encouraging the students to understand the difference between subject and citizen. She took students on field trips to the New York Children's Court and various tenements and markets in the city so they could see the problems facing New Yorkers and how the government tried to address them.

After FDR was elected governor in 1928, ER continued to teach three days a week. "I teach because I love it. I cannot give it up." When FDR was elected president, her teaching career (except for an occasional current events class) at the school ended, although her association with it did not. She attended school functions, delivered graduation addresses, gave lectures to alumnae living in the Washington area, and arranged for Todhunter students to visit the White House. ER finally left the school entirely in 1938.

To have met a progressive educator was more of a treat for me than meeting someone who had had White House connections. But the names of Lorena Hickock and Dickerman's New Canaan housemate Nancy Cook were unknown by the high school faculty to the present author's knowledge. Much later news reports told of Hickock's willing her personal papers to the FDR Library in Hyde Park, New York, part of the US National Archives. Her donation was contained in 18 filing boxes that, according to the provisions of her Will, were to be sealed until ten years after her death, which was on 1 May 1968. Early in May 1978, Doris Faber became perhaps the first person to open these boxes and found that they contained 2,336 letters from Mrs. Roosevelt to Lorena, most of them dated in the 1930s and continuing right up to Mrs. Roosevelt's death in 1962.

A key passage from just one early 12-page handwritten missive to Lorena from Eleanor sheds light on their relationship: "Goodnight, dear one. I want to put my arms around you and kiss you at the corner of your mouth. And in a little more than a week now – I shall! [Doris Faber, *The Life of Lorena Hickok, E.R.'s Friend* (1980)]. It is not universally accepted by historians that the two were romantically connected. Although some lesbians today claim her as a fellow lesbian, no proof has been advanced.

Dickerman's *New York Times* obituary (18 May 1983) reported her death at the age of 93 at Crosslands, a retirement community in Kennett Square, Pennsylvania. It ended, "She taught at the Todhunter School in Manhattan from 1922 to 1927, when she was named principal. After the merger with the Dalton Schools, she served as associate principal until 1942. Miss Dickerman is survived by two sisters, Katherine Boger of Kennett Square and Margaret Levenson of Stamford, Connecticut. Plans for a memorial service in New Canaan are to be announced."

Mrs. Roosevelt and Ms. Dickerman

Dilley, Whitney Crothers

Dilley, the present author's student (NCHS '83) in creative writing, smiled upon hearing on the first day her class met that no one can teach you how to write creatively. Then, to laughter, she heard that her teacher was going to try.

> First, there will be no textbook.
> Second, on the teacher's desk will be an in-basket and anything submitted is to be picked up from an out-basket the next day the class meets.
> Third, students can write nothing at all, or they can write to the point that their other classes will suffer; and
> Fourth, anything submitted is to be as if by someone else . . . and selections written by parents or others are not permitted.

For example, Marie Antoinette might turn in a selection on Monday, receiving a 2.8 the following day; then be revised and on Wednesday resubmitted by Mary Todd, receiving a 3.5; then rewritten and on Friday resubmitted as Adolf Hitler, receiving a 3.9 (out of 4.0, although 4.0's would rarely if ever be given); and only when satisfied with the grade should the student confess that he or she was the author and wanted just the highest grade recorded.

New Criticism, a literary theory that was popular then, emphasized "close reading" and understanding how meaning and structure are closely connected. Examples of really bad sonnets were given, and students who thought they were excellent were amazed to learn they had praised authentic sonnets by Shakespeare that critics agreed were weak. In short, if someone's pseudonymous submission was signed with the name of the student most in the class might think would be the best, they would find out. The 2.0's, 3.0's, and 3.9's were totaled and graded on the curve, which encouraged quantity as well as quality.

Miss Crothers stood out in accumulating points and getting a 4.0 on a final test, although others received higher quarterly grades. She wrote a first-rate documented research paper (with "all the according to's") on "Hare Krishna and the Lure of Cults."

After graduating as a member of New Canaan High School's Class of '83, she studied at Oberlin College and Brown University, earning a doctorate in Comparative Literature at the University of Washington in 1998.

She surprised few when her biography of Ang Lee, *The Cinema of Ang Lee: The Other Side of the Screen*, received critical praise. Lee was the filmmaker who directed *Brokeback Mountain* as well as *Ice Storm* (about two dysfunctional New Canaan families who were trying to deal with tumultuous political and social changes of the early 1970s, and their escapism through alcohol, adultery, and sexual experimentation).

Dr. Dilley lives and teaches in Taipei, Taiwan, with husband Larry Dilley and daughter Emma Judith.

She is an associate professor in the English Department at Shih Hsin University, a media/film school.

Dorato, Fedora

As co-owner with Fernando in New York City of Variety Recording Studio, and working in Connecticut half the year, I thought it would be good business for him to choose a restaurant where he could take staff members or clients to eat. He chose Fedora's on West 4th Street in Greenwich Village.

Fedora's sister Norma worked down the street on 46th Street from us at *Variety*, and once in awhile we would take to the other mail that had been mis-addressed.

Her restaurant was moderately priced, had clients that included nearby New York University students and faculty members with their wives. It was known as "the oldest family-owned restaurant in New York City."

When her husband **Henry Dorato** was still alive, he told me how **Mayor Jimmy Walker** had been a customer when Prohibition was being enforced. When a lieutenant and some cops got by the speakeasy's peephole in the front door, they rushed upstairs and there was the Mayor!

When the lieutenant was asked what he wanted, he blabbered something to the mayor to the effect that he was trying to find the men's room, then fled with his squad.

Carl Sandburg had been a customer because a relative took him there. Edward Albee lived just across the street (4th Street) when he wrote *Zoo Story*. Jerry Herman, Lauren Bacall, Gilbert Price, and other showbiz people were frequently there rather than at nearby expensive places.

From the 1960s on, Fedora's was my hangout. It was here where I ran after cops chased me during the June 1969 Stonewall uprising. On the 2nd night, I found helmeted tactical policemen there, and at a certain point I and a guy next to me threw a garbage can that he set fire to. When a cop came running in our direction, I fled to Fedora's. I learned much later that one of her waiters had actually been arrested, put in a paddy wagon, and taken to jail. That waiter denied this.

It was one of the few places from which I could make a phone call from a rotary pay phone; order prawns Florentine and deviled eggs à la Russe; and find nothing new (although she laughed when anyone noted that in all the years the only thing she ever changed were burned-out light bulbs).

Gabe Stulman, when Fedora was almost 90, obtained the Dorato family's and Community Board 2's approval to lease the place. In 2011, he turned the place into a casual but much more expensive place, so the mainly gay clientele that had been paying less than $20 for full-course dinners now found Cornish Hen and Quail for three times that.

Dubin, Heather

Few of my former New Canaan students and fellow teachers knew that I was one of **General Dwight D. Eisenhower**'s adjutant general's chief clerks from 1944 until the surrender in 1945.

Greenwich Village's *Villager* (11 November 2013) contained the following article by **Heather Dubin**:

> Warren Allen Smith made it through World War II in the Army without firing a rifle.
>
> Wearing a crisp yellow, collared shirt with black slacks, the U.S. Army veteran, born Oct. 27, 1921, gave a riveting interview at his West Village apartment earlier this week about his eclectic past.
>
> Smith, a gay atheist, is originally from Minburn, Iowa, population 328.
>
> "In my little town, they painted a barn yellow because the kid was not drafted," he said. "It was strange if you weren't in the Army."
>
> Smith completed one year of college at the University of Northern Iowa in Cedar Falls, where he studied English literature, music and journalism before he was drafted in 1942. Raised a Methodist, Smith became an Emersonian at school, and started a humanist club there. His interest in atheism grew as a faculty sponsor of the club was also an atheist.
>
> "I joined the Unitarians in Des Moines – I'm still a dues-paying member," Smith noted. "They joke about me because I've never attended."
>
> Smith began his military career at Fort Knox for basic training. Later at Fort Dix, his educational experience and ability to type 113 words per minute landed him in company clerk training instead of soldier training.
>
> There were 300 new men every 13 weeks for training, and the Army was in dire need of clerks.
>
> "When I was actually sent abroad, I was the acting first sergeant because nobody could keep the records," Smith said. "I was a company clerk, and I didn't know how to clean a gun."
>
> His journey overseas started from a Hudson River dock, and it was harrowing. All the men on his ship received a medal for crossing the Atlantic Ocean successfully; Smith used his hands to demonstrate how the ship zigzagged to avoid submarines.

Once they arrived in Liverpool, the men were put on an overnight train to Southampton. Smith recalled that the shades were pulled down, and they could not see England at all.

Their next step was to board another ship, and in an hour they were on Omaha Beach in Normandy. Smith explained that there were huge iron structures on the beach that prevented tanks from coming in, and there was a hill, which is why the Nazis also could not reach them.

As the company clerk, Smith was responsible for bringing along his cohorts' files.

"I'm the one with all the records of the 250 men with my group – otherwise everyone wouldn't have benefits today," he said.

Smith and his company had to walk through the water to get to the beach, holding their rifles overhead to keep them from getting wet. He confided that none of the other men knew that Smith had no idea how to clean, much less use, his rifle.

Smith could not recall anyone helping him carry the records he put in a bag. However, he said he could have ordered someone to do so. When they reached the top, they were there for a day or so in the rain, and slept in pup tents.

"The fact that I was in a war didn't sort of dawn on me," he said. "I was an English major – but hadn't read any World War I stories."

Another part of Smith's job was to lead "Reveille" for daily calisthenics.

"In the morning I had to exercise people," he said. "I was not gay, you could not be gay, I didn't know I was gay."

Smith relocated to anther spot for a few weeks. There were no Nazis around since they were already falling back toward Paris. Since he was a quick typist, Adjutant General Floyd W. Brown recruited Smith for Supreme Headquarters. Brown told him, "Get in the Packard," and they, too, headed toward Paris.

"We tried to drive to Reims and there were no signs. The Germans had taken them all down," Smith recounted. "We couldn't get into Paris because the Germans were still there."

Smith said the adjutant general was "swearing like mad at the chauffeur," and recalled that he thought to himself he was collecting good material to write about.

They finally made it to Reims, 80 miles outside Paris, and happened upon an empty building where the Germans previously had been staying. The phones worked, so they moved in. Smith was there was from 1944 until the end of the war in 1945.

Future President Dwight D. Eisenhower, then supreme commander of the Allied Forces and a five-star general, transferred Smith's office to the Little Red School, which was the largest school in town. Smith worked five doors down from Eisenhower — they did not interact — and the Germans signed their surrender to the Allies in a room five doors in the other direction.

Smith's job at Supreme Headquarters was to ensure every soldier in Europe received his mail.

"By that time there was a million of them," he said. Smith focused on getting people their mail the next day, and called his section "Morale Builders."

"I've talked with veterans, and asked them, 'What was the best part of your service?'" Smith said. "I got them to say, 'Oh, mail call.'" While he admitted to slightly exaggerating, Smith was serious about soldiers wanting to forget everything the war came with.

Smith also took orders for General George S. Patton for tanks and soldiers, plus rations, such as beer, shirts and shoes.

"We were not the Home Depot, but we were the Army Depot," he joked.

Every general was sending his section orders, and they had to check for supplies that were usually in England.

"If the beer supply went down, we could also get champagne from France," he said.

Smith also learned ethics at this time.

"There were some colonels who would steal stuff from other colonels," he added. "We knew who the liars were.

"I went to work every morning at 8 a.m., and I left work around 5 p.m. Being in the Army, if you were in Supreme Headquarters, was not like being in one of General Patton's units – not at all," he said.

There were 200 women who also did clerical work at Supreme Headquarters. Smith became friends with one of them, Corporal Fuqua. The two joined forces to provide 24-hour assistance to help a segregated unit of black American soldiers, who were holding the line in the Battle of Bastogne, to secure ammunition and enforcement.

"That was an important battle because there was nothing between the Nazis and Paris at this point, except a black group," he said. "They built bridges and were cooks."

Smith received two medals for his efforts during this period, one for the Battle of the Atlantic, the other for the Battle of Bastogne.

One day, Smith secured a jeep from a post office and drove with a friend to Verdun to see if he could find a record of his father, who had served in World War I, earned two Purple Hearts and fought in the Battle of Verdun. He found his name, and on the way back, someone took a shot at Smith and his friend in the jeep.

"We didn't have any guns. We were enjoying the countryside," he said.

Smith stepped on the gas, and, as it turned out, that was as close to combat as he got. Smith speculated it was probably a French Nazi sympathizer. Men and women who were caught helping the Germans were forced to shave their heads, he noted.

Smith does not attribute his assignment in World War II to luck, but said he simply had the right skill set.

"We all get prepared in different ways to handle life, and I handled it mainly by skills," he said. "It wasn't luck. You don't succeed by luck, it's all work."

According to Smith, he picked up this mindset from the adjutant general.

"But my experience was positive," he continued. "If you interview any other veterans, I don't think you're going to find that."

After the war, Smith returned to the University of Northern Iowa on the G.I. Bill, followed by a Masters of Arts at Columbia University in English literature, where his adviser was Lionel Trilling, the famed literary critic. To get to New York, Smith cashed in the train ticket his parents bought him, and hitchhiked his way instead.

"I got there pretty quickly," he said.

During his first week at Columbia in 1948, Smith met Fernando Vargas, a sound engineer, who would become his partner for 40 years until his death. Smith had not realized he was gay until then.

"When we went to my room, that's when the mystery was solved," he said.

Smith became a high school English teacher, first in Manhattan and then in New Canaan, Connecticut. He taught for 32 years. Starting in 1977, for more than a decade, he spent summers in the Caribbean working as a journalist. In the 1950s, Smith was also a book review editor at a humanist magazine, and later became the book review editor at *The Humanist*.

Currently, he is a columnist for *The Pink Humanist,* an international online journal.

In 1961, he and Vargas founded Variety, a recording studio. One of their first customers was Marvin Hamlisch, a young composer and conductor, who brought in Liza Minnelli, an actress and singer, when she was a high school junior. The couple did the soundtrack for Minnelli, who sang over the music.

A prolific writer, Smith has written eight books since turning 80, including a three-part autobiography.

He has been adopted by eight kids who all call him "Dad." They are from other countries, and have lived in New York. Smith refers to the eight as his "modern family," and said the kids are from dysfunctional families. Together, they have formed a bond that transcends race and sexuality.

"All eight are straight, and all eight know about me," he said. "Things have changed over the years. Kids today, their peers sometimes say, say, 'I wish my dad were gay.'"

Duncan, James

Mr. Duncan, the principal of Minburn High School, was one of my math teachers. In 9th grade he encouraged us to add, subtract, and multiply in our head. In math we were encouraged to add, subtract, and multiply in their heads. I never learned why, but he knew that 45 times 45 is 2,025 and 85 times 85 is 7,225. If identical numbers ending in 5 are multiplied by each other, the answer always ends in 25, Mr. Duncan explained. You then add one at the beginning of the first number, for example changing 4 to 5 in the 45 times 45 example, obtaining 5 times the 4 just underneath to get 20. Put the 20 with the 25 and you have 2,025.

At Drake University Mr. Duncan had graduated with an interest in philosophy as a teenager, and when he arrived in Minburn as the school's principal he seemed to think it was Athens. Boys had to learn how to throw the shot-put and javelin, jump the hurdles, and race short as well as long distances. In history and many other subjects, the students had two textbooks in order to compare their contents.

My interest in money, being a Des Moines *Register* and *Tribune* paper boy for the entire town, led me while in 10th grade to enter a high school contest at Iowa State University in Ames, winning first prize for an essay about a subject I had never studied: economics. In 9th grade I had scored on the Iowa Every Pupil Test as being the 39th best student in the entire state in algebra. Other of my classmates won even more laurels, and everyone credited Mr. Duncan.

Duncan became my main role model, my inspiration for becoming a teacher.

Edwards, Paul

Having never taken a university college course in philosophy, except for Corliss Lamont's about humanism at Columbia and Horace Kallen's about aesthetics at The New School, I signed up under my Allen Windsor pseudonym to take an introductory course in philosophy at The New School for Social Research taught by Paul Edwards.

The course was not for credit, and Edwards smiled at the end that he knew my name but not what I looked like. I was head of a secular humanism group that he later headed.

So many students wanted to attend his 1995 Prometheus Books Lecture Series that Tim Madigan was able to talk a department chairman into allowing Edwards to use the college's large amphitheater. I was chosen by Prometheus Books to moderate the meeting at which he lectured on **Sigmund Freud** and **Wilhelm Reich.**

Of Edwards's *Encyclopedia of Philosophy* (1967), the new *Oxford Companion to Philosophy* states, "There has been nothing since to compare with it" and it is "superior in every way to all its predecessors" going back all the way to the compendia of 6th Century Cassiodorus.

Tim, who stayed with me when he came to the city from Rochester, took me with him when he visited. We expected to see the same dirty dishes, pots, and pans piled up in his kitchen. The wine Paul offered was in glasses that had merely been rinsed. On every visit, if Paul got worked up, he'd excuse himself to go into one of the three bathrooms and utter/scream the Reichian shriek: a blood-curdling sound that apparently released his (as well as some of our) emotions. He was negatively critical about two philosophers: **Martin Heidegger** (about whom in 2004 he acerbically wrote *Heidegger's Confusions*) and noted philosopher **Sidney Hook**, clapping his hands with joy when relating that upon his death in 1989 Hook – they once shared an office at NYU – hadn't made page one of *The Times*).

Sometimes Edwards would treat us at a Viennese restaurant on 72nd Street, but when that went out of business he'd take us across the street, from his exclusive residence at the Apthorpe, to a Greek diner, always ordering scrambled eggs because a severe dental problem made it painful for him to bite down on food.

Ilse, Reich's wife, knew of my friendship with composer David Amram and Edwards, for Reich's secretary and I shared school meetings together and e-mailed from time to time after she no longer taught German. Amram and Edwards were surprised that I knew Ilse and always inquired about her health.

When she taught German at NCHS, few knew about Ilse's illustrious past. When her biography of Reich came out (in 1970 while school was on), I was first in line to obtain an autographed copy. In 1991 and at other times, we conversed and wrote about how her being a Friend/Quaker and my being a nominal Unitarian/humanist overlapped – we had in common a non-theological humanities humanism that emphasized working (deeds, not just words) for a more humane society.

Upon Edwards's death, **Dr. Timothy Madigan**'s and my going into the 4-bedroom apartment that *philosophe* **Dr. Paul Edwards** had ($1,800/month rent-controlled, for he'd lived in 6-G several decades – in April 2011, a much smaller 2 bedroom, 2½ bath 6-F was selling for $6,195,000). Tim, an ethics prof at St. John Fisher in Rochester, NY, and I went inch-by-inch through the cluttered place, searching for chapters of Paul's unfinished book. One by one, the chapters were located in various boxes on shelves, on the floor, and where you'd never expect them to be – then, Tim had to put everything in order and edit the book. *God and the Philosophers* could never have been published this month if we'd been unable to locate even one box with disks or typed material! Paul's system of answering mail was to throw it on the floor, separating what he didn't want (which remained there for months) and putting the rest in piles.

I had never before met the two Russians, one a Lukoil attorney who was concerned as to the cost of storing several thousand books in the extensive library. Although Paul's treasures were his extensive opera LPs, I advised that they had been extensively used, often with old needles, and would be valuable only for nostalgia lovers or those who knew Paul.

Picture of one of Reich's commercial orgone boxes

The funeral – When Warren asked the teenage Haitian son who adopted him to photograph an event, Ligardy Termonfils happily said yes. Wherever they went, it seemed memorable. This time, Ligardy helped throw a New School University professor into the Hudson River (long before Ligardy was selected as a freshman member of that university's basketball team).

In his Last Will and Testament, Paul Edwards – an atheist who like Tim and me was in the Bertrand Russell Society – directed that his ashes be thrown into the Hudson River, a place near his apartment. Shown below are four of the professor's friends, after which the jar containing his cremains was scattered behind us (and the wind blew some back into our faces).

Ashes, away!

(Photo by Ligardy Termonfils, taken from the overhead bridge)

Warren and Ligardy with four of Prof. Edwards's acquaintances.

Ellis, Royston

Ellis, a British-born poet, novelist, and travel author, was born in Pinner, England, on 10 February 1941.

He dropped out of school in 1957, bummed around Soho and the jazz club scene, all the time writing poetry. He had his first volume of poems about the new generation of freeloving, rock 'n' rolling teenagers published in 1959; made his poetry popular by terming it "rocketry". And he performed his poems to rock music on TV and stage shows around England, appearing with rock groups such as Cliff Richard and the Shadows, then read his poetry backed in 1960 by The Beatles before they became famous.

A 1960s account of Ellis's poetry reading and biography was printed in *Mersey Beat*. Ellis is described as being "Britain's foremost exponent of 'Beat Poetry'."

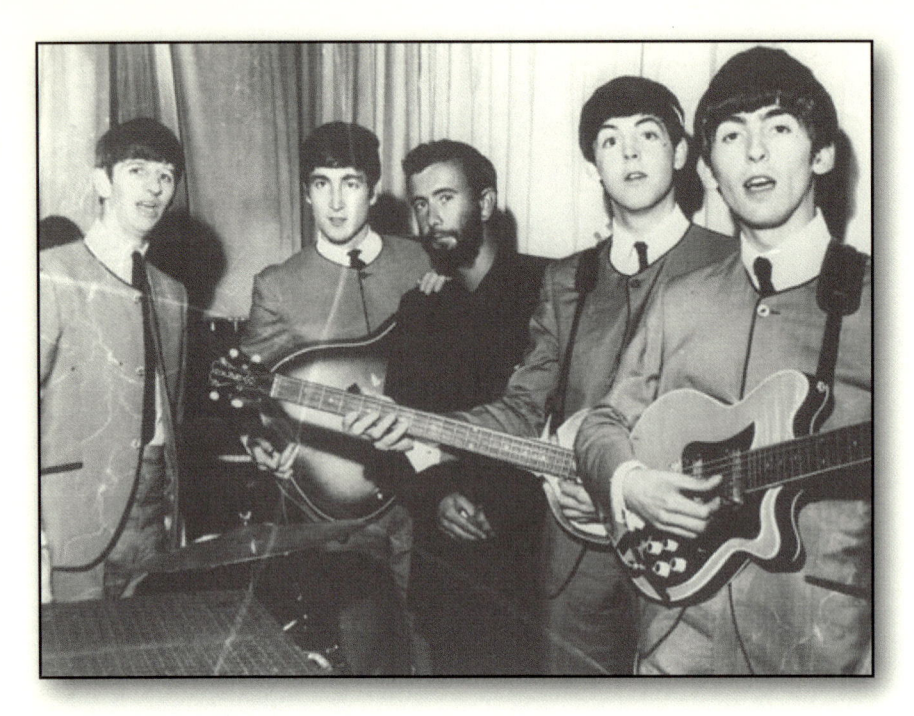

Ellis (center) in Liverpool was backed by the Beatles.

Ellis and John Lennon, both interested in the American Beat poets, bonded and spent time together at 3 Gambier Terrace with Stuart Sutcliffe and others. Lennon said of Ellis that he was "the converging point of rock'n'roll and literature," and Ellis said of Lennon, "I was quite a star for them at that time because I had come up from London and that was a world they didn't really know about."

His main musician, with whom he appeared at London's Mermaid Theatre to great acclaim in July 1961, was the then seventeen-year old Jimmy Page. Ellis gave readings in Moscow at the invitation of Yevgeni Yevtushenko.

Steve Turner, in *Cliff Richard, The Biography* (1993), describes how as a sixteen-year-old Ellis left school and toured with the Beatles – Ellis suggested the spelling (not Beetles, which they had chosen), convincing them they were part of the Beats, the individuals who were unfairly being beaten down because they were unconventional. At performances, the Beatles provided the music and Ellis provided the rocketry (poetry read to rock 'n' roll).

Speaking on a BBC telecast about the Beatles, Ellis said

> On 28 October 2006, Royston wrote to me, "[Have] just seen this extraordinary recollection of me by Paul McCartney. Seems John Lennon claims I turned the Beatles on to drugs. (Benzedrine nose inhalers) and now

Kiss. Surely someone should do a show on Kiss['s] hidden influences of me on the Beatles."

Ellis showed John Lennon and Paul McCartney how to break down a Benzedrine nose inhaler and sniff the strips inside to produce a mild high. Lennon later recounted in *International Times.*

"The first dope, from a Benzedrine inhaler, was given to the Beatles (John, George, Paul, and Stuart) by an English cover version of Allen Ginsberg - one Royston Ellis, known as 'beat poet' . . . . So, give the saint his due".

The Beatles immortalized him in the song "Paperback Writer."

When eighteen years old, Ellis wrote *Driftin' With Cliff,* in which he described life on the road with Britain's top pop singer, Cliff Richard. Turner described Royston as

> Britain's first teenage pundit, an Allen Ginsberg of suburban London. The fact that he wore a beard and had worked as an office boy, duster salesman, gardener, milk-bottle washer, building labourer, and farm hand by the age of eighteen helped confirm the image. . . . His first volume of poems, *Jiving to Gyp,* was dedicated [to Cliff Richard], and he was soon asked by television programmes to explain what teenagers were all about. He ended up with his own series, "Living For Kicks," in which he explored the controversial issues of the day such as pep pills and sex before marriage.

Ellis appeared in *Wonderful Life* (1963, a movie with Cliff Richard) and starred in a TV drama in *Sinhala* (1998).

Ellis met up with Cliff Richard after 44 years when they had tea together in a hotel near Ellis's home in Sri Lanka during Cliff's visit for a concert in Colombo in February 2007. Parenthetically, he became a born-again Christian. Ellis was anti-organized religion.

A cogent musical commentator – his 1961 paperback *The Big Beat Scene* still stands up as an appraisal of early British rock 'n' roll – met the fledgling Beatles (in May 1960). McCartney has recalled,

> The first time we ever heard about gayness was when a poet named Royston Ellis arrived in Liverpool with his book *Jiving With Gyp.* He was a Beat poet. Well, well! Phew! You didn't meet them in Liverpool. And it was all 'Break me in easy, break me in easy.' It was all shagging sailors, I think. We had a laugh with that line."

"One in every four men is homosexual," Ellis told McCartney, according to Barry Miles's *Paul McCartney* (1998): "So we looked at the group! One in every four! It literally meant one of us is gay. Oh, fucking hell, it's not me, is it? We had a lot of soul-searching to do over that little one."

The "one" was their manager, Brian Epstein, who in 1962 signed a management contract with them for twenty-five per cent of their gross receipts, after a certain threshold was reached and after he got them a recording contract.

Ellis met McCartney by chance again in the bar of Le Bristol Hotel in Paris in October 2006, and McCartney recited a line to him from his favourite poem by Royston: "Break me in easy, break me in easy." They swapped stories about the past and promised to meet up again in Sri Lanka.

McCartney's biographer wrote of the Beatles and Ellis:

> "Polythene Pam" was another of John's songs written in India and originally destined for the *White Album*. It was inspired by Stephanie, a girlfriend of the Beat poet Royston Ellis, whom the Beatles backed at Liverpool University in 1960. On 8 August 1963, the Beatles played at the Auditorium in Guernsey, the Channel Islands. Ellis was working as a ferryboat engineer on the island and invited John to come back to his flat. John told *Playboy*: "I had a girl and he had one he wanted me to meet. He said she dressed up in Polythene, which she did. She didn't wear jackboots and kilts, I just sort of elaborated. Perverted sex in a Polythene bag. Just looking for something to write about." Royston Ellis told Steve Turner: "We all dressed up in them and wore them in bed. John stayed the night with us in the same bed." Paul remembered meeting Royston in Guernsey: "John, being Royston's friend, went out to dinner with him and got pissed and stuff and they ended up back at his apartment with a girl who dressed herself in Polythene for John's amusements, so it was a little kinky scene. She became Polythene Pam. She was a real character." John: "When I recorded it I used a thick Liverpool accent because it was supposed to be about a mythical Liverpool scrubber dressed up in her jackboots and kilt."

Lennon wrote about the Polythene Pam incident:

> "Polythene Pam: That was me, remembering a little event I had with a woman in Jersey, an island off the French coast. A poet, England's answer to Allen Ginsberg, a beatnik that looked like a beatnik who was from Liverpool, took me to this apartment of his in Jersey. This was so long ago. This is all triggering these amazing memories. So this poet took me to his place and asked me if I wanted to meet this girl, Polythane Pam, who dressed up in polythene. Which she did. In polythene bags. She didn't wear jack boots and kilts – I just sort of elaborated – and no, she didn't really look like a man. there was nothing much to it. It was kind of perverted sex in a polythene bag. But it provided something to write a song about".

Bill Harry, founder of the Liverpool music paper that publicized what became known as the *Mersey Beat*, wrote of Ellis:

Early in 1960 John Lennon, Stuart Sutcliffe, Rod Murray and I had been to Liverpool University to listen to a poet called Royston Ellis. We later retired to 'Ye Cracke' pub in Rice Street to discuss the evening. The topic of conversation was that Royston was copying the San Francisco poets rather than composing works in the British tradition. We felt that any creative person should really base their work on their own experiences rather than copying someone else's and the discussion led us to decide to work creatively on what we knew best – and that was life in Liverpool. We decided to call ourselves 'The Dissenters' and made a vow that we would work creatively to make Liverpool famous.

Harry confirmed that the Beatles backed Ellis at a place called the Jacaranda:

I reviewed the book *Big Beat Scene* by Royston Ellis, one of the first-ever books about the British music scene. It began: "Royston Ellis, a bearded teenager who made a name for himself on the television programme 'Living for Kicks', visited Liverpool last year. Appearing at Liverpool University's 'Festival of the Arts' where he recited his poetry, he was threatened by students who wanted to set fire to his beard. Later, he recited 'poetry-to-rock' at the Jacaranda coffee club, Slater Street, backed by the Beatles."

John Lennon, Stuart Sutcliffe, Rod Murray and I went to see Royston at his University recital and later retreated to our local art college pub Ye Cracke where we made a decision to call ourselves the Dissenters and use our creative skills to make Liverpool famous. We all got on with Royston and he did recite his poetry at the Jacaranda, backed by the Beatles – and he also stayed for a brief time at the Gambier Terrace flat.

Harry describes Ellis's *Big Beat Scene* as "one of the first books to be published about the British music scene.

John would do it with his music, Stuart and Rod with their painting and me with my writing. In some ways I suppose that could have been the spark that ignited my creation of *Mersey Beat*. The four of us also used to hang around a coffee bar called The Jacaranda in Slater Street, run by an ebullient character called Allan Williams. On the top floor attic of the building, which housed the 'Jac', was a young man selling second-hand albums. I used to chat to him and bought a copy of the 'Picnic' soundtrack. He was aware that I'd been assistant editor of *Pantosphinx*, the University charity magazine, and told me that Frank Hesselberg, who owned the Frank Hessy music store, had asked him to edit a magazine called 'Frank Comments' but he didn't know how to go about it – would I do it with him?

Ellis left England in 1962, "having somehow become a spokesyouth for Britain's mods, rockers, and beatniks, a role I felt I had outgrown," he has said. He lived in the Canary Islands (the setting of his first novel, *The Flesh Merchants*), then from 1966 to 1980 in Dominica, Windward Islands (setting of his million-copy bestsellers such as the historical novel, *The Bondmaster*, which pseudonymously he wrote as Richard Tresillian). It described the lives and loves of 19th century West Indian whites and the workers on their estates. In Dominica, in addition to being the real estate developer for the Marquis of Bristol and a Reuters correspondent, he edited *The Educator*, a journal editorially favorable to the Premier, Edward LeBlanc.

Festivals of the World: Trinidad is a children's book.

In the 1980s, again as Richard Tresillian, he wrote a best-selling series, *Fleshtraders*, again about 19th century miscegenation and adventures, this time set in Mauritius.

Asked in 1991 about philosophic humanism, Ellis wrote,

> Since the age of 14, I have not known exactly what I am, nor do I care, having decided at the age of 14 that it was not god who created man but man who created god. My first book, Jiving to Gyp (gyp means hell) published when I was 18, contained raunchy atheistic poems.

Ellis in Sri Lanka, with friends

Since 1980 he has lived in Sri Lanka and covered the Indian Ocean by writing guide books. *India By Rail* (1993), an insider's view, tells how 7,000 trains operate throughout India. He also has written *The Story of Tea* as well as travel books and articles about Mauritius, Sri Lanka, and the Maldives.

In June 2010, *The Big Beat Scene*, his book that had been out of print for almost half a century, was published. It contained a new Foreword and Afterword by the author.

From: Paul McCartney by Barry Miles 1998

PAUL: The first time we ever heard about gayness was when a poet named Royston Ellis arrived in Liverpool with his book *Jiving With Gyp*. He was a Beat poet. Well, well Phew! You didn't meet them in Liverpool. And it was all 'Break me in easy, break me in easy ...' It was all shagging sailors, I think. We had a laugh with that line. John became quite friendly with Royston. One thing he told us was that one in every four men is homosexual. So we looked at the group! One in every four! It literally meant one of us is gay. Oh, fucking hell, it's not me, is it? We had a lot of soul-searching to do over that little one.

We'd heard that Brian was queer, as we would have called him, nobody used the word 'gay' then. 'He's a queer.' 'Yes. He's all right, though.' We didn't hold that against him. We didn't really know much about it, there were certain people around but they tended to be the slightly older guys on the scene from what we knew. There wasn't much talk amongst us and our friends about anything like that. Brian was quite a well-known gay, I think. We would go down late-night drinking clubs that we hadn't had access to. They were probably gay clubs, now I think about it, but it actually didn't occur to us at all, there were rather a lot of men there, that's all. But no one ever propositioned me. There was never any bother. Pubs would stay open through Brian's influence, which was fine by us. It meant we could get a drink late at night, fantastic! And the police wouldn't bust us, fantastic! In fact, this is where we started to see the seamier side of society, because the policemen would often come round and have a drink with us. There was a lot of that.

Then we got down to London and Brian had his contacts in the gay scene. People would say, 'How are your boys, Brian?' 'Well, they're doing rather well, they just had a hit.' 'Oh, marvellous, do put them on my show!' So obviously that didn't hurt us.

On 24 January 1962, the Beatles signed a management contract with Brian. He was to get 25 per cent of their gross receipts after a certain threshold was reached, but first he had to get them a recording contract. There were many anxious weeks spent waiting for Brian to come up with the goods. John and Paul would wait in the Punch and Judy café opposite Lime Street station (so called because they used to

---

Dear Warren:

Just seen this extraordinary recollection of me by Paul McCartney. Since John Lennon claims I turned the Beatles on to drugs (Benzedrine nose inhalers) and now this, surely someone should do a study on the hidden influences of R.E. on the Beatles!

love, John
8.10.04

Ferra, Max

Max

When a fellow engineer, **Max Ferra**, told Fernando about a vacant apartment in his building in midtown on 45th Street, Fernando and I checked it out. It was up on the 4th floor, and when you entered you were in the combination kitchen/bathroom. In fact, like many other buildings in Hell's Kitchen at that time a board over the bathtub served as the kitchen table. There was a big front room overlooking 45th Street, and a small room in the back.

The building super, to our surprise, was Belgian-born **Marie**, a kindly woman in her 70s or 80s whose ground floor apartment was dank and dark – she might have been one of Herbert Hoover's secretaries (or maybe she was a mistress in the nation's capital, for the stories kept changing).

Things went pretty well. Fernando and I moved from uptown to the apartment that Ferra told us about. Even in 1988, the rent paid to Marin Management for our apartment at 425 West 45th Street was $194.40, only slightly more than we'd been paying back on 103rd. At that time, Fernando had a checking account with New Canaan Bank, one that I handled entirely and always signed his name – he always laughed that he never signed a check. Like his father, he had other people do work for us.

Warren's concern was that we were near the site of "Slaughter on 10th Avenue." A sunken railroad line just to the west was where a Gophers gang used iron spikes to fight guards before looting the boxcars that parked there. A gang called the Westies allegedly shook down anyone in the area. Sailors were required never to pass through the area alone, either coming from or going to their nearby ships.

Anyway, we decided to move because Fernando liked being so close to the recording studio. By this time, Warren was teaching in Connecticut half the year, so he didn't mind taking the small windowless room in the back – Fernando placed a board up the window for him that could have given me fresh air, but I was finicky about noise and complained that someone downstairs was fighting, or the music was too loud, or in one case someone's pet monkey was screaming. Now, Fernando no longer had to take the subway to work, and the rent was something like $100/week for both of us.

Genovese, Kitty

On 13 March 1964, Catherine Susan "Kitty" Genovese (7 July 1935 - 13 March 1964) was a New York City woman who was stabbed to death by Winston Moseley near her home in the Kew Gardens neighborhood of the borough of Queens in New York City.

Two weeks after the murder, a newspaper article reported the circumstances of her murder and the lack of reaction from numerous neighbors. The common portrayal of her neighbors as being fully aware but completely unresponsive has since been criticized as inaccurate. Nonetheless, it prompted investigation into the social psychological phenomenon that has become known as the bystander effect or "Genovese syndrome" and especially diffusion of responsibility.

Genovese's killer, Winston Moseley, was found guilty and sentenced to death on 15 June 1964. That sentence was later reduced to lifetime imprisonment on the grounds that he had not been allowed to argue during the trial that he was "medically insane." Moseley committed another series of crimes when he escaped from custody on 18 March 1968, and then fled to a nearby vacant home, where he held the owners hostage. On March 22, he broke into another home and took a woman and her daughter hostage before surrendering to police. Moseley, who was denied parole for a seventeenth time in December 2013, remains in prison. He is currently one of the longest serving inmates in New York State.

Born in New York City, the daughter of Rachel (née Petrolli) and Vincent Andronelle Genovese, Kitty was the eldest of five children in a lower-middle-class Italian American family and was raised in Park Slope, Brooklyn. Her father, founder of a company that supplied coats and aprons to local businesses, one called the Bay Ridge Coat and Apron Supply Company. After her mother witnessed a murder in the city, the family moved to Connecticut in 1954. Genovese, nineteen at the time and a recent graduate of Prospect Heights High School in Brooklyn, chose to remain in the city, where she had lived for nine years. At the time of her death, she was working as a bar manager at Ev's Eleventh Hour Sports Bar on Jamaica Avenue and 193rd Street in Hollis, Queens. Genovese shared her Kew Gardens, Queens, apartment at 80-20 Austin Street with her partner, Mary Ann Zielonko (on the right):

Genovese had driven home from her job working as bar manager in Ev's Eleventh Hour Club early in the morning of 13 March 1964. Arriving home at about 3:15 a.m., she parked in the Log Island Rail Road parking lot about 100 feet (30 m) from her apartment's door, located in an alley way at the rear of the building. As she walked toward the building, she was approached by Winston Moseley. Frightened, Genovese began to run across the parking lot and toward the front of her building located on Austin Street, trying to make it up to the corner toward the major thoroughfare of Lefferts Boulevard. Moseley ran after her, quickly overtook her, and stabbed her twice in the back. Genovese screamed, "Oh my God, he stabbed me! Help me!" Her cry was heard by several neighbors but, on a cold night with the windows closed, only a few of them recognized the sound as a cry for help. When Robert Mozer, one of the neighbors, shouted at the attacker, "Let that girl alone!" Moseley ran away and Genovese slowly made her way toward the rear entrance of her apartment building. She was seriously injured, but now out of view of any witnesses.

Records of the earliest calls to police are unclear and were not given a high priority by the police. One witness said his father called police after the initial attack and reported that a woman was "beat up, but got up and was staggering around."

Other witnesses observed Moseley enter his car and drive away, only to return ten minutes later. In his car, he changed to a wide-brimmed hat to shadow his face. He systematically searched the parking lot, train station, and an apartment complex. Eventually, he found Genovese who was lying, barely conscious, in a hallway at the back of the building where a locked doorway had prevented her from entering the building. Out of view of the street and of those who may have heard or seen any sign of the original attack, Moseley proceeded to further attack her, stabbing her several more times. Knife wounds in her hands suggested that she attempted to defend herself from him. While Genovese lay dying, Moseley raped her. He stole about $49 from her and left her in the hallway. The attacks spanned approximately half an hour. Afterwards, "Genovese, still alive, lay in the arms of a neighbor named Sophia Farrar, who had courageously left her apartment to go to the crime scene, even though she had no way of knowing that [Mosely] had fled."

A few minutes after the final attack, a witness, Karl Ross, called the police. Police arrived within minutes of Ross' call. Genovese was taken away by ambulance at 4:15 a.m. and died en route to the hospital. Later investigation by police and prosecutors revealed that approximately a dozen (but almost certainly not the 38 cited in the *Times* article) individuals nearby had heard or observed portions of the attack, though none saw or were aware of the entire incident. Only one witness, Joseph Fink, was aware she was stabbed in the first attack, and only Karl Ross was aware of it in the second attack. Many were entirely unaware that an assault or homicide was in progress; some thought that what they saw or heard was a lovers' quarrel or a drunken brawl or a group of friends leaving the bar when Moseley first approached Genovese.

Perpetrator

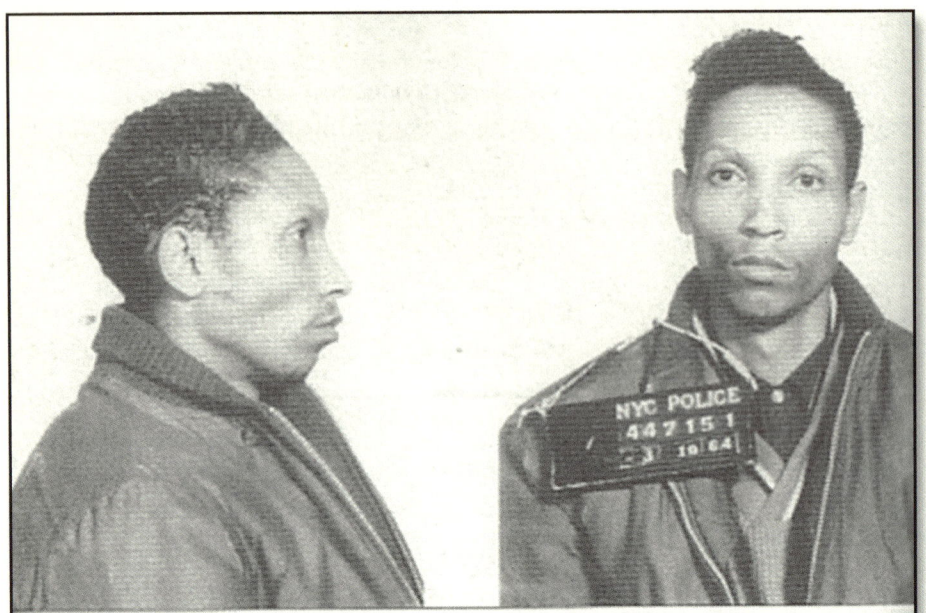

Winston Moseley left his home on the night of March 3, 1964, with the specific intent of randomly killing a woman. Convicted for the murder of Kitty Genovese, he briefly escaped and raped a woman in Buffalo, New York.

Winston Moseley (born 2 March 1935), a then 29-year-old man from South Ozone Park, Queens, was apprehended by police during a house burglary six days after Genovese's murder. At the time of his arrest, Moseley was working as a "Remington Rand tab operator," had no prior criminal record, and was married with two children.

While in custody, Moseley confessed to killing Genovese. He detailed the attack, corroborating the physical evidence at the scene. His motive for the attack was simply "to kill a woman." Moseley preferred to kill women because, he said, "they were easier and didn't fight back." Moseley stated that he got up that night around 2:00 a.m., leaving his wife asleep at home, and drove around to find a victim. He spied Genovese and followed her to the parking lot. He confessed to the murder of not only Kitty Genovese, but also two other murders of women, both involving sexual assaults. He also confessed to committing "30 to 40" burglaries. Subsequent psychiatric examinations suggested that Moseley was a necrophile.

Moseley's trial began on 8 June 1964, and was presided over by Judge J. Irwin Shapiro. Moseley initially pleaded "not guilty," but his plea was later changed by his attorney to "not guilty by reason of insanity." On Thursday, June 11, Moseley was called to testify by his attorney who hoped that Moseley's testimony would convince the jury that he was "a schizophrenic personality and legally insane." During his testimony, Moseley described the events on the night he murdered Genovese, along with the two other murders to which he had confessed and numerous other burglaries and rapes. The jury deliberated for seven hours before returning a guilty verdict on June 11 at around 10:30 p.m.

On Monday, 15 June 1964, Moseley was sentenced to death. When the sentence was read by the jury foreman, Moseley showed no emotion while some spectators applauded and others cheered. When calm had returned, Judge Shapiro added, "I don't believe in capital punishment, but when I see this monster, I wouldn't hesitate to pull the switch myself!" On 1 June 1967, the New York Court of Appeals found that Moseley should have been able to argue that he was "medically insane" at the sentencing hearing when the trial court found that he had been legally sane, and the initial death sentence was reduced to an indeterminate sentence/lifetime imprisonment.

On 18 March 1968, Moseley escaped from custody while being transported back to prison from Meyer Memorial Hospital in Buffalo, New York, where he had undergone minor surgery for a self-inflicted injury. Moseley hit the transporting correctional officer, stole his weapon, and then fled to a nearby vacant home owned by a Grand Island couple, Mr. and Mrs. Matthew Kulaga. Moseley stayed at the residence undetected for three days. On March 21, the Kulagas went to check on the home where they encountered Moseley. He held the couple hostage for over an hour during which he bound and gagged Matthew Kulaga and raped his wife. He then took the couple's car and fled. Moseley made his way to Grand Island where, on March 22nd, he broke into another home and took a woman and her daughter hostage. He held them hostage for two hours before releasing them unharmed. Moseley surrendered to police shortly thereafter. He was later charged with escape and kidnapping to which he pleaded guilty. Moseley was given two additional fifteen-year sentences concurrent with his life sentence.

During the 1970s, Moseley participated in the Attica Prison riots, and late in the decade, obtained a B.A. in sociology in prison from Niagara University. Moseley became eligible for parole in 1984. During his first parole hearing, Moseley told the parole board that the notoriety he faced due to his crimes made him a victim also, stating, "For a victim outside, it's a one-time or one-hour or one-minute affair, but for the person who's caught, it's forever." At the same hearing, Moseley claimed he never intended to kill Genovese and that he considered her murder to be a mugging because "[...] people do kill people when they mug them sometimes." The board denied his request for parole. Moseley remains in prison after being denied parole a seventeenth time in December 2013.

At first, the murder of Genovese did not receive much media attention. It took a remark from Police Commissioner Michael J. Murphy to *New York Times* metropolitan editor A. M. Rosenthal over lunch – Rosenthal later quoted Murphy as saying, "That Queens story is one for the books" – to provoke *The Times* into publishing an investigative report.

The article, written by Martin Gansberg and published on 27 March 1964, two weeks after the murder, bore the headline "Thirty-Seven Who Saw Murder Didn't Call the Police." (It has been variously quoted and reproduced since 1964 with a headline that begins "Thirty-Eight Who Saw ...") The public view of the story crystallized around a quote from the article by an unidentified neighbor who saw part of the attack but deliberated before finally getting another neighbor to call the police, saying, "I didn't want to get involved." Many then saw the story of Genovese's murder as emblematic of the callousness or apathy of life in big cities, and New York in particular.

Science-fiction author and cultural provocateur Harlan Ellison, in articles published in 1970 and 1971 in the *Los Angeles Free Press* and in *Rolling Stone*, referred to the witnesses as "thirty-six motherfuckers" [and stated that they "stood by and watched" Genovese "get knifed to death right in front of them, and wouldn't make a move" and that "thirty-eight people watched" Genovese "get knifed to death in a New York street." In an article in *The Magazine of Fantasy and Science Fiction* (June 1988), later reprinted in his book *Harlan Ellison's Watching*, Ellison referred to the murder as "witnessed by thirty-eight neighbors," citing reports he claimed to have read that one man turned up his radio so that he would not hear Genovese's screams. Ellison says that the reports attributed the "get involved" quote to nearly all of the thirty-eight who supposedly witnessed the attack.

While Genovese's neighbors were vilified by the articles, "thirty-eight onlookers who did nothing" is a misconception. *The New York Times* article begins, "For more than half an hour thirty-eight respectable, law-abiding citizens in Queens watched a killer stalk and stab a woman in three separate attacks in Kew Gardens." However, a 2007 study found many of the purported facts about the murder to be unfounded. The study found "no evidence for the presence of 38 witnesses, or that witnesses observed the murder, or that witnesses remained inactive," Wikipedia reported

Genovese was buried in a family grave at Lakeview Cemetery in New Canaan, Connecticut.

According to *The New York Times*, in an article dated 28 December 1974, ten years after the murder, 25-year-old Sandra Zahler was beaten to death early Christmas morning in an apartment of the building that overlooked the site of the Genovese attack. Neighbors again said they heard screams and "fierce struggles" but did nothing.

Moseley returned for another parole hearing on 13 March 2008, the 44th anniversary of Genovese's murder. The previous week, Moseley had turned 73 years old and had still shown little remorse for murdering Genovese. Parole was denied. Genovese's brother, Vincent, was unaware of the 2008 hearing until he was contacted by *Daily News* reporters. Vincent Genovese has reportedly never "recovered from the horror" of his sister's murder. "This brings back what happened to her," Vincent had said; "the whole family remembers," according to Wikipedia.

After Mrs. Rachel Genovese witnessed a murder in New York City, she and her husband Vincent with their son Vincent moved to New Canaan, Connecticut. The town, called "The Next Station To Heaven," had one of the highest per-capita income figures in the entire state and was chosen for being a safe community with first-rate schools. Kitty, their teenage daughter remained in New York, employed as a bartender.

When teenager Vincent was about to graduate from New Canaan High School, he took advantage of "career day" by asking to visit a police department and hear officers give their advice about his possibly choosing theirs as an occupation. Inasmuch as he was the only student, as he put it, "who wanted to go to jail on career day," the chairman of the English department, Warren Allen Smith volunteered to take him. Because Vincent wanted to visit a larger department, Smith made arrangements with the nearby Norfolk Police Department. On the way, Smith admitted he had been in jail when he was younger than Vincent, had been stopped by the Iowa State Highway Patrol for speeding through his town of 328 and was taken by his father the next morning to the jail, where his father and the sheriff were fellow Masons and enjoyed teaching him a lesson, one that was the first and only time he would ever be incarcerated.

The Norwalk "cops," as Vincent described them, gave valuable advice and encouraged him to consider becoming an officer. Vincent, who was never in any of Smith's classes, chose another profession, however. He did not mention whether he knew his sister Kitty was a lesbian. Smith, "in the closet," never mentioned that during the other 180 days of the school year he lived with his paramour in New York City.

Goldstein, Al

Goldstein (10 January 1936 - 19 January 2013), who once mooned me, I described in Philosopedia.

Goldstein is a fat, angry, vulgarian.

(That's how Goldstein has described himself.)

The Early Years

The son of a New York *Daily Mirror* worker, Alvin Goldstein was once a licensed New York City taxi driver, a student at Pace University in Lower Manhattan, and co-founder with Jim Buckley of a sex newspaper, *Screw*.

His first sexual experience occurred, he has stated, when he was sixteen. His mother had told his uncle to take him to a prostitute.

Goldstein has been married at least three times (Gina, whom he divorced but they had one son, Jordan; Patricia Flaherty, whom he married in 1989 and divorced in 1994; and Christine Ava Maharaj, whom he married in January 2004). Some claim he either had two other wives or married some of them twice.

Screw

In 1968, he and Jim Buckley started *Screw*, the underground magazine with an investment of less than $300. In weeks, its circulation jumped to 150,000 copies per week. Not only did it have smutty photos and what most would call obscene and saucy satire but also it had some in-depth interviews: former Beatle John Lennon; *Blondie's* Debby Harry; actor Jack Nicholson. In Goldstein's words, it was "the first newspaper to have a gay column. We accepted sex ads, we used four-letter words, we've never been euphemist - and that's my pride in the paper."

A 1969 issue of *Screw* included a picture of two men having sexual intercourse.

A 1973 issue (#206) included a picture of Jacqueline Onassis on vacation and in the nude. It sold over half a million copies.

He was arrested at least nineteen times and charged by federal prosecutors on obscenity charges. In 1974 when he insulted then-FBI Director J. Edgar Hoover in print, Goldstein had to face charges in Kansas. When police came to his office, they might find him already dressed in a striped prison outfit, humorously dealing with his threat of being jailed. "I march to my own drummer," he has explained, "and my drummer talks about the one absolute, which is freedom. None of us can be sure what is right, so let's have all voices be heard." In short, Goldstein claims not to be defending pornography per se but defending its right to exist. To *Media Life* (8 August 2003), he explained,

> I'm a crusader. I really believe in the First Amendment, and I use it fully, and I pay a price for that. I keep attacking the villains, the know-nothings, the people who want to take our freedoms away.

Some Views

In one journal, Goldstein is quoted as saying, "I always read Stuart Mill to [my son, Jordan]. I brainwashed him like they do in Catholic school, but instead of reading him the Bible I read from the humanists and the liberals. The real liberals - not the phony New York liberals."

In another journal, however, he is quoted, "I actually see myself as a thoughtful cerebral intellectual. . . . I am very conscious of being a Jew named Goldstein. And I am very proud that my son, who went to Georgetown, a Jesuit college; [of its] 781 students - he finished first. He won the two-year Oxford scholarship. He's there now, and he's accepted for Harvard. So there's a Jewish word, *kvell* - "to be proud."

I am so *haimish* and so bourgeois, and so proud of my son." This shows, Goldstein insisted, that he exemplifies family values.

Some Quotes

"I'm a big fat Jew who doesn't pay retail!"
"Death Before Marriage!"
"I should be an old Jew retired in Century Village, but here I am, with a passion for eating pastrami and eating p*s*y."
"I've always loved food more than sex, so this is really my first love. I've gone from broads to bagels."
"My life has turned to crap. To go from a being a millionaire and then living in a homeless shelter and being rejected by 98% of your friends is horrendous, but I'm a survivor."
"She must be clean. I wash a chicken before I boil it!" (commenting on oral sex)
He left numerous phones messages to a former former secretary, Jennifer Lozinski. "I'll take you down! You loathsome turd. You're a piece of sh*t!"
When asked about his downfall: "The Internet made pornography available for free and I couldn't compete."
"I have the courage of my convictions - all 19 of them."

Some Memories of Goldstein

According to Bill Winter,

Technology also caught up with Goldstein. In November 2003, he ceased publication of *Screw* magazine and filed for Chapter 11 bankruptcy. He said increased competition from the Internet had made magazines like his "an anachronism; we are elephants going to the bone cemetery to die." However, Goldstein promised to relaunch the magazine and focus more attention on an affiliated website. As he planned for the future, his words echoed from the past. "You need fighters like me to battle, because frankly *The New York Times* and the *Washington Post* are not going to fight the fights that I do," he told *Media Life* magazine. "I refuse to be silenced."

Some Trivia
He once ran unsuccessfully for Sheriff of Broward County in Florida.
He was paid $1,200 to be filmed in *I Wanna Be A Porn Star 1*.
In 1985, he was a witness before the Meese Commission that was investigating pornography.

In several movies, he acted as himself: *Inside Deep Throat* (2005); *Porn Star: The Legend of Ron Jeremy* (2001); *Citizen Toxie: The Toxic Avenger IV* (2001); *Sex: The Annabel Chong Story* (1999); *Wadd: The Life and Times of John C. Holmes* (1998).

In 2004, he was arrested on November 28th, allegedly having stolen three books from Barnes & Noble. Bankrupt from numerous lawsuits stemming from harassment charges (started by one of his then-four wives), he lost everything and lived for part of a year in a homeless shelter.

In 2004, Jack Lebewohl, owner of the 2nd Avenue Deli in downtown New York City, gave him a $10/hour job, that of greeting customers. As for trading sex for salami, Goldstein claimed in Greenwich Village's *The Villager* that turning people on to the joys of chopped liver, gefilte fish, and brisket of beef is far more pleasurable than selling the more decadent forms of cheesecake. His duties included greeting customers and showing them to their tables.

He was fired, according to *Times* reporter Andy Newman (6 January 2006), but not before going on record:
"I have not eaten so well since I lived with my mom," said Mr. Goldstein, who was fired after he was found sleeping in the restaurant's basement. Mr. Goldstein, a noted gourmand until a recent stomach-stapling operation, declared the deli's shuttering "almost as sad as the closing of Chock Full O' Nuts," though he added, "I never thought Jack's pastrami was as good as Katz's. It's kosher. It was bland."

When he was 69, his *I, Goldstein* (2006) was published, *Library Journal* wrote, "Though amusing and titillating, this memoir isn't much more than another stab at fame and fortune from a selfish, angry and intermittently funny man." Mike Tribby of *Booklist* wrote, This book, written with former *Screw* associate Friedman, invokes familiar names from Jacob Javits to *Mad* publisher William M. Gaines as it summarizes and justifies a life lived on the cultural barricades. Details about genuine sixties characters, such as porn star John C. Holmes ("Johnny Wadd"), add fascination."

The *Times* reviewer of *I, Goldstein* was one of Goldstein's former employees, Steven Heller, who is the former art director of the newspaper's book review section. For full disclosure, he explained that he had turned down the job of reviewing the book because of the newspaper's cardinal rule that reviewers must not know well the authors they will write about. But he was talked into it because it had been over three decades that he had worked for two years as the magazine's art director.

His review included glimpses of the author:

> Goldstein, in addition to being a porn king, made an art of self-loathing. It pervades *I, Goldstein* and was his most driving and destructive force. Despite his aggressively funny writing style, Goldstein doubted he was truly intelligent. A self-described "bed-wetting stutterer from Brooklyn" and a punching bag for neighborhood toughs, he feared he would become a milquetoast like his father, a photojournalist who exhibited courage in World War II, working alongside the likes of Ernie Pyle, but addressed elevator operators as "sir." (He later toiled in *Screw*'s mailroom.) Goldstein, forever self-conscious about his weight, compensated by making voraciousness the cornerstone of his identity. He describes, touchingly, how as a teenager he was treated by a diet doctor – with whom it turned out his mother was having an affair, because "my father was so inadequate." Thus he entered manhood primed to defy all who crossed him, and he fulfilled this wish, metaphorically flushing hypocrites and incompetents from President Nixon to his auto mechanic in a ceremonial toilet bowl.
>
> Above all, Goldstein really wanted to be somebody. His memoir chronicles the improbable rise of a guy who each year renewed his taxi license just in case he hit the skids, and who was deeply in debt (his Jane Street apartment was stuffed with electronic gadgets bought on credit) but later owned a town house in Manhattan, a mansion in Florida, cars with drivers and millions of dollars' worth of watches. Then came the spiraling downfall: the costly lawsuits, criminal battles and divorces.

Heller also says that Goldstein in 2006 resided in Staten Island in an apartment paid for by the comedian and magician Penn Jillette. The one-time pariah, the host of the pioneering cable TV show "Midnight Blue," who enraged feminists like Andrea Dworkin, now wanders the Manhattan streets: a porn king without a crown, throne, or *Screw*. Goldstein was never as presentable or culturally palatable as Hugh Hefner, and *Screw* was never a beautiful and expensive production like *Playboy*. But had Al Goldstein not dared to create his "sex review," the floodgates of a more expansive and liberating publishing culture might never have opened. As for me, had I not been *Screw*'s art director, and been given the freedom and encouragement to learn my craft, I would not have gotten my job at *The New York Times*.

An Alan Colmes Interview:

Lyle Stuart (seated)   Warren Allen Smith (standing)

Lyle Stuart, who was once an editor for *Mad* and was the noted American independent publisher of controversial books, for years was a special friend of Goldstein. They socialized often and were interviewed several times by Alan Colmes, a liberal radio and television journalist admired by both because of his fairness to those he interviewed.

On one occasion, Stuart took Warren Allen Smith along to the Colmes show for a late-night interview also with Goldstein, who is included in the book. Stuart had published Smith's 1,248 page *Who's Who in Hell,* the thesis of which is that Hell is a theological invention and does not exist, but that if it did his book listed over 10,000 from ancient to contemporary times who would be there. Smith made notes of what transpired:

> Lyle and I arrived early and sat in the station's lobby area, one that had glass doors and allowed us to see who was exiting from the elevator. I didn't know what Goldstein looked like and knew only that he had bought six copies of the $125 book, one for himself and the others for his son - I listed both as atheists, along with Stuart.
>
> It wasn't my first radio or TV interview, but I was nervous about meeting Colmes, who was such a noted interviewer. Lyle left briefly to the men's room, during which time the elevator doors opened, a man exited, saw me inside, dropped his pants, and mooned me. Pulling open the door, he said, "Are you the old fag who's on the program with me?"

Lyle arrived almost at the same time, and because Goldstein was his friend and hadn't heard the insult I said to Lyle, my publisher, as if befuddled, "And is this the handsome buyer of six of my books?"

After that introduction and being rushed into the studio, harnessed by a technician with what it takes to be televised, seated before a microphone, and hurriedly greeted by Mr. Colmes who said we'd be "on" in minutes, I let the two of them talk and didn't cut in until asked something specific.

Colmes expertly guided Lyle and me in our explanations about the book, and I tried to be concise but also be a salesman for the book. It was when Goldstein chimed in about other subjects that the interview suddenly focused on Goldstein, not on my book. It was my introduction as to how, when interviewed, one must remain on camera and stay in the spotlight even if it means being New York pushy. Afterwards, it was too late for me to join them for drinks, although they have thought I was irked. As we departed, Goldstein, with Lyle nodding yes, made me promise to come to his place and be interviewed again.

With much trepidation, I showed up at his suite of *Screw* rooms on the appointed day. He had a cluttered desk, a high-back and regal-like chair, and a beautiful girl sitting nearby. I'm not sure if it was his wife or his secretary, but she phoned for someone in the art department to give me a tour of the many-roomed place. The rent must be humongous, I thought to myself. The employee showed me around each room, particularly a large one in which he as an artist worked. Dildos, penises, teats, erotica of all kinds! In one nondescript room, another employee arranged a microphone, camera, and a chair and made preparations for the interview.

Goldstein, "Uncle Al" the artist called him, arrived with a big smile, a pleasant greeting, apologies for the looks of the room, and then, "Well, old faggot, let's get going!" It wasn't clear if Lyle had told him I am gay or if this was his usual manner of speaking, so again we got off to a bad start.

"You like old faggots?" I asked. Whatever he answered, Iresponded by asking how long he'd had these symptoms. But he went on and on with questions. I was an English teacher in New York? ("Yes, and in Connecticut.") How many students had I had sex with? ("None, whatsoever!") Faculty? ("None, ever, and no administrators.") Married? ("No.") Children? ("No.") Gay? ("Are you? Is this a proposal?")

Then it must have been 45 minutes of questions about my education (U of Northern Iowa and Columbia U), experiences with religion (I emphasized being a Unitarian), atheism (upon first hitch-hiking from Iowa to Manhattan, I had met Charles Smith, editor of *Truth Seeker*, and had talked to him about his atheistic journal). When the time was up, I was given some free copies of *Screw*, told I'd be on their mailing list and would get a year's free subscription, and I got out of there as fast as I could.

Also

Goldstein's company, Milky Way Productions, home of *Screw* and his long-running cable show, *Midnight Blue*, went into bankruptcy in 2004.

Before *Screw* went out of business, Goldstein and Lyle Stuart had a falling out. In one issue, a photo of Hitler and Eva Braun was doctored by putting a photo of Lyle's head on Hitler's body and a photo of the head of Lyle's wife, Carole, on Eva's body. The Stuarts were shocked and angry, and some subscribers reacted by objecting strongly with letters and cancellations of subscriptions.

Goldstein's mansion in Pompano Beach, Florida, with the 11-foot statue of a raised middle finger out back, was sold in June 2004 to pay debts. A documentary was made by James Guardino about Goldstein, and was titled *Goldstein: The Trials of the Sultan of Smut*.

His will specifies that the son may not inherit the father's pornographic business. In short, on the one hand Goldstein comes across as a non-theist and activist atheist, on the other, a cultural Jew.

Harding, Florence

Florence Mabel Kling "Flossie" Harding (previously DeWolfe, 15 August 1860 - 21 November 1924) was the wife of President Warren G. Harding and was the First Lady of the United States from 1921 to 1923.

She was born Florence Kling, the daughter of Amos Kling, a prominent Marion, Ohio, banker, and Louisa Bouton Kling.

As a young girl, she lived in New Canaan.

A White House biography of presidents' wives describes her in detail:

> Daughter of the richest man in a small town – Amos Kling, a successful businessman – Florence Mabel Kling was born in Marion, Ohio, in 1860, to grow up in a setting of wealth, position, and privilege. Much like her strong-willed father in temperament, she developed a self-reliance rare in girls of that era.

A music course at the Cincinnati Conservatory completed her education. When only 19, she eloped with Henry De Wolfe, a neighbor two years her senior. He proved a spendthrift and a heavy drinker who soon deserted her, so she returned to Marion with her baby son. Refusing to live at home, she rented rooms and earned her own money by giving piano lessons to children of the neighborhood. She divorced De Wolfe in 1886 and resumed her maiden name; he died at age 35.

Warren G. Harding had come to Marion when only 16 and, showing a flair for newspaper work, had managed to buy the little *Daily Star*. When he met Florence a courtship quickly developed. Over Amos Kling's angry opposition they were married in 1891, in a house that Harding had planned, and this remained their home for the rest of their lives. (They had no children.)

Mrs. Harding soon took over the *Star*'s circulation department, spanking newsboys when necessary. "No pennies escaped her," a friend recalled, and the paper prospered while its owner's political success increased. As he rose through Ohio politics and became a United States Senator, his wife directed all her acumen to his career. He became Republican nominee for President in 1920 and "the Duchess," as he called her, worked tirelessly for his election. In her own words: "I have only one real hobby – my husband."

She had never been a guest at the White House; and former President Taft, meeting the President-elect and Mrs. Harding, discussed its social customs with her and stressed the value of ceremony. Writing to Nellie, he concluded that the new First Lady was "a nice woman" and would "readily adapt herself."

When Mrs. Harding moved into the White House, she opened mansion and grounds to the public again – both had been closed through President Wilson's illness. She herself suffered from a chronic kidney ailment, but she threw herself into the job of First Lady with energy and willpower. Garden parties for veterans were regular events on a crowded social calendar. The President and his wife relaxed at poker parties in the White House library, where liquor was available although the Eighteenth Amendment made it illegal.

Mrs. Harding always liked to travel with her husband. She was with him in the summer of 1923 when he died unexpectedly in California, shortly before the public learned of the major scandals facing his administration.

With astonishing fortitude she endured the long train ride to Washington with the President's body, the state funeral at the Capitol, the last service and burial at Marion. She died in Marion on November 21, 1924, surviving Warren Harding by little more than a year of illness and sorrow.

Florence met "Wurr'n" – as she pronounced his first name – in 1890 and they married in 1891. They did not have children, but Florence's son lived with them from time to time.

As circulation manager of the *Marion Star* for 14 years, Florence saw that the paper was distributed efficiently and subscriptions were paid up. "Mrs. Harding in those days ran the show," recalled one of her newsboys, Norman Thomas, later the Socialist presidential candidate. "Her husband was the front – it was she who was the real driving power in the success that the *Marion Star* was unquestionably making its community."

Early in 1920, when Harding was still a dark-horse contender for the Republican presidential nomination, she visited Madam Marcia, a noted clairvoyant in the capital, who predicted that her husband was a shoo-in, but added that he would die suddenly in office. Mrs. Harding embarked with her husband on his nationwide "Voyage of Understanding" in the summer of 1923. She was at his side when the President died in San Francisco on 2 August 1923. She refused to allow an autopsy, and opinion has been divided as to whether he died of cardiac insufficiency with congestive heart failure or had died of a heart attack.

Calvin Coolidge succeeded him as the 30th President.

Following the death of President Harding, the former First Lady set about making a new life for herself. Her intention was to remain in Washington, temporarily staying at Friendship, the estate of her best friend, Evalyn Walsh McLean, best known as the owner of the Hope Diamond. However, when Mrs. Harding's long-standing kidney ailment flared up, her friend and the former Surgeon General, Dr. Charles E. Sawyer insisted that she return to Marion for treatment and recovery. She died there of renal failure less than 16 months later, and was buried next to her husband in Marion, Ohio's, Harding Memorial Park.

I was named after the President, and my parents pronounced my name "Wurr'n" as his wife claims he did also. It was 3-time Tony Award nominee Gilbert Price, one of my paramours, who inspired me to pronounce my name WAHrenn.

Heckart, Eileen

Anna Eileen Herbert (29 March 1919 - 31 December 2001) was born in Columbus, Ohio, the daughter of Esther Stark, who wed Leo Herbert. According to Luke Yankee's *Just Outside the Spotlight: Growing Up with Eileen Heckart* (2006), at her own mother's insistence the marriage was arranged so her child would not be born with the stigma of illegitimacy. The child soon afterwards was legally adopted by her grandfather, J.W. Heckart, whose surname she was known by her whole life.

In 1942, she earned her B.A. in drama at Ohio State University, from which she earned an honorary LL.D in 1981.

On 26 June 1943, she married John Harrison Yankee Jr., and they had four children: Mark, Kelly, Philip Craig, and Luke Brian. Heckart was married to Yankee for over five decades until his death in 1997.

The New Canaanite's Broadway career began when she was assistant stage manager and an understudy for *The Voice of the Turtle* in 1943. Her many credits include *Picnic; The Bad Seed* (Golden Globe Award for Best Supporting Actress; nominated Academy Award for Best Supporting Actress); *A View from the Bridge A Memory of Two Mondays*; *The Dark at the Top of the Stairs*; *A Family Affair*; *Barefoot in the Park*; *Butterflies Are Free* (Academy Award for Best Supporting Actress); and *You Know I Can't Hear You When the Water is Running*. *The First Wives Club* (1996) cast received the National Board of Review Award.

Heckart was familiar to television audiences with starring roles in *The 5 Mrs. Buchanans*; *Annie McGuire*; *Out of the Blue*; *Trauma Center, Partners in Crime*; *Backstairs at the White House* (as Eleanor Roosevelt); and guest spots on *The Fugitive, The Mary Tyler Moore Show* as Flo Meredith, a role the carried over to a guest appearance on MTM's spinoff *Lou Grant, Rhoda, Alice* (where she played Alice's meddlesome former mother in-law, Rose Hyatt), *Murder One, Hawaii Five-O, Cybill, The Cosby Show*, among others.

Heckart played two unrelated characters on the daytime soap opera *One Life to Live*. During the 1980s, she played Ruth Perkins, the mother of Allison Perkins, who had kidnapped the newborn baby of heroine Viki Lord Buchanan under orders from phony evangelist and mastermind criminal Mitch Laurence. During the early 1990s, she played the role of Wilma Bern, mother of mobster Carlo Hesser and his identical twin, Mortimer Bern.

She established the "Eileen Heckart Collection" at Ohio State University's Jerome Lawrence and Robert E. Lee Theatre Research Institute, with her notes, copies of scripts, and personal papers. In 2005, the Eileen Heckart Drama for Seniors Competition was established in her memory by Ohio State's Department of Theatre.

Heckart has a Star on the Hollywood Walk of Fame at 6162 Hollywood Boulevard in California.

Her *New York Times* 2 January 2002 obituary was as follows:

> Eileen Heckart, the actress with a smoky voice and toothsome smile who won an Oscar for *Butterflies Are Free*, three Emmys, and a special lifetime achievement Tony, died on Monday at her home in Norwalk, Conn. She was 82.
>
> The cause was cancer, her son Mark said.
>
> One of those ubiquitous actresses who always seemed to be working, Ms. Heckart was perhaps most widely known for her television appearances as Mary Richards's Aunt Flo on the *Mary Tyler Moore* show, for example, or more recently for her recurring role of the mother of the lawyer James Wyler in the ABC drama *Murder One*.
>
> Her best-remembered film roles include the mother of Rocky Graziano in *Somebody Up There Likes Me* (1956) Marilyn Monroe's waitress friend in *Bus Stop* (also 1956), and the overbearing mother of the blind boy in *Butterflies Are Free*, for which she won the Academy Award as best supporting actress in 1972.
>
> Heckart often said in interviews that her heart belonged to the stage and that was where she performed the bulk of her work.

Once on a train ride into Manhattan, we sat together and talked about her son Luke, my student.

Hendrix, Jimmy

Hendrix, a competitor, owned the Electric Lady, which cost more than our studio.

The recording studio's entrance is in the center of the photo, ground floor, of the 3-story building

During his studio's entire existence, **Jimi Hendrix** reportedly liked to be photographed having heterosexual sex.

The Electric Lady was at 52 West 8th Street.

Hirschfeld, Al

Al Hirschfeld often sat at a corner booth at Howard Johnson's on 46th near the studio, seemingly just watching the people go by. But the caricaturist (he called himself a character-ist) was almost as important a player on Broadway as the stars whose physiognomy he so adeptly captured for *The New York Times* and elsewhere.

Hidden in many of the drawings were Ninas, the number of times he had hidden his daughter's name in the drawing.

He drew right up until his final days, dying five months before his 100th birthday. **Gilbert Price** was ecstatic upon seeing his "Timbuktu" caricature. Gilbert is on the bottom right with a hat.

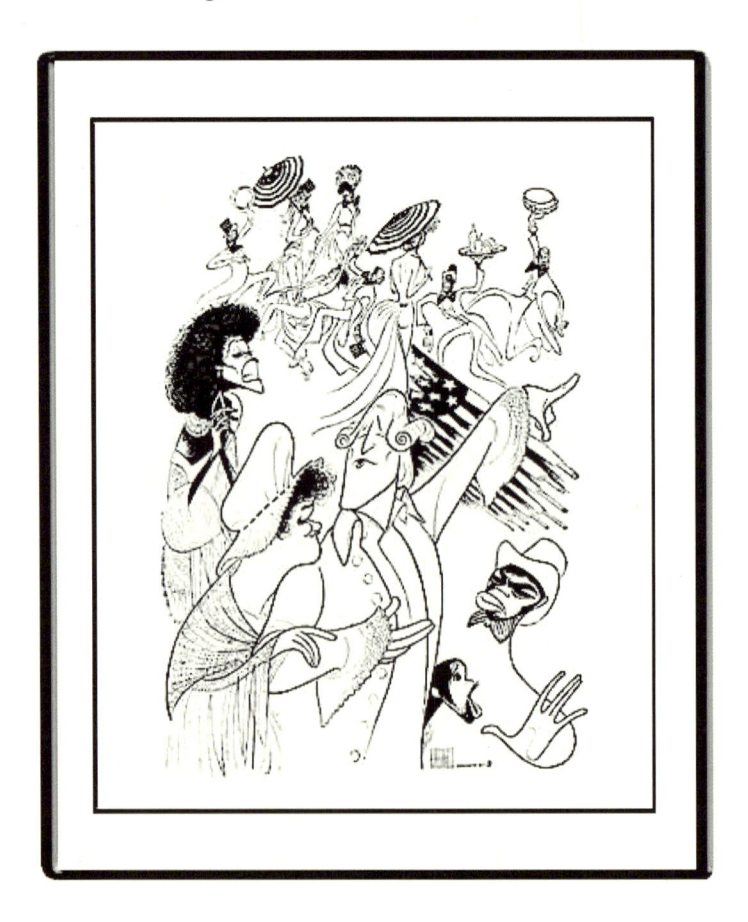

Hoagland, Edward

Photo by Warren Allen Smith

"Who lives on Jane Street now and lived in New Canaan, Connecticut?" the present author asked the member of the American Academy of Arts and Letters in 1992 when as a journalist I attended its annual ceremonial. He suspected some kind of connection but asked with a curious smile if I meant both verbs in the past tense.

No, he learned, and I told about having taught in the Connecticut public school in his town rather than the private school he attended, New Canaan Country.

E-mail friends ever since, he has asked how I have kept getting invitations to attend the ceremonial that is open only to Academy members and their family or friends. In 1956 I was asked by historian Priscilla Robertson, author of *Revolutions of 1848* to be her escort. Her tickets continue to come annually, she had no interest in returning from Kentucky, where her husband was an editor of the *Courier*-Journal, and no one else to Hoagland's or my knowledge has attended for 56 consecutive years.

"Is Frank still the doorman at 31 Jane?" he asked, adding that he had moved to Westbeth in 1970, where he stayed until 1988. No, Frank Shaevlin has long since retired, I told him after first asking a resident, Bruce Camacho, who was a child who grew up in the building.

Edward's father was one of New Canaan's many corporate VIPs. Rebelling against his parents' buttoned-up lives for they expected him to go to Harvard,

Edward joined the circus, getting a job as one of the Ringling Brothers and Barnum & Bailey Circus cat men, tending large lions and tigers in the summers of 1951 and 1952. He did graduate from Harvard in 1954, then sold a novel about his circus experience, *Cat Man* (1955), to his parents' surprise.

Hoagland (21 December 1932 –) then served in the Army for two years, received two Guggenheim Fellowships, wrote a novel about boxing, took nine trips to Alaska and British Columbia, taught at The New School, Columbia University, and other colleges, and in 2005 retired as an English professor from Bennington College in Vermont.

On a postcard after we met, he described his being "a pantheist, but of course I include humankind in the family of nature, for better or worse. Am particularly relieved at the ending of the Cold War because in foreseeable wars we will only be killing ourselves, not that whole wider world."

In my annual visits to the ceremonials, he has been introduced to my guests. One was Dr. Taslima Nasrin (the Bangladesh author with a fatwa, she that extremist Muslims still want to kill). He was amused that I described her as being "the most dangerous woman in the world" for her controversial views on feminism would shake their religious foundation. Another was Ligardy Termonfils, the Haitian-born teenager I have helped raise since he was 11. "You *really* tended lions, Mr. Hoagland? Kids at school won't believe me when I tell them tomorrow!" Hoagland had not heard anyone say something like that in decades, he laughed.

In *Compass Points: How I Lived* (2001), he describes not only having stammered early on but also having been legally blind for several years. After dangerously experimental surgery on his eyes that was successful, he recovered his sight and lost much of his stammering.

The Dictionary of Literary Biography emphasizes his special talent:

> Hoagland's love of solitude and silent observation of wildlife rather than social conversation may have resulted from a severe stammer that still persists. This stammer has, according to Hoagland himself, influenced how he writes: "Words are spoken at considerable cost to me, so a great value is placed on each one. That has had some effect on me as a writer. As a child, since I couldn't talk to people, I became close to animals. I became an observer, and in all my books, even the novels, witnessing things is what counts." His reluctance to speak may account for his desire to write – and be read – and for the sensitive visual, tactile, and olfactory images in his writings.

In *Sex and the River Styx* (2011), Hoagland confirms his humanities humanism with lines like "Heaven is here and the only heaven we have." As to whether God or God's green earth is at center stage, he observes, "If so, one is reminded with some regularity that He may be dying."

He also describes, unlike Henry David Thoreau to whom he has been compared, his youthful partying with hippies. He writes candidly of his past wives and lovers. (Photo in 2014 was taken by Allen Reza at the annual ceremonial of the American Academy of Arts and Letters.)

Fellow Academy members have praised Hoagland highly. John Updike has called Hoagland "the best essayist of my generation." Philip Roth has said he was "America's most intelligent and wide-ranging essayist-naturalist," and Joyce Carol Oates described him evocatively as "our Chopin of the genre."

In moderately good health, Hoagland now lives in the area around Sutton, Vermont, and spends winters in Martha's Vineyard.

Huddleson, Mary Pascoe

The present author's one-time landlady, Mrs. Huddleson was born in 1889 and died in 1966.

She was a dietician who, in New Canaan from 1927 to 1946, edited the *Journal of the American Dietetic Association*. In 1923 and in 1928, Macmillan published her *Food for the Diabetic, What to Eat and How to Calculate It With Common Household Measures*. The foreword was by Dr. Nellis Barnes Foster, an assistant professor of medicine at Cornell University Medical School and Associate Physician at New York Hospital.

She was the wife of psychiatrist James H. Huddleson and the mother of Ellen Huddleson (de la Torre), who later worked in the New Canaan High School's French Department office.

For over a decade I lived in the little white house on the corner of Millport and Lakeview, adjacent to theirs on Millport Avenue, one that she built in order to have a quiet place to edit the journal. When asked by friends if it was a place she could escape from her psychiatrist-husband, I always declined to respond.

She allowed me to rent the house for less than $100/month *if* . . . and . . . *if*: if I promised not to throw wild parties . . . and if my car remained small enough to share the garage with her black Volkswagen Beetle. I had an MGTD roadster and spent weekends in Manhattan's Hell's Kitchen. The smallest house in town, its garage was the house's basement, entered by a short driveway off Millport Avenue. We never had a landlord-tenant problem.

Mrs. Huddleson was a John Birch right-winger who gave me loads of conservative material and once gave me her discarded *Who's Who in America*, in which she was listed. She had a wry sense of humor and, although not overly friendly, sometimes had me over for tea if I would play her grand piano while she sang along.

Doc Huddleson, who had been one of the psychiatrists called to assess the mental health of Bruno Hauptmann, lived much of the time in Oregon. On one of the rare visits to town, I took him to dinner at the Silvermine Tavern, where even after drinks (vodka is not good for you, he said) he remained tight-lipped about the alleged Lindbergh baby's kidnapper except to say his body had tattoos.

In World War I, Mrs. Huddleson served with the Nurse Corps, and she liked to hear my stories about WACs who soldiered with me in World War II. In 1944 and 1945, I was an Adjutant General's Chief Clerk at General Eisenhower's Supreme Headquarters in the Little Red Schoolhouse in Reims, France. Then, I had little or no knowledge that women had been in the Army in my father's war, finding it surprising even to my father who seldom saw a female except in a hospital as a nurse. She liked my telling how when Dad was hospitalized in the Queen of England's palace she came by the room where beds were in rows and columns in a temporary nursing station. When she stopped by his corner bed and asked his name and home state, he surprised her by telling her Iowa but that he had volunteered while working in Saskatchewan. "Well then, you're one of my boys," she smiled. Mrs. H had a regal way about her and, after a short while, changed the subject.

According to a 1919 U. S. Army Medical Department document,

> In August 1919, Miss Pascoe reported to Miss Cooper that better training for Army cooks in health, food preparation, sanitation, and economy was needed in all the Army hospitals. Of the many cooks who served with her in hospitals in France only two had had previous training or experience as cooks either in the Army or civilian life. Miss Pascoe's best mess sergeant had starred on the New York stage. Of her diet kitchen staff, one was a Metropolitan Opera singer, another a big league ball player, and another was a man worth $20 million.
>
> Miss Pascoe, on returning from France in 1919, was asked to speak before the New York Association of Dietitians. She mentioned the quantity of tomatoes in the rations, closing with a vocal outburst against a "scheme of life that had almost drowned me in tomatoes."
>
> She was ashamed and humiliated when a lady in the back of the room chided her by saying that tomatoes were valuable because of their vitamin C. During her service overseas, Miss Pascoe had not had an opportunity to learn of the discovery of vitamin C.

Mrs. Huddleson is buried in the New Canaan Lakeview Cemetery's special section for soldiers, where few other women are buried.

Johnson, Philip Cortelyou

Johnson (8 July 1906 - 25 January 2005), a major American architect and historian, is known for his minimalist Glass House in New Canaan, Connecticut, and for Manhattan's Seagram Building, which he built with the collaboration of Miës van der Rohe.

One biographer, Franz Shulze, has described Johnson's attraction to the Nazi philosophy (writing in a 1939 *The Examiner*, "Reduced to plain terms, Hitler's 'racism' is a perfectly simple though far-reaching idea. It is the myth of 'we the best,' which we find, more or less fully developed, in all vigorous cultures.") and to his homosexuality (Schulze found that Johnson was attracted to the homoerotic undertones of Nazism, "all those blond boys in black leather. . . . He who had sweated and sighed in the arms of lovers hastily picked on the streets of Weimar Berlin . . . could be the most fastidiously self-abnegating puritan in his glass palace in Connecticut.").

In his eighties, Johnson, when interviewed by Hilary Lewis and John O'Connor, stated:

> My philosophical outlook dates from a time and a way of thinking that differs from the liberal, acceptable, politically correct line that we all subscribe to today. To me, Plato was the worst – living the good and the true and the beautiful. There's no such thing as the good or the true or the beautiful. I'm a relativist. I'm a nihilist."

Da Monsta

At the age of eighty-nine, he constructed near the Glass House an all-concrete, blood-red-and-black *Da Monsta*, a "structured warp" which looks more like a sculpture than like a house.

In his words,

> It's non-Euclidean . . . intuitive . . . all wiggly. It hasn't any back and front and sides. . . . I don't know how to describe it, and I'm glad I don't, because then I'd give it a silly name like deconstructivism.

The ceiling is nine feet high in one spot, twenty feet in another. Its lighting is set into the floor, leading him to observe, "If I didn't hate the term, I'd use the word 'spiritual' in this room." He said the structure has a flank and, like a horse, deserves a pat.

The Glass House has been opened to the public through the National Trust for Historic Preservation. Visitors arrive first at *Da Monsta*, which contains two rooms. The first is a reception area and waiting room. The second is a video room, where visitors can watch films and videos on Johnson and his work. These straightforward functions are enclosed in a sculpture, painted bright red and black, which Johnson claimed is a reference to local New England architecture.

The sculpture is a reinforced concrete shell formed using steel mesh, a layer of insulation, sprayed-on concrete, and a waterproof finish of acrylic. The system, which remained sufficiently flexible during construction, allowed for Mr. Johnson to change forms and edges of the shell before it settled into permanent shape. The only two openings to the shell, the glassy entrance and a small window in the waiting area, are non-Euclidean in shape. Johnson claims his influence here came from German Expressionism and the artist Frank Stella. The interior has white walls and a concrete floor.

In his nineties, Johnson posed for the cover of *Out*, a monthly gay and lesbian magazine. Previously, only a few knew that for over three decades he had shared his life with David Whitney, who when a 21-year-old college student had asked to see the Glass House and Johnson liked the idea.

Whitney (who is not related to the New York family that founded the Whitney Museum of Art) moved in the day after he was graduated in 1963 by the Rhode Island School of Design, where he had studied architecture. With Johnson's help, Whitney got a job at the Museum of Modern Art (MoMA), later worked for Leo Castelli, then ran his own art gallery, and became an assistant to Jasper Johns. A performer in Claes Oldenburg's *1965 Happening*, Whitney has said, it was my first nude scene. Everybody wanted to be the star, so I just decided to upstage them all and take my clothes off." The two did not go out socially for their first fifteen years together but, after television star Barbara Walters twitted Johnson in the 1970s, the two began attending functions together.

David Whitney

Whitney became a major figure in the installing of exhibitions as well as in collecting art. Asked in 1996 about their relationship, Johnson told reporters that, although he had some trepidation, "Why not? People know I'm gay, so what am I so scared of?" Johnson was architect of the Cathedral of Hope, a gay and lesbian congregation in Dallas, Texas, that is part of the Universal Fellowship of Metropolitan Community Churches. "I love cathedrals, even though I'm not religious," he said. "Besides, I don't have too much work. Once you're 90, people don't tie you up for long-term projects."

Two months before his 90th birthday, Johnson, described as the cheerleader who had inspired so many young architects, was given a Gold Medal Award by fellow members of the American Academy of Arts and Letters. His reaction to receiving the award, previously received by such as Cass Gilbert, Frank Lloyd Wright, and Ludwig Miës van der Rohe, was, "They made the rest of us look like a flock of pygmies." [*The New York Times*, 11 April 1996]

Selected Johnson Buildings

Glass House, New Canaan, Connecticut (1940)
John de Menil House, Houston (1950)
Four Seasons Restaurant in Mies van der Rohe's Seagram Building,
    New York City (1959)
New York State Theater (home of the New York City Opera and New
    York City Ballet) at Lincoln Center (with Richard Foster; 1964)
Elmer Holmes Bobst Library of New York University (1967-1973)
IDS Center in Minneapolis, Minnesota (1972)
Boston Public Library (1973)

Evangelist Robert Schuller's Crystal Cathedral in Garden Grove, California (1980), re-named Christ Cathedral (Catholic) in 2012

Williams Tower, Houston, (1983)

AEGON Tower, Louisville, Kentucky (Consultant, 1993)

Neuberger Museum of Art at State University of New York at Purchase, New York (1969)

Thanks-Giving Square in Dallas, Texas (1976)

Chapel of St. Basil on the Academic Mall at the University of St. Thomas in Houston, Texas University of Saint Thomas, Texas, with Architect John Manley (1992)

Republic Bank building in Houston, Texas (1983) – re-named Bank of America Center

Museum of Art at Munson-Williams-Proctor Arts Institute in Utica, New York (1960) – listed on the National Register of Historic Places in 2010

190 South LaSalle in Chicago, Illinois – Consultant; John John Burgee Architects (1987)

191 Peachtree Tower, Atlanta, Georgia – Consultant; John John Burgee Architects (1990)

Fort Worth Water Gardens, Fort Worth, Texas (1974)

PPG Place, Pittsburgh, Pennsylvania (1984)

Amon Carter Museum, Fort Worth, Texas (1961, and expansion in 2001)

Puerta de Europa, Madrid (1996), the world's first high leaning buildings

Jones, Matthew Earl

Matt's Uncle James

Matthew Earl Jones, the nephew of actor James Earl Jones, was in my senior English class in 1975 and took me to see his uncle in the Broadway production of *Of Mice and Men*. Jones (Lennie) and Kevin Conway (George) were in the cast with Mark Gordon (Curley); Pamela Blair (Curley's Wife); David Clarke (The Boss); Pat Corley (Carlson); David Gale (Slim); Stefan Gierasch (Candy); Joe Seneca (Crooks); and James Staley (Whit).

Backstage, his uncle (half-brother of New Canaanite Robert Earl Earl Jones) showed us how he takes off his make-up, and I pointed to his dressing room mirror, on which was scotch-taped a New Canaan *Advertiser* sports page article about Matt.

"You some kind of ath-a-lete?" Jones said to his nephew as if in character and still Lennie.

Keating, Edward

Edward Keating (4 March 1956 -), a Pulitzer Prize-winning photographer based in New York City, is a 1974 graduate of New Canaan High School. He has studied political science for two years at American University, and at Columbia University for two years he studied American Literature.

He has spent over 30 years photographing life in the streets and events of the day.

Keating studied with Lisette Model at The New School and currently does regular freelance assignments for major magazines based in NYC including: *Time*, *New York*, *W*, and *Rolling Stone*. In 2002, his photographs accompanied a regular *New York Times* column, "Bending Elbows," by Pulitzer Prize-winning journalist Charlie LeDuff about the city's drinking establishments. He had an article in *New York* (12 Dec 2005) about New York City, "The Abortion Capital of America."

On assignment he has traveled widely, including to the countries of Vietnam, India, Ireland, Albania, Italy, and France. He has exhibited widely and has had one-person shows in the USA, France, and China. He has a close relationship with the photographer, Robert Frank, and was personally responsible in 2009 for bringing Frank to Pingyao, China, where he exhibited his work, *New York City*, alongside Frank's seminal work, *The Americans*.

In addition, Keating in known for his high-end wedding work. As co-creator of "Vows," the weekly wedding column at the *New York Times*, in 1992. According to Director of Photography David Griffin at *National Geographic,* "Vows" and its new journalistic approach to weddings "changed the genre of wedding photography."

The above photo (showing a tea set covered in ash following the attack on the World Trade Towers at a Williamson family apartment on Cedar Street across from the South Tower) won Keating a Pulitzer Prize in Photography in 2002.

He has been on the faculty of The International Center of Photography and The School of Visual Arts, both in New York City.. Keating lives in Manhattan and has two daughters, Caitlin and Emily.

Knaus, Albert ("Al") C. Jr.

Al Knaus, the first of three children born to Albert and Eleanor Knaus, grew up in a middle-class neighborhood of Montclair, New Jersey. He graduated from Montclair High School in 1943, joined the Marines shortly thereafter, and served 34 months as a radio operator with the rank of corporal.

After his discharge, Knaus spent a year as freshman at Rutgers University's extension in Newark while living at home and working part-time for the local dairy. Anxious to continue his education and partake of "campus life," Knaus chose Marietta College in Marietta, Ohio, as the small, Midwestern co-ed school where he would spend the next three years. By the time he graduated with his B.A. degree, he had fallen in love, married a beautiful Pennsylvania girl, Jane Bock, and received admittance to Harvard's Graduate School of Education, where he earned his M.A. in Teaching.

In 1952 he joined the faculty of Friends Academy, a private day school in North Dartmouth, Massachusetts, where he taught English and coached sports for the next five years. By 1957, Knaus decided that public school had more to offer. After a search in Fairfield County, he was offered a position by Principal Norman Hunt at Saxe Junior High School in New Canaan. With Jane and two kids (Lucinda and Bert) in tow, he settled on Parade Hill Road and prepared for a new job and a new baby (David).

After seven years as social studies department chairman, Knaus became eligible for sabbatical leave and sub-sequently flew off to India with his family for a two-year assignment as principal of the American International School of Calcutta. According to him, India was an unforgettable, mostly positive experience which put our kids into small classes with Indian students on scholarships, plus English,

French, Canadians, Germans, and Americans whose fathers were engineers and scientists on assignment from the Ford Foundation, as well as business groups, Peace Corps, and U.S. government officials. Except for Jane, each teacher was hired locally, with some knowledge of western educational methods. His secretary was an Anglo-Indian woman who interpreted the Bengali language when necessary to speak with our custodial staff (a watchman and two bearers) or tradesmen "doing a service."

Returning to New Canaan after a family tour of Europe with 13 bags of luggage, Knaus resumed his teaching at the junior high in the fall of 1968 and moved into a somewhat larger home on Fairty Drive.

Eight years later he took charge of the work-study program at New Canaan High School until his retirement in 1985. During the same period, he became active in local politics, much to the disappointment of First Selectman Charles Kelley and several other Republicans who believed teachers should not be protesting against the Vietnam war. Fortunately for Knaus, who was then Chairman of the Democratic Town Committee, the Board of Education supported his right and that of other teachers to protest outside the classroom.

In retirement Knaus took an interest in portrait painting and rented a small store in South Norwalk's mixed neighborhood, near the Washington Street railroad crossing. Here he got to know numerous street people who often wandered into his studio and posed for an instant photo, which later was converted into an acrylic portrait. During a nine-year period, Knaus painted over 300 portraits for a clientele who could pay for them.

After his wife's retirement in 1992 from teaching at Hindley Elementary School, Darien, the Knauses sold their 16' sailboat and bought a motor home that took them across the country to National Parks in the Southwest and Canada: an adventure they repeated with larger RVs for the next ten years. In between the RV excursions they signed on for many trips throughout Europe, often taking several river voyages via the Danube, Elba, Seine, and Volga, Before entering a more sedentary life back in New Canaan, they ventured into Mexico and Costa Rica.

In September of 2010, Jane was suddenly struck by a deadly strain of leukemia, which was kept dormant with chemo-therapy until June, 2011, enabling Jane and Al to make one last trip of one week in Bermuda.

Following a failed clinical trial with a new drug at NY Cornell-Presbyterian, Jane was brought to a hospice residence in Stamford, where she died on August 6.

In Al's words,

It was a one-year nightmare. After 62 years together, I lost a loving partner and a remarkable teacher. At this writing (March 2012) I must honestly say that life is a lonesome drag which becomes bearable mainly because of long-time friends and my attachments to local groups such as "Staying Put in New Canaan," The United Nations Committee of New Canaan, the YMCA, and the Lapham Center pool hall. I'm also taking photos for different groups and getting back to painting portraits. **I'll be 87 in August 2012, with 53 of those years** spent in New Canaan, where I still abide alone at 59 Fairty Drive. If my feet stop challenging my balance, I might get behind the wheel of my trusty RAV 4 and drive off to . . . oblivion?

Knaus painted *Fernando Vargas and Warren Allen Smith*, the Variety Recording Studio business partners (and paramours), from a photograph.

Fernando Vargas and Warren Allen Smith (1977)

    Medium: Oil on Canvas
    Date: May 1991
    Dimensions: 20" x 16"
    Principal Colors: Blue, Black, Skin Tones, Brown

Krass, Michael

Richard Burton's daughter, Kate, wearing a Krass-designed dress in *Hedda Gabler*

Krass as a New Canaan High School student excelled particularly in English and working with anything connected with drama. He went to William & Mary in Williamsburg, Virginia, where he did extensive theater set and costume design.

Upon graduation, he got positions with Broadway companies and made a name in set designs and making costumes.

In 1996 he was nominated for the Drama Desk Outstanding Costume Design for *Entertaining Mr. Sloane*.

In 1997, he was nominated for the Drama Desk Outstanding Costume Design award for Jean Anouilh's *The Rehearsal*, a work the setting of which was a 1950 chateau in France.

In 1999, *You're a Good Man, Charlie Brown* was a nominee for a Tony Award for Best Revival of a Musical, for which he was the costume designer.

In 2006 he was nominated for a Tony Award for Best Costume Design of *The Constant Wife*, a work the setting of which was a 1920s house on Harley Street in London.

Krass worked in costume design in the following plays: *The Rehearsal* (1997); *A View From the Bridge* (1997-1998); *Getting and Spending* (1998); *You're a Good Man Charlie Brown* (1999); *The Lion in Winter* (1999); *Hedda Gabler* (2001-2002); *An Almost Holy Picture* (2002); *The Man Who Had All the Luck* (2002); *Match* (2004); *After the Fall* (2004); *Reckless* (2004); *Twelve Angry Men* (2004-2005); *'Night, Mother* (2004-2005); *After the Night and the Music* (2005); *The Constant Wife* (2005); and *After Miss Julie* (2009).

From 2004 to 2011, he taught set design and costuming at New York University and has told former teachers Nancy and Ron Russell-Tutty that he loves teaching even more than his design career.

Never his teacher but one who was chairman of the English department, I met Michael one summer in the garment district when I was looking nearby for cloth to use on recording studio walls, and he was looking for cloth to be used on some theatrical job.

In 2012 he went to Russia to design sets and costumes for an opera at St. Petersberg's Kirov Theatre.

Krass lives in New York City.

Longden, Tom

Des Moines Register journalist Tom Longden wrote me up in 2009 as one of "Iowa's Famous Iowans," although I left the Hawkeye State after graduating from Iowa State Teachers in 1948:

Memories Vivid for N.Y. Writer Smith
By Tom Longden

>Warren Allen Smith, an Iowa-born Renaissance man, is a longtime icon in New York City's Greenwich Village. The Minburn native, now in his 80s, has written four books in the past decade and is completing his autobiography, *In the Heart of Showbiz*.
>
>He is a member of Mensa, an international society whose members have IQs in the top two percent of the population.
>
>He is comfortable using a computer, and on any given day knows more about news events in Iowa than many Iowans do.
>
>He has created an online Web site called Philosopedia, with thousands of entries.
>
>http://www.philosopedia.org

McDade, Dorothy

Paul McDade in the 1930s was the Methodist minister in my home town of Minburn, Iowa. His son (Elmer) and daughter (Dorothy McDade) (were among my best friends).

Townspeople, when in a lottery he won a car, believed that surely he had a direct connection with God.

Dorothy McDade Johns and husband Bob

He taught that Wesley was an Arminianist (a believer opposed to the absolute predestinarianism of John Calvin) and a believer in Christian perfection (not just improvement). McDade's sermons, however, are not remembered for explaining theological minutia but, rather, for preaching a common-sense message that encouraged the townspeople to aspire to the highest human ideals, to be good upstanding people, to behave responsibly, to be charitable the Women's Aid Society collected funds for missionaries in order that the Methodist message could be sent to suffering heathens in distant parts of the globe.

Members of the deistic Masonic Lodge often were enrolled in the theistic Methodist Episcopal Church, as it was then known, although the basic tenets of the two were remarkably different. The wooden Methodist pulpit had IHS on its front, a reminder that as Christians we marched in His (Jesus's) steps. The Masonic Lodge did not allow non-members inside, but if somehow you got there you found a well-used pool table, kitchen facilities, some strange looking robes and masonry building tools, and a room with four large chairs in the middle of each wall. Methodists boasted famous members such as General Ulysses S. Grant, Chinese leader Chiang Kai-Shek, and missionary E. Stanley Jones. Masons boasted famous members such as Benjamin Franklin, John Hancock, and ten American presidents before Warren Gamaliel Harding was elected in 1920 by an overwhelming vote in a post-war reaction against President Wilson's international policies. Methodist funerals made reference to God, Jesus, the Holy Ghost, and Heaven. A Mason's funeral often avoided using terms of religiosity, emphasizing the person's character, good works, and deistic belief in the (undefined) Great Architect of the Universe.

When he baptized Harold Gottschalk, Robert Shirley, and me he did it with water from the Dead Sea, and we wondered if it would harm our hair, thinking that the smelly brilliantine hair oil that we wore would counter any bad effects. When Mr. McDade baptized the three of us and the water dribbled down our necks, we laughed and were solemnly scolded by our parents. Dorothy's hair was sometimes curly, Shirley Temple-like, and it glistened because her mother broke an egg on it when she prepared it before washing it. Elmer and I played by using some of his father's formaldehyde to kill ants, then burying them under Coca Cola or Ginger Ale bottle tops. Dorothy and I played in a room with clothes, dressing up and performing as if in a play. Her dad played piccolo, and she played flute, and I accompanied her on the piano. At school, she was my girlfriend. She and I edited a weekly newspaper, The Eye Opener, mimeographing it on her dad's machine. When her family moved to another town, I was devastated.

Bob, her husband, had a foreign sports car, and allegedly Dorothy drove it at 80 miles per hour, maybe more.

Dorothy was a graduate of Iowa State in 1943, and a dietitian at the Woodstock Memorial Hospital for 22 years. According to her obituary, she was the wife of Robert S. Johns; the mother of Robert L. (M. Denise Ward) Johns, Marcia (Anthony) Horvath, and Rebecca (Harold) Keen; cherished grandmother of Alice Johns, Karina (Andy) Carlson, Patrick Horvath, Robert Keen, and James Keen; devoted great-grandmother of Josephine Carlson and Stephanie Carlson; and sister of Elmer (Janny Lou) McDade.

Elmer was a veteran of the Korean War, according to the Ukiah, California, *Daily Journal*, and his son Scott McDade was in the U. S. Coast Guard in San Diego, California.

Madigan, Timothy

Madigan (27 March 1962 -   ) was the Executive Editor (1987–1997) and Editor (1997-1999) of *Free Inquiry*. Also, he was co-editor of *The Secular Humanist Bulletin* until 1997.

He has taught philosophy at several Western New York institutions, including Monroe Community College, Medaille College, Erie Community College, Houghton College, Daemen College, Canisius College, and the State University of New York at Buffalo.

He graduated summa cum laude in 1985 from the State University of New York at Buffalo, receiving his Ph.D. in 1999. In 1999 he became the editorial director for the University of Rochester Press. Currently, he is on the faculty of St. John Fisher College's Religion and Philosophy Department.

Humanist

> Madigan is one of the youngest as well as one of the best-recognized faces in the secular humanist movement, for he has traveled widely and speaks extensively. He has given presentations at Harvard University, Princeton University, Yale University, Louisiana State University, California State University - Northridge, Southeastern Louisiana University, University of South Alabama, Drew University, University of Richmond, Hofstra

University, Youngstown State University, Brock University, University of Minnesota, and Hiram College. He has also spoken at conferences in Moscow and St. Petersburg, Russia; Madrid, Spain; Delphi, Greece; Warsaw, Poland; Amsterdam, The Netherlands; London, England; San Jose, Costa Rica; Toronto, Canada; Edinburgh, Scotland; and Cairo, Egypt.

A Secular Humanist Mentor of the Council for Secular Humanism, Madigan was active in helping establish secular humanist societies throughout the nation. He is an honorary associate of the New Zealand Association of Rationalists and Humanists. Also, he is a member of the American Philosophical Association, the Society for Advancement of American Philosophy, the Bertrand Russell Society (on the board of directors, 1993 - present), the John Dewey Society, the David Hume Society, the International Brontë Society, and the International Primate Protection League. He is Executive Director of the Society of Humanist Philosophers.

Madigan has written "Universalism as Particularism," in which he discusses cynicism, cosmopolitanism, and contemporary humanism.

Interests

A writer on extensive subjects, including the singer Al Jolson, Madigan co-wrote (with Glenn Odden) such plays as *The Knife Before Christmas*, *Unnecessary Roughness*, *Forever Hold Your Piece*, and *Primary Suspect*. He was co-editor of *On the Barricades: The Best of Free Inquiry* (1989); *The Question of Humanism* (1991), and *Toward a New Enlightenment: The Philosophy of Paul Kurtz* (1993). He edited *The Ethics of Belief and other Essays* by W. K. Clifford (1999). Also, he has been associate editor of *Moody Street Irregulars: The Jack Kerouac Newsletter*; and editor of *The Brontë Newsletter*. He is a United States editor of *Philosophy Now* (London).

Views

In "Legor et Legar: Schopenhauer's Atheistic Morality" (*Philo*, Fall-Winter 1998), Madigan states that Nietzsche referred to Arthur Schopenhauer as the first inexorable atheist among German philosophers. "Yet Schopenhauer's philosophy, in particular his discussion of "compassion" as the basis of morality" can serve as a starting point for dialogue among Hindus, Buddhists, Jews, Christians, Muslims, and atheistic humanists, all of whom need to address what Raimundo Panikkar calls "The Silence of God." "Schopenhauer, "this friendless and bad-tempered philosopher," has much to teach about the nature of morality, he writes.

Books by Dr. Madigan

On the Barricades: The Best of Free Inquiry (1989, with Robert Basil and Mary Beth Gehrman)

The Question of Humanism (1993 with David Goicoechea and John Luik)

Toward a New Enlightenment (1993, with Vern Bullough)
Quantitative Research on Effective Schools: A Critique (1993)

Challenges to the Enlightenment: In Defense of Reason and Science (1994, Editor)

The Ethics of Belief and Other Essays by William Clingdon Clifford (1999)

Rational Rituals, or Pay No Attention to That Man Behind the Curtain (1999, Audio CD)

Social Diseases: Mafia, Terrorism, Totalitarianism (Moscow: Russian Humanist Society Press, 2004)

God and the Philosophers (2008, with Paul Edwards)
W. K. Clifford and the Ethics of Belief (Cambridge Scholars Publishing, 2009)

Personal

"Like many people," Madigan has written, "I was named after a relative. But in my case, the relative in question was a Roman Catholic nun, my mother's cousin, Sister Timothy." Nuns, until fairly recently, assumed a male name when taking up the wimple. As a young Catholic, Madigan read in *The Acts of the Apostles* that the biblical Paul "wanted Timothy to accompany him, and he took him and circumcised him because of the Jews that were in those places, for they knew all that his father was a Greek." But then the Church Fathers changed their minds, thanks to a revelation from God, and Christians did not have to have their foreskins removed. Observed Madigan after becoming an atheist, "And after this cruel joke, the guy still honored God? What a schmuck."

In his introduction to W. K. Clifford's *The Ethics of Belief*, Madigan notes that Clifford chose for his epitaph a statement from Epictetus: "I was not, and was conceived; I loved, and did a little work; I am not, and grieve not."

Dr. Madigan signed *Humanist Manifesto 2000*.

Madigan in his Rochester home invites Tim Delaney, a fake Irish "priest," to exorcise all diabolical spirits from *The Humanist*.

Dr. Madigan has visited many philosophers' grave sites:

Samuel Beckett

Jeremy Bentham

Jean-Jacques Rousseau

Jean-Paul Sartre

Voltaire

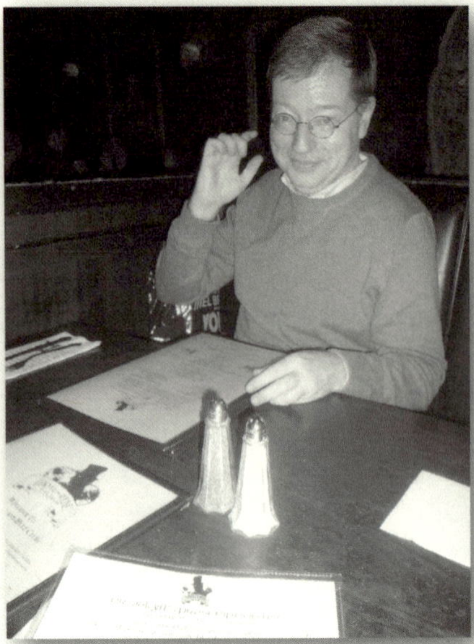

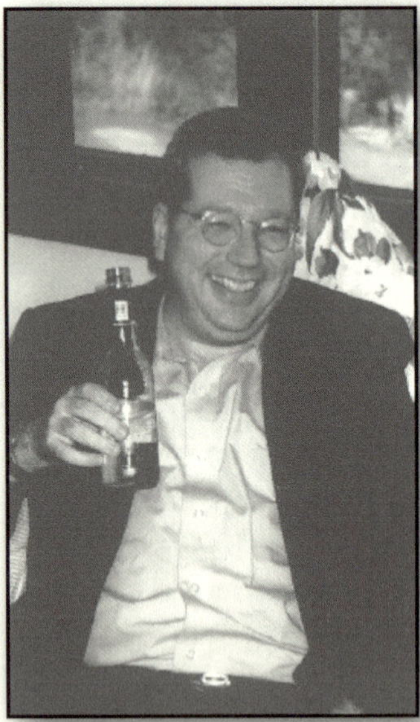

On my 85th birthday, Tim wrote for my festschrift:

> I first met Warren "in the heart of showbiz" when I visited his recording studio on 42nd Street. He was organizing a secular humanist group for New York City subscribers to *Free Inquiry* magazine, which I was helping to edit at the time. This was during the heyday of "the Deuce's" sleazy era and Warren kindly led me – like Virgil leading Dante in *The Inferno* – through many explorations of the area before Mayor Giuliani so unkindly cleaned everything up. It was an historic time.
>
> I have since made it my business to visit Warren as often as I can, and he also visited me in Buffalo and Rochester on several occasions. We've traveled together to various places, from San Jose, Costa Rica, to New Orleans, Louisiana (pre-Katrina) to Minburn, Iowa. He is the perfect traveling companion – always with a quip on his lips, a desire to investigate every nook and cranny, and, best of all, an impeccable sense of direction.

It has been my pleasure to act as Warren's editor on several occasions, particularly when he wrote a regular gossip column for *Free Inquiry*, and I was delighted to be invited by him to write the foreword to his magnum opus, *Who's Who in Hell*. A fascinating compendium of facts, speculations and autobiographical ramblings, the book ranks with *Tristram Shandy* as an unclassifiable, multi-faceted tour de force.

To me, Warren is the quintessential New Yorker – sophisticated, blasé, witty, and never fazed by anything. I have learned more about *the* City from my gallivanting about with him than any other way, and I've seen some sights that very few tourists ever get to see! But I've also had the pleasure – along with my colleague **Dr. David White** – of going across Warren's native state of Iowa with him, seeing his birthplace, his first college, and a good part of the land from whence he came. I have to say, the old song "How You Gonna Keep 'Em Down on the Farm" came to mind. Thank "god" the G.I. Bill brought Warren to the Big Apple, the only place on earth where he truly could be at home.

Warren is my inspiration. Like him, I hope that I too can become a noted sybarite and roué. But the term which most captures him – a term he has spent a good part of his long life exploring – is "humanist." He is a lover of the arts, a freethinker, a social activist, a compassionate and caring humanitarian, and a true friend. Warren Allen Smith is a humanist in every sense of the word. He's even inspired me to write a poem, which I trust captures his fascination with all things Hellish:

There once was fellow named Warren,
Whose life was exciting, not borin'.
He was born in Minburn,
And his "soul" will return
To a land that to Heaven is foreign!

Happy 85th birthday – we'll be celebrating many subsequent ones as well.
Tim

Menschel, Ronay Arlt

Ronay Arlt is the daughter of MacClaire Arlt and Paul T. Arlt, a cartoonist for *The New York Herald Tribune*, where he was an editorial cartoonist from 1951 to 1956.

In the New Canaan High School Class of '60, Arlt was known for her interest in the social studies and the humanities.

She became a graduate of Cornell University and in 1974 married Richard Menschel.

She became Deputy Mayor of New York from 1978 to 1979, just after the time that Mayor Ed Koch's sexuality became an issue. In his 1992 autobiography, *Citizen Koch*, the mayor described his right-hand gal, Ronay, as "a startlingly beautiful woman" who worked for him in Washington and New York and with whom he frequently had dinner.

But no, he had no romantic interest in her or in television game show panelist Bess Myerson. Asked by reporters about his sexuality, his answer was to fuck off, "There have to be some private matters left."

Menschel is the mother of their three daughters. She currently is Chairman of Phipps Houses and previously served as its President and CEO. She is a current trustee of its affiliate, Phipps Community Development Corporation.

Menschel served on the board of the Metropolitan Transportation Authority from 1979 to 1990, focusing on consumer issues and the transit system's station environment, and served as chair of the New York City Advisory Commission for Cultural Affairs from 1984 to 1989.

From 1991 to 1992, she headed the New York City Public Schools Chancellor's Advisory Council on Arts Education.

From 1998 to 2004 Menschel served as a director of the Federal Reserve Bank of New York.

Messerschmidt, Myron

Myron Messerschmidt and Warren Allen Smith
Tutor Ticklers Winners

During my freshman year, my photo appeared seven times in the 1944 yearbook, *Old Gold*.

My hands were photographed playing the auditorium's organ; I was photographed twice playing my trombone; **Myron Messerschmidt** and I in the 1941 yearbook were pictured as winners of that year's Tutor Ticklers show for our piano duo; in the marching band; at a dormitory sing; in the concert band; and as a member of the Romance Language Club.

In Phi Mu Alpha, the honorary music fraternity, Messerschmidt, Class of 1941, was my dad. He played the campanile and, upon retiring, I became his successor and held an open house for any students who cared to climb all the stairs and watch me play.

During World War II, he changed his name to Bob Mitchell and played the organ for Armed Forces Radio. He and his wife later played with the Glenn Miller-Tex Beneke Orchestra They lived in Tucson, Arizona.

319

Miller, Court

Harvey Fierstein, Court Miller, Estelle Getty
in *Torch Song Trilogy* (1982)

Courtland Miller (29 January 1952 - 7 March 1986) was a 1970 New Canaan High School graduate who, without college training, became a successful on-and-off Broadway success in motion pictures straight out of high school.

Drama teachers Nancy and Ronald Russell-Tutty recall working with Miller:

> Court Miller starred in two of Nancy's one-acts the very first fall we arrived at NCHS in 1968. He was the original Snoopy in the musical *You're A Good Man, Charlie Brown* and the gay rabbit in Shirley Jackson's (*The Lottery*) macabre-bizarre retelling of "Hansel and Gretel." With it the year before we arrived in

Connecticut Nancy had won Kentucky's state-wide drama competition held at the University of Kentucky. He did his "Suppertime" song and dance number from *Charlie Brown* the following spring, was seen by an agent in the audience, and was offered the part of Snoopy in the national touring company of the show on the spot! He couldn't take it, however, because he was only seventeen and the producers would have had to hire a full time tutor for anyone under eighteen. He also played a leading role in *Seventeen*, a Broadway hit in the early 50's. We had to fight Peg Sherry "tooth and nail" (as we did until her retirement) to do it!

(I'm sorry, but Peg and Rose, both trained as English and not drama teachers, couldn't direct their way out of a paper bag! I've had to wait 44 years to finally say it, and I'M GLAD!)

We followed Court's career in numerous summer stock productions (with his wife Barbara of the Radio City Music Hall Chorus). We saw them do *The King and I*, *Sweet Charity*, and many others. In New York, Court was a member of "The Paper Bag Players" and later "The Prince Street Players." We also took students to see him Off-Broadway in Eugene O'Neil's *Welded*. And, of course and unfortunately, he later did *Torch Song Trilogy*, which probably led to his untimely death! Such a wasted talent.

Miller was in the following films:

> *Playing for Keeps* (Claiborne) 1986
> *Cat's Eye* (Mr. McCann) 1985
> *The New Kids* (Sheriff) 1985
> *Garbo Talks* (*Romeo and Juliet* Director)
> *Rage of Angels*, a television movie (Ben Bluestone)
> *The 37th Annual Tony Awards*, 1983, a television movie (himself, presenter)

He was the first high-profile actor who contracted and then died of AIDS. He had starred in *Torch Song Trilogy* (1982) in the role of Harvey Fierstein's lover, a history teacher. At his memorial service in what now is the Helen Hayes Theater, Fierstein was the "m.c" and several NCHS faculty members attended. "Court's wife's family and friends sat on one side of the theater and his partner John's family and friends sat on the other, but everyone spoke," observed NCHS graduate Cathy Russell ('73).

At the time of his death from AIDS at the age of 34, according to Nancy and Ronald Russell-Tutty, Miller was living with his partner, John, in Cumberland, Maine.

Mitchell, Kathleen Marie Barndt

Mitchell (9 January 1947 -   ), who was a New Canaan girls physical education coach in three different schools before her retirement, was born in Sellersville, Pennsylvania, was raised in Tylersport, Pennsylvania, and moved to New Canaan in 1968.

Her parents were John Y. Barndt, a factory worker who tested gauges at US Gauge (now Ametek) and during World War II worked in the Philadelphia shipyards. Grace, her mother, was a local seamstress at various factories in the area but basically was a homemaker who was active in her church. They had a son, James, who had been a principal in Wilmington, Delaware, at Mitchell Associates, a design consulting firm, but died in 1990.

In 1964, she graduated from Souderton Area Joint High School in Souderton, Pennsylvania. In 1968, she earned her B.A. in Physical Education and Health from Davis & Elkins College, in Elkins, West Virginia. She earned her M.A. from Fairfield University in 1974 and her M.S. and 6th year equivalency in 1981 in Physical Education at Southern Connecticut State University in New Haven, Connecticut.

In 1973, she married Joseph L. Mitchell of Stamford, Connecticut, a builder of contemporary homes in the area. He also worked in making commercials and movies in the local area. They have had one son, Christopher Joseph Mitchell, born in 1978 and a graduate of New Canaan High School in 1997. A distance runner, he captained cross country, indoor track, and outdoor track teams when a senior. He majored in physics at Rensselaer Polytechnic Institute in Troy, New York, graduating in 2001

At New Canaan High School from September 1968 to June 1989, she taught physical education and health, in addition to coaching volleyball, tennis, and field hockey.

For one year, from September 1989 to June 1990, she taught physical education and health at Saxe Middle school.

For 16 years, from September 1990 to June 2006, she taught physical education at West Elementary School.

In 2006, she retired after having taught 38 years in three different New Canaan schools. Few New Canaan parents of daughters could not have known about Ms. Mitchell.

Asked her special memories of New Canaan, she responded in 2012:

> My husband Joe and I have lived in town for the past 34 years and have seen the town change a great deal. We went from Mom & Pop stores to having some national chain stores taking over Elm St. Rents are so high that local owners are feeling the pinch and gradually are leaving.
>
> I am a member of St. Michael's Lutheran Church in New Canaan, where I have served on Church Council and continue to serve on the Fellowship Committee. In addition to being an active participant in our women's group, I also work with Meals on Wheels and help to serve lunch at the Lapham Community Center. In addition, I substitute teach at the high school and enjoy working out and taking various classes at Stamford Hospital's Tully Health Center. Also, I am actively involved with my alma mater, Davis & Elkins College, as the class agent for the class of 1968.
>
> When I first arrived here in 1968, the schools did not have co-ed physical education classes. A divider in the gym always separated the sexes and was called "the line of demarkation." Female students, in addition to being taught the traditional team sports of field hockey, basketball, and volleyball, were exposed to fencing, ping pong, badminton, and square and folk dancing in order to have a broader experience in their physical education classes. With other female coaches from FCIA schools, we initiated varsity volleyball for girls. We did our own scheduling and officiating and transportation arrangements. Even while coaching tennis we did our own scheduling. When Title IX started, equality began.

Headmaster Harold Kenney would not only find hockey balls and arrows in his backyard from our classes but also would return them to us.

When we hosted opposing girls' tennis teams, they enjoyed the snacks and were amused that we got our cold sodas from one of the many liquor stores in town. Inasmuch as the high school had no tennis courts, we used private courts, even on certain days at the Country Club of New Canaan.

The best part of being at the old high school was the camaraderie of the faculty. The old faculty room was a meeting place and lunch area that I always enjoy. Once at the new, present building, everything died. Now, it is worse. No one sees anyone except those in their department. When in the old building, we knew everyone. Our students were great! I still enjoy subbing and especially enjoy seeing my little elementary kids are grown up!

Mull, Martin

Mull (18 August 1943 -   ), who graduated from New Canaan High School, starred in his own television sitcom, *Fernwood 2 Night*, and became known as a comedian, painter, and recording artist.

An atheist, I describe him as a humanities humanist in Philosopedia:

> Mull was born in Chicago, Illinois, raised from age 2 to 15 in North Ridgeville, Ohio, and moved to New Canaan, Connecticut. He graduated from New Canaan High School, then studied studied painting and went on to graduate from the Rhode Island School of Design with a Bachelor of Fine Arts in 1965 and a Master of Fine Arts (1967) in painting.
>
> His marriage to Kristin Johnson in 1972 ended in divorce in 1978, as did his marriage in 1978 to Sandra Baker. In 1982 he married singer Wendy Mull. He has one daughter, Maggie.
>
> An accomplished painter who has studied in Italy, he has works that have been shown by the Carl Hammer Gallery in Chicago.
>
> Mull made television commercials in the 1980s and 1990s for Michelob (beer), Red Roof Inn (budget-oriented hotels), and others, showing his skill as a comedian. In an episode of the cartoon series, *Dexter's Laboratory*, he was the voice of a lazy robot who had a clueless partner, voiced by Fred Willard. He also voiced the role of the Evil Cad on *Freakazoid!* From 2003 to 2007, he was the voice of Vlad Masters/Vlad Plasmius on *Danny Phantom*.

He has been a guest star in an episode of *The Golden Girls* (1990) and *The Simpsons* (1998). In 2004, he portrayed Gene Parmesan, a private investigator who in ¡*Amigos!* was seen in strange places and in crazy disguises but who never finds anything out.

In addition to painting full-time, Mull has acting credits that in 2008 included *Family Man*; *Two and a Half Men*; *Law and Order: SVU*; *Gary Unmarried*; *The New Adventures of Old Christine*; *The Bonnie Hunt Show*; and, in 2009, in the viral advert *That's Not Fake*. In the animated series *Family Guy*, the name of the elementary school is Martin Mull Elementary.

In a thinly-veiled reference to Mull, fellow comic Ben Stein wrote the following in *Dreemz* (1978):

> July 26, 1977. The comedy variety show I have been working on is finished taping for a few months. I went to the "wrap party" last night at the Bistro restaurant, a fine and fancy place. A lot of my friends from the studio were there . . . .
>
> After an hour, the star of the show [Martin Mull] appeared with his girl friend. He is a funny guy who used to sing at small nightclubs and colleges. He played a role on *Mary Hartman* and then he was killed off. I begged our studio head not to lose him and he was saved for his own show, partly at my pleading request. When we first met, he called me "Ben" and was always full of jokes and pleasantries. When he got on the air, he started calling me "Benny," when he did not pass me without a word. Last night, after he had made it big, he saw me and said, "Well, look who's here." It's a standard line for people when they can't remember someone's name. That ruined the party, even though the Bistro does make pretty good cannelloni.

Mull is not listed in *Who's Who in America* but was in the 1989 *Who's Who in Entertainment*.

Murphy, Karen

Murphy (11 August 1955 –   ), who was born in White Plains, New York, is the daughter of Alice and John Murphy. Her mother was a registered nurse who worked for years at Silver Hill Hospital in New Canaan, and her dad worked as an assistant manager of a bank office in Darien as an expert on retirement plans.

One of six children, three of whom graduated from New Canaan High School, she attended The Boston Conservatory and earned a Theatre Arts degree in 1977 from the University of Massachusetts Boston.

On Broadway, she has been in the following plays:

>*A Little Night Music* (2009 - 2011)
>*9 to 5* (2009)
>*All Shook Up* (2005)
>*42nd Street* (2001-2005)
>*Titanic* (1997-1999)
>*King David* (1997)

She holds a Drama Desk nomination for *My Vaudeville Man,* and she understudied Angela Lansbury in the Broadway revival of *A Little Night Music.* She sang opposite Paul Sorvino at the New York City Opera in *The Most Happy Fella* directed by Philip William McKinley, who replaced Julie Taymor on *Spider Man*, the Broadway musical. At Madison Square Garden's Paramount Theatre she was Mrs. Mops in *A Christmas Carol.*

Off-Broadway, she has appeared in the following:

> *My Vaudeville Man* – Mud Donahue
> (York Theatre)
> *Showtune* – Lead
> (York Theatre)
> *L'Amour the Merrier* – Myself with Steve Ross
> (Kaufmann Theatre)
> *Zombie Prom* – Delilah Strict
> (Variety Arts, New York City)
> *Hysterical Blindness* – Gospel Soloist/Miss Bessmer
> (Van Dam Playhouse)
> *Forbidden Broadway* – Principal
> (Theatre East, New York City)

Murphy has appeared in regional theatre:

> Barrington Stage Company – *No Way To Treat A Lady*
> Cincinnati Playhouse/St. Louis Rep – *Songplay* (by Kurt Weill)
> Geva Theatre, Rochester – *Urinetown*
> Goodspeed Opera House – *Showboat*
> Huntington Theatre Co – *Candide*
> Kansas City Starlight Tour – *The Wizard of Oz*
> Marius Company – *Les Miserables*
> Krieger/Russell, Theatreworks, California – *Kept*
> Pittsburgh CLO – *Bells Are Ringing*
> The Signature, DC – *The Visit*
> TOTS Tour – *White Christmas*
> Westchester Broadway Theatre – *My Fair Lady, Grease, Hello Dolly*

Murphy graduated from New Canaan High School in 1973 and lives in New York City.

On 13 April 2010, Angela Lansbury went on a two-week vacation from *A Little Night Music*, and her role as co-star with Catherine Zeta-Jones was memorably performed by Karen

On that opening night, Catherine Zeta-Jones thanked Karen for her great performance. Karen's friend, Ligardy Termonfils, looks on.

Nasrin, Taslima

"The most dangerous woman in the world" is the way I described Dr. Nasrin in Philosopedia.

Nasrin, who was born in Mymensingh in what then was known as East Pakistan, is the daughter of **Dr. Rojab Ali**, a government physician and practitioner of the Sufi tradition of Islam. Her parents and her family members were all raised as devout Muslims.

In 1984 she graduated in Bangladesh with an M.B.B.S degree (Bachelor of Medicine, Bachelor of Surgery). On the Indian subcontinent, the degree represents having passed a five-year program in a medical college and hospital, after which one does internship in a hospital for a year. In short, the degree is like an M.D. in the United States and elsewhere. Dr. Nasrin could have but did not specialize as a surgeon, which could have resulted in an F.R.C.S had she gone to the Royal College of Surgeons in Britain.

After graduating as a doctor and practicing medicine, she also wrote poetry. Five years into her medical career, she wrote newspaper columns. As a doctor, she treated many 7-or 8-year-old girls who had been raped by male relatives, many 50 or 60 years old, a crime she had also experienced, raped by a relative when she was young.

In her writing, she exposed the sorrow oppressed women universally were experiencing. They were being raped, were victims of drug traffickers, had acid thrown on them, were killed over dowries, and treated as an inferior sex. At first, her editors did not censor her, but when powerful interests were affected by her criticism, her editors' offices were attacked and it became more difficult for her to write freely in her works and speak without being verbally, even physically, attacked.

Typical of her writing is her journalist's account of how the Qur'an prescribes purdah but that doesn't mean women should obey it. In a March 2007 article she suggests discarding the burqa.

2007 and 2008

"India Tells Bangladeshi Writer to Stay Hidden or Leave" was the headline in the 15 February 2008 guardian.co.uk

In short, India - although a secular democracy - has called her a "guest" and not subject to its constitution. She remained confined in a room in an undisclosed place, her only company being a television and her laptop.

At the end of January 2008 and because of her diabetic condition, she was admitted to a hospital because of her high blood pressure. News reports suggested that she was receiving helpful treatment.

On 22 January 2007, Nasrin was forced by extremist Muslim fundamentalists to flee from her apartment in Kolkata, West Bengal, India. She was taken by India's government centre "for her protection" to an undisclosed place in the Delhi area." "Protection" has meant, to some observers, a violation of her human rights in that she is not allowed to leave her room. Alone, as she has described except for "two lizards with wide eyes" over in the corner, she was confined up to the end of 2007.

On 22 April 2007, Karan Thapar of CNN's IBN News asked Taslima if she is trying to change the world. Yes, Nasrin responded, then did not back down when asked the pointed questions that followed. The journalist, in fact, asked what many would find embarrassing questions, and Nasrin responded firmly, truthfully, and inspiringly. "If France's Voltaire, America's Susan B. Anthony, or England's Bertrand Russell were alive, they would be inspired," wrote Warren Allen Smith, who has edited much of what she writes in English.

On 5 May 2007, Nasrin described in India's online Wall Street Journal why, when a child in a patriarchal world, she had had an intense desire to change herself into a boy.

On 9 August 2007, Nasrin was attacked at a publication party for one of her latest books at the press club in Hyderabad, India. Lawmakers and members of the All India Majlis-e-Ittehadul Muslimeen party, threatened her with a chair, hurled a leather case, threw bunches of flowers and other objects while some shouted for her death. Organizers pushed them back, and Nasrin escaped unhurt. In the melee, one of the protesters slapped her, witnesses said. Police reportedly detained the 100 protesters, including the three lawmakers.

As of January 2008, she remained in confinement. To find whether or not she will be granted an extension of her visa or what is being written about her, she consults Google News on her laptop, the only item she took upon leaving Kolkata.

Upon receiving the Simone De Beauvoir Award in Paris, she was unable to attend. For visitors including journalists to see her, she must ask (and is often turned down), she is taken in a vehicle with dark shaded windows to another undisclosed place where she is interviewed by someone who also is taken there in a vehicle with dark shaded windows, after which both are returned, never having known where they have been. Intellectuals around the world have objected according to The Hindu Times and other journals.

French President Nicolas Sarkozy in mid-January 2008 proposed to confer the prestigious Simone de Beauvoir award on her during his visit to India. Indian government officials suggested some other approach, perhaps arranging for her to receive the honor by traveling somewhere else. The Times observed "that the government is likely to renew Nasreen's visa."

On 17 February 2008 when her visa expired, India extended the visa but did not state for how long. Ministry spokesperson Navtej Sarna had said while announcing the extension of the visa, "It is incumbent on those who are welcomed as guests in India that they remain sensitive to India's traditions and do not conduct themselves in a manner that either affects our relations with other countries or cause hurt to our secular ethos."

When Nasreen was told that since she chose to be a rebel and hence should pay the price of her outspokenness, she said "I didn't choose to be a rebel. I only chose to speak the truth. I was targeted because the extremists needed a lone person to target."

2009

In January 2009, FANNY (Freethinking Activist Nonbelieving New Yorkers) welcomed Taslima to New York, where she has applied for citizenship and hopes to live in the city. A dinner at Fedora's in Greenwich Village was attended by FANNY co-directors Dennis Middlebrooks and Warren Allen Smith along with friends.

In October 2008, the homeless Dr. Taslima Nasrin remained in Sweden until she could find a place to reside in New York City. New York University will grant her a year's residency as a visiting scholar when she finds a place and moves permanently to the United States.

In mid-March 2008, concerned that her high blood pressure was not being properly treated, Taslima was forced to choose between dying "caged in a room with two wide-eyed lizards and many black ants" or giving in to the Indian Government's pressures. She sent a press release that against her own wishes she had to leave for medical reasons. Landing the next day in London's Heathrow, she refused to say where she was heading - an Indian reporter thought she was going to Canada. Even after receiving the initial medical help in an undisclosed Swedish hospital, she remained "in an undisclosed place." Friends report that she is much relaxed now, her blood pressure and eye problems are being treated. She had an invitation to speak in July to feminists at the 10th International Interdisciplinary Congress, "Women's Worlds 2008," in Madrid, Spain, and to Mikhail Gorbachev's World Political Forum in Torino, Italy, in November.

In 2009, after speaking on feminism at Indiana University, Taslima is in New York City, where she has a resident scholar's office at New York University.

2010

At a March 2010 conference of atheists in Melbourne, Australia, Taslima received a standing ovation when she spoke about her life as an exile from her birthplace.

Death Threats

In 2007 Terry Sanderson, President of the National Secular Society, on 22 March 2007 sent the following to His Excellency Mr. Kamalesh Sharma, Indian High Commissioner, India House, Aldwych, London Wc2B 4NA:

Death threats to Ms Taslima Nasreen

> We write to seek your assistance in connection with news reports about a threat to Taslima Nasreen who is one of our Society's Honorary associates. We read in the international press that a bounty has been placed on her head by a Muslim cleric in India, Taqi Raza Khan, the president of the All-India Ibtehad Council. Mr Khan is reported to have promised to pay the bounty to anyone who will cut off Ms. Nasreen's head.
>
> We accept that the national executive of the All-India Muslim Personal Law Board do not support him as he implies. We also

recognise that many Muslim leaders have condemned this incitement to murder.

We understand that communal relations are a sensitive issue in India, but we ask that you do all in your power to (a) protect Ms Nasreen from these threats and (b) to bring the full force of the law to bear on those who threaten and incite murder and terror.

We were honoured to host a conference in London only last week at which Taslima Nasreen spoke so eloquently about her life as a woman trying to accommodate her religious background with her desire to live fully in the 21st century free from threats to her human rights, especially her right to life and freedom of expression. India is modernising very quickly and we are thrilled to see its progress. Please encourage your government to put an end to these terrible threats and menaces, and allow Taslima to live unmolested and in peace.

Ms Nasreen is a woman of great courage, fortitude and integrity. If India were to grant her citizenship, as she desires, she would be a credit to your great nation.

Yours sincerely, Terry Sanderson, President

Protests to the Government of India also have been circulated:

http://www.petitiononline.com/taslima/petition.html

In November 2007 after being physically attacked in August by three Muslim members of Hyderabad's parliament, Dr. Nasrin for her safety was forced to move from Kolkata to New Delhi. On 21 November 2007, The British Broadcasting System reported that "police in Calcutta used tear gas and baton charges to control crowds calling for her Indian visa to be cancelled. Rioters blocked roads and set cars alight. At least 43 people were hurt. More than 100 arrests were made. Critics say she called for the Koran to be changed to give women greater rights, something she denies. . . . Wednesday's trouble in Calcutta began after the predominantly Muslim All-India Minority Forum called for blockades on major roads in the city. The group said Ms Nasreen had 'seriously hurt Muslim sentiments.' Many Muslims say her writing ridicules Islam. The army was called out and a night curfew imposed."

Books by Taslima Nasrin – includes poetry, essays, novels, autobiographies, banned books:

http://taslimanasrin.com

Lajja

Lajja is a Bengali word that means "shame." The word connotes the same meaning in Sanskrit, Hindi, and other languages of north India. Originally written in Bangla (Bengali), the book was published in 1993 and has been banned in her native country, the name of which changed in 1971 from West Pakistan to Bangladesh.

The book is dedicated "to the people of the Indian subcontinent" and commences, "Let another name for religion be humanism."

In short, she finds that organized religions are not what they seem to be, and she is particularly critical of the Old Testament's laying down the concept of patriarchy as one of its main tenets. A social system in which the male is the head and descent is traced through the father's side of the family by definition makes females secondary and inferior beings. Let religion be humanistic, she pleads, for females are a part of humanity.

The plot pertains to the lives of four Hindus, members of the Dutta family, who are living in Bangladesh. Sudhamoy is the father, Kiranmoy is the mother, and the children are Nilanjana (his sister's pet name is Maya) and Suranjan, a son. Far away in Ayodhya in the Indian state of Uttar Pradesh, a mosque called Babri is demolished in 1992, and this leads to riots and hatred in Bangladesh as well as in Ayodhya. The novel shows how each of the four reacts to such news, the father feeling that Bangladesh will not harm the Hindu minority and his family, the mother faithfully supporting the father, the son being apathetic, and the daughter becoming angry at her brother's lack of concern for the family's safety. What happens is that as a Hindu minority they were not fairly treated, nationalism became an issue, and the country's secularist approach in government became threatened.

Attacks on Nasrin

Nasrin was attacked in print after writing Lajja (Shame), and hundreds of members of the Council of Soldiers of Islam demanded her death. Religious fundamentalists complained that she had depicted Bangladesh's Hindu minority as having been picked out for revenge by Muslims after the 1992 incident in which a Hindu mob had destroyed the ancient mosque.

A reward of 50,000 taka (£850) was immediately offered to anyone who would kill the thirty-one-year-old former gynecologist, for she could no longer practice medicine.

In December 1993, 5,000 zealots marched through Dhaka, demanding her death. A general strike there resulted in clashes in which one man was killed and more than two hundred were injured.

"She is worse than a prostitute," complained Maulana Azizul Haque, the mullah who has called for her execution. "She demands 'freedom of the vagina.' She says that if a man can have four wives, a woman should have the right to four husbands. Even within marriage, she says a woman should have the right to other men. This is against the Qur'an and Allah. It is blasphemy!"

Although quoted as having said that "the Qur'an should be thoroughly revised," she countered that her purpose was to suggest that "we have to move beyond these ancient texts if we want progress," a comment which deepened the controversy.

Muslim militants say "Nirbachito Kolum," a collection of some of her newspaper columns, is blasphemous, and they publicize her separation after a few years from Bangladeshi poet Rudra Mohammad Shahidullah. Meanwhile, some publishers who fear Muslim fundamentalists stopped picturing pigs in children's books, horse-riding and ballet are kept out because they are symbols of the wealthy, and witches are excluded for fear of satanism and the occult.

Nasrin's Views

Nasrin has been a bold advocate of sexual freedom in her newspaper columns, poems, and novels. Like Salman Rushdie of India, who rallied prominent writers to support her feminism, Nasrin was forced into a life of hiding. She fled to Sweden in 1994 after the twelve nations of the European Union made a formal offer of asylum to the writer. Once there, she said,

The fundamentalists are destroying our society. The silent majority is afraid of them. They will do anything in the name of God. The progressives are not so organized, for they cannot bring together 300,000 people at one time.

As for the Muslim clergy:

The country is infected with them. Their long hair, beards, and robes conceal their insatiable lust for wealth and women.

Interviewed by Mary Anne Weaver for *New Yorker* (12 September 1994), Nasrin was described as "utterly ordinary," a shy Marxist professor and poet who became an atheist at the age of eleven or twelve. She reiterated that she had never, never said the Qur'an (Koran) should be revised:

No, how many times do I have to say it? I've said it over and over again. I said that Shariat law should be revised. I want a modern, civilized law, where women are given equal rights. I want no religious law that discriminates, none, period - no Hindu law, no Christian law, no Islamic law. Why should a man be entitled to have four wives? Why should a son get two-thirds of his parents' property when a daughter can inherit only a third? Should I be killed for saying this?

Bangladesh mullahs, giving no reasons, declared in a separate case that one woman's second marriage was contrary to Islamic law and the unfortunate lady was led to a fundamentalist stronghold where a pit had been dug overnight. She was lowered into the pit and buried waist deep. Then, slowly and methodically, the woman was stoned - a hundred and one times. Her death was said to have horrified even the Dhaka's élite. In another town, a woman who was condemned by a fatwa for adultery was doused with kerosene and burned to death. Women everywhere, Nasrin declared, are humiliated and driven out of their villages by fundamentalist mullahs.

Solidarity

In Stockholm, Nasrin remained secreted for several years. "They've taken everything from me," she said. "My innocence, my youth, now my freedom. I know if I ever go back that I'll have to keep silent, stay inside my house. I'll never lead a normal life in my country, until my death."

Asked in an interview with Sara Whyatt (*Index*, September-October 1994) if she still thought herself a Muslim, Nasrin responded,

> No, I am an atheist. All forms of religion are anachronistic to me. I dream of a world without religion. Religion gives birth to fundamentalism as surely as the seed gives birth to the tree. We can tear the tree down, but if the seed remains it will produce another tree. While the seed remains, we cannot root out fundamentalism.

In *The Guardian* (14 December 1994) when journalist Linda Grant mentioned that Muslim fundamentalists say that humanism is an import from the West, Nasrin responded,

> Humanism is not western or eastern or southern or northern. It is just humanism. They protest against me, but I am surprised that they don't protest against inequality and injustice. What I have done is protested against the system which is against women. I have seen that, in the name of tradition, society wants to keep women in ignorance and slavery. . . . I realised from childhood that women were treated as childbearing machines or decorations, not human beings.

A 1995 poem, "Self Portrait," appears in *New Humanist* (December, 1995) and commences

> I don't believe in God.
>
> I look upon Nature with wondering eyes,
>
> However much I move forward
>
> grasping the hands of progress society's hindrances
>
> take hold of my sleeve
>
> and gradually pull me backwards.
>
> I wish I could walk all through the city in the middle of the night,
>
> sitting down anywhere alone to cry. . . .

It ends

> Throughout the world,
>
> religion has extended its eighteen talons.
>
> In my lone brandishing,
>
> how many of its bones can I shatter.
>
> How much can I rip
>
> discrimination's far-spreading net?

"Taslima," Salman Rushdie wrote in an open letter published in *The New York Times* (14 July 1994), "I know there must be a storm inside you now. . . . You have done nothing wrong. The wrong is committed by others against you. You have done nothing wrong, and I am sure that one day soon you will be free."

In her Oxford Amnesty Lecture of 1995, Nasrin said

> Again I dare to write against male-made religion. I believe that women are oppressed by every religion. If any religion allows the persecution of people of different faiths, if any religion keeps people in ignorance, if any religion keeps women in slavery, then I cannot accept that religion. Freedom for women will never be possible until they cross the barrier of religion and patriarchy.

In 1995, she wrote *The Game in Reverse*. Nasrin has published over 20 books, including Nirbachita Column (1991), which portrays the predicament of women in a male-dominated society.

Humanism

In 1996, Nasrin was elected a Humanist Laureate in the Council for Secular Humanism's International Academy of Humanism. She is an honorary associate of the New Zealand Association of Rationalists and Humanists and is the Vice-Chair of the International Society for Islamic Secularization. She is an honorary member of the Bertrand Russell Society, having been inspired by his Why I Am Not a Christian, and is an activist member of the society's New York City chapter.

At the 1996 Mexico City conference of humanists, Jim Herrick described her as being "an atheist from personal experience. She grew up in a country where people were forced there by the partition of India on religious grounds. She accepted that religion could cause great art, but said that it also did too much damage. She began to apply her powers of observation, analysis and reason to religion and found she could not accept it at all. She used her writings to expose the crimes of religion, which teaches people to hate one another and glorifies poverty. The position of women concerned her and she questioned why women in the East should be deprived of education. Democracy and secularism should be put in practice throughout the world."

Like Antigone and putting family above state, Dr. Nasrin alarmed her friends by returning in 1998 to Bangladesh after a forced four-year exile. She returned with her dying mother, whom she had brought to New York City for medical treatment. Upon her arrival, the religious fundamentalists immediately demanded her death. Again she was forced into hiding; again diplomatic overtures had to be made to rescue her for a return to Sweden. Her plight was described in Free Inquiry (Winter 1998-1999), with letters of support from Sir Arthur C. Clarke, Wole Soyinka, Sir Hermann Bondi, Steven Weinberg, Sir Raymond Firth, Edward O. Wilson, and Mario Bunge.

Included was an interview, "One Brave Woman vs. Religious Fundamentalism," by Matt Cherry and Warren Allen Smith, in which she said:

> When I began to study the Qur'an, the holy book of Islam, I found many unreasonable ideas. The women in the Qur'an were treated as slaves. They were nothing but sexual objects.
>
> I don't find any difference between Islam and Islamic fundamentalists. I believe religion is the root, and from the root fundamentalism grows as a poisonous stem. If we remove fundamentalism and keep religion, then one day or another fundamentalism will grow again. I need to say that because some liberals always defend Islam and blame fundamentalists for creating problems. But Islam itself oppresses women. Islam itself doesn't permit democracy and it violates human rights.
>
> When I was 14 or 15 years old, I found the Bengali translation of the Qur'an, and I learned what God says in the verses. I was surprised to read wrong information about the solar system in the Qur'an - for example, that the sun is moving around the earth and the earth is not moving but standing still because of the support of the mountains.

> [Religion] does not often teach people to love one another. On the contrary, it often teaches them to hate people of a different faith. Religion also leads people to depend on fate and thus lose self-confidence. It unnecessarily glorifies poverty and sacrifice and thus serves the vested interests of the wealthy few. In all countries and through all ages, conscientious people have exposed these unethical aspects of religion and educated people to see religion with the eyes of reason and logic.
>
> Nothing will be achieved by reforming Muslim scriptural tenets. What is needed is a change of the sharia, the code of laws based on the Qur'an. I want a uniform civil code that is equally applicable to men and women.
>
> I am an atheist. I do not believe in prayers. I believe in work. And my work is that of an author. My pen is my weapon.

Amar Meyebela (My Girlhood Days)

The work, published as *Enfance, au Féminin*, 1998, in a translation from Bengali by Philippe Benoît) was immediately banned in Bangladesh because "its contents might hurt the existing social system and religious sentiment of the people and could also create adverse reaction in the country."

It is not a crime, she has argued, to be inquisitive, to demand that those who are responsible for abominable crimes against women, and the very women who are hurt, must not only think about oppression but also must insist that it be stopped:

> I thought it was natural to ask "why." I don't understand why they accepted being beaten by their husbands, being prevented from going outside without permission, being forced to marry somebody and stopping their studies after marriage. I know that this is a very, very difficult situation because if you divorce your husband and try to be independent, you'll be called "prostitute." But, you know, I don't care what people call me. Maybe that is the difference. If you want to be a human being, a good person, you first have to be bad in this society's eyes. If you're not willing to be "bad," you'll never be a truly strong and independent person

Nasrin's poetry, translated into English, can only hint at what it sounds like and means in her native language. The following, however, does suggest her Bengali style:

Special Branch guards

Are on twenty-four hour duty in front of my door.

Who comes and who goes, when I leave, enter the house,

They write down everything on a notebook....

Once I had the body of a queen

Now it's lowly, decrepit, an old house

Plaster falling off

Sad, but true

Taslima Nasrin and Warren at Swing Club, 2005

[For over a decade, Taslima has been Warren's best girlfriend and he has been her best Bengali-to-English editor. The Bangladesh physician (whom some Muslim fundamentalists want to kill because of her writing) has asked Warren to edit her prose, poetry, speeches at UN meetings, or even the wording of a possible acceptance lecture had she won the Nobel Peace Prize 2005. First meeting at a humanist convention in Mexico, he was her guest in Sweden, then she was his guest in Greenwich Village. During a BBC interview when asked where he had met her, for she had had to escape to Sweden and elsewhere, he floored them by responding, "She was hiding in a cave." He took her father and her dying mother to see the Atlantic Ocean at Coney Island, introduced her to Kurt Vonnegut, and is a close friend of her entire family.]

Dr. Nasrin has written, "I met a person in a cave in Mexico. Yes, he was Warren Allen Smith and such a gentleman! It was 1996. I wanted to move to the United

States of America, and because my sister lived in New York I wanted to live in New York with her. **Matt Cherry**, a British humanist and friend of both of us, told me Warren could help me about living in New York. Then I talked with Warren one evening in the lobby of the hotel where we were staying for a humanist congress. Warren was and continues to be so helpful. He attended all my talks in the congress. He has continued to help me whenever I needed it. Time has passed, the months and years have passed. and so many friends disappeared. But Warren did not disappear, he remained as a friend, he helped me correct my speeches and articles and poetry. He helped me to help my nephew and my niece. He helped me to start life in New York. He helped me in each of my difficulties, in my every problem. He laughed with me when I laughed. I feel good because I know that he is always there for me. Wherever I live, whatever I do, I know that Warren will be there for me as a best friend. Love, **Taslima**"

With Steve Lacy

Nasrin's plaintive poetry so appealed to Steve Lacy that he wrote "The Cry," music based on her biting words that he turned into what he called a "jam opera," one performed in 1998 in Washington, D.C. He got the idea in September 1994 after reading her "Happy Marriage" in The New Yorker, for he was inspired by Nasrin's outspoken feminism in the face of Islamic anger concerning her writing. The work in progress, which necessitated protecting her from renewed death threats made by Muslim fundamentalists, was presented in Calais, France, in November 1996. An incident-free world premiere was held in Berlin at the Hebbel Theatre in January 1997, followed by performances at the Women's Festival in Palermo, Italy, in March 1997, and later in Geneva, Bordeaux, Vancouver, Washington (the United States premiere), and Chicago.

Time (the Asian edition) described her as "one of the 20 most influential women in the 20th century," and she became noted throughout the world. As of the end of 1999, Nasrin had moved from her hiding place in Sweden to one in Europe. She signed *Humanist Manifesto* 2000.

She has been called "the most dangerous woman in the world," for she is a major spokesperson against patriarchy. If patriarchy were to be disbanded everywhere and males no longer took precedence over females as laid down in their Bible, the vested interests of Judeo-Christian-Muslim groups would be in jeopardy and religion would be replaced by something humanistic and in keeping with the times.

Impact

"Nasrin is a firm supporter of the Universal Declaration of Human Rights]. Although it was adopted 10 December 1948 by member states of the United Nations, she is but one of many critics who are shocked that signatory nations are not living up to the declaration's demands that human rights be strictly afforded to all humans.

The Woman Without a Country

In 2005 Amnesty France nominated her for the Nobel Peace Prize 2005. Although she did not win, in 2004 she won the UNESCO Prize for Tolerance and Non-Violence. She also has won India's Ananda Award; Bangladesh's Natyasava Award; the European Parliament's Sakharov Prize for Freedom of Thought; the French Government's Human Rights Award; Sweden's PEN's Kurt Tucholsky Prize; the Hellman-Hammett Grant from America's Human Rights Watch; Norway's Humanist Award from Human-Etisk Forbund; and the 1994 Freedom From Religion Foundation's Feminist of the Year Award.

In 2009, along with U. S. Senator from New York Kirsten Gillibrand; lawyer at CUNY School of Law Rhonda Copelon, and Editor-in-Chief of the Huffington Post Arianna Huffington, Nasrin was honored by Feminist Press at their 39th Anniversary Gala Reception. She responded to the large group that had assembled:

I would like to express my heartfelt gratitude to the Feminist Press for honoring me along with such eminent personalities.

I have been fighting for women's rights and freedom in those areas where women are still considered slaves, sexual objects, and child-bearing machines. Women are oppressed because of religion, tradition, culture, and customs.

I believe that no woman is free until all women are free. While you and I tonight are celebrating at this gala event, thousands of women right now, in many countries, are getting beaten and raped, are becoming victims of trafficking, and are selling their body only to earn some money to avoid starving to death.

I have witnessed what miserable lives women in poor countries live. In Muslim countries where patriarchy and religion rule supreme, women are not considered as human beings. Animals are treated better. In rich countries too, I have seen women who are second-class citizens even if they are not physically beaten, just psychologically and socially treated as inferiors.

I strongly believe that education and economic freedom alone are not enough for women to be emancipated. We need to separate state and religion in every country. We need secular societies with a uniform civil code based on equality. Without fighting misogyny, we will never be able to free women.

I dream of a beautiful world where no women will be oppressed. Because of my ideals, I have had to pay a heavy price. I have been living in exile for the last 15 years. I have no other option but to live in exile. Probably I will never be able to return to my home. There is no country in this wide world that I can call my home. Do I really have no home? Well, tonight I feel that I have a home. You who are feminists and progressive humanists who believe in freedom of expression are my home. You are my country, my home.

For a Bengali writer it is difficult to survive in the West, but I am grateful to you for the sympathy, support, and solidarity that you have shown to me.

Tonight's honor has made me all the more committed to my, as well as our, cause. My sincere, sincere thanks to all of you.

2004 in Kolkata

Arefin Shams, in "Are They Waiting For The Cascade of Taslima Nasrin?", wrote in *Blit*

She was a wonderful daughter, a beloved sister, a passionate wife and, above all, a woman with a beautiful mind. Since she was a young girl, she possessed an extra ordinary personality. Like the more than 65 percent women of our male dominated society, she also had to accept the fate of being sexually harassed and secret humiliation. And like most of the females, she kept story of her sufferings – a secret. But her revolutionary thoughts and urge to break the evil shackle of society motivated herself entity and finally inspired to pick pen as her strongest weapon. Thus, Taslima Nasrin was born as a true feminist writer of her age. That is how the lone journey of an unbending crusader starts. And the journey has cost her too much to bear in a lifetime.

When we walk down the lane of history, we find similar instances in century's saga where a different tone was never heard over millions, rather was suffocated. In 1593 an Italian philosopher, astrologer named Giordano Bruno for the first time, informed the world that the sun is nothing but just another star and the entire universe is occupied with endless number of planets orbiting other stars. This was an opposite concept to what the Catholic Church had been preaching for long centuries. He became a national villain instantly and was tried for heresy by Roman Inquisition. The framed charges against him included denial of Trinity, denial of divinity of Christ, denial of virginity of Mary. The inquisition declared him guilty of numerous offenses and in year 1600, Giordano Bruno was burnt at the stake. After his tragic death, he has inspired the dedicated philosophers, educationalists, free thinkers over centuries. Today he is called "a martyr of science ". His theory was misunderstood by his own race and contemporaries, but proved to be truth after his demise. 400 years after this brutal murder, in 2000 Pope John Paul 2 formally made a general apology for the deaths of prominent philosophers and scientists due to inquisition. Now let us come to the present era. In the early 19th century, it was a woman from a high class family named Begum Rokeya

Sakhawat Hossain who initiated the revolutionary steps towards female education and empowerment. Ms. Rokeya had to face numerous hurdles marching towards accomplishing her goals and today we salute Begun Rokeya for her contribution to today's status of women education. If Rokeya deserves heroic appreciation, Taslima Nasrin needs to be worshiped by the females of this country for her selfless service to the cause. She cherished her womanhood, defended her identity as a human and unmasked the brutal face of our society. At the very tender age, Taslima experienced sexual teaching by her maternal uncle while at the age of seven she was raped by her uncle. And the breath taking fact is – Taslima's family was a very pious and rather superstitious one. Besides carrying out the mandatory rituals, her mother used to visit Khaja Baba (a Sufi Man) shrine regularly wearing burqa. Moreover, Taslima was born on 12 Rabiul Awal [the birthday of Prophet Mohammed (pbuh)]. This made her a special child to everyone. But even being and treated special, Taslima was never been spared from sexual harassment and corporal punishment. Taslima or no one is against the true spirit of Islam. Actually when someone sees the religious taboo in the name of rituals, when these taboo and rituals are rather being exploited to torture and demean women, he or she becomes revolutionary against the very religion though that whole package is a misinterpretation of fundamental basics of Islam. That exactly happened. Moreover, when as a child , Taslima was regularly subjected to corporal punishment by her mother now and them. These all hugely affected the child psychology of Taslima and created a lifetime dent in her soul.

The sexual abuse of our females in society at various stages of their life vigorously continuing till date but thanks to Sir Frank Peters for rescuing the nation from the curse of random corporal punishment. He carried out the crucial task of creating social awareness in this regard. Should Bangladesh not be blessed with the presence of Sir Frank Peters, this society might have produced many Taslima Nasrin in future.

Till today the endless number of critics criticized Taslima but never did anyone talked about the pain and Sorrow reflected through the true incidents she had to witness or come across. So, speaking her mind truthfully was possibly her biggest mistake. All male vocals, Mullahs stared accusing Taslima with their velour, making a simple hearted, open minded writer to be the most controversial one. I am not going to enlighten my readers about the literary quality of Taslima's "KO", "Amar Meye Bela" (my girlhood) or any other piece. But what did she write which turned her being such infamous writer? As I said before, in the process of her narration in write ups, she told the truth about her suffering as a girl, as a young lady, as a woman. Eventually, the other side of many people's life came up under the lime light. And a coordinated hate campaign spread like a frenzy. Some people says, Taslima did chase fame. If it is true, then why she published her book "Amar Meye Bela" in 1999, long after being well known? As I said, these are the part of the propaganda by a hate mongering quarter. Don't we condemn the death of atheist poet Humayun Azad? And the present Sheikh Hasina government even conferred Ferdousi Priyovashini with country's one of the highest recognitions named "Ekushey padak" (the honor of 21) for her public confession, declaring herself a Birangana (dishonored) in the 1971 war. Then why a woman like Taslima should be barred from entering her motherland just because of her ideology? Prime Minister Hasina wants to project Bangladesh as a role model of women empowerment. She has already made a non political non elected woman as speaker of the parliament, a political bi-product non elected woman as the leader of the opposition in the parliament. And yet she completely forgets even to utter the name of Taslima Nasrin! Why the entire Bangladeshi nation looks so vengeful? Something like we saw in the so called "Gono Jagoron Mancha" (platform of the mass movement) where the kids to senior citizens, all chanted the slogan for "Death Penalty" irrespective of the person and their conviction. And please note, it was Taslima Nasrin decades before who first wrote demanding the trial of war criminals. Whereas today, in the era of women empowerment and domination, Taslima still lives the pathetic lonely life in exile. And yet none in Bangladesh remembers her.

Before writing this article, I have researched on Taslima Nasrin for quite a long time. I came across an exceptional fact- all three of the men who happened to marry Taslima, became celebrity. Rudra Mohammad Shahidullah, Minar mahmud amd Naimul Islam Khan, All succeeded brilliantly in their professional life after Taslima's appearance in their personal life. So, Taslima's personality is like the touchstone which miraculously transforms someone. If any of her divorces has hurt her much, it was all. But she never attempted to spread hatred against her husbands after the divorce nor did she went to the court. Her husband Naimul Islam Khan must be credited most for the boost of Taslima's career as a writer as he gave a strong platform to Taslima in his daily newspaper "Bhorer Kagoj" (the morning paper). More tragically, two of her three ex husbands committed suicide after their divorce with Taslima. Possibly, the absence of Taslima's magical personality in their personal lives affected them badly.

When the infamous Qaumi Madrasa based radical political front "Hefajot-e-Islam" started massive campaign asking for meeting their 13 points demands to establish Sharia Law, everybody suddenly woke up. Huge demonstration led by women leaders attended by thousands of women took place where the women leaders accused the Hefajot and their demands as insanity. They claimed that Hefajot Leaders were trying to send women status back to the Stone Age. It seemed to me, the shadow of Taslima was everywhere in that demonstration. They talked in the tone of Taslima. And that Hefajot leader Shah Ahmed Shafi? Even after committing so many controversial acts, being termed as "turmeric hujur", at first becoming state level enemy and then govt's friend, Mr. Shafi is still at large with his even larger mouthpiece. Nobody demands to hang him, to punish him or forcing him to exile. If Taslima did a "crime" just narrating her sufferings through pen, then what this Ahmed Shafi has committed? Shouldn't he be forced to have a voyage to the moon as exile in that case? But no, it's male dominated society. Only women like Taslima have no place here. Few years back, I had an opportunity to interact the Blitz Editor, Mr. Salah Uddin Shoaib Choudhury. Whenever any issue related to Taslima came up, the editor was highly appreciating her, as he was her biggest fan. And every time with good reasons and justifications he was saying "If Shirin Ebadi can get the Nobel prize, why not our own Taslima?"

The limbos in our cultural arena are surprisingly remaining tight-lipped on Taslima's home returning issue, possibly to delight any coterie interest. Probably the band of secularists- actually I Should call them mock secularists, are waiting to give a grand farewell to Taslima's dead body. The govt. of Sheikh Hasina surely is waiting impatiently to receive the cascade of Taslima Nasrin, wrap it with national flag and floral wreath and bid her a painful "Home Coming ".

Before I conclude my article, let me remind you that martyr of science Mr. Giordano Bruno's fate. Like his case, shall we have to wait for 400 years to say Sorry to Taslima's ashes? The answer is only known to the priests of our social inquisition.

The writer is a graduate of National University, Bangladesh and presently serving abroad. He is an analyst on local and international issues. E-mail: arefinshams81@gmail.com

Ms. Nasrin spoke in Alexandria, Virginia, at the Women in Secularism conference, 16-18 May 2014.

Nimitz, Chester Jr. and Joan

Nimitz, who became President of Perkin-Elmer, was an officer and submarine commander during World War II and the Korean War. He distinguished himself on a number of occasions and was three times awarded the Silver Star for valor.

Nimitz was born to Chester William Nimitz Sr. and Catherine Vance (née Freeman) Nimitz at the Brooklyn Navy Yard Hospital in Brooklyn, New York, while the couple, with their daughter Catherine Vance "Kate" (born the year before), lived at 415 Washington Avenue, Brooklyn, and Nimitz Sr. was working on the *USS Maumee* at the Brooklyn Navy Yard. He attended the United States Naval Academy at Annapolis, Maryland, graduating with the class of 1936.

On 18 June 1938 Nimitz Jr. married married Joan Leona Labern at the Mare Island Shipyard. She was born in León, Nicaragua, in 1912 to British parents, William Oscar Stonewall and Frances Mary (née Wells) Labern. With her parents she returned to England at the outbreak of World War I in 1914, and was raised in England. Joan came to the United States in 1938 to study dentistry at the University of California Dental School in San Francisco, and met Chester at a cocktail party at Mare Island. She would make news in 1944 when she failed her test to become a United States citizen; two days later she did become a citizen of the U.S.

The couple had three daughters, Frances Mary, Elizabeth "Betsy" Joan, and Sarah Catherine.

Chester Nimitz Jr. retired from the Navy as Rear Admiral in 1957. He joined Texas Instruments, and spent four years there. He later joined Perkin-Elmer Corporation, a manufacturer of scientific instruments based in Norwalk, Connecticut. He became president, chief-executive-officer (CEO) and a director in 1965. In 1969, he was elected Chairman of the Board, serving until retirement in 1980. Also, he was an Honorary Trustee and Honorary Member of the Corporation of the Woods Hole Oceanographic Institution.

The health of Chester and his wife, Joan, deteriorated in later years. Joan was blind, and Chester had lost thirty pounds on account of a prolonged stomach disorder. He also suffered from congestive heart failure.

On 2 January 2002, Chester Nimitz Jr. committed suicide with his wife Joan by ingesting a quantity of sleeping pills in their home at a retirement residence in Needham, Massachusetts. He left a note stating:

> Our decision was made over a considerable period of time and was not carried out in acute desperation. Nor is it the expression of a mental illness. We have consciously, rationally, deliberately and of our own free will taken measures to end our lives today because of the physical limitations on our quality of life placed upon us by age, failing vision, osteoporosis, back and painful orthopedic problems.

Elizabeth Joan, one of Admiral Chester Nimitz Jr.'s two daughters, found the following by the present author on Facebook about her grandfather:

When invited for dinner at my New Canaan High School student Betsy Nimitz's home, I sat across the table from Admiral Chester Nimitz Jr.'s wife and next to Admiral Chester Nimitz Sr.'s wife. When I told my seat-mate that I had been a chief clerk in Reims at SHAEF from 1944 to 1945, down the hall from Ike's office in the Little Red Schoolhouse where Supreme Headquarters was housed and where on 7 May 1945 Nazi commander Alfred Jodl signed the unconditional surrender papers as the representative of Karl Dönitz, Mrs. Nimitz asked where I was from originally. She laughed when she heard I came from near Boone, where Eisenhower's wife Mamie was born in Iowa, saying, "Chester [Sr.] wanted me to come by railroad, not by train, from the East to the West Coast and specifically said I should get off just before I got to the Mississippi River." I asked why, and she laughed, "Oh, he said I wouldn't be able to order and drink alcohol while passing through the dry state of Iowa."

Because he showed such interest in his daughters' newly constructed high school, I invited Admiral Chester Nimitz Jr. to tour the place after the school buses had departed. He was eager to see the new facilities, from the administrative offices to the cafeteria to the physical education department and to the rooms where the academic subjects were taught. When first I called him Admiral, he said just call him Chester and laughed that when he was discharged he had no idea how to get employed and for a time worked at a gasoline station. The observatory was not yet finished, but he remarked that he would like to take an elementary course in astronomy there. The basketball court was big, and he estimated how many could fit in the room. Seeing a big kitchen, he asked, "Is this room called the mess hall?" But he knew the answer. He liked the huge auditorium, the art department, and the place where students could learn about car repairs. He visited one of the toilets once I made sure no students were inside, and he marveled at the new building in which his daughters would be studying.

Finally, I showed him where they would study English. Many of the rooms were complete with a television set over which social studies, English, and other rooms could be shown the same programs. When two students entered my room and consulted the electronic device used by my Adam Smith class to obtain stock quotations of Wall Street corporations, I explained that those in the class or club could come and go throughout the day. They kept track of their stocks and could not buy after the exchange closed, prices had to be verified using copies of *The New York Times* that arrived an hour before classes began, they could use butterfly straddles as well as sell short, but they could not trade in any issues in which their parents has a direct interest. The class taught about investing, banking, law enforcement, taxation, as well as government. Chester asked a student who came in if he could sell PKI (Perkin-Elmer) short and was not at all happy that the boy explained he could, even naked short-sell if the price was in print and it passed the SEC's "tic-test." Although intrigued with the device that plugged in the wall and was paid for by profits made from selling the morning *Times* to faculty members, Chester left somewhat irate concerning my teaching about short-selling despite my telling him that his daughters if they joined the class or club would not be allowed to trade PKI but would have to comply with SEC rules.

Joan and Chester Nimitz are buried at Pleasant Hill Cemetery in Wellfleet, Massachusetts.

Ollendorff, Ilse

Ollendorff (1909 - 19 December 2008), who taught German at New Canaan High School, was the Quaker (Religious Society of Friends) wife of controversial Dr. Wilhelm Reich, the Austrian-American psychiatrist and psychoanalyst, inventor of the orgone box, a one-time member of the Communist Party.

Sexologist Wilhelm Reich with his wife Ilse and their son Peter

Ollendorff, who was Wilhelm Reich's third wife, served as his secretary and laboratory assistant for many years. They had one son, Peter, author of *A Book of Dreams*, a memoir about the close relationship he had with his father, how they would go cloudbusting together, his bewilderment when his father died in prison when Peter was 13 years old.

Ollendorff wrote *Wilhelm Reich: A Personal Biography*, which was a measured description of the scientist she knew so well, one thought to be mad by some and a savior by others.

Following is information about the Reichs in Philosopedia:

Ilse Ollendorff was Wilhelm's third wife. They married in 1946 and divorced in 1951. His first wife, Annie Pink (a psychiatrist he married in 1924 and divorced in 1934), was a former patient. He accused Annie of driving away their two daughters (Eva, born 1924, and Lore, born 1928) by poisoning them against him. His second wife was Elsa Lindenberg, a dancer with whom he had an open marriage from 1933 until their divorce in 1939.

Ilse, who was the mother of Reich's son, Peter (born 1944), wrote *Wilhelm Reich, A Personal Biography* (1969), which was published while she was a teacher of German at New Canaan, High School. Until the book became available, few faculty members knew of her having been married to the controversial sexologist.

Reich, who was born in Dobrzcynica (Dobzau), Galicia, Austria-Hungary. was the son of Leon Reich (who died of pneumonia in 1914) and Cecilie Reich (who died in 1910 during a second suicide attempt). He became a noted as well as controversial psychoanalyst. He received his M.D. at the University of Vienna in 1922.

During World War I, he served from 1915 to 1918 in the Austrian infantry.

A student of Freud, he developed his own theories of neurosis, including a concept about "character armoring" and another about the centrality of "genital" potency. Because of this, and of his radical politics, he was expelled from the International Psychoanalytic Association. The German Communist Party also expelled him, because of his "Trotskyite" book *The Mass Psychology of Fascism* (1933). Moving to the United States he was jailed for several weeks, suspected of being a possible German spy. However, he was one of the first leftists to see the weaknesses of Soviet Marxism, and he developed a following in the 1940s that considered him a genius.

Of the famed Austrian psychiatrist who was hostile to religion, Ollendorff wrote in Philosopedia concerning her ex-husband after his death:

> Reich never belonged to any organized religious community and, until the time he went to prison, he never went to any kind of religious services. I don't know what he would have called himself, probably an agnostic or a humanist. His funeral was secular. He identified with Christ/Jesus the human, and I think he accepted not the Christianity of the Church but the teachings of Jesus. Dr. Elsworth Baker, who in my book was named as the person who gave a brief eulogy at the memorial service and ended with Reich's version of the Lord's Prayer from his *Murder of Christ*, was a psychiatrist who practiced Reich's orgone therapy. He was a devoted "disciple" of Reich, and he organized after Reich's death a group of orgone therapists into the "College of Orgonomy," feuding with all those who in their own way believed they were the only true followers. Baker died a few years ago.

Reich's version of the Lord's Prayer is only different from the original in the start: "Our Love / Life, who art from Heaven," and he substituted "guilt" for debts and in the last two lines "and lead us not into distortion of love, but deliver us from our perversions." He mentions "God-Father is the basic cosmic energy from which all being stems, and which streams through (the) body as through anything else in existence." *Murder of Christ* was written in 1952.

"I don't know," continued Ilse, herself a Quaker, whether he distinguished between Christ the supernatural and Jesus the natural. "I do think that the concept of Christ was for him a universal concept, continuing through the ages, but that Jesus was for him the natural, exceptional human being who, because of his message of love and his understanding of human nature, had to be murdered. I do know that during his imprisonment and until shortly before his death he attended the Protestant services in prison. He sent our son Peter some prayers that he must have found in those services. This 'conversion' seemed to me utterly strange, almost unbelievable in view of his past anti-church attitude. I had, of course, no way to find out why and how this change came about."

In Reich's Federal Bureau of Investigation 12/9/41 file telling of his "custodial detention" by FBI agents and a New York City detective of the 112th Precinct, Reich was brought to his home at 9906 69th Avenue, Forest Hills, Long Island, New York, to the Office of the New York Field Division where he was fingerprinted and photographed.

There, he stated to a special agent "that he was not actually married to Ilse Ollendorf, but that he did reside with her as man and wife, considering her his common law wife." He was described as being 44, male, white, very ruddy complexion, brown eyes, gray hair, 5' 9½" height, 158 lbs. weight, stocky build, Jewish race [sic], Austrian nationality, born Dobzownice, Austria, March 24, 1897, Alien Registration Number 4505146.

Miss Ollendorf was said by Miss Carol Bernard as having helped her secure an $80/month job with Dr. Reich and that after nine months assisting as a technician in his laboratory credited him as being "the best employer that she had ever worked for, that he made her feel as though she were working with him rather than for him." The agents then listed the titles of the 1000 or so books he had. Wrote one agent, Reich "claimed to be of Jewish descent [sic] but advised that he was not of the Jewish religion, stating that he has no religion."

Selected Books:

Die Funktion des Orgasmus (1927); trans., rev. ed. *Genitality* (1980)
Charakteranalyse (1933); trans., 3rd, enlarged ed. *Character Analysis* (1949)
Die Massenpsychologie des Faschismus (1933); trans., rev. ed. *The Mass Psychology of Fascism* (1946)
Die Sexualität im Kulturkampf (1936); trans., rev. ed. *The Sexual Revolution* (1945)
Die Bione (1938); trans. *The Bion Experiments on the Origin of Life* (1979)
The Function of the Orgasm (1942) a "scientific autobiography", no translation of the 1927 book
The Cancer Biopathy (1948)
Listen, Little Man! (1948)
Ether, God and Devil (1951)
Cosmic Superimposition (1951)
People in Trouble (1953)
The Murder of Christ (1953)
Contact with Space (1957)

Packard, Vance

Packard (22 May 1914 - 12 December 1996), a social critic, journalist, and author, was born in Granville Summit, Pennsylvania. He was one of three children of Philip Joseph and Mabel Case Packard. His father worked for Penn State as a superintendent of the college farm.

Following is his entry in Philosopedia:

> On 15 November 1938, Packard married Mamie Virginia Mathews, and they had three children: Vance Philip (born 20 April 42, an archaeologist who retired in 1997 as curator, museum director, and regional director of the Pennsylvania Historical and Museum Commission); Randall Mathews (born 30 May 1945, a historian at Johns Hopkins); and Cynthia Ann (born 5 April 1948, an author and artist). Mrs. Packard taught art in the Darien Public School system in the 1950s.
>
> He received his B.A. at Pennsylvania State University in 1936; his M.S. at Columbia University in 1937; and his Litt. D. at Monmouth College in 1975.
>
> Packard started in 1936 as a reporter for the *Centre Daily Times*, State College, Pennsylvania; became a columnist for the *Boston Record* in 1937-1938; was a writer and editor for Associated Press Feature Service, 1938 - 1941; an editor and staff writer for *American* 1942-1956; and a staff writer for *Collier's* in 1956. From 1941 to 1944, he lectured, reported, and wrote at Columbia University; from 1945 to 1957, he was employed by New York University; and he was a guest lecturer in 18 countries and at several hundred American colleges and universities.

Packard wrote numerous books, but the first to gain international recognition was *The Hidden Persuaders*.

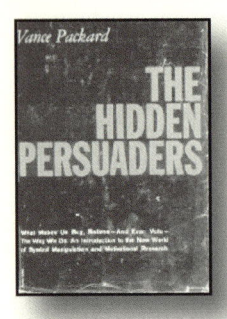

1946 *How to Pick a Mate* – a guide co-authored with Clifford R. Adams, the head of the Penn State's marriage counseling service
1950 *Animal IQ* – a popular paperback on animal intelligence
1957 *The Hidden Persuaders* – a prescient work explaining how advertisers use psychological methods to "persuade" us to buy products, whether or not we really need them
1959 *The Status Seekers* – a work that describes American social stratification and behavior
1960 *The Waste Makers* – a critical study showing how manufacturers plan their products' obsolescence
1962 *The Pyramid Climbers* – a study of how workers and executives conform in order to advance
1964 *The Naked Society* – information as to how computerized programs provide a threat to privacy
1968 *The Sexual Wilderness* – a work describing how male-female relationships changed during the sexual revolution of the 1960s
1972 *A Nation of Strangers* – because of the frequent geographical transfers of corporate executives, employees and corporate heads have become less aware of each other
1977 *The People Shapers* – on the use of psychological and biological testing and experimentation to manipulate human behavior
1983 *Our Endangered Children* – discusses growing up in a changing world, warning that American preoccupation with money, power, status, and sex, ignore the needs of future generations
1989 *Ultra Rich: How Much Is Too Much?* – by interviewing 30 of America's wealthiest men, Packard describes how the rich are different from the rest of us; he proposes a ceiling on transfers of great fortunes and a reworking of tax laws.

Packard lived at 87 Mill Road, New Canaan, Connecticut, and he had a summer home on Martha's Vineyard in Massachusetts.

His activities included the following:

>Member of the New Canaan Planning Commission, 1954-1956
>President, Chappaquiddick Island Association, 1977-1978
>Member of the National Board of the National Book Committee

> Trustee of the Silvermine College of Art in New Canaan
>
> He was the recipient of the Distinguished Alumni Award, Pennsylvania State University, 1961
>
> Outstanding Alumni Award, the Graduate School of Journalism, Columbia University, 1963
>
> He was member of the Society of Magazine Writers (President, 1961)

Vance Packard Jr., one of the present author's students, was required to put onto paper an incident that had just happened in 1960: "Mr. Smith demanded that I give him my yoyo – for no apparent cause – I felt that he did not have the right to confiscate it. America insures that no man may be deprived of life, limb, or property. My reason for this is that the Constitution of the United States says thus. I feel that Mr. Smith was not within his rights to demand my yo-yo." Later, over martinis, his dad and the teacher had a good time discussing teenagers.

Packard was not an active member of any of the organized religious denominations. His daughter Cindy, asked about her father's views, responded,

> My father was not a Congregationalist at all. He rarely attended in New Canaan and, when he did, mortified us with his singing. I'd say he was closest to the Unitarian Universalist mindset, believing in the interdependent web. We had a long conversation late one night when he thought he was dying.
>
> You might want to read Daniel Horowitz' *Vance Packard and American Social Criticism*. It's fairly accurate. As for naming his books, my father was obsessed by titles. He gave each possible title its own index card. Anyone entering the house, from friend to repairman, was handed a set of index cards and asked to rate them.
>
> One of my father's most devious legacies was the Packard Family Realty Trust. While still alive, he gave the big house on the Vineyard to his three children AND their spouses. King Lear meets Dr. Phil. Getting six people to agree on anything is rather like moving a 14 foot cube of jello with a spoon. I'm very close to Randy. Vance is still barbed wire wrapped around marshmallow. Still, we muddle on. And there have been no divorces, which I suspect was what he intended. (e-mail 2 Jan 2008)

Packard died in 1996 at his summer home on Martha's Vineyard in Massachusetts. His cremated ashes were scattered.

Peyton, Tanden

In *Cruising the Deuce*, I describe seeing about six or more who had surrounded a tall person in the extreme darkness of the 14th Street gay Metropolitan Theater, a person who was in the middle of them all. When he left and started feeling for his wallet, I volunteered to hold the exit door open to let light in the area where he'd been, but he found nothing.

I then accompanied him to the men's room to see if his wallet had been discarded in a waste receptacle. Finding nothing, I lent him subway fare in order that he could get home. When he phoned the next day and thanked me and we met, I learned that he was an actor (Tanden Peyton) who had won an Obie and was brother of one of Chicago's best-known football stars, 6' 7" 270-pound **Bubba Smith**. He asked me to help file his taxes (he was a public school teacher using the name **John Smith**). His death certificate listed Jack and Lula English Smith as **Jesse Smith**'s parents, and he was buried in the Lacey (Arkansas) Cemetery 31 August 1986.

When he died of AIDS I helped arrange a memorial where he lived at Manhattan Plaza on 42nd Street. In attendance was his mother and a young nephew, who spoke about how religious his uncle had been, how terrible that his uncle had been accused of being gay, and how he wanted to grow up and be just like his uncle. Gay actors including The Wiz's **Jimmy Justice** sang (I played the piano. We had no time to rehearse), and we kept the truth from the nephew, the deceased's mother, and cousins, all of whom may not even have known that the deceased was also a public school teacher.

Piola, Reyna

In Montevideo, Uruguay, when Mrs. Piola divorced, she brought her daughter Monica and her son Guillermo (Bill) to New Canaan, where she was hired as a Spanish teacher

In 1957, both children were in my classes, and when they invited me home for a Sunday evening dinner I agreed and the occasion became a weekly event. Reyna made instant coffee by placing the desired amount of coffee powder in the cup, then stirred it with a small amount of water until it became syrupy, then added hot water. After the tasty dinners, we watched the Ed Sullivan TV show, which gave the siblings a chance to differ in their judging of the musical acts. I stayed neutral.

I also became like a surrogate dad at a time when they needed one, and when they heard about sons #1 (Fantuzzi) and #2 (Gabriel) – who "adopted" me as their surrogate dad – Guillermo became son #3 and Monica became daughter #1. At New Canaan High School, however, they were just members of my classes. At home, I was the one who checked their homework, gave advice, and was like their dad.

Guillermo Methol, NCHS Class of '58, wrote 29 October 2011:

> WOW, HAVE A FANTASTIC 90th BIRTHDAY!!!!!   Amazing. . . . As the philosopher I'm not, I ask, "What happened"? I, like you, feel the same as I did when I first met you, in that English class, at New Canaan High School in 1964-65! At first I was scared of you because my English wasn't that good; then, I was unhappy with you because you were too demanding and expected "too much" from me, and then I loved you because you were so warm, caring, generous with your time and your knowledge, patient, and most of all, a GREAT FRIEND OF OUR FAMILY! I SO LOOKED FORWARD to our Sunday TV dinners at my house! I'll never forget our trip to Rippey and Perry, Iowa, the breakfast at that lady's farm (historian Priscilla Robertson's, in Kentucky), the MGB you trusted me to drive for a weekend while you were in New York! What incredibly wonderful memories and defining moments of my youth! And, most importantly, as time went by and I grew up and matured, your "expectations" and my efforts to meet them have helped me so much throughout my adult life!
> Thank you Warren. In spite of the fact that I did not stay in touch with you on a regular basis, you made a positive difference in my life and continue to be an example of how to live life to the fullest!
>
> Unfortunately, I won't be there on the 6th. The good news is that I plan to be there on November 12-13-14 with my new young wife (Linda) and hope that we can spend some time together. I have spoken of you so much she can't wait to meet you. I don't know if I'll be able to handle the emotion, but I can't imagine being in NY and not seeing you. Please let me know how we can schedule. I'll contact you in the next couple of weeks and give you more details on our itinerary. Have a wonderful party and I'll be there in spirit!
>
> (30 October 2011) By the way, from Texas I returned to Uruguay and was with my father for the last six months of his life – he died November 11, 2009. Yes,

you left the car with me and you went to NY. My mother was so nervous it was ridiculous. Other than a couple of sudden take offs and a couple of fast curves around the New Canaan countryside, I was so scared that something would happen to it that I actually took very good care of it.

I also just remember a restaurant that you took the whole family to whose image has stayed with me but can't remember the name. It was something like Mill or Pond, or Millpond, but I remember we had dinner outside and there was a creek and beautiful flowers and trees and shrubs all around us. It was beautiful. [The Silvermine Tavern Bed & Breakfast, that was built in 1829]

We are just going for a visit and to show Linda a little about my youth. We plan to take the train to Stamford, rent a car, and drive to New Canaan, Hartford, and drive around and visit all the places I've been. It will be quite nostalgic. Love, Guillermo

Methol, Mónica – Daughter #1; NCHS Class of '57; now a retired teacher in Uruguay

[

26 October 2011] It's actually the 26th, which my computer shows. 6+2 is the same as 2+6. So you see, I'm getting younger (like you....).

Kisses, Monica
8 de Julio 925/802
11100 Montevideo Uruguay

Powell, Mel [Melvin Epstein]

Born in The Bronx to Russian Jewish parents Milton and Mildred Mark Epstein, Melvin (who changed his last name to Powell in 1940) was a jazz pianist as well as a composer of classical music.

Powell (12 February 1923 - 24 April 1998) began playing piano as a child and by 1939 was already working with Bobby Hackett, George Brunies, and Zutty Singleton. He played, composed, and arranged for Benny Goodman in 1941 and 1942; was a member of Glenn Miller's Army Air Force Band in 1943 -1945; and in movies played with other jazz musicians such as Louis Armstrong.

After the war, he married actor Martha Scott in the mid-1940s and their daughter Mary was a student at New Canaan High School. Her English teacher, I allowed students to earn more than one grade for a class project. I gave extra credit for her making 2-track tapes, one track of which was for the student's creative writing, and on the other track some kind of sound effects or music had to be added. Mary composed the words and music for her own song, performed with her guitar using a tape recorder in her class, then recorded her in my New York recording studio at which she received a 45 rpm acetate demo that singer Peggy Lee (her godmother) bought. "It was like getting 4 A's for one assignment!" she exclaimed at the time.

At Yale University, Powell studied with Paul Hindemith and became a member of Yale's composition faculty from 1958 to 1969. In Valencia, California, in 1969, he became the founding dean of the California Institute of the Arts, receiving the Pulitzer Prize in Music for *Duplicates*, a concerto for two pianos and orchestra.

Powell at age 75 died of liver cancer in Sherman Oaks, California, and is buried at the Jamesport Masonic Cemetery, Jamesport, Missouri.

Price, Gilbert

In my autobiography, here is how the teacher met paramour #2:

> The client was early, or at least I had not heard anyone enter the recording studio that morning. What sounded like a fat old opera singer in Studio A turned out to be a personable young black chap whose voice had a timbre that reminded me of **Paul Robeson**'s. We made small talk. I learned that he had toured with **Harry Belafonte's** group from 1961 to 1962, he had come early to be a backup singer for someone, he said he wanted an acting career, and he added that he was going to be in an off-Broadway play, **Langston Hughes**'s *Jericho-Jim Crow*.
>
> "Come see the play," he said, telling me where and when it would open. (I knew about Hughes but not about the play's directors, **Alvin Ailey** and **William Hairston**. Nor did I know about The Sanctuary, a little theater in the basement of a white Presbyterian church at 143 West 13th Street, near the old St. Vincent's Hospital on 7th Avenue.) "Come see my play," he asked again, adding that I could bring a friend (implying that he wondered if I had a companion or wife).
>
> I decided to do just that but, I must confess, I was as interested in knowing more about him as I was in seeing the play. It was not characteristic of me to invite a non-paying client to visit me at the studio where I'd be his accompanist on the piano if there were no sessions booked . . . and we could be alone.

He telephoned not long afterwards. I suggested an early morning meeting when the studio was not booked, he arrived on time, and I found "Old Man River" was an easy song we both knew. He was like a little boy as we rehearsed for a possible recording.

I easily found his key: E-flat.

Although I was not aware, he found the key to what I was thinking.

He was Hughes's protégé, but he had no agent, no accompanist, no contacts, and when he told me *Life* was going to photograph him and he didn't know what to wear, I asked if my new sweater would do. It did.

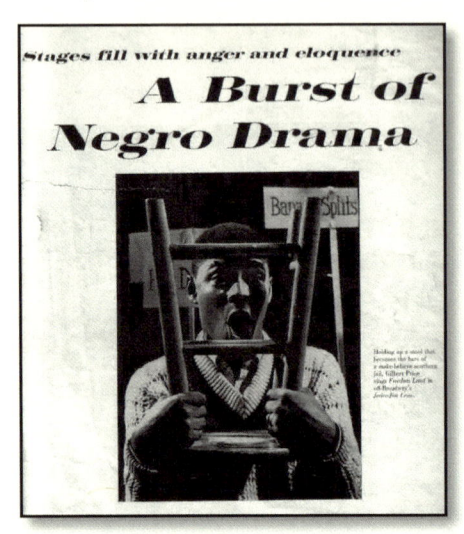

He began spending as much time as he could with me at the studio. On one occasion he jumped up on the Wurlitzer church organ and, once I turned it on, he just departed the physical world and, like a kid pretending to fly an airplane while sitting on a chair, he banged out un-melodic sounds, slipping up onto the upper register to hear how those keys sounded different.

I decided I'd start with 1-4-5 chords, so I placed his finger on a C, then up to an F, up to a G, and back down to C. He repeated this easily. Now I tried a full chord with three fingers: CEG, FAC, GBD, and back to CEG. This he had trouble repeating, so while standing behind him as he sat on the organ bench, with my left hand I played C, while with my right a CEG, then on to an F paired with an FAC, then on to the GBD triad and back to the CEG.

"Know any hymns that use this 1-4-5 pattern of chords?" I asked.

But he couldn't repeat, so now I placed my fingers right above his, and we went through the exercise 3, 4, and 5 times. At some point, he turned around to look me in the eyes and he backed into my arms which were already around him from in back.

If this had been a scene on Broadway, violin music would have slowly increased and ended with a crescendo when our lips met.

In Philosopedia, I wrote the following.

Gilbert Price (10 September 1942 - 2 January 1991)

Price was an American baritone and actor who was one of Langston Hughes's protégés. His first starring role was in Hughes's *Jericho-Jim Crow* (1964), for which he won a Theatre World Award.

He was born in New York City to Leon and Carmen Price, who were nominal Protestants. His father had had some experience in show business, having worked with Redd Foxx as a comic. His mother's mother, whose Caribbean accent Gilbert could imitate accurately, was from St. Kitts. For years, Gilbert thought that "Granny" was from a country in Africa.

The Prices had two other children, Jeanette (Stargill) and Stanley.

When the parents separated, Leon moved to Charlotte, North Carolina, where after his wife died he had three other children with Virginia Patterson Price: a daughter, Tracy Michelle, and two sons, Mark Leon and Don Vincent.

Gilbert Price was educated first in New York City public schools, but he transferred to a Catholic elementary school, his mother believing he would get a stricter education with nuns as teachers. In the elementary school, he converted to Catholicism.

As a teenager, however, he was educated at Erasmus Hall High School in Brooklyn and became a lead singer in their choir, a member of which was Barbra Streisand.

Contents

1 Fly Blackbird (1962)
2 Jericho-Jim Crow (1964)
3 The Roar of the Greasepaint - The Smell of the Crowd (1965)
4 Promenade (1969)
5 Mass (1971)
6 Lost in the Stars (1972)
7 The Night That Made America Famous (1975)
8 1600 Pennsylvania Avenue (1976)
9 Timbuktu (1978)
10 Trivia
11 Final Days

12 External Links
13 You Tube Clips
14 Fly Blackbird (1962)

Gershon Kingsley, the play's conductor, hired Price to sing in the play that premiered 5 February 1962.

Jericho-Jim Crow (1964)

In 1964, the 21-year-old Price starred in a Langston Hughes play, *Jericho-Jim Crow*, which was performed at the Sanctuary Theatre in Greenwich Village for 32 performances.

Price received a Theatre World Award and was featured in a *Life"* article, *"Stages Fill With Anger and Eloquence, A Burst of Negro Drama."* Richard F. Shepard, in *The New York Times*, described the play's depiction of the Negro struggle up from slavery. The book was by William Hairston and Langston Hughes].

The Roar of the Greasepaint - The Smell of the Crowd (1965)

When Anthony Newley was casting for *Roar* upstairs in the Variety Arts Building at 225 West 46th Street in Manhattan, actors at the "cattle call" were given material to speak or sing.

Price got a copy of "Feelin' Good" and raced downstairs to my recording studio, who recalls that

> I cleared Studio A and helped him prep by accompanying him on the piano. We weren't sure whether "Feelin' Good" was going to be a fast or a slow number, but we ran through the song several times, he ran back upstairs, and when he sang Newley exclaimed that he had not been looking for a black, had not wanted a baritone, had not wanted a person of Gil's size, "but you've got the greatest fucking voice I've ever heard!" And Gil got the job. I was the first American to play Newley's song on a piano, I kept telling myself.

The other songs in the play were "Who Can I Turn To (When Nobody Needs Me)?", "A Wonderful Day Like Today," "It Isn't Enough," "Where Would You Be Without Me," "My First Love Song," "Nothing Can Stop Me Now," and "Sweet Beginning."

In London, the play starring Norman Wisdom was not successful. In New York City, Newley performed the role of Cocky, who plays by the rules in life, and Sir (played by Cyril Ritchard), was the one who ignores rules and lives life as he chooses. It ran for 232 performances after opening on 16 May 1965.

Promenade (1969)

Price sang several songs in *Promenade's* chorus: "The Clothes Make the Man"; "The Cigarette Song"; "Two Little Angels"; "Crown Me"; and "All Is Well in the City."

The play was a collaboration of Reverend Al Carmines and Maria Irene Fornes and starred Alikce Playten, Shannon Bolin, and Florence Tarlow. Madeline Kahn was one of the original cast members but left before the cast album was recorded.

It featured Ty McConnell and Price as Prisoners 105 and 106. They escape for a better life, then encounter a variety of unpleasant people.

Mass (1971)

Gilbert performed at Leonard Bernstein's request either at the opening on 8 Sept 1971 at the John F. Kennedy Center for the Performing Arts or in California, or both.

Lost in the Stars (1972)

The play opened as a revival at the Music Box Theater on 30 October 1949 and closed after 273 performances on 1 July 1950. Maxwell Anderson wrote the lyrics to music by Kurt Weill, based on Alan Paton's *Cry, the Beloved Country*.

Price, playing the role of Absalom Kumalo, joked that this allowed him to "die 6 evening and 2 matinee performances per week."

The Night That Made America Famous (1975)

As one of the performers, along with Harry Chapin, Mercedes Ellington, and Delores Hall, Price sang the Harry Chapin lyrics and music at the Ethel Barrymore Theater.

Price received the 1975 Drama Desk Award for Outstanding Featured Actor in a Musical. He also was nominated for the 1975 Tony Award for Best Featured Actor in a Musical.

1600 Pennsylvania Avenue (1976)

Price played the role of Lud in the play that previewed 21 April 1976 and only had 20 performances. His friend, George Faison was co-director with Gilbert Moses. The book and lyrics were by Alan Jay Lerner, and the music was by Leonard Bernstein.

The play flopped, after out-of-town tryouts in Philadelphia and Washington, DC. Critics generally praised Bernstein's score but savaged Lerner's book.

The plot, which was about the White House, showed President and Mrs. John Adams moving in but hiring Lud as the person in charge of the place. When

Thomas Jefferson is elected, the Adamses move but Lud stays. President after elected President arrive, and Lud remains. Eventually, his son takes over. Primarily about race relations, the play mentions Jefferson's alleged affair with a black maid, James Monroe's refusal to halt slavery in Washington, and the problems after the Civil War when Andrew Johnson is impeached.

Timbuktu (1978)

Price starred as the handsome Prince of the Realm, Kasa, The Mansa of Mali in the musical produced by Luther Davis that was directed and choreographed by Geoffrey Holder. It opened 1 March 1978 and closed 10 September 1978 after 243 performances. Set to music by Alexander Borodin, George Forrest, and Robert Wright, the musical comedy was based on "Kismet" by Charles Lederer and Luther Davis.

Timbuktu! was a musical fable based on *Kismet* but in a West African setting, the city of Timbuktu. Fate plays a big part in the story of how Price, the prince, rose to be the king.

Eartha Kitt made a grand entrance, carried on the shoulders of a handsome and muscular former Mr. Universe, Joe Lynn. Amid all the pomp and circumstance, she purred and brought the house down with, "Anything new in town?"

Melba Moore and Ira Hawkins rounded out the cast, Moore in the role of a possible lover for the prince.

Price was a 1978 Tony Award nominee for Best Actor in a Musical, his 4th such nomination. He sang "Stranger in Paradise," "Night of My Nights," "And This Is My Beloved," songs that were familiar to many in the audience. Those in the musical cognoscenti heard a voice with the timbre of a Paul Robeson, something they did not hear from singers Kitt and Moore.

Trivia:

>Price appeared on numerous Ed Sullivan, Red Skelton, and Merv Griffin television shows.

>He had a Canadian show and also one in Australia.

>In 1987 he made an unpublicized trip to Cuba to sing for political prisoners. He was entertained at a party where Castro appeared, and he was surprised that the revolutionary Cuban was graying. The first American entertainer to be allowed into a prison for political prisoners, he performed and talked with many but avoided political subjects. When one prisoner gave him a wad of paper that he took from inside his shoe and placed in Price's hands, he requested that the note be given to a relative of his near Hartford. With Warren Allen Smith, he later drove to the Connecticut address and were unable to find anyone who knew the prisoner's relative - Price concluded the two assumed to be federal agents. A letter to the prisoner's address was returned, "unknown." Friends criticized Price for having acted so dangerously, even daring to bring a rock back as a souvenir from Castro's front yard.

>Political matters did not much interest Price. What angered him, however, was Amiri Baraka's (LeRoi Jones's) once turning him down for a job, saying he wasn't black enough. Jews in show business, he told Smith, a white non-believer, had never treated him badly.

>One of his companions, George Stanton from Canada, was known to have had a police record. Price lived dangerously within subcultural sites. A description of his personal life has been written by Smith and includes memories about Langston Hughes.

Final Days

>After *Timbuktu!* with its weekly paycheck of around $2,000., Price was unable to find employment. He had never before had a regular job, not even temporary work. For a decade he tried, always complaining about agents and about the dearth of jobs for blacks. Warren Allen Smith, his close friend who managed his finances and served as a buffer for those wanting to borrow money, found he began out of necessity footing many of Gil's expenses. When the play ended, Price soon had almost no spending money, although

Smith claimed that except for Price's fixing up an apartment to live with **George Stanton** in Manhattan's West 70s and indulging in drugs, Price was not profligate. For almost a decade he scrounged, giving generously of his talent but unable to help pay the rent where he lived in Harlem with his mother. Receiving an offer to teach at a school in Vienna and with the help of **Joan Grisham** in Hyde Park, NY, he left and told friends he was happy to be in such an artistic and music-appreciating environment. One CD was made in Vienna, a sad one in which Price's powerful voice was accompanied by an oompah-oompah brass band. When Price did not show up at his classes for several days, students went to his apartment and found the body.

My further memories:

> Because in a who's who book of blacks I used my address in Gil's listing to shield him from the curious, *The New York Times* telephoned when Gil died, inquiring about the details. I had no knowledge of his death and decided not to reveal that before going to Europe he had shown me medical papers that indicated he was HIV+. The newspaper's staff eventually informed me about Gil's having been accidentally asphyxiated by a faulty propane heater while he was staying alone in someone's apartment, that of an Austrian who was on a trip to Africa.

> Using his address book, I then arranged a razzledazzle showbiz memorial in the Actors' Chapel. Gil's entire family came. I had not known that Gil had a half-brother, and I met his father for the first time. "Wiz" arranger **Harold Wheeler** played piano, "Timbuktu" director-choreographer **Geoffrey Holder** spoke eloquently and dramatically ("Gil, Gil, I know you're up there looking down at us"), and sportscaster **Dick Schaap** was M.C. The first and last words were by two of Gil's Maryknoll priest-friends, one being **Father Phil Wallace** from Seattle. I supervised the sound, lighting, publicity . . . and tears.

> Individuals listed in Price's address book were notified about the memorial, and one – **Arthur C. Clarke** – sent a large check to Smith which was given to Price's sister, **Jeannette**, so she could go to the gravesite arranged by Austrian actor-friends. At the time, Jeannette was living off New York City welfare checks.

A friend, **Ann Brashear**, found from a friend in Bratislava the following:

> I called to the Vienna cemetery office. **Mr Gilbert Price** (born in 1942) was buried at the Feuerhalle-Simmering cemetery (Simmeringer Hauptstrasse 337, Vienna) in January 1991 in grave No. E11/82.

Repplier-Fockeniers, Judy

Judy, if I recall, once said she might have been related to the author and essayist Agnes Repplier. But inasmuch as she was a newly hired teacher in my English department, I was most impressed by her friendly personality and knowledge, although it was understandable that most were struck by her beauty.

When we both mentioned driving to see our parents, hers in Colorado, mine in Iowa, we discussed taking her Volkswagen. My mother hoped we were a couple. Hers possibly hoped we were not.

Taking turns driving across the country was fun, figuring out where to eat, where to find a toilet, and where to sleep were fun. Nothing was like our formal relationship as teachers. Although I made telephone calls to my "business partner" at the recording studio, she had met Fernando and didn't imagine that we had more than just a business relationship. I didn't suspect that Judy may have had an idea that we could develop more than an educational relationship. In retrospect, neither of us suspected what our parents were wondering.

Reza, Allen

During the summer of 1997, his Aunt **Taslima Nasrin** inquired if I would tutor her brother **Kamal**'s son, **Suhrid**, and instruct him in the humanities. For two months the teenager resided with me. We not only went to musical and dramatic events but also I guided him all over the city when he played in tennis tournaments. He briefly was a ball boy at the U. S. Opens, and he worked to earn his B.A. in physics at Hunter College.

A time came when he was discouraged by his father (**Kamal** [kuhMOLL]) and mother (**Afroza**) [uh FROza] and aunts (**Taslima** [tass LEE ma] and **Yeasmeen** [yazz MEEN] from going to Bangladesh to marry. They disapproved because they felt he should get his degree first. Unknown to most, I helped him get to Dhaka where he wrote that in 2011 he was working hard to have an import and distribution business in order get it started up and running. He was importing cosmetics from California. And in Bangladesh he married **Shornali** [shor NOLL ee]

In 2014, he was trying to get his wife to the States, and he was working on a B.A. in neuroscience at Hunter.

Hunter's first diploma was in the name of **Allen K. Reza** [rhymes with MEZza], for he had taken my middle name and had become the son #5 who adopted me. He interviewed me for over a dozen YouTube videos and, using the GarageBand program, has engineered a society project in which I read aloud my entire book, *Cruising the Deuce*, to be made available to sociology departments worldwide.

Allen, Warren, Ariana Huffington, Unknown, Dennis Middlebrooks – we are seen with Allen's aunt, feminist Dr. Taslima Nasrin, in my apartment.

Allen with his wife, Shornali, in Bangladesh
[rhymes with shor-NALL-ee]

In 2014, Allen accompanied me to the
Annual Ceremonial of the American Academy of Arts
and Letters

In May 2014, Allen went on a camping trip in the Adirondacks, carrying 50 pounds of supplies, seeing raw nature firsthand. Snakes? Water snakes. Venomous snakes? Copperheads and Timber Rattlers. While swimming, he saw 6' or 7' water snakes. "We didn't get in the other's way, and we had the same big thunderstorm New York City had."

Upon returning, he learned that some nearby campers had been afflicted with Lyme Disease (named after Lyme and Old Lyme, Connecticut, where numbers of cases in 1975 were identified).

Has he had enough camping? "No, I expect in June 2014 to go first to Bangladesh, be met by Sharmalim, and my wife, and I will camp and trek in the northern India mountains.

Allen's father (Kamal) and sister (Oendrila)

Rice, John Sr.

Murder Suspect Booked

In 1970, directly across from my house in New Canaan, four members of the Rice family were brutally murdered by John Rice Jr: his mother, Janet Rice, 44; his brother Stephen Rice, 16; his sister Nancy Rice, 14, and his grandmother Edith Fitzpatrick, 73. The murderer, who was never in my classes, I knew because he and his siblings played across the street in their yard. The boy was captured in Arizona.

John Rice Sr., by not coming home from work in December 1970, missed watching his 17-year-old son use an axe, a hammer, a knife, and a necktie to kill his own mother, grandmother, brother, and sister (who was bitten on her breast). The women were discovered unclothed. A police car hid near Lakeview Avenue in case the boy returned to kill his father that night. All night long I listened to the police car's engine that was parked in my driveway.

My student, Ed Keating, remembered the Rice boy as being a bully, one who pleaded guilty by reason of insanity and served almost six years at the Whiting Institute for the Criminally Insane in Middletown, Connecticut.

Upon being released, he moved out of state, his record erased by the State of Connecticut.

Old-timers guess that at some point he must have returned to see where he had committed the murders. As to whether or not he inherited his murdered grandmother's estate has remained a question.

Risom, Jens

Risom (8 May 1916 -   ) was among the first of Scandinavian furniture designers to introduce mid-century modern design in the United States.

Jens (pronounced yenns that almost rhymes with fence) was the son of a prominent architect, Sven Risom, one of the leaders of Nordic Classicism. Jens was trained as a designer at the Copenhagen School of Industrial Arts and Design (*Kunsthåndværkerskolen*) where he studied under Ole Wanscher and Kaare Klint and was a classmate of Hans Wegner and Borge Mogensen.

Moving to Stockholm, he developed a reputation for his work with Nordiska Komaniet and traveled to New York City to study American design. When his work appeared in *Collier's* "House of Ideas" designed by Edward Durell Stone and constructed in front of Rockefeller Center during the 1939 New York Word's Fair, it was highly publicized and led to his teaming with entrepreneur Hans Knoll to launch the Hans Knoll Furniture Company with 15 of the 20 pieces in Risom's "600" line, works like stools and armchairs made from cedar and surplus webbing.

Risom came to the United States in 1938 and became a naturalized citizen in 1944. Drafted in 1943, he served under General George S. Patton until 1945. After the war, he launched his own firm, Jens Risom Design on 1 May 1946. His works were photographed by Richard Avedon and his firms ads included "The Answer is Risom." By the late 1950s the focus was on office, hospital, and library furniture.

Playboy featured him as one of six furniture designers the magazine profiled. President Lyndon B. Johnson chose a Risom chair to use in the Oval Office. Many of Risom's furniture designs are considered modern classics, and his furniture is on display at the Museum of Modern Art, the Yale University Art Gallery, the Brooklyn Museum, the Rhode Island School of Design Museum, and the Cooper-Hewitt National Design Museum.

In 1970, after having run his company for twenty-five years, he sold it to Dictaphone, then relocated from New York to New Canaan, where he launched a consulting service, Design Control.

On 12 January 1939, he married Iben Haderup, and their children are Helen Ann, Peggy Ann (New Canaan High School, graduate of '65), Thomas Christian, and Sven Christian. He has been a trustee of the New Canaan Library.

His daughter, Peggy, was my student at NCHS.

Robeson, Paul Jr.

When Mr. Robeson spoke at the New York Ethical Society, he spoke factually about his father, then showed his continuing love for him.

Afterwards, I told him that his mother once requested Gilbert Price to sing at an event because Gilbert's and her husband's voice was so similar.

On a day when **Emmeline Termonfils**, Ligardy's mother, visited my apartment, from a YouTube video I played Robeson and Gilbert, each singing "Old Man River" from *Showboat* (1936, Jerome Kern - Oscar Hammerstein II).

Ms. Termonfils, who knew that Price was my paramour, said she preferred Price over Robeson Sr., although she agreed that recording mechanisms have greatly improved since Robeson's time.

When we departed from my 10th floor apartment and got on the down elevator, I introduced her to Arnold Schoenberg's great grand-son Arnold Greissle-Schoenberg, informing him that we had just listened to Paul Robeson Sr. and Gilbert Price both sing "Old Man River."

"Robeson was the greatest of his time," Arnold beamed.

Paul Robeson's son died in April 2014.

Robeson, Paul Sr.

Philosopedia includes the following:

Paul Robeson Jr. (2 November 1927 - 26 April 2014)

The only child of the legendary Paul Robeson Sr., Robeson Jr. for twenty years was his father's close aide and archived the vast collection of Robeson Papers. He became a journalist, translator, and lecturer.

First educated in the Soviet Union, Robeson later attended Fieldston, the Ethical Culture high school in New York.

Although his father was accused of being a communist and had his career shattered during the McCarthy era, Robeson Jr. contended that his father's true threat to the American government were his cultural ideas, his explorations of slave culture and its value system. Robeson's studies presented "an alternative value system of an unassimilated, automatically dissident culture" that alarmed the Anglo-Saxon powers, Robeson Jr. told reporters and spoke of his views at a 2005 conference about his father held at Lafayette College in Easton, Pennsylvania.

"He wasn't the communist in the family, I was," he says. "He never joined any party. He, being a great artist, didn't do that. He thought it would destroy his effectiveness. I, being a generation younger and not an artist, felt that the way to be effective was through an organization."

Robeson Jr. says he has been politically independent for 40 years. He contends that "grievous distortions" destroyed the communist movement, which, in any case, had become infiltrated by U.S. agents and ceased to have a useful function to African Americans and labor.

"I regret not a moment of that, even the difficult times, although no one likes being a target," he wrote. In Nation article (20 December 1999), he wrote In the morning of March 27, 1961, Paul Robeson was found in the bathroom of his Moscow hotel suite after having slashed his wrists with a razor blade following a wild party that had raged there the preceding night. His blood loss was not yet severe, and he recovered rapidly. However, both the raucous party and his "suicide attempt" remain unexplained, and for the past twenty years the US government has withheld documents that I believe hold the answer to the question: Was this a drug induced suicide attempt?

Heavily censored documents I have already received under the Freedom of Information Act confirm that my father was under intense surveillance by the FBI and the CIA in 1960 and 1961, because he was planning to visit China and Cuba, in violation of US passport restrictions. The FBI files also reveal a suspicious concern over my father's health, beginning in 1955.

A meeting I had in 1998 adds further grounds for suspicion. In June of that year I met Dr. Eric Olson in New York, and we were both struck by the similarities between the cases of our respective fathers. On November 28, 1953, Olson's father, Dr. Frank Olson, a scientist working with the CIA's top-secret MK-ULTRA "mind control" program, allegedly "jumped" through the glass of a thirteenth-floor hotel window and fell to his death. CIA documents have confirmed that a week earlier Olson had been surreptitiously drugged with LSD at a high-level CIA meeting. It is expected that a New York grand jury will soon reveal whether it believes Olson was murdered by the CIA because of his qualms about the work he was doing. MK-ULTRA poisoned foreign and domestic "enemies" with LSD to induce mental breakdown and/or suicide. Olson's drugging suggested a CIA motive similar to the possible one in my father's case—concern about the target's planned course of action.

In this context, the fact that Richard Helms was CIA chief of operations at the time of my father's 1961 "suicide attempt" has sinister implications. Helms was also responsible for the MK-ULTRA program. In 1967 a former CIA agent to whom I promised anonymity told me in a private conversation that my father was the subject of high-level concern and that Helms and Director of Central Intelligence Allen Dulles discussed him in a meeting in 1955.

The events leading to my father's "suicide attempt" began when, alarmed by intense surveillance in London, he departed abruptly for Moscow alone. His intention was to visit Havana at Fidel Castro's personal invitation and return home to join the civil rights movement. Since the date set by the CIA for the Bay of Pigs invasion fell only four weeks after his arrival in Moscow, the CIA had a strong motive for preventing his travel to Havana.

My father manifested no depressive symptoms at the time, and when my mother and I spoke to him in the hospital soon after his "suicide" attempt, he was lucid and able to recount his experience clearly. The party in his suite had been imposed on him under false pretenses, by people he knew but without the knowledge of his official hosts. By the time he realized this, his suite had been invaded by a variety of anti-Soviet people whose behavior had become so raucous that he locked himself in his bedroom. His description of that setting, I later came to learn, matched the conditions prescribed by the CIA for drugging an unsuspecting victim, and the physical psychological symptoms he experienced matched those of an LSD trip.

My Russian being fluent, I confirmed my father's story by interviewing his official hosts, his doctors, the organizers of the party, several attendees and a top Soviet official. However, I could not determine whether my father's blood tests had shown any trace of drugs, whether an official investigation was in progress or why his hosts were unaware of the party. The Soviet official confirmed that known "anti-Soviet people" had attended the party.

By the time I returned to New York in early June, my father appeared to me to be fully recovered. However, when my parents returned to London several weeks later, my father became anxious, and he and my mother returned to Moscow. There his well-being was again restored, and in September they once more went back to London, where my father almost immediately suffered a relapse. My mother, acting on the ill-considered advice of a close family friend, allowed a hastily recommended English physician to sign my father into the Priory psychiatric hospital near London.

My father's records from the Priory, which I obtained only recently, raise the suspicion that he may have been subjected to the CIA's MK-ULTRA "mind depatterning" technique, which combined massive electroconvulsive therapy with drug therapy. On the day of his admission, my mother was pressured into consenting to ECT, and the treatment began just thirty-six hours later. In May 1963 1 learned that my father had received fifty four ECT treatments, and I arranged his transfer to a clinic in East Berlin.

His Paul Robeson Jr. Speaks to America (1993) and The Undiscovered Paul Robeson: The Early Years, 1898-1939 (2001) described his father's having been a great scholar-athlete-performing artist who became a compelling figure of the 20th century. Robeson's father, son of a Presbyterian minister, had been an escaped slave and his mother, a schoolteacher, a descendent of freedmen. His mother was Eslanda Cardozo Goode (1896 - 1965). The biography tells of his father's cultural scholarship and his becoming outspoken concerning anti-colonial and antifascist forces in society.

To Harlem's New Amsterdam News (2005), Robeson wrote of the two Americas, "the progressive America of Abraham Lincoln's Union and the reactionary America of Jefferson Davis's Confederacy. Presidents Franklin Delano Roosevelt and John F. Kennedy symbolize the progressive tradition, whereas Presidents Ronald Reagan and George W. Bush are the icons of the reactionary tradition. . . ."

Ethical Society Member Recalls Meeting Robeson:

> When New York Society member Warren Allen Smith met Robeson the day he spoke. He told him that his mother once requested that Broadway star Gilbert Price sing at an event because Gilbert's and her husband's voice was so similar.

In April 2014, Smith went to YouTube and, for Emmeline Jean-Baptiste, played Robeson and Smith's paramour Gilbert singing "Old Man River" from Showboat (1936, Jerome Kern - Oscar Hammerstein II):

> https://www.youtube.com/watch?v=cIKozcc0HUk

> https://www.youtube.com/watch?v=eh9WayN7R-s

Leaving on the Greenwich Village co-op's elevator, they met Arnold Schoenberg's great grand-son Arnold Greissle-Schoenberg and told him they had just listened to Paul Robeson Sr. and Gilbert Price both singing "Old Man River."

"Robeson was the greatest of his time," Schoenbeg's great-grandson beamed.

Ross, Peter

For an American success story, and despite life's vagaries, Peter Ross is a prime example.

His grandparents were Mrs. Viola Jenkings Zaratt and Mr. Jacinto Zaratt, and his parents were Mrs. Josefa Cornelia Zaratt Ross and Mr. Sharon Ross

The Rosses had three sons: André (13 September 1963), Joron Armando (31 July 1967), and Peter, who at the time of his birth on 20 September 1965 was named Sha-ron Constantino Ross Jr.

His many varied interests include flora and fauna (he had a flower that was a spider trap), animals (he gave a home to Daisy, his present cat), and computers.

Many in Greenwich Village where he lives call him "the computer man" or "the computer techy."

Ross's entry in Philosopedia:

Peter Ross

Peter Ross (20 September 1965 -), who was born in New York City's Borough of the Bronx, attended PS 92, PS 149, St John's Lutheran School in Queens; Maplewood Elementary School in Huntington Station; Memorial Junior High in Huntington Station; Walt Whitman High School in Huntington Station, Long Island; then SUNY at Stony Brook, Long Island. He majored in computer science and minored in music.

The website he set up for **Dr. Taslima Nasrin** has been visited more than 250,000 times, and he helped teach her how to keep it up-to-date herself.

He designed the website for Fashion Institute of Technology's **Professor Karen Santry**.

Similarly, he set up the website for **Warren Allen Smith's** free online research engine, Philosopedia. It has received over 7,000,000 hits.

A pragmatist, Ross has said that his idea of Heaven is that of being somewhere where he could help people or things, where solutions are the norms and complications are always resolved.

Peter with an Iowa T-shirt in front of 31 Jane Street

Peter on the roof at 31 Jane Street

After working on Wall Street, Peter relaxed at a cafe, necktie in his pocket.

In the United States, Peter has been to all the states on the Eastern coast except Maine; has been to western states such as Nevada and California; has been to the midwestern state of Iowa; to New Jersey, and to Connecticut. He has traveled to England, France, Germany, and Switzerland.

On the Staten Island Ferry

"No, he's not Muslim?"

Peter, in front of the home where John Lennon lived, finds it hard to break out of the habit he learned from being an usher for countless years at Faith Baptist Church, of Coram, Long Island. Strangely, he stated perhaps he would make a great doorman.

Peter answered a Craigslist ad looking for a background singer. He and Canara Price rehearsed with Alan Cove (2nd from the left, a person who had sung with the Belmonts, a lead singer after Dion) for 3 years at the high school on 18th Street between 8th and 9th avenues. Peter is the one on the right.

A private person, Peter knows the present author's strengths and weaknesses better than anyone else listed in this book. He is frugal, he enjoys humor, he is 100% honest.

Russell, Catherine

Russell, star of the longest-running non-musical play, *The Perfect Crime*. She is the daughter of Mildred Russell, who was the coordinator of the career resource center at the high school, and William T. Russell Sr., who was an assistant general counsel of the International Business Machines Corporation in Armonk, New York.

She was in the New Canaan Class of '73.

Russell debuted Off-Broadway in 1980 as Nicola Davies in Stephen Poliakoff's *City Sugar* and has appeared Off-Broadway also in Miss Schumann's *Quartet*; *A Resounding Tinkle*; *The Award and Other Plays*; and *Creeps*.

She also has appeared in *New York* as Masha in *Three Sisters*, Rose in *Incommunicado*, Edie in *The Lunch Girls*, Missy in *Home on the Range*, and Cathy Cake in *Inserts*.

As Margaret Thorne Brent, a role she originated in *The Perfect Crime* in 1987, she has played every performance but four, earning her a spot in the Guinness Book of World Records.

After 10:30 p.m. during *The Perfect Crime* or on her nights off, she has also appeared in *The Queen of the Parting Shot*, *Pas de Deux*, *Stages*, *I'll See You in Hell*; *Guardian Star*, and *Some Enchanted Evening*. She has been in several films, including *Soundman* and *Remedy*.

Kathy by Al Hirschfeld and Patrick Robustelli, the love of her life

Russell teaches acting at New York University, is the General Manager of the Snapple Theater Center and also is one of the executive producers of *The Fantasticks*, playing downstairs in the Jerry Orbach Theater.
For a 13-minute video, a crew followed her for a day. See two videos:

    http://goo.gl/FVAOP

    http://goo.gl/TYvKh

Ms. Russell lives in New York City.

Sasamori, Shigeko

[Niimoto Sasamori, Shigeko]

Miss Shigeko Niimoto Sasamori is one of the 25 disfigured and maimed Hiroshima Maidens whom *Saturday Review* editor **Norman Cousins** (shown in photo) brought to the States for surgery in 1955.

"One third of my body was burned, especially my neck and hands," she told a *New York Times* reporter who wrote her Metropolitan Hospital physician's obituary (5 August 1999).

"Dr. Simon and his colleagues operated on me more than a dozen times. I was then able to marry and give birth to a son."

One poignant memory was that of her being introduced by me to another student, Betsy Nimitz, grand-daughter of Admiral Chester A. Nimitz Sr., about whom Shigeko had never before heard.

On 6 August 1945 in Reims while at work in the Little Red Schoolhouse, we all got the answer as to whether now that the war was over in Europe we might get transferred to the Pacific Theatre of Operations. What we found was that a 5-ton atomic bomb had been dropped on Hiroshima and 40,000 were killed instantly.

Another 100,000 would die from the effects of wounds and radiation sickness. On the one hand, this was horrible. On the other, it meant that I would get discharged from the Army much sooner. I was offered a promotion to Warrant Officer if I would remain in the Army, but I chose to get discharged after having served 3½ years.

Years later, **Norman Cousins** arranged to bring to the States twenty-four "Hiroshima Maidens" for plastic surgery to help repair the disfiguration they suffered. **Shigeko Niimoto** lived at his New Canaan house, and I became her English teacher.

Shirley, Robert

Shirley (17 September 1921 -) is the son of Walter Scott Shirley and Gladys Rhoda Shirley, farmers who lived near Minburn, Iowa.

After graduating from Minburn High School in 1939, he served in the United States Navy from 1943 to 1946, obtaining the rank of Lieutenant Junior Grade.

In 1943, he received his B.A. at the University of Iowa, followed in 1948 by an MBA. from Harvard University, and in 1965 a Ph.D. from the University of Utah.

From 1964 to 1985, he taught accounting and other business subjects in Corvallis, Oregon, at Oregon State University.

Asked about religion, Shirley told me, a fellow elementary and secondary school friend, that he was baptized by Methodist minister Paul McDade when a teenager in Iowa but is inactive. The main influences in his life, according to Shirley, were his mother, McDade, teacher Jim Duncan, and farmer Clarence Hill. When I asked him if he was a member of some organized religion, he said he was not. So when I asked him to choose from six pairs of names as to which he would prefer spending three hours of discussion, in case that were possible, he chose the following:

1. Grant Wood and Michelangelo

2. Henry Ford and Warren Buffett

3. Confucius and Jesus

4. Gautama and Jean-Paul Sartre

5. Irving Berlin and John Lennon

6. Pope Benedict and Billy Graham

Shirley chose the pairs in the above order, adding that he does not believe in any afterlife. He chose Abraham Lincoln and Winston Churchill as the two individuals over time that he has found the most inspiring. He found Plato, as reflected in his dialogues, to be the most inspiring philosopher he has read, and he liked the character of Socrates.

Shirley, I surmised, is a free thinking Protestant, one who keeps an inquiring mind regarding religion and as he studies all of the major religions.

Shirley and his wife, Ann K. Shirley, have retired in Corvallis with their daughter, Debbie A. Shirley.

In his retirement, Shirley has traveled extensively abroad and in the United States.

A son, Scott J. Shirley, who lives in Corvallis, Oregon, has written that his father is alive. But Robert Shirley in 2014 has not kept in touch with his fellow classmates, which they find pathetic (uninspiring).

Smith, Ruth Marion and Harry Clark

Harry Clark Smith
Warren and Pal

Smith, Harry Clark (13 February 1887 – 18 February 1975)

Smith, Ruth Marion Miles (7 February 1891 – 1 June 1975)

Warren, Ruth, and Harry
Rippey, Iowa

Smith, a grain dealer who was born in Waukee, Iowa, played third base for the Portland farm team of Chicago Cubs in the 1910s and had a .400 batting average. During the winters, he was employed to oversee snowbound grain elevators in Saskatchewan – at one point, he claimed to be the champion chess player in Saskatoon.

Wounded in the Battle of Verdun while fighting in World War I with the 33rd Infantry Division, Smith was hospitalized at the Buckingham Palace barracks and received the Purple Heart medal. When Queen Mary visited the American soldiers and inquired where he had come from, she was surprised at his mention of having worked in Saskatchewan and said, "Why, then, you're one of my boys!"

Again wounded by a German plane which swooped down over the trenches, Smith later received a second Purple Heart.

The founder of the first American Legion chapter in Iowa, Smith was secretary of the Masonic Lodge in Minburn , then a town of 328. He managed the Clark Brown Grain Elevator from 1920 until 1938, then moved to Rippey to manage another of their grain elevators. He became Mayor of Rippey.

I knew little about cousins on Dad's side. When landscape architect **Ken Smith** with his wife **Priscilla McGeehon Smith** (textbook publisher consultant) were searching for their grandfather's grave in Waukee, Iowa, they found the stone for Clark Smith (9 Feb 1848) was near that of my grandfather Spencer J. Smith (1843 - 1923). With a little research, they learned that the two were brothers from Aylmer, Ontario, who as logrollers on the Mississippi River had volunteered into the U. S. Army. Spencer was too young, but Clark was allowed to enlist because he was over 6' 2" (then rejected because he was too young).

My dad had once introduced me to the Waukee postmaster (Lyle Clark Smith, Clark's son), but it was on my mother's side that I had many cousins, who grew up in South Dakota, Minnesota, and Michigan.

Ken and his wife now are neighbors (80 Warren Street, near 1 World Trade Center), and we have had breakfasts together, after which they walk to his landscape architecture office at 450 West 31st Street. Ken (with the Philip Johnson glasses) is the Iowa-born designer who changed downtown Des Moines, renaming Nollen Plaza to Cowles Commons.

Ken Smith and Priscilla McGeehon, cousins

Stone, Peter

I met Stone in Rochester while he was pursuing a degree and we were attending a Bertrand Russell Society conference. Although I was one of the society's officers, it was Stone who was an expert about Russell.

In Philosopedia, I wrote of Stone, who was born in 1971:

> At Pennsylvania State from 1991 to 1993, he taught calculus, analytic geometry, and Critical Thinking in the Social Sciences. He graduated Magna Cum Laude with honors in 1993 from Pennsylvania University. His Senior Honors Thesis was "Towards the Empowerment of Labor: The Allende Experience."
>
> In 1996 he received his M.A. from the University of Rochester's Department of Political Science, specializing in political philosophy, positive political theory, and methods.
>
> In the University of Rochester's Department of Political Science, he was a teaching assistant, an instructor, and an adjunct assistant professor from 2001 to 2003, teaching contemporary political theory, law and authority, game theory and the law, anarchism, and applied data analysis.
>
> Stone attended graduate school in political science at the University of Rochester, receiving his M.A. in 1996 and his Ph.D. in 2000. His dissertation was entitled "The Luck of the Draw: Revisiting the Lot as a Democratic

Institution." He taught a number of courses at Rochester until 2003, when he moved to Stanford University.

There, he became an Assistant Professor of Political Science and went on sabbatical starting in 2007. His current research interests include theories of justice, democratic theory, rational choice theory, the philosophy of social science, and the philosophy of Bertrand Russell.

In 1990, Stone joined the Bertrand Russell Society and has served on its Board of Directors since 1996. In addition to serving as Secretary of the Society and Board and as editor of the *Bertrand Russell Society Quarterly*, Stone is a founding member of both the Greater Rochester Russell Set (GRRS) and the Bay Area Russell Set (BARS). He frequently lectures on Russell.

Asked in 2006 if any political or philosophic labels characterize his present views, Stone replied,

- I greatly admire Bertrand Russell, Noam Chomsky, and John Dewey. All three embody the sort of principled life of the public intellectual to which I aspire. I once heard Russell described as possessing a "liberal anarchist, leftist, and skeptical atheist temperament." I can only hope to be worthy of such a description myself.

As of May 2013, Dr. Stone is Ussher Lecturer in Political Science at Trinity College, Dublin

Political Science Dept.
University of Rochester
Rochester, NY 14627
August 27, 1996

Dear Warren:

Forgive my tardiness in responding to you. I was pleased to hear that you had voted for Noam Chomsky, and even more pleased when Don Jackanicz informed me that Chomsky had accepted the BRS's offer of an honorary membership. He will be a fine addition to our already prestigious list, and perhaps he'll even be willing to come to one of our meetings. I am a longtime admirer of his philosophical and political writings, and would be honored to meet him.

As for your questions, I do not believe in any form of supernatural existence. I looked up "naturalism" in the dictionary, and found that it was "the view of the world which takes account only of natural elements and forces, excluding the supernatural or spiritual." I think this is an excellent description of my views, provided that one does not construe "spiritual" too broadly.

I have no reason to believe there is an afterlife, and therefore I don't. My practical attitude is that of Woody Allen's father in "Hannah and Her Sisters" (great movie, by the way). When confronted by his son's desire to know what happened after death, his response was, "When I'm dead, I'm dead...I'll worry about it then."

Philosophically, I'm definitely an agnostic. For all practical purposes, however, I'm an atheist. Without any evidence of the existence of God or the supernatural, I must for practical purposes assume there is no God or supernatural realm of which to speak.

I was born in 1971. At the moment, I'm a graduate student at the University of Rochester, studying political science. I'm active around various left-wing causes, and politically I consider myself an anarchist. I'm not quite sure where you'd go to find out more information about me (except my mother, of course).

I hope this tells you what you want to know. I'm quite happy to go on record about my beliefs. If I wasn't, I'd probably have to wonder what was wrong with them.

Hopefully, I'll see you at next year's BRS meeting. Until, then, enjoy this life, for it may well be the only one we have.

Yours Very Sincerely,

Peter Stone

Stuart, Carole and Lyle

Lyle Stuart (seated; Warren Allen Smith, standing), who was once an editor for *Mad* and was the noted American independent publisher of controversial books, for years was a special friend of Al Goldstein. They socialized often and were interviewed several times by Alan Colmes, a liberal radio and television journalist admired by both because of his fairness to those he interviewed.

On one occasion, Stuart took me to the Colmes television show for a late-night interview with Goldstein. The show was about Stuart's having published my 1,248 page *Who's Who in Hell*, the thesis of which is that Hell is a theological invention and does not exist . . . but that, if it did, my book listed over 10,000 from ancient to contemporary times who would be there.

I made notes of what transpired at the 1999 interview, notes that Stuart published in my *In the Heart of Showbiz Volume* 1 (NY: Barricade Books, 2000).

Stuart and I arrived early at Fox News Radio and TV and sat in the station's lobby area, one that had glass doors and allowed us to see who was exiting from the elevator. I didn't know what Goldstein looked like and knew only that he had bought six copies of my $125. book, one for himself and the others for his son, Jordan. My book listed both as atheists, along with Stuart.

It wasn't my first radio or TV interview, but I was nervous about meeting Colmes, who was such a noted interviewer. When Stuart left to use the men's room, the elevator doors opened, a man exited, saw me inside, dropped his pants, and mooned me. Pulling open the door, he said, "Are you the old fag who's on the program with me?" In 1999, Goldstein was 66, 14 years my junior.

Stuart arrived almost at the same time, and, because Goldstein was his friend and he hadn't heard the insult, I said to my publisher, as if befuddled, "And is this the handsome buyer of six of my books?"

After that introduction and being rushed into the studio, harnessed by a technician with what it takes to be televised, seated before a microphone, and hurriedly greeted by Mr. Colmes, who said we'd be "on" in minutes, I let the two of them talk and didn't cut in until asked something specific.

Colmes expertly guided Stuart and me in our explanation about the book, and I tried to be concise but also be a salesman for the book. It was when Goldstein chimed in about other subjects that the interview suddenly focused on Goldstein, not on my book. It was my introduction as to how, when interviewed, one must remain on camera and stay in the spotlight even if it means being New York-pushy. After the interview, it was too late for me to join them for drinks, although they could have thought that maybe I was irked. As we departed, Goldstein, with Stuart nodding yes, made me promise to come to his magazine office and be interviewed again.

With much trepidation, on the appointed day I showed up at his suite of *Screw* rooms. He had a cluttered desk, a high-back and regal-like chair, and a beautiful girl sitting nearby. I wasn't sure if it was his wife or his secretary, but she phoned for someone in the art department to give me a tour of the many-roomed place. The rent must be humongous, I thought to myself.

The employee showed me around each room, particularly a large one in which he worked as an artist. Dildos, penises, teats, erotica of all kinds were prominent. In one nondescript room, another employee arranged a microphone, camera, and a chair, preparing for the interview.

Goldstein, "Uncle Al" the artist called him, arrived with a big smile, a pleasant greeting, apologies for the looks of the room, and then, "Well, old faggot, let's get going!"

It wasn't clear if my publisher had told him I am gay, for this had nothing to do with my book, or if this was Goldstein's usual manner of speaking. So again we got off to a bad start.

"You like old faggots?" I asked. Whatever he answered, I responded by asking how long he'd had these symptoms. But he went on and on with questions. I was an English teacher in New York? ("Yes, and in Connecticut.") How many students had I had sex with? ("None, whatsoever!") Faculty? ("None, ever, and no administrators.") Married? ("No.") Children? ("No.") Gay? ("Are you? Is this a proposal?") You're a vet? ("Yes, as an acting first sergeant, I led my company onto Omaha Beach in 1944. In Reims I became one of General Eisenhower's adjutant general's chief clerks in Supreme Headquarters from 1944 to the end of the war in 1945. Oh, and I'm a veteran of the Stonewall uprising in 1969.")

Then it must have been 45 minutes of questions about my education (U of Northern Iowa and Columbia U), experiences with religion (I emphasized being a Unitarian and non-believer). Goldstein showed real interest in hearing that upon first hitch-hiking from Iowa to Manhattan, I had met Charles Smith (1887-1964), editor of the atheist journal, *Truth Seeker*, and had joked to the very serious scholar that we Smiths might be related.

When the time was up, I was given some free copies of *Screw*, told I'd be on their mailing list and would get a year's free subscription. I got out of there as fast as I could.

Did Goldstein remain friends with Lyle Stuart and his wife Carole? No, not after Goldstein published a photo of Stuart and his wife's faces on Adolf Hitler's and Eva Braun's bodies.

Did I ever see or talk with Goldstein again? No chance in hell!

Sukarno, Rukmini

Rukmini Sukarno at Carnegie Hall before she went to prison

In my last website post, I posed the following question:

• Which dictator's daughter, during a New Canaan teacher's summer job in a recording studio, when it came to paying her bill of $5,000, said, seriously, "Do you take gold?"

Ms. **Rukmini Sukarno** (born around 1943) is a daughter of Indonesian **President Sukarno** (6 June 1901 - 21 June 1970). An opera singer, she lived in Rome in the 1960s. There, she met and married the American film actor **Franklin Latimore Kline** (28 September 1925 - 29 November 1996). Their son, **Chris Kline**, reportedly is a journalist.

Her husband once arranged a concert for her at Carnegie Hall, dubbing it *Fiesta Mundo* (World Party).

I not only was an NCHS English teacher but also I co-owned a major independent recording studio in Times Square: **Variety Recording Studio**, just off Broadway on 46th Street "in the heart of showbiz" (which also is the title of my 3-volume autobiography).

During school summer sessions, I spent days managing the studio and my partner (**Fernando Vargas**, also my paramour) managed late-afternoons and evenings. We worked with **Robert Whitehead** (*After the Fall*, 1964; *Medea*, 1982); **Arthur Miller** (cues for *After the Fall*, 1964); **Paddy Chayevsky** (*Joseph D*,

1964), **David Amram** (music for *Joseph D*, 1964); and **Hal Prince** (*Fiddler on the Roof*, 1964).

Marvin Hamlisch brought **Liza Minnelli** in 1963, when she was a junior at Scarsdale High School, to record a track for *Best Foot Forward*, her first dub.

For **Jerry Bock**, Vargas recorded tracks for his "Fiorello" (1959) and "Fiddler on the Roof" (1964).

For jazz great **Sun Ra and his Arkestra**, we completed master acetates from 1961 to 1990.

Ms. Sukarno was a beauty, and her two guards although friendly were tense. When I made out the $5,000 statement for the tapes to be used three hours hence for a performance at which she would sing in Spanish at Carnegie Hall that evening, she didn't want a receipt and asked, seriously, if the studio accepted gold.

The program was only three hours away, and the guards suggested we bring the tapes, put them on the tape machines, and listen to the program for free, then pick the tapes up and she would return the following day with cash.

We could go anywhere we wanted backstage and had the best seats in the house. She sang partly in Spanish and her band was first-rate. What a surprise, to hear an Indonesian singing Spanish. She claimed to speak eight languages.

Well, I got snookered!

The event was over, would not be repeated, and she no longer needed the tape!

If we could have found an address, we would have turned her over to Dun & Bradstreet. By the late 1970s, she was the sole owner of Frankenburg Import-Export Ltd., a Kansas corporation registered in Mexico as a middleman-supplier of steel products to that country. In December 1978, Petroleos Mexicanos, "Pemex," Mexico's national oil company, accepted her bid to supply some 93,000 meters of steel oil field pipe, and in March 1979 forwarded Frankenburg-Kansas a purchase order requesting various types and quantities of pipe for which Pemex was willing to pay approximately $5.2 million.

In March 1986 and later editions, *The New York Times* reported that upon her conviction on felony charges, she had surrendered to the authorities, was held in $500,000 bail, and was jailed in Houston, Texas. Convicted of misapplication of $5.6 million in fiduciary funds, she was sentenced to 14 years and a $10,000 fine. After her indictment, she moved to Mexico but was deported in 1984 and returned to Houston, where she was arrested. Free on $250,000 bail, she disappeared.

In a recent e-mail to the District Attorney who had convicted and had her jailed, I learned that she still is on the loose.

Termonfils, Ligardy

Termonfils, the son of Lima Charles-Pierre and Emmeline Termonfils, was born in Haiti. His father was one of Baby Doc Duvalier's bodyguards and was captain of one of Haiti's volleyball teams. Ligardy's mother is the daughter of Marie Yva Termonfils Volmar (15 October 1935 - 2 June 2006).

Separating from her husband, Ligardy's mother moved to Brooklyn, New York, where she brought her 9-year-old son. Ligardy's father was assassinated in 2004 in Haiti.

Ligardy (pronounced as if spelled LeGardy) volunteered for the genographic project of *National Geographic*, which revealed that his DNA test showed that he is descended from M168, the name for the study's earliest genetic reference, a man who lived 50,000 years ago when approximately only 10,000 humans existed.

He volunteered as a photographer to record the event of philosopher Paul Edwards's ashes being thrown into the Hudson River. A student at Halsey Middle School 296 and then at Thomas Jefferson High School in Brooklyn, he participated by accompanying me and photographing the event.

In 2007, Ligardy applied to and was accepted at Washington Irving High School, where he studied art and the basic curriculum.

After receiving a top grade during college-level art classes at the Fashion Institute of Technology (FIT), he was awarded a scholarship to take art classes.

In 2009, he had passed three of FIT's college-level courses and two college-level courses at Parsons New School For Design.

In June 2010, the 6' senior at Gramercy Arts High School graduated with a total average of 91, excelling in art and the social sciences.

Ligardy wearing my Eisenhower jacket and medals

I had one service stripe; 2 overseas service bars; the American Campaign Medal; the European-African-Middle Eastern Theater Ribbon with two Bronze Battle Stars; a Good Conduct Medal; and a World War II Victory medal.

Self Portrait, Fire Spirit

Donated to the Forest Park Museum in Perry, Iowa

In 2011 he finished his freshman year as an art major at Parsons The New School for Design. One of his works, inspired by the phoenix and showing how he has risen from the ashes of a difficult childhood, is called *Fire Spirit*.

In September 2011, he started his sophomore year studying animation at the Academy of Arts University in San Francisco.

Ligardy's father, **Lima** (on the left), with four of the other Haitian Presidential Guards.

Ligardy and Emmeline, his mother, the day I met them, 26 August 2004.

Just as I thought my Father did not leave me something after his death, I met Warren Allen Smith. He was the greatest thing that happened to me. He is like a father to me. He is also my best friend. I love this man very much. Thank you for every thing being a tutor, father and friend.

My son, the California model

My dad the retired Cub and I didn't talk much about sports, but he knew **Bob Feller**'s dad and I was on a Radio WHO program with Feller (playing my accordion) at the time he was chosen by the Cleveland Indians when he was a senior at Van Meter High School.

Ligardy's dad listened to him when he chose **LeBron James** at the time James left the Cleveland Cavaliers, who on 11 July 2014 announced that he is returning to Cleveland. James, now 29 years old, is described in *The New York Times* (12 July 2014) as "widely regarded as the greatest basketball player of his generation," and by Mike Lupica in the *Daily News* (12 July 2014) as "the best player on the planet and the best teammate at his word."

James will be returning to Ohio where his wife **Savanna Brinson** and sons **LeBron James Jr.** (born 6 October 2004) and **Bryce Maximus** (born 14 June 2007) are.   [Photo is on the cover of *Sports Illustrated*.]

419

Tyrrell, Susan

Susan Creamer (18 March 1945 - 16 June 2012) was SuSu in my class and became **Susan Tyrrell** in the movies.

Her father, Jack Creamer (a William Morris agent who once had promised to take her to Sardi's), died of a bee sting before he could take her. So I took her there, after which in a 1972 John Huston movie, *Fat City,* she received an Oscar nomination and was called "the greatest lush since Ray Milland."

(Surely I didn't order anything but food!)

On a visit to New Canaan, she refused to get out of the car, asking a student to have me visit her in the car "I hate everything New Canaan," she exclaimed.

SuSu specialized in odd roles, such as playing frightful characters and prostitutes. In 2000, she contacted a rare blood disease that led to the amputation of both her legs. She continued working as an actress, in scenes that showed only her upper body, until her death in 2012.

Ultra Violet

Isabelle Collin Dufresne (Ultra Violet in the large hat, with **Taylor Mead** (star of the Andy Warhol movie, *Taylor Mead's Ass*) died 14 June 2014 at Manhattan Hospital. Mead died 8 May 2013.

I hadn't heard her arrive, and when I saw her sitting in the engineer's chair at the recording studio's console, she volunteered to explain, "I wait for Hal and Hosea. Songwriters Contact."

Detecting the French accent, I responded something in French. She responded, "You have BE-n in FRAWNss?"

"Oui, sur la plage d'Omaha dans dix-neuf quarante-quatre."

Usually, mention of 1944 gets positive reactions from French people, but she continued looking at a script. "I am Isabelle. Ultra Violet. Born Grenoble. I left when 16. I do not know Reims."

I was elated to meet her and saw her and Taylor Mead years later when a Warhol statue was installed in lower Manhattan.

Vargas, Fernando

Vargas was the son of Manuel Elias Vargas Cordero, a department store owner, and Elena Zamora Paniagua. Their children were Aura Vargas de Moreno, Eugenia Vargas Zamora, Nery Vargas Zamora, Elena Vargas Zamora, and Otto Vargas Zamora. Fernando was the last-born.

When 16 and a student at Colegio Los Angeles in San José, Vargas earned his best grades in biology and history, his weakest in religion and English.

His father owned a large department store, in which as a teenager he worked and was allowed to handle money. His youth was spent excelling in sports, riding a bicycle, visiting relatives in Cartago, Heredia, and Alajuela, and spending time near Teatro Melico Salazar and the Parque Central, the park on Calle 14 that he knew the best.

His hard-working mother supervised several servants and looked after her large family. When her husband died, a big tomb was constructed at Cementerio Obreros, for he was an important person who once had dreams of becoming President. MANUEL ELIAS VARGAS CORDERO was written on the tomb, which had an angel atop. Later, members of the family were to be buried there next to Father and Mother.

Fernando, Elena, and Elena Zamora Paniagua

On 3 May 1946, at the passport office Fernando received his passport and on 22 May 1946 he, his sister Elena, and his mother arrived in Miami. His Alien Registration Receipt Card was #6312922. Quickly, Selective Service on 3 December 1946 gave him a registration card that showed he had green eyes, was white, had brown hair, was 5' 7", and weighed 132.

When he was 8 months older than 17, Vargas arrived at 175 Claremont Avenue, New York City. His mother, sister, and he lived in a one-bedroom apartment between 123rd and 125th Street near the International House and the Manhattan School of Music. It was just west of Harlem, and he and his sister were not allowed to walk in the neighborhood, which their mother thought was dangerous. Little by little, they were allowed to go together around the immediate neighborhood. Much of his time was spent watching TV or going shopping with his sister for groceries or supplies. In the evenings they eventually got tired of supervising him and allowed him to go out alone. He spent lots of time around the corner at Grant's Tomb, 122nd Street.

Almost every time that he went to Grant's Tomb and walked around Riverside Park, he found people who were Columbia University professors, students, and professional types. Also, as was the case at Parque Central near his home in San José, he noticed some younger and older males who were looking for sex. Although they were relatively rare at Parque Central, they were quite numerous in that section of Riverside Park. If you sat on a park bench alone here, someone might sit down next to you and, if you just sat in a slouched position, your hands clasped behind your head, someone would unzip your pants and play with you.

His first introduction to sex had been when he was an altar boy. A Catholic priest, who pretended it was accidental, touched his crotch. Asking a childhood friend whose family was German and imported toys if the priest had ever pulled his pants down to see his penis, he found that had happened to him, also. The German boy was a best friend, was heavier, and was easily beaten in races. But on one occasion his friend claimed he had something bigger than Vargas did and, bragging, pulled out his *pene* and *testículos*. Then, his friend had put one of Vargas's hands on his own crotch, which felt good, and he reciprocated. Not knowing whether to tell an older brother or anyone else, he decided he might get in trouble both with the church and his family and said nothing.

Between Riverside Drive and the Hudson River, the park was extensive. There was a tennis court, a skating area, and there was a big sports area before you got as far downtown as 96th Street. Whatever transpired while cruising the area, he had to make sure he got home before 10 p.m.

Harold Bonilla, who was Costa Rica's consul in the city, accidentally met him in the park and asked him to move in with him nearby on 103rd Street. It was not difficult to obtain Fernando's mother's approval, for here was a person who wrote history books, was a Catholic, and mentioned that he might be able to get him a job and schooling.

Now exactly 20, finding no jobs but not having to pay any rent, Vargas moved in. But when "Major" Bonilla was at work, Vargas hung out in the nearby Riverside Park.

Just up from 103rd Street one day in September 1948, he saw a college student sitting alone. The guy was friendly, said hello, and Vargas's response sounded to the stranger as if he were French. What transpired that day, the first week in which the stranger had arrived on the GI Bill to study English at Columbia University, is to be continued by Warren Allen Smith in a biography/autobiography of their 40 years together, one that is tentatively called *In The Heart of Showbiz*.

Smith, whom he met soon after arriving in New York City, has in detail described their meeting and their forty years together:

Bonilla helped Vargas get a job in Manhattan's Garment District, one in which he used a sewing machine to stitch garments and was paid by the piece.

But in 1949 Vargas moved from Bonilla's place with me to a furnished room on 109th Street, where their Austrian landlady, Sophie Likar, liked us so much she allowed us alone of her various renters to share her refrigerator. I now had earned my M.A. at Columbia – Vargas took a photo after Eisenhower handed me the sheepskin – and began teaching English at Bentley School on 86th Street.

I answered an ad for Vargas that led to his being interviewed by R. E. L. Lab, where he made a favorable impression on Edwin Armstrong after being coached about how to weld a certain item. Hired, he found Armstrong avuncular and confiding his problems. Telling Armstrong he lived on 109th near Columbia, he learned that his boss taught there and in 1913 had discovered regeneration. With talk about amplifiers, feedback, and oscillators, the work turned out to be educational and enjoyable, particularly when Edwin – they soon were on a first-name basis – told of being paid only $1 by Columbia but was earning money from his patents. He allowed the military to use royalty-free his findings about FM – frequency modulation – but when the war ended RCA claimed that they, not he, had invented it and they were suing each other. Edwin complained that he became nearly bankrupt from defending his patents, that his wife had left him in the middle of all this, and in 1953 his licenses and patents would all expire. He did not confide everything all at once, but on some days when agitated he would tell bits and pieces about having made the first portable radio and advanced AM radio and on other days he was like a friendly uncle.

In 1954, Armstrong dressed neatly, walked to a 13th story window, and jumped out. His body hit a third story overhang. Vargas was devastated. Later, Armstrong's wife settled with RCA for over a million dollars.

Vargas then studied electrical engineering at RCA Labs in Greenwich Village, West 4th and Greenwich Street, receiving a certificate in a year.

When Major Bonilla told us that a 1½ room apartment adjacent to his own on 103rd Street was vacant (and had once been lived in by a mistress of Costa Rican President Rafael Calderón Guardia), the two moved into their first apartment together.

Upon hearing from one of his many gay friends that Audiosonic Recording Studio was looking for someone who knew about electrical engineering, Vargas applied for the job at the Brill Building on Broadway and was hired as a temporary the same day by Bob Guy, the studio's owner.

When one of the engineers mentioned that there was a vacant 2 ½ room apartment at 425 West 45th in Hell's Kitchen, Vargas and I moved into

Apartment 3FW where the rent of $194.40/month was only slightly more than the one back on 103rd Street.

By 1961, Audiosonic was floundering. Guy, the bi-sexual owner, was kiting checks and had put a prima donna trick on the payroll, Vargas complained. Fellow engineer Joe Cyr warned that they might all need to look for a job somewhere else. Vargas's and others' paychecks began to bounce and, at a quickly called meeting the owner said, yes, the place was bankrupt, he was sorry the paychecks were no good, and Eaton Factors that was owed money was going to shut the place down.

Cyr and Vargas, explaining this to Smith, suggested the three together might try to salvage the company by working with Eaton Factors. It was agreed that the three would be equal owners of a Sub-Chapter S corporation that would be set up. Space at Variety Arts, a major rehearsal building on 46th Street, became available. With many difficulties, the three not only founded Variety Sound Corporation but also included Guy as a partner because he had contacts with all the clients and would include Ad-Lib, his company that made radio jingles for stations.

In April of 1961, Variety Sound Corporation was formed. Smith and Vargas also started Variety Recording Service, a d/b/a that separated Variety Sound Corporation's recording income from Vargas's wholly owned dub-cutting business. The agreement with Guy included the stipulation that only Smith could sign checks, and eventually it was arranged that Guy would exchange his one-fourth interest in Variety Sound for his entire Ad-Lib company. With Guy no longer associated with the business, Variety continued profitably until Vargas's death in 1989.

Corliss Lamont came early one morning to our 103rd Street Manhattan apartment to speak with Smith. Finding Vargas wearing red pajamas, he said, "Oh, your roommate rooms with the Devil?" It was Vargas's first introduction both to a Columbia University professor and to a bona fide naturalistic humanist.

On another occasion Vargas attended Charles Francis Potter's humanist "church," laughing at the lecture on the joys of sex. But astronomy, not religion or academic philosophy, was his major diversion. A nominal member of the Bertrand Russell Society, he was only mildly interested in the various philosophers. For its founding meeting in 1989, he allowed the New York Chapter of Secular Humanists to meet in his recording studio and became its first member.

To have lived a great life, no matter how long, is life's purpose, he believed. To that end he mastered acetate disks, using his own inventive modification of a Scully lathe and being one of the few in the Greater New York Area who could operate such a machine; recorded Broadway plays, working with Arthur Miller (*After the Fall*, 1964), Paddy Chayevsky (*Joseph D*, 1964], Robert Whitehead (*After the Fall*, 1964; *Medea*, 1982), Hal Prince, *Fiddler on the Roof*, 1964;

David Amram (*Joseph D*, 1964); worked with internationally known songwriters and performers (he recorded Liza Minnelli's first demo record, at which Marvin Hamlisch was accompanist in 1963); worked with songwriter Jerry Bock on "Fiorello" (1959) and "Fiddler on the Roof" (1964); completed master acetates from 1961 to 1990 for Sun Ra, arguing over wine with him about mysticism; and was well-known among a who's who of Broadway and Latino musicians and artists.

As a business executive, Vargas produced a collector's LP of "Costa Rica's Caruso," Manuel Salazar; sang "I-gotta-be-me," and fearlessly ventured on life's less-traveled roads.

He died six months after being diagnosed with having Kaposi's sarcoma in the lungs, was resigned to his condition, and spent much of his final and painful weeks studying the latest developments in astronomy. Up to 2007, over 25,000,000 had died of AIDS, and in 2007 an estimated 33,000,000 adults and children were living with HIV/AIDS.

A portion of his cremains were scattered in the Hell's Kitchen and Times Square neighborhoods of New York City, where he had spent most of his life. Another portion was saved to be mixed with my own. The bulk was returned to Costa Rica, where I personally placed his cremains in the family above-ground tomb next to his father (Elias) and mother (Elena) at San in Costa Rica. In his honor, an Agua Buena support group was formed.

Riverside Drive Park Bench

Vargas and Smith
Painting by Al Knopf

Fernando with Ambassador Mario Echandi, who later became President of Costa Rica.

Costa Rican Consul Harold Bonilla with Fernando

VARIETY

March 22-28, 1989

OBITUARIES

FERNANDO VARGAS

Fernando Vargas, 60, recording studio exec and cofounder of Variety Sound Corp., died Feb. 20 in New York of cancer.

A native of Costa Rica, Vargas came to the U.S. in 1946 to study electrical engineering at RCA Institutes in New York. His first job in the business was at REL Labs, where he welded wires. He worked with Maj. Edwin Howard Armstrong, who invented the receiver that led to the development of FM radio.

At Audiosonic Recording, he engineered sessions for such musicians as Jerry Bock and Paul Simon.

In 1961 Vargas helped found Variety Sound Corp. The company's Broadway demos and cues include Arthur Miller's "After The Fall," Larry Grossman's "Grind," Robert Whitehead's "Medea" and John Guare's "The House Of Blue Leaves."

The studio has worked with artists such as David Amram, Sun Ra, Tiny Tim, Tito Puente and Paquito de Rivera.

Vargas also was v.p. at AAA Record Plating and co-owner of AAA Recording Studio.

WHO'S WHO IN ENTERTAINMENT

VARGAS, FERNANDO RODOLFO, recording studio executive, b San Jose, Costa Rica, Sept. 22, 1928, came to U.S., 1946. s. Elias and Elena (Zamora) V.; student, RCA Inst., 1954. Engr. Audiosonic Rec. N.Y.C., 1953-61; exec. dir. Variety Sound Corp., N.Y.C., 1961-88, co-owner, engr. Variety Rec. Studio, 1986-88; v.p. AAA Record Plating, N.Y.C., 1986-88; co-owner AAA Rec. Studio, 1980-88. Avocations: electrical engineering, astronomy. Office: Variety Rec. Studio 130 W 42d St #551 New York NY 10036

The above-ground Vargas Tomb in San José, Costa Rica, into which I placed Fernando's cremains.

Warhol, Andy

Seeing Warhol all alone during an intermission at the Palace, Fernando Vargas and I pretended not to know who he was and, approaching, asked him to settle an argument we two were having about something in the play.

Warhol responded until the buzzers were heard for the audience to return to their seats.

He genuinely struck us as being lonely.

Warm, Anna and Michael Roedel

A seasoned teacher of literature and writing from Darien, Connecticut, Ms. Warm once wrote, "I became an atheist in Methodist Sunday School when, one day, I looked around and said to myself, incredulously, 'These kids are buying this?' Also, I hated the Welch's grape juice communions." Not only did she and I share many views about organized religions, but also we are Mensans.

Upon retiring to her ranch in New Mexico, and later returning to Connecticut, Ms. Warm has continued to tutor and travel.

As English department chairman, I recommended in 1969 that Ms. Warm be hired, and she taught 34 years at New Canaan High School. She also tutored extensively.

Knowing me as a personal friend, she and her husband – Michael Roedel – invited Ligardy Termonfils and me to their ranch in Mission, New Mexico, for two successive summers. Neither of us had ever before or since seen so many American Indians.

Roedel is a professional wildlife biologist with extensive experience as a birder across the southern states. In recent years he has served as the State Ornithologist for Tennessee.

After they disposed of their ranch, they moved to Norwalk, Connecticut. We go to Broadway plays, have dinners together, and I credit the two as being just the right mature couple to help me be a dad for the father Ligardy never had.

Weschler, Anita

Anita in her studio, with abstract hexes and a nude statue of José Limón

In *Who's Who in Hell*, I wrote the following:

Weschler, Anita (1903 – 2000)

Weschler, a sculptor, is known for her representational statues and groups. She studied at the Parsons School of Design and graduated from the National Academy of Design. She also studied with Laessle at the Pennsylvania Academy of Fine Arts and with William Zorach at the Art Students League. One of her life-size works, *The Humanist* (1955), received national notice when a photograph in *Look* showed the statue being carried on the back of the diminutive sculptor, a feat made possible because it was the first such to be made out of lightweight, unbreakable glass fibers and plastic resins. It depicts a man of ambiguous race, two arms outstretched, one for giving, one for receiving. *The Humanis*t (#6, 1956) described the work and Weschler's artistic philosophy. Her sculpture includes multi-figure groups, single figures, portraits, constructions, collages, and stone collages. She has used such media as bronze, aluminum, cast stone, stone, durastone (hydrocal), wood, plastic, plaster, terra cotta, and fiber glass. Her paintings include "organic abstractions" (synthetic glazes on panels), "translucencies" (plastic resins, abstractions backlighted in shadow box frames); and "linear abstractions" (works on paper).

Her work is in the public collections of the Whitney Museum in New York City; Yale University in New Haven, Connecticut; Brandeis University; Wichita State Museum; and a variety of other United States as well as foreign collections, both private and public. Her sculpture has been commissioned by the United States Treasury Department, and various portraits were commissioned by the U.S. Post Office in Elkin, North Carolina. Ten life-size portrait heads in bronze are in the Institute for Achievement of Human Potential, Philadelphia, Pennsylvania. She has had forty one-person shows nationwide. Weschler has been a delegate to the US Committee of the International Association of Art, on the board of directors of the Sculptors' Guild, and on the executive committee of the Federation of Modern Painters and Sculptors. She is the author of a book of poems, *Nightshade*, the recipient of many awards including the Audubon Artists Medal of Honor, and is a fellow of the MacDowell Colony and Yaddo.

Weschler, who since her youth has considered herself an atheist and a deist. She is an honorary member of the Secular Humanist Society of New York. Her husband, Herbert Solomon, also was a freethinker. Her *The Humanist*, a life-size statue, was donated in 1995 by Warren Allen Smith to the Council for Secular Humanism, at the time of the dedication of the Center for Inquiry building in Amherst, New York. Visiting art experts have said it is noteworthy for its texture and symbolism.

"A statue," Weschler often declared, "should be touched," an outlook frowned upon by gallery and museum guards. Shown a photo of Nobel Prize-winning biochemist **Herbert Hauptman** speaking at the Center for Inquiry's dedication ceremony while, just behind, someone had placed a hat atop *The Humanist*, Weschler laughed appreciatively. She lived to be 97.

She and her husband, **Herbert Solomon**, fortunately did not notice as I photographed them leaving their Waverly Street apartment building.

Solomon, Herbert E. (1902–1995)

Solomon, a freethinker, was a financial analyst in New York City, a fiercely independent thinker, one whose mental acuity always led him to be quietly amused by the claims of believers.

Other memories: Anita refused to be referred to as Mrs. Solomon. Herb and I always just called her Anita. Others were expected to call her Ms. Weschler. When I learned that she'd named her work *The Humanist*, and I was working on the magazine of the same name, it was only natural that I would request an interview. When I showed up, however, she was mostly flirtatious and sensed that I knew nothing about the world of sculpture. But then she told of her interest in **Friedrich Nietzsche** and **John Dewey** and other left-leaning nonbelievers. When she described her philosophic outlook, she said she was a deist.

I smiled that I didn't know any deists were still alive – well, maybe I wasn't that blunt – but detected she was really a typical independent and a freethinker entirely uninterested in labels.

Upon several occasions at the annual ceremonial of the American Academy of Arts and Letters, I drove her home because she was too tipsy. She blamed several sculptors for not nominating her for membership in the Institute (as the 200-member organization was called before it merged with the 50-member Academy). Chaim Gross's studio was adjacent to hers, and they were friends – but when he got nominated, she felt she was a better sculptor who just didn't have pull with members like **Louise Nevelson** (to whom she once introduced me as if I were her lover) – her and Nevelson's parents apparently arrived as immigrants on the same ship. She saw Nevelson as a great sculptor, of course.

Anita always detested homosexuals, specifically citing those (like **Paul Cadmus**) who had not nominated her and those whom she described as preferring "the junkyard school of art." She introduced me, for example, to the New York University prof who obtained his materials like bumpers and parts of cars from garbage dumps – I hesitated telling her that he had sculpted a beautiful work of art for the main Haitian cathedral. At one Academy ceremonial (I've attended annually for over 5 decades as a journalist, and she always attended because someone gave her a guest ticket), she told me that one English teacher I'd brought as my guest (**David Maier**) looked porcine.

Another year, she asked if the teacher I'd brought was gay (a retired Marine colonel, **Matt Coyle**), he was quite insulted). Any females I brought as guests she detested (and she clearly had had the hots for me from the first day we met). Those were the days I was glad I was in the closet.

Toward the end of his life, Herb and I were unable to get her out of an agreement she once signed donating all unsold works to Syracuse University, with which she never had any connection. The first lawyer she disapproved of because of his hair style and the fact he lived only a few blocks away from her. The second lawyer agreed with Herb and me that the agreement could be legally stopped or she could just donate all unsold works now, with her and my working on a list of museums across the country. That lawyer worked for a big firm that specialized in such matters, and she thought he would charge too much. Herb, who was Wall Street-smart, was as disappointed as I was.

One mysterious point: she donated her correspondence to Syracuse with the stipulation that it not be opened until after all who might be mentioned were dead. Because she and Herb lived in Greenwich Village during the roaring 20s I always wondered if maybe she was trying to cover up any bohemian lovers. Just before he died, Herb showed me an article in a science magazine that discussed homosexuality's being inherited, not something chosen as a lifestyle. Perhaps he believed the non-scientific view.

Anita and Herb didn't live extravagantly but did have a great place in Bucks County, which I visited several times – it was here that her kiln baked the statue as well as the hexes and other works of hers that I own. The first time I visited, they had a big argument and she was not allowed to return upstairs until she did some kind of cleaning downstairs. I stayed out of the fight and Anita was devastated at being treated so brusquely. When once I drove them in a rented car to the old shed where some of her unsold art was stored, at a hardware store we had to rent one of those big cutters to cut the padlock off – no one had been in the room for decades, and Syracuse probably wouldn't even want to pay to dump the stuff into a garbage dump. But during the many times I visited at their Waverly Place apartment, all was fun and laughter. Herb loved to recharge batteries instead of buying new ones. Anita was deft at opening wine bottles as well as imbibing. If they took me to a restaurant, I made sure I didn't order anything on the menu that was more expensive than what they'd ordered – they were that kind of a couple! And I do miss them.

If I could have found time, I should have gone to Syracuse University to see if I could read the correspondence. I also suspect they've sold all the art, all but the statue of José Limon. Herb and I worried that this would happen. Anita seemed not to want ever to give anything away for free, which is an admirable trait, but Herb and I thought her work deserved to be in dozens of museums. Some is in an Israeli museum. I have one of the few existing copies of her book of poetry, *Nightshade*, inscribed to me as an esteemed friend and fascinating person.

Sweet Blues, an electric painting by Anita Weschler that I donated to the Forest Park Museum in Perry, Iowa.

Wheeler, Harold

At televised awards ceremonies, when the recipients talk too long, it's Harold Wheeler (born St. Louis, Missouri, 14 June 1943 -) who strikes up the band.

He was Gilbert Price's accompanist, and he did not charge him. I got him the street-level apartment at a house near mine on 45th Street. When just divorced, and short of funds, he hoped I would buy his Renault. He became the first Broadway band conductor (for Burt Bacharach's *Promises, Promises* (1968), married Hattie Winston (they have one child), and since 2005 he has worked on *Dancing With The Stars*.

Wheeler stood next to me when arsonists burned my recording studio, and one report stated that the two of us were caught in the fire.

At Gilbert Price's memorial, he played an emotional dirge. True, I had a semi-crush on this exceptionally talented pianist.

Wittman, Bill

At Variety Recording, Fernando and I found potential engineers visited almost daily to see if they could be hired. Joe Cyr, our original partner, told them that we had no vacancies. But, he told **William Zaum**, he could be a gofer for two weeks, no pay, someone to make errands, a person to go'fer coffees. Most job-seekers returned to their recording studio schools to obtain new leads, but Bill stayed. At the end of two weeks, he was hired.

First, he was curious. Second, he learned quickly anything Joe showed him. Third, he looked the part.

Whether the client was new made no difference. If it was Sun Ra, David Amram, or old clients, Bill was particularly liked. He knew the contemporary sound scene, and he was a natural.

William Zaum changed his name to **Bill Wittman**, and after years of being our chief engineer he has kept in touch. In 2011 he had been married to **Barbara** for 36 years and his son **Ian** was a third year resident in emergency medicine at NYU Medical Center and was getting married in April.

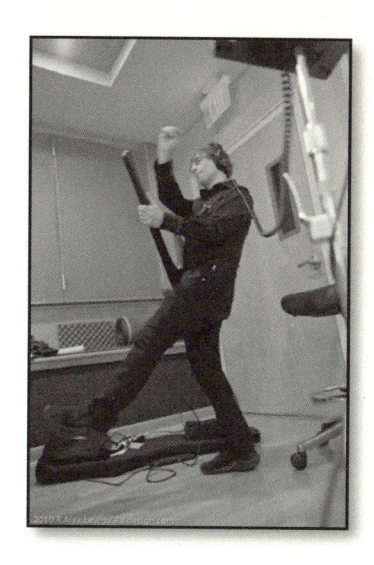

In 2014 he plays bass guitar in Cyndi's band (as well as functions as "musical director"). Her band opened for **Cher** on her "Dressed to Kill Tour" around the U.S. and Canada, as it had twelve years prior.

In Brooklyn, Bill (on the right) shared the stage with **Cyndi Lauper** and **Liza Minnelli**.

From the stage looking out at the audience:

Yankee, Luke

Yankee (7 February 1960 -), the son of **John Harrison Yankee Jr.** and **Eileen Heckart**, who won an Academy Award for *Butterflies are Free* and is a member of the Theatre Hall of Fame, was born in Stamford, Connecticut. Their two other sons are Philip (deceased in 2005) and Mark (who currently resides in Norwalk, Connecticut). After graduating from New Canaan High School in 1978, he attended the Juilliard School of Drama and New York University, where he received a B.A. in Drama and Literature in 1982.

Yankee has directed, produced, taught, lectured, and acted throughout the country and abroad. He has run two regional theatres, serving as Producing Artistic Director of the Long Beach Civic Light Opera in Long Beach, California, and the Struthers Library theatre in Warren, Pennsylvania.

Yankee's credits include the following:

Broadway – Assistant Director
> *Grind* starring Ben Vereen (as assistant to Harold Prince); *The Circle* with Rex Harrison and Glynis Johns *Light Up the Sky* with Peter Falk; New York City Opera's *Brigadoon* with Tony Roberts, and *Real Estate* with Sada Thompson.

Off-Broadway – Director
    Promenade Theatre, New York City –
        High Infidelity with John Davidson and Morgan Fairchild
        York Theatre, New York – Chekhov's *Cherry Orchard* with
        Penny Fuller and Cynthia Nixon.

Regional Theater – Director
        Nite Club Confidential with Barbara Eden; *Private Lives* with David Canary; *The King and I* with Lee Meriwether; *Driving Miss Daisy* with Eileen Heckart; *Man of La Mancha* with John McCook; *Love Letters* with Ed Asner, Joanna Gleason, John Rubinstein, Sally Struthers, and former California Governor Pete Wilson; the southeastern premiere of David Mamet's *Oleanna* (Carbonnell Award nomination as Best Director); the 30th anniversary revival of *Waiting for Godot* at the Coconut Grove Playhouse; a bi-lingual tour of *Cyrano De Bergerac,* and productions of *Sweeney Todd, The Road To Mecca, Painting Churches, Lost in Yonkers, A Little Night Music, Gypsy,* and *Lend Me A Tenor,* among others.

Yankee's writing credits include the highly acclaimed memoir, *Just Outside the potlight: Growing up with Eileen Heckart* (Random House 2006; Foreword by Mary Tyler Moore) and *A Place At Forest Lawn (*co-written with James Bontempo; Dramatists play Service 2008.) Other plays include *The Jesus Hickey* (which he directed in Los Angeles, starring Harry Hamlin) and *The Last Lifeboat.* The screenplay version of *The Last Lifeboat* was one of ten scripts selected for the 2012 *Plume & Peillicule* workshop in Switzerland and was the only American screenplay chosen out of more than 150 entries worldwide. He spent five years touring internationally with his one-man shows, *Diva Dish* and *Diva Dish: The Second Helping* which he has performed in theatres, at universities and on more than 25 cruises around the world.

As a director and producer of special events, Yankee has worked with Quincy Jones, Stephen Sondheim, Alec Baldwin, Noah Wyle, Annette Bening, Neil Simon, Barry Manilow, Debbie Allen, Dick Clark, Bill Pullman, John Guare, Roma Downey, Patti Austin, August Wilson, Alfre Woodard, and Betty White in theatres ranging from Radio City Music Hall to the *Crystal Symphony* cruise ship. Luke has also produced a number of special events and trade shows for the Mattel Toy Company.

As a filmmaker, Yankee wrote and directed the short film, *Help Is On The Way*, starring Lois DeBanzie. He also created *E.H. On Film: An Eileen Heckart Retrospective* and *Barbara Eden: Still Dreaming*. He also created and hosted the seminar series, *Conversations On Craft*, where he interviewed prominent people in the entertainment industry about their careers, with the proceeds from ticket sales going to charity. His guests included Edward Asner, Mark Rydell, Michael Learned, Marc Cherry, and David Lee.

In addition, Yankee has taught and guest-directed extensively at colleges, universities, and conservatories throughout the United States and abroad, including five years at the American Academy of Dramatic Arts, Northwestern, Ohio State University, the American Musical and Dramatic Academy, California State University – Long Beach, University of New Mexico, University of California – Irvine, the Folkwang Hochschule (in Essen, Germany); and three years on the faculty of Columbia College-Hollywood.

For the past 15 years, he has been a panelist and guest instructor at the William Inge Theatre Festival, where he has performed with Marybeth Hurt, Holland Taylor, George Grizzard and Carole Cook, among others. He is also a member of their Advisory Board.

His theatre acting credits include *Our Town* at the American Shakespeare Theatre with Fred Gwynne, the U.S. premiere of *The Greeks* at The Williamstown Theatre Festival with Gwyneth Paltrow, Blythe Danner, Christopher Reeve, and Celeste Holm and *The Dream Watcher* with Eva LeGallienne.

In film and television, he has appeared in *The Hiding Place* with Julie Harris, *Ragtime* with Elizabeth McGovern, *Evergreen* with Armand Assante, and *The Equalizer* with Jim Dale. He spent six years as casting director for the Los Angeles based, syndicated TV spot, *Hero In Education*.

Yankee currently lives in Long Beach, California, with his domestic partner, Don Hill, a professor of theatre at the University of California, Irvine.

5

From Twilight to Dusk

As a youth I lived "the good ol' days" of growing up during the Great Depression, when grasshoppers were a plague in parts of the Midwest. In a word, twilight finds me observing how pathetic life has become for Earth's creatures.

Five years ago, I had no intention of retiring nor, now 93, still have no such intention. But neither had I imagined it would be necessary to write a complaint to my co-op building's superintendent (**Scott Casazza**) the following:

> 21 May 2014
>
> Today when the doorman telephoned that Allen Reza was downstairs and coming up to accompany me to the American Academy of Arts and Letters, I put my door against the kitchen shutter to keep it open as well as help cool the room.
>
> A fellow shareholder, Mr. Michael Blazer in 10-F literally kicked my door and screamed "Keep your fucking door closed. You've been told many times. It's a fire hazard. I'll report you and get you thrown out."
>
> "I will report you for damaging my property," I replied in a normal voice, and he said something to the effect of "go ahead."
>
> Scott, I am giving you this copy for a follow-up. I am leaving now for the ceremonial. At some point, please check the door to see if there is visible damage.
>
> Mr. Reza is one of the 25 and growing ethicists that have formed as the result of the *New York Times* ethicist column who are in solidarity with his column about the "Cat Man." I will see 31 Jane's former tenant, Academy Member **Edward Hoagland**, author of *Cat Man,* and tell him about this as well as let him know that the names of 31 Jane Street Board Members and others who were involved will be printed in full in my forthcoming book.

As described above, *The New York Times* article about "Cat Man" has led me to spend my final years in a studio apartment that has not changed, but two of my neighbors have. One banged wildly on my door and threatened to sue me because I caught her blatantly lying and fingering another neighbor as being the one who reported my allowing my cat to roam the corridor without my being with the cat at all times (although I have supervised the cat's twelve years of playing for up to ten minutes outside my apartment – the feline was never alone). This I found bordered on the clinical, as does the other neighbor whom she snookered, neither of whom to my knowledge has been warned that such behavior is prohibited by our lease's stated right for shareholders to enjoy peace and quiet.

The 2012 elected Board of Directors for 31 Jane Street Tenants Association, that heard the above two shareholders' views and did not hear me in person, although I specifically asked the chairperson to be heard in person, were Alvin Alunan (4-G); Karen S. Lavine (18-D); Andrew Seibert (17-C); James Schmidt (8-H); Erin Shippee (9-F, Chairperson); and Fred Tripp (8-F). All are volunteers, so any blame rests entirely with Key. Two former members (Lavine, Schmidt) are no longer on the Board.

It is not clear how long the co-op Board of Directors has hired Key, but I would favor hiring another company. Soon! When I was on the Board with **Peter Foster** (below, who today is the lawyer who is my alternate Executor), we may have used Key.

A conversation that I had with **Arthur C. Clarke** at the Hotel Chelsea where he stopped briefly on his way back from the Mayo Clinic to Sri Lanka was both inspiring and non-inspiring. "Will we live to see organized religions' demise," I asked. "I was surprised," he responded, that on January 1st in 2001, I woke up, and it was 2001." We both expressed concern that religion, which he once described as "the most malevolent of all mind viruses," would lead to domination by one of the religious groups and the resultant deaths that would reduce the worldwide human population to fewer than a million by 3001. His room surely was not wired, but we did not say the word Islam. "I don't expect to wake up in

3001," I smiled. Arthur lived to be a little over 90 despite his frailties. I'm going on 94, despite mine. Bertrand Russell, whom we both admired, lived to be 97.

My extensive writing and getting published has been dependent upon my having Peter Ross, a computer technician. Not to be overlooked is that his physical problems include having, in 2013, the need for a pacemaker, which he is learning to live with. Also not to be overlooked is that he suffers from clinical depression. Appointments are seldom met on time, resulting in further deadline problems. On the one hand he stopped smoking cigarettes altogether, but in 2014 a mutual friend reported that he was seen smoking, at which time he saw no reason not to smoke despite physicians' concern.

Working with one who is depressed has required my careful choice of words – at one point, he angrily threw his phone on the floor and walked out of one of our many several-hour work sessions. To pay for his $75/hour jobs, I have always covered his apartment expenses. At times he was several thousand dollars ahead, and at other times he was several thousand dollars behind. He earned little from clients, accepted being on welfare, and received food supplements from government sources. When mentioning that he once had his own business and property such as a truck but now is depressed and always low on resources, he became more depressed. Since we met in 2001, I made sure he had the Apple computers and devices he needed, and he insured that my own Apple computer and devices were in good working order. Being dependent upon one computer technician with a serious life-threatening case of depression has been anything but relaxing. But his mature input, for example, not to include a logo from *The New York Times Magazine* was positive and mature, and his input has resulted in my often writing more precisely. His honesty is 100%. His loyalty in putting up with my weaknesses is 100%.

Writing entries for Philosopedia about individuals younger than I am who have died is an unusual way for me to relax.

Also, it has been relaxing, having grown old, to reflect on my life as death approaches. I am comfortable with my mortality and take responsibility for how I have handled life's challenges Fernando, who admired Frank Sinatra's enunciation and phrasing, and I clearly, as Sinatra sang, "did it our way."

Although I usually look forward, in the present work I have enjoyed looking back into my past.

It is what it is.

Obituary

Warren Allen Smith, a teacher, editor, businessman, and author, died on _____date_____ of happiness.

He was born 27 October 1921 in Minburn, Iowa, the son of a South Dakota homesteader's daughter and an Iowa-born (Waukee) grain dealer who had been a scout for the Chicago Cubs' Portland farm team. Drafted into the U.S. Army (1942-1946), he landed on Omaha Beach (1944) and became a Chief Clerk of the Adjutant General's Office in the Little Red Schoolhouse, Reims, France. In 1948, he received his B.A. from the University of Northern Iowa, and in 1949 with Professor Lionel Trilling as his advisor received his M.A. from Columbia University.

Smith taught at a private progressive school in Manhattan (Bentley, 1950-1954); at New Canaan (Connecticut) High School (1954-1986); and Teachers College, Columbia University (1961-1962).

In the 1950s he was book review editor of *The Humanist*, wrote reviews for *Library Journal*, and under the name Lvcretivs founded the Hvmanist Book Clvb.

In 1961 with Costa Rica-born Fernando Rodolfo de Jesus Vargas Zamora, he founded Variety Recording Studio, a major independent company in Times Square's 42nd Street and Broadway, advertising it as being "in the heart of showbiz." Their clients included Afro-Carib Records, David Amram, Black Roots of Dominica, Jerry Bock, Sammy Cahn, Franz Casseus; Ray Charles; Paddy Chayevsky; Celia Cruz; Des Moines YMCA Bell Ringers; Loretta Devine; Fantuzzi; Sammy Fields; Bob Fosse; Garifuna de Honduras; Hal Gordon; Grand Cayman Barefoot Man; John Guare; Marvin Hamlisch; Athena Hosey; Peggy Lee; Maurice Levine; Lorna Luft; Mary Martin; Carmen McCrae; Arthur Miller; Liza Minnelli; Earl Monroe; Mary Powell; Elvis Presley Music; Gilbert Price; Harold Prince; Tito Puente; Sun Ra; Paul Simon (Jerry Landis); Jimmy Smits; Susan Tyrell; United Jewish Appeal; Ultra Violet; Vangellis (Evangelos Odysseas Papathanassiou); Sarah Vaughan; Harold Wheeler; Robert Whitehead; Stefan Wolpe; and Stevie Wonder.

Smith was paramour of and business parter with Fernando Rodolfo de Jesus Vargas Zamora from 1948 until his death in 1989.

Smith was paramour of and personal agent – from 1963 until his death in 1991 – for Gilbert Price, three-time Tony Award nominee.

In 1971 he was a co-founder of Taursa, a mutual fund he named by combining Taurus and Ursa. From 1967 to 1993, he was chairman of the international Mensa Investment Club.

His articles about philosophy and literature were published in numerous international journals, including *The Villager* (New York); *The New Canaan Advertiser* (Connecticut); *The Educator* (Dominica); *Gay and Lesbian Humanist* (United Kingdom); *Philosophy Now* (United Kingdom); and *Pink Humanist* (international). Authors who corresponded with him or cited their correspondence with him included Barrows Dunham; Corliss Lamont; Thomas Mann; George Santayana; John Steinbeck; and William Carlos Williams. He wrote book jacket blurbs or forewords for books by sci-fi writer Isaac Asimov and a biography about Premier Edward O. LeBlanc of the Commonwealth of Dominica. Sci-fi writer Arthur C. Clarke corresponded from 1991 to 2004.

Seven of Smith's works (five different titles, and a 3-volume autobiography) were published after he reached the age of 80. *Who's Who in Hell* was a 1,264-page biographical listing of over ten thousand philosophic subjects and documented names of non-believers. *Celebrities in Hell* included biographical listings of people whose belief systems have run against the grain. *Gossip from Across the Pond* is a collection of a decade of his columns in the United Kingdom's *Gay & Lesbian Humanist*. *Cruising the Deuce* described Times Square Manhattan grind houses and the subculture that flourished on 42nd Street in the 1940s to 1980s. *In the Heart of Showbiz, A Triography*, was an autobiography in three volumes.

As a spokesperson for Bangladesh dissident Taslima Nasrin, he edited several of her autobiographical and poetry works and helped start her online web page. When the governments of Bangladesh and West Bengal banned two of her books, Smith posted them on the web for reading or downloading for free.

Smith was an activist member of Act Up (and was in the June 1969 Stonewall Uprising in Greenwich Village); the Bertrand Russell Society (a board member from 1977 until 2014); FreethinkersNY (a co-founder); Mensa (1964 until his death); the New York Society for Ethical Culture; the Rationalist Press Association (United Kingdom); and the Unitarian Society.

He leaves no survivors.

31 Jane Street, where I wrote all my columns and books

Waukee, Iowa, Cemetery

SPENCER SMITH
1843 AYLMER, ONT. 1923 WAUKEE, IA
HOTELIER & FOUNDER OF WAUKEE

MARTHA SCHAEFFER SMITH
1848   1916

MABEL SMITH WOOLEY

HARRY CLARK SMITH
1887 WAUKEE IA - 1975 RIPPEY IA
3RD BASE PORTLAND FARM TEAM
CHICAGO CUBS
GRAIN DEALER MINBURN RIPPEY

RUTH MILES SMITH
1891 - 1975

WARREN ALLEN SMITH
1921 MINBURN IA
SECULAR HUMANIST

What do we *know* about Russia? If we are to make policy decisions on the basis of facts rather than guesswork, we must turn to our scholars for information. Scholars themselves need to know which areas have been explored by their colleagues and what topics most urgently require further investigation. This book is the first major attempt by a non-governmental group to analyze the results of our study of Russia in eleven fields since World War II.

The study of Russia presents a fascinating challenge to the American scholar, precisely because of the difficulties that surround it. Data are always incomplete, often deliberately deceptive. Gregory Grossman, author of the chapter on economics, compares the economist's work on Soviet Russia to that of the archaeologist who must reconstruct a whole civilization from a few fragments of pottery—except that the fragments, at least, are genuine. The record of American scholarship is impressive, despite these difficulties. But much remains to be done.

The contributors to this book urge more research in certain fields and greater collaboration between the specialists in these fields and those in which more work has been done. The sputniks, the discussions of the Soviet educational system, the strength of the Communist movement in Asia, the newly-emphasized Communist policies of foreign aid and foreign trade—all have combined to force us to realize the need for learning everything we can about Soviet Russia, past and present.

Specialists and non-specialists alike will find in AMERICAN RESEARCH ON RUSSIA a guide to our present knowledge and a clear indication of the most serious gaps that remain to be filled.

American Research on Russia

EDITED BY HAROLD H. FISHER

American Research on RUSSIA

INDIANA UNIVERSITY PRESS
Bloomington

Copyright © 1959 by Indiana University Press
Manufactured in the United States of America
Library of Congress catalog card number: 59-10870

PREFACE

A GREAT DEAL of research on Russia has been done in the United States since World War II. This is a matter of common knowledge, but many of those who have been doing this research have little or no notion of what has been accomplished in fields of specialization adjacent to their own. Others who are not specialists but for one reason or another are interested in Russia, the Soviet Union, and the Communist movement, have even less reason to know what subjects have been investigated, what has been written about these subjects, and where these writings may be found. At the same time, the lack of this information makes it difficult to know the topics on which further investigation is most urgent or most promising. Furthermore, without knowledge of what studies have been made, it is impossible to make the best use for general education and public enlightenment of the truly impressive scholarly work of the last few years. The essays in this book are intended to provide this information, first, by reviewing American research on Russia during the years since World War II and, secondly, by indicating some of the topics on which further research would benefit the specialist and the nonspecialist and add to our knowledge of an important area.

The essays were written at the suggestion of a subcommittee of the Joint Committee on Slavic Studies of the American Council of Learned Societies and the Social Science Research Council. This Subcommittee on the Review of Russian Studies has conducted a general survey of Russian studies in the United States, which has covered not only research but also the organization and development of Russian area studies and the impact of these studies on general education.* A complementary survey of library problems and needs has been made by a committee of the Association of Research Libraries. The purpose of these surveys is to present information on recent experience and to stimulate thought, provoke discussion, and draw out suggestions regarding the direction and methods of Russian studies during the next decade.

The authors of the eleven essays in this book prepared their first drafts as discussion papers for a conference held under the auspices of the Joint Committee at Cambridge, Massachusetts, January 30-31, 1958, in conjunction with the tenth anniversary of the Russian Research Center of Harvard University. The draft of each paper was read and commented on by specialists in the respective fields and, in most cases, by at least one other scholar in the discipline who was not a Russian specialist. The authors have taken into account these comments and the Cambridge discussions, but the final versions are the views of the individual authors.

The introductory chapter by Dr. Philip E. Mosely is based on an address made at the Cambridge conference. Dr. Mosely, now Director of Studies at the Council of Foreign Relations, was formerly Director of the Russian Institute of Columbia University, and is one of the founders of Russian area studies in the United States and a leader of great influence in their growth. His observations on interdisciplinary, cooperative, and group re-

* The reports on education will be published in a volume on *The Study of Russia in American Education* (Indiana University Press).

search, on government and privately sponsored research projects, and on the peculiar difficulties and achievements in this field of scholarship are based on a wide acquaintance with the work of the individuals and institutions which have accomplished so much in the study of Russia.

As will appear, the authors place the principal focus of their essays on research by American scholars outside the government. They also discuss the different kinds of research that have been done in their disciplines, and refer to certain titles that illustrate these trends or are otherwise significant. None of the contributors attempts to cover all research done in his field or to present a comprehensive bibliographical survey of that research. They all, however, suggest topics, periods, and methods to which more attention should be given.

The writers have approached their subjects in a variety of ways. Some have surveyed the work in their fields by topics, others by major works; some have listed a good many titles, others only a few which they considered representative. Some have given more and some less attention to published articles and to studies in progress. Some have had more occasion than others to refer to work done before World War II, to research by other than American scholars, and to studies made under government contract. All have dealt to some extent with topics of both the Imperial and the Soviet period, the amount of attention being determined by the amount of research, which, in turn, has been largely determined by the nature of the discipline. For example, in such disciplines as economics, political science, and social relations, the analysis of pre-Soviet materials has been considered by most of the contributors to be the business of the historian, and the review of historical research refers to several studies of this type.

Most of the essayists have discussed area-oriented interdisciplinary research and discipline-oriented individual research together. Since much research has been done under the sponsorship of the various Russian area programs, considerable emphasis has been put on an integrated outlook in the study of Russian society through drawing upon the insights and techniques of several disciplines. Sometimes this has turned out very well; sometimes not so well. The evidence is not sufficient to determine whether the occasionally unsatisfactory result is due to something inherent in the "integration" approach or to failure, as yet, to solve some of the problems involved in this seemingly promising method. In the meantime there has been a substantial increase in the research done in the spirit and according to the rules of traditional discipline study. The essays do not examine the relative merits of the integrated and the non-integrated method, but the reviews of what has been accomplished and the suggestions of what needs to be done indicate that both methods should be encouraged.

The eleven fields surveyed—history, geography, political science, economics, social relations, philosophy and religion, literature, linguistics, music, fine arts, and science—do not include all the fields of specialization in which work on Russia has been or is being done. No separate surveys have been made of the research done on the history and structure of Russian and Soviet education, or on painting, sculpture, choreography, and the dramatic arts. Some reference is made to these aspects of Russian life in the essays, but the absence of separate surveys is an indication that very little research has been done in these fields. Some investigations have been made of and much has been written about Soviet education, especially since Soviet scientists and technologists made such a sensational demonstration of the high quality of their work, and some of these studies are mentioned in the chapters on history, social relations, and science.

In conclusion I know that I speak for the contributors in acknowledging the assistance of Professor C. E. Black of Princeton University and Mr. John M. Thompson of the Social Science Research Council, chairman and staff assistant of the Subcommittee on the Review of Russian Studies, in the preparation of these essays. I wish also to express the thanks of the participants in this undertaking to the scholars who commented on the original drafts of the papers and especially to the Subcommittee on Grants of the Joint Committee on Slavic Studies, whose generous aid made this publication possible.

H. H. F.

CONTENTS

1. The Growth of Russian Studies   PHILIP E. MOSELY   1
2. History   JOHN S. CURTISS   23
3. Economics   GREGORY GROSSMAN   34
4. Political Science   JOHN A. ARMSTRONG   50
5. Philosophy and Religion   GEORGE L. KLINE   66
6. Social Relations   ARTHUR S. BARRON   77
7. Science   JOHN TURKEVICH   103
8. Geography   W. A. DOUGLAS JACKSON   113
9. Literature   EDWARD J. BROWN   123
10. Linguistics   FRANCIS J. WHITFIELD   139
11. Music   ROBERT M. SLUSSER   151
12. Architecture and Minor Arts   PAUL WILLEN   164

13. Postscript HAROLD H. FISHER   176

    Notes   187

    Index   233

CONTRIBUTORS

JOHN A. ARMSTRONG is associate professor of political science at the University of Wisconsin and the author of *Ukrainian Nationalism 1939-1945*, and *The Soviet Bureaucratic Elite: A Case Study of the Ukrainian Apparatus*.

ARTHUR S. BARRON studied at the Russian Institute of Columbia University and received his doctorate in sociology at Columbia. Formerly with the Research Institute of America, he is now on the staff of CBS News.

EDWARD J. BROWN is professor of Russian at Brown University and attended the Fourth International Congress of Slavists in Moscow in September, 1958. He is the author of *The Proletarian Episode in Russian Literature, 1928-1932*.

JOHN S. CURTISS is professor of history at Duke University and has written two studies of the position of the Orthodox Church in modern Russia, *Church and State in Russia* and *The Russian Church and the Soviet State*, as well as a brief interpretation of *The Russian Revolutions of 1917*.

HAROLD H. FISHER is professor of international relations at San Francisco State College. He was an officer of the American Relief Administration during its operations in eastern Europe after the First World War and during the Russian famine of 1921-23. He was for many years professor of history and chairman of the Hoover Institute and Library at Stanford University.

GREGORY GROSSMAN is associate professor of economics at the University of California, Berkeley, and the author of articles on the Soviet economy.

CONTRIBUTORS

W. A. DOUGLAS JACKSON is associate professor of geography at the University of Washington and has written on Russian agricultural geography.

GEORGE L. KLINE is assistant professor of philosophy at Columbia University. He has translated V. V. Zenkovsky's *A History of Russian Philosophy* and has selected, translated, and written an introduction for a series of essays published under the title *Spinoza in Soviet Philosophy*.

PHILIP E. MOSELY is director of studies at the Council on Foreign Relations. He served with the Department of State during the Second World War and was director of the Russian Institute at Columbia University from 1951 to 1955. He is the author of *Russian Diplomacy and the Opening of the Eastern Question in 1838 and 1839* and has written extensively on Soviet foreign policy and international affairs.

ROBERT M. SLUSSER studied at the Russian Institute of Columbia University. From 1953 to 1956 he was associate director of the Research Program on the U.S.S.R. of the East European Fund, and since that time he has been co-director of A Study of Soviet Treaties at the Hoover Institution, Stanford University.

JOHN TURKEVICH is professor of chemistry at Princeton University. His avocation is the study of the development of Soviet science. He has frequently served as a consultant to the government and has contributed a number of significant articles in this field.

FRANCIS J. WHITFIELD is professor of Slavic languages and literatures and chairman of that department at the University of California, Berkeley. He has written *A Russian Reference Grammar* and prepared a one-volume abridgment of Prince Mirsky's *History of Russian Literature*.

PAUL WILLEN is an architecture student at Pratt Institute, Brooklyn. He also studied at the Russian Institute of Columbia University and has been on the staff of Radio Free Europe. He has written articles on Soviet and East European affairs and prepared for the Free Europe Press a volume entitled *Satellite Agriculture in Crisis*.

American Research on Russia

Philip E. Mosely

1. THE GROWTH OF RUSSIAN STUDIES

I

THE FIRST BEGINNINGS in the continuous and systematic study of Russia by American scholars date back to the years before 1914, when the United States was groping toward an understanding of its emerging role in world politics, and therefore felt a need to enlarge its intellectual horizons beyond the traditional fascination with the literature, the arts, and the history of western Europe and the Mediterranean. And this was the decade in which Tolstoy and Chekhov, Stanislavsky and Diagilev, Musorgsky and Tchaikovsky became familiar and exciting spirits throughout the West, returning to the older centers of science and culture the new and challenging gifts of a Russian renaissance. Prior to these years, it is true, talented individuals—Eugene Schuyler and George Kennan (uncle of George F. Kennan), among them—had sporadically "discovered" Russia for Americans, but the "naturalization" of Russian studies could begin only with their anchoring in universities and their curricula. By 1914 there were three chairs of Russian language and literature—at Harvard, Columbia, and California—and courses in Russian history were being taught at California and Harvard.

A new stage in the study of Russia began with the dramatic and perplexing events of the Russian Revolution. The emergence of an entirely new and, for the West, unforeseen system of ideas and power aroused an unceasing if unfocused curiosity about Russia's origins and much speculation about its future. The same upheavals also brought to our shores a number of talented Russian scholars who, together with American-born scholars, did much, during the 1920's and 1930's, to nourish a slow but steady development of Russian studies, primarily in the traditional fields of history and literature. During these two decades a few American-trained scholars, not more than a dozen or so, were also equipping themselves for research and teaching, through systematic training in the Russian language and in their disciplines as applied to Russian studies. By 1937, when access to the Soviet Union became almost impossible, most of them had benefited, and benefited greatly, from varying periods of intensive research and direct experience in Russia.

Meanwhile, several modest steps were being taken to establish a wider framework for scholarly work related to Russia. In 1934, on the initiative of the American Council of Learned Societies and with the support of the Rockefeller Foundation, a first and very useful experiment was launched in the improved teaching of the Russian language. Three intensive summer courses, held at Columbia, Harvard, and Berkeley, helped lay to rest one persistent bogy, proving that with the right methods a reading knowledge of Russian can be acquired in a relatively few months. This experience, and the materials and methods developed from it, provided a springboard for the war-time and postwar programs for the intensive teaching of Russian. For the head start of Russian area studies in the intensive teaching of the language, scholars in this field are deeply indebted to the efforts of the American Council of Learned Societies and particularly of Mortimer Graves, its executive secretary.

The ACLS, through Mortimer Graves, also took the first

initiative in providing a focus through which the opportunities and needs of Russian studies could be studied and presented in a wider setting, by appointing, in 1938, a Committee on Slavic Studies.* In reviewing the prospects and requirements for this infant field of study, the committee emphasized the importance of intensive language training and of building up research materials on a systematic basis. It pointed out some of the major gaps in our research personnel and resources, and outlined some of the main requirements for the effective study of Russia, for example, the need for economists and political scientists, geographers and sociologists equipped in this field. As a stimulus to the setting up of college courses on Russian history and literature it arranged for the preparation and publication of a 1,500-item selected *List of Works on Slavic Civilizations, in West European Languages,* and followed this with a 500-item basic list of Russian books essential to college teaching in this field. To fill some of the gaps in library resources, it undertook the offset reprinting of several scarce books of special importance to research training, and it encouraged the ACLS to set up an extensive and very useful Russian reprint program, conducted mainly through the University of Michigan Press. Through an intellectual offshoot, the Russian Translation Project, conducted in 1942-48 by a devoted editor, W. Chapin Huntington, some twenty-five important Russian books of political, economic, and intellectual history, as well as geography and political science, were translated, carefully edited, and published in English.

From its inception the Committee on Slavic Studies, without in any way depreciating the cooperation and hospitality which the editors of the *Slavonic and East European Review* (London) had always shown their American colleagues, had stressed the need for an American journal to serve as a focus and stimulus to

* George R. Noyes, chairman, 1938-39; Samuel H. Cross, chairman, 1939-46; Philip E. Mosely, chairman, 1947-48; others members for varying terms: Geroid T. Robinson, Alfred Senn, Ernest J. Simmons, Marvin Farber, Francis J. Whitfield.

research and publication, and in 1939 it undertook to establish the *American Slavic and East European Review*, with assistance from the Curt H. Reisinger Foundation. After drawing up a comprehensive list of some 300 people teaching in the Slavic field, the committee arranged for this constituency to nominate and then elect a board of editors, who then elected Samuel H. Cross as the first editor of the *Review*. Plans for a first issue had been completed, and the articles and reviews received or promised, when, in December 1940, Cross received a heart-rending cable from Sir Bernard Pares. Because of the savage fire-bombing of London, the *Slavonic and East European Review* had been crippled and Pares asked his American colleagues to carry on the *Review* until the war was over. Naturally, there could be only one response, and therefore the war-time issues of the American *Review* bear the title and numbering of its British elder brother.

During the period until 1941 most studies by American scholars dealt with the history and literature of Russia prior to 1917. One prominent exception was the work of Samuel N. Harper and of several of his pupils at the University of Chicago; a beginning was also being made at Harvard and Columbia in the fields of political science and economics. However, with a few exceptions most of the efforts to study contemporary Soviet Russia were carried on, not by university scholars, but by talented journalists, such as William Henry Chamberlin and Louis Fischer. Some of the "schoolmen" felt, however, that a systematic study of contemporary foreign civilizations was both possible and necessary, and in the years 1938-41 there was some discussion of setting up Russian and other "area programs." Several of these proposals had a markedly linguistic flavor, assuming that the study of the history, institutions, and culture of Russia should proceed from a perfect mastery of the language, both printed and spoken. On the other hand, the organized social science disciplines, except history, were then unsympathetic to the concept of area studies;

for them, a discipline could only be universal in validity, and "area studies," largely untried as yet, seemed of doubtful scholarly value or promise. Still, many future Russian specialists received indispensable fellowship support from 1924 on through the programs of the Social Science Research Council, in addition to fellowships provided by the ACLS.

Another difficulty sometimes hampered Russian studies in their early development. Sometimes the general public, and occasionally even college administrators, found it hard to believe that Russia could be the subject of objective teaching and research. Scholars interested in studying Russia not infrequently were asked: "Are you for it or against it?" As a result of an unrelenting emphasis upon careful and systematic research achievement, this naive assumption that in one way or another one must be "for" or "against" has been almost completely dissipated. Today any conscientious scholar can state his strong attachment to the liberal values of our free society and at the same time calmly pursue his researches to their own factual conclusions, however discomforting these may be to him and his readers.

II

The cataclysm of World War II, in shaking the world, also shook up the small world of Russian studies. The national interest, indeed, the national survival, brought new needs and demanded urgent and accurate answers to many difficult questions. One requirement, which some scholars foresaw many months before the national government, was to provide at least small numbers of people trained in languages, from Japanese and Burmese to Urdu and Swahili, and versed in the history and culture of many peoples in many distant parts of the world. The ACLS Committee on Language Instruction in the Emergency, created within a few days after Pearl Harbor, did yeoman service, with support from the foundations, in identifying scarce resources in teachers and informants and in filling many gaps in teaching materials and methods. Although the teaching of more than forty "unusual" languages was eventually introduced or strengthened under this program, Russian, with its head start, was the first to be taught, from late January 1942, in a new "super-intensive" course, first at Cornell and then elsewhere.

It was also clear from the start of hostilities that the knowledge of a "strange" language must be backed by at least some familiarity with the culture and institutions, customs and thought-patterns, of the peoples studied, and again it was a Russian Area Program, also at Cornell, which pioneered in the first area studies program, with the support of the Rockefeller Foundation. At first government agencies insisted stoutly that there was no possible utility in these and similar "boondoggling" programs, but by 1943, convinced by experience of the crucial need for interrogators, intelligence specialists, liaison and military government personnel, the Army and Navy set about developing numerous Area Studies Training Programs of their own on a scale which dwarfed the modest efforts of the ACLS, the foundations and universities. From these programs, and from the experience the Army and Navy area students had subsequently gained in many far-flung corners of the globe, came the inrush of able, enthusiastic, and mature young men and women who made the new postwar programs a dynamic addition to our educational and research resources. From this war-time experience have come also the excellent postwar language schools of the Army and Air Force, as well as continuing programs of the services for training groups of selected officers in the universities' area programs.

The central authorities of a government waging war around the globe needed expert area information on an entirely new and unprecedented scale. Was the entire Japanese nation inspired by a *kamikaze* psychology? How could the Arabs of the Maghreb be persuaded to contribute to an early Allied victory? How could friction be minimized between the masses of American servicemen and their friendly but often exasperated host peoples in Britain, France, and elsewhere? Clyde Kluckhohn, Ruth Benedict, and their colleagues proved by their incisive studies that it was possible, working at a distance and relying on the raw materials at hand, to analyze the Japanese institutional and psychological structure to great effect. The same desperate need for accurate information and reliable forecasts also applied to our relations with the Soviet Union.

Although Russia was an ally, its rulers were even less communicative than in peace-time when it came to supplying information needed in Washington to make vital decisions or establish painful priorities. Yet it was important to know whether Murmansk and Vladivostok could actually handle great amounts of supplies and equipment, or whether the upshot of meeting the vast Soviet demands would be to leave scarce shipping riding idle in roadsteads for many weeks while other fronts were starved of supplies. How far could the unoccupied areas of the U.S.S.R. feed the people and the army, and how much food should the United States and Canada supply? And what were Soviet intentions toward the not yet occupied countries of east central Europe? Was Tito likely to be a national or a Muscovite Communist? The range of questions was almost infinite, the research resources sadly limited, and the conviction grew among the overworked area specialists that systematic steps must be taken after the war to plug these gaps in the arsenal of national policy.

Among many agencies which attempted to provide informed answers—ranging from "hard" answers on logistics to "soft" ones on intentions and attitudes—the Research and Analysis Branch of the Office of Strategic Services rendered pre-eminent services. Geroid T. Robinson served as the Chief of R & A, U.S.S.R., with John S. Curtiss and Abram Bergson as his immediate assistants. Despite the glamorized notions which have gathered about some of the activities of OSS, the work of R & A was a real research slugging match, mustering the inadequate data as carefully as possible, and interpreting them with the combined analytical techniques of historians, economists, sociologists, oil and food specialists, and engineers. The answers, demanded with a deadline attached, were cranked into the machinery of state, which spewed forth its crucial decisions of policy and operations. The field of inquiry was, if anything, wider-ranging, more recalcitrant, and more poignant in its meaning for human lives than even the broadest academic program of today. The R & A experience showed that analysts of many different skills not only could but must work in harness to accomplish many types of research. While neither R & A nor the present area programs have broken down the walls which separate the social sciences, they have broken through many new channels of mutual comprehension and cooperation. Thus the determination to establish graduate programs of interdisciplinary teaching and research on Russia and the U.S.S.R. grew out of both prewar hopes and war-time urgencies.

Just as the war came to a close, farsighted university administrators and foundation officials were debating the meaning of the United States' world-wide contacts and responsibilities and the ways in which the universities could help promote a new level and range of information and understanding of distant areas and unfamiliar peoples. Because of the prewar pioneering in the Russian field, and because of the availability of a small reserve of senior scholars in a variety of disciplines, the field of Russian studies was better equipped than most others to press forward in this new initiative, and in the first two years after the war five new or enlarged programs received substantial university-plus-foundation support for greatly strengthened work in Russian studies. Returning enriched in mind by their war-time experiences, both teachers and students plunged with enthusiasm and conviction into this challenging experiment.

In the rapid growth of Russian studies after 1945, organized channels of research effort, interpreting to universities and foundations the needs as the scholars saw them, again played an active part. The main difference now was that the social sciences were adding their backing to the continuing contributions of the humanities. It was, for example, the World Areas Research Committee of the Social Science Research Council which in 1946 laid down the basic criteria for defining an adequate graduate program of area studies: five disciplines or more, working closely together, intensive language training, substantial library resources, administrative recognition of the program within the system of instruction. The SSRC program of postwar "reconversion" fellowships enabled many area specialists to turn from wartime service to productive research during their transition back to academic pursuits. The SSRC program of Area Research Fellowships, inaugurated in 1947, for the first time gave specific recognition to the opportunities and needs in this field. At the end of 1946 the *American Slavic and East European Review* surveyed its role afresh and adopted new policies, emphasizing new areas of interest. Under the editorship of Ernest J. Simmons and John N. Hazard, it has both reflected and stimulated a rapidly growing maturity of research. The Committee for the Promotion of Advanced Slavic Studies, Inc., inspired and guided by R. Gordon Wasson, has made many contributions to research and publication, with special attention to the culture and history of pre-Soviet Russia and to the needs of Slavic linguistics.

In 1947 the ACLS Committee on Slavic Studies was enlarged and strengthened by becoming the Joint Committee on Slavic Studies, appointed concurrently by the ACLS and the SSRC. A major part of its work has been to improve and broaden the flow of published research materials in many ingenious ways, to make west European repositories more accessible to scholarly use, to recommend the completion of the Cyrillic bibliography of the Library of Congress, to expedite the distribution of Library of Congress duplicates, to encourage the publication of the Library's *Monthly List of Russian Accessions* and the parallel bibliographies on east central Europe. A special concern of the Joint Committee has been the establishment and operation of the *Current Digest of the Soviet Press,* an invaluable tool for both teaching and research.

The Joint Committee has also advocated successfully the enlargement of programs for the support of research training, for advanced research leaves and other grants-in-aid. Under four successive chairmen and with a membership reflecting the insights of several disciplines, the Joint Committee has labored long and hard to strengthen the resources of Slavic studies. The Inter-University Committee on Travel Grants has moved energetically, once the barriers were lowered in 1954, to enlarge the opportunity for scholars to see something of the Soviet Union at first hand and, under the U.S.-Soviet cultural exchange agreement of January 1958, to enable American graduate students to take advantage of the opportunity to do research in the Soviet Union, while arranging reciprocal opportunities for advanced Soviet students in American universities. Finally, no review of Slavic studies can fail to pay tribute to the many and great contributions which the Library of Congress, wisely advised by Sergius Yakobson, Chief of its Slavic and Central European Division, has made and is making to the advancement of this field of research.

III

Russian area studies may be experimental, but there is nothing unique or mysterious about their purpose or their methods. The function of area studies is the same for Russian studies as for the study of China or Japan, India, the Moslem world, Africa, or Latin America. Their educational purpose is to help people see a society, a system of power, or an economy, or all three interacting together as they do in real life, and to see them both in their interconnections and as a whole.

In an age of scientific specialization this is not an easy task. As our various disciplines have broken away, since the eighteenth century, from their stern parent, Moral Philosophy, they have often tended to emphasize their separateness from each other, the unique validity of their exclusive methodologies, and even the mutual incomprehensibility of their vocabularies. The area studies approach can, as I see it, help to pull the fissiparous disciplines back together again, not by administrative fiat but by a common dedication to the study of a single civilization or area. Like all educational enterprises, this is a difficult and never finished one, but the effort to see any human society and see it whole is in itself an exciting experience in self-education.

Viewed in this perspective, area studies are not a real innovation, a "sport," within education. For several centuries the interdisciplinary study of ancient Greece and Rome provided the central core for the training of minds in the West, and classical training has today a high prestige in Britain and France. In addition to mastering grammar and vocabulary, a student of the classics must understand the philosophy and logic, the literature and history, the political, economic, and social institutions, the religious beliefs and military strategies of the ancient world, and, above all, the interconnections among them. The peculiar feature of classical studies is that they deal with a civilization which in its fully developed form seemed relatively stable for several centuries and which can no longer be studied *in situ* today. In contrast, area studies aim to study and interpret living societies, all of which are developing, some slowly, some tempestuously, but none without profound implications for the future of mankind.

In the few years since 1945 a number of factors have favored the emergence of Russian area studies as a relatively strong segment within the widening field of area studies. For one thing, no one can go far in studying Russia without realizing how closely different aspects of its life interact. The Soviet leadership aims to create a monolithic system, embracing potentially all activities. What happens in the economy interacts with, and is affected by, changes in the structure of political power. Literature is influenced strongly by the changing demands of the ruling party and in turn reflects changes in the purposes and expectations of the Party. This factor of interaction, which is displayed in varying degrees in both Soviet and earlier Russian development, makes it natural for students of Russia to attempt to apply a coordinated or multidisciplinary approach, more so than would be easy in analyzing a highly dispersed system with many interacting centers of power or resistance.

A further advantage in the impetus given to Russian studies has been that one major and not very difficult language opens up the study of the principal forces and actions of the system of power and the economy. The languages of the non-Russian peoples unlock other cultures and problems for study, and there is an encouraging widening of our research focus to include study of the non-Russian peoples. In this field, as well as in comparing these forces and factors with what is happening within the Soviet-dominated satellite countries, there are many urgent themes of research. Nevertheless, unlike the situation in Far Eastern, Moslem, and Indic studies, the beginning specialist on Russia can accomplish a great deal after learning one principal language well, and this has made possible a relatively short period of basic area training, compared with the study of most other non-European areas.

The challenge of Soviet secretiveness has certainly added a special zest to research in the Russian field. If the Soviet leadership should open up many more aspects of its system to easy study, perhaps scholars would not feel to the same degree the challenge to probe the obscurities of Soviet data, to piece together the confusing and conflicting figures on the growth of the Soviet economy, to penetrate the workings of the Communist Party and the political police. To the student of the Soviet system the excitement of discovering the bits and pieces and fitting them into meaningful patterns is as stimulating as a similar task is to the archaeologist, except that new "artifacts" are turned out every day by the Soviet press and radio instead of being dug laboriously out of ancient ruins or kitchen middens. The unceasing effort of research is spurred on by the need to analyze, urgently and objectively, what the Soviet system is, how it is evolving, and how the Soviet leaders use their growing power, at home and abroad.

To meet this need, Russian area studies centers and institutes have endeavored, within the limits of trained personnel and budgets available, to provide an essential framework for systematic research, backed by growing but far from adequate facilities. They have elaborated programs of necessary research, identifying gaps and encouraging promising students to fill them. They have trained, far better than was possible before the war, substantial numbers of teachers, government officials, and journalists. Like scholars in other fields they have worked hard to build a solid body of verified knowledge. When solid data fail, they point out the role of projection and conjecture, thus widening the areas of systematic and verifiable knowledge and diminishing gradually the necessity to rely on personal hunches and insights, however inspired. That great strides have been made in building up this body of knowledge and that much more must be done is confirmed in the reports that follow.

Merely to accumulate research bricks, however workmanlike each may be, is to stop far short of our duty to scholarship and to an informed public opinion. Area studies offer a special opportunity to work out a systematic framework of interrelated concepts to explain the strengths and weaknesses, the forces and the resistances, of the society under study, and ultimately to predict within broad limits the directions in which it is moving. Some important efforts have been made to analyze the broad structures and dynamics of the Soviet system, but more efforts are needed. Remembering the influence which personal and political predilections exercised in the 1920's and 1930's on the interpretation of Soviet events, postwar scholars have understandably preferred to prove their mastery of method and to leave the more massive enterprises until later. In the next decade, I predict, students of Russian affairs will be better equipped to devote more attention to the dynamic aspects of the Soviet society and system, and they will be the more encouraged to do so if that society, after appearing almost frozen for so long, continues to display signs of gradual change.

IV

Because area study programs strive, however imperfectly, to look at a society or a system of power as a whole, they have a special opportunity and duty to pioneer in projects of multidisciplinary research. In this part of our research there have been some notable efforts and some solid achievements. The Harvard Russian Refugee Interview project showed that scholars of different disciplines can work together fruitfully, learning a great deal from each other and about each other's methods in the process. If the successive steps from raw data to broad conclusions about the nature of the Soviet system proved not quite as simple and direct as had been assumed in the beginning, both the experience and the products of this project have added a great deal to the realism of Russian studies.

The study of Russia in Asia, carried on at the University of Washington, has brought together scholars of several disciplines and of very different if contiguous areas, and its results, for both Russian and Chinese studies, are of great interest. A somewhat different, more contemporary, study of Russian and Asian interactions is progressing favorably at the University of Southern California, and Stanford and Columbia have been hospitable to work in this difficult field.

The studies of the RAND Corporation on the Soviet economy have shown the great importance of intensive full-time research in a stimulating and self-critical environment, if we are to plumb successfully the mysteries of deceptive or self-deceptive Soviet statistics. Similarly, the studies of Soviet politics at RAND, by Nathan Leites and others, have opened up new techniques of analysis and emphasized the need for more experimental approaches. The War Documentation Project of Columbia University attempted to bring several disciplines to bear on the study of the behavior of the Soviet population under German occupation, as a means of investigating the impact of Soviet rule on the people governed. The studies of the Massachusetts Institute of Technology on the working of Soviet society, on the economies of the east European satellites, and on Soviet education have similarly brought together a wide variety of skills and professions.

While our scholars have learned a little about interdisciplinary research, there is, I am sure, no single or preordained pattern to serve as a guide. A new pattern has to be worked out, by trial and error, for each new major problem. Russian studies, nevertheless, have developed a substantial body of scholars who have learned to work together, combining their different skills and insights to tackle problems which would leave an individual researcher dazed and helpless. Side by side with interdisciplinary efforts, cooperative research of a more customary variety has also been practiced on a fairly wide scale. In the Research Program on the U.S.S.R., a part of the East European Fund, Inc., some of the ablest of the ex-Soviet scholars worked closely with American-trained scholars expert in their own fields; the new arrivals learned a great deal about Western standards of research and American scholars learned much about life and research within the Soviet Union. In a related field the Mid-European Studies Center of the Free Europe Committee, Inc., brought together much systematic information on east central Europe. Working under a still different pattern, the Institute for the Study of the U.S.S.R. in Munich offers an outlet for research talents among the ex-Soviet refugees. Its resources could be utilized to greater advantage by west European and American research workers. The Research Program on the History of the Communist Party of the Soviet Union is similarly an attempt to identify our resources and fill some of the gaps in the study of the Soviet system of power and ideology.

Interdisciplinary, or as I prefer to call it, multidisciplinary research is neither an open sesame nor a nostrum. It is not a prescription which can be filled by rote. It can be very rewarding if it allows time for individual minds to understand and adopt the underlying concepts and apply the methods of related fields of work. Unless the economist is paired with a sociologist or a social psychologist it is going to be difficult for him to measure the role of incentives and deterrents within a Soviet scale of satisfactions. Similarly a student of Soviet ideology needs a long background of Russian history and a sensitivity to what is "façade" and what is a genuinely motivating force in Soviet statements of value. Meanwhile, the student of Russia has strong incentives to open up channels of communication with his colleagues in other disciplines and to help some of the ablest students press on from the multidisciplinary program of training to build effective habits of multidisciplinary research as their abilities mature.

V

If present trends continue, American scholars will find increasing opportunities to do research in Soviet libraries, to consult Soviet colleagues on problems of common research interest, and perhaps to make some use of archival and statistical collections. Perhaps there will be some opportunities to do archaeological field work, perhaps later, ethnographic studies. Other types of field studies, such as are widely practiced in our own society, seem remote today. Any type of study and research in the Soviet Union is going to be expensive, and is going to require much greater proficiency in understanding and speaking Russian than most of our scholars have acquired. Whatever the cost, ways and means must be expanded to give our area specialists a firsthand experience of Soviet life. During the postwar years, those senior scholars who had done research in prewar Russia have been more and more distressed as they watched the growing number of people who must study Russian subjects without ever having lived in Russia and among Russians. They often wondered whether a high standard of realistic understanding could be maintained indefinitely under conditions of isolation. The new opportunity for research in the Soviet Union must be utilized to the full, and reciprocal hospitality extended freely and cordially to Soviet scholars, if our resources are to expand in quality as well as quantity.

In order to meet more effectively the growing demands which are placed on Russian and Slavic studies, our field of study needs even more research opportunities than it now offers. Much more must be done to strengthen our research collections, and efficient and rapid means must be found to reproduce unique or rare books at low cost. If this obstacle can be removed, research opportunities can be expanded rapidly and brought within reach of many score of able young scholars who now feel cut off from the resources of the few major repositories. Our field needs many more oppportunities for people already engaged in teaching to return to major centers or to go to the Soviet Union or other countries of eastern Europe in order to carry on their research systematically. Younger scholars, with good research skills and research ambitions, should be able every third year to go where they can pursue their research interests full-time and in a stimulating environment, and not be forced to let that research skill wither for lack of adequate research time and research resources. We need more encouragement and support for the publication of the best research studies. A useful program to this end is being carried on by the SSRC Grants-in-Aid program, but more can profitably be done, perhaps through endowing prizes to finance the publishing of the best studies.

Much more can and must be done to study the history and literature, the social and cultural conditions and prospects of the non-Russian peoples constituting almost one-half of the population of the Soviet Union. As our students gain a firm footing in Russian studies, a few of the ablest are adding to their tool kits a knowledge of one or more non-Russian languages of the Soviet Union. In particular Soviet studies need more researchers who can do original work in the history and culture of Ukraine and the Baltic states, of Georgia and Armenia, Azerbaijan and Central Asia. Because of their own multi-ethnic origins, American scholars are perhaps especially interested in the very different situations and forces which shape the relations among the various nationalities in the Soviet Union. To what extent are the Russian language and a basic Soviet culture being accepted as a convenience and a means of vertical mobility? In what measure do national cultures subsist or develop further within a common ideological and political framework? What are the effects of industrial development and geographical mobility on long-settled peoples? Even some of the basic facts are obscure. Perhaps, for example, the census of 1959 will at least open the way to a fuller description of the new patterns of ethnic settlement and occupations.

An important task which has hardly been tackled at all is the comparative study of Communist systems, their economies, their political organizations, and the channels of communication between different layers of the population and among different nationalities. This type of study, resting first on intensive investigations of these problems within the Soviet Union and the countries of east central Europe, should be enlarged to a comparative examination of social and political dynamics in the Soviet Union and Communist China, and North Korea and North Vietnam should not be overlooked. Many concepts and insights can be sharpened by applying acquired research skills to similar problems elsewhere within the bloc. Here a genuinely cooperative effort on a substantial scale is needed.

Perhaps we need to undertake "bloc-wide" studies of the operations of the Communist Parties, which, despite a common ideology and a common reliance on totalitarian dictatorship, show today some significant differences. Do we know which of these differences are really important and which are transitional? In the various systems there are presumably some differences in the composition and intellectual inheritance of the elites and in the methods of communication between them and the peoples they rule. What is meant by the "communization" of culture in each Communist-ruled country, and what social and cultural factors favor or resist it? The events of 1956 in Poland and Hungary showed how superficial the penetration of the popular psychology had been. What is the role of simulated and "guided" voluntarism? And how far are controls tempered to fit different national conditions? These and many other subjects invite intensive comparative study today.

VI

Building on a modest but strong prewar foundation, Russian and Soviet studies, since the war, have attracted a strong core of able graduate students. To a remarkable extent unequal twin challenges—a difficult field of investigation and the emergence of a bipolar world—have recruited a considerable share of the pick of the crop. During these years several new fields, in addition to history, literature, and language, have matured to a high level of achievement. Economics has had a startling growth in the scope and effectiveness of its researches. The study of political institutions and ideology has advanced greatly. Sociology has made a good beginning. International relations, dealing with actions and aims of Communist states and parties, has made a strong place for itself in teaching, research, and policy study. Much remains to be done, however, not only in more or less established fields of investigation, but especially in the study of geography and natural resources, of psychology and mass cultural changes, of law and institutions, of propaganda and education, and of the various institutional and psychological channels through which the Communist leadership exerts its influence upon the peoples it rules and outside the bloc. Many solid achievements, as well as great unfilled needs, are described in the following chapters.

Scholars working in the Russian field can review with some confidence the healthy way in which, on the whole, they have taken in their stride the adjustment to the polarization of power in world politics. One can imagine situations in which serious damage could have been done, from within and without the academic community, to the integrity and self-respect of the scholar-citizen. In fact, however, the basic effect of this polarization has been to lend greater urgency and inspire greater efforts to advance Russian studies. The spirit of scholarly endeavor, the ambition to serve our democracy by striving for objectivity of analysis, has been a strong armor against the risk of non-scholarly and even anti-scholarly interference.

Some people argue that the expansion of Russian studies has been a by-product of the "cold war." As a matter of record, several of the basic decisions to develop this field of study more effectively were taken before the outlines of the postwar division of the world had become clear. In 1945-47, in planning the first major steps, American students of Russia hoped that we could have, if not intimate, at least regular and continuing intercourse with Soviet scholars in related disciplines. The planning of Columbia's Russian Institute, for example, included provision for inviting a visiting historian from the Soviet Union. In 1947 Ernest J. Simmons visited Moscow, armed with a basketful of useful proposals for scientific cooperation and cultural exchanges. These and other proposals, even if rebuffed by Soviet officialdom, testify to the desire, on the part of our leading scholars and institutions, to enter into mutually beneficial cultural and academic exchanges even as the cold peace was turning into a cold war. And this desire remains strong today. Russian studies have not become a permanent part of the academic landscape because of the cold war or despite it. They are here because it became clear by 1945 that Russia is one of the great powers, with a powerful system of its own, with a great impact in world politics. Scholars and academic statesmen realized that we needed to learn far more about Russia, to study it more tenaciously and more systematically than we had previously studied any other system of power.

An important by-product of the development of Russian and Soviet studies has been the strengthening of the research function within government. This has been accomplished in large part by younger scholars who have gone from the area centers into government research posts; within government their reputation stands high and they have made valuable contributions to the background of policy, some also in the formulation and execution of policy. Government agencies have come to feel that they can benefit a great deal in meeting their responsibilities through sending selected officers to the major centers for advanced training in research, and they have done so on a substantial scale. Finally, many individual scholars, in their personal capacities, have been called on by government agencies to advise them. The strength and flexibility of our democratic system is illustrated by the way in which, from the founding of the Research and Analysis Branch of the Office of Strategic Services in 1941, and the many other war-time demands for the expert services of area specialists, there has been a steady strengthening of systematic research within government, often paralleling that done in the university centers. The interchange of research experience and sometimes of research materials has been beneficial to both.

One of the strengths of Russian studies is that, whatever fears and hopes its practitioners feel as citizens, they have worked long and hard to make sure that their conclusions are founded on solid research. Compared with the value-laden judgments and predictions emanating from many non-research sources, the sober findings of our Russian area specialists stand up well. No one, even the detached scholar, can or wants to live and work without expressing his deep-felt values as a member of a democratic society. But, by stating those values explicitly, he can go on to fulfill his special role, that of strengthening the democratic world, helping it to take better informed and more farsighted decisions, by providing it with the best fund of systematic knowledge which he can work out, without regard to whether he or others like or dislike his findings.

A scholar has a special duty to be vigilant against his own preconceptions and preferences and to be willing constantly to test his previous conclusions against new evidence or data previously neglected. In this way he serves both as a scholar and as a citizen. As a citizen he takes part in many non-research activities. As a scholar he always returns to that central purpose of making his research as nearly objective as possible, not by renouncing values, but by making them explicit through his self-disciplined effort to rise above them as he studies and analyzes a system which, very different from our own in its values, constitutes, in the world of today, a dynamic and challenging focus of power.

John S. Curtiss

2. HISTORY

I

A STRIKING FEATURE of historical studies in the United States before 1917 was the very slight interest in Russia. American students who worked in the field of European history turned chiefly to England and France, and to a lesser degree to Germany and Italy. The vast area east of the Elbe and the Adriatic was largely *terra incognita*. Eugene Schuyler's work on Peter the Great remained an isolated landmark for thirty years.[1] Archibald Cary Coolidge vigorously promoted Russian history at Harvard University, and took the initiative in building up one of the first large libraries in this field.[2] His student, Robert J. Kerner, produced an outstanding bibliography of Slavic Europe.[3] A few years earlier another student of Coolidge, Frank A. Golder, had published his volume on Russian expansion on the Pacific.[4] At about the same time, Samuel N. Harper of Chicago was investigating Russian life and politics on the spot in the company of Bernard Pares.[5] George Kennan had aroused special interest in one aspect of Russian life, the exile system, and ten years later Senator Beveridge wrote eloquently of Russian imperialism for the *Saturday Evening Post*.[6] There was little demand for Russian history, however, among university administrators, professors, or students.

It was the events of the First World War and the revolutions of 1917 that definitely brought Russia into the forefront of American interest. During this period a considerable number of Americans were present in Russia in various capacities and, as our citizens realized their ignorance of this now vital area, the ground was prepared for scholarly work. The events of the Russian civil war did much to stimulate the growth of Russian studies in this country, as Russian scholars, uprooted by the revolutionary turmoil, began to make their way to our shores to find places in academic life. In addition, a small band of young men, after serving in various missions in Russia during the immediate postwar period, returned home with some knowledge of the language and the people and entered academic life. Thanks largely to these two sources, Russian historical studies in the United States began to develop and it became possible to train graduate students in the field. Nevertheless the progress was far from rapid, as few students took the trouble to learn the language and there were few academic opportunities for scholars in the field of Russian history.

Able journalists helped to supply the need for historical works, with little competition from the academic historians. By 1941, however, the second generation of historians in the Russian field, chiefly trained in this country, had begun to reach respectable proportions, only to have their historical studies almost completely cut short by the demands of World War II.

Russian historical studies in the United States before 1945 were thus limited, both in volume and in scope. There was a considerable flow of memoirs of Russians who had fled their homeland, among them Kokovtsov, Rodzianko, Sazonov, and Kerensky. Among the Americans who published their memoirs of experiences in Russia were Ambassador D. R. Francis, Major General William S. Graves, and Raymond Robins. The Economic and Social History of the World War sponsored by the Carnegie Endowment for International Peace published a dozen very useful volumes on various aspects of Russia's participation in the conflict, written by competent Russians.[7] Furthermore, valuable works were produced by men who were not professional historians: Louis Fischer's *The Soviets in World Affairs* (2 vols., 1930) and W. H. Chamberlin's *The Russian Revolution* (2 vols., 1935) are notable examples.

The historical monographs of the period between the World Wars deal with both the Imperial and the Soviet period. In the former group are studies of limited aspects of Russian foreign policy,[8] and on a wide variety of domestic problems.[9] For the postrevolutionary period there have been studies of the famine of 1919-23, of Soviet policy in the Arctic, of the economics of the First Five-Year Plan, and of the development of the Red Army; and works on the Soviet government, the church, the Revolution, and foreign policy.[10] Work was also done on the intellectual history of the two periods.[11]

II

When the Second World War ended the number of Americans interested in Russia had greatly increased. Many who had learned to use Russian during the war took up the study of Russian history and institutions at the newly established university centers for area studies. Russian specialists who had been in government service returned to academic life. In a few years these developments were reflected in the publication of increasing numbers of books and articles dealing with the entire range of Russian history.

The most impressive general works to appear since World War II are the three volumes of George Vernadsky—*Ancient Russia, Kievan Russia,* and *The Mongols and Russia*—and Michael T. Florinsky's two-volume *Russia: A History and an Interpretation*.[12] Shorter studies have dealt with the Slavs and the history of early Russia;[13] with the rule of the boy Tsars Ivan and Peter; with British travelers in eighteenth-century Russia; and with Siberia.[14] Many of the writings on the last century of the Tsars have dealt with aspects of Russian intellectual history, and especially the Marxist movement and its leaders in Russia.[15] In addition, there have been monographs on Alexander I, Speransky, the reformed Russian law courts, the school system, the end of the Georgian monarchy, and the Socialist Revolutionary Party during the revolution.[16] In the realm of foreign affairs there have been works on Alaska and on Russian policy in Asia; on Russia and Europe from 1789 to 1878; on the Baltic question; on Tsarist policies during the war; and on Russian influence in the Balkans.[17]

Among the books dealing with the Soviet era two that treat the revolutions of 1917 are in the form of memoirs.[18] Apart from college textbooks, with which this essay is not concerned, a number of general interpretations of the Soviet regime have been published which are at least partly historical in character.[19] There are also several studies devoted to various aspects of the political and social system.[20] An important group of studies has been concerned with the workings of the Soviet regime in certain local areas: the Ukraine, Turkestan, Transcaucasia, and Belorussia.[21] In addition, there are accounts of the Russian Orthodox Church, an analysis of the Vlasov movement, and several studies of Soviet historiography.[22] Attention should likewise be called to the significant treatises, many of which are historical in character, in the fields of political science, economics, literature, and social relations.[23] A good many historians have been drawn to the study of Russian-American relations. A number have concentrated on the period immediately following 1917,[24] while others have selected a broader period or have emphasized relations during World War II.[25] Several studies have also been written on other aspects of Russian foreign policy.[26]

In addition to the above works by American authors during

the period under consideration, another group of books has become available through the Translation Project of the American Council of Learned Societies. These are works by Soviet authors, a few of which are of special interest to historians. Research by recent refugees from the Soviet Union, some of which is historical in character, has been made available in English by the Research Program on the U.S.S.R. Of particular interest to historians of the Soviet period will be the studies which are being prepared under the auspices of the Research Program on the History of the Communist Party of the Soviet Union.

Brief mention should also be made of the work of British, European, and Asian scholars, in order to place recent American scholarship in its proper setting. Significant historical studies published abroad have dealt with the period before 1917, but the principal interest has inevitably been in the Soviet period. The contribution of Canadian, British, and European scholars has indeed been so extensive that space does not permit a discussion of individual authors and works. These can be followed, however, in the various Canadian and European journals devoted to the field of Russian studies.[27] Well-informed studies of various aspects of Russian affairs have also been published by specialists in Turkey and India.[28] At the same time, there is a growing interest in Russian history on the part of Japanese scholars.[29]

III

Impressive as is this list of achievements, one is even more impressed by the opportunities and needs for further work in this field. Much more has been written about the early Russian Marxists than about their predecessors, the liberals and radicals of the mid-nineteenth century. We have no satisfactory treatment of Petrashevsky, Chernyshevsky, or the Land and Liberty Society. No one has produced monographs on the Imperial administration, the censorship, the nobility, the *zemstvos*, the merchant class, or the towns. Little or nothing has been written on the taxation system, the liquor problem, foreign trade, or the development of the railways. Russian military history remains to be written. We lack satisfactory biographies of most of the Tsars, to say nothing of statesmen and politicians like Gorchakov, Miliutin, D. A. Tolstoy, Plehve, Stolypin, and Sazonov. There are no effective studies of the political parties such as the Mensheviks, the Cadets, the Octobrists, and the Union of the Russian People. There is no good history of the Revolution of 1905. The Duma as a whole has not been properly studied. Little has been done on the Ukraine, the Caucasus, Siberia, and the Baltic states under the Tsars or on the major Russian cities. There are no comprehensive studies of Tsarist foreign policy in the nineteenth and twentieth centuries.

Some may object that sources are lacking for many of these topics: few memoirs are available; there were no parliamentary debates before 1906; a free press did not exist. Nevertheless, the Russians expressed themselves abundantly, in spite of the censorship, and much source material has been printed in historical journals. We have in this country magnificent libraries that contain extensive collections of Russian books and periodicals.[30] In addition, there are the resources of the European libraries to supplement ours. Finally, it may be possible in the future to have access to Soviet libraries and archives. Much of the pre-Soviet period is no longer particularly controversial, and Soviet authorities may be willing to permit research by American scholars.

One may ask whether Americans can add significantly to work already being done by Soviet historians. Much historical writing has indeed been done in the U.S.S.R., of which a great deal, especially since 1934, displays abundant documentation and analysis of evidence. Certain Soviet historians, whose skill and scholarly ability are unquestioned, have produced excellent studies dealing with early Russia up to the middle of the nineteenth century. On the other hand, Soviet historical writings on the last one hundred years are rarely satisfactory to Western scholars.

The chief criticism is that they are subject to censorship by the Communist Party, which rejects findings at variance with the prevailing Party line and imposes the obligation to support its objectives. Furthermore, Soviet historians do not normally have access to archives in Western countries and are not always in touch with the achievements of Western scholarship. For these reasons, American historians feel that they cannot be satisfied with the conclusions of Soviet historians, but must themselves study the evidence and draw their own conclusions.

In studying the Soviet period students encounter greater difficulty than in research on the earlier years. Decision-making has become increasingly secretive; there is not the give-and-take of party politics; and speeches in the Supreme Soviet are remarkably similar in content. The press, which is fully controlled by the Communist Party, is used as a medium to propagate ideas sponsored by the Party and to eliminate opposing influences and ideas. When a prominent Communist is "relieved" of his duties, he does not publish his memoirs. Nevertheless, by patient, intelligent reading of Soviet periodicals and books, a surprising amount can be learned, as the excellent monographs published in this country show. The present difficulties of studying the Soviet system are no greater than in the last decade and may even be somewhat less. The importance of learning as much as possible about the Soviet regime is greater than ever.

A substantial amount of work is at present in progress, in the form of doctoral dissertations or of postdoctoral studies. Among these are monographs dealing with various governmental institutions of the Imperial regime, such as the administration, the political police, the bureaucracy, the army, and the First Duma. Studies are being made of various aspects of social and political thought in Russia, including the views of conservatives like Karamzin and Pobedonostsev, the Slavophiles, Herzen, Mikhailovsky, and Chernov. The careers of such prominent figures as Witte and Nicholas II are also being studied. Other projects analyze groups outside the government, among them the Congresses of Representatives of Trade and Industry, the United Nobility, the intelligentsia, and the Old Believers. A few works discuss Russia's foreign relations before 1917—with the Balkans, Iran, and Korea, as well as with the Dutch in the seventeenth century.

Many more scholars are at work on the period from 1917 to the present. Studies of the Provisional Government of 1917 and of the Russian peasant in revolt are in process. A relatively large number of investigations deal with Marxist ideology in Soviet Russia, chiefly as expressed by individual leaders of the 1920's and 1930's. Other subjects under study are the consolidation of the Soviet system in central Asia, the decline of the Jewish community in the U.S.S.R., and the NKVD. The problems that are presently being studied in the field of Soviet foreign relations include Allied intervention in southern Russia in 1919, the establishment of the Comintern, and various aspects of relations between the Soviet regime and Germany, Great Britain, and France. Other investigations discuss Russia at the Paris Peace Conference, and Russia and the League of Nations. Still others concern Soviet dealings with Japan, China, and India.

In spite of these undertakings, however, the catalog of important problems that still require study is long. The several studies of national minorities in the U.S.S.R. have rarely extended beyond 1927, and most of them stop with 1921 or 1922. It is highly important to know how these peoples have fared since then. Moreover, other nationalities, such as the Armenians, the Georgians, the Caucasian mountaineers, the Baltic peoples, the Yakuts, to mention only a few, should be investigated. This should be attempted in spite of the inevitable obstacles in a police state. There is need for a careful and thorough study of the fate of several important religious bodies under Soviet rule, such as the Baptists and the Moslems. An up-to-date treatment of Soviet education, as well as of the health system, would be of value. The whole field of Soviet military history has hardly been touched. Additional problems that might be considered with advantage include the history of individual Soviet cities or of individual industries, and the history of Soviet labor. Undoubtedly the list could be extended further.

Soviet foreign relations should be another fruitful field for research. There is need of a whole series of monographs on Soviet relations with individual countries: Great Britain, France, Germany, Italy, Finland, Poland, Turkey, Iran, Afghanistan, Japan, and China after 1927 are examples. Soviet relations with Yugoslavia also need further study. It also seems likely that the list will increase, with the inclusion of such countries as the Arab states, India, Indonesia, some of the new countries of Africa, and possibly some Latin American states. A monograph on the U.S.S.R. and the United Nations is near completion, but studies are needed of the role of the Soviet Union in the various councils and commissions of the United Nations and in its specialized agencies. Finally, the whole question of the relations between the Soviet Union and the other members of the Soviet orbit offers interesting problems in contemporary history.

IV

There is good reason to expect that in the course of the next generation these and many other specific problems will receive the attention of careful research. There is less cause to be optimistic, however, regarding the achievements of American scholars in examining the broader issues raised by Russian history. In the quarter of a century since the study of Russian history began to attract increasing attention from American scholars, historians in the United States have given relatively little thought to the meaning of Russian history. The predominant assumption appears to have been that Russia was following the same path as western Europe in the march toward democracy. It had for various reasons been delayed in its progress along this path, to a greater degree but in much the same way as Germany and Italy had been delayed by comparison with Britain and France. But can it not be just as readily maintained, for instance, that Russian society has always been distinct from the societies of western Europe, despite many intimate ties in space and time, and that the institutions and values of a fully modern Russia will be significantly different from those generally accepted as the basis of the "Atlantic" states?

The questioning and discussion of such assumptions is an important task for historians, and it is a weakness of American scholarship in Russian history that problems of this type are not more generally debated. The exploration of interpretive questions might serve to enrich the work of a new generation of scholars, and might have a significant bearing on their evaluation of Russian personalities and events.

One approach to general problems of this character is that provided by periodization. We have heard a great deal concerning periodization from Soviet historians in recent years, although their debates have been determined as much by politics as by scholarship. This is nevertheless an important subject, for the division of history into periods is fundamentally a question of interpretation. In the case of Russian history, a typical issue in need of further debate is the analogy frequently made between the Russian revolutions of 1917 and the French Revolution of 1789. It is often maintained that the Russian events were simply the French Revolution taking place at last in eastern Europe, and indeed it is tempting to contrast the Old Regime with the New in Russia as in France. Yet just as good a case can be made for 1861 as the dividing line in Russia between the agrarian and the industrial era, or between autocracy and the beginnings of self-government. Such choices are not only of theoretical interest, but in this instance would have a significant bearing on one's evaluation of the last years of the empire.

Another means of locating Russia's proper place in European and world history is the comparative method. Much has already been written about the relationship of Russia to Europe. One suspects that much could also be learned by comparing the development of modern Russia with that of Turkey, Japan, and perhaps other Asian states. The comparative method has many pitfalls, but it remains an essential approach to the understanding of any society. All scholars use this approach in some measure in the study of a foreign country, whether they realize it or not, and a more systematic and comprehensive application of this method in the case of Russia might well produce valuable insights.

Finally, it must be acknowledged that the interest of American historians in Russia has focused largely on political and intellectual developments. Apart from a few outstanding volumes in the field of economic history, there has been little interest in what might very vaguely be called Russian society. This attitude also underlies much American thinking about Russia. Political developments and foreign policy are often discussed without reference to the social and economic forces which form an inseparable part of any national scene. These forces are particularly significant for an understanding of Russia, because it is specifically these aspects that are so different from those familiar to American historians. Many of the limitations of American historical work on Russia may be explained by its two-dimensional approach. It is true that social and economic history requires a type of source material far less accessible than that needed for political or intellectual history, and this may to some extent explain this shortcoming in American historiography. If new opportunities for research in the Soviet Union are opened up in the years to come, it should be possible to probe into the many aspects of Russian society that remain unexplored. This would help to round out our understanding of Russian history, and would also encourage the development of interpretations embracing the totality of the Russian experience.

Gregory Grossman

3. ECONOMICS

I

THE AMERICAN STUDENT of the Soviet economy has been performing a complex role in the last ten or twelve years. As an economist working on a particular economic system, he has been concerned with comparative studies, specific institutions, their interrelationship, their antecedents, their evolution, and—last but not least—their impact upon the functioning and achievements of the Soviet economy. As a student of the Soviet Union, he has contributed—whether much or little is for others to say—to the progress of cognate areas of Soviet studies and to integral conceptions of the Soviet society and polity. His government has often called upon him to serve as an intelligence analyst, or justified its support of aspects of his research from the standpoint of some ultimate (fortunately, often very "ultimate") intelligence value. And whether he wished it or not, his work has had political implications in the world arena.

If we had the Russian penchant for marking jubilees, we should have taken note in 1957 of the tenth anniversary of the publication of a symposium entitled "Appraisals of Russian Economic Statistics."[1] While that collection of essays certainly was not the beginning of serious research in the United States on the Soviet economy, and while the contributors did (and still do) represent a rather wide range of opinion, the appearance of the symposium may well be regarded as having ushered in a new, postwar phase in study of the Soviet economy. Thumbing now through its pages, one is both comforted and disturbed by the realization that its topics—measurement of Soviet economic growth, structure of national income—are still among the main concerns of our research, and its statistical and conceptual problems are still with us. True, we now know (or think we know) much more about the Soviet economy than we did then, and there are now many more of us sharing the knowledge. Our answers have raised more questions; we know our tools better, and we trust them less; we dispose of more data, but we dispel fewer doubts. This, I suppose, constitutes scholarly progress.

It is not only, however, the distance we have traveled that prompts us to take our bearings anew. The terrain itself has changed markedly of late, and in several respects it is not as forbidding as it once was. Some of these changes are too well known to be more than enumerated here: the partial relaxation of secrecy on the part of the Soviet Union, resulting especially, from the economist's standpoint, in the publication of statistical compilations and other factual information; the possibility of traveling in the U.S.S.R., visiting libraries there, obtaining microfilms, establishing personal contacts and maintaining correspondence; and so forth. Other newly created opportunities are less frequently listed. They include: insights into the Soviet economic system through experienced Polish eyes, now that the Poles are more communicative and less constrained; glimpses of Soviet economic problems reflected in the Polish and Yugoslav attempts at institutional reform; the possibility of interviewing a more recent group of refugees from the satellite countries; and lastly, the bare inception of Soviet-American debates contained in the newly manifested readiness of Soviet economists to join the issue directly.[2]

II

Without trying to draw a sharp line between description and explanation, or between measurement and interpretation, we must recognize that the problems of data in the Soviet economic field have been no less serious than the problems of explanation and interpretation. Much of the economist's work has, therefore, been directed first to answering the questions "What?" and "How much?" before he can try to answer the questions "How?" and "Why?"

The necessity of creating its own data has left a definite stamp on the character of this branch of economics. Because the data were otherwise not readily available, or where available, not reliable, or at least had to be checked, the economist has had to dig up the basic figures and to combine them into assimilable and digestible aggregates. In moments of complacency he has compared himself with the archaeologist; probably a wishful thought, since the latter does not have to contend with deliberately deceptive materials.

Digging, whether literal or figurative, is at once ennobling and degrading. It develops one's insight, one's sense of order and proportion. But it also conduces to pedantry, to search for search's sake, to dodging larger issues, and—through an excessive spirit of competition against one's sources—to the possibility of denigrational bias. Digging takes time and energy at the expense of analytical study. It may block broader perspectives. Last but not least, it may have tended to alienate the economist from his fellow students in other disciplines, who could not share his excitement over exhuming statistical fragments and possibily even regarded it as a sign of intellectual narrowness.

Hence the partial relaxation of statistical secrecy by the U.S.S.R. is welcome for more than its own sake. Yet, withal, the economist need not be ashamed of the results of the intensive digging that dominated the first postwar decade of research. His estimates of the basic figures (index numbers are something else again, as we shall see) by and large have been closely confirmed by the statistical handbooks, which began to appear in 1956, and even by data released earlier. Indeed, it is perhaps not absurd to suggest that the success of Western students in reconstructing basic Soviet figures may have contributed to the Soviet decision to publish the data in the form of organized compilations.

Lest the reader get an unduly optimistic impression, it must also be mentioned that much important information has not yet found its way into the statistical handbooks. Such basic and, one may add, nonmilitary items as the absolute size of the grain crop,* the size and composition of the agricultural labor force, and the amount of money in circulation, to name but a few, must still be estimated from fragmentary or indirect evidence. More significantly, the mere assembling of previously scattered or unpublished figures between the covers of a few statistical abstracts in no way enhances their reliability, meaningfulness, or comparability. These problems remain as acute and time-consuming as ever.

Most of the digging, however, has not been an end in itself, but has served as a first phase for one of three types of study: construction of index numbers, compilation of national accounts, and industry studies. In the construction of index numbers—temporal series and international comparisons on production and real earnings, prices and costs, and productivity—and in the construction of national accounts, postwar American research on the Soviet economy has accomplished its most impressive volume of work, completed or well on the way. As a result, the main dimensional outline, independent of Soviet claims, of the growth in output and productivity since 1928 (over-all and by major sectors), of the movement in prices and wages, and of the structure of the economy and certain flows within it during a number

* Since this was written absolute data on the grain harvests in 1953 and 1958, and thereby through percentage links with other years of the 1950's as well, have been released (*Pravda*, December 16, 1958).

of "benchmark years" has emerged or is in the process of emerging. Considering the shortage of qualified personnel and the paucity and intractability of the data, this is a decade's achievement that economists—most of them American, but many of them west European—need not be ashamed of.

It would be quite impossible to subject such a large amount of quantitative work to a systematic review within the compass of this brief paper. In fact, I shall not attempt even to cite systematically all major work of this kind. Rather I shall confine myself to some general remarks regarding such studies.

(a) The results of index number studies for a country like the U.S.S.R., where the temporal and international differences in economic structure are pronounced, may be expected to vary significantly with the regimen of weights and other formal statistical properties.[3] Clear conception and exposition of the method employed by the author of any such attempt are therefore mandatory. Fortunately, this has been the case with most American work on index numbers for the Soviet economy.

(b) It follows from this, considering the different purposes for which the indices are wanted and the formidable problems of data, that a multiplicity of methods (formulae, weighting regimens) of constructing index numbers is often necessary and desirable. However, a consequence of the variety of methods used is that tests of mutual consistency are not always possible. Instead, tests of the validity of the individual computations must often rest largely on conclusions with regard to the representativeness of the sample on which they are based and the appropriateness of the formal methods of their construction.

(c) This relativism in the meaning of indices not only tends to hinder the putting together of a coherent picture of the Soviet economy over time and in relation to other economies, but may also tend to impede communication between the economist and other students of the Soviet Union, as well as between the economist and the general public. At times it seems to have hampered understanding even between economists. Similar problems arise with respect to cross-sectional accounts, whose meaning is entirely relative to the standard employed (e.g., efficiency standard, welfare standard).[4]

(d) Conceptual problems apart, and notwithstanding all the digging and piecing together, nearly all attempts at measuring the performance of the Soviet economy have, of course, been faced by serious limitations on data, especially with regard to the secret sectors. Without trying to minimize the difficulty, we may note that the limitation need not always be as severe as might be assumed at first glance, if only because data on *both* rapidly growing and slowly growing sectors and items have been withheld by the Soviets, the former generally for reasons of strategic security, the latter for reasons of prestige. Thus it is possible, at least for some subperiods and for broad sectors of the economy, that the sample of items (e.g., industrial commodities) available to us may not be too unrepresentative of the whole. Moreover, we may suspect a tendency toward inverse behavior (at least over short periods) between the secret areas at the two extremes, the lag in the low-priority items releasing the resources that permit the rapid advance in the high-priority items.

Attempts to circumvent secrecy by the deflation of current ruble magnitudes through the use of price indices[5] run into the difficulty that in the secret sectors the price indices, if at all constructible, are among the least reliable, and the current ruble figures are among the least credible. On the other hand, certain tests of plausibility can be applied to the price indices, and tests derived from the logic of double-entry bookkeeping to the ruble values. Hence this approach is certainly valuable when applied and interpreted with circumspection.

Another method of circumventing secrecy (or unreliability, or nonmeasurability) of data on output is by estimating changes in output from changes in input. (This method is, of course, applicable to international as well as to temporal comparisons.) The input-output relation may be assumed to be linear homogeneous over time or space, or may be estimated from the non-Soviet environment or from Soviet experience during less secret periods. By means of this general method, estimates have been made of the growth of industrial output, by Shimkin and by Seton (Oxford); of the magnitude of Soviet industrial output in relation to American, by Shimkin; of the growth of construction, by Powell; of agricultural output, by Johnson.[6] Although the postulate with regard to the input-output relation is rarely entirely satisfactory, although the method is at times not without recognizable statistical bias, and although the concrete meaning of the result is not always clear (which limits its use for analysis), input-derived estimates are unavoidable in some cases, and provide welcome alternative estimates in other cases. The possibility of undertaking further estimates of this nature by utilizing such input data as total caloric consumption, use of electric power for drive purposes, volume of goods carried by transport, and so forth, may be worth considering.

(e) Major statistical studies based on extensive digging are very costly and time-consuming. I am thinking not so much of the monetary expense as of the time of the senior research personnel and of the qualified junior staff. Personnel resources are scarce, their training is slow, and their attrition rate is substantial. True, the cost in lost opportunity for other kinds of work is not necessarily as great as the input of labor may suggest: some of the junior researchers are not qualified, and some of the senior personnel may not be inclined, to pursue anything but such statistical studies. Nonetheless, it is clear that there are points in all such projects where the incremental returns begin to decline, at the extensive as well as the intensive margins. The question may be legitimately raised at appropriate junctures whether additional statistical coverage, precision, or variety will add as much to our understanding of the Soviet economy as would an alternative use of the same scarce resources in a different line of investigation, such as (to pick an example) analysis of the how-and-why variety.

In raising this question, I am looking at the problem from the standpoint of the subject as a whole. I do not mean to question the individual's right to pursue research according to his own inclinations. Nor do I mean to suggest that the yardstick to be applied to returns and costs is not an ambiguous one.

(f) Lastly, there is the question of timeliness, which derives largely from the relationship of Soviet studies to the national interest. The implications are twofold: (i) Time as such, apart from money and research resources, cannot be entirely dismissed in the balancing of returns and costs (as discussed in the paragraph above). It is hardly necessary to add that this is not an argument for undue haste and sloppiness. (ii) Continual consideration should be given to bringing up to date and revising past statistical work as fuller, more accurate, and more recent information becomes available.

III

Less has been done by way of intensive and rounded monographic work on individual segments of the economy (such as industries, sectors, or regions) than has been accomplished in the accumulation of data. To qualify fully for this category, a study must be at once descriptive, historical, statistical, and analytical, and must investigate nearly every major facet of the segment and relate it to the rest of the economy.

I know of only three completed industry studies, in the full sense of the term: Jasny's on prewar agriculture, Gardner Clark's on steel, and Hunter's on transportation.[7] In addition, a small number of monographs inquire into a more limited range of problems with respect to individual industries; Shimkin on minerals, Hardt on electric power, Blackman on locomotives, and Sosnovy on housing are good examples,[8] though of varying scope and length. The extant industry studies are only a beginning of what could be done and, for a better understanding of the Soviet economy, probably should be done.

No regional economic studies, except minor ones, have been published in the period under review, to my knowledge. The limited number of substantial industry studies, major or otherwise, and the lack of major regional studies can be explained only in part. True, for the years from the middle thirties to the early fifties, the data for individual industries and regions are few. The local press for certain regions is meager, and for some years entirely lacking, while non-Russian languages present an additional barrier to the American student. In some industries the technology may be too unfamiliar and the range of outputs too great and varied to attract a mere social scientist. On the other hand, trade journals and (to a smaller extent) the local press are available in considerable volume for most years, and are not entirely lacking even for the lean years. The recent publication of Soviet regional and sectoral statistical handbooks has greatly added to these materials.

Regional and sectoral monographs are desirable not only—perhaps not even primarily—in themselves, but also as avenues of approach to an understanding of the system as a whole, and to greater knowledge of the how-and-why as well as of the what-and-how-much of the Soviet economy. It would be especially useful if the monographs covered a considerable range of industries and regions in terms of their politico-economic characteristics (priority rating, expansion or stagnation, and so forth). Of course, there would be little point in aiming at a complete set of such monographs. Even if, by dint of great cost and effort, all regions, industries, and sectors were to be represented, completeness in terms of conceptual design and up-to-dateness is never attainable anyway. Often yet another study of the same segment of the economy will contribute more than an expedition into virgin territory.

Nonagricultural labor is a case in point. Solomon Schwarz's

book,[9] the outstanding work in the field, deals essentially with the prewar period; its discussion of the postwar situation is brief and, in some respects, outdated. It would seem, particularly in view of the important developments since Stalin's death, that there is now room for a more up-to-date monograph on Soviet labor as a segment of the economy.[10] On the other hand, the updating of Bergson's statistical inquiry into the structure of Soviet wages,[11] which ends at a point even more remote in time (1934), must wait until a considerable further relaxation of Soviet secrecy takes place. However, a nonstatistical inquiry into the Soviet wage system is probably now feasible, and would be very welcome.

Another such segment is finance, where coverage has been relatively good, thanks particularly to the work of Holzman and Powell,[12] but where much interesting work remains to be done. This is also true with regard to foreign trade, on which much has been published in short pieces, but almost nothing in breadth and depth, at least for a decade.

No comprehensive economic history of any period or subperiod of the Soviet era, not to mention an economic history of the whole era, has been produced by American scholarship in the last decade. Indeed, there is hardly anything that the student can be referred to for a book-length synoptic survey of the evolution of the Soviet economy, except two British works by Baykov and Dobb,[13] both now out of date in several respects. Not only would a competent history of the entire Soviet era, or of the Plan era alone, be highly welcome, but much would be gained by the preparation of comprehensive and competent studies of shorter periods, for example, the NEP, the First Five-Year Plan and collectivization period, the war years (1941-1945), and the postwar reconstruction period.

It need hardly be added that a study of Soviet industrialization by the comparative historical method would also be timely. Such a study would presumably distinguish the elements and features that have been specifically Soviet in this development from those which have close analogues in other historical experiences of rapid industrialization. By the same token such a study would also facilitate the construction of a dynamic model of the Soviet economy, to which reference is made below.

While the shortage of materials is serious for some periods, I believe that even for the war and the postwar reconstruction periods enough data are available in this country for a useful, though more or less tentative, historical analysis. For the years prior to 1930, the availability of material can hardly be called a limiting factor. Thus there must be other reasons for the almost total lack of such works. In some cases the economist has been waiting—often, but not always, justifiably—for the completion of the massive statistical inquiries into the growth of the Soviet economy, and in some cases he has been preoccupied with their compilation. But it is perhaps also true that the American economist, because of his training and experience, feels more at home with a statistical approach than with a historical one, which often overflows into political and social realms. These he tends to consider as outside his domain. And as to the economic history of prerevolutionary Russia, this vast realm the economist (with a few conspicuous exceptions, such as Gerschenkron and Volin) has left to his gracious but somewhat undisciplined colleague, the historian.

IV

Most of us will agree that what-and-how-much cannot be divorced from how-and-why. But if we have already taken considerable strides in describing and measuring the Soviet economy, the task of understanding and explaining it still lies as a steep trail before us—or rather several trails, which, if we blaze them well, should merge into a general model of the Soviet economic system. The several paths that might take us there are partial models pertaining to identifiable sectors or processes within the Soviet economy. (I use the word "model" here broadly, as a comprehensive and internally consistent explanation of the interrelationship of economic variables and of the behavior of economic agents, without necessarily implying a formal mathematical model.)

We need the model or models for insight into the essential operating and evolutionary characteristics of the Soviet economy, apart from and in addition to our grasp of the organizational and institutional picture. We need to know the *Wirtschaftssystem* as well as the *Wirtschaftsordnung* in order to be able to evaluate the performance of the economy, the significance of reforms such as the mid-1957 reorganization of industry, and the potential for change.

Slowly, we have begun to ascend some of the trails. The greatest progress has been made with regard to a model of the industrial enterprise, particularly in the work of Berliner, Granick, and others.[14] A considerable foundation toward a model of the *kolkhoz* has been laid, thanks to the work of a number of students in this country (Volin, Jasny, Dinerstein,[15] and others) and abroad (especially Alec Nove in London). On the other hand, little is known about the operating principles of other basic economic units: the store, the bank, the *stroika* (construction project), and those twins that have so far lurked in the penumbra of our studies, but which may, in fact, be very significant on the Soviet economic scene—*snab* and *sbyt* (supply and sales organizations).

These are, or would be, theories of the Soviet firm. We can, perhaps, apply to the Soviet scene, with certain adaptations, the Western theories of the household, especially since the abolition of rationing and of some of the restrictive labor decrees. But above and beyond these theories, we need a good analytical study, possibly leading to a model, of the Soviet planned-and-command economy. A fundamental obstacle that may be encountered in the construction of such a model or theory is a lack of systematic and orderly relationship between variables, at least at certain points. But whether this obstacle is insurmountable or not we shall not know until we have tried to build the model.

Very little has been done, in the United States or elsewhere, to investigate systematically the likely elements of such a model: the planning system, "project-making" and technological policy, the price and wage structure, the supply system, the roles of administrative fiat and of economic calculation, and so forth. Thus, apart from incidental or short pieces, there is as yet no study of Soviet planning. The same holds true for the supply system. Admittedly, meaningful information on these topics is hard to acquire. Yet whether the handicap is insuperable cannot be determined until the available data are looked into carefully. (In this connection, some information might be obtained from Soviet defectors, as well as Poles, Hungarians, and East Germans who are now in, or accessible to, the West.)

The aspect of planning known as "project-making" (i.e., engineering design) is a small, moderately explored enclave within this broad *terra incognita*, thanks to a lively Soviet controversy that attracted considerable attention in the West.[16] On technological policy—probably a significant element in the prospective model—some information has been collected and assessed in the same context, and in connection with some of the industry studies already referred to.[17] Here the problem of data is characterized by a plethora of material in the economic and technical literature; the difficulty lies in systematization and digestion. There seems to be general agreement that a thorough study of Soviet technology as, among other things, an autonomous force in the economic picture is now overdue.

That "the meaning of Soviet prices will rise to plague us in almost every study involving rubles"[18]—the last two words are virtually redundant—has been recognized for a long time, but we are still being plagued. The only two books with the phrase "Soviet prices(s)" in the title, both by Jasny,[19] are primarily descriptive and statistical. An analytical investigation of the principles of Soviet price formation and of their effects on the planning and operation of the economy remains to be made.

The recent flood of inquiry by Soviet economists into their own price system, oriented also toward the question of meaningfulness but, of course, from a radically different theoretical basis, should provide considerable new information on the problem. Several studies of the Soviet price structure and system, from different angles, are now in progress in this country, but it will doubtless be some time before the plague is conquered (or kills the patient).

In the meantime, current ruble magnitudes—whether "established" or "adjusted,"[20] as the circumstances may warrant—must be used. The strictures that have been lately raised against "adjusted rubles," and the debate that followed,[21] seem to me to have sharpened our appreciation of the conceptual and theoretical difficulties involved in the manipulation of ruble magnitudes, but not to have undermined the conceptual framework of Bergson's national accounts or Hodgman's index of industrial production, the two studies that have been criticized on this ground.[22]

Lastly, we need a *dynamic* model of the Soviet economy, a "theory of Soviet economic development" to explain the "socialist accumulation" and the specific form of "creative destruction" carried on by the Soviet regime-entreprenuer. In fact, as I have already noted, we do not even yet have a good account of *"wie es eigentlich gewesen"*—of what has and has not been accomplished, and of the qualitative and quantitative role played in the Soviet process of expansion by the various elements, such as capital investment, the transfer of labor, the training of skills, the taking over of technology, and—last but not least—the source of the drive and the mechanism of its transmission. Some valuable work on several such dynamic elements has been done;[23] much more remains to be done, particularly by way of fitting the elements together and rounding out the picture.

It is perhaps not surprising that something as sophistic, exegetic, and arid as post-1930 Soviet economic theorizing has attracted little attention from American economists, who in any event have rarely possessed the background to appreciate and assess the finer points of Marxism-Leninism-Stalinism; nor have they always been convinced of its great relevance to their analysis of the Soviet economy. Soviet economics of the twenties, particularly the great industrialization debates, is something else again. But even this literature, despite the wealth of material and the implications for a theory of economic development in general, has attracted relatively little attention in the United States, Erlich's work being the notable exception.[24]

Without either deploring or defending this neglect of Soviet economic theory, it seems likely that now, with Soviet economists theorizing (in print) much more, and somewhat more sensibly, than a few years ago, interest in what they are saying will increase on this side of the curtain.

As to ideology, this is another area which the economist has, by and large and, to my mind, unfortunately, left to the other disciplines.[25]

V

The completion of the several major extragovernmental statistical projects now under way—the Bergson-RAND deflation of national accounts to obtain a derived picture of physical growth, 1928-1955; direct measurement of Soviet economic growth by the National Bureau of Economic Research;[26] the study by the RAND Corporation of ruble-dollar ratios for purposes of international "deflation"[27]—in addition to the already published, though sometimes more impressionistic and tentative, work along these lines, will constitute a great advance in measurement. Without bringing the work of measuring to an end, it will probably mark the transition from one phase to another in American studies of the Soviet economy. Thanks in part to the digging and statistical foundation-laying, and in part to the change in environment mentioned at the beginning of this paper, students of Soviet economy will be, if they are not already, in a position to shift their emphasis from description and measurement to (what should be no less satisfying to the social scientist) analysis, cognition, interpretation, and explanation. As I have tried to point out, despite the large number of studies that have been produced in the last decade—a record that we need not be ashamed of—we still know little about what makes the Soviet economy and its components tick, what are (to continue the metaphor) its mainspring, escapement, and balance wheel. Statistical studies alone, indispensable as they are, will not give us answers to these questions. Careful empirical work, quantitative and nonquantitative, together with imaginative and perspicacious building of theories and models, "which [in Kaplan's words] we can test, revise, and then apply," may do so.

This calls for monographic studies of industries, sectors, regions, periods, and problems; and, of course, simultaneously trying our hand on the theoretical and model-building plane. Among other things it probably requires a high degree of communication not only within the field (which we have already), but also with contiguous fields in economics and in Soviet studies, and with scholars engaged in studying the other parts of the Communist world. The mechanics of this communication, however, falls outside the purview of this paper.

Needless to say, should the field develop in this direction, its requirements in research materials, in well-trained personnel, and in intellectual focal centers will assuredly not decline. It is difficult to conceive a situation during the coming decade in which the study of the Soviet economy will not elicit scholarly curiosity, or will not be in the national interest. The study of the Soviet economy is approaching not the end of its road but a challenging crossroads, with a broad and inviting panorama beyond.

John A. Armstrong

4. POLITICAL SCIENCE

I

AN EXAMINATION of the progress and prospects of Russian area research in political science is complicated by the fact that political science itself, as a scholarly discipline, is hard to define.[1] The discipline has developed pragmatically rather than from a single school of thought or central theory. While there is general agreement as to the central place of some fields of study in political science, others are peripheral or, frequently, shared with other disciplines. Consequently, in this survey it seems best to consider subjects of Soviet area research to be parts of political science if corresponding subjects are commonly treated by American political scientists who are not area specialists.

It must, however, be recognized that wide differences between the Soviet system and the Western constitutional systems that constitute the main object of consideration for most political scientists mean that Soviet area research in political science must omit, or place slight emphasis on, certain topics customarily handled by the discipline, while greatly expanding or emphasizing the treatment of others which have a special relevance for the Soviet scene. For example, the studies of parliamentary organization, procedure, and tactics which form such a large part of our research on the American, British, and French governments can have little if any counterpart in Soviet studies.[2] Direct studies of public opinion, largely dependent on polling techniques, can scarcely be applied to the Soviet Union. Conversely, the totalitarian nature of the Soviet system, in which politics is the key to the understanding of vast ranges of society, means that the political scientist specializing in the Soviet area must be concerned with a large number of subjects which, in the study of Western societies, are customarily left to the sociologist, the economist, or the philosopher.

Anyone considering the state of political science research on the Soviet Union is immediately impressed with the brief period of time in which such research has been carried on. Prior to World War II, the principal contributions of political scientists to this field were sections on the Soviet Union in works on comparative government and studies of international affairs dealing in part with Soviet or Communist policy.[3] Two general treatises on government, Walter R. Batsell's *Soviet Rule in Russia* (New York, 1929) and Bertram W. Maxwell's *The Soviet State* (Topeka, 1934), together with Waldemar Gurian's *Bolshevism: Theory and Practice* (New York, 1932) were pioneering works. The historian Samuel N. Harper also made a number of contributions to the study of Soviet politics.[4]

The intensive development of Soviet area programs immediately after the war included very considerable attention to political science; the bulk of research since that time is attributable at least in part to these programs. Since the area programs were designed to overcome rapidly the alarming shortage in the United States of trained personnel and verified knowledge concerning the Soviet Union, they were undertaken with a considerable sense of urgency. After a decade in which some of the most immediate needs in this regard have been met, it may now be useful to consider the research record of the last ten years and to suggest changes in the nature and direction of political science area research appropriate to the long-term development of this field.

II

Any review of research in political science must necessarily be selective. To be sure, a comprehensive list of works on the U.S.S.R. by American scholars who consider themselves to be professional political scientists, though lengthy, would be of manageable proportions. It would be quite misleading, however, to consider the various subjects without reference to research and publications by foreign scholars, by scholars in other disciplines, and, in certain cases, by nonscholars. Consequently, examples of important books will be considered, regardless of their authorship, while specific articles, except for the most significant or illustrative, will not be mentioned. References to work in progress must also be limited, both because of the frequent difficulty of estimating in advance its nature and value, and because much of this work, especially that comprised in Ph.D. dissertations, is never completed, or completed only after a very long time. In general, all citations in the following pages are illustrative. They are by no means intended as a comprehensive catalogue, which would include many other valuable studies, particularly those prepared by or for government agencies.[5]

Ideology. Whether under this heading, or under the more customary rubric of "political theory," this is one of the core subjects of traditional political science. In dealing with this topic, the political scientist, usually concerned primarily with very recent developments, is obliged to deal with a much greater chronological span. This is true also of ideological studies by political scientists in the Soviet area. While most of the studies —too numerous to list—of Marxist and Russian political thought before the 1917 Revolution have been written by scholars in other disciplines, Alfred G. Meyer's *Marxism: The Unity of*

Theory and Practice (Cambridge, Mass., 1954), is an example of a professional political scientist's work.[6] The same author's book, *Leninism* (Cambridge, Mass., 1957), deals with the ideological background of the Soviet system, a topic also treated by scholars in other disciplines—for example, the historians Bertram Wolfe and Leonard Schapiro.[7] On the whole it seems that the pre-Leninist period and Leninism have been dealt with fairly adequately, and that no special concentration of effort on these subjects is needed.

Less adequately treated is the Stalinist period. Nathan Leites' *A Study of Bolshevism* (Glencoe, Ill., 1953) is an attempt to classify a wide range of Soviet Communist doctrine. Stalin's own political theory, however, has never been subjected to a full-scale analysis by a professional political scientist, a historian, or a philosopher. There are, to be sure, numerous shorter works on aspects of Stalin's thought, especially those by Geroid T. Robinson[8] and George Morgan.[9] Trotsky's life through the 1917 Revolution has been treated comprehensively by Isaac Deutscher.[10]

Reflections of the central ideology in related fields have keen interest for the political scientist. This is especially true for philosophy, where the principal work on the Stalinist period so far completed has been done by the Catholic priests Henri Chambre,[11] Gustav Wetter,[12] and I. M. Bocheński.[13] A recent study by Herbert Marcuse[14] represents a different philosophical viewpoint. In historiography, the reflection of ideological developments is portrayed in *Rewriting Russian History: Soviet Interpretations of Russia's Past* (ed. Cyril E. Black; New York, 1956). A somewhat similar analysis of developments in psychology is presented in Raymond Bauer's *The New Man in Soviet Psychology* (Cambridge, Mass., 1952). Similar studies for other intellectual spheres, whether written by political scientists or others, would be extremely useful.

On the whole, the study of ideology appears to have received fairly adequate attention, with impressive results in terms of completed research. Nevertheless, the rapid ideological developments since Stalin's death mean that this subject must continue to be subjected to close study and reinterpretation.

Power. The heart of political science research, according to many, if not most, members of the profession, lies in the study of power relationships.[15] Because the U.S.S.R. is a totalitarian dictatorship, power is an even more important subject for Soviet area study than it is for investigations of Western systems. Scholars in all disciplines are concerned with this problem, but its direct examination is particularly appropriate for the political scientist.

The most extended study of power relationships in the early years of the Soviet regime is Edward H. Carr's *A History of Soviet Russia* (5 vols.; New York, 1951-58). The period of the Revolution, the civil war, and to a lesser extent the struggle for power in the 1920's seems to be increasingly the province of the political historian, however, since, for this relatively remote period, a sufficient body of documentary and other source material is available to permit the writing of definitive studies.[16]

To the political scientist (and to a considerable extent the sociologist), then, falls the especially difficult task of analyzing power relationships in the obscure period since 1930. Here the Soviet area specialist can be of great use to his fellow political scientists by providing an interpretation of totalitarianism in a modern industrial society. A number of brilliant over-all studies have been completed in the last twelve years.[17] On the other hand, monographs on this subject have been fewer, and of uneven quality. In some cases, the lack of sufficient theoretical background and the inability of the authors to relate their findings to broader interests of political science—defects which some perceptive senior scholars in other branches of political science regard as the most serious confronting area research—have limited the value of the available monographs. Many studies have been reports originally prepared for government agencies.[18] The shortage of monographs on Soviet power relations is unfortunate, for in spite of the brilliance of many of the more general works, further progress in analysis would appear to depend on the development of the necessary foundation of specialized studies.[19]

The complexity of the problem of power relationships requires a slightly more detailed examination of special facets of this subject. One important topic, treated at length, of course, in the general studies and the particular subject of Nemzer's pioneering article mentioned above (see note 19), is the study of the organization and operation of the central Party apparatus.[20] Except for Sidney Harcave's study,[21] the operation and histories of the territorial Party organizations have received less attention, though as Khrushchev's triumph in June 1957 (achieved partly through the support of provincial Central Committee members) showed, power relationships at this level can be of crucial importance. This lack is particularly unfortunate in view of the existence of a vast body of newspaper and other material on the regional Party organizations, frequently far more detailed and more revealing than available sources on the central organization. The gap in intensive examination of the territorial Party organizations has been partially filled, however, by Merle Fainsod's study of the Smolensk Party, governmental, and police apparatuses, based on a unique body of documentary material seized by the Germans in 1941.[22]

Closely related to the topics just discussed are the problems of the composition and circulation of members in the ruling groups of the Soviet Union, and of Party membership in general. Little has been done on these topics, except as a part of general studies, though the same materials available for an examination of regional Party organizations have invaluable information on the composition and circulation of the elite as well. However, several studies of this nature are in preparation.[23]

Since World War II, the study of civil-military relations has been an increasingly important subject for political science. The relationship between the Soviet Army and the Party has occupied a number of scholars. In addition to Nemzer's study cited above, Zbigniew Brzezinski's *Political Controls in the Soviet Army* (New York, 1954) contributes to the topic. Raymond Garthoff's *Soviet Military Doctrine* (Glencoe, Ill., 1954), while only peripherally concerned with political relations, is valuable for background.[24] Among earlier works, D. Fedotoff White's *The Growth of the Red Army* (Princeton, 1944) and Erich Wollenberg's *The Red Army* (London, 1938), are still important. Many other significant aspects of the political role of the Soviet Army remain to be treated, however. Relationships between high-level military and political figures have scarcely been considered. The role of the army as an occupying force in eastern Europe and elsewhere needs detailed analysis.

Unlike the military, the police system is seldom considered a subject of investigation for political scientists in Western countries. The prominent role of the Soviet police has, however, made it a prime object for analysis by students in the Soviet area, in spite of the extreme difficulty of obtaining reliable information. Two recent works discuss the political ramifications of the police system;[25] a Columbia Ph.D. dissertation will deal primarily with earlier aspects of the problem.[26] A number of revealing studies of the role of the police terror in the Soviet political system have been made; Zbigniew Brzezinski's *The Permanent Purge* (Cambridge, Mass., 1956) is an outstanding example. Nathan Leites and Elsa Bernaut in *Ritual of Liquidation* (Glencoe, Ill., 1954) approach the subject from a somewhat different standpoint, while F. Beck and W. Godin in *Russian Purge and the Extraction of Confession* (New York, 1951) present a remarkably detached analysis of the operation of the Soviet terror apparatus, especially since the book is in part based on the authors' experiences as victims of the system. These studies exhaust much of the reasonably reliable material on this topic. However, Fainsod's analysis of the Smolensk documents is particularly revealing on police activities.[27]

Certain special topics in political science which have received little attention in Soviet area studies should be mentioned. Political psychology, brilliantly investigated by a few political scientists such as Harold Lasswell, faces almost insurmountable obstacles in the Soviet field because of the inability of investigators to conduct personal analyses of political figures, except for occasional defectors.[28] The somewhat greater accessibility of Soviet leaders at the present time might make possible some indirect approaches to this type of study. A second special subject, political control of communications, has received more attention.[29] Nevertheless, monographic studies of particular media would be highly useful.

Administration. Public administration is a central subject of political science. If all its ramifications—city and regional planning, local administration, etc.—are considered, it is probably the most developed branch of the discipline. Moreover, it is one in which comparative techniques are particularly appropriate. Comparison of administrative organization or practices under different systems of government frequently reveals the "marginal" effectiveness of the arrangements under consideration.

At first glance, the purposes and extent of Soviet bureaucratic operations appear too foreign to American values and practice to be of much utility for comparative purposes. Closer inspection shows, however, that there are certain administrative problems common to both advanced technological societies. Detailed examination of the Soviet experience may be of the utmost significance, if only to indicate errors (such as organizational "gigantism") to be avoided, or means which must be rejected if values are not to be corrupted.[30] Here, then, is a subject in which intensive study in the Soviet area might contribute greatly not only to a deeper understanding of the Soviet system, but to an increase in knowledge of practical importance for American institutions.

It is rather surprising that comparatively little systematic monographic investigation has been conducted on this subject.

General treatments, particularly those by Merle Fainsod and Julian Towster,[31] provide the framework for understanding Soviet administration from the political science standpoint. In his legal studies, John N. Hazard has devoted much attention to the rules and laws affecting Soviet administration, and to administrative practice as well. But most of the detailed analysis of the operation of the Soviet administration has been carried on by economists, and has only partial or indirect relevance for public administration.[32]

Law. Political scientists customarily confine themselves to the study of constitutional (public) law, except in so far as private law impinges upon political questions. The hazy line between the two types of law in a basically nonconstitutional state makes this distinction of little importance in the study of the U.S.S.R. Moreover, several of the scholars most concerned with the political and social implications of Soviet legal institutions are by training lawyers, and consequently interested in the whole range of Soviet law. Particularly important in this respect has been the work of John N. Hazard[33] and Harold Berman.[34] Several students of these scholars have already made minor contributions to the literature on Soviet law, and their research production may be expected to increase. Two émigré scholars have also made notable contributions to the study of the Soviet legal system: Vladimir Gsovski in *Soviet Civil Law* (2 vols.; Ann Arbor, 1948-49) and George C. Guins in *Soviet Law and Soviet Society* (The Hague, 1953). Soviet law will continue to require close attention, especially since it will doubtless undergo considerable change as a result of the altered political conditions in the U.S.S.R. General direction of this subject appears to be in highly competent hands, however, and no special concentration of effort upon it seems to be required.

Nationalism. The study of national movements is a subject which is rather difficult to place in the spectrum of political science, for it impinges upon the fields of ideology, power relationships, and international relations. Since nationalism is usually a complicating factor in international relations, it has customarily been studied by political scientists mainly interested in that field. In spite of the somewhat indeterminate nature of the subject, it has given rise to some of the most important recent publications in political science,[35] though the subject received a somewhat greater concentration of attention in the 1930's.

Because the U.S.S.R. is a multinational state, and particularly because national differences have played a prominent role in the struggle for power within it, studies of nationalism have been of special importance for the Soviet area political scientist. Most of the studies of Russian nationalism have been written by historians and deal primarily with the pre-Soviet period. The most important study of Russian nationalism in the Soviet period is Frederick C. Barghoorn's recent *Soviet Russian Nationalism* (New York, 1956). There is, however, room for a number of monographic studies of recent manifestations of Russian nationalism, particularly in the occupied Soviet Union during World War II; in the emigration in general; and the use of Pan-Slav ideology by the Soviet regime. Studies of the use of the Russian Orthodox Church as a political arm of the Soviet government would also be useful.[36] Material on all these topics is relatively easy to obtain.

Of the non-Russian nationalities, the Ukrainians have received the greatest attention. A series of monographic studies was initiated by the political scientist John S. Reshetar's *Ukrainian Revolution, 1917-1920* (Princeton, 1952), and followed by the present writer's *Ukrainian Nationalism, 1939-1945* (New York, 1955). Most of the intervening period is the subject of a Ph.D. dissertation (Columbia University, history) being prepared by Michael Luther. A longer period is covered by Basil Dmytryshyn's *Moscow and the Ukraine* (New York, 1956). There is certainly room for more specialized works, but as in other studies of nationalism, there is in this field a special danger of overenthusiastic and partisan efforts to draw conclusions going beyond the available evidence.

Very little has been done on the other European nationalities under Soviet rule. Nicholas Vakar's *Belorussia* (Cambridge, Mass., 1955) provides some information on the recent period. No truly scholarly studies of the Baltic nationalities during World War II have been published, though ample material is available. The other European groups—Moldavians, Finnic peoples—probably do not warrant full-scale studies, though smaller studies would be useful.

The picture is much the same as far as the Georgians and the Armenians are concerned, though these nations are much more important. Much more work has been done on the Moslem nationalities. The historian Richard Pipes' *The Formation of the U.S.S.R.* (Cambridge, Mass., 1954) is most useful on the Turkic groups. A political scientist, Alexander Park, has done a comprehensive study of the Central Asian Turkic peoples in the early period of the Soviet regime.[37] Olaf Caroe's *Soviet Empire: The Turks of Central Asia and Stalinism* (London, 1953) and Walter Kolarz' *Russia and Her Colonies* (New York, 1952) deal with Asian nationalities of the U.S.S.R. The British *Central Asian Review* has published a number of valuable short studies.

On the whole, the field of nationalism appears to have been fairly well developed, and the remaining gaps, while numerous, are at least well defined. A general study of nationality conflict in the U.S.S.R. is much needed, but should probably await the production of more monographs.

International Relations. This subject, which has steadily grown in importance in the general discipline of political science, has been especially significant in Soviet area studies, where it has occupied the attention of nearly half of the political scientists. This is, of course, due to the fact that the immediate concern of Americans with the Soviet Union arises primarily from the influence of that country in international affairs. In this connection, the work of the Council on Foreign Relations in sponsoring analyses of the Soviet impact on international relations is outstanding.[38] Philip E. Mosely, supervisor of the more recent research activities of the Council, has himself contributed what is undoubtedly the most important body of analytical articles on Soviet foreign relations.[39]

A recent tendency of political scientists investigating the foreign affairs of other countries has been to concentrate on such questions as the role of public opinion in policy formation; the process of policy formation within the government; the organization, personnel, and administration of foreign affairs; and techniques of diplomacy. All of these subjects are almost inaccessible to foreigners studying Soviet foreign relations. From his close personal contact and exhaustive study of printed materials, Frederick C. Barghoorn was able to make a contribution to the knowledge of forces behind Soviet policy formation.[40] At the present time, Professor Barghoorn is undertaking an extensive examination of the role of cultural relations, an aspect of Soviet foreign policy which is rapidly increasing in importance.

Memoirs, rather than research publications, remain one of the principal sources of information concerning Soviet diplomacy; but their value can be much enhanced by skillful assembling and editing, as in the case of *Negotiating with the Russians* (ed. by Raymond Dennett and Joseph E. Johnson; Boston, 1951). Still, much can be done, especially on the organization and personnel of the Soviet diplomatic service.[41]

Little need be said here about the extensive work of collecting and publishing Soviet documents related to foreign affairs, except to note that this effort, generally made by historians, provides an indispensable base for further analysis.[42] These collections are, of course, especially important for the study of Soviet relations with the major powers, and a number of comprehensive studies have been made of the pre-1941 period, where documentation is relatively plentiful.[43] It is unfortunate that full-scale analyses have not been completed on such important and relatively accessible topics of the postwar period as Soviet activities in the United Nations; Soviet attitudes toward atomic energy and disarmament; and the Paris Peace Conference.

Soviet relations with the satellite (and former satellite) countries of eastern Europe have been the subject of numerous books and shorter studies. Among the most important are Hugh Seton-Watson's *East European Revolution* (New York, 1956) and Adam B. Ulam's *Titoism and the Cominform* (Cambridge, Mass., 1952). Many more specialized studies of the imposition of the Soviet system upon the east European countries are needed, however.[44]

Almost as important as the study of the relation of the Soviet regime to its satellites is the problem of the link between the U.S.S.R. and Communist Parties which have not attained power. Important studies have been made of the west European Communist Parties, particularly those by Gabriel Almond,[45] Mario Einaudi,[46] and Ossip K. Flechtheim.[47] David T. Cattell's *Communism and the Spanish Civil War* (Berkeley, 1955) and *Soviet Diplomacy and the Spanish Civil War* (Berkeley, 1957) devote special attention to tracing the connection between Soviet policy and Spanish Communist activities. Careful studies of Comintern and Cominform activities in the European area would be especially useful.

The field of Soviet and Communist policy in the Far East is distinguished by the number of scholars who combine Russian area specialization with intimate knowledge of the language and politics of one or more Asian countries. Among them may be mentioned Paul S. Langer and Rodger Swearingen, *Red Flag in Japan* (Cambridge, Mass., 1952); Benjamin Schwartz, *Chinese Communism and the Rise of Mao* (Cambridge, Mass., 1951); Peter Tang, *Communist China Today* (New York, 1957); Allen S. Whiting, *Soviet Policies in China, 1917-1924* (New York, 1954); and James W. Morley, *The Japanese Thrust into Siberia*,

1918 (New York, 1957).[48] A similar combination of Russian and Middle Eastern specialization is perhaps even more difficult, but is especially needed at the present time.

The foregoing survey of research in the international relations field indicates that the need for specialized works is far from being met, especially in relation to Communist activities outside the Soviet Union. Undoubtedly the most urgent practical requirement of the field at the present time, however, is for an over-all study of Soviet foreign policy since the outbreak of World War II. Such a work is needed not only as a textbook, but to provide a central point for general consideration of the subject, and to point the way for further specialized research. It is probably no exaggeration to say that such a book is the greatest single need in Soviet area studies today.

III

A significant accomplishment of scholarship on the Soviet area has been the sponsorship of a large body of writing by émigrés from the U.S.S.R. Many useful articles have been produced, usually based upon the writer's personal experience or contacts, on such subjects as the police system, concentration camps, Soviet personalities, and Communist Party intrigues. Together with the extensive information collected in oral interviews,[49] this material constitutes a most important source for further analysis of the Soviet political system.

One of the greatest contributions of area studies to the growth of scholarship in the United States has been the fostering of an interdisciplinary approach. In Russian studies particularly, a willingness to transcend traditional approaches rooted in the methodology of individual disciplines has made research both intellectually exciting and fruitful in results. One does, however, often hear the complaint that area specialists who have established such a high degree of communication among themselves have failed to present their findings in such a way as to make them of maximum value to other political scientists. It is said that area specialists do not have the necessary background in theory; are unfamiliar with recent methodological advances; and disregard political developments outside their own area.

The best answer to these criticisms, if they really are significant, is the caliber of the future scholarship by area specialists who are also political scientists. If the scholar is of high intellectual competence and possesses a sound background of training, the direction of his interest is of secondary importance. In this field, as in others where basic research is involved, it would be self-defeating to prescribe subjects for investigation, for often the seemingly most remote topics ultimately have the greatest relevance for practical interests, as well as for the general advance of knowledge.

With full awareness of the overriding importance of individual choice of research interests, it does appear worth while to suggest three fields in which Soviet area research would be especially relevant for political science in general: (1) The study of power relationships in the Soviet totalitarian system should go a long way toward clarifying the general role of power in advanced technological societies. As Franz Neumann pointed out, the extreme or crisis situation often reveals trends or phenomena which are obscured in the "normal" configuration.[50] (2) The study of Soviet administration would be useful because of this circumstance, and also because the administrative experience of any country the size of the Soviet Union is bound to be relevant for other countries. (3) Unraveling the obscure but essential connections between the Soviet regime and foreign Communism is vital to an understanding of international relations in our time. But to be relevant to the discipline as a whole, such research must be reported in a manner which will make it available for comparative purposes. Fortunately, political science, unlike some disciplines, has little recondite terminology or highly elaborated theory which must be mastered as a prerequisite to communication with one's colleagues. Even if some area specialists now lack acquaintance with methodology, classic political theory, or the literature of other fields of political science, such deficiencies can be overcome with relatively little difficulty.

The need for more monographic research, stressed earlier, seems at first glance to conflict with the objective of making Soviet area investigations more relevant to the discipline of political science as a whole. But there is no reason why monographic research, if properly conceived and reported, may not both contribute to the advancement of the body of knowledge on the Soviet area and be relevant to the political science discipline. Monographs on such subjects as composition of the elite, local administration, and ties between the U.S.S.R. and foreign Communists, if properly related to broader problems in the field, should be of great interest to professional political scientists.

IV

As one looks back over the past twelve years, the progress made in the study of Soviet politics appears nothing short of phenomenal. Professional students of politics are now able to draw on a reliable and systematic body of knowledge concerning the U.S.S.R. Granting all the difficulties of exploiting Soviet materials, however, an immense field for investigation remains. During the past five years this field has very considerably expanded because of the heightened tempo of change in Soviet political conditions, and particularly the increase in material made available in the Soviet Union. To this is added the possibility of limited direct observation of Soviet conditions. Moreover, many of the students trained since the war are now approaching the status of established scholars; as a result the field is equipped with a competent staff. Consequently, there is a good prospect for still more rapid development of Soviet area research in political science during the next decade.

George L. Kline

5. PHILOSOPHY AND RELIGION

I

WHILE AMERICAN SCHOLARS have made important contributions to the exploration and illumination of Russian and Soviet philosophy and religion, several of the basic studies have been written by Europeans. This must be borne in mind not only in reviewing the present state of research, but in considering future needs. It is perfectly true, for example, that no definitive study of Soviet philosophy has yet been produced in this country. However, while a brilliant study in this field would always be welcome, the need does not seem so pressing in the light of the existing works by such European scholars as Bocheński, Wetter, and Acton.

There would seem to be two principal reasons for the preponderance of European scholars among students of Russian and Soviet philosophy. First, most—though not all—of the European students of the subject are of Russian or western Slav origin (Zenkovsky, Lossky, Vysheslavtsev, Weidlé, Koyré; Masaryk, Bocheński). A majority of them received their philosophic training in Russian universities; thus they began with a special knowledge of, and interest in, Russian philosophy, together with a general philosophic competence. Second, institutional support for teaching and research in this area has been stronger in western Europe than in the United States. As an instance, the only chair of the history of Russian philosophy outside the Soviet Union is held by Professor Wetter at the Pontifical Oriental Institute in Rome.

Philosophy and religion have often been regarded as closely linked (e.g., among Russian thinkers of the nineteenth and early twentieth centuries—Leontyev, Solovyov, Berdyaev, Bulgakov, Frank); but they have often been regarded as quite distinct, even opposed (e.g., by contemporary Soviet writers). In any case, for purposes of organizational clarity and convenience, these two fields will be treated separately in the present review.

II

The last decade has seen the publication of a number of solid general works on Russian and Soviet philosophy, supplementing and, to a degree, correcting the still valuable work of Masaryk.[1] Professor Zenkovsky's monumental *History of Russian Philosophy* is the major study.[2] Professor Lossky's shorter work is useful for its exposition and criticism of Russian religious thinkers.[3]

Of recent works devoted to individual thinkers and tendencies in Russian thought, we may note the studies by Hepner, Bowman, Hare, and Haimson.[4] Hepner's book on Bakunin and Revolutionary Pan-Slavism is broader than its title would indicate; it has a good deal to say, for example, about Belinsky, Schelling, Hegel, and "dialectical nihilism." Bowman explores Belinsky's successive attachments to Schelling, Fichte, and Hegel, and his later impassioned repudiation of Hegelian impersonalism. Hare's study focuses upon the historical views of nineteenth-century Russian thinkers, offering relatively little exposition or analysis of their ethical, social, or aesthetic theory. Both Bowman and Hare provide copious and well-translated excerpts from such thinkers as Belinsky, Herzen, Chaadayev, and Leontyev. Haimson's book is an exemplary essay in intellectual-institutional-political history; it deals with philosophy only in passing.

None of the works mentioned thus far treats *Soviet* philosophy in any detail. Of full-length studies devoted exclusively to Soviet dialectical materialism, Professor Wetter's is the most comprehensive.[5] Indeed, its exhaustively detailed exposition makes the book difficult reading for the nonspecialist in philosophy. A more accessible book is the admirably concise critical study by Professor Bocheński.[6] It is to be hoped that the publication of the already completed English translation of this work will not be long delayed.

Marxist-Leninist social and political philosophy is perceptively analyzed in the recent works of Professors Mayo and Maček.[7] Both are models of vigorous criticism, although Mayo addresses himself to a somewhat more sophisticated audience than does Maček, who is concerned with the ways in which Marx, Engels, and Lenin were interpreted and exploited by their political offspring. Both studies are well organized and crisply written.

A work by a younger American scholar, quite different in intention from these two, is Stanley W. Moore's recent volume.[8] Unlike Mayo and Maček, Moore concentrates upon exposition, rather than upon analysis and criticism. But he offers a connected account, often with a real gain in clarity, of what Marx, Engels, and Lenin actually asserted on various economic, social, and political questions.

Of broader philosophic scope, and written from a firm foundation in general philosophy, is Professor Acton's annihilating critical study.[9] Strictly speaking, this work does not fall within the scope of a review of Russian studies, since Acton, who does not read Russian, bases himself upon non-Russian or translated Russian sources. However, it is too important a work to omit upon such slender grounds. And Acton's professional competence and perspective more than make up for his lack of familiarity with the

Russian originals. Such studies by non-Slavicists are not only to be welcomed, but invited.

An excellent brief critique of Marxist-Leninist ontology, epistemology, and social philosophy—as yet available only in Russian —is *The Philosophic Poverty of Marxism* by the late Professor Boris Vysheslavtsev, published under the pseudonym "Petrov."[10]

American scholars have published several other books and a number of articles dealing with Soviet philosophy. Professor Meyer's volume on Leninism,[11] a companion to his earlier study of non-Russian Marxism, represents a solid critical contribution. Like the studies by Moore and Maček, it is concerned primarily with social and political philosophy, but it throws fresh light on a number of questions of Marxist-Leninist doctrine in these areas.

Professor Marcuse's recently published study offers a useful and perceptive, though rather technical, historical-cultural analysis and critique of Soviet philosophy.[12] It focuses upon political, social, and ethical theory, but touches upon questions of logic and dialectic. In general, this work represents a valuable supplement to the primarily analytical studies of Vysheslavtsev, Mayo, Acton, and others. Professor Robinson has made a careful analysis of an important phase of Stalinist social and political philosophy.[13] The interesting studies of Leites are not discussed here since they fall within the scope of the review of political science and ideology.[14]

Kline has published three articles of a general nature; a brief survey of the history of Russian (including Soviet) philosophy; a more detailed review of Soviet philosophy since the death of Stalin; and a concise study of Soviet ethical and social theory.[15] He has also contributed a study of the place and influence of Spinoza in Russian and Soviet philosophy, which includes translations of representative samples of Soviet scholarship on Spinoza.[16]

In the field of logic and the philosophy of science, no major study has yet appeared. Alexander Philipov has published a brief monograph on formal logic and dialectic and the ways in which both have been exploited for political ends in the Soviet Union.[17] Questions of logic and philosophy of science are treated in passing by Bocheński, Wetter, Mayo, and Acton.

A detailed historical examination of the development of the Soviet philosophy of the natural sciences during the formative (and relatively uninhibited) years 1922-29 is provided by David Joravsky in an unpublished doctoral dissertation.[18] Joravsky is a historian and his study falls under the category of intellectual and institutional history rather than philosophy; but it touches competently upon philosophic questions at many points. Joravsky has also published articles and reviews dealing with Soviet histories of science and bibliographies of logic.

A certain amount of material on the philosophy of the biological sciences is included in Kline's study of Darwinism and the Russian Orthodox Church.[19] Professor Wetter has completed a monograph on Soviet philosophy of the biological sciences, *Der dialektische Materialismus und das Problem der Entstehung des Lebens: Zur Theorie von A. I. Oparin* (Munich-Salzburg-Cologne, 1958).

There have, as yet, been no substantive studies of Russian or Soviet aesthetic theory, although a brief monograph on this subject by Philipov has been edited for possible publication in English.

In the field of religion and the church, American scholars, including those of Russian origin, have produced a number of valuable studies. Professor Curtiss has written two comprehensive and thoroughly documented historical accounts.[20] Professor Timasheff has contributed an illuminating short book on the subject, and offers many perceptive remarks in his later, more general study.[21] Professor Spinka's history of the Church and its Patriarchs under the Soviet regime, though less exhaustive than the works of Curtiss, has the advantage of being up-to-date and extremely concise.[22]

A limitation of these studies is their exclusive consideration of the Russian Orthodox Church, to the neglect of schismatic (Old Believer), Roman Catholic, Protestant, Jewish, and Mohammedan groups. This is also true of most articles in the field, e.g., Professor Inkeles' excellent brief survey of family and church in the postwar U.S.S.R.[23]

In the field of Russian religious beliefs, attitudes, and values, less work has been done.[24] Both Zenkovsky and Masaryk, especially the former, offer copious material on Russian philosophy of religion and philosophical theology. In addition to the late Professor G. P. Fedotov's study of *The Russian Religious Mind*, there have been valuable anthologies: e.g., the anthology of Solovyov's writings edited by S. L. Frank (London, 1950), and the recent German-language anthology edited by Bubnoff.[25]

III

Philosophy is a discipline in which it is always helpful, and sometimes essential, to know one's intellectual antecedents. This is particularly true of the relation between Soviet and nineteenth-century Russian social and political philosophy. For example, it is difficult, if not impossible, to understand the Bolshevism of Lenin, Trotsky, and Stalin without a knowledge of the radical nihilism of Bakunin and Chernyshevsky, Nechayev and Tkachov. For this reason, among others, most of the following suggestions will be aimed at deepening and broadening our knowledge of nineteenth- and early twentieth-century Russian philosophic thought.

A preliminary point requires clarification. Would it not be desirable, someone might urge, to set up as a major project the production of a "definitive" history of Russian philosophy? Upon reflection, such a task seems less than essential; the works of Zenkovsky, Masaryk, *et al.*, whatever their minor shortcomings, are adequate. And our far from limitless scholarly energies should be channeled into studies which would involve less duplication of effort and at the same time promise a richer intellectual harvest.

In sum, it does not seem worth while to probe exhaustively into the history of Russian metaphysics, epistemology, or philosophy of science. This conclusion flows from the very nature of Russian (and, to a considerable degree, Soviet) philosophizing. From the late eighteenth century to the present day, Russian philosophers have been primarily concerned with questions of ethics, social and political philosophy, and philosophy of history. Compared to their German, French, and English counterparts, they have devoted much less attention to logic, theory of knowledge, and metaphysics. The relation of the individual to society, the problem of good and evil in individual and social life, the meaning and direction of historical development, the relation of national to universal culture—rather than the nature of being and knowledge, or the presuppositions of science—have been the major foci of their philosophic interest.

It thus seems obvious that at least two kinds of comprehensive study are called for: one focusing upon Russian (including Soviet) ethical and social theory,[26] a second upon Russian (including Soviet) philosophy of history. No one has yet undertaken a full-scale study of Russian philosophy (or philosophies) of history. Such questions receive peripheral consideration in recent works by Riasanovsky and MacMaster, and somewhat fuller treatment in Hare's book, as well as in the earlier study by Chyzhevsky.[27] Isaiah Berlin has written a stimulating essay on Tolstoy's philosophy of history.[28] But a major gap remains in the exploration of Russian philosophies of history, which might profitably be filled, either by one comprehensive study, or by a series of short monographs—e.g., on the Slavophile philosophy of history, on Chaadayev, on Kareyev.[29]

There is an urgent need for a series of monographs devoted to the philosophic views of Herzen, Pisarev, Lavrov, Mikhailovsky, Lunacharsky, Bogdanov, Struve, and many other thinkers. James Billington's monograph, *Mikhailovsky and Russian Populism* (Oxford, 1958), is a substantial and conscientious study, but its chief emphasis falls upon personal and institutional history rather than upon the history of ideas.[30]

As indicated above, the field of Russian and Soviet aesthetics and philosophy of art has been little studied. There is room for a good critical monograph, or perhaps two or three of them, in this area.[31] Here again, nineteenth-century doctrine (Chernyshevsky, Dobrolyubov, Pisarev, Tolstoy) illuminates and sets in perspective recent Soviet developments.

It would also be useful to have several additional studies of particular Western philosophers as they have influenced, and been interpreted by, Russian and Soviet thinkers. A study of Hegel in Soviet philosophy, for example, would be a valuable supplement to Chyzhevsky's book, which deals only with pre- and non-Soviet thinkers (see note 27). This might also be done for Kant, Schopenhauer, Feuerbach, Nietzsche, and perhaps Herder and Schelling. Among political and social philosophers, one thinks of de Maistre (whose doctrinal similarities to Tolstoy are emphasized in Berlin's study), St.-Simon, Fourier, and Proudhon. Studies of Kant, de Maistre, Herder, Schelling, Schopenhauer, and Nietzsche would naturally focus upon the nineteenth century. Those devoted to Hegel, Feuerbach, St.-Simon, Fourier, and Proudhon might profitably include both pre- and post-revolutionary developments.

As a logical extension of such analyses, there is need for a series of comparative studies of Western and Russian thinkers.[32] A number of interesting combinations come readily to mind: e.g., Leontyev and Nietzsche, Lavrov and Mill, Mikhailovsky and Spencer. Due regard should, of course, be paid to contrasts and oppositions, as well as to similarities.

More ambitious comparative studies—of entire philosophic schools or of general constellations of cultural values and beliefs —might eventually be carried out, but only by investigators whose linguistic, philosophic, and historical equipment was truly exceptional. A pioneer study along these lines is Dr. Sarkisyanz's work on messianic and chiliastic ideas and attitudes in Russia and the Moslem, Hindu, and Buddhist East.[33] Even a linguist as accomplished as Sarkisyanz, who commands Russian and Persian, in addition to German, French, and English, has had to rely heavily on translated sources.

Of more restricted scope, but of at least equal promise, is a suggestion put forward by Professor Alfred Meyer concerning the exploration of particular concepts, or groups of related concepts, in Russian philosophic thought. He has himself made the beginnings of such an exploration of the concept of culture.[34] Concepts like "progress," "duty," "consciousness," "conscience," "truth-justice" [*pravda*], could be similarly analyzed. Such a series of limited studies might eventually be brought together in a general dictionary or encyclopedia of Russian and Soviet philosophy.

With respect to the recent Soviet period, philosophy has been a sterile field. However, some of the younger Soviet philosophers (men in their early and middle twenties) have recently turned with enthusiasm and competence to the more technical branches of logic, logistic, and philosophy of science: *viz.*, mathematical logic, axiomatization, proof theory, formalized languages, information theory, "thinking machines." As yet these men have published almost nothing; but when their work begins to appear, it should be carefully studied.

Finally, there is need for a series of good English translations of some of the important works of nineteenth-century Russian thought, e.g., Lavrov's *Historical Letters*. Even more pressing from the viewpoint of pedagogy and popularization is the need for a series of anthologies drawn from the works of Herzen, Pisarev, Lavrov, Mikhailovsky, and others.[35]

The most obvious lacunae in research on religion in Russia (both before and after 1917) result from the lack of attention paid to religious groups and institutions other than the Russian Orthodox Church—schismatic Old Believers, Roman Catholics,

Protestants, Jews, Armenians, Moslems, Buddhists. This is understandable in view of the historically privileged position of the Orthodox Church, under both Soviet and Tsarist regimes, and the fact that more than two-thirds of the churched population has always been Orthodox. But substantial monographs could profitably be devoted to each of the major non-Orthodox faiths. There may be difficulties with sources, particularly in the case of the Lutherans (in Soviet Latvia and Estonia), the Armenians, and the various sects of Old Believers. But—as an example—with regard to current Protestant (Baptist) groups, there are the files of the journal *Bratskii Vestnik*. And the possibility may develop of on-the-spot observation and interviewing of leaders and ordinary churchgoers of all sects.

A topic of great current interest is the degree and kind of religious conviction among Soviet young people, especially young intellectuals. Such an investigation verges upon the domain of sociology, social psychology, and perhaps cultural anthropology; and it would involve extensive field work. But neither of these considerations seems a sufficient reason for refusing to undertake such a study. Unsystematic observations and inquiries among young Soviet intellectuals in 1956 and 1957 on the part of several scholars suggest that the results might be most illuminating.

In the field of philosophical theology and philosophy of religion, monographs on men like Solovyov, Leontyev, Rozanov, Bulgakov, Frank, and Shestov are needed. It would be valuable, too, to have anthologies from the writings of these and other religious thinkers, on the model of the Solovyov anthology edited by Frank, or general source books bringing together selections from several writers, like that of Bubnoff referred to above (note 25).[36]

IV

The present situation and future prospects for research in Russian philosophy and religion give no cause for discouragement or dismay. Solid and informative works have been published during the past decade; there is every reason to expect that even better ones will be published during the next. But a word of warning and suggestion is in order. The number of scholars working in these fields is extremely small, and many of them are already advanced in years. The assuring of a *Nachwuchs,* a scholarly "younger generation," is an urgent problem, and one made difficult by the paucity of universities offering graduate courses in Russian philosophy or religion.

Many of the works referred to in this report were produced either by members of history departments or by persons without academic affiliation. This is not in itself alarming; but it indicates a need for closer cooperation between departments of philosophy (and religion) and Russian area programs. Courses in various aspects of Russian intellectual history are offered at Brandeis, California, Chicago, Columbia, Cornell, Harvard, Michigan State, and Wellesley, with students drawn from a variety of disciplines. But these are, for the most part, *lecture* courses. Competent young scholars dedicated to a study of Russian philosophy or religion are much more likely to emerge from an advanced *seminar* on an appropriate topic. And thus far, such seminars are disquietingly few and far between.

Arthur S. Barron

6. SOCIAL RELATIONS

I

THE ACHIEVEMENTS of American behavioral scientists in the field of Russian studies have been noteworthy.[1] They have made significant progress in at least four major areas. The basic institutions of Soviet society have been described with special reference to their structure and functioning. Salient features of Soviet national character have been identified and related to the social structure. Sharp insights have been gained into Soviet demography. A preliminary methodology for the study of totalitarian systems has been developed, and both the special and the general aspects of Soviet totalitarianism have been examined. Almost no work, however, has been done on Russian society before 1917 or on the prerevolutionary origins of such continuing problems as urbanization, industrialization, and the changing composition of the elite.

This accomplishment is the work of a very few people. There are probably no more than thirty sociologists in this country with professional training in Russian studies. In the behavioral sciences as a whole, there are perhaps no more than a hundred with such training. There are several reasons for this: limited opportunities for field work or experiment in Soviet studies, the unavailability of many primary source materials, the difficulty of Russian language training, the lack of opportunities for academic employment, and the failure of some behavioral science departments in universities to recognize Russian studies as a legitimate field of specialization.

In addition, Soviet studies, by their very nature, are removed from the main currents of the behavioral sciences in the United States. They represent, in fact, a dramatic departure from traditional American sociology. That tradition has stressed empirical techniques—questionnaires, IBM tabulation, content analysis, interviewing, the whole paraphernalia of survey research. But American sociologists working on the Soviet Union have relied mainly on the techniques which have dominated European sociology—library research, the use of historical documents, the construction of ideal types and theoretical models. Moreover, traditional American sociology has been largely concerned with "small" problems, with rigorously delimited phenomena, with issues of such scope that they could be explored in the laboratory. It has not generally dealt with society as a whole. Students of Soviet society, on the other hand, have been very much concerned with the vast problems of social structure, with exploring society as a totality. Finally, traditional American sociology has not much emphasized the study of ideology, the functioning of political institutions, or the problem of social change. In Soviet studies these issues have predominated.

In very general terms, the behavioral sciences in this country have used four broad approaches in their study of the Soviet Union.* These have followed each other in roughly chronological order, though there is naturally much overlap.

First on the scene was what might be termed the *partisan* school of Soviet studies. The work done in this early period was

---

* What Daniel Bell refers to as the "Kremlinology" approach is not included. This approach seeks to explain Soviet society primarily in terms of the political jockeying for power that takes place among the men in the Kremlin.

less scientific than propagandist. Its purpose seems to have been less to understand the workings of Soviet society than to demonstrate either its superiority or its inferiority to Western society.[2] Monographs and articles produced in this period were marked by naïveté and special pleading.

Next there emerged the *institutional* or *cultural* school. Here the emphasis was placed on an accurate description of Soviet institutions. Some attempt was made to outline their functions and interrelations, but, on the whole, the main concern was with structure.[3]

A preoccupation with *social psychological* factors and with the Soviet Union as a *social system* characterized a third stage in the development of sociological studies of the U.S.S.R. Here the emphasis has clearly been on interrelations, not only of institutions, but of personality and social structure. In the tradition of structural functional analysis, this approach attempts to study the Soviet Union as a going concern, to determine the functional and dysfunctional interrelations which characterize Soviet social structure, personality, and culture.[4]

Finally, an approach has developed which attempts to view the Soviet Union in the broader context of *totalitarianism* generally. This school moves in the direction of a genuine comparative sociology. The emphasis is on distinguishing between those factors of Soviet society which reflect totalitarianism as it has been known elsewhere, those which reflect unique Bolshevik contributions to totalitarianism, and those which merely reflect changes in social structure characteristic of a rapidly industrialized society in the twentieth century. Scholars of this school are less concerned with the Soviet Union as such than they are with Soviet phenomena as representing more universal trends in social change and social structure.[5]

A review of the literature follows.* Before moving to a dis-

---

* Because of security considerations, government works were not generally available. This is unfortunate since government research, particularly in the realm of strategic intelligence, is sophisticated and relevant to behavioral

cussion of specific works, however, three general observations will be made. First, it should be noted that the great bulk of these studies are remarkably free from ideological bias. High standards of scholarship have prevailed: Soviet sources are used for facts; quotations are accurate; full attention is given to context. On the other hand, the authors cannot help being ideologically engaged. For one thing, their results are frequently used in a cold war context by journalists, government officials, and action agencies. For another thing, research problems are often defined in terms of their political connotations. No matter how objectively conducted, for example, study of the Soviet system supported by the Air Force tends to have distinct ideological implications.

Second, while these studies have not produced many general propositions useful in the study of human society as a whole, they have nevertheless made some contributions to the theory and methodology of behavioral science. For example, the work of Margaret Mead and Rhoda Métraux at the American Museum of Natural History on studying a culture at a distance represented a significant innovation, and the two-volume study of Soviet communications compiled under the direction of Margaret Mead at the M.I.T. Center for International Studies revealed new methodological techniques.[6] Similarly, Nathan Leites' utilization of Soviet texts (writings, speeches, and pronouncements) as source materials and Barrington Moore's study of the role of social classes in industrialization reflected novel approaches of some significance.[7] At the same time, practical contributions have clearly been made to our understanding of various aspects of Soviet society and to comparative social science, particularly in the substantive areas of social change, stratification, and totalitarianism. Subsequent work and further refinements and interpretation of the data already collected promise to yield additional basic insights.

---

science. On the other hand, it is probably safe to say that much of it is tied directly to the daily twists and turns of the cold war.

Finally, these studies have sometimes tended to neglect problems which relate most clearly to the central and distinctive features of Soviet society. Several such problems come immediately to mind: the nature and implications of Soviet planning, the sociology of occupations in the Soviet Union, the objectives and chief features of the Soviet educational system (including the position of science and technology), and the Soviet Union as a special case of the change from peasant to industrial society. Such gaps undoubtedly reflect in part the inaccessibility of data. In part, however, they may also stem from an overattachment to the theoretical and methodological preoccupations of American behavioral science.

II

Demography. At one time Soviet social statistics were excellent. Precise data on population, the labor force, the social composition of the Party, abortion, divorce, and other topics were readily available to Western scholars. As long ago as the late twenties, however, the Soviet government began to withdraw such information. Soon Soviet social statistics became almost impossible to obtain. Accurate census data, for example, have not been available since 1939.

Considering the obstacles, American research has done an excellent job in throwing light on Soviet population trends. Basic data have been compiled.[8] The dynamics of Soviet population growth have been analyzed. Long-range projections of population growth, especially of the labor force, have been charted.[9] For the early period of Soviet development, excellent sources are available on migration, urbanization, and work force.[10] The validity of certain inferential techniques of demographic analysis has been established. It has been demonstrated, for example, that Soviet literacy rates can be used to arrive at population data.[11] An excellent study of Soviet professional manpower has been made.[12] This study is especially valuable because it relates population data to social structure. It provides genuine insight into Soviet techniques of mobilizing segments of the population for the attainment of the regime's goals. Finally, attention has been given to the special role of women in the Soviet work force.[13]

National Character.[14] Research on national character has typically sought to answer three questions: What are the modal personality patterns in a given society? What are the determinants of these patterns? What role do these patterns play in culture and social structure? Recent work in the United States in the field of Russian national character has, however, been mainly concerned with a delineation of modal personality patterns. Much less attention has been paid to determinants, or to the interaction of personality and social structure.

Utilizing the techniques and concepts of anthropology, sociology, clinical psychology, and psychoanalysis, various students have sought to delineate the personality patterns comprised in Russian national character.[15] Despite some inconsistency in the findings, the results tend to converge.[16] This would seem to provide an indirect measure of validity.

Attempts have also been made to explore the personality characteristics of the Soviet elite. Leites views the Bolshevik's behavior as essentially a "reaction-formation" against the behavior of the nineteenth-century intelligentsia. According to Leites, two principal drives explain Bolshevik character: preoccupation with death and latent passive homosexual impulses. The working out of these impulses is traced by Leites in his analysis of Bolshevik behavior. Submergence in the Party, for example, is viewed as a defense against fear of death; hostility toward the external world is seen as a reaction to the fear of being passive.

In addition to attempting a delineation of modal Russian personality patterns, Soviet specialists have also sought to describe the norms of Soviet behavior as they are defined by the regime. Specifically, an attempt has been made to identify what constitutes "socially required' behavior in the Soviet Union. For example, Bauer has successfully traced the changes in the image of man and his behavior which have characterized Soviet psychology at various stages in its development.[17] These changes are seen as a reflection of basic transformations in Soviet ideology and social structure. According to Bauer, the Soviets have shifted from an image of man as "a creature of the forces of environment," to one of man as being controlled neither by heredity nor by environment, but "an activist, the source of his own error and evil, capable of self-initiation." In the process of this shift the concept of consciousness has been given new emphasis and prominence.

Mead has sought to define what is expected of Soviet citizens in response to authority. She and her associates carefully document the regime's insistence on discipline, purposeful behavior, and seriousness. A major contribution of her study is a demonstration that the regime has different expectations of behavior for persons occupying different statuses in Soviet society.

Several writers have pointed out that there does not seem to be a very good "fit" between the personality structure of the Russian, on the one hand, and the structure and expectations of the regime, on the other. Inkeles suggests that there is a "fairly massive degree of incongruence" between the modal personality patterns of Soviet citizens and the regime, and specifies at least five major areas of incongruence.[18] In much the same vein, Dicks sees a "salient divergence" between the Soviet system and Russian personality. The coercions and deprivations of the regime are interpreted by the Russian as "withdrawal of love and nurturance." This creates unconscious rage and also inner guilts. The end result is an increase in the atmosphere of "persecutory anxiety and diffuse fear."

Bauer has attempted to explain the phenomenon of disaffection in terms of a lack of congruence between personality and the requirements of the regime.[19] He sets himself the problem of explaining why certain external conditions influence some individuals to disaffection, but not others. According to Bauer, different personality types tend to play different political roles. When the external situation is such that one cannot play a political role which is "congenial" to one's personality, disaffection results.

Several criticisms can be leveled against these studies of Russian national character. An insufficient attempt, it would seem, has been made to relate findings in Russian national character studies to other work done in academic psychology. Though the continuities seem obvious, little effort has been made, for example, to analyze Bolshevik behavior in terms of the authoritarian personality concept.[20] Sufficient attention has not been paid to areas of congruence between Russian personality and Soviet social structure. The development of Russian character—its roots in child-rearing practices, education, and history—has scarcely been examined.[21] Sociocultural factors have received little emphasis in the analysis of Russian character: the literature has been overbalanced in the direction of psychoanalysis.

Theories about Russian national character are too often static and descriptive; little attention has been paid to the problem of change. The notion of variability in Russian national character has been seriously neglected. Because a standard analytic scheme for the delineation of personality patterns is lacking, several crucial dimensions of personality have been unexplored. Nowhere in the literature, for example, is the Russian's concept of self dealt with; extremely little attention has been paid to his typical forms of expressive behavior, his methods for resolving conflict, and so forth.

Public Opinion and Mass Communications. For obvious reasons, American scholars have been unable to conduct surveys of opinion among Soviet citizens. On the other hand, extensive and systematic research has been conducted on the attitudes of *former* Soviet citizens (i.e., defectors) as part of the Harvard Project on the Soviet Social System.[22]

A major attempt has been made to evaluate popular reaction to the Soviet system as it now stands.[23] Perhaps the most significant finding to emerge is that the Soviet citizen approves many of the basic institutional forms of Soviet society. By and large, he sanctions the welfare aspects of the Soviet system, government ownership and control of the economy (except agriculture), and accomplishments in the military and technological realm.

Hostility is focused on police terror and absolutism. A desire for more personal autonomy is particularly intense in the areas of career and family life. No feature of Soviet life seems to be more detested than the collective-farm system, except, perhaps, the secret police.

Attitudes of Soviet citizens toward the West reflect the extensive program of anti-Western propaganda conducted by the Soviet government. The intensity and vituperativeness of this campaign have been well documented.[24] Apparently, the campaign has had a great deal of success in shaping the attitudes of Soviet citizens toward the West, and toward the United States in particular.[25]

No academic study of the impact of American propaganda on the attitudes of Soviet citizens has been made.[26] An assessment has been made of the regime's response to Voice of America broadcasts, but no measure is available of how our message gets through to the public.[27]

The formal structure of the Soviet mass communications system and the Bolshevik theory of public opinion and mass communications have been definitely described by Inkeles.[28] Attention is directed in this study to the special role played by "personal oral agitation" and radio nets in the Soviet communication process. Inkeles concludes that the Soviets have vast and effective resources for the mobilization of public opinion.

Perhaps the chief feature of Soviet mass communications is the degree to which they are controlled by the regime. Various aspects of the Soviet system of control have been studied.[29] The mechanics of Soviet press censorship have been described in detail.[30] Soviet concern for ideological "purity" in science has resulted in the censorship of scientific papers.[31] The ability of the regime to blunt hostility through control of "Letters to the Editor" columns in the press has been analyzed.[32]

Understandably, little work has been done on informal communication patterns in the Soviet Union, though two notable exceptions come to mind. An analysis of word-of-mouth communication has been made.[33] This system serves as a substitute for formal communication among the lower classes; it supplements formal communication for the upper class. Word-of-mouth serves the latent function of releasing tension. Participation in it cannot be regarded as a measure of disaffection, however. That exposure to Soviet media reflects the system of stratification has also been demonstrated.[34] Four channels of communication exist: mass official, aesthetic official, personalized official, and covert. An individual's class position determines his degree of participation in each. High involvement in the system (not necessarily support) leads to high participation in covert channels.

This brief review of the research accomplished in the field of Soviet public opinion and mass communications reveals certain gaps. The effectiveness of content analysis in the study of Soviet communication has been demonstrated,[35] yet little use of the technique has been made. More attention might be paid to the comparison of Soviet media. It would be fruitful, for example, to compare the provincial press with the metropolitan press on specific issues; to compare what the Soviet government tells its own people with what it tells foreigners; or to compare the differences in the Soviet "line" aimed at various foreign countries.

More needs to be done on the structure and functioning of informal communication channels. An analysis of the Soviet humor magazine *Krokodil* might reveal a great deal about current strains and tensions in Soviet society.

Virtually no assessment has been made of Soviet television. The implications of the continued popularity of the Russian nineteenth-century literary classics in Soviet society have not been sufficiently explored, though good initial work has been done on this.[36] Finally, no systematic attempt has been made to ascertain the extent to which the Communist Party has to take public opinion into account in its policy decisions.

Methodology. A most ambitious and complex methodological guide to the study of totalitarian societies as social systems has been prepared.[37] Within the framework of structural functional analysis, this guide attempts to chart the basic setting, components, and operations of a totalitarian social system. Its purpose in doing this is to arrive at a theoretical scheme suitable for the analysis of complex totalitarian systems. In this connection, two major contributions are made. First, the student is provided with an inclusive set of factors which must be encompassed in any thorough analysis of a totalitarian social system. Second, he is alerted to crucial areas of interrelatedness. His ability to interpret and predict behavior is increased.

This study represents a valuable tool in the study of totalitarian systems. Its major drawback would seem to be too much concern with the institutional framework, with structure. Others (e.g., Inkeles) have demonstrated the usefulness of analyzing Soviet society in terms of a series of operating characteristics or "themes." Such themes (e.g., "creating and maintaining myths," "planning and controlling," "rigidity-flexibility," "terror") cut across institutional lines and give stability or continuity of form and structure. Use of these themes as an organizing principle enables the student to deal with the dynamics of Soviet society more successfully than when institutions are used as the focus.

Soviet specialists have also developed useful special techniques for the study of Soviet society. A persuasive theoretical justification for the use of Soviet literature as primary data in developing sociological insights into Soviet society has been made by Simmons.[38] Excellent illustrations of the use of this technique have been given.[39] Profound insights into the mechanics of the Soviet system of class stratification have been derived from a careful study of Soviet novels.[40] A sensitive understanding of the career patterns of local Party secretaries has been obtained through an analysis of postwar Soviet literature.[41]

Analysis of both nineteenth-century Russian literature and official literature, accompanied by the application of psychoanalytic techniques, has produced an assessment of Bolshevik character, structure, and personality by Leites, who has also made an attempt to isolate a code of Soviet behavior which will be useful in prediction.[42]

A critical review has been made of methodological techniques and theoretical approaches to Soviet society.[43] This review defines the major problems which exist in the analysis and prediction of Soviet behavior and evaluates the attempts made to solve them. It emphasizes the ideological and national character approaches, but does not deal effectively with the social system approach. It also gives scant attention to the problem of social change.

A brilliant paper has been written on the difficulties in distinguishing "within-system" changes in the Soviet Union from changes in the system itself.[44] In spite of a few errors in historical facts, this paper is a genuine contribution to an understanding of the nature of social change in the Soviet Union.

Finally, several methodological and control studies based on the Harvard Project contribute to general methodological sophistication regarding such matters as control for sampling bias, distortion of response as a measure of hostility, comparison of interviews and questionnaires, the reliability of coding techniques, and validity.[45]

Much additional work remains to be done, of course. Additional indirect techniques for getting at phenomena inaccessible to ordinary techniques should be devised. The study of career lines, for example, might be developed to an extent which would enable us to arrive at a solid understanding of the social composition of various classes and occupations in the Soviet Union.

A critical review of the broad assumptions about society in general which have a direct impact on how Soviet behavior is interpreted seems in order. Considerable attention, for example, should be devoted to an assessment of the validity of the general assumption that increased education produces a tendency toward greater freedom in a society, toward "mellowing" of totalitarian regimes. A review of Communist semantics is needed. What do the Communists really mean when they speak of "freedom," "class," "peace," etc.? A refinement of techniques for the isolation of areas of strain and tension in Soviet society is needed. A study of conflicts in various Soviet professions may provide valuable insights here. This technique has already proved useful in an analysis of conflict within the Soviet medical profession.[46] Techniques for isolating what is specifically *Soviet* about Soviet society, as opposed to that which is Russian or merely a response to rapid industrialization, must be developed.

Social Problems. Marxist doctrine maintains that social problems flow from capitalism. Since the Soviet Union is a "classless," "socialist" society, social problems are not supposed to exist. The truth is, of course, that they do exist. Even the regime's strict censorship of information cannot hide this fact. Still, because of the regime's suppression of the facts, there have been extremely few studies of Soviet social problems. There are, of course, many journalistic exposés of such problems, but very little serious sociological work.

Definition is a problem in itself. What should be considered a "social problem" in the Soviet Union? Should slave labor camps, for example, be viewed as a form of social disorganization—or rather as a special form of totalitarian control? There is an ambiguity here of definition and frame of reference which clouds the sociological study of such issues.

Hazard has documented the trend of Soviet criminal law toward increasing severity and support of the concept of individual responsibility during the prewar period. Field has reviewed and evaluated reports in the Soviet press of juvenile delinquency and drunkenness.[47] When forced to admit the existence of such problems, the Communists have offered two explanations, both of which leave Marxist theory intact. Such issues are explained either in terms of "capitalist encirclement" or of "remnants of capitalism" in the minds of individual backsliders. As Field points out, however, the more likely explanation lies in a reaction to the boredom, scarcity, and unflagging tempo which characterize Soviet society.

Much more information, obviously, is needed on Soviet social problems. A careful content analysis of crime stories in the Soviet press would help fill in the details. A similar analysis should be made of Soviet criminal cases as reported in legal sources. From the standpoint of the sociology of knowledge, it would be helpful if the changing images of crime, guilt, and law which have characterized Soviet legal thought over the years were carefully traced and related to the social structure.[48]

Considerable attention should be devoted to an analysis of the nature, extent, and causes of social disorganization in the Soviet Union. A concern with social problems, as such, will not suffice. These must be related to structural factors in Soviet society which make for disorganization. The focus should be, not on individual problems, but rather on the broader sociological factors which cause them. Of course, an attempt should be made to determine which aspects of social disorganization are similar in Soviet and Western societies, which are uniquely Soviet, which reflect totalitarianism generally. Naturally, this kind of approach requires that the examination of Soviet social problems be taken out of a purely political context and placed in a more genuinely sociological framework.

Nationality. Much evidence has been collected on the deliberate destruction of national cultures in the U.S.S.R. by the Soviet regime. Russification of national arts and culture has been demonstrated.[49] Russian control of the Party bureaucracy and government in districts where minority groups predominate has been documented.[50] The dynamics of Sovietization of nationality groups, the actual liquidation of national minorities, the Soviet view of "two world camps" as an especially intense and virulent form of Russian nationalism have been explored in detail.[51]

There is disagreement concerning the effect of Russification on the stability and cohesiveness of Soviet society. Some regard the problem of non-Russian national consciousness as a secondary one.[52] They concede that such national consciousness still exists in the Soviet Union but do not view it as a major source of tension or strain. Through the use of survey research techniques in some instances, they demonstrate that social class, rather than nationality, plays the central role in determining attitudes toward the regime. Their view seems to be that such nationalistic feeling as remains is insufficient to motivate revolt, passive resistance, or sabotage, and that time is on the side of the regime since younger members of nationality groups seem far more reconciled to it than do older members, and since there is considerable intermarriage.

Others, however, regard national consciousness as a major source of strain and tension in the Soviet system[53] and as a serious threat to the cohesiveness and stability of the Soviet regime.

Obviously, further research is needed to clarify the issue. Two major gaps in our knowledge need to be filled. First, information on the process of acculturation is almost totally lacking. Second, insufficient examination has been made of Soviet nationalism in the sphere of international politics. Study of the organizational structure of Communist Parties, for example, might well reveal sources of strain between the Communist Party of the Soviet Union and national Communist Parties.

The Family. Soviet policy toward the family has gone through two major stages. Up to the thirties, the regime sought to smash the family as a social institution. Since the thirties, it has sought to stabilize and strengthen it. This has been well documented.[54] Various explanations have been offered for this shift in policy: (1) a desire to compensate for population losses, (2) a desire to have the family act as a "transmission belt" of authoritarian norms, (3) an attempt to control and restrict vertical social mobility, (4) a desire to restore stability to Soviet society, to place social relations on a stable basis adequate to the demands of a large-scale industrialized, stratified, and authoritarian society, (5) pragmatic recognition of the inherent resistance of family relations to planned social change, and of the indispensability of the family in social organization. Unfortunately, little attempt has been made to determine the relative importance of these explanations.

Still less attention has been paid to description of the Soviet family as a functioning social institution. Geiger has made a major study, however,[55] based on interviews and questionnaires of Soviet defectors. This study develops a number of findings concerning the relations between the value and behavior patterns of the urban Slavic family and the larger social system and concerning the functional or dysfunctional significance of these relations for the regime.

According to Geiger, the Soviet family places very great emphasis on education and occupational mobility. Parents in *all* social classes have high aspirations for their children. Adverse material living conditions have a corrosive effect on family solidarity, but experience with political terror enhances solidarity. The family provides a center for anti-regime sentiment, a haven in an atmosphere of distrust, unless directly attacked by the regime. But by and large, Slavic parents are likely to bring up children who are loyal to the existing social order.

Inkeles in his study of the Soviet family has sought to modify those theories of child-rearing which maintain that parents are unable to transmit new value orientations during periods of rapid social change, but instead transmit the old values or surrender this function to others.[56] On the basis of the Russian experience, Inkeles argues that parents can transmit the values of the emerging social order to their children, even if these values conflict with their own. They are motivated in this by a desire to insure the "happiness" or "adjustment" of their children in the social system.

Differences in attitudes between generations have been dealt with by Rossi.[57] According to her, young people are better adjusted to the regime than their elders. The young tend to blame *aspects* of the system, rather than the system itself, for any sources of dissatisfaction. They lay more stress on Soviet achievements, and give greater support to the regime, than do older persons. But, being more involved in the regime, they also expect more from it.

Gaps in research on the Soviet family are a lack of information on peasant and minority families, child-rearing techniques and values, images of romance in Soviet values and literature, divorce, authority patterns in the family, and the impact of state boarding schools on personality and family solidarity.

Stratification. The concept of stratification has been heavily emphasized in the study of Soviet society. It would be fair to say that the Harvard Project, for example, viewed social class as a major integrating concept. Most other Soviet specialists have also stressed its importance in explaining the functioning of Soviet society and the attitudes and behavior of Soviet citizens. The fact that Soviet society has a well differentiated class system* marked by extreme differences in income, status, power, and style of life has been demonstrated.[58] Special attention has been paid

* Though there is disagreement in the listing of the various social classes, most specialists would probably agree that any list should differentiate the Party elite, the intelligentsia, the middle bureaucracy, skilled workers, unskilled workers, peasants, and slave labor.

to the privileged position of the Soviet elite.[59] Interesting comparisons have been made between the style of life, privileges, and outlook of the Soviet intelligentsia and the bourgeoisie of nineteenth-century Europe.

Most specialists point to an increasing rigidity in the Soviet stratification system. Vertical social mobility in the Soviet Union, they feel, is on the decline. Such factors as the changing social composition of the Party and managerial group, tuition fees, the Labor Reserves, a declining rate of economic expansion, the introduction of uniforms for the various ranks in many Soviet occupations, the exercise of parental influence in obtaining special privileges for children in education and jobs, and the regime's announced intention to create special boarding schools for the children of the Soviet elite are cited as evidence of a brake on social mobility.

In addition, a very careful statistical study by Feldmesser has demonstrated that, despite the announced intention of the regime, advantages due to status have persisted in the Soviet Union: "the occupational chances of persons of toiler origin improved under the Soviets, but *not* at the expense of those of non-manual origin."[60]

In the realm of values it has been shown that "organized inequality" has constituted a part of official ideology since 1934. At the same time, there has been an attempt to preserve the official myth of the "classless society." This has created a certain degree of strain and tension. It has been argued by Moore, however, that the emergence of a well differentiated class system was inevitable in the Soviet Union, since social inequality is a "functional prerequisite" of any industrialized society.[61]

Interesting comparisons can be drawn between the Soviet and American systems of stratification. Inkeles finds the Soviet system "open," "universalistic," and characterized by an emphasis on "achieved status."[62] These criteria also accurately describe the American system.

In both societies class position serves as a determinant of educational opportunity. On the other hand, considerable evidence is offered by Feldmesser to indicate that "status privilege in access to higher education is *more* pronounced in the United States than in the Soviet Union."[63] According to Feldmesser, children of manual background in the U.S.S.R. have roughly twice as good a chance of attending college as children of similar background in America.

No studies have been made of comparative social mobility, though Feldmesser argues that mobility is, and will probably remain, higher in America.[64] He maintains that private business offers a channel for talent not found in Russia, and that American emphasis on "social justice" ensures the continuance of such opportunity.

Finally, prestige ratings of various occupations are found to be highly similar in the United States and the U.S.S.R.[65] This reflects universal features of the occupational structure in industrialized societies. Some variability does exist, however, in the ratings of agricultural and service occupations.

Broadly speaking, it seems clear that the American and Soviet systems of stratification show great similarities. In most essentials they are alike. The major differences, of course, relate to the greater significance of political criteria in the U.S.S.R.

In addition to analyzing the objective features of the Soviet class system, Soviet specialists have also studied salient subjective factors. By and large, these studies indicate a lack of "class consciousness" among Soviet citizens.[66] This does not mean that cleavages do not exist. Lower classes feel somewhat more deprived than other classes and verbalize more hostility. The intelligentsia evidence some feeling of "guilt" about special privileges and advantages. On the whole, however, inter-class feelings are "amicable."

Three explanations are offered for this lack of class consciousness: (1) Because of the rapid vertical mobility which has characterized Soviet society, the membership of the various classes is still heterogeneous. As the classes become more homogeneous, more of a class point of view should emerge. (2) The totalitarian controls of the regime prevent any kind of political coalescence along class lines. (3) The various classes focus all their hostility on the Party, thus reducing the chances for class cleavages.

The last explanation, however, seems to beg the question. It fails to take account of the fact that the Party may constitute a social class in is own right, a point of view recently and persuasively set forth by Milovan Djilas, for example.[67] Failure to examine the Party in these terms is a major failing of previous studies of the Soviet stratification system.

Another major gap is the failure of American sociologists to spell out the implications of the Soviet experience for the values which characterize the American class system. Though considerably less free than American society, Soviet society may prove to have more equality in several respects. This seems to be the case with access to higher education, for example. How compatible is equality with freedom? Does political freedom necessarily imply inequality? These are questions which would bear further examination.[68]

Other topics which suggest themselves for further research are the role played by Soviet purges in the stratification system, the degree of success achieved in giving manual labor special status and prestige in the U.S.S.R., the techniques used to resolve the ideological and social contradictions inherent in an ideology embracing both "classlessness" and "organized inequality," the emergence of a managerial elite in the Soviet Union, and the impact of this group on Soviet values and on the regime itself.

Industrial Sociology. Industrial sociology is a much neglected field in Soviet studies. Data are difficult to collect. Problems of the kind that are customarily studied in this country—human relations, communications, absenteeism, turnover, labor strife—have not been as important in the Soviet Union.

A major theme in the work accomplished thus far by American specialists has been the degree of autonomy enjoyed by Soviet managers. In his study of management in the Soviet industrial firm, Granick has indicated that a "considerable independence of decision-making" is left to the manager of the Soviet enterprise.[69] Among Soviet managers, Granick argues, much "entrepreneurial-type" ideology survives. Employing Weber's definition of bureaucracy, Granick also maintains that less bureaucracy exists in large Soviet firms than in comparable firms in the United States. Obviously, there is some evidence to the contrary. The Soviet press itself stresses the need to make inroads on "crippling bureaucracy" in industry. The recent steps toward decentralization in industrial planning and administration in the U.S.S.R. probably reflects in part a genuine concern with bureaucracy. Finally, in comparison with managers in the United States, Soviet managers have so little say in such fundamental matters as pricing, wages, capitalization, and quantity of output that greater bureaucracy would seem inevitable in the Soviet system.

Some scholars, of course, do emphasize the formal bureaucratic features of the Soviet enterprise.[70] Perhaps there has been an overemphasis on such features. If so, Granick's contribution is a welcome corrective.

After studying the formal structure and functioning of the Soviet firm, Berliner has also stressed the entrepreneurial activities of the manager.[71] These activities are numerous and significant. Faced with a rigid Plan, with scarcities, and with severe punishment for failure (or very generous rewards for success), the Soviet manager is forced to live by his wits. His activity in deceiving the Party, in using *"blat"* or "pull," and generally in evading the formal requirements of the regime is persuasively detailed.

The tensions which characterize the relations between Party representatives and the Soviet plant manager have been excellently discussed in the collective work by Bienstock, Schwarz, and Yugow.[72] This study makes it plain that the workers have long since been left out of the power equation in the Soviet enterprise. It is especially valuable for its treatment of the role of the collective farm manager and of the functioning of the collective farm enterprise. These are both subjects which have received extremely little attention.

The role of forced labor as a "massive social and economic fact" in Soviet society has been well documented.[73] Such studies have dealt satisfactorily with the extent of forced labor and its contribution as a form of terror and as a source of cheap labor for special tasks of capital construction. Although data are scarce, these topics and the latest attitude of the regime toward forced labor deserve further investigation.

Several important gaps remain to be filled. The nature and effectiveness of incentives, as opposed to coercions, have scarcely been touched in an analysis of the motivations and accomplishments of the Soviet labor force. The emergence of a managerial elite, its values, and its impact on Soviet society have not been carefully examined, though there has been a great deal of journalistic speculation on this. The effect on the Soviet regime of increased material well-being and further economic advancement has not been studied, though these factors may well have profound consequences.[74]

Soviet experience, if any, with testing, training, human relations and the like has not been evaluated. Finally, shifts in the modes of legitimization of industrial authority in the U.S.S.R. have not been analyzed.

Social System. Analysis of social systems seeks to identify the operating parts of a society, to determine the functional interdependence of the parts, and to determine the repercussions produced in the total system by a change in any of its parts. Assuming that the general relationships between the parts have been determined, it should be possible to predict roughly the nature and extent of change in the system.

Three themes have predominated in the analysis of the Soviet Union as a social system: the structure and functioning of Soviet institutions viewed as an interrelated whole, the Soviet Union as a special type of totalitarian social system, and the potentialities for change in the Soviet system.

The most ambitious attempt to describe the structure and functioning of Soviet society as an interrelated whole is the Harvard Project on the Soviet Social System.[75] A study has been published which sets forth the major findings of the Harvard Project in nontechnical terms.[76] In addition to identifying the major operating characteristics of the system, this study attempts to calculate the impact of these characteristics on the individual Soviet citizen and on specific Soviet groups. A summary evaluation of the strengths and weaknesses of the system is made.

The Harvard approach seems, however, to lack a unifying concept, a basic organizing principle.[77] Several "operating characteristics," "formal institutions," and "adjustive mechanisms" are identified. But no attempt is made to gauge relative weights, importance, or significance. No priorities are established. From the Harvard analysis, it is difficult to determine which aspects of the system are likely to act more as independent than as dependent variables, which are likely to have the greatest impact on other parts of the system, and which serve as the "motor force" of the system. The dynamics of the system as a going concern are spelled out, but little insight is given into the sources and potentialities of change. Moreover, it is difficult to assess the regime's capacity for survival, since the Harvard Project does not provide a measure of those characteristics that are essential to its maintenance or of those that can be modified without a change in the nature of the system itself.

Paradoxically, this deficiency stems from the Project's major strength—its emphasis on social psychological factors. Most previous studies have stressed the political aspects of the Soviet system. The Harvard study strikes out in a fresh direction. Yet in view of the dominance of the political factor in Soviet society (i.e., the centralized control which the regime exerts over all aspects of life), the Project fails to explore this factor adequately.[78]

A more general and less sociologically penetrating study of the Soviet social system has been produced at the M.I.T. Center for International Studies.[79] This study focuses on conventional institutions. It leans heavily on historical and purely descriptive materials and makes little effort to demonstrate interrelationships or to include social psychological data. It does, however, demonstrate an appreciation for the central role of power and command in Soviet society.[80]

Several studies have been written of aspects of the Soviet Union as a special type of totalitarian social system. A careful analysis has been made of the role of the purge in the Soviet system.[81] Both the functional and dysfunctional consequences of the purge for the system as a whole are described.

As a corrective to theories which perhaps overemphasize raw power factors in explaining Soviet behavior, a study has been made of the "totalitarian mystique" as a factor in the motivation of Soviet leaders.[82] The concept of mystique goes beyond formal ideology in the sense that it is common to *all* totalitarian societies. The substantive content of the mystique is described.

The role of individual indoctrination and training in the development of the totalitarian elite in Soviet society has been described.[83] A solid analysis of the Soviet Union's ability to mobilize its educational institutions along totalitarian lines has been made.[84]

The attempts of the regime to stamp out religion have been discussed, and the fundamental incompatibilities of religion and totalitarianism have been explored.[85] Soviet specialists have not, however, assessed the potentialities of Communist ideology to meet "religious" needs of individuals and groups. A major question is the extent to which "totalitarian mystique" can serve some of the basic psychological functions of religion.

Many of these studies of Soviet totalitarianism suffer, incidentally, by not specifying which aspects of Soviet totalitarianism are unique and which are found in other totalitarian societies. This is definitely a problem for further research.

Several studies of the potentialities for social change in the Soviet system have been made. Wolfe maintains that Soviet totalitarianism exerts such pervasive and crushing control over its population that no essential change in the system is possible from within.[86]

An effort has been made to differentiate between the various levels on which change can occur, and has occurred, in the Soviet Union.[87] Five levels of change are identified, but little attempt is made to determine at which level a given change is operating.

After defining three basic modes of power in any society (i.e., traditional, rational-technical, political), Moore attempts to determine which mode the Soviet Union will come to emphasize most in the future.[88] He shows that the predominance of any one mode limits the range of workable alternatives for the solution of other problems. Moore views the Soviets as ultimately striking a new balance between rational and traditionalist elements. In another study, he discusses the limitations of directed social change in Soviet society.[89]

Two major studies have attempted to describe patterns of change in the Soviet Union since the founding of the regime. Timasheff views all social changes in the Soviet Union as the working out of conflict between the new institutions and national Russian traditions.[90] Inkeles sees three major phases of change: the heroic phase (up to 1924), the phase of building new institutions (up to 1934), the phase of stabilization of the new society (since 1934).[91] According to Inkeles, the major determinant of the tempo and direction of social change has been "the differential adaptability of social organization to consciously directed change." This factor has produced different rates of change in different areas of the society. Far from reflecting consciously planned direction, Soviet social changes reflect such factors as unanticipated consequences of planned change, reaction to external threats, and the resistance of basic institutions to change.

In terms of gaps, studies of social change in the Soviet Union have failed to take sufficiently into account irrational factors, the impact of events in other countries (particularly in the Soviet orbit) on Soviet affairs, and the role played by ideology in the behavior of the Soviet elite.

III

It is hoped that in the years ahead continued progress in American sociological study of the Soviet system can be achieved and that more American sociologists will be attracted to this field. Basing themselves on the solid foundations that have been laid, American behavioral scientists should be able increasingly to concentrate on problems that relate to what is most central and distinctive in the Soviet system. Most attention should be paid to matters that reflect the new modes of organizing life, governing people, and administering institutions that are at the heart of Soviet society. Emphasis on how the Soviet system is functioning in its key features, and with what consequences, is also likely to yield in the long run the most useful knowledge for sociology as a whole. In this regard, the selection of problems for study should be guided less by the methodological and theoretical concerns of contemporary American sociology than by a desire to undertake an accurate and realistic accounting of what is taking place in Soviet society.

John Turkevich

7. SCIENCE

I

IT MUST BE ACKNOWLEDGED from the outset that scholarly investigation of the progress of science in Russia has been very limited. This is due to a variety of causes. At universities and research centers, fields such as history, art, literature, politics, and economics are well established. Scholarly work in these fields is assured by an organization of professorships, graduate studies, extensive library collections, publications, and recognition for the successful scholar. By contrast, the history of science is a relatively new field and until recently has not enjoyed comparable support.

As for the scientist himself, he finds little of the time or atmosphere necessary for delving into a description, philosophy, or history of scientific achievements. The ever-pressing demand on the scholar in the sciences to take an active part in the unfolding of the physical and biological world circumscribes his interest in the past. His primary interest in earlier accomplishments is to find a basis for his own scientific explorations. The individual successes of his scientific predecessors have been for the most part consolidated, and their personalities and national environments have faded out in this process. Only here and there in the structure of the sciences do traces remain of the great personalities, when laws and theories have come to be known by their names; and of the national environment, when chemical elements are named after the country of their discoverer. Certainly the historical sequence of discoveries is but dimly recognized in a science. The increasing amount of factual knowledge required of the student of science has resulted in the gradual disappearance of courses in the history of individual sciences. This has been followed by the omission of historical questions in examinations for advanced degrees.

Most scientists lack knowledge of the historical threads which led to the development of their science and of the personalities that contributed to its growth. Aside from a small group of historians of science, few professional scientists are interested in scholarly work on the history of their science. Moreover, historians of science are more often concerned with static science, such as classical Greek science, or the scientific knowledge of the Chinese or Arabs, or of the French during the Revolution. General histories of science usually end with the opening of the twentieth century.

In view of the fact that American and Soviet science came to fruition during the twentieth century, it is not surprising that there has been little formal scholarly work in their histories. Similarly, our universities have paid little attention to the relation between government and science. It must be recognized, however, that the number of people qualified for work in the study of Soviet science is limited by rather special requirements. The scholar must have a command of the Russian language, and there are relatively few scholars who can use Russian. In addition, the specialist in this field must have sound knowledge in more than one branch of science. Finally, he must find moral and financial support for what is still a rather exotic branch of scholarship. In these days when universities and research institutes find it difficult to finance studies in such established fields as Soviet literature, language, politics, and economics, it is small wonder that scholarship in the history and sociology of Soviet science hardly exists in the formal traditional sense, but is carried on in large measure by amateurs like the present writer, who work on the subject in their spare time and cherish it as a hobby. The limited amount of formal scholarship is supplemented by a surprisingly large number of studies by such amateurs. Their productivity reflects in part the general interest on the part of the American people in the Soviet scene.

II

Americans began to take an interest in Russian science half a century ago. An article was written on Pavlov's studies in physiology as early as 1909.[1] This interest has had its ups and downs. The plight of the Russian intellectual during the civil war and the early years of the Soviet regime evoked sympathetic interest from the American scientist. This resulted in a number of articles on Russian science.[2]

In the late twenties and during the thirties relations were established between Soviet science and that of the West. Scientific information flowed, through the medium of journals, between this country and the Soviet Union. Tables of contents and abstracts of individual articles were given in a Western language in all important Russian journals. Three prestige journals, the *Comptes rendus* of the Academy of Sciences of the U.S.S.R., the Soviet *Journal of Physics,* and the *Physiocochemica Acta,* were published in the languages of western Europe. Organizations like VOKS in the Soviet Union and American-Russian committees encouraged contacts between scientists of the two countries and aided in the exchange of scientific literature. A number of American scientists undertook studies in Soviet research centers, and individual Soviet postdoctoral students studied in the United States. With the establishment of these normal relations and in the absence of startling discoveries in the Soviet Union, little was published in this period on Soviet science.

World War II again aroused sympathy in American scientific

circles for the Soviet scholar, working in a country half conquered and widely devastated by the Germans. The various committees for cultural and scientific relationships with the U.S.S.R. carried on as best they could under war conditions. These activities soon came to an end when the Soviet government dropped an Iron Curtain and made "anti-cosmopolitanism" the order of the day. The flow of journals was impeded. A language barrier was set up when the Soviet journals discontinued the use of Western languages in their tables of contents and abstracts, and the Academy of Sciences of the U.S.S.R. suspended the publication of the three prestige journals in Western langauges. Few American scholars visited Soviet laboratories, and there were no Soviet scientific visitors in this country. In the meantime, interest in the U.S.S.R. and matters Russian was unfortunately sometimes viewed in the United States with suspicion, as symptomatic of sympathy for the Communist cause.

The genetics controversy in the Soviet Union, raising as it did the fundamental issue of government control of scientific inquiry, again turned the attention of the general public to the Russian scientific scene. A number of studies were published on the subject of Stalinism and freedom of scientific research.[3] Some of our scientific and educational leaders concluded that a country that indulged in such an inquisition of science as in the Lysenko case could not have an effective science. The public readily accepted the verdict that all science was dead in the Soviet Union. With this acceptance, interest in the technological achievements of the Russians again decreased. However, the steady advance of Soviet achievement in military fields—atom bombs, hydrogen weapons, missiles, and ultimately the visible evidence of this progress in the *sputniks*—all this revived an interest which was less sympathetic to than apprehensive of the accomplishments of Soviet science. This interest was coupled with an awareness both of the strong emphasis on science and mathematics in the Soviet schools and of the large number of technically trained graduates being produced by the Soviet educational system. The American public now became eager to know answers to a number of questions concerning Soviet science and education.

What is the record of accomplishment of the U.S.S.R. in the various individual fields of science? What is the prognosis for the future development of science in the Soviet Union? What are the elements that assured the Soviets success in space science, where their distinction is indisputable? Is this due to better organization, more effective exploitation of their scientists, stronger motivation, or smoother liaison with the military? Does their educational system have unusual features? Will they be able to continue to turn out a large number of scientists and engineers? How good are their scientists and engineers? Partial answers to these questions may be found in scholarly work published in the U.S.S.R., but American scholars have not yet answered them.

Scholarly activity in this country has not produced a history of Russian or Soviet science. This is not surprising, for there is no systematic or complete history of Russian science in the Russian language. On the other hand, there are abundant secondary sources for such a history.[4] Furthermore, in 1947, to mark the thirtieth anniversary of Soviet rule, a number of studies were published on the progress of individual fields of science in the Soviet Union,[5] and on January 5-11, 1949, a special session of the Academy of Sciences of the U.S.S.R. was devoted to reports on "The History of the Natural Sciences." These and other materials could serve as sources for a general history of this subject; yet only a handful of studies have appeared in this country on the history of Russian science.[6]

Several biographies of Russian scientists, and one autobiography, have been published in the United States. An authoritative Soviet biography of M. V. Lomonosov (1711-65) has been translated under the auspices of the Russian Translation Project of the American Council of Learned Societies.[7] Lomonosov, the great scientist, poet, teacher, grammarian, and founder of the University of Moscow, is certainly a towering figure in the development of Russian science. Professor Posin has written a fictionalized biography of D. I. Mendeleev (1834-1907), and there is a life of Pavlov (1849-1936) by Babkin.[8] There has also appeared in the United States an interesting autobiography by V. N. Ipatieff (1867-1953), one of the leading chemists of the last decades of the Empire and of the early Soviet regime, who not only carried out important work on high pressure catalysis but after the October Revolution was active in organizing chemical research and industry in the newly established Soviet state. He later emigrated from Russia to the United States and became a leader in American chemistry and the petroleum industry. His autobiography is a valuable contribution to our knowledge of Russian and Soviet science of the twentieth century.[9]

The organizational aspect of Soviet science is of particular interest.[10] To some, the unusual strength the Soviet Union has shown in the missile field and the conquest of space has seemed to reflect the excellent organization of these projects, effective liaison between pure science and industry, and a clear understanding of the role of scientific research on the part of government leaders. This understanding is surprising in view of the genetics controversy. The organization of the Soviet Academy of Sciences has been the subject of recent research,[11] and attention has been called to the important statement by Academician Kapitsa on the problems associated with the organization of basic research in modern society.[12] Work has also been done on the position of Soviet scientists and on scientific training in the U.S.S.R.[13]

Russian publications contain a good deal of material on the nature of the planning carried out by Soviet administrators. Obviously some of the planning was badly conceived, and there have been some crude efforts to impose Marxist or Stalinist dogmas on the development of science. As a result, such disciplines as genetics and theoretical chemistry have all but vanished from the Soviet scientific scene. On the other hand, planning must have been well carried out in the nuclear energy and missile fields. Students of the relation of government to science might well study this aspect of Soviet science.[14] In recent years the present writer has conducted an undergraduate seminar on "Government and Science" at the Woodrow Wilson School of Public and International Affairs at Princeton University, and he has become convinced of the value of such studies and of the need to extend them to Soviet science.[15] The relationship between science, on the one hand, and Marxism-Leninism-Stalinism, on the other, has begun to engage the attention of Russian specialists and will be a fruitful field of work for many years to come.[16] The issues involved transcend the Soviet scene. In the genetics controversy and the subsequent repercussions in other fields, the whole question of the freedom of the individual to pursue scientific work came into focus. Professor Zirkle has contributed a valuable volume to the literature of this subject.[17]

Soviet accomplishments in natural science have attracted general interest in recent years. Typical of this interest was the symposium on "Soviet Science" held at the Philadelphia meeting of the American Association for the Advancement of Science on November 27, 1951.[18] General appraisals of Soviet science have appeared, both in the published proceedings of this symposium and in more recent publications.[19] Brief accounts are available of Soviet work in several disciplines in the natural sciences, and in mathematics.[20] There have also been several studies of Soviet medicine.[21] Needless to say, scholars in many specialized fields draw on the results of Soviet research, which may be followed in the abstracting publications of the various branches of science.

Closely related to the problem of studying Soviet science is that of translation. Scholars acquainted with the Russian language now have the aid of dictionaries specializing in several technical fields. There is also a textbook for specialists in science interested in learning the Russian language.[22] Interest in Russian science has far outstripped the linguistic knowledge of American scientists, however, and the translation of current Soviet materials has become a major undertaking.

In the late thirties a group of American petroleum companies privately circulated translated tables of contents, abstracts, and complete translations of certain select articles in Soviet journals dealing with hydrocarbon and petroleum chemistry. This enterprise lasted for about eight years under the direction of Dr. J. C. Tolpin. After World War II, John and Ludmilla Turkevich organized and edited a *Guide to Russian Scientific Periodical Literature*. It was published for the Atomic Energy Commission by the Brookhaven National Laboratory. The guide came out as a monthly for five years, 1948-52, when its support was withdrawn by the Atomic Energy Commission in Washington. The functions of the guide were taken over in a more extensive but somewhat diffuse way by the *Monthly Index of Russian Accessions,* published by the Library of Congress at Washington.[23] At the present time there is increasing activity in the complete translation of certain scientific journals. In the United States 54 Soviet scientific and technical journals are now being translated into English and 128 are being abstracted.[24] Similar translation programs, although on a smaller scale, are being undertaken in Australia, Canada, Great Britain, and India. In these countries, as in the United States, the government plays a major role in this enterprise.[25] Important Soviet articles relating to the ideology and organization of the natural sciences also appear in translation in the *Current Digest of the Soviet Press*.

No review of this subject would be complete without mention of the very considerable attention that has been devoted to Soviet science in Great Britain and western Europe. British scientists have been interested in this subject for many years, and have produced a number of important studies.[26] In recent years German scholarship has also turned to this field of study, with the publication of at least two outstanding works on the relationship between ideology and the natural sciences in the U.S.S.R.[27] At the same time a semiannual journal, *Osteuropa-Naturwissenschaft*, was established in Stuttgart in 1955 under the editorship of Arnold Buchholz with the purpose of following current Soviet scientific trends. A similar function is performed in the field of medicine by the *Review of Eastern Medical Sciences*, published in Munich under the editorship of H. Schulz. Finally, it should be noted that a number of general descriptive works by Soviet scientists have been translated into English by the Foreign Languages Publishing House in Moscow.[28] While there is a strong element of propaganda in these publications, an informed and discriminating reader can learn much from them.

III

From what has been said, it is clear that in this, as in so many other fields relating to Russia, there are many opportunities for new research. A single general volume on Russian science both before and since the October Revolution would be most useful. Authoritative biographies remain to be written of those outstanding Russian scholars who have won a permanent place in the history of science. Interesting studies could be made of the lives and contributions of the many Russian-born scientists who, like Ipatieff, emigrated to the United States and western Europe. Included in such a list would be the mathematicians Tamarkin and Lefschetz, the physicists Gamow and Zworikin, the chemist Kistiakowsky, the biologist Dobzhanski, the microbiologist Waksman, the airplane designers Sikorsky and Seversky, the engineer Timoshenko, and many others.

It would be well, also, to encourage the study of developments in the individual disciplines of the natural sciences, as well as the related fields of mathematics, medicine, and technology. Such studies would depend in some degree on finding scholars who combine scientific training with knowledge of Russian. In at least one instance, however, two scholars with complementary skills have joined forces with great success to produce a study of this sort,[29] and this pattern may well be applicable to other cases. Similar results might also be achieved through conferences and symposia.[30]

The study of the role of science in the Soviet Union also provides a challenging new approach to certain general problems in which the social scientist needs the help of the scientist. To what extent, for example, does Marxism in the abstract, as well as the more specific doctrines of Leninism and Stalinism, and perhaps later formulations, form a part of Soviet scientific thought? Why has one discipline been very largely dominated by ideology, while others appear to be as free from ideological restraints as they are in the West? Are those that appear to be free, really free? Is it possible that in certain disciplines, vital to military strength, national interest has won out over ideology? To what extent have the disciplines that are relatively free from ideological controls provided a place of refuge for those who might have preferred to work in such persecuted fields of study as biology, psychology, and philosophy? What can the organization of science teach us about the relationship between scholarship and politics in the Soviet Union? Many other questions of this character come to mind as one contemplates the problems posed by Russian science, and it is hoped that this challenge will be taken up by political scientists and sociologists, as well as by those scholars trained in the natural sciences who are concerned with the social role of their discipline.

W. A. Douglas Jackson

8. GEOGRAPHY

I

UNTIL WORLD WAR II, the attention of American geographers, if measured in terms of their output, was focused primarily on the United States. The advantages for research afforded by the great wealth of material available, both in libraries and in the field, attracted them to study their own geographical milieu. Yet, in spite of the difficulties associated with research on foreign areas, due either to lack of data in this country or to the financial burden imposed by field study abroad, some parts of the world did receive firsthand investigation by American geographers. Latin America, relatively close at hand, provided a fertile field, and geographers from the United States made substantial contributions to our knowledge of the lands and peoples south of the Rio Grande. Japan and China, to some extent, also came in for study by American geographers. On the other hand, Europe and its colonies were for the most part left to competent European geographers. Little attention was directed toward the Soviet Union and the geographical impact of the revolutionary changes that were occurring in that vast territory. In fact, in the prewar period only two American geographers devoted any significant amount of time to study of the Soviet Union.[1]

World War II stimulated the interest of geographers in the Soviet Union, as well as in other areas to which they had previously paid little attention. Foundation support, which has grown steadily since 1948, has done much to encourage and facilitate this development by enabling geographers to increase their familiarity with foreign languages and cultures, thus giving rise to an expanding number of young specialists capable of undertaking competent research on foreign areas. Yet, however rapid the growth of interest in the rest of the world, American geography in Russian studies remains essentially an underdeveloped discipline. In view of the Soviet Union's prominence in world affairs, the lack of attention given Soviet geography is altogether regrettable. Too few geographers are writing about the largest and most complex political unit in the world, and their numbers are increasing at much too slow a rate. There is not, therefore, a large body of geographical literature upon which a balanced discussion of past development in the field can be based.

II

Practically all of the writing on the geography of the Soviet Union belongs to the postwar period. It consists of several general works and a small collection of articles, published mainly in the two major professional geographical journals, the *Geographical Review* and the *Annals* of the Association of American Geographers. Monographs are lacking. A review of the literature should also include, however, a brief reference to the major works of persons in closely related fields; while they are not geographers, their work does in part reflect geographical techniques or method in presentation.

The general works, without exception, are descriptive in nature and traditional in organization and treatment. *The Basis of Soviet Strength* by Cressey, an expansion of the relevant chapters in his general study on Asia, is designed primarily for college use. It has the distinction of being the first general study written by an

American on the geography of the Soviet Union. In a popular vein is his later publication entitled *How Strong is Russia?*[2]

In a somewhat different category is Shabad's *Geography of the USSR: A Regional Survey*. Organized regionally, as its title implies, the book relies heavily on Soviet sources for descriptions of economic and political changes. This survey, which is primarily factual, constitutes a valuable handbook for reference use. Shabad's special contribution, included in the earlier part of the book, is his use of electoral districts, as published in *Pravda*, to arrive at generalized postwar population figures.[3]

Unlike Shabad, Mirov deals almost exclusively with the elements of the natural environment in his *Geography of Russia*.[4] The summaries of the regional associations of climate, topography, soils, and vegetation are good though brief, lacking the detail found in Berg's monumental study of natural regions. These four works, then, constitute the general literature on the geography of the Soviet Union.

American geographers have also been active in making available to the profession translations of several of the better Soviet studies. Under the editorial guidance of Morrison and Nikiforoff, Berg's work has been translated and published in the United States. A companion volume, the prewar economic geography of the U.S.S.R. by Balzak, Vasyutin, and Feigin, was edited by Harris. Though Marxist in interpretation and now considerably out of date, it was the most detailed, systematic economic geography available at that time and has constituted a valuable addition to the literature in English on the economic-geographic changes in the Soviet Union up to 1939.[5] Currently, Suslov's detailed study of the physical geography of the Asiatic part of the Soviet Union is being prepared for publication in English.[6]

It is natural that American geographers should want translations of the better Soviet works; in a sense, these studies represent source materials for both student and teacher alike. American geographers have also turned to western Europe for assistance.

Perhaps the best general survey of the geography of the Soviet Union is by the German geographer, Leimbach, now in the process of being translated and revised at the University of Maryland for use in its overseas geography teaching program. Thiel's descriptive regional study of the Soviet Far East has already been revised and translated.[7] Of the French works, Jorré's text, although less thorough than Leimbach's, has been used rather extensively in the translated edition in American universities where courses on the geography of the Soviet Union have been offered. George's work, still untranslated, has less merit because of a lack of objectivity. Two British books, by Gregory and Shave, and by Gray, are marred by serious factual errors.[8] Since most of the general studies are now somewhat out of date, a need exists for one or more new American texts on the geography of the Soviet Union. John A. Morrison has such a book in preparation.

A review of the entire periodical literature, limited in extent though it may be, cannot be attempted here. However, because some articles tend to focus upon a small number of related topics of an economic-geographic nature and thus reveal the special interests of current American writers, they deserve special comment.

The studies on regionalization and regional development by Morrison, Shabad, and Shimkin not only are basic but constitute a significant contribution to our knowledge of the geographical spread of Soviet development.[9] Morrison, examining territorially the conflict of economic principle with the nationality principle in the prewar Soviet attempts to redraw internal boundaries, detected a trend toward realism in the establishment of administrative areas based on the practical requirements of administration. Shabad, on the other hand, concerned with the Soviet concept of economic regionalization, found that Soviet ideology and economics were major factors in bringing about the existing regional structure. Somewhat different, too, is Shimkin's study, which deals solely with the impact of industrialization from 1926 to 1950 on the pattern of regional development; he attempts to assess the possible effects of Soviet plans and of the greater utilization of underdeveloped human and physical resources on the future economic geography of the country.

Harris's urban study reflects an awareness of the impact of industrialization under prewar Five-Year Plans on the growth and function of cities. His method of analysis illustrates how techniques used to study phenomena in the United States might effectively be applied to similar phenomena in the Soviet Union, given the necessary data.[10] Selecting cities of over 100,000 in population according to the 1939 census, and using the 1935 per capita value of industrial production for those cities in terms of 1925-27 prices, Harris arrived at a four-type functional classification of cities which brought rather favorable comment from Soviet geographers.[11]

The lack of postwar data on agricultural land use, such as were available before the war by minor civil divisions, has tended to limit the scope of agricultural geographic research. From time to time geographers have participated in symposia dealing with Soviet agriculture, and while they have contributed to an over-all understanding of the problems under consideration, their papers have, nevertheless, been of a survey type, reflecting the frustration that arises from the necessity of having to use only the limited materials available.[12] On the other hand, where more information has generally been available, as with some of the major projects undertaken by the Soviet government to increase agricultural production by altering the traditional patterns of land use, geographers have been able to arrive at definite conclusions as to their geographical feasibility. Jackson's studies of agricultural conditions in the dry steppe are critical of Soviet efforts to expand widely the basis of dry farming, although he sees a possibility of limited success for the current virgin and idle land scheme through the extensive sowing of drought-resistant durum wheat.[13] Attempts to expand irrigation in central Asia through further use of the not-too-abundant waters of the Amu Darya, and the need for and problems associated with irrigation in southeast Russia, have been critically analyzed by Field.[14] Rodgers has applied standard geographic techniques to the study of land use in the non-chernozem (non-black earth) between Moscow and Leningrad.[15]

Other topics which have been studied by geographers vary considerably. The theory of the "urge to the sea" has been effectively refuted by Morrison.[16] Taskin has examined the economic implications of the falling level of the Caspian Sea, due to evaporation and the diversion of Volga River water;[17] and Rodgers has mapped and analyzed changing patterns in the Soviet pulp and paper industry.[18]

Of studies in related fields which employ in part a geographical approach, only those more widely used by geographers need be mentioned. Shimkin's study of Soviet minerals is exhaustive, reflecting a careful job of recording and analyzing Soviet resources, production, and consumption. Volin's monograph on agriculture offers an especially valuable discussion of crop geography, and his dot maps of distributions in 1938 are extremely useful. Somewhat different in scope are the agro-climatological studies by Nuttonson, published by the American Institute of Crop Ecology. These incorporate systematized data on temperature, precipitation, and length of growing season for selected stations in the Soviet Union as well as their North American analogues. Lorimer's population study, in both text and maps, provides valuable information on growth and changes.[19]

This is not the place to attempt a thorough inquiry into the reasons why geography represents an underdeveloped discipline in Russian studies. However, some of the factors responsible for retarding its growth must be recognized if a path to future progress is to be found.

Most of the current writers bring to their study a solid grounding in geography, as well as a certain degree of familiarity with the language and culture of the Russian area. Much of the writing which appears in the professional journals, therefore, is based on primary or Soviet source materials, and clearly reveals the efforts of American geographers to rise above a mere recording of facts concerning Soviet geographical development. But, as indicated previously, there are too few trained geographers attempting the study of Soviet growth and change.

The question that immediately arises, then, is a simple one. Why are so few geographers attracted to pursuing advanced work on the Russian area? Perhaps the answer lies in the fact that they are overwhelmed and repelled by the considerable amount of time and energy they must expend in order to gain familiarity with the language and culture of the area, over and above that required to gain competence in their own discipline. It is not likely, therefore, that the geographer who has himself specialized in the Russian area will find at any one time that he has more than a handful of students studying under his guidance. The mortality rate, too, is high.

Young geographers who wish to build a sound foundation in the geography of the Soviet Union must have access to the training afforded by an area program, which provides valuable opportunity for interrelated study in several disciplines. It is possible, at present, to combine training at the graduate level in both geography and the Russian area at only a few institutions. The alternative compels the geographer to undertake at some point in his graduate work an intensive program of area and language training at one of the major centers of Russian study away from his home university. Neither of the two major eastern centers for Russian studies, Harvard and Columbia, has participating geographers, supported by solidly established geography departments. These centers attract the greatest number of students interested in the Soviet Union, but there can be no contact with the geographical approach, a contact which might stimulate some students to develop, simultaneously with their area specialization, a sound foundation in this discipline. Such centers, therefore, should be encouraged to broaden their programs to include training in geography.

Field work has always been an important method of geographical research, but during the last twenty years it has been impossible to undertake field work in the Soviet Union, although brief travel is now permitted. Inability to travel extensively and to study at first hand the area of interest cannot but have a dampening effect on the morale and work of the geographer. At the same time, the lack of readily available quantitative data, necessary to meaningful geographical analysis, has resulted in a spotty literature on the Soviet area. Geographers have worked, it could be said, where they have been permitted to work.

It would be quite inaccurate, however, to paint an altogether gloomy picture for geographical research on Russia. Data have been scarce, it is true, but geographers have also suffered, to some extent, from unfamiliarity with the source materials that are available in the libraries of this country or elsewhere. The publication by the Library of Congress in 1951 of a two-volume bibliography on the geography of the Soviet Union was an important step in the right direction.[20] Periodic revision of the bibliography would be beneficial, too, in view of the significant increase in the volume of material published in the Soviet Union and now available in the United States. The appearance within recent years of up-to-date, detailed atlases of the Soviet Union, as well as *oblast* maps showing *raion* subdivision, and the issuing once again of statistical handbooks augur well for future geographical research and writing.

III

Any program aiming at the establishment of a more significant place for geography in Russian studies must recognize, first of all, that the basic need is to train more students. Interest in the geography of the Soviet Union among American students might be stimulated if the stronger departments of geography throughout the country gave more attention to the Soviet Union as a region. On the other hand, the major centers for Russian study should make every effort possible to expose their students to geography.

Not to be ignored is the need to stimulate contacts between American and Soviet geographers; such contacts might lead to opportunities for travel and research inside the Soviet Union, although it is doubtful that extensive field study there will become possible in the near future.

As was noted, geographical research in the past has been spotty and fragmentary. Therefore, more broadly conceived studies, both regional and topical, are required if the contribution of the geographer to the Russian area is to grow substantially. Particularly needed is the development of a conceptual frame of reference, or a philosophy of Soviet geographical change and growth, within which American geographers might work. The latter, in this connection, might do well to explore more fully, however unrewarding they may seem to be, the theories which Soviet geographers have advanced concerning their own work. Certainly, the frequent and insistent attempts in the Soviet Union to create rational, functional regions, whether administrative, economic, industrial management, or agricultural, warrant closer scrutiny in order to assess the existing stage of development, as well as to gain some insight into the ultimate goal and patterns to be achieved.

Systematic topical studies also hold great promise, not only in terms of the study of specific phenomena, but also as related to other phenomena and to the geographic whole. American geographers, as a rule, have tended to give more attention to the economic aspects of Soviet geography, for the most part ignoring the physical. Perhaps this is as it should be, since the work of Soviet physical geographers is in general useful, while economic geography has been largely neglected by Soviet scholars. American geographers might then direct their efforts to any number of economic topics and related problems. What, for example, are the relationships among resources, which constantly need re-evaluating in the light of new discoveries and changing technology, manpower, population, and industrial growth and location? What is the role and function of the city?—a subject which increasingly is attracting the attention of the Soviet geographer. Is there a hierarchy of places and how are these linked by expanding Soviet transportation facilities? Can Soviet agriculture meet the demands of a rapidly growing population, which is becoming increasingly urbanized? In what manner is the city affecting the utilization of the lands of the neighboring *kolkhozes* and *sovkhozes*?

At the same time, political and administrative geography represents a field much neglected by both Soviet and American geographers. Careful examination of pertinent geographic, political, and economic materials and data may yield fruitful studies. How and to what extent does the Soviet political-administrative map reflect Soviet political, economic, and geographic reality? What territorial functions do the subordinate administrative units perform? How closely do the national territories reflect national groupings and how significant is the political-administrative boundary?

Soviet cartographic techniques, exemplified in the newer Soviet atlases, have made important progress within recent years, and open up a large and complex field of study, which also demands attention.

If any of the foregoing suggestions have validity, there should be realized over the next five or ten years a greater volume and range of geographical writing in the United States on the Soviet Union. Indeed, the serious deficiencies in the literature must be overcome if geography is to play a significant role in any program of concentrated Russian studies, and if it is to demonstrate that it does truly have a point of view and an approach capable of making a major contribution when brought to bear full force on the Soviet area. The challenge exists, and there is much to be done.

Edward J. Brown

9. LITERATURE

I

THE PURPOSE of the present review is to assess the value of research in literature since 1945 as a contribution to our understanding of Russia, and to indicate its gaps and shortcomings and the most profitable lines of development for the future. We have not, of course, confined our attention to Soviet literature alone, but have considered also the most important research on Russian literature of the nineteenth century and even earlier; indeed, Soviet literature can hardly be understood, nor can research in it be properly evaluated, without constant reference to its roots in the past.

Much has been accomplished in the years since the first Russian area program was set up at Cornell University in 1943. Academic training in Russian, the training of specialists for teaching and research, and integrated area programs had received little attention up to that time; and Russian literature, both old and new, offered a rich field for American scholars. Since 1945 major studies on all aspects of Soviet life have been added to the excellent but limited material which existed at that time. In the field of Russian and Soviet literature the performance of the last ten years is impressive: the number of monographs and essays, both published and unpublished, is striking and their general quality is high. Moreover, the major institutions during this time have trained many new people in the techniques of research and writing. For example, at Columbia University twenty-one Ph.D. degrees and over eighty M.A. degrees have been awarded in the field of Slavic languages and more than half of these were in Russian and Soviet literature. Such figures hold promise of a great increase in research activity and publication in the near future.

The main purpose of our review has not been to outline accomplishments in the field of literature, but rather to locate lacunae and to emphasize shortcomings—in short, to point out not so much what has been done as what has not. In everything that follows, it is assumed that the reader is aware of the great progress in this field since 1945.

II

A number of general works on the history and criticism of Russian literature have been made available to the teacher and student, among them Whitfield's one-volume abridgment of Prince Mirsky's *History of Russian Literature*,[1] a new edition of an old book. Except for a very brief section on Soviet literature, this edition does not claim to add anything to the original work of Mirsky, which was completed in 1926. In addition to Mirsky, we have Marc Slonim's extensive two-volume history of Russian literature from the earliest times.[2] In either of these works the student will find a treatment of the main facts and even of subsidiary facts and personalities in Russian and Soviet literature. Yet neither book is completely satisfactory as a reference work for the scholar or as an introduction to the field for the sophisticated American student. Mirsky's book is extremely valuable for its original and stimulating, though at times highly personal, critical interpretations of certain authors and periods; but Mirsky is not always adequate in his treatment of intellectual and ideological backgrounds, and without this, much of Russian literature remains unilluminated. Figures of great moment for literature such as Stankevich, Belinsky, Herzen, Mikhailovsky, and many others are given only a few scant pages in this otherwise fine work.

There is wide agreement on the need for a general work in literary history and criticism. But what is the condition of the field with regard to specialized works on particular topics and individual figures? And have we at our disposal the scholarly monographs and dissertations upon which general studies must be based? As a matter of fact, many works on individual writers of the pre-Soviet period have appeared during the last ten years, works which vary widely in their approach and scholarly purposes and which range from Simmons' lengthy and definitive biography of Tolstoy[3]—a work that made available to the American reader much new material on the writer's life and thought—to a number of brief but interesting and thoroughly readable biographies and critical studies that have appeared recently in book form—most of them, it is true, not by Americans. For example, in Britain David Magarshack has brought out two books on Chekhov as well as biographical studies of Turgenev and Gogol, along with his growing list of translations of the Russian classics;[4] Janko Lavrin has published a series of useful introductory works on Pushkin, Gogol, Tolstoy, Goncharov, and other writers;[5] and W. H. Bruford[6] and Ronald Hingley[7] have each published a book-length study of Chekhov. A book on Belinsky has already appeared,[8] an older work on Dostoyevsky has been reissued in a revised edition,[9] and books on several other writers are in the making.

It should be mentioned that some extremely important research on the earliest period of Russian literature has been accomplished in the United States. An outstanding example of cooperative, interdisciplinary scholarship is *La Geste du Prince Igor'*,[10] to which the principal contributors were Roman Jakobson, Henri Grégoire, Marc Szeftel, and George Vernadsky. Another work which should be mentioned, also a cooperative enterprise, is *Russian Epic Studies*,[11] edited by Roman Jakobson and Ernest J. Simmons. Articles on literature of the seventeenth century have frequently appeared in our journals, William E. Harkins of Columbia being one of the chief contributors of work on this period. Horace W. Dewey of the University of Michigan has worked in the medieval field on linguistic, legal, and literary problems.

We are not well supplied, however, with detailed, systematic, original and primary research on particular periods in the history of Russian literature; on many important nineteenth-century authors; on successive trends, both intellectual and stylistic; or on the important literary works themselves. It is true that our literary journals have carried excellent original articles on rather special and limited topics: the style of Bunin; certain types of symbolism in Dostoyevsky; various urges within him, including the matricidal and the parricidal; the technique of the "interior monologue" in Tolstoy; the interpretation of Gogol's story "The Nose," to mention only a few. These studies constitute a valuable body of research. Still, there is at present no major study of Tolstoy's *War and Peace* by an American scholar, though this lack will soon be corrected by the forthcoming appearance at Columbia of a dissertation on this topic.[12] A brief study of Dostoyevsky's novelistic technique in *The Brothers Karamazov* was published in 1957,[13] and a larger work on the novel is now in preparation at Columbia as a doctoral dissertation.[14] Two interesting articles on *Oblomov* have recently been published; but Goncharov's peculiar world as reflected in his fiction has lain fallow for many years, and Mazon's monumental work, which appeared in 1914, settled nothing finally.[15] The student of Russian literature and the teacher have been waiting for investigation and original discussion of the great literary works of the nineteenth century, the books which bulk so large in the intellectual experience of Russians, both Soviet and pre-Soviet.

We are not better off with regard to particular periods, trends, and schools of thought in Russian literature. Apart from Chyzhevsky's provocative book *On Romanticism in Slavic Literature*,[16] the study of Russian romanticism has not yet passed beyond the stage of annotated stereotypes. The "natural school" must be discussed in lectures on Russian literature, but we do not yet know exactly what it was and are learning only gradually;[17] the idealistic philosophers of the thirties are barely visible to us through a haze of established and impenetrable generalizations. The "men of the sixties" and their great antagonist Dostoyevsky offer opportunities that are still far from being exhausted.[18]

It has frequently been pointed out that the field suffers from an absence of comparative studies that would throw light on the interrelationships of Russian thought and writing with western European cultural and intellectual movements. Despite the contributions in this area of such productive scholars as Waclaw Lednicki[19] and of younger men like George Gibian,[20] there is still no work for the period since Pushkin that is comparable to Ernest J. Simmons' *English Literature and Culture in Russia* for the period up to Pushkin.[21] Many rich fields in pre-Soviet literature are yet to be exploited by American scholarship.

Perhaps we should remind ourselves that there is no need to look for new and remote areas of research, to study figures of secondary importance, or to discover unexpected or recondite topics in the work of the major figures. With us, hardly anything has already been done. The relatively few works so far made available—excellent though they are—have not settled anything for all time, and all signs indicate that our younger scholars are prepared and eager to do a job of reinterpretation on many topics, figures, and periods. We need not look far afield for problems to investigate concerning any Russian author; we can begin almost anywhere.

It should be emphasized again that much research is in progress at the moment this is written, and that this work will in the near future result in filling some of the gaps noted here. A number of works on Russian literature of the nineteenth century have recently appeared: Seduro's *Dostoyevsky in Russian Literary Criticism*;[22] Poggioli's *The Phoenix and the Spider*,[23] a collection of interesting critical essays; and the *Letters of Gorky and Andreev*, edited by Peter Yershov.[24] Among recently completed dissertations one should mention the study of Mayakovsky's early poetry by Lawrence Stahlberger (Harvard); "Sterne's Influence on the Early Tolstoy," by Peter Rudy (Columbia); "Symbolists' Criticism of Gogol," by Zoya Yurieff (Radcliffe); "Between Image and Idea: the Poetry of Blok," by Franklin Reeve (Columbia); "Viazemsky's Literary Criticism," by G. Ivask (Harvard); "Dostoyevsky's Underground Man," by Robert Jackson (California); and two studies of Herzen, by Allen McConnell (Columbia) and Martin Malia (Harvard). Dissertations are now in progress on the *Znanie* group of writers (Lydia Weston Kesich, Columbia), on Tyutchev (Richard Gregg, Columbia), and on Karamzin (Henry M. Nevel, Columbia); and postdoctoral research is now well advanced on a study of Gogol by Leon Stilman of Columbia, a study of Dostoyevsky's influence in France by Rufus Mathewson of Columbia, a work on Stankevich and his circle by Edward J. Brown of Brown University, a study of the Natural School of the 1840's by Kenneth Harper of the University of California at Los Angeles, a study of Leskov's literary technique by Hugh McLean of Harvard, and a biographical study of Leskov by William B. Edgerton of Indiana University.

In turning to research in literature of the Soviet period, we find that we are well served with works of both a general and a particular nature. There are two general histories dealing with the Soviet period: Marc Slonim's *Modern Russian Literature*,[25] and Gleb Struve's *Soviet Russian Literature, 1917-1950*,[26] books which provide information on all aspects of Soviet literature. A number of valuable insights on relations between Russian literature of the past and of the Soviet period are provided in *Con-*

tinuity and Change in Russian and Soviet Thought, edited by Ernest J. Simmons, a collaborative effort not devoted specifically to literature which seeks constants in the intellectual history of Russia, both old and new.[27] A similar effort to bridge the past and present is found in Rufus Mathewson's recently published dissertation, *The Russian Positive Hero: An Inquiry into the Aesthetics of Radicalism* (New York, 1958).

Research on specific topics in the field may be conveniently treated under three classifications: (1) studies of Soviet-Marxist literary policy, theory, and criticism; (2) studies of literature as social documentation; and (3) literary-critical studies. Under the first heading we should mention a number of works published by the Columbia University Press, among them *The Proletarian Episode in Russian Literature,*[28] which examines the period from 1928 to 1932, when the Stalinist authorities finally eliminated all trace of independence from Party doctrine in Soviet literature, being forced in the end to liquidate their own proletarian organization as a hotbed of dissidence. Luckyj's *Literary Politics in the Soviet Ukraine*[29] is an excellent study of the struggle for an independent national literature which makes use not only of all pertinent published materials but also of the unpublished diaries and letters of one of the leading participants in the events of that day. Both of these works were originally written as dissertations at Columbia University. Another book that is concerned with literary politics and policies, among other things, is *Through the Glass of Soviet Literature,*[30] edited by Ernest J. Simmons, an interesting and sometimes very able series of research papers in which the emphasis is on the use of Soviet literature and literary criticism as valid documentation of Soviet life. A large number of excellent Master's essays on kindred topics have been produced in past years at Columbia, some of which have already been published as articles in scholarly journals; another series will soon appear in book form.

Among studies of Soviet-Marxist criticism we might mention

Deming Brown's dissertation—soon to be published—on Soviet criticism of American literature, and Burton Rubin's dissertation —now in progress—on Plekhanov and Russian Marxist literary criticism. These studies will greatly enrich our resources in this field, since they give much indispensable background and historical information on current Soviet attitudes and ideas about the nature and function of literature.

We have been weakest in the production of genuine literary and critical studies. Victor Erlich's excellent *Russian Formalism*,[31] a study of literary criticism in the early twenties, is a fine exception. Ernest J. Simmons has just published a study of the works of Fedin, Leonov, and Sholokhov, which shows, by detailed analysis of their major novels, how these writers created works of enduring literary merit within the framework of Party dictation.[32] The four volumes so far published in the series, Harvard Slavic Studies,[33] have presented a number of interesting articles on Soviet literature.

There is no doubt among those who know the field that American research on Soviet literature represents a solid accomplishment. In the course of investigating literature, literary life in the Soviet Union, Marxist literary theory, and Soviet literary practice, our scholars have been able to throw light on all aspects of Soviet life, and their work on literature is regarded as useful by scholars in other disciplines. However, since it is our policy not to dwell overlong on positive accomplishments, we shall proceed immediately to point out some faults, defects, and shortcomings.

One sweeping criticism of research in this field over the last ten years is that a great deal of time and talent has been invested in the painstaking and detailed study of a stunted growth: Soviet literature. Even if one grants the assumptions that underlie such a criticism, we must still reply that basic research had to be done in order to establish certain facts that could not be taken for granted. If today Soviet literature is not as much of an "enigma wrapped in a mystery" as it was ten years ago, if today we know much more than we once did about the real meaning of such terms as "proletarian literature," "socialist realism," "the positive hero," it is largely because so much work has been done in the interval that we can, on some things, speak with knowledge. We have taken great pains to document thoroughly the now known and admitted fact that the Communist authorities, after a brief literary revival in the twenties, deliberately and consciously inhibited the production of literature, replacing it as far as possible with propaganda and educational materials in the forms usually employed by literature: the novel, the play, the poem. Once this was convincingly demonstrated, we studied in meticulous detail the methods and processes of control: we have investigated VAPP, RAPP, VAPLITE;[34] we have studied the Writers' Union; and we have examined the careers of Soviet literary men in order to discover not so much what they wrote as why they had to write it. We have studied Soviet criticism less as criticism than for its political motivation and content. And we now know in great detail how conformity to political directives was imposed on Soviet literature. An indispensable labor was performed and the ground was cleared of many misconceptions that were widespread in 1945.

This approach to Soviet literature has been criticized on the ground that, owing partly to the severe limitations of Soviet literature itself, much research effort has been concentrated not on literary production but on literary theory, literary organization, and literature as social documentation. The charge has been made that literary scholarship has impinged unduly on other disciplines and at times has been almost indistinguishable in its approach and purpose from the work of the historian or the political scientist.

In the absence of poems, plays, and novels giving honest, direct, and immediate literary formulation to the raw material of Soviet life, American scholarship has often been reduced to political and social analysis of the voluminous product which has gone under the name of Soviet literature. The use of Soviet literature as social documentation has yielded some good results, but these results have always to be evaluated with the greatest care, since the literature we study is perhaps the one literature in Europe least likely, except by accident, to reflect the real experience of actual people.

In defense of the political and sociological analysis of Soviet literature it has been said that since the "area" approach to Russian studies involves integration and cross-fertilization of the disciplines, the research in literature of an area program ought to grow out of and contribute to the whole study of a given area. In the Columbia Russian Institute area program and in other such programs, for instance, literature of the Soviet period has been emphasized. Problems have been studied, the solution of which would be of value to the social and political historian as well as to the historian of literature in general. It has been pointed out that this "sociological" approach to literary research is a widely accepted one, that it has yielded much of value, and that it is entirely valid if it is not allowed to obstruct or obscure other possible avenues of research, which might not so readily enter into an area program.

Perhaps the issues involved here should be defined more closely. It would seem that there are at least two possible approaches to the study of literature in its relation to a given society: (1) the study of literature as a source of information about the society which produces it; and (2) the study of social conditions as factors which influence the form and content of literature. Either approach is a valid one for Soviet literature, but it may be well to keep the distinction in mind. The first approach—the use of literature as social documentation—has only a limited usefulness when applied to Soviet literature, since that literature was reduced during the Stalin period to the status of a government-controlled educational and propaganda tool. The study of this controlled literature tells us very little about actual social conditions in the Soviet Union, though it does give us much information about the state of mind of the Soviet government, and its programs and policies at any given moment. The second approach makes use of information already at hand concerning social conditions in order to understand and interpret the literature. It is obvious that this approach is necessary and inevitable in the study of Soviet literature, and that we cannot begin to understand the latter without using information gleaned from the work of social scientists, or literary scholars engaged in similar investigations.

Perhaps this distinction should also be kept in mind when we consider the place of literature in an area program. However, the sociological approach obviously does not exhaust the possibilities of literary study, even in an area program. One might very well question whether there is really any conflict between the study of literature for its purely aesthetic and literary values, and the use of that literature in the total, integrated study of a given area from the viewpoint of several disciplines. Is it not the purpose of an integrated area program that *all* points of view should be represented, including that of the literary specialist? Might not studies of literary form and content, the critical analysis of aesthetic standards as revealed in the literature of a nation, contribute an ingredient to area programs that those programs sometimes lack? The study of literature—not only as social documentation but for its own sake—is a source of direct and immediate contact with the most sensitive, conscious, and articulate section of any society, and only a literary specialist can make this contribution.

At the same time, the peculiar nature of Soviet society demands from the literary scholar a historical perspective and a political sophistication that can scarcely be compared to the equipment that is considered necessary for the study of the literatures of western Europe. The research of the last ten years on the relation of Soviet literature to Soviet society has been indispensable as a part of the groundwork for a study of Soviet literature as literature. Moreover, the sociological or political approach to Soviet literature must continue to play its part in our future research, for we must keep ourselves informed about the changing nature of the political controls that are imposed upon the creative impulse of Soviet artists. Equipped with this growing knowledge about the place of the writer in Soviet society, the American literary scholar will find great and exciting opportunities awaiting him in the field of Soviet literature.

Perhaps the most immediate need is for monographs on key figures and leading schools of thought in Soviet literary history. Studies are called for on LEF, the Perevaltsy, the Constructivists, and the Serapion Brothers. Even the Proletcult has yet to be studied as a literary movement. The list of writers whose works must be examined more closely before we can generalize about the Soviet period is a long one, and includes most of the leading figures in Soviet literature. Curiously enough, since Kaun's biography, published in 1931, there has been almost no serious work by American scholars on so important a figure in Soviet literature and politics as Maxim Gorky.[35]

We know from the research of the past ten years how seriously the development of Soviet literature has been stunted by political regimentation, but the glimpses we have gotten since 1955 into literary life below the surface of the officially printed page make it clear that, even in Soviet society, literature continues to serve in some measure as a vehicle for the transmission of human values that resist the corrosive force of totalitarianism. Such symptomatic books as Dudintsev's *Not by Bread Alone*, the works in the two volumes of *Literaturnaya Moskva*, and Pasternak's *Doctor Zhivago* open to the student new vistas of study on the interaction between the Soviet literary artist and the society in which he lives. This challenge will call forth all the ingenuity of the scholar experienced in studying the social content of

Soviet literature and all the literary insight of the scholar who is trained in formal criticism. Together they can make a contribution of unusual significance.

III

No attempt has been made to spell out in detailed terms the research needs of our field, though some specific suggestions have been made. There seems to be wide agreement that a general work of literary analysis and criticism is sorely needed for Russian literature. Such a work would not replace, but supplement, the histories we now have, with greater emphasis on actual literary production as a revelation of Russian intellectual life of the nineteenth and twentieth centuries. The intimate connection of literature in Russia with ideas and ideology makes such a work indispensable.

Before such a work can be written, much preliminary work remains to be done on individual writers and critics and on certain periods in Russian intellectual history. The just completed Jubilee Edition of Tolstoy in ninety volumes is ground waiting to be tilled; the complete works of Belinsky, recently published, offer new and interesting material that ought to be investigated; the work of Chekhov has been neglected by American scholarship, although Chekhov not only was an important innovator and influence in European literature generally, but offers a free commentary on Russian intellectual and social life at the turn of the century. There is a long list of topics awaiting our interest and our scholarly labor.

We have remarked on the lack of comparative studies and on the importance they hold for us. Men now at work in the field recognize the futility of studying Russian literature in isolation from its sources and close relatives in western Europe. An interesting and fruitful line of endeavor would be the study of Russian culture—even in its most particularist and Slavophile moments—as a significant peripheral branch of European culture.

Russian writers are placed in clearer perspective when understood as part of a larger cultural and intellectual pattern. The idea now has gained wide acceptance that every specialist in Russian literature must to some extent also be a comparativist.

What has already been said about research in Soviet literature indicates one direction in which we ought to move. A more general suggestion, applicable to Russian literature before the Revolution as well as since, arises out of the nature of Soviet scholarship. The quantity of literary research that has appeared in the Soviet Union is enormous. One of its most commendable achievements has been the publication of such series of literary archival materials as *Literaturnoye Nasledstvo, Zvenya,* and the *Letopisi* of the State Literary Museum; and the publication of scholarly editions of such writers as Belinsky, Chekhov, Chernyshevsky, Dobrolyubov, Gogol, Gorky, Herzen, Nekrasov, A. N. Ostrovsky, Pushkin, Saltykov-Shchedrin, and Leo Tolstoy. All this material has been a boon to specialists on Russian literature everywhere. Along with this documentary material Soviet scholars have likewise published a great deal of original research, some of which is of very high quality. The requirements of Soviet Marxist orthodoxy, however, have so influenced the bulk of Soviet literary scholarship that the resultant interpretation of Russian literature suffers from an imbalance unacceptable to most scholars who do not share the Soviet Marxist faith. This situation presents two basic challenges to students living beyond the confines in which this faith is imposed: to help restore the balance by working on topics that are neglected by Soviet scholars, and to strive to correct misinterpretations wherever the requirements of Soviet orthodoxy lead Soviet scholars to conclusions that are open to question.

Quantitative examples of this imbalance can be seen in Matsuev's recent bibliography of literature and literary scholarship published in the Soviet Union from 1938 to 1945. Works written by and about Gorky fill thirty-nine pages of this book, and the list for Mayakovsky fills twenty-one pages, while Turgenev gets only four and a half pages and Goncharov only one. In the whole period from 1938 to 1945 Matsuev lists only two articles published in the Soviet Union on S. T. Aksakov, four on Fet, nine on Tyutchev, three on A. K. Tolstoy, three on Apollon Maikov, eight on Pisemsky, six on Stankevich, and none at all on Alexander Blok, Balmont, Vyacheslav Ivanov, Merezhkovsky, the Slavophiles, and a host of Soviet writers whose names disappeared from the Soviet press in the 1930's. Among critics the bibliography on Chernyshevsky fills seven pages; while Apollon Grigoryev gets two articles; Druzhinin, one; and Annenkov, Leontyev, and N. K. Mikhailovsky, none at all.[36]

These merely quantitative comparisons give only a partial indication of the gaps in published Soviet scholarship and the wealth of opportunities for significant research on Russian literature that await the American scholar. Some of the gaps have already attracted American specialists, as shown by references made above to research in progress or recently completed, and likewise by such books as Oleg Maslennikov's study of Bely and the Symbolist poets[37] and Zavalishin's recent work on early Soviet writers.[38] Among the numerous possibilities for group research it has been suggested that a seminar might be held on "Continuity and Change in Russian and Soviet Literature," from which there might emerge a series of research papers that would establish the modality of literary succession or invention in the old and the new. Studies of the element of dissent in the works of nearly all the prominent Soviet writers might yield information on the pattern of "inner revolt" in the total development of Soviet literature. Despite the relaxation of controls since the death of Stalin and the rehabilitation of many Soviet writers whose names could not previously be mentioned in print, there are still numerous figures and aspects of Soviet literature that can be discussed in print only outside the Soviet Union, among them such significant writers as Remizov, Pilnyak, and Zamyatin.

The Frenchman studying English literature or the Englishman studying French literature must overcome great handicaps of language and cultural experience before he can hope to match the research of native scholars. Naturally, the Englishman, Frenchman, or American studying Russian literature must overcome the same handicaps; but their freedom from the subtle network of controls over scholarly research in the Soviet Union gives their work a potential importance far greater than that of any research the English and French may produce on each other's literature. As long as this situation lasts, foreign scholars must continue their effort to fill the gaps and correct the imbalances wherever they can in the structure of literary scholarship on Russia. But as they work they can hope that the unnatural importance of their own research on Russian literature will eventually disappear, along with present-day barriers in the Soviet Union to full freedom of inquiry and communication.

Francis J. Whitfield

10. LINGUISTICS

I

A MOST IMPORTANT ASPECT of American study of Russian linguistics since World War II has been the increase in opportunities for scholars in the field to maintain contact with each other and to carry on a profitable exchange of ideas. Near the beginning of the period, for example, at the Stanford meeting of the Modern Language Association in 1949, the first meeting of the Slavic and East European "Group II," devoted specifically to linguistics of the area, took place. Neither of the papers delivered at that meeting was concerned primarily with Russian linguistics—or, indeed, with linguistics in the narrow sense.[1] The topics discussed were the original homelands of the Balts and of the Slavs—problems in which linguistics assumes the function of an auxiliary science. But it was made clear at the meeting that the choice of these general subjects reflected the intention of the organizers and participants to inaugurate the new discussion group with emphasis on the broad implications of linguistic research, the interrelations of such research within the Slavic and East European field, and its relations with other disciplines. Subsequent developments—not merely within the Modern Language Association—have confirmed this setting, even extending the frames of research in the field.

This catholic approach is one of the valuable traditions of American Slavistics, inherited from the pioneers of Russian studies in this country. In spite of every practical reason for confining their attention to the Russian field, interpreted narrowly, and in spite of no little pressure to do so, these early workers succeeded in clearing the ground for the broad developments in Slavic studies that followed the end of the last war. The importance of this inheritance cannot be overstressed. Professor George Y. Shevelov of Columbia, in reviewing this report, has commented:

> There may be no deep insight into either the structure of Modern Russian or its history without knowledge of the other Slavic languages. This is the only guarantee against one-sidedness, naive exaggerations based on insufficient knowledge, and premature generalizations by amateurs. Neither adequate research nor high-level teaching of Russian is thinkable without mastering the data on at least some of the other Slavic languages. Concentration on Russian linguistic studies alone would not only be shortsighted from the point of view of orientation in the entangled inter-Slavic relations, but would mean a depreciation of Russian studies themselves. . . . The emphasis on Russian, very much in vogue now under the influence of *sputniks*, but always basically sound, would turn out to be unfortunate if it led to a neglect of other Slavic languages, at least as an auxiliary means for better understanding of Russian. These considerations, of course, do not imply that the study of Russian should be comparative. What is important is knowledge of the other Slavic languages, not necessarily their explicit use in any particular piece of research.

To such a broad conception of its responsibilities, the Modern Language Association group has been attached from its very beginnings, and, together with other organizations of a related character, it has provided much needed forums for linguists working in the Slavic and East European area. Thus, gradually, one of the first prerequisites for rapid, efficient exchange of information concerning research in Russian linguistics has been attained. In this connection, particular mention should be made of such a meeting as the Conference of American and Canadian Slavicists, held at Ann Arbor, June 27-29, 1953. This congress, with one session devoted entirely to Russian linguistics and another to Slavic linguistics in general, offered special advantages that cannot be duplicated in meetings where non-Slavic studies occupy the greater part of the available time. The desirability of establishing a regular schedule of such Slavic congresses should be given serious attention in any program for strengthening the position of Russian linguistics in this country.

Two years after the Stanford meeting, and two years before the Ann Arbor Conference, "in view of the rapid development of Slavic studies in America," as the masthead explained, an entire number of the linguistics journal *Word* (Volume 7, Number 2) was devoted primarily to articles and reviews in the field of Slavic linguistics. It is pertinent, in such an essay as this, to note that this important event was made possible by a generous grant from the Committee for the Promotion of Advanced Slavic Studies, n.c. In the following year, the same Committee supported the founding of a special journal, *Slavic Word*, appearing annually as a fourth number of *Word* and serving as a central organ for American studies in Slavic linguistics and—in the small measure possible—as a place where Slavicists abroad could present their work to an American audience. The editors' introduction may be quoted to illustrate their conception of the activity to be reflected in, and encouraged by, the new journal, and to emphasize once again the lively contacts with other parts of the field and with other disciplines that have characterized the healthy growth of Russian linguistics in this country over the past dozen years:

> In the principal American centers of Slavic studies, scholars are actively engaged in a systematic description of contemporary Slavic languages, making full use of the recent methodological achievements in structural linguistics and such cognate fields as cultural anthro-

pology, theory of social interaction, symbolic logic, communication theory, sound analysis, etc. This synchronic approach is being supplemented by a more profound enquiry into the historical phonology and grammar of different Slavic languages, their genetic interrelations, and their affinities with adjacent tongues. Here again, the rich accumulation of experience gained in structural analysis, areal studies, and contiguous historical disciplines will be put to full use.

The robust optimism of this manifesto would, of course, have sufficiently identified its principal composer and the leading spirit behind the journal, even if Roman Jakobson's pervasive influence had not been evident throughout this and the following issues. There have been, and will be, other occasions for appreciating the extent and the quality of his exceptional contribution to the development of American Slavistics, but even in a brief report of this kind it should not go unmentioned.

In all, four numbers of *Slavic Word* appeared—all with the aid of the Committee for the Promotion of Advanced Slavic Studies, n.c. In addition, the same Committee supported the separate publication of two significant monographs in the field, issued as supplements to *Word* in 1951 and 1953: Karl Menges's *Oriental Elements in the Vocabulary of the Oldest Russian Epos, The Igor' Tale*—continuing the new phase of *Igor'* studies inaugurated by the great collective volume of text, translations, and commentary that was published in New York shortly after the war[2]—and Yury Šerech [—Shevelov]'s *Problems in the Formation of Belorussian*.

The demise of *Slavic Word*, after its fourth issue (1955), involved serious consequences for the well-being of Russian studies in this country. Neither general linguistic reviews nor the growing number of journals, series, and yearbooks devoted to Slavic studies as a whole and involving many disciplines can fill the gap. These other outlets have, indeed, in varying degrees, tended to reflect the generally increased activity in Slavic linguistics, both in the quantity and in the quality of the research they have published in the field.[3] At the same time they cannot, by their nature, fulfill the functions of a journal devoted exclusively to Slavic linguistics.

II

The picture of research opportunities in Russian linguistics over the past decade is, in general, a cheering one. Conditions have improved for fruitful cooperation of scholars in the field and for exchange of information on the results of their work. Long-term projects, reflecting some of the most advanced positions in contemporary American and European linguistics, have attracted able Ph.D. candidates and young postdoctoral scholars and furnished an important part of their training. The gradual spread of Russian studies over the country has involved an increasing number of university centers in the promotion of Slavic linguistic research. If it has been necessary to record an occasional disappointment and setback, still a heartening example has been given of what can be accomplished with the timely application of appropriate stimuli.

The use that has been made of improved research conditions and the exploitation of new areas of research and new methods have, on the whole, well justified the efforts and hopes of those who took the lead in these developments. Inevitably, given the extraordinarily rapid growth of the field during the period under consideration, and given the very ambitious and all-embracing program under which the work has been planned, many of the expected results are observable only in part. Theoretical mappings of extensive areas of inquiry, preliminary methodological discussions, progress reports, and studies of sample problems selected from a larger nexus constitute a good proportion of the evidence that Russian linguistic studies are advancing with ever greater momentum.

Lest this report be taken to overemphasize certain newer aspects of linguistic research, it should be stated clearly that there is no intention to minimize more conservative approaches. Projects which apply new methods and try to pave new ways deserve particular support, but in any branch of science no single approach can guarantee an absolutely adequate and complete cognition of reality. Every method, by its own nature, disregards certain aspects of reality. It is very important, therefore, not to rely on one method alone in any scholarly investigations, Slavic linguistics included.

A conspicuous example of the application of modern techniques to questions of basic theoretical importance is to be found in the collective research project supported by the Rockefeller Foundation and dealing with intensive X-ray and sound-spectrographic study of Russian speech sounds, making possible the calculation of relations between their motor and acoustic aspects. The results of these studies that have so far appeared, and the refined distinctive-feature analysis that they have helped to make possible, have already had far-reaching effects, not merely on Russian and on Slavic linguistics, but on general linguistic theory.[4]

Work is in progress using similar techniques of statistical communication theory on Russian phonemic complexes, vocabulary, and connected text. In this connection might also be mentioned the ground-breaking *Russian Word Count and Frequency Analysis of Grammatical Categories of Standard Literary Russian*, prepared by Harry H. Josselson (Detroit, 1953), which, beyond its immediate results, suggests further statistical work that will be required from other premises and other points of view.

Structural studies of Russian radical, derivational, and inflexional morphemes, of morphophonemic alternations, and of devices of word-composition are being undertaken and are already represented by a number of exploratory articles that promise a fresh contribution to the analysis of Russian sign-structure in its expression aspect. Content-analysis of morphological categories, sign-classes, and constructions in Russian, cutting across traditional and often theoretically indefensible boundaries of morphology, syntax, and semantics, hold similar promise of having basic implications for linguistics, extending far beyond the Russian field. Work on the semantic spectra of such categories as aspect and tense in Russian, for example, again illustrates the function that Russian studies have assumed of bringing into the core of linguistic research phenomena that have in the past tended to receive only marginal attention in this country.

At the meeting ground of linguistic and literary studies, where are located such subjects as the formation of literary languages and their peculiar characteristics in relation to other usages, the devices of poetic language, and the many other problems of stylistics, research plans in our field again warrant the expectation that, with proper encouragement, American Slavic linguistics will stake out territories still relatively unfamiliar to general linguistic research in this country. This expectation is strengthened by the friendly collaboration of scholars representing different traditions and by their generous contribution to the training of a new generation of American research workers and teachers. Various possible lines of such research, making use of sophisticated synchronic and diachronic techniques, are indicated in programmatic articles like Jakobson's "Kernel of Comparative Slavic Literature"[5] or Šerech [—Shevelov]'s "Toward a Historical Dialectology: Its Delimitation of the History of Literary Language."[6]

Significant also is the readiness of workers in Russian linguistics—perhaps in part because of the very newness of the discipline in this country—to establish contact with other disciplines that must be called on for aid in any vigorous program of linguistic investigation. Already noted in connection with phonetic and phonemic studies, this characteristic is equally evident in such current research as that on machine translation from Russian (which also has basic theoretical implications of great importance) and is well exemplified by the already mentioned collective volume on the *Igor' Tale*, along with the several supplementary studies that it has inspired. Comparative work involving connections between the Slavic and Baltic languages, particularly associated with long-range research projects at the University of Pennsylvania, is another instance of this "open" aspect of our studies, further exemplified by current research on contacts between Russian and languages that are in neither the Slavic nor the Baltic family.

It may, then, fairly be claimed that, within the general expansion of Russian studies in the last decade, linguistics has had a significant share in the training of able young scholars and teachers, the development and application of new research methods, and the awakening of interest in an increasing number of universities. Here, as in other aspects of Russian studies, progress was largely made possible through the farsighted planning and effective cooperation of the universities and the foundations and through the devotion and skilled leadership of the senior scholars in the field. Moreover, Russian linguistic studies have benefited, not only from the rapidly growing concern with Russian studies as a whole, but also from lively contemporary developments in American linguistics.

The picture is gratifying on the whole. But it must be added that our linguistic studies are still only in the beginning of their healthy growth. A number of important and challenging projects lie ahead. For example, there have been no studies at all of a comprehensive nature in Slavic historical phonology and grammar; almost no studies in dialectology; no important studies on etymology and onomastics; no studies in synchronic comparative phonology and grammar of the Slavic languages (except H. Rubenstein's *A Comparative Study of Morphophonemic Alternations in Standard Serbo-Croatian, Czech and Russian* [Ann Arbor, 1950]); and very few on the history of the Slavic literary languages. We have been promised numerous and ground-breaking studies in the structure of Modern Standard Russian, but so far almost nothing in this field has come out.[7]

If the potentialities of the field are to be realized, intelligent planning, efficient use of the resources accumulated, and continued cooperation of institutions and individual scholars are all badly needed. Specifically, lines of effective communication among scholars in the field must be assured. Among other problems, mention has been made of the need for a central outlet for the publication of research and the review of current Slavic linguistic work both here and abroad. It also devolves on those concerned with maintaining favorable conditions of research to investigate means of providing regularly scheduled congresses for specialists in the field.

III

In considering future research needs and the encouragement of specific lines of research, wisdom dictates that we be guided by the successful beginnings that can now be recorded. The organic growth of Russian linguistic studies in America over the last decade reflects in large part the precept and example of scholars committed to the belief that only basic research over a broad field of inquiry can make a healthy climate for work of permanent significance. The most important investigations of the Russian language have accordingly been carried on in the vanguard of present-day linguistic studies and have run parallel with analyses of closely related languages. An understanding of the need for such a setting for research, and an appreciation of its long-term value, are prerequisites for the proper encouragement of Russian linguistics, just as they are for the encouragement of any other area of linguistic studies.

In common with those other areas, the Russian field shares, by its very nature, certain general conditions of development. Common sense and a reasonable concern for the efficient use of limited personnel will require that priority be given to research that can be better done here than elsewhere. Put the other way, caution should be exercised in the planning of work for which indispensable firsthand materials are available mainly in the Soviet Union, at least until opportunities are afforded for prolonged study and field work abroad. Mere restatements of well-worked problems in modern Russian grammar, for instance, so far as they are based on no particularly new or "American" methodology and rely primarily on secondary sources or, in studies of the spoken language, on a limited number of accidentally available informants, would represent unsound and wasteful use of our resources. Other important limitations to be considered are those imposed when the investigator's native language is not Russian.

On the other hand, American scholars enjoy peculiarly rich opportunities for research in areas that are ignored or underdeveloped in the Slavic countries. The application of new techniques of linguistic analysis to the Russian language has already been cited several times as an example. Many problems of a politically sensitive nature in the Soviet Union, like the influence of jargons on modern Russian, the influence of Russian on the other languages of the U.S.S.R. and vice versa, peculiarities of propaganda language, or Western influences in Russian, require the unbiased treatment of free scholarship and promise rich returns both for their own sake and for their obvious implications outside the field of linguistics.

Ten years ago, a national conference on the study of world areas, held under the sponsorship of the Committee on World Area Research of the Social Science Research Council, observed the need for an improved Russian-English dictionary. It may not be inappropriate to suggest here that a study should be made of the resources available for a large-scale, cooperative project, exploiting modern techniques of bilingual lexicography, to provide a dictionary fitted to the needs of American scholars.

As in other fields of Russian studies, there has been some tendency in linguistics, with notable exceptions, to weigh the balance heavily on the side of contemporary subject matter. Despite an awareness of the largely unexplored comparative and historical fields and despite some outstanding achievements in attacking them, scholars in linguistics have oriented much of their work toward synchronic description. Yet both diachronic and synchronic comparative studies, which have suffered from considerable shortcomings in the Soviet Union, offer opportunities for American-trained scholars to make important contributions. Structural interpretation of linguistic developments and historical dialectology have already been cited as examples of promising research fields where investigators who are unhampered by political bias or pressure and are armed with modern methods of analysis may expect to find rewarding topics and may help significantly in deepening our knowledge of Russian civilization and history.

In commenting on this report, Professor Shevelov has pointed out that the development of Slavic studies in general and Slavic linguistics in particular under present world conditions is important to assure American contributions to this branch of science, to strengthen the prestige of the United States in the cultural field, and to ensure a solid basis for the vitally important spread of a knowledge of the Russian language. In addition, achievements in Slavic linguistic studies may easily become a matter of cultural export to countries of Asia, Africa, and Latin America. These countries are beginning to teach Slavic languages and literatures. Assistance in providing teaching staff, textbooks, and other aids is or will soon be wanted. Naturally, first glances are turned to Russia. But American Slavic linguistics may have some advantages in comparison with Russia. It can supply these countries with Slavicists and Slavistics with no political implications; it can offer more modern methods and better technical equipment; the English language is familiar in many of these countries. And the only real advantage of Russia, the unlimited number of native speakers, can be partly countered by the fact that America also has many persons with both English and a Slavic language as native languages.

Consolidation of the gains achieved during the period under

review, maintenance and improvement of the conditions that have made those gains possible, increased attention to the relatively neglected portions of the comprehensive program lying behind Russian linguistic studies in America from their inception, and increased awareness of where American research can render best and most efficient service—these would seem to be desiderata on which all responsible workers in the field find themselves in agreement. A candid view of the foundations that have been laid and a no more than moderately optimistic appreciation of future opportunities give good reason for hope in the increased prestige and importance of Russian linguistics in America in the years ahead.

Robert M. Slusser

11. MUSIC

I

As USED IN THIS ESSAY, the term "Russian music" refers primarily to music composed in pre- and post-1917 Russia. In a historical sense, however, "Russian music" includes the work of *all* those composers who received their training and spent their formative years in Russia, regardless of whether they left Russia after the 1917 revolutions. Thus, Rachmaninoff and Stravinsky, who lived abroad after 1917, must be considered "Russian" composers, as well as Prokofiev, who emigrated but returned, and Miaskovsky, who never left Russia. Music in the Soviet Union today is still under the strong influence of the work of the pre-revolutionary generation of composers, the émigrés as well as those in Russia. For example, music written by Stravinsky since 1930, despite the official ban on its performance or reproduction in the Soviet Union, is the subject of avid study among Soviet composers, and thus forms one of the basic influences helping to determine the future direction of "Russian music." Moreover, the work of the émigré composers is rooted to a considerable extent in the specifically Russian cultural and musical milieu in which they were trained. The term "Russian music" is therefore used in a historical and organic, as well as a political and geographic, sense. "Soviet music," on the other hand, refers specifically to music composed in post-1917 Russia.

While this essay deals primarily with work done in the United States, musicology is an international discipline, with its oldest and best established centers outside the United States; it has therefore been necessary to take into account not only studies completed in the United States but also publications in English from other countries, as well as those in European languages.

This is a survey of writing about music, not a survey of the music itself. The story of the popularization of Russian music in the United States is a long and extremely interesting one, but no attempt has been made to tell it here, except as it finds partial reflection in books and articles.

In the field of Russian area studies, Russian music has so far figured only as a small and obscure frontier province, seldom visited and imperfectly explored, whereas in the world of music it is an important and strategically located territory. Inevitably, therefore, the major share of the task of studying Russian music has been carried out by critics, commentators, scholars, and professional writers whose primary concern is with music. In evaluating the work done, this fact must be kept in mind.

II

In the final analysis, most of the writing about music, from journalistic criticism to scholarly studies, reflects and is based on the standard repertoire. Furthermore, a firsthand knowledge of the music itself is a prerequisite to any serious study of the subject. A consideration of what Russian music is performed and recorded is therefore a necessary preliminary to our inquiry.

Russian music has long formed an essential part of the standard repertoire. Works by most of the major composers of nineteenth- and early twentieth-century Russia are performed almost as frequently in New York, Paris, and Rome as in Leningrad and

Moscow. In their treatment of post-1917 composers, however, the Soviet Union and the West diverge sharply; whereas in the West works written under the Soviet regime gain acceptance only after overcoming the double obstacle of unfamiliarity and ideological strangeness, in the Soviet Union it is precisely these works which constitute the major part of the repertoire.

Consequently, the student dependent on concert performances alone for his knowledge of Russian music would inevitably miss the greater part of the music currently being composed in the Soviet Union. To some extent this situation can be remedied by the use of recordings. Thanks to the technological revolution wrought by the invention of the long-playing record, not only is most of the standard repertoire available on records,[1] but many Soviet works seldom or never played in the West can be heard.[2] Although the coverage is by no means complete, it seems likely that in the course of time most works of major importance will become available in recorded form.

It remains true, nevertheless, that music is a field in which direct observation and study are of primary importance. It is therefore to be hoped that among the American students who will be visiting and studying in the Soviet Union in coming years will be some with an interest and training in music.

Published works on music include both general and scholarly studies. The subjects represented in both categories closely conform to the prevailing taste in performance—with few exceptions, the composers dealt with are those whose works are most popular.

The books on Russian music which have been published in English over the past forty years present few novelties. There are a number of surveys and historical studies, biographies of a relatively few composers or performers, and a considerable body of criticism and appreciation.[3] From the standpoint of the Russian area specialist, most of these works leave much to be desired. An adequate knowledge of the Russian background is often lacking, and when scholarly standards are met, they tend naturally to be those of the musician rather than of the area specialist. Most of the more solid works are by a handful of writers who for many years have specialized in the study of various aspects of Russian music.

Some of the most valuable publications from the standpoint of scholarship reflect the tastes and initiative of a few individual publishers rather than any broad popular interest. Since books in this category usually represent a financial risk, their number is limited and what has been published is only a small fraction of what would be desirable from the standpoint of Russian area studies. We are given Tchaikovsky's *Diaries,* but not his extensive and valuable correspondence; Stravinsky's *Autobiography* and *Poetics of Music,* but almost nothing on his talented contemporary, Scriabin; Rimsky-Korsakoff's autobiography, but none of César Cui's critical writings; an excellent documentary biography of Musorgsky, but nothing on such seminal figures as Glinka and Dargomyzhsky.[4] In view of the limited sales such works can be expected to have, however, Russian area specialists should no doubt be grateful for what has been vouchsafed, rather than complain about what is withheld. It must be recognized, nevertheless, that the documentary and scholarly materials on Russian music published commercially, despite their value, do not in themselves provide an adequate basis for serious musicological or area-study analysis of Russian music. Moreover, such analysis presupposes both a technical preparation in music and the ability to use source materials in Russian or other Slavic languages.

There are only a few works which deal with the relationship between music and the system of political controls in the Soviet Union, mainly written by journalists who specialize in Soviet topics.[5] A few books in this category represent defenses of the policies of the Communist Party.[6] Such works, useful as *prima facie* evidence, must be treated with due caution as contributions to scholarship.

Russian music has a definite place in all standard works of musical reference. Whether the place is adequate and whether the treatment is sound are questions, however, which the Russian area specialist will wish to raise.

It is encouraging, therefore, to be able to report that the basic work of musical reference in the English language—*Grove's Dictionary of Music and Musicians,* now in its fifth edition—presents an admirable example of professional musical scholarship judiciously but unobtrusively aware of the major factors which have determined the evolution of Russian music. In smaller musical reference handbooks, one finds varying degrees of comprehension of the special problems of Russian music.[7] With *Grove's* available as a standard, however, the Russian area specialist need experience no great alarm concerning the basic reference data being used by musical scholars.

At the same time, this is not to say that Russian area specialists can rest satisfied with what has been provided by the editors of works of musical reference. Such editors necessarily treat Russian music as a component of music as a whole and only to the extent they consider justified by its intrinsic importance. While this approach produces reasonably good results for the pre-Soviet period, it is less satisfactory for post-1917 Russian music. It is the Soviet period of Russian music which most urgently requires documentation and elucidation, since here Russian music diverges most significantly from the practices and standards of the West. It is exactly the music of this period, however, which engages the attention of Western scholars least, whether because it is not felt to be of value as music or because professional writers on music tend to regard with distrust any subject involving political considerations. Thus the complex phenomena of Soviet music, especially those related to its enforced subordination to the political goals of the Communist Party, are not treated adequately in any standard Western reference handbook on music. A real need for Russian area specialists, therefore, is the compilation of accurate reference data on the major aspects of contemporary

Russian music—its educational institutions, its composers and performers, its theoretical postulates, and the major stages of its evolution.

Students of contemporary Russian music will find much useful information on their subject in the musical journals of the West In the United States and Great Britain there are more than a dozen such journals, ranging from small news bulletins to scholarly and specialized musicological publications. If one adds journals published in western Europe, one has an extensive and varied group upon which to draw.

While reserving for separate treatment the strictly musicological journals, it can be said that the information provided in the specialized music press consists generally of three types of material, occurring singly or in combination: (a) reviews of performances of new compositions, (b) reports and reviews of performances by Soviet musicians in the West or by Western musicians in the Soviet Union, and (c) general articles and editorials on the state of Soviet music, the relation between Communist Party controls and music, and similar topics.[8]

Writers in the British and western European journals tend to stress purely musical considerations, with a corresponding neglect or underestimation of political factors, while writers in the American journals often show a greater awareness of the latter element, but with only a vague conception of the actual techniques and purposes of the system of political controls. Used with caution, however, and interpreted against the background of a fuller knowledge of Soviet political factors than is usually available to professional writers of music, the articles and reviews in musical journals are an invaluable aid to research.

A relative newcomer to the field of social and humanistic studies, musicology is now firmly established in the United States and other Western countries.[9] It is legitimate, therefore, to survey its achievements in the field of Russian music and to measure them against the potential significance of the subject.

Available evidence points to the conclusion that musicology, not only in the United States but in the West generally, does not consider Russian music, whether pre- or post-Soviet, to be a major field of inquiry. Articles on problems of Russian music, particularly of the post-1917 period, seldom appear in musicological journals,[10] while graduate dissertations in musicology on any aspect of Russian music have been few and far between.[11]

That this situation is not peculiar to the United States is suggested by a recent survey of musicological activities in West Germany since 1945,[12] and by the announced schedule of the Seventh Congress of the International Musicological Society,[13] both of which lack any indication of concern with Russian music.

Several possible explanations for this situation come to mind. In the first place, the professional world of music has evidently lost interest to a considerable extent in the music currently being composed in the Soviet Union, perhaps believing that it possesses neither the untrammeled experimentalism of earlier Russian music nor a healthy organic relation to the central current of Western music. Lacking such interest, Western musicologists apparently feel little stimulus to investigate the current Soviet musical scene, despite its significance as a battleground of art and politics, nor do they feel the need to study Russian music of earlier periods, even though it forms one of the major sources of contemporary Western music.

Secondly, the science of musicology appears to be predominantly concerned with studying the evolution and characterization of the Germanic component of Western music. The majority of American graduate dissertations in musicology, for example, deal with some aspect of Germanic music.

Thirdly, the language barrier undoubtedly contributes to the neglect of Russian music by Western musicologists. With few exceptions, articles and books on the subject are by men linked to Russian studies by some personal connection. There appears to be little realization in the professional schools of music of the need to train young scholars to work in Slavic language sources.

Finally, it seems evident that the inescapable presence of political considerations in the very center of modern Russian music has led some Western musicologists to view the field as somehow less "scholarly" than other branches of musicology in which political considerations are either entirely absent or are at a safe historical distance.

Whatever the reasons, the fact remains that professional musicology in the West, including the United States, has hardly begun to devote serious attention to the study of Russian music. It is furthermore clear that there has been little effective collaboration between professional scholars and departments of music and Russian area specialists.

During the last decade the field of Russian studies has grown up about the musicologist and the professional writer on music without their noticing it. Conversely, the specialist in Russian affairs has paid little attention to developments in Russian music.

An exception to this general picture is a study on Soviet music and musicians now being conducted by Stanley D. Krebs, a Ph.D. candidate at the University of Washington. His project includes "investigation, analysis and reporting of Soviet music, Soviet literature and criticism on music, and the phenomenon of the identification of creative activity with the Soviet state," to quote from Mr. Krebs' own definition of his study.

A full-length study of Soviet music by a refugee scholar—*Music under the Soviets*, by Andrei Olkhovsky, a former professor at the Kiev Conservatory—reflects firsthand knowledge of the subject in many of its aspects.[14] Including an extensive bibliography and an index of composers and compositions, it is the most comprehensive treatment of the subject now available in English.

Special mention should be made of the excellent work being done by the *Current Digest of the Soviet Press* in publishing translations of important articles on Communist Party policy in the field of music. With few exceptions, however, the *Current Digest* does not publish translations of articles on purely musical subjects.

An attempt to correlate data from the two chief fields involved in any study of Soviet music—art and politics—was made in a recent article by the author of the present report.[15] The inclusion of this article in a symposium surveying developments in the Soviet Union since the death of Stalin was in itself a noteworthy sign of an awakening interest in the subject among Russian area specialists.

III

The general picture which emerges from our survey is as follows: first, Russian music of the period before 1917 has established a strong place in the musical consciousness of the Western world. It is widely and frequently performed, and enjoys broad popularity. In regard to post-1917 Russian music, it is necessary to distinguish between the two channels into which it has split. With few exceptions, the music now being composed in the Soviet Union has ceased to be a subject of concern or a creative stimulus to the musicians and composers of the West. The work of the émigré composers, however, continues to exert a major influence, not only in the West but also in the Soviet Union.

Second, there is a considerable volume of writing and publishing on certain aspects of Russian music. General as well as scholarly books and articles are numerous on those composers whose works are most frequently performed. Much of what is published is useful for the purposes of scholarship, although it does not fully serve those purposes, either as to the depth of penetration of particular topics or the range of subjects covered.

Third, professional American and Western musicology has

so far hesitated to come to grips with the special problems of Russian music—its relation to the music of other areas and periods, its contemporary milieu, and its significance for the West.

Fourth, Russian area specialists have up to now devoted little attention to Russian music, despite its intrinsic importance as a major component of Russian culture, a seminal force in Western intellectual life, and a crucial area of the interaction of art and politics in the Soviet system. There are signs, however, of an awakening interest in the subject and a realization of its potential significance on the part of Russian area specialists.

IV

If the contention is granted that Russian music is a subject worthy of scholarly investigation, one may well ask who is to be considered responsible for its study. Is it desirable to add another to the already extensive list of subjects with which the Russian area specialist is concerned? Would it not be possible to leave music in the hands of the professional musicians, critics, and musicologists?

For reasons already discussed, it seems probable that, for at least the near future, musicologists and writers on music in general will not fully meet the need of area specialists for scholarly study in the field of Russian music, particularly of the Soviet period. Even if the musicologists and their associates should increase the degree of their attention to Russian music—a development greatly to be desired—there are still many problems in the field which can be adequately explored and illuminated only by the Russian area specialist, who is trained to evaluate the elements of Russian and Soviet intellectual and cultural life and who has the necessary background of language and area experience.

What are some of these problems? The following list is intended to be suggestive rather than exhaustive.

(1) *Historical subjects.* From the viewpoint of the Russian area specialist, the major historical problems relating to music

center around its role as a significant component of Russian cultural and intellectual life. In this regard, a number of important specific subjects await examination: the origins of Russian opera and its relationship to the institution of serfdom, the close tie between music and literature in the operas of Serov, the influence on the evolution of mid-nineteenth-century Russian music of the concepts of the *Narodniki*, to name only a few. In addition, a most useful general study would be a survey of the evolution of Russian music from the reign of Catherine II to the Bolshevik Revolution. Such a survey would be immensely helpful in illuminating many aspects of the development of Russian culture.

In addition, biographical and critical studies of most of the key figures in Russian music are urgently needed. While satisfactory studies exist of some of the most popular composers—Tchaikovsky, Musorgsky, Rachmaninoff—there is nothing, or next to nothing, on such men as Balakirev and Borodin, Scriabin and Taneev, Miaskovsky and Khachaturian. Particularly valuable would be critical studies of the life and work of composers whose activity spans the transition from pre- to postrevolutionary Russia, such as Prokofiev and Glière. In the works of such men it is possible to trace the direct impact of politics on music, and in the degree to which politics has influenced their work, one can read the auguries for the future of music in the Communist system.

(2) *Subjects in political science.* An analysis of the evolution of political controls over Soviet music could be expected to shed fresh light on the general problem of the nature and purpose of such controls in Soviet cultural life. Moreover, since music has proved singularly resistant to Communist Party dominance—thereby forcing the Party to develop new techniques and concepts in attempting to control it—such an analysis would have special significance. A comparative study of the system of controls in music and painting should have value for a fuller understanding of the parallel system in literature, which has so far received the major share of attention from Russian area specialists.

A critical study of the concepts and practices of the Soviet Union's most influential musicologist and theorist, B. V. Asafiev, would contribute greatly to our knowledge of the interrelation between the Soviet intellectual elite and the Communist Party. In his life and writings Asafiev spanned the wide gamut from the experimentalism of the 1920's (when he enthusiastically welcomed Stravinsky's most radical innovations) to the "socialist realism" of the 1940's (when he lent the weight of his authority to the Party's dictates in the field of music). The stages in Asafiev's intellectual evolution present an epitome of the forced marriage between aesthetics and political imperatives in Soviet culture.

A highly significant process, to which comparatively little attention has been paid in the West, is the extension of Soviet controls and conceptions in music (and other artistic fields) to the vassal nations of eastern Europe. These countries, each with its own more or less well established musical tradition, are now being forcibly assimilated into the Soviet cultural pattern. Studies of the transition taking place would sharpen our understanding of the Communist dynamic and the interaction of cultural and political factors in the Communist system.

(3) *Subjects in aesthetics and philosophy.* A historical study of the development of genres in Russian music—the symphony, the opera, the song—would help to distinguish those evolutionary processes organic to music itself (e.g., the emergence of a specifically Russian symphonic tradition) from those which have their origin in political considerations (e.g., the decline of chamber music in the Soviet Union and the concomitant rise of the "mass song").

One of the most creative periods in Russian music is that covering approximately the years 1895-1925. The close relation between the musical aesthetics developed during these years and other branches of Russian culture is generally recognized (for example, the relation between the music of Scriabin and symbolist poetry). What may not be as fully realized, however, is the extent to which the artistic impetus generated in Russia during this period still constitutes one of the major creative forces in modern Western culture. In choreography, for example, a field which is most intimately related to music, the strongest single influence in America today is that of George Balanchine, an émigré artist whose outlook and aesthetic system were developed in late nineteenth- and early twentieth-century Russia. The debt modern American music owes to this generation of Russian musicians will be apparent if one adds the names of Koussevitsky, Horowitz, Pyatigorsky, and Milstein, to mention only a few. A full study of this key problem in contemporary aesthetics would require the collaboration of scholars in a number of fields, but Russian area specialists have a special opportunity and responsibility to explore the origins and first stages of a movement which is now of significance throughout the Western world.

Successfully to carry out the study of problems such as these, it is clear, will require closer collaboration between musicologists and Russian area specialists. Bridges must be built, in the construction of which both sides will have their assigned task—a greater degree of attention to the role and significance of music on the part of Russian area specialists, and among musicians and musicologists, a greater degree of awareness of the special problems and opportunities presented by the study of Russian music as part of Western cultural and intellectual life.

Paul Willen

12. ARCHITECTURE AND MINOR ARTS

I

It may be safely stated at the outset that of all the images by which we commonly identify the basic character of a civilization the most powerful single image is probably the one created by architecture—in which both the aesthetic and the functional genius of a people are embodied. The Parthenon of ancient Greece, the Colosseum of imperial Rome, the Gothic cathedral of medieval Europe, and our own glass-enclosed skyscrapers are familiar examples of this type of identification.

Curiously enough, the Soviet—or Communist—civilization has not as yet produced a striking visual image of this kind, and its present leaders have repudiated the monumental Palace of Soviets by which Stalin had once hoped to fix a place for himself, and the civilization he wrought, in architectural history. The complete failure of the Soviet society to produce an indigenous style may be taken, incidentally, as one indication of their continuing dependence on western Europe for the fundamental ideas by which their allegedly independent civilization is being built.

The absence of a single architectural image for Soviet Communism does not, however, mean that the study of Soviet architecture is useless to us in our efforts to determine the essential character of its culture. In their effort to appear independent of western Europe, the Soviet architects have evolved a rather stuffy and eclectic architecture based on a variety of styles popular in Europe between the fourteenth and nineteenth centuries. The neo-classic façades which have resulted—in so sharp a contrast with the gleaming concrete structures of the postrevolutionary era—unquestionably bear some relationship to the authoritarian character of the Soviet regime; and, likewise, the rigid and formal planning concepts adopted by the Soviet architects in the mid-1930's surely are not unrelated to the fixed and hierarchal concepts of social structure which are held by the Soviet political theorists.

At the same time the limits of this type of symbolic analysis should be recognized. In our modern technological age styles are transplanted and reproduced with such ease that adoption of a given style can disguise (deliberately or otherwise) as much as it can reveal. Soviet architectural style, for example, rejects modern technology as an influence; yet it would be wrong to conclude from this that the Soviet leaders, who determined this style, are averse to modern technology. We find Yugoslav architects employing the same concepts of modern design now prevalent in most of western Europe; and yet it would be equally hazardous to conclude from this that the "inner feeling" of Yugoslav Communism is therefore radically different from the "inner feeling" of Soviet Communism. These variations in architectural style are certainly of importance—as significant perhaps as the bold stand made by modern architecture in both Poland and Hungary in the period of Communist "take-over" following World War II, when Polish and Hungarian architects fought, with some success, the introduction of Stalinist-style extravagance—but they must be handled with caution.

At the same time these complexities should not paralyze the

student in his attempts to utilize architecture as a barometer of Soviet civilization. Certainly the striking contrast between the avant-garde architecture of early postrevolutionary Russia and the heavy neoclassical architecture of Stalinist Russia is of more than passing historical significance; and certainly the slight modification of this overbearing monumentalism in the post-Stalin era deserves close observation. The deep surprise felt by many American visitors to the Soviet Union, on discovering the ornate Soviet style, underlines the pertinence of studying these reflections of changing Soviet attitudes.

American (and Western) scholarship in Russian architecture has thus far been extremely limited. Several excellent studies of prerevolutionary art have appeared in English, most notably George Heard Hamilton's *The Art and Architecture of Russia*, published in 1954.[1] This book has been well received, and it is regrettable that nothing of comparable stature has appeared for the period since 1917.

The reason for this lack of interest in Soviet art and architecture is not difficult to find. The field is a very specialized one, demanding the skills of a trained architect or art historian—few of whom have, for aesthetic reasons, deemed Soviet works of sufficient interest to merit close inspection, to say nothing of extended study.

In the 1920's, when Russian architects were lurching boldly ahead toward new artistic horizons, this was not true; and American specialists, such as Alfred Barr, now the director of collections for the Museum of Modern Art, made special trips to Russia to see Soviet architecture at first hand.[2] Several English architects also kept a close watch on Soviet developments, as well as one or two Frenchmen.[3] Frank Lloyd Wright went to Russia in 1937, and wrote extensively of his impressions.[4] Talbot Hamlin of Columbia University also wrote on the subject, describing the philosophy and prospects of Soviet architecture.[5] Many German architects worked closely with the Russians, participating directly in their planning.

But in the late 1930's, with the virtual extinction of modern architecture in the U.S.S.R., this interest on the part of Westerners largely disappeared. Articles appeared in architectural journals, sadly or indignantly describing the mounting extravagance and tastelessness of Soviet architecture,[6] but there were no firsthand reports, and very little detailed study. Soviet architecture had, for all practical purposes, isolated itself from the main stream of modern aesthetic thought, and the lack of genuine curiosity which Western architects felt (and still feel) about their Russian colleagues was as natural as the intense curiosity (to which there is much testimony) which Soviet architects feel about Western developments.

Perhaps the decline in professional interest in Russia helps to explain the relatively small amount of scholarly attention paid to Soviet architecture since 1946. Scholarship (in the strict sense of the word) has been limited to the work of three Americans, none of whom has produced a first-rate and complete study. These are Arthur Voyce, who published *Russian Architecture* (New York, 1948), Maurice Frank Parkins, *City Planning in Soviet Russia* (Chicago, 1953), and the present writer, whose study, "Soviet Architecture in Transformation, a Study in Ideological Manipulation," was completed as a Master's essay at the Russian Institute of Columbia University in 1953.[7]

The books by Voyce and Parkins both contain interesting material, but neither volume comes to grips with the major issues posed by the aesthetic changes which occurred in Soviet architecture. In accepting the return to classicism in the thirties as a natural reaction to the intense modernism of the earlier period, Voyce oversimplifies what was a very complex historical process. Parkins, for his part, assumes a degree of continuity in the Soviet approach which the material he has assembled tends to belie. Voyce's book lacks some of the necessary scholarly apparatus.

Parkins' volume, on the other hand, is well documented, and contains an excellent annotated bibliography.

Indeed, in some respects city planning is of greater importance than architecture, since the problems are practical rather than aesthetic and Soviet policy could not so easily indulge itself in the fantasies which seized architecture in the 1930's. Furthermore, here the problems are primarily organizational, and in this field the Soviets have shown themselves considerably more adroit than in the humanities.

The Master's essay by the present writer attempts to deal with the broad questions of long-range change which are not treated by Voyce and Parkins. It traces the major developments, describes the different architectural organizations, summarizes crucial debates, notes important personalities, delineates different styles, and assembles the key governmental decrees and decisions. But it is handicapped by its heavy concentration on purely ideological considerations, in accord with the general goals set for the work, as well as by the author's insufficient knowledge of the complex history of twentieth-century architecture. Much has happened since it was written which would lead the author to modify some of his early conclusions.

Thus there is today no single reliable and thorough study of Soviet architecture; this subject remains a gap in the growing body of American scholarship on Russia.[8] The importance of the subject should not be exaggerated. Soviet architecture conceals as much as, if not more than, it reveals; and the very dearth of interesting or original architecture (as well as of painting, interior design, landscape architecture, graphic design—indeed, all the visual arts) reflects its relative insignificance in the total Soviet picture. Genuinely aesthetic discussions have not been heard in almost a generation; even Khrushchev's 1955 criticism of Stalinist architecture was phrased entirely in economic terms. But insofar as the almost complete destruction of creativity in architecture—

replaced by a mediocre and monotonous monumentality—is itself significant, it does deserve at least one serious full-length study, or at the very least, continuing observation by an experienced scholar. The materials for such a study exist in abundance, and Soviet architects themselves are now accessible, many of whom lived through the years of the greatest aesthetic storms (there have been no architectural purges to speak of).

Such a study could be undertaken in one of two ways: either by encouraging a student with an artistic bent, who is now engaged in Russian area training, to specialize in this field, or by offering a grant to a recognized art historian to make a full-scale study. There are six different realms into which research might profitably be directed:

(1) The great outburst of talent in Russian architecture in the 1920's—associated with the term "constructivism"—is not unknown to Western students. However, its real place in the history of the Russian arts has not yet been documented and assessed. Frequently these early achievements are attributed to the strange and chaotic atmosphere of the immediate postrevolutionary years; however, there are some students who feel that this creative surge was primarily Russian, rather than Soviet, in character and that, as in literature, the theater, and the plastic arts, many of its origins can be traced to prerevolutionary times. Hamilton closes his fine book with the following comment:

That the future [post-World War I] held promise of Russia's increasing participation with Western Europe in the foundation of modern art as we have come to know it and in the development of a particularly Russian revision of that art, there can be no doubt.[9]

An account of the partial fulfillment, in the 1920's, of this promise, and of the subsequent destruction of the "magnificent talents" (Hamilton's term) which Russia exhibited in the first three decades of this century has still to be written. Such an account would conclude an important chapter in the history of Russian art and aesthetics, a chapter for which 1917 was not the decisive year, but which spanned the whole brilliant period from 1900 to 1930.

(2) The crucial years in Soviet architecture, as in so many other fields, were 1928-33. Those were the years in which fundamental decisions were made, in which the Soviet leaders apparently sensed (with amazing intuitive grasp, feeling their way from month to month) that there was something incongruous about modern technological architecture in the new totalitarian state—in spite of the fact that this was the very period in which the building of Russia's extraordinary technological apparatus was being so ruthlessly begun. Lunacharsky delivered an astounding speech on this problem; so did a number of other leaders. Behind the scenes, Kaganovich reorganized the architectural cadres, advancing unknown young men over respected veterans, well before these young men had the faintest notion of why the veterans had to fall. Many architects fought back, and never did accept the new doctrines; countless others yielded. A depth-study of these few years might offer new clues. The documentary material is extensive, including many periodicals, pamphlets, decrees, competition awards, and a number of books, including one full-length Soviet study published a year or two ago.[10]

(3) This writer's essay ended with the year 1936, leaving the intervening years virtually untouched by American scholarship. In architecture very little has happened in these years, except for Khrushchev's 1955 denunciation of Stalinist excesses (in the direction of costly ornamentation); but a cursory study should be made, simply to complete the picture. Particular attention might be paid to reports of abortive attempts in 1944-45 by certain Soviet architects to return to a more simple and human style.

(4) Any further study of Soviet architecture should be undertaken by someone who has actually seen the buildings in their natural setting. This is not merely for aesthetic reasons, but to gain some sense of how people live and work in these enormous and overwrought buildings—how they react to them. Neither

Parkins nor Voyce, nor this writer, could say much on this subject, beyond speculation based on their own limited experience. (Voyce was permitted to spend thirty days in the U.S.S.R. in 1958 and received a friendly reception from Soviet officials and in Soviet institutions concerned with architecture, city planning, and related matters.) The gleaming surfaces of modern architecture, their bold geometric forms, their light-weight walls and free forms, their vast expanses of glass and daring use of exposed steel, have become so much a part of the accepted landscape of the non-Soviet world that it is difficult to imagine that fully one-third of the world's population is growing up today in a milieu utterly barren of these effects.

(5) The field of city planning (of such increasing importance in the West) definitely requires further investigation on the part of American students of Soviet Russia. City planning spans a large horizon—from the aesthetic problems of architecture to the administrative problems of municipal government—and thus provides an excellent view of a wide variety of social policies. Parkins' book neither exhausts the available sources nor offers an analytic foundation by which to judge Soviet policy and practice. In the light of the importance of planning in the U.S.S.R., and in the context of increasing American use of city planning principles, this area would seem a logical one for further research.

(6) The most important task, however, is not one of research, but of evaluation and interpretation. Assuming a certain connection between architectural style and the "inner core" of a civilization, what can be honestly and accurately said about the significance of the monumentalism of Soviet architecture? The omnipotence of the state is one easy answer; and yet the problem seems to lie deeper. Why, in spite of Soviet emphasis on technology, has the regime rejected a technologically inspired architecture? Or is it really correct to reduce modern architecture to technology; is there rather something basically ideological in its nature? Is there something inherently democratic about modern

architecture—simple, direct, functional, utterly incapable of pomp and awesomeness—which the Soviet leaders consider of more importance than any technological consideration? Comparisons with the architecture of Nazi Germany and Fascist Italy, as well as with that of Tito's Yugoslavia and Peron's Argentina, might be profitable.

11

The minor visual arts in the Soviet Union have been characterized by the same developments and trends which we noted in our discussion of architecture. Russian achievements prior to the revolution had brought the country into international artistic preeminence, producing such figures as Kandinsky, Tatlin, Gabo, Pevsner, and Chagall, among others. Although many of these individuals left the country soon after the Revolution, their influence was felt, and indeed nurtured, by Russian artists throughout the 1920's. Magazines employed a bold, imaginative layout, with a great use of color, varied types, montage photography, and superimposed drawings and copy; art exhibits reflected every new movement of European art, including the cubism and expressionism then current. The impact of modern art was evident in posters, book jackets, furniture design, and even in the formal insignia of state. In the 1930's a complete reversal occurred. Posters lost their dazzling color; magazine layout became stodgy and formal; and "realism" became the order of the day in art. Specifically, in each field, this is what happened:

Interior decoration: large formal rooms, frequently with high ceilings, separate treatment of architecture and interior design, rejection of the modern concept of flowing space and flexible partition, little attention to the natural properties of materials, heavy use of wallpaper and formal decorative devices such as moldings, little appreciation of sunlight and direct exposure through the use of glass, heavy carpeting, and huge picture frames.

Furniture design: heavy "Victorian" furniture, lavishly upholstered and decorated, dark wood stains to add to the massive effect, tables covered with "elegant" embroidery, symmetrically arranged flowers, and frequent use of overwrought chandeliers.

Landscaping: formal gardens, axial arrangements, frank imitations of Versailles, Villa d'Este, and other famous seventeenth-century baroque attempts to force nature into a strong, precise human pattern on a large scale, and formal and symmetrical distribution of statues, fountains, walks, and so forth.

Book and magazine layout: again, extremely conservative practices in every field, although with far less lavishness of product; straightforward, unimaginative typography, avoiding both the elaborate styles of the nineteenth century and the imaginative innovations of the twentieth; emphasis on easy readability, as in children's textbooks, rather than on attractiveness of style.

Industrial design: here the Soviets have also taken a conservative approach, either following a completely utilitarian technique (giving no expression to the functional aesthetic implied in the manufactured product, an approach which has revolutionized industrial design in the West over the past twenty-five years) or following a conservative Western precedent—as in the case of automobiles, TV sets, etc.

The sole possible exception to Soviet conservatism in industrial design is in advanced scientific and military apparatus—rocketry, jet aviation, and so forth—where the Russians seem to have followed some of our most daring leads, from the aesthetic as well as the scientific point of view. This field seems to occupy a special place in the Soviet aesthetic world. The principles which prevail in Soviet architecture—notably adherence to the past—could hardly be transferred to the aesthetic side of the design of a jet airplane. However, it is interesting to note that the building which houses Russia's first atomic energy plant was constructed according to the archaic principles of Stalinist architecture. The reconciliation of these two phases of Soviet life—revolutionary science and a reactionary aesthetic—must pose as many problems to the alert Soviet administrator as they do to Western students.

Western research in this field is virtually non-existent, although there has been much informal reporting on the subject from Western travelers. In regard to source materials, however, there is little need for extended work. The evidence is largely pictorial and exists in such abundance that the student need hardly lift a finger to uncover it. Every recent visitor to the Soviet Union may offer his own comments based on firsthand observation.

This vast material must, however, be organized by a competent student, and each of the tentative summary statements put forward above must be confirmed, disputed, or modified, as the case may be. This job is primarily one of collection and arrangement. The contrast with prevailing Western practices and standards will be so marked and clear-cut that little interpretive analysis will be necessary at the first stage of the proposed study. Where the contrast is not marked, as in the field of advanced scientific apparatus (and there are other such exceptions to the general rule, especially if one includes the east European countries and certain non-Russian areas of the U.S.S.R. itself), special evaluation will be required.

After such a fact-finding survey has been completed, the data should be turned over to a sociologist or a social psychologist for further study. The problems are no longer essentially aesthetic, but sociological. In the visual arts this is even truer than in architecture, where certain pseudo-aesthetic ideas are occasionally presented in Soviet work and discussions. But with regard to interior decoration, for example, the problems are practical, intimate, and between the planner and the individual. The key questions which should be asked are:

(1) What is the way of life fostered by this particular type of visual experience? What might the Soviet planners have in mind?

What is the actual result of their decisions? What are the day-to-day consequences of such a visual atmosphere—so seemingly stifling to Westerners accustomed to the light, airy, free-flowing designs and insignia of our life?

(2) How can modern technological activities be conducted in an atmosphere characterized by these archaic formalities and outdated designs? The delicate lace and embroidery, the stuffed sofas, the small windows, the heavy window frames, the ornate lampshades—how do these fit into a life so full of the sharp precision of modern machinery and space orbiting?

These questions have deep ramifications which concern our total evaluation of Soviet life and culture. It may indeed be discovered—with the aid of sociological and psychological research and insights—that although modern visual design springs from industrial life, many phases of modern design inhibit the most efficient behavior in an industrial state. In other words, the sophisticated modern design of the West, based on the machine, may be inimical to the labor discipline so necessary for efficient utilization of the machines. In any case, it is possible that certain Soviet leaders have reasoned this way, and it would be well worth while to examine critically this and alternative suppositions. The study of Soviet visual design may offer some valuable clues to our discussion of the total Soviet culture—particularly the relative importance of its authoritarian and scientific components.

Harold H. Fisher

13. POSTSCRIPT

As I HAVE READ these reports of what has been done and as I look back over the years during which I have had the privilege of watching the development of Slavic studies in this country, I have been struck by the effects of the changes in the motivation of these studies and in the atmosphere in which and the methods by which they have been carried on. I propose to comment on motivation, atmosphere, and methods and to offer six "theses" for the consideration of those who will be making the new record during the next ten years.

In this field of research, as in every other, scholars hope to add to the store of knowledge. To this end they use the methodology of the discipline in which they have been trained in accordance with the principles of intellectual or, as it is sometimes called, academic freedom. The denial of this freedom by the Communists has, of course, affected Russian research by Soviet scholars. It has also affected Russian research by Americans through the restriction or prohibition of library research and field work by foreigners in the U.S.S.R. Soviet policy with respect to cultural exchange has shifted since the 1920's from encouragement to discouragement and back again as the Communist general line has shifted from soft to hard and hard to soft. Individuals and institutions interested in this field are doing their best during the present (1959) soft turn in the Party line to develop the exchange of scholars, students, and materials, but it will not be wise to base our future plans on the belief that the Communists are being won over to our view of intellectual freedom and that their present policy will continue indefinitely.

In our own country during the first decade after the Second World War intellectual freedom was under attack. The quality of Russian research, as the essays in this book show, did not suffer. This was due to the integrity of those who guided or did the research and to the support they received from their own institutions and the interested foundations. But no field of research can be wholly insulated from pressures of this kind whenever they arise, as they do from time to time in our society. Graduate and postgraduate research have their roots in the undergraduate courses which produce young scholars, and all scholars are affected by the general climate of opinion prevailing in the colleges and universities. In their investigation of the effects of the general tension on social science teaching in colleges and universities during what they call "the difficult years," Messrs. Lazarsfeld and Thielens found that the topics most often avoided as dangerously controversial were Communism, Soviet Russia, and Red China, and that the teachers interviewed "often complained of problems in obtaining and using materials needed for their writing and research. Leading the list, of course, are books and pamphlets dealing with Russia and Communism which cannot be obtained or are considered too risky to use."[1]

I am not going to discuss the causes of these tensions or of the changes in the Communist Party line but I should like to make two points that have a bearing on future Russian research.

(1) The Communists may change their policies regarding cultural exchanges, as they have in the past, and prohibit or

effectively discourage research by foreign non-Communists in the U.S.S.R. We should take this possibility into account and not allow our collecting of research materials to decline, but on the contrary we should expand collecting especially in those disciplines in which, as these reports show, more research needs to be done.

(2) The academic mind is under less stress now than during "the difficult years," but this is no guarantee that it will remain so. In fact, it seems to me not only possible but likely that tensions may again be generated as competition between different political and social systems intensifies, regardless of how seemingly peaceful coexistence turns out to be. This possibility ought not to be a matter of indifference to those who will be doing research during the next ten or fifteen years. The best, perhaps the only, way to prepare for this possibility is to create among those who teach and do research in this and other similarly exposed areas a sense of common purpose and mutual support in the exercise of the principles of intellectual freedom which, with private initiative and public support, have made possible the splendid achievements of higher education in the United States in the last sixty years.

Russian research is not self-supporting; it must be considered sufficiently worth while to persuade some people to want to do it and others to want to encourage and help them. The number of persons so persuaded and the amount of moral and material help given them have been determined by two influences. One was an appreciation of Russian culture, an interest in the history, literature, and institutions of Russia, and a belief that a knowledge of these matters was rewarding to those who gained it. A second influence has been an awareness of the growing revolutionary power that originated in Russia, its nearness, thanks to the revolution in communications, and its challenge to our way of life.

Russian activities in the North Pacific in the early years of the last century no doubt disturbed others besides John Quincy Adams, but the American academic community seems not to have been much aroused by these remote affairs or by de Tocqueville's famous prophecy about the two great and growing nations "marked out by the will of Heaven to sway the destinies of half the globe," the one whose principal instrument was freedom, the other servitude. And when Commodore Matthew Calbraith Perry warned of the inevitable mighty battle between the "antagonistic exponents of freedom and absolutism" which would decide "whether despotism or rational liberty must be the fate of civilized man," it appears to have made very little impression on the members of the American Geographical and Statistical Society to whom he gave the warning, and it made no impression at all on the *New York Daily Times,* which did not get around to publishing it until a hundred years later on March 6, 1956.

Two men who, at the turn of the present century, used their considerable influence to establish the study of Russia in American universities were moved, it would appear, by a great liking for the Russian land, Russian culture, and certain qualities of Russian national character which have won the warm admiration of many other Americans. Archibald Cary Coolidge and Charles R. Crane may have had a premonition of the role a nation with such a reservoir of talent would be bound to play. They were certainly aware of and may have been influenced by George Kennan's *Siberia and the Exile System* and by the sympathies of the "American Friends of Russian Freedom" for the pre-Marxist revolutionaries. Probably they read Albert J. Beveridge's rather florid appreciation of Russian achievements as an imperial power and his startled interpretation of Pobedonostsev's exclamation, "Russia is no state; Russia is a world!," but it does not appear that Coolidge and Crane encouraged Russian studies as being required in the national interest. They seem to have believed that the study of Russia, and interestingly enough of the Near East and the Far East, was rewarding and important in itself and that young Americans should have the opportunity to discover this.

The fact that the study of Russia, past and present, has been rewarding and seemed important to many suggests that it should be made possible for more young people to find this out, and what is more, that it is necessary to do this if we hope to achieve the larger quantity and higher quality of research recommended by the contributors to this volume. This is particularly true of those fields of specialization in which much less has been done than in history, literature, and political science. If students who are drawn to such disciplines as economics, sociology, anthropology, philosophy, geography, fine arts, education, and the sciences are to contribute to our knowledge of Russia, they must be enabled to find out that the exercise of these disciplines in the Russian field gives rewards that are worth the extra effort required. These young students will not make this discovery if we merely increase the number of courses in Russian history, literature, comparative government, or comparative "isms," though this would help. It would be even more helpful if those who are teaching in the Russian field and especially those who are training future researchers and teachers made a special effort to inform themselves and then to inform their students why these undermanned sections of the Russian field are interesting and why some knowledge of them is valuable not only to the area specialist but to those whose major interest lies in a discipline which does not have an area focus.

The intellectual satisfactions of Russian area study ought never to be lost sight of, but they are by no means the only motive for work in this field. One need not take at face value the resolution of the Twentieth Congress of the Communist Party of the Soviet Union that "the emergence of socialism from within the bounds of a single country and its transformation into a world system is the main feature of our era," but one should not pretend that this transformation, which might well perplex both Marx and Lenin, is a transitory phenomenon of interest only to historians. A system, as the Communists call it, which in less than fifty years has transformed Russia, has been imposed on a third of the world's population living on a fourth of the earth's surface and commanding about a third of the world's production, and has made some impressive and ominous advances in science and technology calls for study on its own account. Such a study must begin with the Russian area, where the system began and developed, and it should include all the fields of specialization reviewed in this book and some that are not. And it must take into account other areas in which Communists are trying to transplant and adapt an alien order.

Those who direct or support Russian research in the academic world and those who do research and transmit its results all help to form public opinion, but they are also influenced by the prevailing climate of opinion, which is the product of many forces, among them the international situation, economic conditions, technological developments, the current line of the Communist Party, and the policies of the Administration in Washington. The climate of opinion about Russia has changed several times since 1917, reflecting in part the sharp changes in the Communist line. Russia has been viewed as the victim of crackpots and criminals whose cruel depredations were one of the costs of war. Russia has been regarded as the scene of a national revolution which, because it was long overdue, had gone to extremes from which it would swing back as radical policies proved unworkable and as the admirable qualities of the Russian national character prevailed. This happy outcome seemed nearer realization when Soviet Russia, after some disturbing incidents, was on our side in the Second World War. Then suddenly when the war was over and the main trend of Soviet policy became clear, the atmosphere changed again. The urge to diabolize replaced the temptation to eulogize. "Know the enemy" was added to the traditional motives for research in fields relating to national security.

And now the climate of opinion is changing once more. Public opinion has been stirred and confused by the unfolding of Khrushchev's policies in the U.S.S.R., in Europe and the Middle East, and in outer space, by the lengthening shadow of Maoist China, by polemics over revisionism, dogmatism, and literary treason, by atomic threats, impressive production figures, and a modest resumption of cultural exchange. This disturbed atmosphere has led to much soul-searching, shrill and often uninformed denunciations of our whole educational system, and demands for crash programs to close the gap.

Two aspects of this agitation are of concern to Russian research. One, which affects other areas equally, is the current tendency to stress the physical sciences to the detriment of the humanities and the social sciences. Another problem is that since the Second World War the government has taken an increasing interest in stimulating research on the Soviet Union. I am concerned lest in recognizing the necessity for government research and more emphasis on science, we assume that the more government research we have, the less private enterprise research we need. I am convinced that the contrary is true. Of course we need government-directed intelligence and scientific research of the highest quality, and our needs will increase during the coming years. At the same time, to maintain the high quality of government research and to meet the increasing need for trained minds, we must enlarge the scope of private training and research untrammeled by the exigencies of pressing issues or shifts in official policy.

A number of thoughtful people have come to the conclusion that what the Communists now call "the socialist world system" should not be looked upon as just a resourceful and wicked conspiracy aimed at world domination, but as a method of organizing society in the age of industrialism. This view stresses the achievements of the Soviet Union in economic development, political power, and technical and social progress. The Communists appear to be accomplishing this by combining a remarkable operational flexibility with an inflexible retention of a power monopoly exercised by the Communist Party through a totalitarian despotism which shows no immediate signs of disintegrating, withering away, or mellowing.[2]

With this view I agree, but I should like to add that events seem to indicate that the further the socialist world system is extended, the more difficult appear to be the problems of rigid, centralized control. It seems to me unlikely that problems of this character can be solved by operational flexibility alone. This suggests that with or even without further extension of the system, these control problems may profoundly modify the relations of the members of the system with each other and inevitably with the rest of the world.

With this proviso, my first thesis is: That the Communist movement should not be regarded merely as a new formula of revolt and a new and efficient method of oppression, which it is, but also as a movement firmly and powerfully established in the Soviet Union and dedicated to the promotion throughout the world of a form of social organization evolved in Russia. This implies due emphasis in teaching and research on both the undeniable accomplishments and the undeniable costs of the Communist system. It implies study both of the relation of some of the features of this system to Russia's past and of Soviet Russia's inheritance from the achievements of Imperial Russia.

Second, that there is need today for more emphasis on interpretive writing on Tsarist and Soviet Russia to supplement the impressive body of monographic studies now available. To the extent that much monographic work has been based on assumptions drawn from west European or American experience, it would be useful to test new interpretations based on the unique factors in Russia's development and on comparative studies of conditions in the non-Western world.

Third, that studies of contemporary Russia cannot be separated from the Communist movement and that since the Communist movement is transnational and interactive, special efforts should be made to have liaison with and, where possible, to cooperate in studies of other areas where Communist rule has been set up or where the achievements of the Communists have great attraction.

Fourth, that the greatest contributions to knowledge and the public interest will be made if the results of research in relevant disciplines are integrated, or at least interrelated. This does not mean the substitution of group research for individual research, for which there is no substitute. The work of the individual scholar will nevertheless be enriched by knowledge of what has been done and of the methods used in other disciplines. This implies "the timely application of appropriate stimuli," as Professor Whitfield puts it, to those fields of specialization in which, as these essays show, more research might well be done. It also implies patient and continued effort to work out ways to maintain interdisciplinary contact and to integrate the contributions of the different disciplines when integration will give a deeper understanding of what is being investigated.

Fifth, that the results of research in the Russian field should be transmitted to the people of this country through general education and the various media of communication in order to provide the basis for informed discussion of issues of great moment to us all. This means more cooperation with teachers and other agents of enlightenment who, because of distance from centers of research or lack of access to the products of research, are sometimes out of touch with work being done in this field.

Sixth, that the advancement of research as well as the public interest are best served by the maximum exchange of views of those doing research and the maximum availability of research materials. This means making the most of inventions that facilitate the communication of materials and ideas. It also means the expansion of exchanges already begun with countries in which Slavic studies have long been established like France, Britain, and Germany, with countries where such studies have been more lately initiated such as Japan, Turkey, and India, and with the countries of the Soviet orbit.

Most of the suggestions made by others and by me in this book are a lot easier to propose than to effect. They are, in fact, aspirations. They demand patience, which most scholars have, time and money, which they have not—at least not enough—and a capacity for cooperation. What is most needed, perhaps, is a realization that the intention to deepen and disseminate knowledge of Russia and the Communist movement during the next decade is more than a worth-while form of academic enterprise; it is a proposal to test the resourcefulness and integrity of scholarship in applying the principles of intellectual freedom to the fateful and controversial issues of our century.

NOTES

2. HISTORY

1. *Peter the Great* (2 vols.; New York, 1884).
2. See especially his address to the American Historical Association in December, 1895, entitled "A Plea for the Study of the History of Northern Europe," *American Historical Review*, II (October, 1896), 34-39.
3. *Slavic Europe: A Selected Bibliography in the Western European Languages* (Cambridge, Mass., 1918).
4. *Russian Expansion on the Pacific, 1641-1850* (Cleveland, 1914).
5. *The Russia I Believe In: The Memoirs of Samuel N. Harper, 1902-1941* (Chicago, 1945).
6. George Kennan, *Siberia and the Exile System* (2 vols.; New York, 1891); Albert J. Beveridge, *The Russian Advance* (New York, 1904).
7. This series was edited by Sir Paul Vinogradoff until his death in 1925, and thereafter by Professor Michael T. Florinsky, who contributed a valuable summary volume: *The End of the Russian Empire* (New Haven, 1931).
8. Frederick S. Rodkey, *The Turco-Egyptian Question in the Relations of England, France, and Russia, 1832-1841* (Urbana, 1924); William L. Langer, *The Franco-Russian Alliance, 1890-1894* (Cambridge, Mass., 1929); B. P. Thomas, *Russo-American Relations, 1815-67* (Baltimore, 1930); Vernon J. Puryear, *England, Russia and the Straits Question, 1844-1856* (Berkeley, 1931); Philip E. Mosely,

NOTES TO PAGE 25

Russian Diplomacy and the Opening of the Eastern Question in 1838 and 1839 (Cambridge, Mass., 1934); A. Lobanov-Rostovsky, *Russia and Asia* (1st ed., New York, 1933; 2nd ed., Ann Arbor, 1951); Leonid I. Strakhovsky, *The Origins of American Intervention in North Russia* (Princeton, 1937), and *Intervention in Archangel* (Princeton, 1944); Sergius Yakobson, "Russia and Africa," *Slavonic and East European Review*, XVII (1938-39), 623-37; XIX (1939-40), 158-74; R. P. Churchill, *The Anglo-Russian Convention of 1907* (Cedar Rapids, 1939); C. E. Black, *The Establishment of Constitutional Government in Bulgaria* (Princeton, 1943).

9. Geroid T. Robinson, *Rural Russia Under the Old Regime* (New York, 1932; new ed., 1949); George Stewart, *The White Armies of Russia: A Chronicle of Counter-Revolution and Allied Intervention* (New York, 1933); A. G. Mazour, *The First Russian Revolution, 1825* (Berkeley, 1937); Douglas K. Reading, *The Anglo-Russian Commercial Treaty of 1734* (New Haven, 1938); Alfred Levin, *The Second Duma: A Study of the Social-Democratic Party and the Russian Constitutional Experiment* (New Haven, 1940); John S. Curtiss, *Church and State in Russia: The Last Years of the Empire, 1900-1917* (New York, 1940); Robert J. Kerner, *The Urge to the Sea: The Course of Russian History* (Berkeley, 1942); Raymond H. Fisher, *The Russian Fur Trade, 1550-1700* (Berkeley, 1943); G. V. Lantzeff, *Siberia in the Seventeenth Century: A Study in Colonial Administration* (Berkeley, 1943).

10. H. H. Fisher, *The Famine in Soviet Russia, 1919-1923: The Operation of the American Relief Administration* (New York, 1927); T. A. Taracouzio, *Soviets in the Arctic: An Historical, Economic, and Political Study of the Soviet Advance into the Arctic* (New York, 1938); Calvin B. Hoover, *The Economic Life of Soviet Russia* (New York, 1931); D. Fedotoff White, *The Growth of the Red Army* (Princeton, 1944); Samuel N. Harper, *Civic Training in Soviet Russia* (Chicago, 1929), and *Making Bolsheviks* (Chicago, 1931); W. R. Batsell, *Soviet Rule in Russia* (New York, 1929); Matthew Spinka, *The Church and the Russian Revolution* (New York, 1927); Nicholas S. Timasheff, *Religion in Soviet Russia, 1917-1942* (New York, 1942); Paul B. Anderson, *People, Church, and State in Modern Russia* (London, 1944); J. Bunyan and H. H. Fisher, *The Bolshevik Revolution, 1917-1918: Documents and Materials* (Stanford, 1934); Elena Varneck and H. H. Fisher, *The Testimony of Kolchak and Other Siberian Materials* (Stanford, 1935); James Bunyan, *Intervention, Civil War, and Communism in Russia, April-*

December, 1918: Documents and Materials (Baltimore, 1936); Olga H. Gankin and H. H. Fisher, *The Bolsheviks and the World War: The Origin of the Third International* (Stanford, 1940); Kathryn Davis, *The Soviets at Geneva: The U.S.S.R. and the League of Nations, 1919-1933* (Geneva, 1934); W. L. Mahaney, Jr., *The Soviet Union, the League of Nations and Disarmament: 1917-1935* (Philadelphia, 1940).

11. Anatole G. Mazour, *An Outline of Modern Russian Historiography* (Berkeley, 1939; 2nd ed., Princeton, 1958); F. C. Barghoorn, "The Russian Radicals of the 1860's and the Problem of the Industrial Proletariat," *Slavonic and East European Review* (American Series, II), XXI (March, 1943), 57-69; Michael Karpovich, "Klyuchevski and Recent Trends in Russian Historiography," *ibid.*, 31-39, and "A Forerunner of Lenin: P. N. Tkachev," *Review of Politics*, VI (July, 1944), 336-50.

12. Vernadsky: (New Haven, 1943, 1948, 1953); Florinsky: (2 vols.; New York, 1953).

13. Alexander A. Vasiliev, *The Russian Attack on Constantinople in 860* (Cambridge, Mass., 1946); Samuel H. Cross, *Slavic Civilization through the Ages* (Cambridge, Mass., 1948); William K. Medlin, *Moscow and East Rome: A Political Study of the Relations of Church and State in Muscovite Russia* (Geneva, 1952); Douglas M. Dunlop, *The History of the Jewish Khazars* (Princeton, 1954); Francis Dvornik, *The Slavs: Their Early History and Civilization* (Boston, 1956); and Jerome Blum, "The Beginnings of Large-scale Private Landownership in Russia," *Speculum*, XXVIII (1953), 781-790, "The *Smerd* in Kievan Russia," *American Slavic and East European Review*, XII (1953), 125-29, and "The Rise of Serfdom in Eastern Europe," *American Historical Review*, LXII (1957), 807-36.

14. C. B. O'Brien, *Russia under Two Tsars, 1682-1689* (Berkeley, 1952); Peter B. Putnam (ed.), *Seven Britons in Imperial Russia, 1698-1812* (Princeton, 1952); J. R. Masterson and H. Brower, *Bering's Successors, 1745-1780* (Seattle, 1948); Marc Raeff, *Siberia and the Reforms of 1822* (Seattle, 1956); Donald W. Treadgold, *The Great Siberian Migration* (Princeton, 1957).

15. David Hecht, *Russian Radicals Look to America, 1825-1894* (Cambridge, Mass., 1947); Bertram D. Wolfe, *Three Who Made a Revolution* (New York, 1948); Frederick C. Barghoorn, "D. I. Pisarev: a Representative of Russian Nihilism," *Review of Politics*, X (April, 1948), 190-211; Nicholas V. Riasanovsky, *Russia and the West in the Teachings of the Slavophiles* (Cambridge, Mass., 1952);

Hans Kohn, *Panslavism: Its History and Ideology* (Notre Dame, 1953); Leopold H. Haimson, *The Russian Marxists and the Origins of Bolshevism* (Cambridge, Mass., 1955); Donald W. Treadgold, *Lenin and His Rivals: The Struggle for Russia's Future, 1898-1906* (New York, 1955); Michael B. Petrovich, *The Emergence of Russian Panslavism, 1856-1870* (New York, 1956); Alfred G. Meyer, *Leninism* (Cambridge, Mass., 1957); George Fischer, *Russian Liberalism: From Gentry to Intelligentsia* (Cambridge, Mass., 1958); James H. Billington, *Mikhailovsky and Russian Populism* (Oxford, 1958).

The variety of interest in Russian intellectual history is reflected in the essays in Ernest J. Simmons (ed.), *Continuity and Change in Russian and Soviet Thought* (Cambridge, Mass., 1955); and Hugh McLean, Martin E. Malia, and George Fischer (eds.), *Russian Thought and Politics* ("Harvard Slavic Studies," Vol. IV; Cambridge, Mass., 1957), dedicated to Professor Michael Karpovich.

16. Leonid I. Strakhovsky, *Alexander I of Russia* (New York, 1947); Marc Raeff, *Michael Speransky: Statesman of Imperial Russia, 1772-1839* (The Hague, 1957); Samuel Kucherov, *Courts, Lawyers, and Trials under the Last Three Tsars* (New York, 1953); William H. E. Johnson, *Russia's Educational Heritage: Teacher Education in the Russian Empire, 1600-1917* (Pittsburgh, 1950); David M. Lang, *The Last Years of the Georgian Monarchy, 1658-1837* (New York, 1957); Oliver H. Radkey, *The Agrarian Foes of Bolshevism* (New York, 1958).

17. Stuart R. Tompkins, *Alaska: Promyshlennik and Sourdough* (Norman, Okla., 1945); Edward H. Zabriskie, *American-Russian Rivalry in the Far East: A Study in Diplomacy and Power Politics, 1895-1914* (New York, 1946); M. N. Pavlovsky, *Russian-Chinese Relations* (New York, 1949); David Dallin, *The Rise of Russia in Asia* (New Haven, 1949); A. Lobanov-Rostovsky, *Russia and Europe, 1789-1825* (Durham, N. C., 1947), and *Russia and Europe, 1825-1878* (Ann Arbor, 1954); Walther Kirchner, *The Rise of the Baltic Question* (Newark, Del., 1954); George A. Lensen, *Russia's Japan Expedition of 1852 to 1855* (Gainesville, Fla., 1955); C. Jay Smith, Jr., *The Russian Struggle for Power, 1914-1917: A Study of Russian Foreign Policy during the First World War* (New York, 1956); Charles Jelavich, *Tsarist Russia and Balkan Nationalism: Russian Influence in the Internal Affairs of Bulgaria and Serbia, 1879-86* (Berkeley, 1958).

18. Simon Liberman, *Building Lenin's Russia* (Chicago, 1945) and William Reswick, *I Dreamt Revolution* (Chicago, 1952).

19. Nicholas S. Timasheff, *The Great Retreat: The Growth and Decline of Communism in Russia* (New York, 1946); Frederick L. Schuman, *Soviet Politics at Home and Abroad* (New York, 1948), and *Russia Since 1917* (New York, 1957); Barrington Moore, Jr., *Soviet Politics: The Dilemma of Power* (Cambridge, Mass., 1950); David J. Dallin, *The Changing World of Soviet Russia* (New Haven, 1956).

20. Oliver H. Radkey, *The Election to the Russian Constituent Assembly of 1917* (Cambridge, Mass., 1950); Richard Pipes, *The Formation of the Soviet Union: Communism and Nationalism, 1917-1923* (Cambridge, Mass., 1954); George Barr Carson, Jr., *Electoral Practices in the U.S.S.R.* (New York, 1956); Zbigniew Brzezinski, *The Permanent Purge: Politics in Soviet Totalitarianism* (Cambridge, Mass., 1956).

21. John A. Armstrong, *Ukrainian Nationalism, 1939-1945* (New York, 1955); John S. Reshetar, Jr., *The Ukrainian Revolution, 1917-1920* (Princeton, 1952); Basil Dmytryshyn, *Moscow and the Ukraine, 1918-1953* (New York, 1957); A. G. Park, *Bolshevism in Turkestan, 1917-1927* (New York, 1957); F. Kazemzadeh, *The Struggle for Transcaucasia, 1917-1921* (New York, 1951); Nicholas P. Vakar, *Belorussia: The Making of a Nation* (Cambridge, Mass., 1956).

22. R. P. Casey, *Religion in Russia* (New York, 1946); John S. Curtiss, *The Russian Church and the Soviet State* (Boston, 1953); Matthew Spinka, *The Church and Soviet Russia* (New York, 1956); George Fischer, *Soviet Opposition to Stalin* (Cambridge, Mass., 1952); George Barr Carson, Jr., "Changing Perspectives in Soviet Historiography," *South Atlantic Quarterly*, XLVII (April, 1948), 186-95; Sergius Yakobson, "Postwar Historical Research in the Soviet Union," *Annals of the American Academy of Political and Social Science*, CCLXIII (May, 1949), 123-33; Anatole G. Mazour and Herman E. Bateman, "Recent Conflicts in Soviet Historiography," *Journal of Modern History*, XXIV (March, 1952), 56-68; Alfred A. Skerpan, "Modern Russian Historiography," *Kent State University Bulletin (Research Series I)*, XL (October, 1952), 37-60; C. E. Black (ed.), *Rewriting Russian History: Soviet Interpretations of Russia's Past* (New York, 1956).

23. These publications are discussed in other chapters in this volume.

24. John A. White, *The Siberian Intervention* (Princeton, 1950); Robert P. Browder, *The Origins of Soviet-American Diplomacy*

(Princeton, 1953); Robert D. Warth, *The Allies and the Russian Revolution* (Durham, N. C., 1954); Betty Miller Unterberger, *America's Siberian Expedition, 1918-1920* (Durham, N. C., 1956); George F. Kennan, *Russia Leaves the War* (Princeton, 1956), and *The Decision to Intervene* (Princeton, 1958).

25. Pauline Tompkins, *American-Russian Relations in the Far East* (New York, 1949); Max M. Laserson, *The American Impact on Russia: Diplomacy and Ideology, 1784-1917* (New York, 1950); Thomas A. Bailey, *America Faces Russia: Russian-American Relations from Early Times to Our Day* (Ithaca, 1950); William A. Williams, *American-Russian Relations, 1781-1947* (New York, 1952); William H. McNeill, *America, Britain, and Russia: Their Co-operation and Conflict, 1941-1946* (London, 1953); Herbert Feis, *Churchill—Roosevelt—Stalin: The War They Waged and the Peace They Sought* (Princeton, 1957).

26. Harriet L. Moore, *Soviet Far Eastern Relations, 1931-1945* (Princeton, 1945); David J. Dallin, *Soviet Russia and the Far East* (New Haven, 1948), and *Soviet Espionage* (New Haven, 1955); Rodger Swearingen and Paul Langer, *Red Flag in Japan: International Communism in Action, 1919-1951* (Cambridge, Mass., 1952); Robert C. North, *Moscow and Chinese Communists* (Stanford, 1953); Allen S. Whiting, *Soviet Politics in China, 1917-1924* (New York, 1954); John N. Kautsky, *Moscow and the Communist Party of India* (New York, 1956); Henry Wei, *China and Soviet Russia* (Princeton, 1956); David T. Cattell, *Communism and the Spanish Civil War* (Berkeley, 1955), and *Soviet Diplomacy and the Spanish Civil War* (Berkeley, 1957); George Lenczowski, *Russia and the West in Iran, 1918-1948* (Ithaca, 1949); Gerhard L. Weinberg, *Germany and the Soviet Union, 1939-1941* (Leiden, 1954); Alexander Dallin, *German Rule in Russia, 1941-1945* (New York, 1957); Robert J. Alexander, *Communism in Latin America* (New Brunswick, 1957); Xenia J. Eudin and H. H. Fisher, *Soviet Russia and the West, 1920-1927: A Documentary Survey* (Stanford, 1957); Xenia J. Eudin and Robert C. North, *Soviet Russia and the East, 1920-1927: A Documentary Survey* (Stanford, 1957); Gerald Freund, *Unholy Alliance* (New York, 1957); Clarence J. Smith, *Finland and the Russian Revolution, 1917-1923* (Athens, Ga., 1956); Anatole G. Mazour, *Finland between East and West* (Princeton, 1956).

27. *Canadian Slavonic Papers* (Toronto, 1956 ff., annual); *Est et Ouest* (Paris, 1949 ff., semimonthly); *Slavic and East-European Studies* (Montreal, 1956 ff., quarterly); *Europe de l'Est et Union*

Soviétique (Paris, 1957 ff., quarterly); *Jahrbücher für Geschichte Osteuropas* (Munich, 1953 ff., quarterly); *Osteuropa* (Stuttgart, 1951 ff., monthly); *Revue des Etudes Slaves* (Paris, 1921 ff., annual); *Die Slavische Rundschau* (Munich, 1956 ff., bimonthly); *Slavonic and East European Review* (London, 1922 ff., semiannual); *Soviet Studies* (Glasgow, 1949 ff., quarterly); *Die Welt der Slaven* (Munich, 1956 ff., quarterly).

28. For example: A. N. Kurat, *Isvec Kirali XII Karl 'in Türkiyede Kalisi ve bu siralarda Osmanli Imparatorlugu* [The residence in Turkey of King Charles XII of Sweden and the Ottoman empire at that time] (Istanbul, 1943), and *Rusya Tarihi* [History of Russia] (Ankara, 1948); M. N. Roy, *The Russian Revolution* (Calcutta, 1949); and M. R. Masani, *The Communist Party of India: A Short History* (New York, 1954).

29. See Peter Berton, Paul Langer, and Rodger Swearingen, *Japanese Training and Research in the Russian Field* (Los Angeles, 1956).

30. There is a valuable description of Russian collections in American libraries in Charles Morley, *Guide to Research in Russian History* (Syracuse, 1951).

3. ECONOMICS

1. *Review of Economics and Statistics*, XXIX, No. 4 (November, 1947).

2. See the reply to *Fortune* by E. Varga, *ibid.* (July, 1957); to G. Warren Nutter in *New Times*, June 15, 1957; to J. P. Hardt in *Elektrichestvo* (1957); to David Granick and to the Joint Economic Committee (U.S. Congress) in *Voprosy Ekonomiki*, XI (1957); and by academician Ostrovityanov to various critics of the Soviet index of industrial production in *The Times* (London), February 6, 1958. That this constitutes a definite policy, at least on the part of the Academy of Sciences of the U.S.S.R., is indicated in *Voprosy Ekonomiki*, XI (1957), 160.

3. Where the regimens of weights are drawn from years at different stages of industrialization, this index number phenomenon is now often referred to as the "Gerschenkron effect." For striking illustrations of the "effect," see Alexander Gerschenkron, *A Dollar Index of Soviet Machinery Output, 1927-28 to 1937* (Santa Monica: The RAND Corporation, 1951), chap. 4.

4. See Abram Bergson, *Soviet National Income and Product in*

1937 (New York, 1953), chap. 3, on the nature of the alternative standards.

5. This is essentially the approach of both Naum Jasny in his growth study, *The Soviet Economy during the Plan Era* (Stanford, 1951), and of the Bergson-RAND project currently in progress.

6. Demitri B. Shimkin, *Minerals: A Key to Soviet Power* (Cambridge, Mass., 1953), chap. IX; Francis Seton, *The Tempo of Soviet Industrial Expansion* (Manchester, 1957); Raymond P. Powell, *A Materials-Input Index of Soviet Construction, 1927/28 to 1955* (The RAND Corporation, Parts I and II, RM-1872 and RM-1873, 1957); D. Gale Johnson, *A Study of the Growth Potential of Agriculture of the USSR* (The RAND Corporation, RM-1561, 1955).

7. Naum Jasny, *The Socialized Agriculture of the USSR* (Stanford, 1949); M. Gardner Clark, *The Economics of Soviet Steel* (Cambridge, Mass., 1956); Holland Hunter, *Soviet Transportation Policy* (Cambridge, Mass., 1957).

8. Shimkin, *op. cit.;* John P. Hardt, *Economics of the Soviet Electric Power Industry* (Research Studies Institute, Air University [mimeographed], 1955); James H. Blackman, *Transport Development and Locomotive Technology* ("Essays in Economics," No. 3, Bureau of Business and Economic Research, University of South Carolina, 1957); Timothy Sosnovy, *The Housing Problem in the Soviet Union,* Research Program on the U.S.S.R. (New York, 1954).

9. Solomon M. Schwarz, *Labor in the Soviet Union* (New York, 1951). At this point note should also be made of Walter Galenson's major statistical study, *Labor Productivity in Soviet and American Industry* (New York, 1954).

10. A helpful start in this direction is Jerzy Gliksman's *Postwar Trends in Soviet Labor Policy* (The RAND Corporation, P-754, 1955), and various articles by the same author.

11. Abram Bergson, *The Structure of Soviet Wages* (Cambridge, Mass., 1946).

12. Franklyn D. Holzman, *Soviet Taxation* (Cambridge, Mass., 1955); Raymond P. Powell, "Soviet Monetary Policy" (Ph.D. dissertation, University of California, 1952). Mikhail V. Condoide's *The Soviet Financial System* (Columbus, 1951) is less analytical.

13. Alexander Baykov, *The Development of the Soviet Economic System* (Cambridge, England, 1946); Maurice Dobb, *Soviet Economic Development since 1917* (New York, 1948). These two books are sometimes also thought of as basic textbooks. As such, they seem

to be much less in use in this country than the standard (and only) American textbook: Harry Schwartz, *Russia's Soviet Economy* (2d ed., New York, 1954).

14. Joseph S. Berliner, *Factory and Manager in the USSR* (Cambridge, Mass., 1957); David Granick, *Management of the Industrial Firm in the USSR* (New York, 1954). See also Gregory Bienstock et al., *Management in Russian Industry and Agriculture* (New York, 1948); Alexander Vucinich, *Soviet Economic Institutions* (Stanford, 1952); and relevant sections of Raymond A. Bauer et al., *How the Soviet System Works* (Cambridge, Mass., 1956). At this point may be also mentioned the helpful survey, based on secondary sources, of "The Organization of Economic Activity in the Soviet Union" by Andrew G. Frank (*Weltwirtschaftliches Archiv*, 78:1 [1957], 104-156).

15. Lazar Volin's numerous articles; Naum Jasny's *Socialized Agriculture, op. cit.* and many articles; Herbert Dinerstein, *Communism and the Russian Peasant* (Glencoe, Ill., 1955).

16. See Norman Kaplan, "Investment Alternatives in Soviet Economic Theory," *Journal of Political Economy*, LX, No. 2 (April, 1952), 133-44; and Gregory Grossman, "Scarce Capital and Soviet Doctrine," *Quarterly Journal of Economics*, LXVII, No. 3 (August, 1953), 311-43, as well as the literature cited in footnote 1 thereof. For more recent developments, see also A. Zauberman, "A Note on Soviet Capital Controversy," *ibid.*, LXIX, No. 3 (August, 1955), 445-51.

17. E. g., Gardner Clark, *op. cit.*, Blackman, *op. cit.* Also note Granick's work on technological choice in the metalworking industry still in progress with interim reports by him in "Economic Development and Productivity Analysis: the Case of Soviet Metalworking," *Quarterly Journal of Economics*, LXXI, No. 2 (May, 1957), 205-33, and "Organization and Technology in Soviet Metalworking: Some Conditioning Factors," *American Economic Review*, XLVII, No. 2 (May, 1957), 631-42.

18. Norman Kaplan, "Arithmancy, Theomancy, and the Soviet Economy," *Journal of Political Economy*, LXI, No. 2 (April, 1953), 110. The paragraph from which the quotation is taken is a plea for "a model of the Soviet economic system, a theory of 'perfect Soviet socialism' ...," with which the present author substantially agrees.

19. Naum Jasny, *The Soviet Price System* (Stanford, 1951) and *Soviet Prices of Producers' Goods* (Stanford, 1952).

20. For the meaning of these terms and their use see: Bergson, *Soviet National Income and Product in 1937, op. cit.*; Bergson and Hans Heymann, Jr., *Soviet National Income and Product, 1940-48* (New York, 1954); Oleg Hoeffding, *Soviet National Income and Product in 1928* (New York, 1954).

21. See *Soviet Studies,* October, 1956, and subsequent issues.

22. Bergson's studies in question are essentially the books by himself and his associates cited in note 20 above; Donald R. Hodgman, *Soviet Industrial Production, 1928-1951* (Cambridge, Mass., 1954), and "A New Production Index for Soviet Industry," *Review of Economics and Statistics,* XXXII, No. 4 (November, 1950), 325-338.

23. For example, many of the contributions to Abram Bergson (ed.), *Soviet Economic Growth* (Evanston, 1953); Norman Kaplan, *Capital Investments in the Soviet Union, 1924-1951* (The RAND Corporation, RM-735, 1951); Walter Galenson, *op. cit.*; Nicholas DeWitt, *Soviet Professional Manpower* (Washington, 1955).

24. Alexander Erlich, "Preobrazhenskii and the Economics of Soviet Industrialization," *Quarterly Journal of Economics,* LXIV, No. 1 (February, 1950), 57-88, and "Stalin's Views on Soviet Economic Development," in Ernest J. Simmons (ed.), *Continuity and Change in Russian and Soviet Thought* (Cambridge, Mass., 1955). A book-length study on the industrialization debates is now under preparation by the same author. Another postwar American publication on the economic theorizing of the twenties is Adam Kaufman, "The Origin of the 'Political Economy of Socialism'," *Soviet Studies,* IV, No. 3 (January, 1953), 243-72.

25. See, for example, the valuable recent study of the ideologies of industrialism in prerevolutionary Russia and in the postwar Soviet orbit by a sociologist: Reinhard Bendix, *Work and Authority in Industry* (New York, 1956), esp. chaps. 3 and 6.

26. "Study of Soviet Economic Growth," National Bureau of Economic Research, Inc., under the direction of G. Warren Nutter (originally under Raymond W. Goldsmith).

27. Under the supervision of Norman M. Kaplan, and with the collaboration of the Stanford Research Institute.

4. POLITICAL SCIENCE

1. A brief preliminary version of this paper was presented and discussed at a meeting of Soviet area specialists during the convention

of the American Political Science Association, New York, September, 1957.

2. Such topics are, of course, appropriate for the study of certain pre-Soviet Russian political institutions; indeed, one of the earliest scholarly works on Russia by an American, Samuel N. Harper's *The New Electoral Law for the Russian Duma* (Chicago, 1908), dealt with such a theme. In general, coverage of Tsarist political institutions is part of the general treatment of Russian history prior to the Revolution, and is not reviewed in this paper. Three works now in progress which promise to be of special interest to the student of comparative politics should, however, be mentioned: Marc Szeftel's "The Political Institutions of the Russian Constitutional Monarchy (1905-1917)"; C. E. Black's "The Founding of the Modern Russian State: The Administrative Reforms of Peter the Great;" and Serge Levitsky's "Studies in the Procedure of the Russian Duma."

3. A notable example of books in the first category is Malbone W. Graham, *New Governments of Eastern Europe* (New York, 1927).

4. See especially *Civic Training in Soviet Russia* (Chicago, 1929) and *The Government of the Soviet Union* (New York, 1938).

5. For a comprehensive list of studies published by American scholars in the Soviet area field since 1947, and of work now in progress, see *Soviet Studies in the United States: A Survey of American Social Science Research on Soviet Russia, 1947-1957* (prepared in mimeographed form by the External Research Staff, Department of State).

6. Meyer's work on Marxism deals largely with non-Russian schools of Marxist thought. A number of other books on Marxism are discussed in the section on political philosophy in the chapter reviewing research in Russian and Soviet philosophy and religion.

7. Bertram D. Wolfe, *Three Who Made a Revolution* (New York, 1948); Leonard Schapiro, *The Origin of the Communist Autocracy* (Cambridge, Mass., 1955).

8. "Stalin's Vision of Utopia," *Proceedings of the American Philosophical Society*, XCIX, No. 1 (January 27, 1955), 11-21.

9. "Stalin on Revolution," *Foreign Affairs*, XXVII, No. 2 (January, 1949), 175-214.

10. *The Prophet Armed: Trotsky, 1879-1921* (New York, 1954). Deutscher is preparing a continuation of this treatment of Trotsky; Sidney Heitman is preparing a history Ph.D. dissertation on Bukharin (Columbia University); another dissertation (J. E. Flaherty, "The Political Career of Nicholas Bukharin") was completed at New York

University in 1954. For information on dissertations in the Soviet field, I am indebted to the Research Program on the Communist Party of the Soviet Union, for which Kermit Mackenzie prepared a comprehensive list.

11. *Le Marxisme en Union Soviétique* (Paris, 1955).
12. *Dialectical Materialism: A Historical and Systematic Survey of Philosophy in the Soviet Union* (New York, 1958).
13. *Der Sowjetrussische dialektische Materialismus (Diamat)* (Bern, 1950).
14. *Soviet Marxism* (New York, 1958).
15. Most of the studies of "political behavior" fall under this heading. Essentially, however, "behavioral" studies are an approach or a method rather than a distinct subject matter, and consequently will not be considered separately here.
16. An important study of this nature, now nearing completion, is Robert V. Daniels' "A History of Opposition in the Russian Communist Party."
17. Julian Towster, *Political Power in the USSR* (New York, 1948); Barrington Moore, Jr., *Soviet Politics: The Dilemma of Power* (Cambridge, Mass., 1950); Boris Meissner, *Russland im Umbruch* (Frankfurt a.M., 1951); Merle Fainsod, *How Russia Is Ruled* (Cambridge, Mass., 1954); Raymond Bauer, Alex Inkeles, and Clyde Kluckhohn, *How the Soviet System Works* (Cambridge, Mass., 1956); John N. Hazard, *The Soviet System of Government* (Chicago, 1957).
18. The historian Sidney Harcave's study, *The Structure and Functioning of the Lower Party Organizations in the Soviet Union* (Technical Research Report Number 23 of the Human Resources Research Institute Project, "An Analysis of the Soviet Social System," Maxwell Air Force Base, Alabama, 1954); a study of the political indoctrination system of the Soviet Army prepared by the political scientist Louis Nemzer for the Department of the Army; Herbert Dinerstein, *Communism and the Russian Peasant,* and Dinerstein and Leon Gouré, *Moscow in Crisis* (the latter two studies published in a single volume, Glencoe, Ill., 1955).
19. A few solidly based articles of a monographic nature should be noted. See especially Louis Nemzer's "The Kremlin's Professional Staff," *American Political Science Review,* XLIV (March, 1950), 64-85; and Merle Fainsod's "Controls and Tensions in the Soviet System." *ibid.,* XLIV (June, 1950), 266-82.

20. This topic is to be the subject of a book-length monograph being written by Mark Neuweld: "The Central Organization of the Communist Party of the Soviet Union."

21. See note 18.

22. Merle Fainsod, *Smolensk under Soviet Rule* (Cambridge, Mass., 1958). See also John A. Armstrong, *The Soviet Bureaucratic Elite: A Case Study of the Ukrainian Apparatus* (New York, 1959); and a dissertation by M. Rywkin being prepared for the Department of Public Law and Government, Columbia University, on the Uzbek Party organization.

23. In addition to those mentioned in note 22 above, two British Ph.D. candidates are treating the subject: T. H. Rigby, "The Selection of Leading Personnel in the Soviet State and Communist Party," University of London; and S. Utechin, "The Formation of the Ruling Class in the Soviet Society," Oxford University.

24. The numerous studies of Soviet strategical doctrine, while of special interest to the political scientist analyzing international relations, are in themselves too peripheral to political science to be discussed here.

25. Otto Heilbrunn, *The Soviet Secret Services* (New York, 1956) and Robert Slusser and Simon Wolin, *The Soviet Secret Police* (New York, 1957).

26. Ernest V. Hollis, Jr., "Police Systems of Imperial and Soviet Russia, 1700-1938" (Department of Public Law and Government).

27. See note 22.

28. The psychologist, Raymond Bauer, has used the techniques of political psychology in his composite "portrait" of a Party secretary in *Nine Soviet Portraits* (New York, 1955).

29. See especially Alex Inkeles, *Public Opinion in Soviet Russia* (Cambridge, Mass., 1951); and a European study, Bruno Kalnins, *Der sowjetische Propagandastaat* (Stockholm, 1956). An earlier work is Arthur W. Just, *Die presse der Sowjetunion: Methoden diktatorischer Massenführung* (Berlin, 1931).

30. Naive or illiberal efforts to glorify the Soviet experience as something to be adopted wholesale have tended to obscure the practical advantages to be derived from the study of Soviet administrative practice. Apparently the Labor administrators in Great Britain did draw heavily on the Soviet experience, without being "corrupted" by it.

31. See note 17.

32. See especially David Granick's *Management of the Industrial Firm in the USSR* (New York, 1954). Among other "management" studies are Alexander Baykov, *The Development of the Soviet Economic System* (New York, 1947); Alexander Vucinich, *Soviet Economic Institutions* (Stanford, 1952); and Joseph S. Berliner, *Factory and Manager in the USSR* (Cambridge, Mass., 1957).

33. *Soviet Housing Law* (New Haven, 1939); *Law and Social Change in the USSR* (Toronto, 1953).

34. *Justice in Russia* (Cambridge, Mass., 1950); *Soviet Military Law and Administration* (Cambridge, Mass., 1955).

35. For example, George M. Kahin, *Nationalism and Revolution in Indonesia* (Ithaca, 1952).

36. The helpful study by John S. Curtiss, *The Russian Church and the Soviet State* (New York, 1953), deals chiefly with the period before 1935.

37. *Bolshevism in Turkestan, 1917-1927* (New York, 1957). Mary Kilbourne Matossian has published two articles on Soviet Armenia and has completed studies, as yet unpublished, on the Communist Party of Armenia and the impact of Soviet policies in Armenia.

38. Among these studies, Henry L. Roberts' *Russia and America* (New York, 1956) is especially important.

39. Among the most significant are: "Soviet Policy in the UN," *Proceedings of the Academy of Political Science*, XXII, No. 2 (January, 1947), 28-37; "Dismemberment of Germany: The Allied Negotiations from Yalta to Potsdam," *Foreign Affairs*, XXVIII, No. 3 (April, 1950), 487-98; "The Occupation of Germany: New Light on How the Zones Were Drawn," *ibid.*, XXVIII, No. 4 (July, 1950), 580-604; "Soviet Exploitation of National Conflicts in Eastern Europe," in *The Soviet Union: Background, Ideology, Reality*, ed. by W. Gurian (Notre Dame, 1951), pp. 67-84; "Soviet Foreign Policy: New Goals or New Manners?," *Foreign Affairs*, XXXIV, No. 4 (July, 1956), 541-53; "The Soviet Union and the United States: Problems and Prospects," *Annals of the American Academy of Political and Social Science*, CCCIII (January, 1956), 192-98; (co-author) "The Moscow-Peking Axis in World Politics," in *Moscow-Peking Axis: Strengths and Strains*, by Howard L. Boorman and others (New York, 1957), 198-227.

40. In his *Soviet Image of the United States* (New York, 1950).

41. A proposed history dissertation by Eugene Magerovsky (Columbia University) will examine this subject for the 1920's, when

much more material was made available. For a good summary of the meager available information on the formulation of foreign policy in the Soviet Union, see David T. Cattell's chapter in Philip W. Buck and Martin B. Travis, Jr., *Control of Foreign Relations in Modern Nations* (New York, 1957), pp. 656-84.

42. The most important collections dealing directly with the U.S.S.R. are Jane Degras' *Soviet Documents on Foreign Policy* (London, 1951-1952) and *The Communist International, 1919-1943* (London, 1956———); Xenia J. Eudin and Harold H. Fisher, *Soviet Russia and the West, 1920-1927*, and Xenia J. Eudin and Robert C. North, *Soviet Russia and the East, 1920-1927* (both Stanford, 1957). In addition, of course, the British, American, and German diplomatic documents have been invaluable as sources on Soviet policy.

Among sources on Communist parties outside the U.S.S.R. as auxiliaries of Soviet foreign policy, the Canadian Royal Commission to Investigate Disclosure of Secret and Confidential Information to Unauthorized Persons, *The Report of the Royal Commission* (Ottawa, 1946) and the Australian Royal Commission on Espionage, *Report of the Royal Commission on Espionage* (Sydney, 1955) are outstanding.

Jan Triska and Robert M. Slusser are completing a two-volume work "The Soviet Government as a Treaty Partner: 1917-1957," which will contain an annotated calendar of treaties and an analysis of Soviet theory and practice of treaty-making. See also the article by Triska and Slusser, "Treaties and other Sources of Order in International Relations: The Soviet View," *The American Journal of International Law*, LII, No. 4 (October, 1958), 699-726.

43. The principal work is Max Beloff's *The Foreign Policy of Soviet Russia, 1929-1941* (2 vols.; London, 1947-49). Among studies on special questions may be mentioned Gerhard L. Weinberg, *Germany and the Soviet Union, 1939-41* (Leyden, 1954) and David T. Cattell, *Soviet Diplomacy and the Spanish Civil War* (Berkeley, 1957).

W. L. Mahaney, *The Soviet Union, the League of Nations, and Disarmament* (Philadelphia, 1940); and T. A. Taracouzio, *The Soviet Union and International Law* (New York, 1935) and *War and Peace in Soviet Diplomacy* (New York, 1940) were early and relatively successful efforts to examine Soviet policies toward international organization and law.

Alexander Dallin's *The German Occupation of Russia* (London, 1957) carries the story of German-Soviet relations through the war period. Boris Meissner's *Russland, die Westmächte, und Deutschland* (Hamburg, 1954) is an examination of Soviet policy toward Germany since the closing period of the war.

Two studies dealing with Soviet war-time foreign relations, though written by scholars not connected with the Soviet area field, deserve special mention: Herbert Feis's *Churchill—Roosevelt—Stalin* (Princeton, 1956) and William H. McNeill's *America, Britain, and Russia* (London, 1953). Both are based primarily on the important body of memoir material concerning negotiations during the war.

44. Important studies of this type now in progress are Paul E. Zinner's "Communist Strategy and Tactics in Czechoslovakia from 1924 to 1952" and Richard V. Burks, "Communism in the European East."

45. *The Appeals of Communism* (Princeton, 1954).

46. M. Einaudi and others, *Communism in Western Europe* (Ithaca, 1951).

47. *Die KPD in der Weimarer Republik* (Offenbach a.M, 1948). There are, in addition, other useful works, such as Angelo Rossi's *Physiologie du parti communiste français* (Paris, 1948); and Franz Borkenau's *The Communist International* (London, 1938), together with later studies by the same authors.

48. On the somewhat different problem of direct Soviet-Chinese relations, the important survey *Moscow-Peking Axis: Strengths and Strains* (New York, 1957) by Howard Boorman et al., and the numerous articles on border problems by William B. Ballis should be noted. See also R. C. North, *Moscow and Chinese Communists* (Stanford, 1953) and J. H. Kautsky, *Moscow and the Communist Party of India* (New York, 1956).

49. Particularly by the Harvard Refugee Interview Project. Continued efforts are needed to secure the most important testimony of the émigrés before it is lost forever through their deaths.

50. "Approaches to the Study of Political Power," *Political Science Quarterly*, LXV (June 1950), 161-80.

5. PHILOSOPHY AND RELIGION

1. T. G. Masaryk, *The Spirit of Russia*, trans. E. and C. Paul (2 vols.; New York, 1955; original German edition, 1913).

2. V. V. Zenkovsky, *A History of Russian Philosophy*, trans. G. L. Kline (2 vols.; New York and London, 1953; original Russian edition, Paris, 1948, 1950).

3. N. O. Lossky, *History of Russian Philosophy* (New York, 1951).

4. Benoit-P. Hepner, *Bakounine et le panslavisme revolutionnaire: Cinq essais sur l'histoire des idées en Russie et en Europe* (Paris, 1950); Herbert E. Bowman, *Vissarion Belinski (1811-1848): A Study in the Origins of Social Criticism in Russia* (Cambridge, Mass., 1954); Richard Hare, *Pioneers of Russian Social Thought: Studies of Non-Marxian Formation in Nineteenth-Century Russia and of Its Partial Revival in the Soviet Union* (London and New York, 1951); Leopold H. Haimson, *The Russian Marxists and the Origins of Bolshevism* (Cambridge, Mass., 1955).

5. Gustav A. Wetter, *Dialectical Materialism: A Historical and Systematic Survey of Philosophy in the Soviet Union* (New York, 1958).

6. I. M. Bocheński, *Der sowjetrussische dialektische Materialismus (Diamat)* (Bern, 1950; 2nd ed., 1956). It should be noted that Wetter, Bocheński, and Zenkovsky are all members of religious orders. However, this fact does not adversely affect the objectivity of their studies. Even Wetter, who offers the fullest "confession of faith," is careful to place it in a separate chapter at the end of his study.

7. H. B. Mayo, *Marxism and Democracy* (New York, 1955); Josef Maček, *An Essay on the Impact of Marxism* (Pittsburgh, 1955). Marxist-Leninist political and social theory is competently discussed by two recent British writers: John Plamenatz in *German Marxism and Russian Communism* (New York and London, 1954); and, more briefly, R. N. Carew Hunt in *The Theory and Practice of Communism* (London, 1950). To be noted also: Max G. Lange, *Marxismus Leninismus Stalinismus: Zur Kritik des dialektischen Materialismus* (Stuttgart, 1955).

8. Stanley W. Moore, *The Critique of Capitalist Democracy: An Introduction to the Theory of the State in Marx, Engels, and Lenin* (New York, 1957).

9. H. B. Acton, *The Illusion of the Epoch: Marxism-Leninism as a Philosophical Creed* (London, 1955).

10. B. Petrov (Vysheslavtsev), *Filosofskaya Nishcheta Marksizma* (Frankfurt am Main, 1952; 2nd ed., 1957). For an exposition and evaluation of this study, see G. L. Kline, "A Philosophical Critique of Soviet Marxism," *The Review of Metaphysics*, IX (1955), 90-105.

11. Alfred G. Meyer, *Leninism* (Cambridge, Mass., 1957).

12. Herbert A. Marcuse, *Soviet Marxism: A Critical Analysis* (New York, 1958).

13. Geroid T. Robinson, "Stalin's Vision of Utopia," *Proceedings of the American Philosophical Society*, XCIX, No. 1 (January 27, 1955), 11-21.

14. While its main focus is intellectual and cultural history, the Festschrift for Professor Michael Karpovich, *Russian Thought and Politics*, ed. Hugh McLean, Martin E. Malia, and George Fischer ("Harvard Slavic Studies," Vol. IV; Cambridge, Mass., 1957), contains several articles touching on philosophy (e.g., those by Malia and Barghoorn). Russian philosophy and religion are ably discussed, in a broad cultural context, by Wladimir Weidlé in his *Russia, Absent and Present* (New York, 1952; original French edition, 1949).

15. G. L. Kline, "Russian Philosophy" in *Dictionary of Russian Literature*, ed. William E. Harkins (New York, 1956), pp. 288-300; "Recent Soviet Philosophy," in *Annals of the American Academy of Political and Social Science*, CCCIII (1956), 126-38; "Current Soviet Morality" in *Encyclopedia of Morals*, ed. V. T. A. Ferm (New York, 1956), pp. 569-80. The last work represents a preliminary and highly condensed version of part of a book (now in progress) on Russian ethical and social theory.

16. G. L. Kline, *Spinoza in Soviet Philosophy* (London and New York, 1952).

17. Alexander Philipov, *Logic and Dialectic in the Soviet Union* (New York, 1952), with preface by Ernest Nagel. Kline has reviewed the Soviet literature in this field for the *Journal of Symbolic Logic* and for *Mathematical Reviews*, and has translated technical papers in probability theory and mathematical logic.

18. David Joravsky, "Soviet Marxism and the Philosophy of Natural Science, 1922-1929: The Rejection of Positivism" (doctoral dissertation, Columbia University, 1957).

19. G. L. Kline, "Darwinism and the Russian Orthodox Church" in *Continuity and Change in Russian and Soviet Thought*, ed. Ernest J. Simmons (Cambridge, Mass., 1955), pp. 307-28.

20. John S. Curtiss, *Church and State in Russia, 1900-1917* (New York, 1940); *The Russian Church and the Soviet State, 1917-1950* (New York, 1953).

21. N. S. Timasheff, *Religion in Soviet Russia, 1917-1942* (New York, 1943); *The Great Retreat* (New York 1946). Professor Timasheff brings his account into the postwar period in a long article on "Religion" in *The Soviet Union*, ed. Waldemar Gurian (Notre

Dame, 1951). He also has ready for publication a manuscript on "Religion and Antireligion in Russia since the Revolution."

22. Matthew Spinka, *The Church in Soviet Russia* (New York, 1956).

23. Alex Inkeles, "Family and Church in the Postwar U.S.S.R.," *Annals of the American Academy of Political and Social Science*, CCLXIII (1949), 33-51.

24. A pioneer study of religious beliefs and attitudes, based on the testimony of recent Soviet émigrés, is Ivan London and N. Poltoratsky, "Contemporary Religious Sentiment in the Soviet Union," published in *Psychological Reports*, Monograph Supplement 3, (1957).

25. Nicolai von Bubnoff, *Russische Religions-Philosophen* (Heidelberg, 1956). This volume contains selections from Ivan Kireyevsky, Leontyev, Rozanov, Nesmelov, Ye. Trubetskoy, and Shestov.

26. Kline has undertaken the first study, which is now nearing completion. See note 15.

27. Nicholas V. Riasanovsky, *Russia and the West in the Teachings of the Slavophiles* (Cambridge, Mass., 1952); Robert E. MacMaster, "Danilevski: Scientist and Panslavist" (a Harvard dissertation, currently being reworked for book publication in 1959 or 1960); Dmitri Chyzhevsky, *Gegel' v Rossii* [Hegel in Russia] (Paris, 1939); for Hare, see note 4.

28. Isaiah Berlin, *The Hedgehog and the Fox: An Essay on Tolstoy's View of History* (New York, 1953).

29. Professor Peter K. Christoff is working on a study of nineteeth-century Slavophilism which will deal with such questions. It will also include translations of brief works by several Slavophile thinkers.

30. Another study of Mikhailovsky, by Mendel, is now in progress. Robert Belknap of Columbia has undertaken a study of Lunacharsky. Professor Frederick Barghoorn's Harvard dissertation on Pisarev (1941) deserves to be reworked for publication as a monograph. This is also true for Mrs. Miriam Haskell Berlin's Harvard dissertation on Nechayev and Tkachev (1957), although both of these studies straddle the border regions where philosophy, intellectual history, and political science converge.

31. Burton Rubin has a dissertation in progress at Columbia on the Marxian aesthetics of Plekhanov.

32. Kline has undertaken two such comparative studies: of Bugayev

and Whitehead (with special attention to ontology, cosmology, and philosophy of science), and of Bogdanov and Dewey (with special attention to theory of knowledge and experience). The essay on Bogdanov and Dewey will appear as an article or pair of articles in the *Journal of the History of Ideas;* that on Bugayev and Whitehead as a series of articles in the *Review of Metaphysics.* The author hopes eventually to publish both essays as a short book under the title, "Comparative Studies in Russian and Anglo-American Philosophy."

33. Emanuel Sarkisyanz, *Russland und der Messianismus des Orients: Sendungsbewusstsein und politischer Chiliasmus des Ostens* (Tübingen, 1955).

34. Alfred G. Meyer, "Historical Notes on Ideological Aspects of the Concept of Culture in Germany and Russia" and "The Use of the Term Culture in the Soviet Union," printed as appendices to *Culture: A Critical Review of Concepts and Definitions,* ed. Clyde Kluckhohn and A. L. Kroeber (Cambridge, Mass., 1952). pp. 207-12 and 213-17.

35. Though not well edited, an example of this type of anthology is *The Political Philosophy of Michael Bakunin: Scientific Anarchism,* ed. G. P. Maximoff (Glencoe, Ill., 1953).

36. An anthology of Rozanov's writings has reportedly been prepared in French for publication in 1959 or 1960.

6. SOCIAL RELATIONS

1. This study is primarily concerned with work done by sociologists, psychologists, and anthropologists, but the contributions of students in other relevant disciplines are also discussed. It is of some interest to sociologists and Russian area specialists that one of the first American scholars to write about the Russian revolutions with some firsthand knowledge was the sociologist Edward Alsworth Ross, who published *Russia in Upheaval* (New York, 1918), *The Bolshevik Revolution* (New York, 1921), and *The Russian Soviet Republic* (New York, 1923).

2. See some of the articles in a symposium of the *American Sociological Review,* IX, No. 3 (June, 1944), for examples of work in this vein.

3. See Alexander Vucinich, "The Structure of Factory Control in the Soviet Union," *ibid.,* XV, No. 2 (April, 1950), 179-86, for an example of this approach.

4. For example, *How the Soviet System Works* by Raymond Bauer, Alex Inkeles, and Clyde Kluckhohn (Cambridge, Mass., 1956).

5. For example, *Totalitarianism: Proceedings of a Conference Held at the American Academy of Arts and Sciences, March, 1953*, ed. Carl J. Friedrich (Cambridge, Mass., 1954).

6. Margaret Mead and Rhoda Métraux (eds.), *The Study of Culture at a Distance* (Chicago, 1953).

7. Nathan Leites, *A Study of Bolshevism* (Glencoe, Ill., 1953); Barrington Moore, Jr., *Soviet Politics: The Dilemma of Power* (Cambridge, Mass., 1951).

8. Frank Lorimer, "Recent Population Trends In the Soviet Union," *American Sociological Review*, IX, No. 3 (June, 1944), 219-22; and *The Population of the Soviet Union* (New York, 1947).

9. Warren Eason, "Population and Labor Force" in *Soviet Economic Growth*, ed. Abram Bergson (Evanston, 1953), pp. 101-26; and *Trends and Prospects of the Soviet Population and Labor Force* (the RAND Corporation [mimeographed], appendix B, December 17, 1952).

10. Nicholas Timasheff, *The Great Retreat* (New York, 1946); and Eugene Kulischer, "Recent Migration in the Soviet Union," *American Sociological Review*, IX, No. 3 (June, 1944), 223-28.

11. Eugene Kulischer and Michael Roof, "A New Look At The Soviet Population Structure of 1939," *American Sociological Review*, XXI, No. 3 (June, 1956), 280-90.

12. Nicholas DeWitt, *Soviet Professional Manpower* (Washington: National Science Foundation, 1955).

13. David Heer, "Differences Between Men and Women in Occupational Placement and in Attitudes toward Occupations," The Harvard Project (see note 22).

14. The author's evaluation of studies of Russian national character borrows heavily from two papers: Alex Inkeles and Daniel J. Levinson, "National Character: The Study of Modal Personality and Socio-cultural Systems," reprint of chapter 26 from G. Lindzey (ed.), *Handbook of Social Psychology*, II (Cambridge, Mass., 1954); and Daniel Bell, "Ten Theories in Search of Reality: The Prediction of Soviet Behavior in the Social Sciences," *World Politics*, X, No. 3 (April, 1958), 327-65.

15. E. Hanfman and H. Beir, "Psychological Patterns of Soviet Citizens: A Survey of Clinical Psychological Aspects of the Soviet

Defection," The Harvard Project; Henry Dicks, "Observations on Contemporary Russian Behavior," *Human Relations*, V, No. 2 (1952), 111-76; Nathan Leites, *A Study of Bolshevism* (Glencoe, Ill., 1953); H. Roseborough and H. Phillips, "A Comparative Analysis of the Response to a Sentence Completion Test of a Matched Sample of Americans and Former Russian Subjects," The Harvard Project; Raymond Bauer, *The New Man in Soviet Psychology* (Cambridge, Mass., 1952); Margaret Mead, *Soviet Attitudes toward Authority* (New York, 1951). The work done in this field has exclusively emphasized the character of the Great Russians. It is a failing of the field in general that none of these studies has explored personality patterns among members of the minority nationality groups of the Soviet Union.

16. Dicks stresses Russian "orality;" others do not. Hanfman fails to find a dominant need in Russians for submissiveness; Dicks does, etc.

17. Bauer's study, *The New Man in Soviet Psychology*, represents an outstanding contribution to the sociology of knowledge. Nowhere else in sociological literature is the interaction between a system of knowledge and political, ideological, and economic requirements so sensitively traced. As a matter of fact, because of its unique emphasis on the relation between ideology and social structure, the whole field of Soviet studies contains much valuable material for the study of the sociology of knowledge.

18. Bauer, Inkeles, and Kluckhohn, *How the Soviet System Works* (see note 4).

19. Raymond Bauer, "The Developmental History of the Political Attitudes of Individuals toward the Soviet Regime," The Harvard Project.

20. An exception is Edward Shils' essay, "Authoritarianism: 'Right' and 'Left,'" in *Studies in the Scope and Method of the Authoritarian Personality*, ed. Richard Christie and Marie Jahoda (Glencoe, Ill., 1954), pp. 24-49.

21. Geoffrey Gorer's swaddling hypothesis (dubbed "diaperology" by some critics) notwithstanding. See Gorer, *The People of Great Russia* (London, 1949).

22. The Harvard Project was sponsored by the United States Air Force and conducted by the Russian Research Center of Harvard University. During 1950 and 1951 interviews were conducted and questionnaires administered to Soviet émigrés in Europe and the United States. The project gathered data from 329 extended life-

history interviews, including detailed personality tests; 435 supplementary interviews; almost 10,000 questionnaires on special topics; 2,700 general questionnaires; and 100 interviews and tests administered for control purposes to a matched group of Americans. To date, over fifty specialized unpublished studies, about thirty-five published articles, and a summary book (see note 4) have emerged from the project. An over-all evaluation of this project is to be found in our discussion of the "Soviet Social System" later in this paper.

23. D. Gleicher and I. Caro, "Patterns of Ideological and Value Orientation among Former Soviet Citizens," The Harvard Project.

24. Frederick C. Barghoorn, *The Soviet Image of the United States: A Study in Distortion* (New York, 1950).

25. American sociologists will be amused (and appalled) to learn of the Soviet image of American sociology. See J. K. Musgrave, "Soviet Evaluation of American Sociology," *American Sociological Review*, XIV, No. 1 (February, 1949), 137-43.

26. Government studies have undoubtedly been made, but are not available to the public.

27. Alex Inkeles, "The Soviet Attack on the Voice of America: A Study in Propaganda Warfare," *American Slavic and East European Review*, XII, No. 3 (October, 1953), 319-42.

28. Alex Inkeles, *Public Opinion in Soviet Russia: A Study in Mass Persuasion* (Cambridge, Mass., 1953).

29. For an analysis of the situation in one medium, see John Rimberg, *The Soviet Film Industry* (New York, 1956).

30. Merle Fainsod, "Censorship in the U.S.S.R.," *Problems of Communism*, V, No. 2 (March-April, 1956), 12-19; and Leo Gruliow, "How the Soviet Newspaper Operates," *ibid.*, 3-11.

31. Ivan London, "The Scientific Council on Problems of the Psychological Theory of Academician I. Pavlov: A Study in Control," *Science*, CXVI, No. 3002 (July 11, 1952), 23-27.

32. Alex Inkeles and Kent Geiger, "Critical Letters to the Editors of the Soviet Press: Social Characteristics and Interrelations of Critics and the Criticized," *American Sociological Review*, XVIII, No. 1 (February, 1953), 12-22; and "Critical Letters to the Editors of the Soviet Press: Areas and Modes of Complaint," *ibid.*, XVII, No. 6 (December, 1952), 694-703.

33. Raymond Bauer and David Gleicher, "Word-of-Mouth Communication in the Soviet Union," *Public Opinion Quarterly*, XVII, No. 3 (Fall, 1953), 297-310.

34. Peter Rossi and Raymond Bauer, "Some Patterns of Soviet

Communications Behavior," *ibid.*, XVI, No. 4 (Winter, 1952-53), 653-65.

35. Harold Lasswell and Sergei Yakobson, "May Day Slogans in Soviet Russia, 1928-43," *Language of Politics*, ed. Harold Lasswell (New York, 1949), pp. 233-97; Nathan Leites, "The Third International on Its Changes in Policy," *ibid.*, pp. 298-333; and Nathan Leites and I. de Sola Pool, "The Response of Communist Propaganda to Frustration," *ibid.*, pp. 334-68.

36. G. Denicke, "Links With the Past in Communist Society" (Washington: Series 3, No. 84, External Research Staff, Department of State, 1952).

37. Irwin Sanders, *Final Technical Report, Research for Evaluation of Social Systems Analysis* (Prepared for the Officer Education Research Laboratory, Air Force Personnel and Training Research Center, Maxwell Air Force Base, Alabama, by Associates for International Research, Cambridge, Mass. [mimeographed], September 15, 1957).

38. In the introduction to Ernest J. Simmons (ed.), *Through the Glass of Soviet Literature* (New York, 1953).

39. In addition to the examples cited below, see many of the articles included in *ibid.*

40. Kathryn Feuer, "Evidences of Class Stratification and Social Mobility in Postwar Soviet Literature" (Master's thesis, Columbia University, 1954).

41. Vera Dunham, "The Party Secretary in Postwar and Post-Stalinist Soviet Literature" (unpublished paper for the Research Program on the History of the Communist Party of the Soviet Union).

42. See note 7 and Nathan Leites, *The Operational Code of the Politburo* (New York, 1951).

43. John Reshetar, *Problems of Analyzing and Predicting Soviet Behavior* (Garden City, 1955).

44. Bertram Wolfe, "The Durability of Soviet Despotism," *Commentary*, XXIV, No. 2 (August, 1957), 93-104.

45. Edith Bennett, "The Relationship of Age to Other Demographic Characteristics of the PPQ Sample"; David Gleicher, "The Meaning of Distortion: A Note on the Causes and Correlates of Hostility toward the Soviet Regime"; Edward Wasiolek, "Responses of Former Soviet Citizens to a Questionnaire vs. Life History Interview"; Daniel Rosenblatt, "Technical Report on Coding and

Reliability Studies"; Babette Whipple, "Munich-New York Comparisons as Validity Tests of the PPQ"; all are papers of the Harvard Project.

46. Mark Field, "Structural Strain in the Role of the Soviet Physician," *American Journal of Sociology*, LVIII, No. 5 (March, 1953), 493-502.

47. John Hazard, "Trends in the Soviet Treatment of Crime," *American Sociological Review*, V, No. 4 (August, 1940), 566-76; Mark Field, "Drink and Delinquency in the U.S.S.R.," *Problems of Communism*, IV, No. 3 (May-June, 1955), 29-37.

48. See Harold J. Berman, *Justice in Soviet Russia: An Interpretation of Soviet Law* (Cambridge, Mass., 1952), for some analysis in this vein.

49. Michael Luther and John Reshetar, "The Genesis of Soviet Nationality Policies," The Harvard Project; Timasheff, *The Great Retreat* (see note 10); Michael Pap, "The Ukrainian Problem" in *Soviet Imperialism: Origins and Tactics*, ed. Waldemar Gurian (Notre Dame, 1953), pp. 43-74.

50. John Reshetar, "National Deviation in the Soviet Union," The Harvard Project.

51. Frederick Barghoorn, *Soviet Russian Nationalism* (New York, 1956).

52. *Ibid.*; George Fischer, *Soviet Opposition to Stalin: A Case Study in World War II* (Cambridge, Mass., 1952); Gillian, Rosow, and Reshetar, "The Nationality Problem in the Soviet Union: The Ukrainian Case," The Harvard Project; Irving Rosow, "Educational Patterns in the Soviet Union," The Harvard Project; Reshetar, "National Deviation in the Soviet Union" (see note 50).

53. Pap, "The Ukrainian Problem" (see note 49); Merle Fainsod, *How Russia Is Ruled* (Cambridge, Mass., 1953).

54. Timasheff, *The Great Retreat* (see note 10); William Petersen, "The Evolution of Soviet Family Policy," *Problems of Communism*, V, No. 5 (September-October, 1956), 29-35; Berman, *Justice in Soviet Russia* (see note 48).

55. Kent Geiger, "The Solidarity of the Urban Slavic Family under the Soviet System," The Harvard Project.

56. Alex Inkeles, "Social Change & Social Character: The Role of Parental Mediation," *Journal of Social Issues*, XI, No. 2 (1955), 12-23.

57. Alice Rossi, "Generational Differences in the Soviet Union," *The Harvard Project*.

58. Alex Inkeles, "Stratification and Mobility in the Soviet Union," *American Sociological Review*, XV, No. 4 (August, 1950), 465-79; Nicholas Timasheff, "Vertical Social Mobility in Communist Society," *American Journal of Sociology*, L, No. 1 (July, 1944), 9-21; Robert Feldmesser, "Some Observations on Trends in Social Mobility in the Soviet Union and Their Implications," *The Harvard Project*; Feuer, "Evidences of Class Stratification and Social Mobility" (see note 40); Gabriel Grasberg, "Problems of Stratification," *The Harvard Project*; Kassof, Inkeles, Feldmesser, and Grasberg, "Stratification and Mobility in the Soviet Union: A Study of Social Class Cleavages in the U.S.S.R.," *The Harvard Project*; David Dallin, *The Changing World of Soviet Russia* (New Haven, 1956).

59. W. W. Kulski, "Classes in the 'Classless' State," *Problems of Communism*, IV, No. 1 (January-February, 1955), 20-28; Hugh Seton-Watson, "The Soviet Ruling Class," *ibid.*, V, No. 3 (May-June, 1956), 10-15; Barrington Moore, Jr., "The Communist Party of the Soviet Union, 1928-1944," *American Sociological Review*, IX, No. 3 (June, 1944), 267-78.

60. Robert Feldmesser, "The Persistence of Status Advantage in Soviet Russia," *American Journal of Sociology*, LIX, No. 1 (July, 1953), 19-27.

61. See note 7.

62. Bauer, Inkeles, and Kluckhohn, *How the Soviet System Works* (see note 4).

63. Robert Feldmesser, "Social Status and Access to Higher Education, A Comparison of the U. S. and the Soviet Union," *Harvard Educational Review*, XXVII, No. 2 (Spring, 1957), 92-106.

64. See note 58.

65. Alex Inkeles and Peter Rossi, "National Comparisons of Occupational Prestige," *American Journal of Sociology*, LXI, No. 4 (January, 1956), 329-39.

66. Alex Inkeles, "Images of Class Relations among Former Soviet Citizens," *Social Problems*, III, No. 3 (January, 1956), 181-96; Grasberg, "Problems of Stratification" (see note 58).

67. Milovan Djilas, *The New Class* (New York, 1957).

68. Robert Feldmesser of Brandeis University is grappling with these issues. For an initial statement, see his work cited in note 63.

69. David Granick, *Management of the Industrial Firm in the U.S.S.R.* (New York, 1954).

70. See, for example, the article by Vucinich cited in note 3.
71. Joseph Berliner, *Industrial Management in the U.S.S.R.* (Cambridge, Mass., 1957).
72. Gregory Bienstock, Solomon M. Schwarz, and Aaron Yugow, *Management in Russian Industry and Agriculture* (New York, 1944).
73. David Dallin and Boris Nicolaevsky, *Forced Labor in Soviet Russia* (New Haven, 1947); Barrington Moore, Jr., *Terror and Progress in the U.S.S.R.* (Cambridge, Mass., 1954).
74. There is a theory (especially pronounced in the work of Isaac Deutscher) that once industrialization has been fully achieved and a reasonable standard of living obtained, social forces will come into being which will conflict with the regime and will tend to change it. The change will take the direction either of greater "liberalization" or of Bonapartism. It will be engendered by a more politically conscious working class and by a managerial elite desiring stability, security, wealth, etc. All this is debatable, of course. The approach is interesting, though, as a kind of "reverse Marxism" (i.e., wealth and privilege leading to greater freedom).
75. Instead of studying conventional institutions such as the family, church, army, etc., the Harvard Project identified eight basic "operating characteristics": "Creating and Maintaining Myths," "Planning and Controlling," "Problem Solving, Over-commitment of Resources, and Storming," "Refusal to Allow Independent Concentrations of Power," "Terror and Forced Labor," "Informal Adjustive Mechanisms," "Rigidity-Flexibility," "Caution at Major Risks in Foreign Affairs." As with conventional institutions, however, the analysis emphasized interrelatedness, adjustive mechanisms, functional and dysfunctional, etc.
76. Bauer, Inkeles, and Kluckhohn, *How the Soviet System Works* (see note 4).
77. Again, this discussion borrows heavily from Daniel Bell's analysis of several theories of Soviet behavior (see note 14).
78. For an example of the use of the power and command variable in an analysis of Soviet institutions and ideology, see D. Tomasic, "Interrelations between Bolshevik Ideology and the Structure of Soviet Society," *American Sociological Review*, XVI, No. 2 (April, 1951), 137-48.
79. W. W. Rostow, *The Dynamics of Soviet Society* (Cambridge, Mass., 1953). This study also seeks to specify strengths and weaknesses in the system.
80. For a sophisticated analysis of the relation of terror and

monopoly of control to other features of the Soviet system, see Barrington Moore, Jr., *Terror and Progress in the U.S.S.R.* (see note 73), and Merle Fainsod, *How Russia Is Ruled* (Cambridge, Mass., 1955).

81. Zbigniew Brzezinski, *The Permanent Purge* (Cambridge, Mass., 1956). This study, incidentally, contains an excellent definition of totalitarianism: ". . . a system where technologically advanced instruments of political power are wielded without restraint by centralized leadership of an elite movement, for the purpose of effecting a total social revolution, on the basis of certain arbitrary ideological assumptions proclaimed by the leadership, in an atmosphere of coerced unanimity of the entire population."

82. Alex Inkeles, "The Totalitarian Mystique: Some Impressions of the Dynamics of Totalitarian Society," The Harvard Project.

83. Mark Field, "The Academy of the Social Sciences of the Soviet Union," *American Journal of Sociology*, LVI, No. 2 (September, 1950), 137-41.

84. George S. Counts, *The Challenge of Soviet Education* (New York, 1957).

85. Nicholas Timasheff, *Religion in Soviet Russia, 1917-1942* (New York, 1942).

86. Wolfe, "The Durability of Soviet Despotism" (see note 44).

87. Marshall Shulman, "Is the Soviet Union Changing?," *Problems of Communism*, V, No. 3 (May-June, 1956), 16-23.

88. Moore, *Terror and Progress* (see note 73).

89. Moore, *Soviet Politics* (see note 7).

90. Timasheff, *The Great Retreat* (see note 10).

91. Alex Inkeles, "Social Changes in Soviet Russia," The Harvard Project.

7. SCIENCE

1. F. G. Benedict, "Russian Research in Metabolism," *Science*, XXIX (March 5, 1909), 394-95.

2. Alexander Petrunkevich, "Russia's Contribution to Science," *Transactions of the Connecticut Academy of Arts and Sciences*, XXIII (1920), 611-41; A. Hrdlička, "Scientific Work in Russia," *Science*, LV (June 9, 1922), 618-19; H. J. Muller, "Observations of Biological Science in Russia," *Scientific Monthly*, XVI (May, 1923), 539-52; V. Kellogg, "Relief for Russian Scientists," *Science*, LVIII

(October 5, 1923), 264-65; W. Seifriz, "Science in Russia Today," *Scientific Monthly*, XXVI (May, 1928), 433-48.

3. For example, Julian S. Huxley, *Heredity East and West: Lysenko and World Science* (New York, 1949).

4. P. P. Lazarev, *Ocherki po Istorii Russkoi Nauki* [Essays in the history of Russian science] (Moscow, 1950); T. I. Rainov, *Nauka v Rossii XI-XVII vekov* [Science in Russia from the eleventh to the seventeenth centuries] (Parts 1-3; Moscow, 1940); I. S. Galkin, ed., *Rol' Russkoi Nauki v Razvitii Mirovoi Nauki i Kulturi* [The role of Russian science in the development of world science and culture] (3 vols.), in the *Uchenye Zapiski Moskovskovo Gosudarstvennovo Universiteta* [Learned Papers of Moscow State University], Nos. 91-92, 103-104, 106-107 (1946).

5. Academy of Sciences of the U.S.S.R., *Yubileinyi Sbornik Posvyaschchenny Tridtsatiletiyu Velikoi Oktyabr'skoi Sotsialisticheskoi Revolyutsii* [Jubilee anthology dedicated to the thirtieth anniversary of the great October socialist revolution] (2 vols.; Moscow, 1947). Volume one reviews progress in mathematics; physics, geophysics, and astronomy; and chemistry. Volume two covers geology, mineralogy, and soil sciences; biological sciences; history; and language and literature.

6. For example, V. A. Riazanovsky, *Razvitiye Russkoi Nauchnoi Mysli XVII-XIX st.* [The development of Russian scientific thought from the seventeenth to the nineteenth centuries] (New York, 1949); A. Lipski, "The Foundation of the Russian Academy of Sciences," *Isis*, XLIV (1953), 349-54.

7. B. N. Menshutkin, *Russia's Lomonosov* (Princeton, 1952).

8. Daniel Q. Posin, *Mendeleyev: The Story of a Great Scientist* (New York, 1948); Boris P. Babkin, *Pavlov: A Biography* (Chicago, 1949), written in exile by a former student; see also the special issue of the *Bulletin*, XXIV (1929), of the medical faculty of the Battle Creek (Mich.) Sanitorium, in honor of the eightieth birthday of Pavlov; V. N. Boldyrev, "Academician I. P. Pavlov," *American Journal of Digestion Diseases and Nutrition*, I (December, 1934), 747-54.

9. V. N. Ipatieff, *The Life of a Chemist* (Stanford, 1946); see also his "Modern Science in Russia," *Russian Review*, II (Spring, 1943), 68-80.

10. A study of scientific research and development in the Soviet

Union is currently being undertaken by the Center for International Studies at M.I.T. for the National Science Foundation.

11. Alexander Vucinich, *The Soviet Academy of Sciences* (Stanford, 1956); George C. Guins, "The Academy of Sciences of the USSR," *Russian Review*, XII (1952), 269-71; Iakov Budanov, "Tekhnicheskiye Instituti v SSSR" [Technical institutes in the U.S.S.R.], No. 26 in the Mimeographed Series of the Research Program on the U.S.S.R. (New York, 1952).

12. W. W. Leontief, Sr., "Scientific and Technological Research in Russia," *Russian Review*, IV (1943), 70-72.

13. Nicholas DeWitt, *Soviet Professional Manpower* (Washington, 1955); Alexander G. Korol, *Soviet Education for Science and Technology* (Cambridge, Mass., 1957); Leon Trilling, "Soviet Engineering Education," *Aviation Week*, LXV (August 20, 1956), 50-63, and (September 3, 1956), 58-79; John Turkevich, "The Soviet's Scientific Elite," *The Saturday Review of Literature*, XXXIX (March 24, 1956), 60-62, "Soviet Science and Education," in *The Challenge of Soviet Industrial Growth* (Princeton, 1957), 25-45, and "The Scientist in the USSR," *Atlantic Monthly*, CCI (January, 1958), 45-49.

14. V. P. Marchenko, *Planirovaniye Nauchnoi Raboty v SSSR* [The planning of scientific work in the U.S.S.R.] (Munich, 1953), prepared under the auspices of the Institute for the Study of the U.S.S.R.

15. For two excellent studies of this problem in the United States, see Don K. Price, *Government and Science* (New York, 1954); and A. Hunter Dupree, *Science in the Federal Government* (Cambridge, Mass., 1957).

16. L. S. Feuer, "Dialectical Materialism and Soviet Science," *Philosophy of Science*, XVI (April, 1949), 105-24; David Joravsky, "Soviet Views on the History of Science," *Isis*, XLVI (March, 1955), 3-13, and his "Soviet Marxism and Biology before Lysenko," *Journal of the History of Ideas*, XX, No. 1 (January, 1959), 85-104; and Gustav Wetter, "Dialectical Materialism and Natural Science," *Soviet Survey*, No. 23 (January-March, 1958), 51-59. See also the doctoral dissertation of David Joravsky on "Soviet Marxism and the Philosophy of Natural Science, 1922-1929: The Rejection of Positivism" (Columbia University, 1957), and the following papers prepared under the auspices of the Research Program on the History of the Communist Party of the Soviet Union: Maxim M. Mikulak,

"Soviet Philosophical-Cosmological Thought"; Stanislaw Kownacki, "Dialectical Materialism and Soviet Theoretical Physics"; and Michael Samygin, "Terror in the Academy of Sciences."

17. Conway Zirkle (ed.), *Death of a Science in Russia* (Philadelphia, 1949).

18. *Soviet Science*, arranged by Conway Zirkle and Howard A. Meyerhoff, and edited by Ruth C. Christman (Washington, 1952).

19. Russell L. Ackoff, "Scientific Method and Social Science: East and West," *ibid.*, 48-56; Lazar Volin, "Science and Intellectual Freedom in Russia," *ibid.*, 85-99; Conway Zirkle, "An Appraisal of Science in the USSR," *ibid.*, 100-108; John Turkevich, "The Progress of Soviet Science," *Foreign Affairs*, XXXII (April, 1954), 430-39, "Soviet Science in the Post-Stalin Era," *Annals of the American Academy of Political and Social Science*, CCCIII (January, 1956), 139-51, and "How Good is Russian Science?" *Fortune*, LV (February, 1957), 117-21.

20. Theodosius Dobzhansky, "Russian Genetics," *Soviet Science*, 1-7; W. Horsley Gannt, "Russian Physiology and Pathology," *ibid.*, 8-39; Ivan D. London, "Russian Psychology and Psychiatry," *ibid.*, 40-47; J. S. Joffe, "Russia's Contribution to Soil Science," *ibid.*, 57-69; John Turkevich, "Soviet Physics and Chemistry," *ibid.*, 70-79; J. R. Kline, "Soviet Mathematics," *ibid.*, 80-84; Raymond A. Bauer, *The New Man in Soviet Psychology* (Cambridge, Mass., 1952); G. L. Stebbins, "New Look in Soviet Genetics," *Science*, CXXIII (April 27, 1956), 721-22; M. J. Ruggles and A. Kramish, *The Soviet Union and the Atom* (Santa Monica, 1956).

21. Edward Podolsky, "Some Achievements of Soviet Medical Research," *Russian Review*, VI (Autumn, 1946), 77-83; and Saul Herner, "American Use of Soviet Medical Research," *Science*, CXXVIII, 3314 (July 4, 1958), 9-15. There are also several books on medicine: Henry E. Sigerist, with Julia Older, *Medicine and Health in the Soviet Union* (New York, 1947); I. Lazarévitch, *La Médicine en U.R.S.S.* (Paris, 1953); and especially Mark G. Field, *Doctor and Patient in Soviet Russia* (Cambridge, Mass., 1957).

22. Andrew R. MacAndrew (comp.), *A Glossary of Russian Technical Terms Used in Metallurgy* (New York, 1953); Ludmilla Ignatiev Callaham, *Russian-English Technical and Chemical Dictionary* (New York, 1957); Eugene A. Carpovich, *Russian-English Atomic Dictionary* (New York, 1957); James Perry, *Scientific Russian* (New York, 1951).

23. U. S. Library of Congress, *Bibliography of Translations from Russian Scientific and Technical Literature* (monthly); Special Libraries Association, *Translation Monthly;* Great Britain, Department of Scientific and Industrial Research, *Translated Contents List of Russian Periodicals* (monthly). See also A. E. Stubbs, "The Dissemination of Knowledge of Soviet Scientific Works in Western Countries," *Proceedings* of the Association of Special Libraries and Information Bureaux (London), IX (November, 1957), 333-40; and National Science Foundation, *Providing U.S. Scientists with Soviet Scientific Information* (Washington, 1958).

24. Translations are listed in U. S. Library of Congress, *East and East Central Europe: Periodicals in English and Other West European Languages,* comp. by Paul L. Horecky and Janina Wojcicka (Washington, 1958).

25. R. E. O'Dette, "Russian Translation," *Science,* CXXV (March 29, 1957), 579-85; and S. A. Wilde, "On Scientific Russian: Its Study and Translation," *American Scientist,* XLVI, No. 3 (September, 1958), 222-25.

26. For example, J. G. Crowther, *Science in Soviet Russia* (London, 1930); *Soviet Science* (Harmondsworth, England, 1942); P. H. Hudson and R. H. Richens, *Genetics in the Soviet Union* (Cambridge, England, 1946); Eric Ashby, *Scientist in Russia* (London, 1947).

27. Arnold Buchholz, *Ideologie und Forschung in den Sowjetischen Naturwissenschaft* (Stuttgart, 1953); and Gustav A. Wetter, *Der Dialektische Materialismus und das Problem der Entstehung des Lebens: Zur Theorie von A. I. Oparin* (Munich-Salzburg-Cologne, 1958).

28. For example, A. E. Fersman, *Twenty-five Years of Soviet Natural Science* (Moscow, 1944); S. I. Vavilov, *The Progress of Soviet Science* (Moscow, 1951).

29. M. J. Ruggles and A. Kramish, cited above in note 20.

30. See, for example, the extensive attention to Russian science in Mary A. B. Brazier (ed.), *The Central Nervous System and Behavior* (New York, 1958), pp. 23-231, resulting from a conference sponsored by the Josiah Macy, Jr., Foundation.

8. GEOGRAPHY

1. Professor John A. Morrison, at the University of Chicago, and Professor George B. Cressey, at Syracuse University.

2. George B. Cressey, *The Basis of Soviet Strength* (New York, 1945); *How Strong Is Russia? A Geographical Appraisal* (Syracuse, 1954).

3. Theodore Shabad, *Geography of the USSR: A Regional Survey* (New York, 1951). His research on Soviet population, undertaken while with the RAND Corporation, was issued under the title: *Population of Major Cities of the USSR* (Santa Monica: RAND Corporation, 1952). Shabad's technique for arriving at estimates of the 1947 and 1950 Soviet population allowed for a margin of error, as he himself acknowledged, but it is doubtful if the author anticipated so wide a margin as was revealed by the publication of *Narodnoye Khozyaistvo S.S.S.R.* [National economy of the U.S.S.R.] (Moscow, 1956).

4. Nicholas Tiho Mirov, *Geography of Russia* (New York, 1951).

5. L. S. Berg, *Natural Regions of the USSR* (New York, 1950); S. S. Balzak, V. F. Vasyutin, and Ya. G. Feigin, *Economic Geography of the USSR* (New York, 1949).

6. S. P. Suslov, *Fizicheskaya geografiya SSSR, Azyatskaya chast'* [Physical geography of the U.S.S.R., Asiatic part] (Moscow, 1954).

7. Werner Leimbach, *Die Sowjetunion; Natur, Volk und Wirtschaft* (Stuttgart, 1950); Erich Thiel, *Sowjet-Fernost; eine Landes- und Wirtschaftskundliche Ubersicht* (München, 1953); *The Soviet Far East* (New York, 1957); see also Heinrich Hassman, *Oil in the Soviet Union: History, Geography, Problems* (Princeton, 1953).

8. Georges Jorré, *The Soviet Union, the Land and Its People* (New York, 1950); Pierre George, *U.R.S.S., Haute-Asie, Iran* (Paris, 1947); James S. Gregory and D. W. Shave, *The USSR: A Geographical Survey* (London, 1944); G.D.B. Gray, *Soviet Land: the Country, Its People and Their Work* (London, 1947).

9. John A. Morrison, "The Evolution of the Territorial-Administrative System of the USSR," *The American Quarterly on the Soviet Union*, I, No. 3 (October, 1938), 25-46; Theodore Shabad, "The Soviet Concept of Economic Regionalization," *The Geographical Review*, XLIII, No. 2 (April, 1953), 214-22; also his "Political-Administrative Divisions of the USSR," *The Geographical Review*, XXXVI, No. 2 (April, 1946), 303-11; Demitri B. Shimkin, "Economic Regionalization in the Soviet Union," *The Geographical Review*, XLII, No. 3 (October, 1952), 591-614.

10. Chauncy D. Harris, "The Cities of the Soviet Union," *The Geographical Review*, XXXV, No. 1 (January, 1945), 107-21; for his study of the Soviet city as a center of assimilation, see "Ethnic

Groups in Cities of the Soviet Union," *ibid.*, XXXV, No. 3 (July, 1945), 466-73.

11. *Izvestia Vsesoyuznovo Geograficheskovo Obshchestvo* [Journal of the All-Union Geographical Society], LXXIX, No. 2 (1947), 218.

12. George B. Cressey, "The Geographic Base for Agricultural Planning," pp. 334-36, in "Soil Conservation in the USSR," *Land Economics*, XXV (1949), 333-64; Chauncy D. Harris, "Soviet Agricultural Resources Reappraised," *Journal of Farm Economics*, XXXVIII, No. 2 (May, 1956), 258-73.

13. W. A. Douglas Jackson, "The Virgin and Idle Lands of Western Siberia and Northern Kazakhstan: A Geographical Appraisal," *The Geographical Review*, XLVI, No. 1 (January, 1956), 1-19; "Durum Wheat and the Expansion of Dry Farming in the Soviet Union," *Annals of the Association of American Geographers*, XLVI, No. 4 (December, 1956), 405-10. In progress are additional studies by Jackson, involving Soviet experience with wheat culture in the non-chernozem zone of the north European part of the country and attempts to expand agriculture generally in eastern Siberia and the Soviet Far East. Jackson's studies are to be combined with other unpublished studies of agricultural change in a monograph on Soviet agricultural geography.

14. Neil C. Field, "The Amu Darya: A Study in Resource Geography," *The Geographical Review*, XLIV, No. 4 (October, 1954), 528-42; "The Role of Irrigation in the South European USSR in Soviet Agricultural Growth" (Ph. D. dissertation, University of Washington, 1956).

15. Allan L. Rodgers, "The Pasture—Small Grains—Livestock Region of North European Russia," in *Proceedings* of the Eighth General Assembly and Seventeenth International Congress of the International Geographical Union (Washington, 1952), pp. 662-67.

16. John A. Morrison, "Russia and Warm Water, A Fallacious Generalization and Its Consequences," *Proceedings*, U. S. Naval Institute, LXXVIII, No. 11 (November, 1952), 1169-79.

17. George A. Taskin, "The Falling Level of the Caspian Sea in Relation to the Soviet Economy," *The Geographical Review*, XLIV, No. 4 (October, 1954), 508-27.

18. Allan L. Rodgers, "Changing Locational Patterns in the Soviet Pulp and Paper Industry," *Annals of the Association of American Geographers*, XLV, No. 1 (March, 1955), 85-104.

19. Demitri B. Shimkin, *Minerals, A Key to Soviet Power* (Cambridge, Mass., 1953); Lazar Volin, *A Survey of Soviet Russian Agriculture*, U.S. Department of Agriculture, Agriculture Monograph No. 5 (Washington, 1951); Michael Y. Nuttonson, *Ecological Crop Geography of the Ukraine and the Ukrainian Agro-Climatic Analogues in North America*, American Institute of Crop Ecology (Washington, 1947); *Agricultural Climatology of Siberia, Natural Belts, and Agro-Climatic Analogues in North America*, American Institute of Crop Ecology (Washington, 1950); *Wheat-Climate Relationships and the Use of Phenology in Ascertaining the Thermal and Photo-Thermal Requirements of Wheat*, American Institute of Crop Ecology (Washington, 1955); Frank Lorimer, *The Population of the Soviet Union: History and Prospects*, League of Nations (Geneva, 1946).

20. *Soviet Geography: A Bibliography*, Part I, USSR Geography by Subject; Part II, Administrative, Natural and Economic Regions (Washington: Library of Congress Reference Department, 1951).

9. LITERATURE

1. D. S. Mirsky, *A History of Russian Literature, Comprising a History of Russian Literature and Contemporary Russian Literature*, edited and abridged by Francis J. Whitfield (New York, 1949).
2. Marc L. Slonim, *The Epic of Russian Literature, from Its Origins through Tolstoy* (New York, 1950); and *Modern Russian Literature* (New York, 1953).
3. Ernest J. Simmons, *Leo Tolstoy* (Boston, 1946).
4. David Magarshack, *Chekhov, A Life* (London, 1952); *Chekhov the Dramatist* (New York, 1952); *Turgenev, A Life* (New York, 1954); *Gogol* (New York, 1957).
5. Janko Lavrin, *Tolstoy: An Approach* (New York, 1946); *Pushkin and Russian Literature* (London, 1947); *N. V. Gogol, 1809-1852: A Centenary Survey* (London, 1951); *Goncharov* (New Haven, 1954).
6. W. H. Bruford, *Chekhov and His Russia* (London, 1947).
7. Ronald Hingley, *Chekhov, a Biographical and Critical Study* (London, 1950).
8. Herbert Bowman, *Vissarion Belinski, 1811-1848: A Study in the Origins of Social Criticism in Russia* (Cambridge, Mass., 1954).

9. Avrahm Yarmolinsky, *Dostoevsky: His Life and Art* (2nd ed., revised and enlarged; New York, 1957).

10. Henri Grégoire, Roman Jakobson, Marc Szeftel, *La Geste du Prince Igor', épopée russe du douzième siècle* (New York, 1948).

11. Roman Jakobson and Ernest J. Simmons (eds.), *Russian Epic Studies* (Philadelphia, 1949).

12. Kathryn Feuer, "Tolstoy's Literary Method in *War and Peace*."

13. Ralph E. Matlaw, *The Brothers Karamazov: Novelistic Technique* (Musagetes, No. 2; The Hague, 1957).

14. Robert Belknap, "The Narrative Structure of *The Brothers Karamazov*."

15. André Mazon, *Un Maître du roman russe: Ivan Gontcharov* (Paris, 1914).

16. Dmitri Chyzhevsky, *On Romanticism in Slavic Literature* (Musagetes, No. 1; The Hague, 1957).

17. We are helped by articles such as Kenneth Harper's "Criticism of the Natural School in the 1840's," *American Slavic and East European Review*, XV, No. 3 (October, 1956), 400-14.

18. An excellent piece of German scholarship is A. Rammelmeyer, "Dostojevskijs Begegnung mit Belinskij," *Zeitschrift fur slavische Philologie*, XXI (1952), 1-21; 273-92.

19. Waclaw Lednicki, *Russia, Poland and the West: Essays in Literary and Cultural History* (New York, 1954).

20. George Gibian, *Tolstoy and Shakespeare* (The Hague, 1957).

21. Ernest J. Simmons, *English Literature and Culture in Russia, 1553-1840* (Cambridge, Mass., 1935). Mention should also be made of Ludmilla Turkevich's study, *Cervantes in Russia* (Princeton, 1950).

22. V. Seduro, *Dostoevsky in Russian Literary Criticism, 1846-1956* (New York, 1957).

23. Renato Poggioli, *The Phoenix and the Spider* (Cambridge, Mass., 1957).

24. P. Yershov (ed.), *Letters of Gorky and Andreev, 1899-1912* (New York, 1957).

25. Marc L. Slonim, *Modern Russian Literature* (New York, 1953).

26. Gleb Struve, *Soviet Russian Literature, 1917-1950* (Norman, Okla., 1951). A revised and enlarged edition has appeared more recently in German translation: *Geschichte der Sowjetliteratur* (Munich, 1957).

27. *Continuity and Change in Russian and Soviet Thought*, edited with an introduction by Ernest J. Simmons (Cambridge, Mass., 1955).

28. Edward J. Brown, *The Proletarian Episode in Russian Literature, 1928-1932* (New York, 1953).

29. George Luckyj, *Literary Politics in the Soviet Ukraine, 1917-1934* (New York, 1956).

30. *Through the Glass of Soviet Literature*, edited with an introduction by Ernest J. Simmons (New York, 1953).

31. Victor Erlich, *Russian Formalism; History—Doctrine* (The Hague, 1955).

32. Ernest J. Simmons, *Russian Fiction and Soviet Ideology: Introduction to Fedin, Leonov, and Sholokhov* (New York, 1958).

33. *Harvard Slavic Studies*, I-IV (Cambridge, 1953-1957). The four volumes published up to the time this is written contain interesting material on Gorky, Soviet war poetry, and Ukrainian literature, as well as articles on Dostoevsky, Bunin, and other figures.

34. Initials used in referring to the proletarian writers' groups of the thirties.

35. Alexander Kaun, *Maxim Gorky and His Russia* (New York, 1931).

36. N. Matsuev, *Khudozhestvennaya Literatura, Russkaya i Perevodnaya, 1938-1953 gg. Bibliografiya* [Artistic literature, Russian and translated, 1938-1953, a bibliography] I (1938-1945) (Moscow, 1956).

37. Oleg Maslennikov, *The Frenzied Poets: Andrey Biely and the Russian Symbolists* (Berkeley, 1952).

38. V. Zavalishin, *Early Soviet Writers* (New York, 1958).

10. LINGUISTICS

1. Alfred Senn, "The Original Homeland of the Baltic People," and Roman Smal-Stocki, "The Original Homeland of the Slavic People." See *Publications of the Modern Language Association of America*, LXV (1950), 63.

2. *La Geste du Prince Igor'*. . . . Texte établi, traduit et commenté sous la direction d'Henri Grégoire, de Roman Jakobson et de Marc Szeftel, assistés de J. A. Joffe (*Annuaire de l'Institut de philologie et d'histoire orientales et slaves*, Tome VIII, New York, 1948). Professor Shevelov, in his comments on the present essay, has observed:

"The only field in which American Slavic research in linguistics has yielded significant results has been the examination of the *Igor' Tale* and contiguous problems. But . . . this field less than any other meets the justified requirement . . . that American Slavic linguists concentrate their efforts primarily on those questions which cannot be adequately studied in the Slavic countries. The problem of the *Igor' Tale*, which has been raised in Moscow to an issue of Russian national pride and patriotism, is a problem which, whatever may be the endeavors and intentions of American scholars, is doomed to be dependent, not guiding, and is bound to move in channels and along lines set in Moscow."

3. This record of periodical and monographic publication cannot, however, stand comparison with the contributions of some other non-Slavic countries, such as France, Germany, and Sweden.

4. See E. Colin Cherry, Morris Halle, and Roman Jakobson, "Toward the Logical Description of Languages in Their Phonemic Aspect," *Language*, XXIX (1953), 34-46.

5. In *Harvard Slavic Studies*, I (1953).

6. *Orbis*, III (1954), 43-57.

7. I am indebted to Professor Shevelov for his suggestion of some of the major studies that remain to be undertaken.

11. MUSIC

1. As of February, 1958, the coverage of the major pre-1917 Russian composers whose works are available on long-playing records could be characterized as follows: Balakirev, good; Borodin, good; Cui, poor; Dargomyzhsky, poor; Glazunov, fair; Glinka, fair; Ippolitov-Ivanov, fair; Liadov, good; Musorgsky, excellent; Rimsky-Korsakov, excellent; Rubinstein, fair; Scriabin, good; Taneev, fair; Tchaikovsky, excellent.

The situation with regard to the leading post-1917 émigrés can be characterized as follows: Gretchaninoff, nothing; Rachmaninoff, excellent; Stravinsky, excellent.

2. Post-1917 Russian (Soviet) composers whose works are currently available on long-playing records include the following: Fikret Amirov; Arno Babadzhanian; Nikolai Chaikin; Boris Chaikovsky; Reinhold Glière (many works); Otar Gordelli; Vera Gorodskaia; Dmitri Kabalevsky (many works); Basil Kalinikov; Kara Karaev; Aram Khachaturian (many works); Karen Khachaturian; Tikhon Khrennikov; Alexis Machavariani; Nikolai Medtner; Nikolai Mias-

kovsky (several works); Aleksandr Mossolov; Gavril Popov; Nikolai Rakov; Lazar Sarian; Yuri Shishakov; Aleksandr Spendiarov; Otar Taktakishvili; Armen Tigranian; Sergei Vassilenko; and Vladimir Vlassov. Recordings of compositions by two post-1917 composers—Sergei Prokofiev and Dmitri Shostakovich—rival in number and variety those of the most popular pre-1917 or émigré composers.

3. Only a few general historical surveys of Russian music have been published, none entirely adequate. M. Montagu-Nathan's *A History of Russian Music* (New York, 1914), good for its time, is now out of date. M. D. Calvocoressi's *Survey of Russian Music* (New York, 1944) is a competent brief introduction. The most recent one-volume treatment, R. A. Leonard's *History of Russian Music* (New York, 1956), is reasonably satisfactory although the author makes no direct use of Russian language sources and omits any musical citations.

Biographical coverage is highly uneven. No full-length biographical or critical studies of the following composers have been published in English in the last forty years: Balakirev, Cui, Dargomyzhsky, Glazunov, Ippolitov-Ivanov, Glinka, Khachaturian, Liadov, Rebikov, Serov, and Taneev. The most recent book on Borodin (by G. E. H. Abraham) is over twenty years old; on Nikolai and Anton Rubinstein (by Catherine Drinker Bowen) over fifteen; on Scriabin (by Alfred J. Swan) over thirty. Except for translations of studies first published in the Soviet Union, there are no books in English on Miaskovsky and Prokofiev. On Gretchaninoff, there is only the composer's autobiography, *My Life* (New York, 1952).

The situation with regard to a few Russian composers is better. Musorgsky has been the subject of several excellent books. The biography by M. D. Calvocoressi (New York, 1951), not to be confused with earlier studies (1919 and 1946) by the same author, is a work of fundamental importance; it overshadows the French study by Rostislav Hofman (Paris, 1952) and the German biography by Oskar von Riesemann, translated by Paul England (New York, 1929). Of particular value is *The Musorgsky Reader*, ed. Jay Leyda and Sergei Bertensson (New York, 1947), a biography in letters and documents.

On Rachmaninoff there are a number of excellent studies. The most recent is the biography by Sergei Bertensson and Jay Leyda (New York, 1956). Also valuable are John Culshaw's *Rachmaninov, the Man and His Music* (London, 1950), V. I. Seroff's *Rachmaninoff* (New York, 1950), and to a lesser extent the older studies by Antoni Gronowicz (New York, 1946, a translation) and W. R. Lyle (London, 1939). The composer's *Recollections* (London, 1934, translated from the German) are still indispensable.

The only good study of Rimsky-Korsakoff available is the one by G. E. H. Abraham (London, 1945). There is an excellent translation, however, of the classic autobiography, *My Musical Life*, based on the revised 3rd Russian edition (New York, 1942). In addition, two of the composer's technical treatises are available in English translation: *Principles of Orchestration*, ed. Maximilian Steinberg (3rd ed.; London, 1938) and *Practical Manual of Harmony*, translated from the 12th Russian edition by Joseph Achron (New York, 1930).

On Shostakovich, surprisingly enough, there is only one non-Soviet work, the useful study by V. I. Seroff (New York, 1943), which includes material provided by the composer's aunt, Nadejda Galli-Shohat. The more recent book by I. I. Martynov (New York, 1947) is a translation of a Soviet study.

The list of books on Stravinsky and his music is a long one. Of prime importance are the composer's autobiography (first published in French; English translation, New York, 1936) and his *Poetics of Music* (French edition 1942, English edition 1947, both Cambridge, Mass.). A bibliography to 1940 has been compiled by Paul David Magriel in *Bulletin of Bibliography*, XVII, No. 1 (January-April, 1940), 8-9; No. 2 (May-August, 1940), 31-33.

As is perhaps inevitable in the case of such a protean artist, whose career is still unfolding, none of the many useful studies so far published can claim to be definitive. The following volumes may be mentioned: Rollo H. Myers, *Introduction to the Music of Stravinsky* (London, 1950); Eric Walter White, *Stravinsky's Sacrifice to Apollo* (London, 1930); V. M. Beliaev, *Igor Stravinsky's "Les Noces"* (London, 1928); and Merle Armitage's *Stravinsky* (New York, 1936). European studies include the following: Italian, Alfredo Casella (Brescia, 1947); Belgian, Paul Collaer (Brussels, 1930); German, Herbert Fleischer (Berlin, 1931); Swiss, Leon Oleggini, *Connaissance de Stravinsky* (Lausanne, 1952), and C. R. Ramuz, *Souvenirs d'Igor Stravinsky* (Paris, 1929); and French, André Schaeffner (1931) and Boris Schloeser (1929). The composer's son has published *Le Message d'Igor Stravinsky* (Paris, 1948).

Less extensive is the published literature on Tchaikovsky. The composer's *Diaries* have been made available in translation (New York, 1945). The best biography, a model of musicological research and style, is Herbert Weinstock's *Tchaikovsky* (New York, 1943), which supersedes the biography by the composer's brother, M. I. Tchaikovsky, *Life and Letters of Peter Ilich Tchaikovsky* (New York, 1924, an abridged translation). A popular biography, *Beloved Friend*, by Catherine Drinker Bowen and Barbara von Meck (New York, 1937), deals primarily with the relation between the composer and his patroness, Madame Nadejda von Meck. Other useful studies are those by G. E. H. Abraham (new ed.; London, 1949), A. Gronowicz (New York, 1946), and E. Evans (rev. ed.; New York, 1935). The best critical studies of the music are by Eric Blom, dealing with the orchestral works (London, 1927; new ed., 1948), and by G. E. H. Abraham (New York, 1946). The somewhat oddly titled book, *Russian Symphony: Thoughts about Tchaikovsky* (New York, 1947), is a translation of a volume of essays on Tchaikovsky by various Soviet musicians and writers, including B. V. Asafiev, Dmitri Shostakovich, and Yuri Keldysh.

To some extent the deficiencies in biographical and critical studies which have been pointed out above are remedied by shorter treatments of individual composers available in collective volumes. Thus, the able and industrious English critic G. E. H. Abraham has dealt with the Soviet composers Shostakovich, Prokofiev, Khachaturian, Knipper, Shebalin, Kabalevsky, Dzerzhinsky, and Shaporin in his book, *Eight Soviet Composers* (London, 1946), and with some of the major nineteenth-century composers in *On Russian Music* (New York, 1939) and *Studies in Russian Music* (London, 1935). The same writer has collaborated with M. D. Calvocoressi in *Masters of Russian Music* (New York, 1936). Less scholarly, but useful, is the book by V. I. Seroff, *The Mighty Five* (New York, 1948), dealing with the nineteenth-century pleiade around Musorgsky.

A number of valuable documentary translations from Soviet musical politics are given in Nicolas Slonimsky's *Music Since 1900* (3rd ed.; New York, 1949). Useful summary articles by the same author are "Development of Soviet Music" in *Research Bulletin on the Soviet Union*, II, No. 4 (April 30, 1937), 31-36, and "The Changing Style of Soviet Music" in the *Journal of the American Musicological Society* (hereinafter cited as *JAMS*), III (1950) 236-55.

As part of the Russian translation project of the American Council of Learned Societies, translations were undertaken of two standard Soviet historical works on music, B. V. Asafiev's *Russkaya Muzyka ot Nachala XIX Veka* [Russian music from the beginning of the nineteenth century] (Moscow, 1930) and Nikolai Findeisen's *Ocherki po Istorii Muzyki v Rossii s Drevneishikh Vremyon do Kontsa XVIII*

Veka [Essays on the history of music in Russia from the earliest times to the end of the eighteenth century] (Moscow, 1928-1929). Owing to lack of funds, the work by Asafiev was put out in paper covers with a minimum of editorial revision, while that by Findeisen was left in manuscript. (On the whole music translation project and on the deficiencies of the Asafiev translation, see the review by Judah A. Joffe, *Music Library Association Notes*, XII, No. 1, 2nd series (December, 1945).

Other translations of Soviet studies, undertaken commercially, include, in addition to those mentioned previously in this note: I. V. Nestyev on Prokofiev (New York, 1946) and A. A. Ikonnikov on Miaskovsky (New York, 1946).

A unique place in Western studies of music in Russia during the past four decades is occupied by two magistral works by the Swiss scholar, R. A. Mooser. His *magnum opus*, a landmark in musicology but apparently almost unknown to Russian area specialists, is *Annales de la musique et des musiciens en Russie au 18e siècle* (3 vols.; Geneva, 1948-1951). This "monumental assemblage of source materials" (E. O. D. Downes in *JAMS*, IX [1956], 47) has been severely criticized, however, by a musicologist who specializes in Slavic music for "disparag[ing] the whole Russian past, disposing of it as a state of barbarism," and as a "truly monumental work . . . on the crazy Italian eighteenth century," rather than a study of *Russian* music (review by Alfred J. Swan, *JAMS*, I [1949], 51-52). Mooser's three volumes are nevertheless a mine of information for anyone concerned with the origins of modern Russian culture.

On a less imposing scale but equally indispensable for the period is the same author's *L'opéra-comique français en Russie au XVIIIe siècle* (Geneva, 1951); for a review, with valuable data on the author's background and sources, see *JAMS*, IX (1956), 46-47.

Of the few other serious scholarly historical studies may be mentioned Elsa Mahler's *Altrussische Volkslieder aus den Pečoryland* (Basel, 1951) and C. Stief's *Studies in the Russian Historical Song* (Stockholm, 1953). Studies of this caliber by American scholars are conspicuously lacking.

4. The works which fall in this category are included in note 3.

5. The 1948 decree on music by the Communist Party, for example, gave rise to an extensive discussion. Alexander Werth's *Musical Uproar in Moscow* (London, 1949) retains its value as a record of the debate. Juri Jelagin's *Taming of the Arts* (New York, 1951), although it deals primarily with the theater, is of great interest

for the light it casts on the situation of music and musicians in the Soviet system. An unclassifiable but noteworthy book is Truman Capote's *The Muses Are Heard: An Account of the Porgy and Bess Visit to Leningrad* (New York, 1956).

6. The publication of various Soviet studies in translation has been mentioned in note 3. One may add I. F. Boelza's *Handbook of Soviet Musicians* (London, 1942); A. D. Bush's *Music in the Soviet Union* (London, 1944); R. Moisenco's *Realist Music* (London, 1949); and the same author's *Twenty Soviet Composers* (London, 1942).

7. Most of the articles in *Grove's* make careful use of Soviet materials. Facts are used without accompanying propaganda, and Soviet evaluations, where used, are generally counterbalanced by quotations from Western critics. Of the smaller music handbooks, perhaps the only one which calls for separate mention is Percy Scholes' *Oxford Companion to Music* (Oxford, 1938).

8. The following articles may serve as examples of the three types of material mentioned: (a) Reviews of Shostakovich's Violin Concerto in *Music Review*, November, 1956; *Music Times*, October, 1956; *Musical Opinion*, April, 1956; *Musical America*, January, 1956; *Saturday Review of Literature*, January 14, 1956; *Time*, January 9, 1956. (b) Reviews of the performances of *Porgy and Bess* in Moscow and Leningrad in *Etude*, March 15, 1956; *Musical Courier*, March 1, 1956; *Saturday Review of Literature*, January 14, 1956; *Musical America*, January 15, 1956. For Soviet musicians in the United States, "The Soviet Invasion of Our Concert Halls," *Reporter*, March 22, 1956. (c) Walter Howard Rubsamen, "Political and Ideological Censorship of Opera," 1941 (read at the American Musicological Society Annual Meeting, 1941); see the same author's review of several books on Russian music in *JAMS*, IV (1951), 268-72; Marc Soriano, "Les Problèmes de la musique et le Marxisme," *La Pensée*, new series, No. 56 (1954), 77-88; Robert C. Tucker, "Music in the Soviet Union," *Musical Opinion*, March, 1955; J. Briggs, "Soviet Party Line in Song," *New York Times*, June 17, 1956, Section 2; editorial, "Reform from the Bottom," *Musical America*, LXXVI, No. 9 (July, 1956), 4; I. Stern, "A Violinist's Look at Russia," *New York Times*, July 8, 1956, Section 2; Y. Arbatsky, "Soviet Attitude towards Music: An Analysis Based in Part on Secret Archives," *Musical Quarterly*, XLIII (July, 1957), 295-315; Jean-Michel Hayos, "Art et communisme," *Schweizerische Musikzeitung*, XCVIII, No. 7-8 (July 15, 1958), 293-96.

9. The results of a survey of musicological resources and studies in

the United States sponsored by the committee in musicology of the American Council of Learned Societies (appointed in 1929) were published in W. O. Strunk's *State and Resources of Musicology in the United States* (American Council of Learned Societies Bulletin No. 19, 1932). Later bibliographies sponsored by the committee include *Report on Publication and Research in Musicology and Allied Fields in the United States, 1932-1938* (Washington, 1938) and *A Bibliography of Periodical Literature in Musicology and Allied Fields* (A.C.L.S. Bulletins No. 1, 1938-1939, and No. 2, 1939-1940). Musicological studies suffered some interruption during World War II, but were resumed with new vigor thereafter, with the establishment of a central organ, *The Journal of the American Musicological Society (JAMS)*, and the broadening of general interest in music and musicology.

10. The following titles will serve as characteristic examples of the articles on Russian music in specialized musicological journals: Alfred J. Swan, "The Nature of the Russian Folk-song," *Musical Quarterly*, XIX (1943), 499-503; idem, "Old Byzantine and Russian Liturgical Chant," *Bulletin of the American Musicological Society*, No. 8 (1945), 22-23; idem, "Harmonizations of the Old Russian Chants," *JAMS*, II (1949), 83-86; Bruno Nettl, "Ukrainian Polyphonic Folksongs," abstract in *JAMS*, VII (1954), 167-68; Alfred J. Swan, "Russian Liturgical Music and its Relation to Twentieth-century Ideals," *Music and Letters*, XXXIX, No. 3 (July, 1958), 265-74. Mention should also be made of the article by Dragotin Cvetko, "The Renaissance in Slovene Music," in the British *Slavonic and East European Review*, XXXVI, No. 86 (December, 1957), 27-36.

11. In the course of making this survey, the author has compiled a list of American master's essays and doctoral dissertations in musicology concerned with some aspect of Russian music (based principally on the bibliographical works cited in note 9, on annual lists of doctoral dissertations in musicology for 1953-1954, 1955, and 1956 in *JAMS*, and on *A List of Doctoral Dissertations in Musicology and Allied Fields* [Denton, Texas, 1951]). Since 1920, a period of almost forty years, only nine master's essays and nine doctoral dissertations in musicology have dealt with Russian music; one dissertation is still in progress. Moreover, only twelve of the forty institutions in the United States which sponsor doctoral degrees in music are represented in this list, and there is no indication of systematic attention to the study of Russian music in any institution.

12. Harald Heckmann, "Musikwissenschaftliche Unternehmun-

gen in Deutschland seit 1945," *Acta musicologica*, XXIX, fasc. ii/iii (1957).

13. Prospectus of the Congress, Cologne, June, 1958. Compare the report on the 1956 Congress in Hamburg (Gesellschaft für Musikforschung, *Bericht über den internationalen musikwissenschaftlichen Kongress Hamburg 1956* [Kassel and Basel, 1957]), from which it would appear that although the Congress found time to explore such esoteric topics as "The Gilds of Blind Musicians in Japan" and "Robber Folk Songs in the Tatra Mountain Area," no one at the Congress spoke on any subject connected with Russian music.

14. Andrei Olkhovsky, *Music Under the Soviets: The Agony of an Art* (New York, 1955).

15. Robert M. Slusser, "Soviet Music since the Death of Stalin," *Annals of the American Academy of Social and Political Science*, CCCIII (January, 1956), 116-25.

12. ARCHITECTURE AND MINOR ARTS

1. George Heard Hamilton, *The Art and Architecture of Russia*, (Baltimore, 1954). Other volumes on this subject in English include C. G. E. Bunt, *Russian Art from Scyths to Soviets* (New York, 1956); Tamara Talbot Rice, *Russian Art* (Baltimore, 1949); D. Talbot Rice (ed.), *Russian Art* (London, 1935); D. R. Buxton, *Russian Medieval Architecture* (Cambridge, England, 1934); G. K. Lukomsky, *History of Modern Russian Painting* (London, 1945); Arthur Voyce, *The Moscow Kremlin* (Berkeley, 1954). Voyce has also prepared a volume on "The Russian Decorative Arts and Crafts." As in other fields, Soviet scholars of the arts have contributed some basic research on earlier historic periods. One Soviet history has been translated into English: M. Alpatov, *The Russian Impact on Art* (New York, 1950). This book is increasingly useful the more remote it becomes from contemporary problems.

2. Alfred Hamilton Barr, Jr., "Notes on Russian Architecture," *The Arts*, XV, No. 2 (February, 1929), 99-105. For Barr's later observations on a related topic, see his "Is Modern Art Communistic?," *New York Times Magazine*, December 14, 1952, pp. 22-23, 28-29.

3. Robert Byron, "The Russian Scene, I. The Foundations," *Architectural Review*, LXXI, No. 426 (May, 1932), 174-200; and Edward Carter, "Soviet Architecture To-day," *ibid.*, XCII, No. 551 (November, 1942), 107-14.

4. Frank Lloyd Wright, "Architecture and Life in the U.S.S.R.," *Architectural Record*, LXXXII, No. 4 (October, 1937), 58-63.

5. Talbot Faulkner Hamlin, "Style Developments in Soviet Architecture," *American Quarterly on the Soviet Union*, I, No. 1 (April, 1938), 17-21. See also his later articles on "The Development of Russian Architecture," *Magazine of Art*, XXXVIII, No. 4 (April, 1945), 128-32; No. 5 (May, 1945), 180-85.

6. See, for example, Lionel Brett, "The Architecture of Authority," *Architectural Review*, XCIX, No. 593 (May, 1946), 131-34.

7. An article utilizing some material from Paul Willen's Master's essay is his "Soviet Architecture: Progress and Reaction," *Problems of Communism*, III, No. 1 (January-February, 1954), 24-34. For a discussion of recent problems in Soviet architecture, see the same author's "New Era in Soviet Architecture?," *ibid.*, V, No. 4 (July-August, 1956), 29-33; and H. A. Meek, "Retreat to Moscow," *Architectural Review*, CXIII, No. 675 (March, 1953), 143-51.

8. For additional British articles useful in tracing the history of Soviet architecture, see David Arkin, "Architecture," *Art in the U.S.S.R.*, ed. C. G. Home (London, 1935), pp. 12-26; Peter Blake, "The Soviet Architectural Purge," *Architectural Record*, CVI, No. 3 (September, 1949), 127-29; Arthur Link, "Soviet Architecture," *Soviet Cultural Relations Journal*, Spring, 1949, pp. 31-32; Berthold Lubetkin, "The Russian Scene, II. The Builders," *Architectural Review*, LXXI, No. 2 (May, 1932), 201-8.

9. Hamilton, *The Art and Architecture of Russia*, p. 266.

10. M. N. Tsapenko, *O Realisticheskikh Osnovakh Sovetskoi Arkhitektury* [Concerning the realistic bases of Soviet architecture] (Moscow, 1952).

13. POSTSCRIPT

1. Paul F. Lazarsfeld and Wagner Thielens, Jr., *The Academic Mind: Social Scientists in a Time of Crisis* (Glencoe, Ill., 1958), 97-98, 219-20.

2. Marshall D. Shulman, "Changing Appreciation of the Soviet Problem," *World Politics*, X, No. 4 (July, 1958), 509. Also Harold J. Berman, "The Devil and Soviet Russia," *The American Scholar*, XXVII, No. 2 (Spring, 1958), 147-52, and Alex Inkeles, "The Challenge of a Stable Russia," *The Antioch Review*, XVIII, No. 2 (Summer, 1958), 133-44.

INDEX OF AUTHORS

Abraham, G.E.H., 225 n.3, 226 n.3
Achron, Joseph, 226 n.3
Ackoff, Russell L., 217 n.19
Acton, H.B., 66, 68, 69, 70, 203 n.9
Aleggini, Leon, 226 n.3
Alexander, Robert J., 192 n.26
Almond, Gabriel, 62
Alpatov, M., 231 n.1
Anderson, Paul B., 188 n.10
Arbatsky, Y., 229 n.9
Arkin, David, 232 n.8
Armitage, Merle, 226 n.3
Armstrong, John A., 191 n.21, 199 n.22
Asafiev, B.V., 227 n.3, 228 n.3
Ashby, Eric, 218 n.26

Babkin, Boris P., 108, 215 n.8
Bailey, Thomas A., 192 n.25
Ballis, William B., 202 n.48
Balzak, S.S., 115, 219 n.5
Barghoorn, Frederick C., 59, 61, 189 n.11, 189 n.15, 204 n.14, 205 n.30, 209 n.24, 211 n.51
Barr, Alfred Hamilton, Jr., 166, 231 n.2
Bateman, Herman, 191 n.22
Batsell, W.R., 51, 188 n.10
Bauer, Raymond A., 53, 83, 84, 195 n.14, 198 n.17, 199 n.28, 207 n.4, 208 n.15, 208 n.17, 208 n.18, 208 n.19, 209 n.33, 209 n.34, 212 n.62, 213 n.76, 217 n.20
Baykov, Alexander, 43, 194 n.13, 200 n.32
Beck, F., 56
Beir, H., 207 n.15
Beliaev, V.M., 226 n.3
Belknap, Robert, 205 n.30, 222 n.14
Bell, Daniel, 78, 207 n.14, 213 n.77
Beloff, Max, 201 n.43
Benedict, F.G., 214 n.1
Bennett, Edith, 210 n.45
Berg, L.S., 115, 219 n.5
Bergson, Abram, 7, 43, 47, 48, 193 n.4, 194 n.5, 194 n.11, 196 n.20, 196 n.22, 196 n.23, 207 n.9
Berlin, Isaiah, 72, 73, 205 n.28
Berlin, Miriam Haskell, 205 n.30
Berliner, Joseph S., 45, 97, 195 n.14, 200 n.32, 213 n.71
Berman, Harold J., 58, 211 n.48, 211 n.54, 232 n.2
Bernaut, Elsa, 56
Bertensson, Sergei, 225 n.3
Berton, Peter, 193 n.29
Beveridge, Albert J., 23, 179, 187 n.6
Bienstock, Gregory, 98, 195 n.14, 213 n.72
Billington, James H., 72, 190 n.15

INDEX

Black, C.E., 53, 188 n.8, 191 n.22, 197 n.2
Blackman, James H., 41, 194 n.8, 195 n.17
Blake, Peter, 232 n.8
Blom, Eric, 227 n.3
Blum, Jerome, 189 n.13
Bocheński, F.M., 53, 66, 68, 70, 203 n.6
Boelza, I.F., 229 n.6
Boldyrev, V.N., 215 n.8
Boorman, Howard L., 200 n.39, 202 n.48
Borkenau, Franz, 202 n.47
Bowen, Catherine Drinker, 225 n.3, 227 n.3
Bowman, Herbert E., 67, 203 n.4, 221 n.8
Brazier, Mary A.B., 218 n.30
Brett, Lionel, 232 n.6
Briggs, J., 229 n.8
Browder, Robert P., 191 n.24
Brower, H., 189 n.14
Brown, Deming, 130
Brown, Edward J., 128, 223 n.28
Bruford, W.H., 125, 221 n.6
Brzezinski, Zbigniew, 56, 191 n.20, 214 n.81
Bubnoff, Nicolai von, 205 n.25
Buchholz, Arnold, 111, 218 n.27
Buck, Philip W., 201 n.41
Budanov, Iakov, 216 n.11
Bunt, C.G.E., 231 n.1
Bunyan, J., 188 n.10
Burks, Richard V., 202 n.44
Bush, A.D., 229 n.6
Buxton, D.R., 231 n.1
Byron, Robert, 231 n.3

Callaham, Ludmilla Ignatiev, 217 n.22
Calvocoressi, M.D., 225 n.3, 227 n.3
Capote, Truman, 229 n.5
Caro, I., 209 n.23
Caroe, Olaf, 60
Carpovich, Eugene A., 217 n.22
Carr, E.H., 54
Carson, George Barr, Jr., 191 n.20, 191 n.22
Carter, Edward, 231 n.3

Casella, Alfredo, 226 n.3
Casey, R.P., 191 n.22
Cattell, David T., 62, 192 n.26, 201 n.41, 201 n.43
Chamberlin, William Henry, 4, 25
Chambre, Henri, 53
Cherry, E. Colin, 224 n.4
Christie, Richard, 208 n.20
Christman, Ruth C., 217 n.18
Christoff, Peter K., 205 n.29
Churchill, R.P., 188 n.8
Chyzhevsky, Dmitri, 72, 73, 127, 205 n.27, 222 n.16
Clark, M. Gardner, 41, 194 n.7, 195 n.17
Collaer, Paul, 226 n.3
Condoide, Mikhail V., 194 n.12
Coolidge, Archibald Cary, 23, 179
Counts, George S., 214 n.84
Cressey, George B., 114, 219 n.2, 220 n.12
Cross, Samuel H., 3n., 4, 189 n.13
Crowther, J.G., 218 n.26
Culshaw, John, 225 n.3
Curtiss, John S., 7, 70, 188 n.9, 191 n.22, 200 n.36, 204 n.20
Cvetko, Dragotin, 230 n.10

Dallin, Alexander, 192 n.26, 201 n.43
Dallin, David J., 190 n.17, 191 n.19, 192 n.26, 212 n.58, 213 n.73
Daniels, Robert V., 198 n.16
Davis, Kathryn, 189 n.10
Degras, Jane, 201 n.42
Denicke, G., 210 n.36
Dennett, Raymond, 61
Deutscher, Isaac, 53, 197 n.10, 213 n.74
Dewey, Horace W., 126
DeWitt, Nicholas, 196 n.23, 207 n.12, 216 n.13
Dicks, Henry, 83, 208 n.15, 208 n.16
Dinerstein, Herbert, 45, 195 n.15, 198 n.18
Djilas, Milovan, 96, 212 n.67
Dmytryshyn, Basil, 59, 191 n.21
Dobb, Maurice, 43, 194 n.13
Dobzhansky, Theodosius, 217 n.20
Downes, E.O.D., 228 n.3

INDEX

Dunham, Vera, 210 n.41
Dunlop, Douglas M., 189 n.13
Dupree, A. Hunter, 216 n.15
Dvornik, Francis, 189 n.13

Eason, Warren, 207 n.9
Edgerton, William B., 128
Einaudi, Mario, 62, 202 n.46
Erlich, Alexander, 48, 196 n.24
Erlich, Victor, 130, 223 n.31
Eudin, Xenia J., 192 n.26, 201 n.42
Evans, E., 227 n.3

Fainsod, Merle, 55, 56, 58, 198 n.17, 198 n.19, 199 n.22, 209 n.30, 211 n.53, 214 n.80
Fedotoff White, D., 56, 188 n.10
Fedotov, G.P., 71
Feigin, Ya.G., 115, 219 n.5
Feis, Herbert, 192 n.25, 202 n.43
Feldmesser, Robert, 95, 212 n.58, 212 n.59, 212 n.63, 212 n.68
Ferm, V.T.A., 204 n.15
Fersman, A.E., 218 n.28
Feuer, Kathryn, 210 n.40, 212 n.58, 222 n.12
Feuer, L.S., 216 n.16
Field, Mark G., 90, 211 n.46, 211 n.52, 214 n.83, 217 n.21
Field, Neil C., 118, 220 n.14
Findeisen, Nikolai, 227 n.3, 228 n.3
Fischer, George, 190 n.15, 191 n.22, 204 n.14, 211 n.52
Fischer, Louis, 4, 25
Fisher, Harold H., 188 n.10, 189 n.10, 192 n.26, 201 n.42
Fisher, Raymond H., 188 n.9
Flaherty, J.E., 197 n.10
Flechtheim, Ossip K., 62
Fleischer, Herbert, 226 n.3
Florinsky, Michael T., 25, 187 n.7, 189 n.12
Francis, D.R., 24
Frank, Andrew G., 195 n.14
Freund, Gerald, 192 n.26

Galenson, Walter, 194 n.9, 196 n.23
Galkin, J.S., 215 n.4
Galli-Shohat, Nadejda, 226 n.3

Gankin, Olga H., 189 n.10
Gannt, W. Horsley, 217 n.20
Garthoff, Raymond, 56
Geiger, Kent, 92, 209 n.32, 211 n.55
George, Pierre, 116, 219 n.8
Gerschenkron, Alexander, 44, 193 n.3
Gibian, George, 127, 222 n.20
Gleicher, David, 209 n.23, 209 n.33, 210 n.45
Gliksman, Jerzy, 194 n.10
Godin, W., 56
Golder, Frank A., 23
Gorer, Geoffrey, 208 n.21
Gouré, Leon, 198 n.18
Graham, Malbone W., 197 n.3
Granick, David, 45, 97, 193 n.2, 195 n.14, 195 n.17, 200 n.32, 212 n.69
Grasberg, Gabriel, 212 n.58, 212 n.66
Graves, William S., 24
Gregg, Richard, 128
Gray, G.D.B., 116, 219 n.8
Grégoire, Henri, 125, 222 n.10, 223 n.2
Gregory, James S., 116, 219 n.8
Gronowicz, Antoni, 225 n.3, 227 n.3
Grossman, Gregory, 195 n.16
Gruliow, Leo, 209 n.30
Gsovski, Vladimir, 58
Guins, George C., 58, 216 n.11
Gurian, Waldemar, 51, 200 n.39, 204 n.21, 211 n.49

Haimson, Leopold H., 67, 68, 190 n.15, 203 n.4
Halle, Morris, 224 n.4
Hamilton, George Heard, 166, 169, 231 n.1, 232 n.9
Hamlin, Talbot Faulkner, 166, 232 n.5
Hanfman, E., 207 n.15, 208 n.16
Harcave, Sidney, 55, 198 n.18
Hardt, John P., 41, 193 n.2, 194 n.8
Hare, Richard, 67, 72, 203 n.4
Harkins, William E., 126, 204 n.15
Harper, Kenneth, 128, 222 n.17
Harper, Samuel N., 4, 23, 51, 187 n.5, 188 n.10, 197 n.2

Harris, Chauncy D., 115, 117, 219 n.10, 220 n.12
Hassman, Heinrich, 219 n.7
Hayos, Jean-Michel, 229 n.8
Hazard, John N., 9, 58, 90, 198 n.17, 211 n.47
Hecht, David, 189 n.15
Heckmann, Harald, 230 n.12
Heer, David, 207 n.13
Heilbrunn, Otto, 199 n.25
Heitman, Sidney, 197 n.10
Hepner, Benoît-P., 67, 203 n.4
Herner, Saul, 217 n.21
Heymann, Hans, Jr., 196 n.20
Hingley, Ronald, 125, 221 n.7
Hodgman, Donald R., 47, 196 n.22
Hoeffding, Oleg, 196 n.20
Hofman, Rostislav, 225 n.3
Hollis, Ernest V., Jr., 199 n.26
Holzman, Franklyn D., 43, 194 n.12
Home, C.G., 232 n.8
Hoover, Calvin B., 188 n.10
Horecky, Paul L., 218 n.24
Hrdlička, A., 214 n.2
Hudson, P.H., 218 n.26
Hunt, R.N. Carew, 203 n.7
Hunter, Holland, 41, 194 n.7
Huntington, W. Chapin, 3
Huxley, Julian S., 215 n.3

Ikonnikov, A.A., 228 n.3
Inkeles, Alex, 71, 85, 87, 93, 101, 198 n.17, 199 n.29, 205 n.23, 207 n.4, 207 n.14, 208 n.18, 209 n.27, 209 n.28, 209 n.32, 211 n.56, 212 n.58, 212 n.62, 212 n.65, 212 n.66, 213 n.76, 214 n.82, 214 n.91, 232 n.2
Ipatieff, V.N., 108, 111, 215 n.9
Ivask, G., 128

Jackson, Robert, 128
Jackson, W.A. Douglas, 117, 220 n.13
Jahoda, Marie, 208 n.20
Jakobson, Roman, 125, 126, 142, 145, 222 n.10, 222 n.11, 223 n.2, 224 n.4
Jasny, Naum, 41, 45, 46, 194 n.5, 194 n.7, 195 n.15, 195 n.19

Jelagin, Juri, 228 n.5
Jelavich, Charles, 190 n.17
Joffe, J.A., 223 n.2, 228 n.3
Joffe, J.S., 217 n.20
Johnson, D. Gale, 40, 194 n.6
Johnson, Joseph E., 61
Johnson, William H.E., 190 n.16
Joravsky, David, 70, 204 n.18, 216 n.16
Jorré, Georges, 116, 219 n.8
Josselson, Harry H., 144
Just, Arthur W., 199 n.29

Kahin, George M., 220 n.35
Kalnins, Bruno, 199 n.29
Kaplan, Norman, 195 n.16, 195 n.18, 196 n.23, 196 n.27
Karpovich, Michael, 189 n.11, 190 n.15, 204 n.14
Kassof, Allen, 212 n.58
Kaun, Alexander, 134, 223 n.25
Kautsky, John N., 192 n.26, 202 n.48
Kazemzadeh, Firuz, 191 n.21
Kellogg, V., 214 n.2
Kennan, George, 1, 23, 179, 187 n.6
Kennan, George F., 1, 192 n.24
Kerensky, Alexander, 24
Kerner, Robert J., 23, 188 n.9
Kesich, Lydia Weston, 128
Kirchner, Walther, 190 n.17
Kline, G.L., 203 n.10, 204 n.15, 204 n.16, 204 n.19, 205 n.26, 205 n.32
Kline, J.R., 217 n.20
Kluckhohn, Clyde, 7, 198 n.17, 200 n.34, 207 n.4, 208 n.18, 212 n.62, 213 n.76
Kohn, Hans, 190 n.15
Kolarz, Walter, 60
Korol, Alexander G., 216 n.13
Kownacki, Stanislaw, 217 n.16
Koyré, Alexander, 66
Kramish, A., 217 n.20
Krebs, Stanley D., 158
Kroeber, A.L., 206 n.34
Kucherov, Samuel, 190 n.16
Kulischer, Eugene, 207 n.10
Kulski, W.W., 212 n.59
Kurat, A.N., 193 n.28

INDEX

Lang, David M., 190 n.16
Lange, Max G., 203 n.7
Langer, Paul, 62, 192 n.26, 193 n.29
Langer, William L., 187 n.8
Lantzeff, G.V., 188 n.9
Laserson, Max M., 192 n.25
Lasswell, Harold, 57, 210 n.35
Lavrin, Janko, 125, 221 n.5
Lazarev, P.P., 215 n.4
Lazarévitch, D., 217 n.21
Lazarsfeld, Paul F., 177, 232 n.1
Lednicki, Waclaw, 127, 222 n.18
Leimbach, Werner, 116, 219 n.7
Leites, Nathan, 15, 53, 56, 80, 82, 88, 207 n.7, 208 n.15, 210 n.35, 210 n.42
Lenczowski, George, 192 n.26
Lensen, George A., 190 n.17
Leonard, R.A., 225 n.3
Leontief, W.W., Jr., 216 n.12
Levin, Alfred, 188 n.9
Levinson, Daniel J., 207 n.14
Levitsky, Serge, 197 n.2
Leyda, Jay, 225 n.3
Liberman, Simon, 190 n.18
Lindzey, G., 207 n.14
Link, Arthur, 232 n.8
Lipski, A., 215 n.6
Lobanov-Rostovsky, A., 188 n.8, 190 n.17
London, Ivan D., 205 n.24, 209 n.31, 217 n.20
Lorimer, Frank, 118, 221 n.19, 207 n.8
Lossky, N.O., 66, 67, 203 n.3
Lubetkin, Berthold, 232 n.8
Luckyj, George, 129, 223 n.29
Lukomsky, G.K., 231 n.1
Luther, Michael, 59, 211 n.49
Lyle, W.R., 225 n.3

McAndrew, Andrew R., 217 n.22
Maček, Josef, 68, 69, 203 n.7
Mackenzie, Kermit, 198 n.10
MacMaster, Robert E., 72, 205 n.27
Magarshack, David, 125, 221 n.4
Magerovsky, Eugene, 200 n.41
Magriel, Paul David, 226 n.3

Mahaney, W.L., Jr., 189 n.10, 201 n.43
Mahler, Elsa, 228 n.3
Malia, Martin, 128, 190 n.15, 204 n.14
Marchenko, V.P., 216 n.14
Marcuse, Herbert A., 53, 69, 204 n.12
Martynov, J.J., 226 n.3
Masani, M.R., 193 n.28
Masaryk, T.G., 66, 67, 71, 202 n.1
Maslennikov, Oleg, 137, 223 n.37
Masterson, J.R., 189 n.14
Mathewson, Rufus, 128, 129
Matlaw, Ralph E., 222 n.13
Matossian, Mary Kilbourne, 200 n.37
Matsuev, N., 223 n.36
Maximoff, G.P., 206 n.35
Maxwell, Bertram W., 51
Mayo, H.B., 67, 69, 70, 203 n.7
Mazon, André, 126, 222 n.15
Mazour, Anatole G., 188 n.9, 189 n.11, 191 n.22, 192 n.26
McConnell, Allen, 128
McLean, Hugh, 128, 190 n.15, 204 n.14
McNeill, William H., 192 n.25, 202 n.43
Mead, Margaret, 80, 83, 207 n.7, 208 n.15
Meck, Barbara von, 226 n.3
Medlin, William K., 189 n.13
Meek, H.A., 232 n.7
Meissner, Boris, 198 n.17, 202 n.43
Mendel, Arthur P., 205 n.30
Menges, Karl, 142
Menshutkin, B.N., 215 n.7
Métraux, Rhoda, 80, 207 n.6
Meyer, Alfred G., 52, 69, 74, 190 n.15, 197 n.6, 203 n.11, 206 n.34
Meyerhoff, Howard A., 217 n.18
Mikulak, Maxim M., 216 n.16
Mirov, Nicholas Tiho, 115, 219 n.4
Mirsky, D.S., 124, 221 n.1
Moisenco, R., 229 n.6
Montagu-Nathan, M., 225 n.3
Moore, Barrington, Jr., 80, 94, 101, 191 n.19, 198 n.17, 207 n.7, 212 n.59, 213 n.73, 214 n.80, 214 n.88, 214 n.89

Moore, Harriet L., 192 n.26
Moore, Stanley W., 68, 69, 203 n.8
Mooser, R.A., 228 n.3
Morgan, George A., 53
Morley, Charles, 193 n.30
Morley, James W., 62
Morrison, John A., 115, 116, 118, 218 n.1, 219 n.9, 220 n.16
Mosely, Philip E., 3n., 61, 187 n.8
Muller, H.J., 214 n.2
Musgrave, J.K., 209 n.25
Myers, Rollo H., 226 n.3

Nemzer, Louis, 55, 56, 198 n.18, 198 n.19
Nestyev, J.I., 228 n.3
Nettl, Bruno, 230 n.10
Neumann, Franz, 64
Neweld, Mark, 199 n.20
Nevel, Henry, 128
Nicolaevsky, Boris, 213 n.73
North, Robert C., 192 n.26, 201 n.42, 202 n.48
Nove, Alec, 45
Noyes, George R., 3n.
Nutter, G. Warren, 193 n.2, 196 n.26
Nuttonson, Michael Y., 118, 221 n.19

O'Brien, C.B., 189 n.14
O'Dette, R.E., 218 n.25
Older, Julia, 217 n.21
Olkhovsky, Andrei, 158, 231 n.14

Pap, Michael, 211 n.49, 211 n.53
Pares, Bernard, 4, 23
Park, Alexander G., 60, 191 n.21
Parkins, Maurice Frank, 167
Pavlovsky, M.N., 190 n.17
Perry, James, 217 n.22
Petersen, William, 211 n.54
Petrov, see Vysheslavtsev
Petrovich, Michael B., 190 n.15
Petrunkevich, Alexander, 214 n.2
Philipov, Alexander, 69, 70, 204 n.17
Phillips, H., 208 n.15
Pipes, Richard, 60, 191 n.20
Plamenatz, John, 203 n.7
Podolsky, Edward, 217 n.21
Poggioli, Renato, 128, 222 n.23

Poltoratsky, N., 205 n.24
Pool, I. de Sola, 210 n.35
Posin, Daniel Q., 108, 215 n.8
Powell, Raymond P., 40, 43, 194 n.6, 194 n.12
Price, Don K., 216 n.15
Puryear, Vernon J., 187 n.8
Putnam, Peter B., 189 n.14

Radkey, Oliver H., 190 n.16, 191 n.20
Raeff, Marc, 189 n.14, 190 n.16
Rainov, T.I., 215 n.4
Rammelmeyer, A., 222 n.18
Ramuz, C.R., 226 n.3
Reading, Douglas K., 188 n.9
Reeve, Franklin, 128
Reshetar, John S., Jr., 59, 191 n.21, 210 n.43, 211 n.49, 211 n.50, 211 n.52
Reswick, William, 190 n.18
Riasanovsky, Nicholas V., 72, 189 n.15, 205 n.27
Riazanovsky, V.A., 215 n.6
Rice, D. Talbot, 231 n.1
Rice, Tamara Talbot, 231 n.1
Richens, R.H., 218 n.26
Riesemann, Oskar von, 225 n.3
Rigby, T.H., 199 n.23
Rimberg, John, 209 n.29
Roberts, Henry L., 200 n.38
Robins, Raymond, 24
Robinson, Geroid T., 3n., 7, 53, 69, 188 n.9, 204 n.13
Rodgers, Allan L., 118, 220 n.15, 220 n.18
Rodkey, Frederick S., 187 n.8
Roof, Michael, 207 n.11
Roseborough, H., 208 n.15
Rosenblatt, Daniel, 210 n.45
Rosow, Irvine, 211 n.52
Ross, Edward Alsworth, 206 n.1
Rossi, Alice, 93, 212 n.57
Rossi, Angelo, 202 n.47
Rossi, Peter, 209 n.34, 212 n.65
Rostow, W.W., 213 n.79
Roy, M.N., 193 n.28
Rubenstein, H., 146
Rubin, Burton, 130, 205 n.31
Rubsamen, Walter Howard, 229 n.8

INDEX

Rudy, Peter, 128
Ruggles, M.J., 217 n.20
Rywkin, M., 199 n.22

Samygin, Michael, 217 n.16
Sanders, Irwin, 210 n.37
Sarkisyanz, Emanuel, 73, 74, 206 n.33
Schaeffner, André, 226 n.3
Schapiro, Leonard, 53, 197 n.7
Schloeser, Boris, 226 n.3
Scholes, Peter, 229 n.7
Schulz, H., 111
Schuman, Frederick L., 191 n.19
Schuyler, Eugene, 1, 23
Schwartz, Benjamin, 62
Schwartz, Harry, 195 n.13
Schwarz, Solomon M., 42, 98, 194 n.9, 213 n.70
Seduro, V., 128, 222 n.22
Seifriz, W., 215 n.2
Senn, Alfred, 3n., 223 n.1
Seroff, V.I., 225 n.3, 226 n.3
Seton, Francis, 40, 194 n.6
Seton-Watson, Hugh, 62, 212 n.59
Shabad, Theodore, 115, 116, 219 n.3, 219 n.9
Shave, D.W., 116, 219 n.8
Shevelov, George Y., 140, 142, 145, 149, 223 n.2, 224 n.7
Shils, Edward, 208 n.20
Shimkin, Demitri B., 40, 41, 116, 118, 194 n.6, 194 n.8, 219 n.9, 221 n.19
Shulman, Marshall D., 214 n.87, 232 n.2
Sigerist, Henry E., 217 n.21
Simmons, Ernest J., 3n., 9, 20, 87-88, 125, 126, 127, 129, 130, 210 n.38, 221 n.3, 222 n.11, 222 n.21, 223 n.27, 223 n.30, 223 n.32
Skerpan, Alfred A., 191 n.22
Slonim, Marc, 124, 128, 221 n.2, 222 n.25
Slonimsky, Nicolas, 227 n.3
Slusser, Robert M., 199 n.25, 201 n.42, 231 n.15
Smal-Stocki, Roman, 223 n.1
Smith, C. Jay, Jr., 190 n.17, 192 n.26
Soriano, Marc, 229 n.8

Sosnovy, Timothy, 41, 194 n.8
Spinka, Matthew, 70, 188 n.10, 191 n.22, 205 n.22
Stahlberger, Lawrence, 128
Stebbins, G.L., 217 n.20
Steinberg, Maximilian, 226 n.3
Stern, J., 229 n.8
Stewart, George, 188 n.9
Stief, C., 228 n.3
Stilman, Leon, 128
Strakhovsky, Leonid I., 188 n.8, 190 n.16
Strunk, W.O., 230 n.9
Struve, Gleb, 128, 222 n.26
Stubbs, A.E., 218 n.23
Suslov, S.P., 115, 219 n.6
Swan, Alfred J., 225 n.3, 228 n.3, 230 n.10
Swearingen, Rodger, 62, 192 n.26, 193 n.29
Szeftel, Marc, 125, 197 n.2, 222 n.10, 223 n.2

Tang, Peter, 62
Taracouzio, T.A., 188 n.10, 201 n.43
Taskin, George A., 118, 220 n.17
Tchaikovsky, M.J., 226 n.3
Thiel, Erich, 116, 219 n.7
Thielens, Wagner, Jr., 177, 232 n.1
Thomas, B.P., 187 n.8
Timasheff, Nicholas S., 70, 101, 188 n.10, 191 n.19, 204 n.21, 207 n.10, 211 n.49, 211 n.54, 212 n.58, 214 n.85, 214 n.90
Tolpin, J.C., 110
Tomasic, D., 219 n.78
Tompkins, Pauline, 192 n.25
Tompkins, Stuart R., 190 n.17
Towster, Julian, 198 n.17
Travis, Martin B., Jr., 201 n.41
Treadgold, Donald W., 189 n.14, 190 n.15
Trilling, Leon, 216 n.13
Triska, Jan, 201 n.42
Tsapenko, M.N., 232 n.10
Tucker, Robert C., 229 n.8
Turkevich, John, 110, 216 n.13, 217 n.19, 217 n.20
Turkevich, Ludmilla, 110, 222 n.21

Ulam, Adam B., 62
Unterberger, Betty Miller, 192 n.24
Utechin, S., 199 n.23

Vakar, Nicholas P., 60, 191 n.21
Varneck, Elena, 188 n.10
Vasiliev, Alexander A., 189 n.13
Vasyutin, V.F., 115, 219 n.5
Vavilov, S.I., 218 n.28
Vernadsky, George, 25, 125, 189 n.12
Vinogradoff, Paul, 187 n.7
Volin, Lazar, 44, 45, 118, 195 n.15, 217 n.19, 221 n.19
Voyce, Arthur, 167, 231 n.1
Vucinich, Alexander, 195 n.14, 200 n.32, 206 n.3, 213 n.70, 216 n.11
Vysheslavtsev, Boris, 66, 69, 203 n.10

Warth, Robert D., 192 n.24
Wasiolek, Edward, 210 n.45
Weber, Max, 97
Wei, Henry, 192 n.26
Weidlé, Wladimir, 66, 204 n.14
Weinberg, Gerhard L., 192 n.26, 201 n.43
Weinstock, Herbert, 226 n.3
Werth, Alexander, 228 n.5
Wetter, Gustav A., 53, 66, 67, 68, 70, 203 n.5, 203 n.6, 216 n.16, 218 n.27
Whipple, Babette, 211 n.45

White, Eric Walter, 226 n.3
White, John A., 191 n.24
Whitfield, Francis J., 3n., 124, 184, 221 n.1
Whiting, Allen S., 62, 192 n.26
Wilde, S.A., 218 n.25
Willen, Paul, 232 n.7
Williams, William A., 192 n.25
Wojcicka, Janina, 218 n.24
Wolfe, Bertram D., 53, 101, 189 n.15, 197 n.7, 210 n.44, 214 n.86
Wolin, Simon, 199 n.25
Wollenberg, Erich, 56
Wright, Frank Lloyd, 166, 232 n.4

Yakobson, Sergius, 10, 188 n.8, 191 n.22, 210 n.35
Yarmolinsky, Avrahm, 222 n.9
Yershov, Peter, 128, 222 n.24
Yugow, Aaron, 98, 195 n.14, 213 n.72
Yurieff, Zoya, 128

Zabriskie, Edward H., 190 n.17
Zauberman, A., 195 n.16
Zavalishin, V., 137, 223 n.38
Zenkovsky, V.V., 66, 67, 71, 202 n.7, 203 n.6
Zirkle, Conway, 109, 217 n.17, 217 n.18, 217 n.19
Zinner, Paul E., 202 n.44